BUILDINGS

FOR

SMALL ACREAGES

FARM, RANCH & RECREATION

BUILDINGS FOR SMALL ACREAGES

FARM, RANCH & RECREATION

James S. Boyd, Ph.D.

Revised by
Carl L. Reynolds, Ph.D.
Associate Dean
The University of Wyoming,
Laramie

Interstate Publishers, Inc.
Danville, Illinois

BUILDINGS FOR SMALL ACREAGES

Farm, Ranch & Recreation

Second Edition

COPYRIGHT © 1996 BY INTERSTATE PUBLISHERS, INC.
All rights reserved. Printed in the U.S.A.

Library of Congress Catalog Card No. 93-79032

ISBN 0-8134-2973-0

1 2 3 4 5 6 7 8 9 10   02 01 00 99 98 97 96

Order from
Interstate Publishers, Inc.
510 North Vermilion
P.O. Box 50
Danville, IL 61834-0050
Phone: (800) 843-4774
Fax: (217) 446-9706

Notice To the Reader

TABLE OF CONTENTS

Introduction

When the original author of this text, James S. Boyd, wrote the introduction in 1978, he predicted accurately that more and more people would be moving to small acreages. The trend is still as evident today as it was then. At the same time, the trend has been that plans for these small-acreage operations are more and more limited in availability.

The purpose of this book is to insure that plans for use by small rural-acreage residents are preserved and readily available. Plans range for low-cost residential and recreational housing to all types of housing for the common types of livestock found on these small acreages. In addition, the book includes a wide variety of plans for fencing, feeding, and handling equipment.

Many of the housing and equipment plans fit the needs for large operations as well. For those who do not find plans in this text to fit their needs, the addresses of sources of plans from each state university as well as the USDA are listed in the appendices.

Included are many other miscellaneous plans as well, with the notion that many of these enhance the "country living" comforts to which people living on small acreages aspire.

Carl L. Reynolds

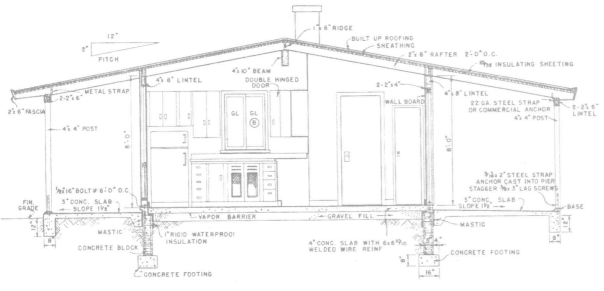

SECTION A-A

CABINS

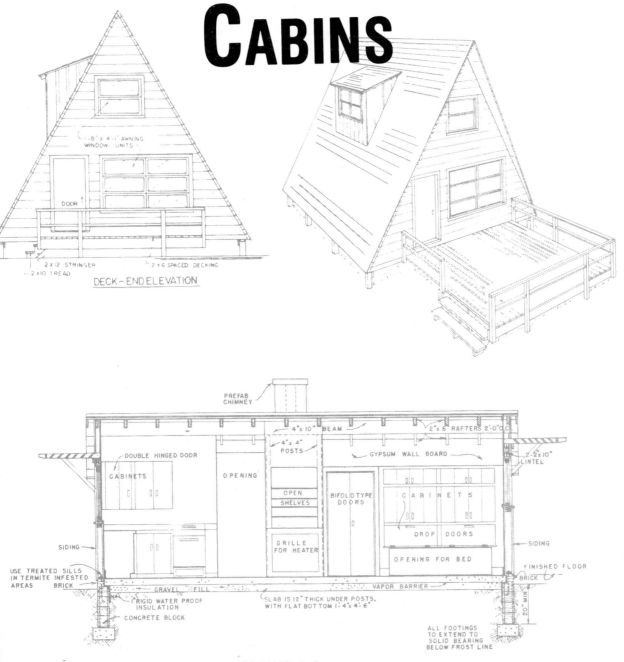

DECK-END ELEVATION

SECTION B-B

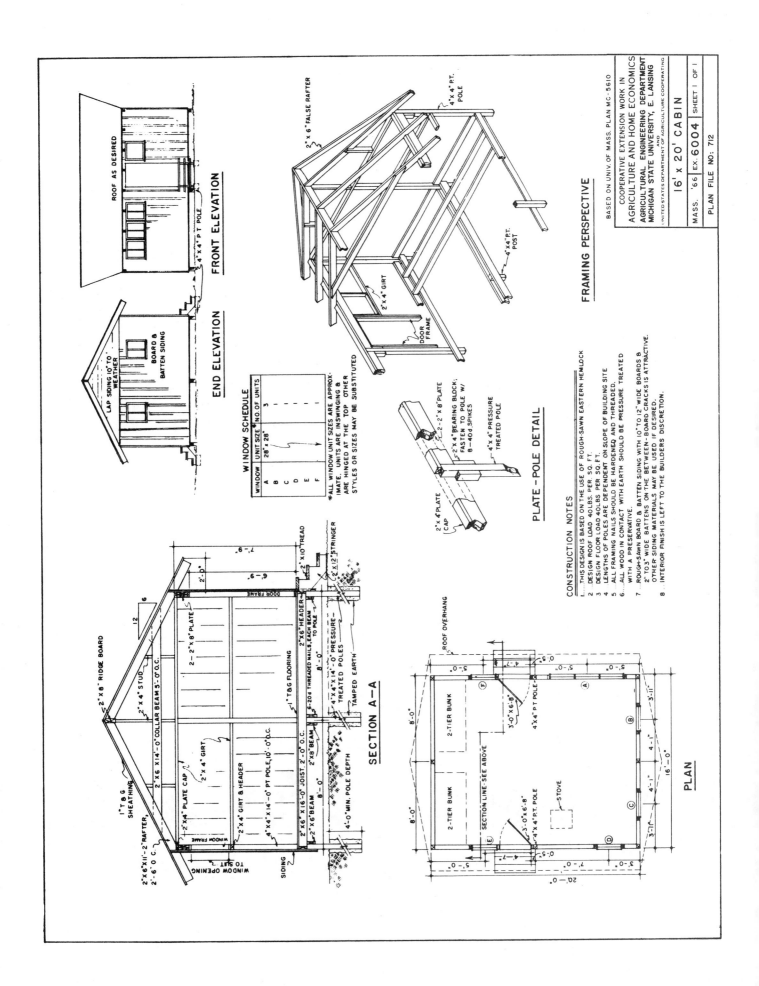

FRONT ELEVATION

ROOF AS DESIRED

4"X 4" P.T. POLE

END ELEVATION

LAP SIDING 10" TO WEATHER

BOARD & BATTEN SIDING

FRAMING PERSPECTIVE

2"X 6" FALSE RAFTER

4"X 4" P.T. POLE

4"X 4" P.T. POST

2"X 4" GIRT

DOOR FRAME

WINDOW SCHEDULE

WINDOW	UNIT SIZE*	NO. OF UNITS
A	28"x 28"	3
B		—
C		—
D		—
E		—
F		—

*ALL WINDOW UNIT SIZES ARE APPROXIMATE. UNITS ARE INSWINGING & ARE HINGED AT THE TOP OTHER STYLES OR SIZES MAY BE SUBSTITUTED.

PLATE - POLE DETAIL

2"x 4" PLATE CAP

2-2"x 8" PLATE

2"x 4" BEARING BLOCK; FASTEN TO POLE W/ 8-40d SPIKES

4"X 4" PRESSURE TREATED POLE

CONSTRUCTION NOTES

1. THIS DESIGN IS BASED ON THE USE OF ROUGH-SAWN EASTERN HEMLOCK.
2. DESIGN ROOF LOAD 40 LBS. PER SQ. FT.
3. DESIGN FLOOR LOAD 40 LBS. PER SQ. FT.
4. LENGTHS OF POLES ARE DEPENDENT ON SLOPE OF BUILDING SITE.
5. ALL FRAMING NAILS SHOULD BE HARDENED AND THREADED.
6. ALL WOOD IN CONTACT WITH EARTH SHOULD BE PRESSURE TREATED WITH A PRESERVATIVE.
7. ROUGH-SAWN BOARD & BATTEN SIDING WITH 10" TO 12" WIDE BOARDS & 2" TO 3" WIDE BATTENS ON THE BETWEEN - BOARD CRACKS IS ATTRACTIVE. OTHER SIDING MATERIALS MAY BE USED IF DESIRED.
8. INTERIOR FINISH IS LEFT TO THE BUILDERS DISCRETION.

BASED ON UNIV. OF MASS. PLAN MC-5610

COOPERATIVE EXTENSION WORK IN
AGRICULTURE AND HOME ECONOMICS
AGRICULTURAL ENGINEERING DEPARTMENT
MICHIGAN STATE UNIVERSITY, E. LANSING
AND
UNITED STATES DEPARTMENT OF AGRICULTURE COOPERATING

16' x 20' CABIN

| MASS. '66 | EX. 6004 | SHEET 1 OF 1 |

PLAN FILE NO: 712

SECTION A-A

2"X 6"X 11'-2" RAFTER
2'-6' O.C.

1" T&G SHEATHING

2"x 6" RIDGE BOARD

12

6

2"X 4" STUD

2"X 6"X14'-0" COLLAR BEAM 5'-0" O.C.

2"X 4" PLATE CAP

2-2"x 8" PLATE

7'-9"

6'-9"

2'-0"

2"x10"TREAD

2"x12"STRINGER

DOOR FRAME

2"X6"HEADER

2"X6"X14'-0" PRESSURE TREATED POLES

6-20d THREADED NAILS EACH BEAM

8'-0"

4"X4"X14'-0" PT POLE

1" T&G FLOORING

2"X 6" GIRT

2"X 4" GIRT

2"X 6"X16'-0" JOIST 2'-0" O.C.

4"X4"X14'-0" PT POLE 10'-0"O.C.

2"X8"BEAM

2"X6" BEAM

4'-0" MIN. POLE DEPTH

8'-0"

2"X 4" GIRT & HEADER

WINDOW FRAME

SIDING

WINDOW OPENING TO SUIT

TAMPED EARTH

PLAN

16'-0"

20'-0"

ROOF OVERHANG

5'-0"

5'-0"

5'-0"

3'-11"

8'-0"

2-TIER BUNK

2-TIER BUNK

2-TIER BUNK

SECTION LINE-SEE ABOVE

STOVE

3'-0"X 6'-8"

3'-0"X 6'-8"

4"X 4" P.T. POLE

4"X 4" P.T. POLE

4"X 4" P.T. POLE

F

A

B

C

D

E

3'-0"

5'-0"

5'-0"

7'-0"

4'-1"

4'-1"

4'-7"

4'-7"

0'-5"

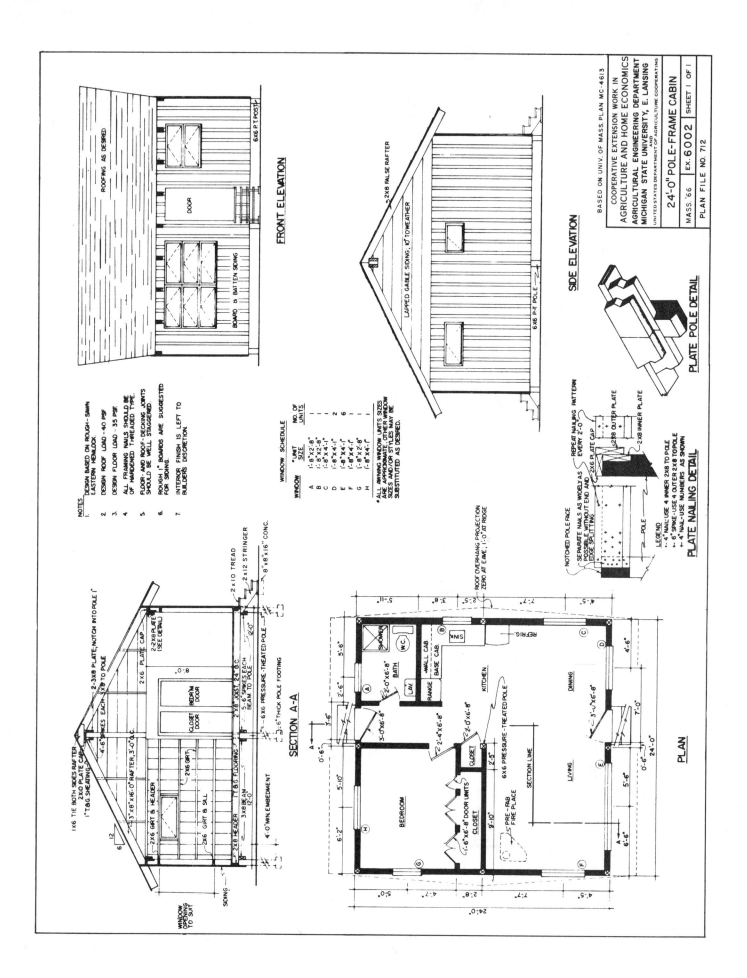

FRONT ELEVATION

SIDE ELEVATION

PLATE POLE DETAIL

PLATE NAILING DETAIL

SECTION A-A

PLAN

NOTES

1. DESIGN BASED ON ROUGH-SAWN EASTERN HEMLOCK

2. DESIGN ROOF LOAD - 40 PSF.

3. DESIGN FLOOR LOAD - 35 PSF.

4. ALL FRAMING NAILS SHOULD BE OF HARDENED THREADED TYPE.

5. FLOOR- AND ROOF-DECKING JOINTS SHOULD BE WELL STAGGERED.

6. ROUGH 1" BOARDS ARE SUGGESTED FOR SIDING.

7. INTERIOR FINISH IS LEFT TO BUILDERS DISCRETION.

WINDOW SCHEDULE

WINDOW	"UNIT" SIZE	NO. OF UNITS
A	1'-6"X2'-8"	1
B	1'-8"X2'-8"	1
C	1'-8"X4'-1"	2
D	1'-8"X4'-1"	6
E	1'-8"X4'-1"	1
F	1'-8"X4'-1"	1
G	1'-8"X2'-8"	1
H	1'-8"X4'-1"	1

* ALL AWNING WINDOW UNITS SIZES ARE APPROXIMATE. OTHER WINDOW SIZES AND/OR STYLES MAY BE SUBSTITUTED AS DESIRED.

BASED ON UNIV. OF MASS. PLAN MC-4613

Cooperative Extension Work in
AGRICULTURAL AND HOME ECONOMICS
AGRICULTURAL ENGINEERING DEPARTMENT
MICHIGAN STATE UNIVERSITY, E. LANSING
AND
UNITED STATES DEPARTMENT OF AGRICULTURE COOPERATING

24'-0" POLE-FRAME CABIN

MASS. '66 | EX. 6002 | SHEET 1 OF 1

PLAN FILE NO. 712

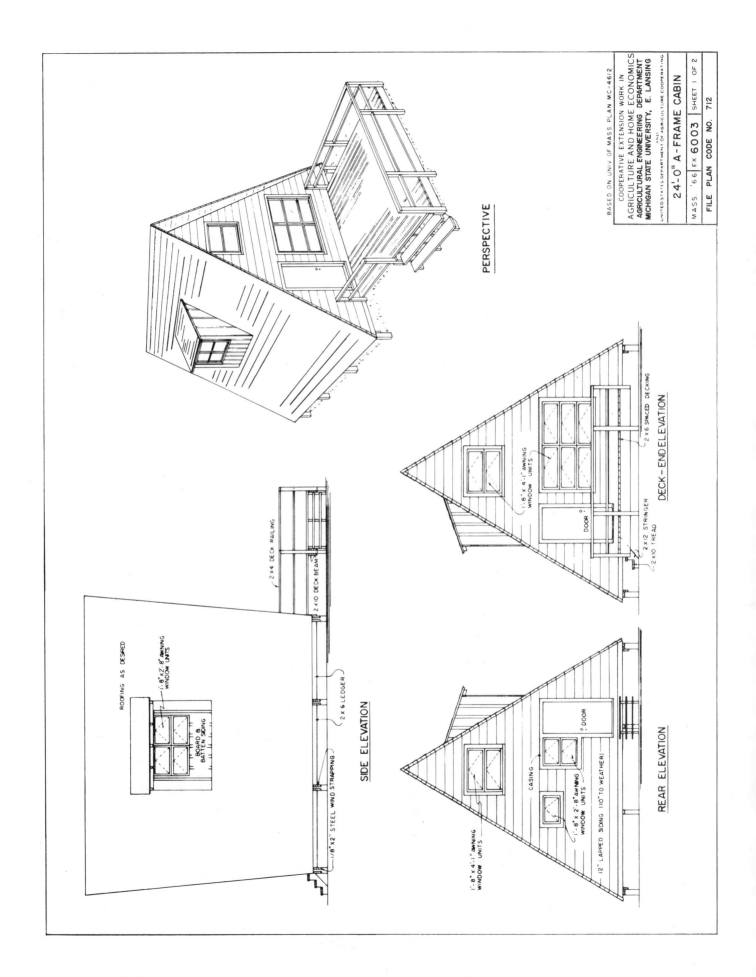

PERSPECTIVE

DECK-END ELEVATION

2 x 6 SPACED DECKING

1'-8" x 4'-1" AWNING WINDOW UNITS

DOOR

2 x 12 STRINGER

2 x 10 TREAD

REAR ELEVATION

1'-8" x 4'-1" AWNING WINDOW UNITS

CASING

DOOR

1'-8" x 2'-8" AWNING WINDOW UNITS

12" LAPPED SIDING (10" TO WEATHER)

SIDE ELEVATION

ROOFING AS DESIRED

1'-8" x 2'-8" AWNING WINDOW UNITS

BOARD & BATTEN SIDING

1/8" x 2" STEEL WIND STRAPPING

2 x 4 DECK RAILING

2 x 10 DECK BEAM

2 x 6 LEDGER

BASED ON UNIV OF MASS PLAN MC-4612

COOPERATIVE EXTENSION WORK IN
AGRICULTURE AND HOME ECONOMICS
AGRICULTURAL ENGINEERING DEPARTMENT
MICHIGAN STATE UNIVERSITY, E. LANSING
AND
UNITED STATES DEPARTMENT OF AGRICULTURE COOPERATING

24'-0" A-FRAME CABIN

MASS. '66 | EX 6003 | SHEET 1 OF 2

FILE PLAN CODE NO. 712

5

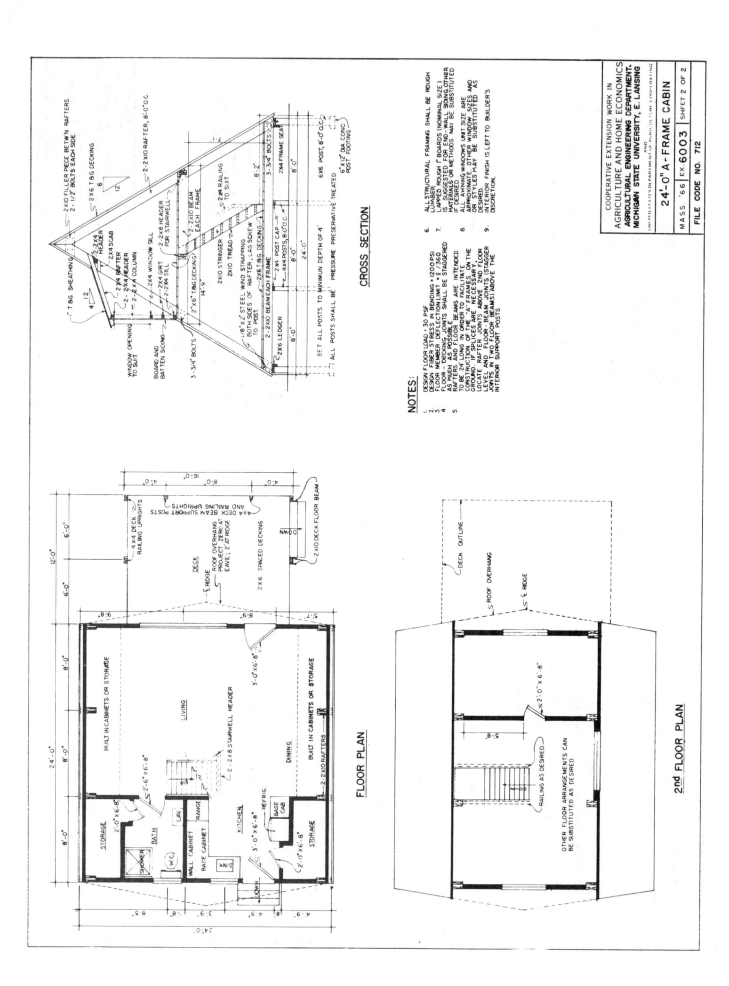

CROSS SECTION

FLOOR PLAN

2nd FLOOR PLAN

NOTES:

1. DESIGN FLOOR LOAD = 30 PSF
2. DESIGN FIBER STRESS IN BENDING = 1200 PSI
3. FLOOR MEMBER DEFLECTION LIMIT = ℓ/360
4. FLOOR – DECKING JOINTS SHALL BE STAGGERED AS MUCH AS POSSIBLE
5. RAFTERS AND FLOOR BEAMS ARE INTENDED TO BE 24' LONG IN ORDER TO FACILITATE CONSTRUCTION OF THE "A" FRAMES ON THE GROUND. IF SPLICES ARE NECESSARY, LOCATE RAFTER JOINTS ABOVE 2ND FLOOR LEVEL AND FLOOR – BEAM JOINTS (STAGGER JOINTS IN TWO FLOOR – BEAMS) ABOVE THE INTERIOR SUPPORT POSTS

6. ALL STRUCTURAL FRAMING SHALL BE ROUGH LUMBER
7. LAPPED ROUGH 1" BOARDS (NOMINAL SIZE) IS SUGGESTED FOR END– WALL SIDING OTHER MATERIALS OR METHODS MAY BE SUBSTITUTED IF DESIRED
8. ALL AWNING WINDOWS UNIT SIZE ARE APPROXIMATE. OTHER WINDOW SIZES AND OR STYLES MAY BE SUBSTITUTED AS DESIRED.
9. INTERIOR FINISH IS LEFT TO BUILDER'S DISCRETION.

COOPERATIVE EXTENSION WORK IN
AGRICULTURE AND HOME ECONOMICS,
AGRICULTURAL ENGINEERING DEPARTMENT.
MICHIGAN STATE UNIVERSITY, E. LANSING
UNITED STATES DEPARTMENT OF AGRICULTURE COOPERATING

24'-0" A-FRAME CABIN

MASS. '66 | EX. 6003 | SHEET 2 OF 2

FILE CODE NO. 712

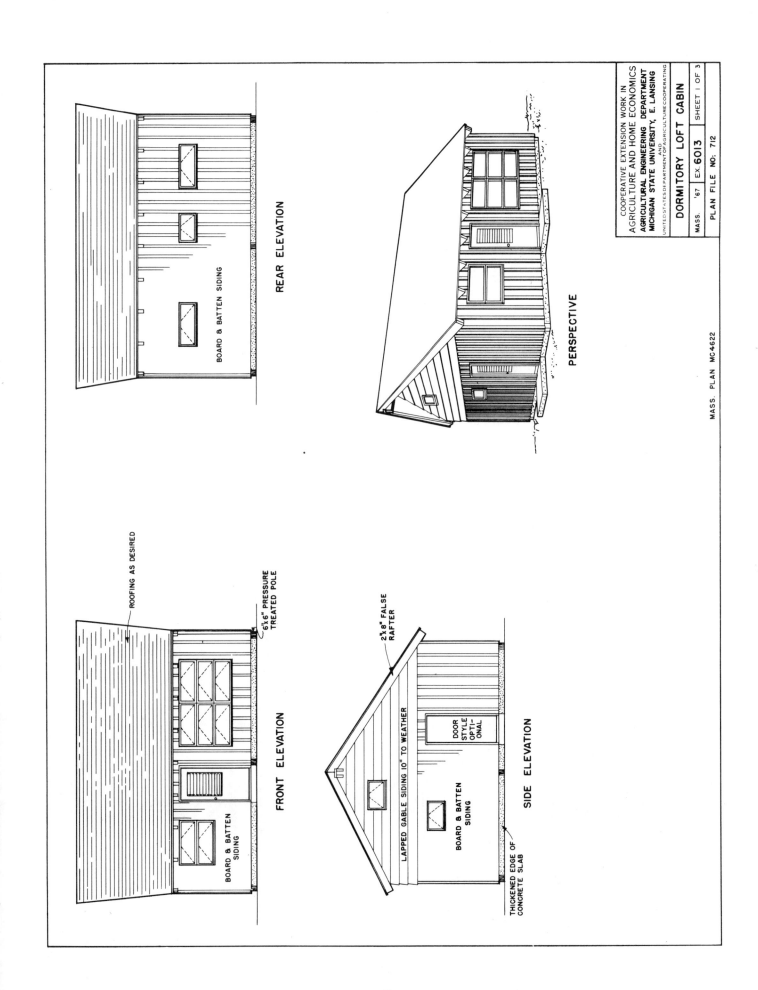

BOARD & BATTEN SIDING

REAR ELEVATION

PERSPECTIVE

ROOFING AS DESIRED

6"x 6" PRESSURE TREATED POLE

BOARD & BATTEN SIDING

FRONT ELEVATION

2"x 8" FALSE RAFTER

LAPPED GABLE SIDING 10" TO WEATHER

DOOR STYLE OPTI- ONAL

BOARD & BATTEN SIDING

THICKENED EDGE OF CONCRETE SLAB

SIDE ELEVATION

COOPERATIVE EXTENSION WORK IN
AGRICULTURE AND HOME ECONOMICS
AND
AGRICULTURAL ENGINEERING DEPARTMENT
MICHIGAN STATE UNIVERSITY, E. LANSING
UNITED STATES DEPARTMENT OF AGRICULTURE COOPERATING

DORMITORY LOFT CABIN

MASS. '67 | EX. 6013 | SHEET I OF 3

PLAN FILE NO: 712

MASS. PLAN MC4622

7

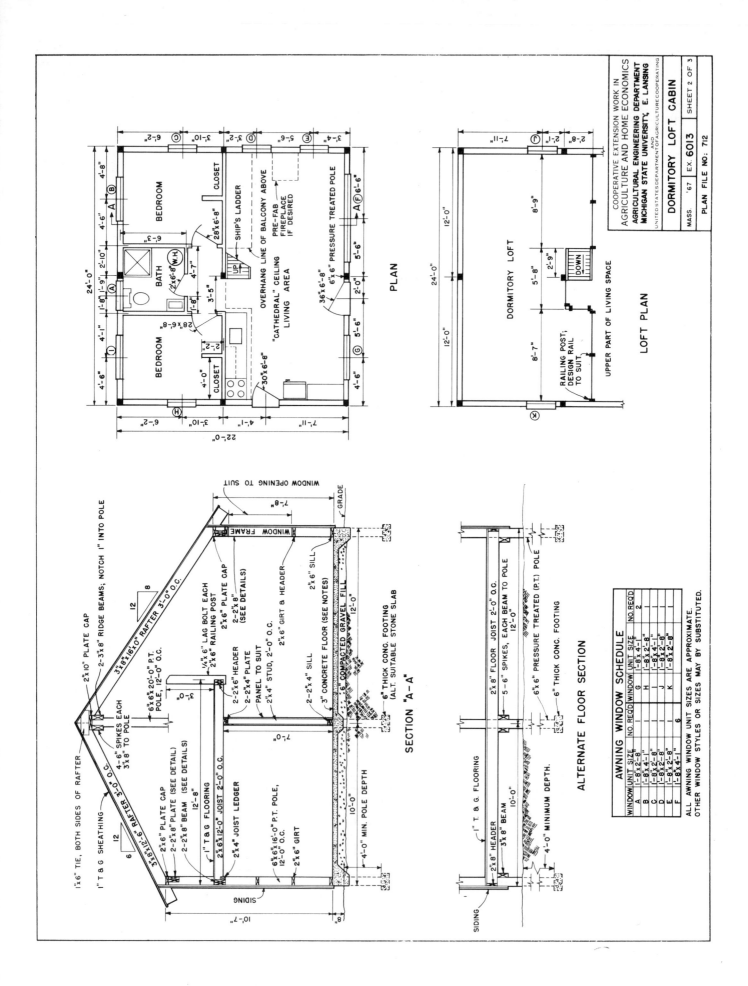

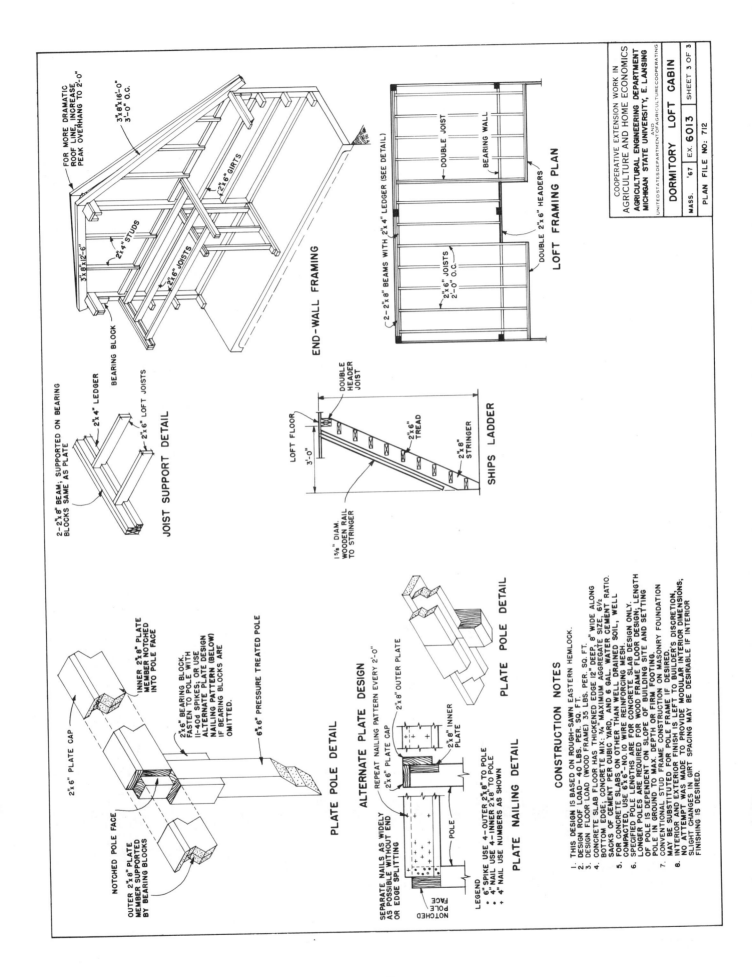

FOR MORE DRAMATIC ROOF LINE, INCREASE PEAK OVERHANG TO 2'-0"

3"x8"x16'-0" 3'-0" O.C.

2"x6" GIRTS

3"x8"x12'-6"

2"x4" STUDS

2"x6" JOISTS

2"x6" JOISTS

BEARING BLOCK

END-WALL FRAMING

DOUBLE JOIST

BEARING WALL

2-2"x8" BEAMS WITH 2"x4" LEDGER (SEE DETAIL)

2"x6" JOISTS 2'-0" O.C.

DOUBLE 2"x6" HEADERS

LOFT FRAMING PLAN

2-2"x8" BEAM; SUPPORTED ON BEARING BLOCKS SAME AS PLATE

2"x4" LEDGER

2"x6" LOFT JOISTS

JOIST SUPPORT DETAIL

DOUBLE HEADER JOIST

LOFT FLOOR

3'-0"

2"x6" TREAD

2"x8" STRINGER

1 5/8" DIAM. WOODEN RAIL TO STRINGER

SHIPS LADDER

2"x6" PLATE CAP

INNER 2"x8" PLATE MEMBER NOTCHED INTO POLE FACE

2"x6" BEARING BLOCK. FASTEN TO POLE WITH 11-40d SPIKES; OR USE ALTERNATE PLATE DESIGN NAILING PATTERN (BELOW) IF BEARING BLOCKS ARE OMITTED.

6"x6" PRESSURE TREATED POLE

NOTCHED POLE FACE

OUTER 2"x8" PLATE MEMBER SUPPORTED BY BEARING BLOCKS

PLATE POLE DETAIL

PLATE POLE DETAIL

REPEAT NAILING PATTERN EVERY 2'-0"

2"x6" PLATE CAP

2"x8" OUTER PLATE

2"x8" INNER PLATE

POLE

ALTERNATE PLATE DESIGN

2"x6" PLATE CAP

2"x8" OUTER 2"x8" TO POLE

NOTCHED POLE FACE

SEPARATE NAILS AS WIDELY AS POSSIBLE WITHOUT END OR EDGE SPLITTING

LEGEND
• 6" SPIKE USE 4—OUTER 2"x8" TO POLE
+ 4" NAIL USE 4—INNER 2"x8" TO POLE
+ 4" NAIL USE NUMBERS AS SHOWN

PLATE NAILING DETAIL

CONSTRUCTION NOTES

1. THIS DESIGN IS BASED ON ROUGH-SAWN EASTERN HEMLOCK.
2. DESIGN ROOF LOAD—40 LBS. PER. SQ. FT.
3. DESIGN FLOOR LOAD (WOOD FRAME) 35 LBS. PER. SQ. FT.
4. CONCRETE SLAB FLOOR HAS THICKENED EDGE 12" DEEP, 8" WIDE ALONG BOTTOM EDGE; CONCRETE MIX: 3/4" MAXIMUM AGGREGATE SIZE, 6 1/2 SACKS OF CEMENT PER CUBIC YARD, AND 6 GAL. WATER CEMENT RATIO.
5. FOR CONCRETE SLABS ON OTHER THAN WELL DRAINED SOIL, WELL COMPACTED, USE 6"x6"—NO.10 WIRE REINFORCING MESH.
6. SPECIFIED POLE LENGTHS ARE FOR CONCRETE SLAB DESIGN ONLY. LONGER POLES ARE REQUIRED FOR WOOD FRAME FLOOR DESIGN; LENGTH OF POLE IS DEPENDENT ON SLOPE OF BUILDING SITE AND SETTING OF POLE IN GROUND TO MAX. DEPTH OR FIRM FOOTING.
7. CONVENTIONAL STUD FRAME CONSTRUCTION ON MASONRY FOUNDATION MAY BE SUBSTITUTED FOR POLE FRAME IF DESIRED.
8. INTERIOR AND EXTERIOR FINISH IS LEFT TO BUILDER'S DISCRETION. NO ATTEMPT WAS MADE TO PROVIDE MODULAR INTERIOR DIMENSIONS; SLIGHT CHANGES IN GIRT SPACING MAY BE DESIRABLE IF INTERIOR FINISHING IS DESIRED.

COOPERATIVE EXTENSION WORK IN AGRICULTURE AND HOME ECONOMICS
AGRICULTURAL ENGINEERING DEPARTMENT
MICHIGAN STATE UNIVERSITY, E. LANSING
AND
UNITED STATES DEPARTMENT OF AGRICULTURE COOPERATING

DORMITORY LOFT CABIN

MASS. '67 EX. 6013 SHEET 3 OF 3

PLAN FILE NO: 712

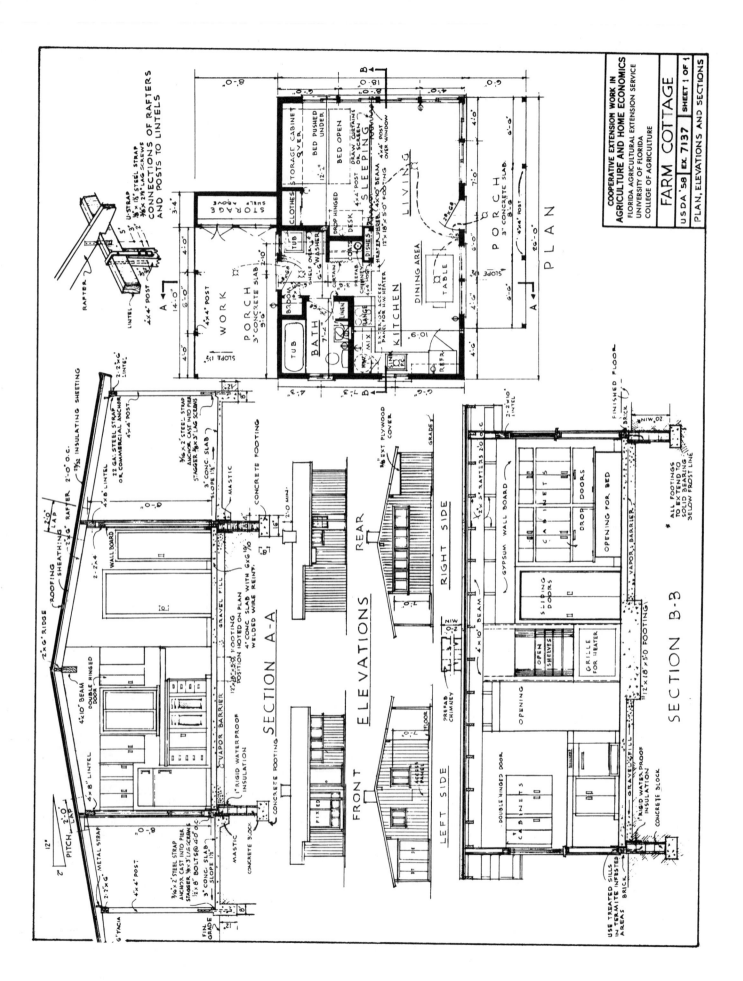

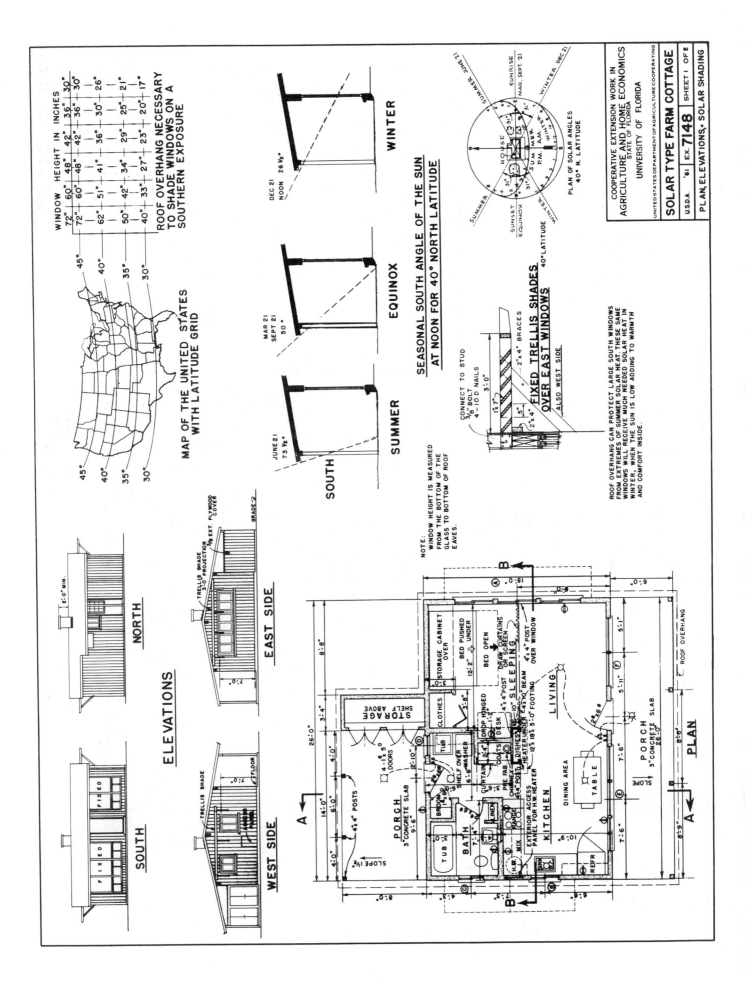

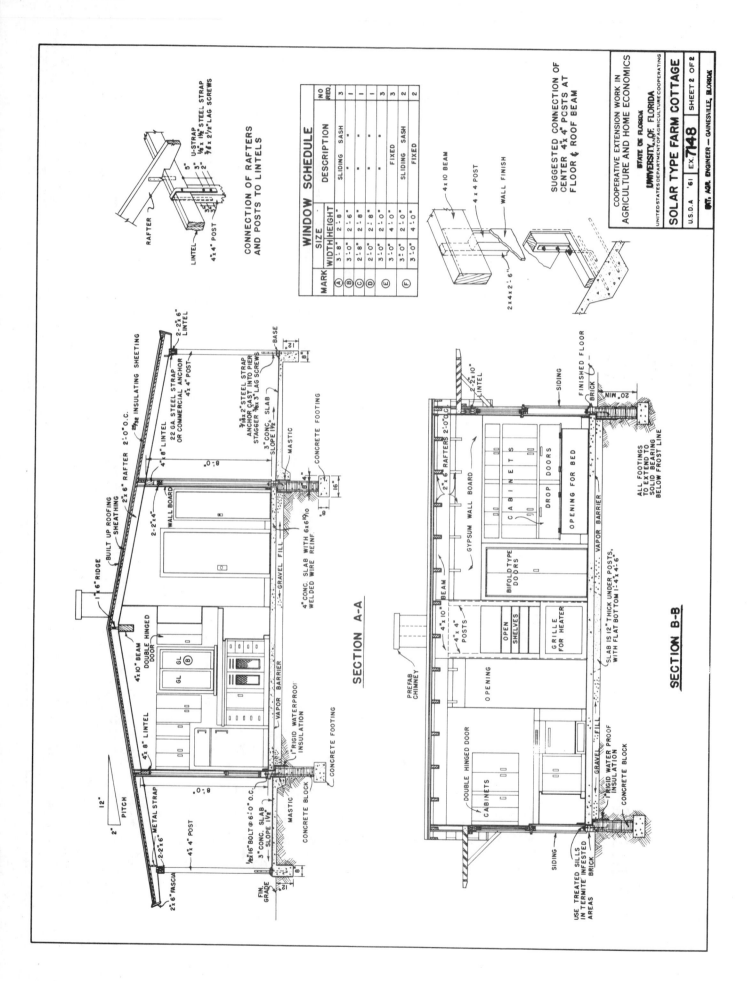

CONNECTION OF RAFTERS
AND POSTS TO LINTELS

WINDOW SCHEDULE

MARK	SIZE WIDTH	HEIGHT	DESCRIPTION		NO REQ'D.
A	3'-8"	2'-8"	SLIDING	SASH	3
B	3'-0"	2'-6"	"	"	1
C	2'-8"	2'-8"	"	"	1
D	2'-0"	2'-0"	"	"	1
E	3'-0"	4'-0"	FIXED		3
F	3'-0"	2'-0"	SLIDING	SASH	2
	3'-0"	4'-0"	FIXED		2

SUGGESTED CONNECTION OF
CENTER 4"x 4" POSTS AT
FLOOR & ROOF BEAM

SECTION A-A

SECTION B-B

COOPERATIVE EXTENSION WORK IN
AGRICULTURE AND HOME ECONOMICS
STATE OF FLORIDA
UNIVERSITY OF FLORIDA
UNITED STATES DEPARTMENT OF AGRICULTURE COOPERATING

SOLAR TYPE FARM COTTAGE

U.S.D.A. '61 | EX. 7148 | SHEET 2 OF 2

EXT. AGR. ENGINEER — GAINESVILLE, FLORIDA

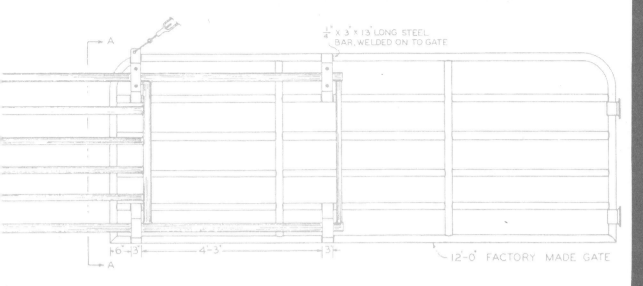

¼" X 3" X 13" LONG STEEL BAR, WELDED ON TO GATE

12'-0" FACTORY MADE GATE

FENCES AND GATES

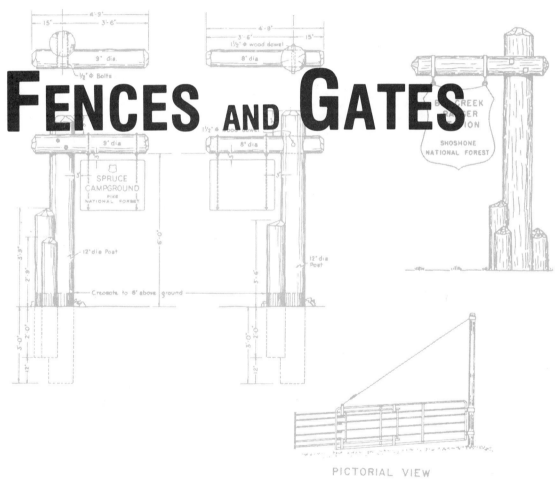

PICTORIAL VIEW

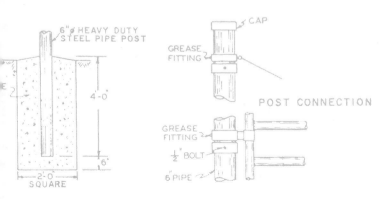

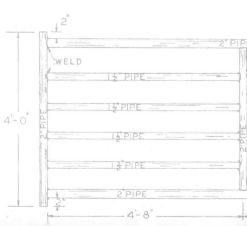

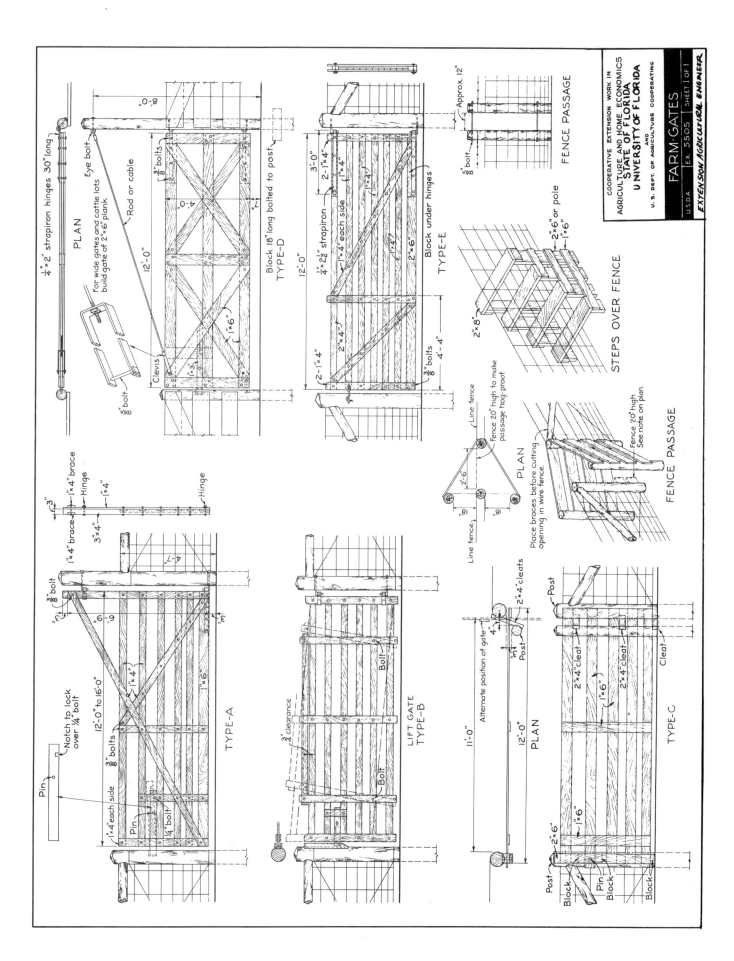

COOPERATIVE EXTENSION WORK IN
AGRICULTURE AND HOME ECONOMICS
STATE OF FLORIDA
UNIVERSITY OF FLORIDA
AND
U.S. DEPT. OF AGRICULTURE COOPERATING

FARM·GATES

U.S.D.A. | EX. 5505 | SHEET 1 OF 1

EXTENSION AGRICULTURAL ENGINEER.

PLAN

FENCE PASSAGE

$\frac{1}{4}$"×2" strapiron hinges 30" long

Eye bolt

Rod or cable

For wide gates and cattle lots build gate of 2"×6" plank.

Clevis

$\frac{5}{8}$" bolt

12'-0"

8'-0"

$\frac{3}{8}$" bolts

Block 18" long bolted to post
TYPE-D

4'-0"

12'-0"

Approx. 12"

$\frac{5}{8}$" bolt

3'-0"

2-1"×4"

$\frac{1}{4}$"×2$\frac{1}{2}$" strapiron

1"×4" each side

1"×4"

1"×4"

2"×6"

Block under hinges

TYPE-E

2"×4"

1"×6"

2-1"×4"

$\frac{3}{8}$" bolts

4'-4"

1"×3"

STEPS OVER FENCE

2"×8"

2"×6" or pole

1"×6"

Line fence

Fence 20" high to make passage hog-proof

2'-6"

18"

18"

PLAN

Place braces before cutting opening in wire fence.

Line fence

Fence 20" high.
See note on plan.

FENCE PASSAGE

TYPE-A

1"×4" brace

Hinge

1"×4"

1"×4" brace

3"×4"

Hinge

3"

4'-7"

$\frac{3}{8}$" bolt

9'-0" to 9'-6"

1"×4"

Notch to lock over $\frac{1}{4}$" bolt

Pin

1"×4" each side

$\frac{3}{8}$" bolts

Pin

$\frac{1}{4}$" bolt

12'-0" to 16'-0"

LIFT GATE
TYPE-B

$\frac{3}{4}$" clearance

Bolt

1"×6"

Bolt

Alternate position of gate

4"

Post

Post

2"×4" cleats

11'-0"

12'-0"

PLAN

TYPE-C

Post

2"×4" cleat

1"×6"

2"×4" cleat

Cleat

2"×6"

1"×6"

Post

Block
Pin
Block

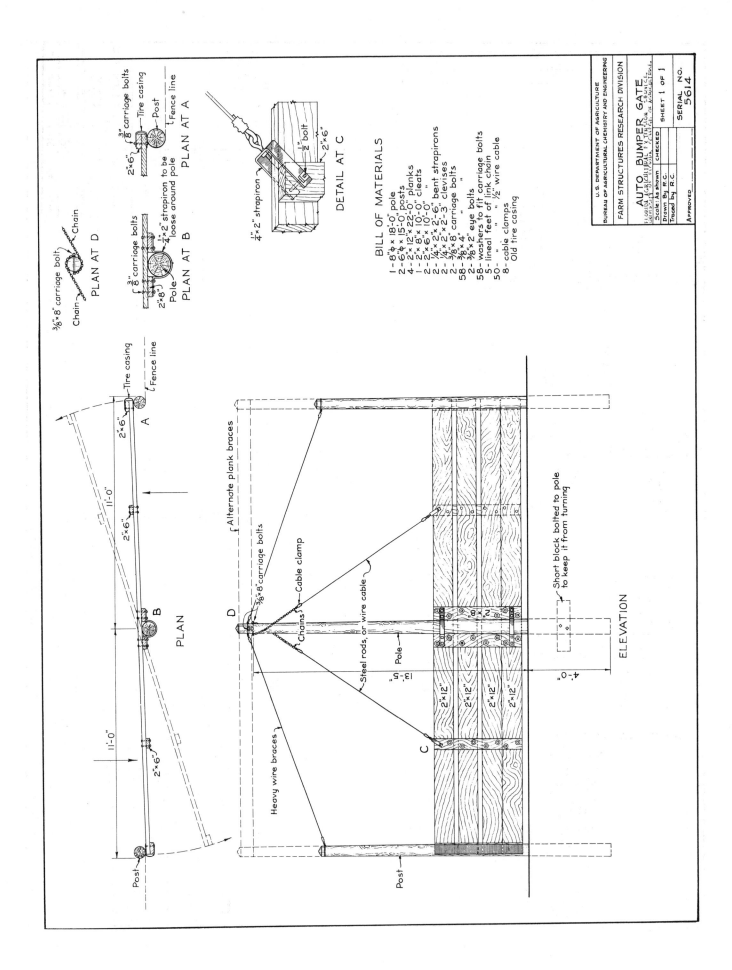

PLAN AT A

PLAN AT D

PLAN AT B

DETAIL AT C

BILL OF MATERIALS

1— 8"Φ x 18'-0" pole
2— 6"Φ x 15'-0" posts
4— 2"x 12"x 22'-0" planks
1— 2"x 8"x 10'-0" cleats
2— 2"x 6"x 10'-0"
2— ¼"x 2"x 2'-6" bent strapirons
2— ¼"x 2"x 2'-3" clevises
2— ⅜"x 8" carriage bolts
58— ⅜"x 4"
2— ⅜"x 2" eye bolts
58— washers to fit carriage bolts
5— lineal feet of link chain
50— ½" wire cable
8— cable clamps
Old tire casing

PLAN

ELEVATION

U.S. DEPARTMENT OF AGRICULTURE
BUREAU OF AGRICULTURAL CHEMISTRY AND ENGINEERING
FARM STRUCTURES RESEARCH DIVISION

AUTO BUMPER GATE
FLORIDA AGRICULTURAL EXTENSION SERVICE
UNIVERSITY OF FLORIDA, COLLEGE OF AGRICULTURAL

Scale: As shown   CHECKED   SHEET 1 of 1
Drawn By R.C.
Traced by R.C.
Approved _____   SERIAL NO. 5614.

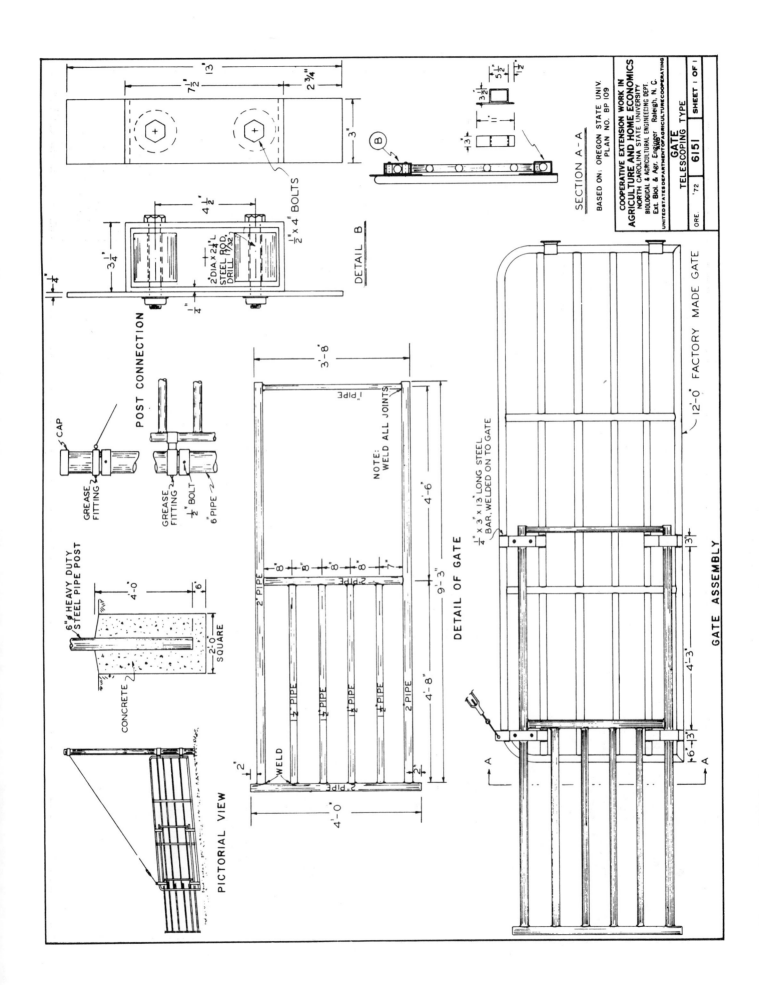

13"
7½"
2¾"
3"

¼ x 4" BOLTS

DETAIL B

3¼"
4½"
¼"
¼"

2"DIA x 2¼"L STEEL ROD, DRILL ¹³/₃₂"

POST CONNECTION

CAP
GREASE FITTING

GREASE FITTING
½" BOLT
6"PIPE

6"∅ HEAVY DUTY STEEL PIPE POST

4'-0"
6"
CONCRETE
2'-0" SQUARE

PICTORIAL VIEW

5½"
1½"
3½"
11"
3"

SECTION A-A

BASED ON: OREGON STATE UNIV.
PLAN NO. BP 109

COOPERATIVE EXTENSION WORK IN
AGRICULTURE AND HOME ECONOMICS
NORTH CAROLINA STATE UNIVERSITY
BIOLOGICAL & AGRICULTURAL ENGINEERING DEPT.
Ext. Biol. & Agr. Engineer   Raleigh, N. C.
UNITED STATES DEPARTMENT OF AGRICULTURE COOPERATING

GATE
TELESCOPING TYPE

ORE.   '72   6151   SHEET 1 OF 1

3'-8"
1"PIPE

NOTE: WELD ALL JOINTS

4'-6"
9'-3"
8" 8" 8" 8" 7"

2" PIPE
1½ PIPE
1½ PIPE
1½ PIPE
1½ PIPE
2 PIPE
2 PIPE

4'-8"

2"
2"
WELD
2 PIPE
4'-0"

DETAIL OF GATE

12'-0" FACTORY MADE GATE

¼" x 3" x 13" LONG STEEL BAR, WELDED ON TO GATE

3"
4'-3"
6'-3"
A
A

GATE ASSEMBLY

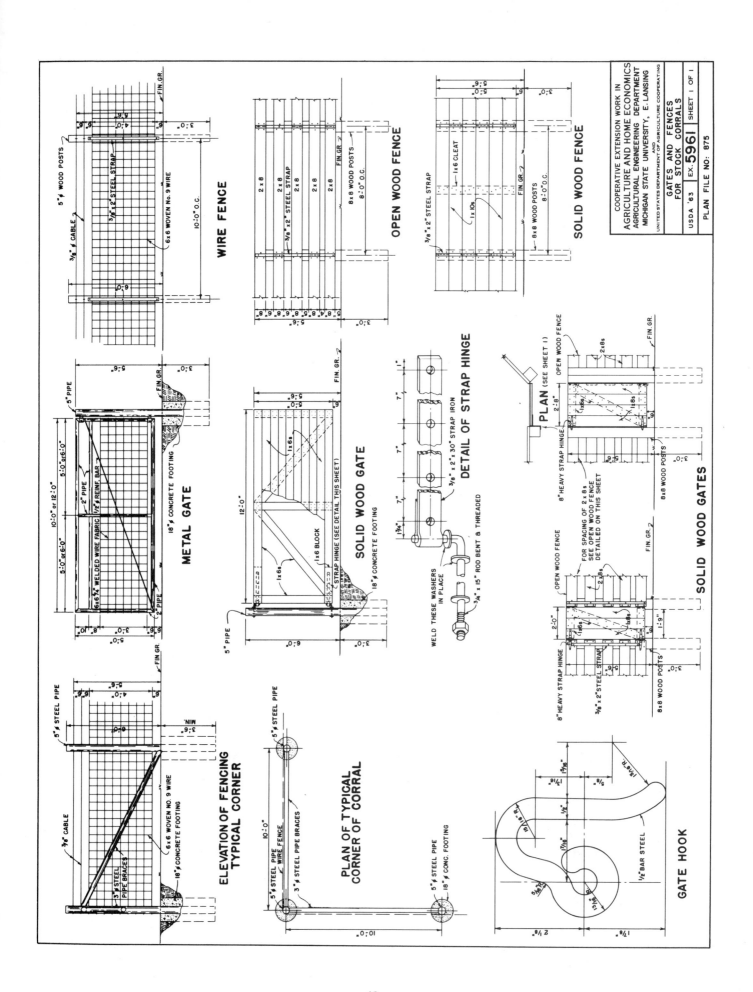

WIRE FENCE

OPEN WOOD FENCE

SOLID WOOD FENCE

METAL GATE

SOLID WOOD GATE

DETAIL OF STRAP HINGE

PLAN (SEE SHEET 1)

SOLID WOOD GATES

ELEVATION OF FENCING TYPICAL CORNER

PLAN OF TYPICAL CORNER OF CORRAL

GATE HOOK

COOPERATIVE EXTENSION WORK IN
AGRICULTURE AND HOME ECONOMICS
AGRICULTURAL ENGINEERING DEPARTMENT
MICHIGAN STATE UNIVERSITY, E. LANSING
AND
UNITED STATES DEPARTMENT OF AGRICULTURE COOPERATING

GATES AND FENCES
FOR STOCK CORRALS

USDA '63 | EX. 5961 | SHEET 1 OF 1

PLAN FILE NO: 875

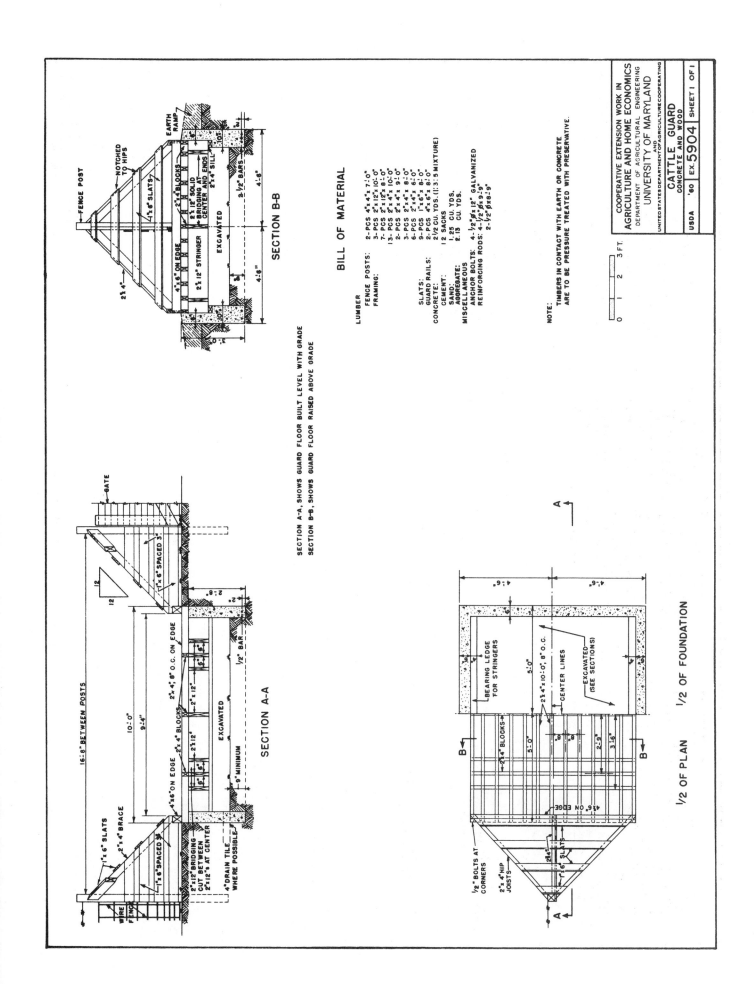

SECTION B-B

SECTION A-A

SECTION A-A, SHOWS GUARD FLOOR BUILT LEVEL WITH GRADE
SECTION B-B, SHOWS GUARD FLOOR RAISED ABOVE GRADE

1/2 OF PLAN   1/2 OF FOUNDATION

BILL OF MATERIAL

LUMBER

FENCE POSTS:	2-PCS 4"x4"x 7'-0"
FRAMING:	3-PCS 2"x12"x10'-0"
	7-PCS 2"x12"x 8'-0"
	13-PCS 2"x4"x10'-0"
	2-PCS 2"x4"x 9'-0"
	3-PCS 2"x4"x 8'-0"
	6-PCS 2"x4"x 6'-0"
	9-PCS 1"x6"x 8'-0"
SLATS:	9-PCS 4"x6"x 8'-0"
GUARD RAILS:	2 1/2 CU. YDS.(1:3:5 MIXTURE)
CONCRETE:	
CEMENT:	12 SACKS
SAND:	1.25 CU. YDS.
AGGREGATE:	2.13 CU. YDS.
MISCELLANEOUS	
ANCHOR BOLTS:	4-1/2"∅x12" GALVANIZED
REINFORCING RODS:	4-1/2"∅x9'-9"
	2-1/2"∅x8'-9"

NOTE:

TIMBERS IN CONTACT WITH EARTH OR CONCRETE
ARE TO BE PRESSURE TREATED WITH PRESERVATIVE.

0 1 2 3 FT.

COOPERATIVE EXTENSION WORK IN
AGRICULTURE AND HOME ECONOMICS
DEPARTMENT OF AGRICULTURAL ENGINEERING
UNIVERSITY OF MARYLAND
AND
UNITED STATES DEPARTMENT OF AGRICULTURE COOPERATING

CATTLE GUARD
CONCRETE AND WOOD

| USDA | '60 | EX.5904 | SHEET 1 OF 1 |

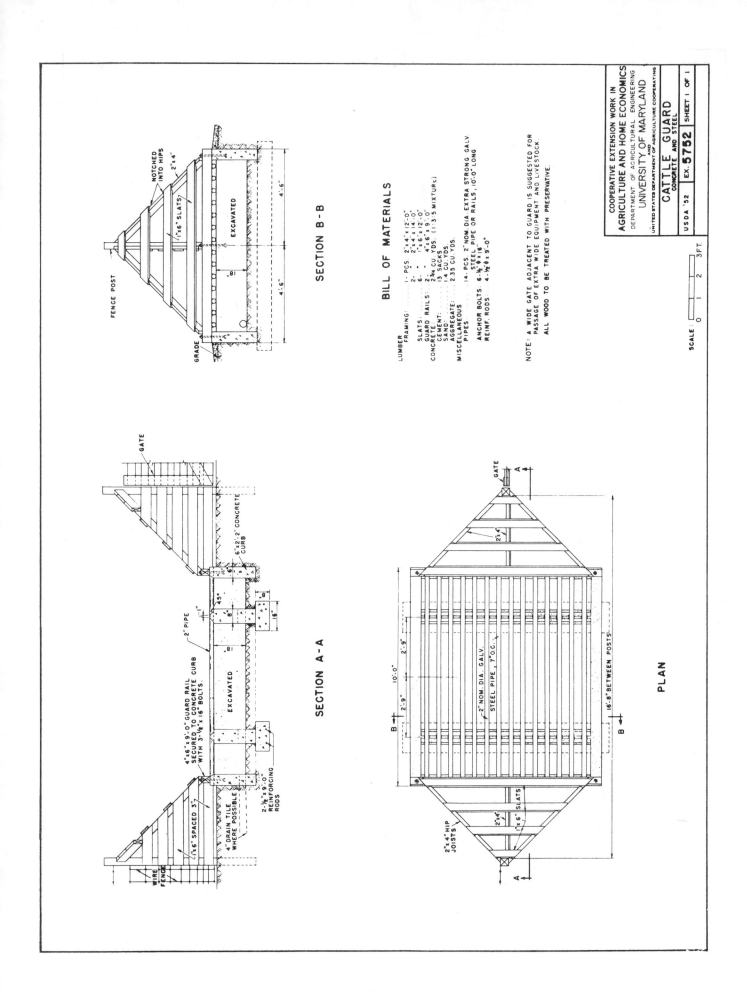

SECTION B - B

FENCE POST

NOTCHED INTO HIPS

2"x 4"

1"x 6" SLATS

EXCAVATED

GRADE

4'-6"   4'-6"

18"

BILL OF MATERIALS

LUMBER
  FRAMING: 1 - PCS. 2"x 4"x 12'-0"
  SLATS: 2 -   -   2"x 4"x 12'-0"
  GUARD RAILS: 6 -   -   1"x 6"x 12'-0"
CONCRETE   2¾ CU. YDS. (1-3-5 MIXTURE)
  CEMENT: 13 SACKS
  SAND: 1.4 CU. YDS.
  AGGREGATE: 2.35 CU. YDS.
MISCELLANEOUS
  PIPES: 14 - PCS. 2" NOM. DIA. EXTRA STRONG GALV.
                       STEEL PIPE OR RAILS, 10'-0" LONG
  ANCHOR BOLTS: 6 - ½"∅ x 16"
  REINF. RODS: 4 - ½"∅ x 9'-0"

NOTE: A WIDE GATE ADJACENT TO GUARD IS SUGGESTED FOR
      PASSAGE OF EXTRA WIDE EQUIPMENT AND LIVESTOCK.
      ALL WOOD TO BE TREATED WITH PRESERVATIVE.

SECTION A - A

GATE

6"x 2'-2" CONCRETE CURB

4"x 6"x 9'-0" GUARD RAIL
SECURED TO CONCRETE CURB
WITH 3-½"x 16" BOLTS.

2" PIPE

45°

6"   8"   1"

8"   18"   16"

EXCAVATED

2-½"x 9'-0"
REINFORCING
RODS

4" DRAIN TILE
WHERE POSSIBLE

1"x 6" SPACED 3"

WIRE FENCE

PLAN

GATE

2"x 4"

2'-9" 2'-9"

10'-0"

2" NOM. DIA. GALV.
STEEL PIPE, 7" O.C.

16'-8" BETWEEN POSTS

2"x 4" HIP
JOISTS

1"x 6" SLATS

2"x 4"

COOPERATIVE EXTENSION WORK IN
AGRICULTURE AND HOME ECONOMICS
DEPARTMENT OF AGRICULTURAL ENGINEERING
UNIVERSITY OF MARYLAND
AND
UNITED STATES DEPARTMENT OF AGRICULTURE COOPERATING

CATTLE GUARD
CONCRETE AND STEEL

USDA '52   EX. 5752   SHEET 1 OF 1

SCALE: 0   1   2   3FT

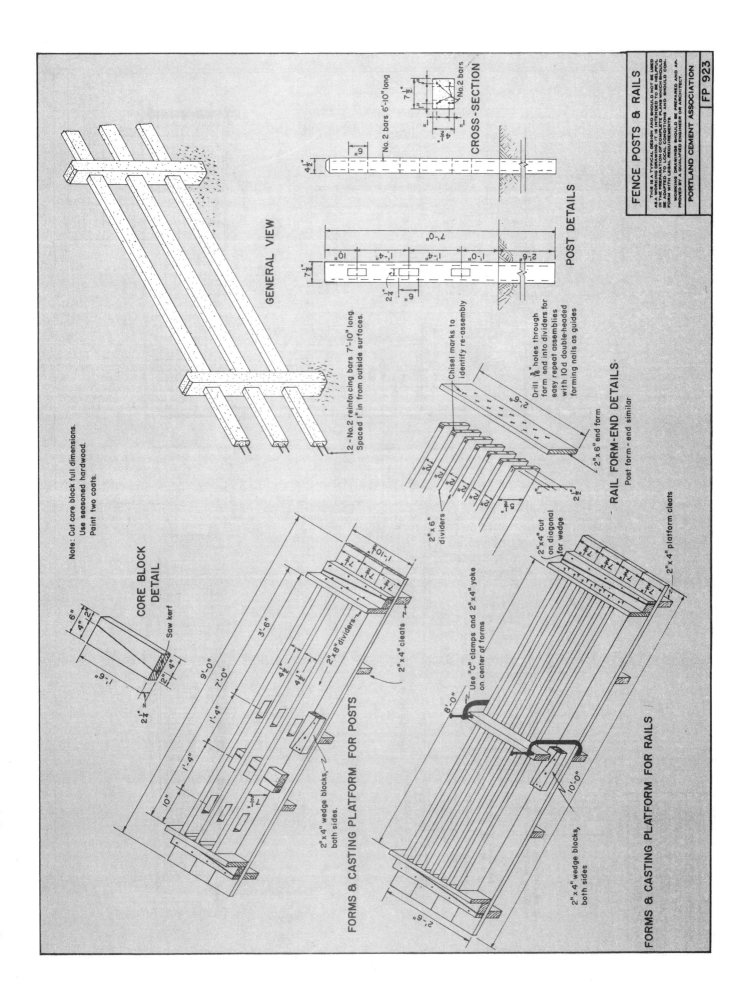

GENERAL VIEW

Note: Cut core block full dimensions.
Use seasoned hardwood.
Paint two coats.

2 - No.2 reinforcing bars 7'-10" long.
Spaced 1" in from outside surfaces.

CORE BLOCK DETAIL

Saw kerf

FORMS & CASTING PLATFORM FOR POSTS

2" x 4" wedge blocks, both sides.

2" x 8" dividers

2" x 4" cleats

FORMS & CASTING PLATFORM FOR RAILS

Use "C" clamps and 2" x 4" yoke on center of forms

2" x 4" wedge blocks, both sides

2" x 4" cut on diagonal for wedge

2" x 4" platform cleats

RAIL FORM-END DETAILS
Post form - end similar

2" x 6" dividers

Chisel marks to identify re-assembly

Drill ³⁄₁₆" holes through form end into dividers for easy repeat assemblies with 10d double-headed forming nails as guides

2"x 6" end form

POST DETAILS

No.2 bars 6'-10" long

CROSS-SECTION

No.2 bars

FENCE POSTS & RAILS

THIS IS A TYPICAL DESIGN AND SHOULD NOT BE USED AS A WORKING DRAWING. IT IS INTENDED TO BE HELPFUL IN THE PREPARATION OF COMPLETE PLANS WHICH SHOULD BE ADAPTED TO LOCAL CONDITIONS AND SHOULD CON-FORM WITH LEGAL REQUIREMENTS.
WORKING DRAWINGS SHOULD BE PREPARED AND AP-PROVED BY A QUALIFIED ENGINEER OR ARCHITECT.

PORTLAND CEMENT ASSOCIATION

FP 923

21

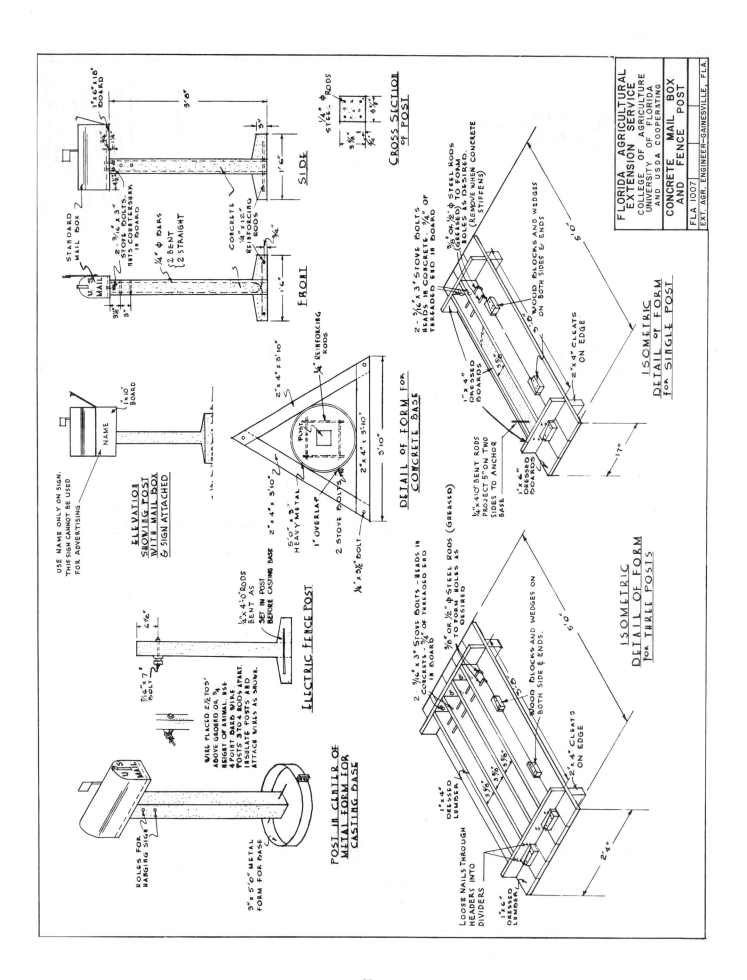

FLORIDA AGRICULTURAL
EXTENSION SERVICE
COLLEGE OF AGRICULTURE
UNIVERSITY OF FLORIDA
AND USDA COOPERATING

CONCRETE MAIL BOX
AND FENCE POST

FLA 1007

EXT. AGR. ENGINEER-GAINESVILLE, FLA.

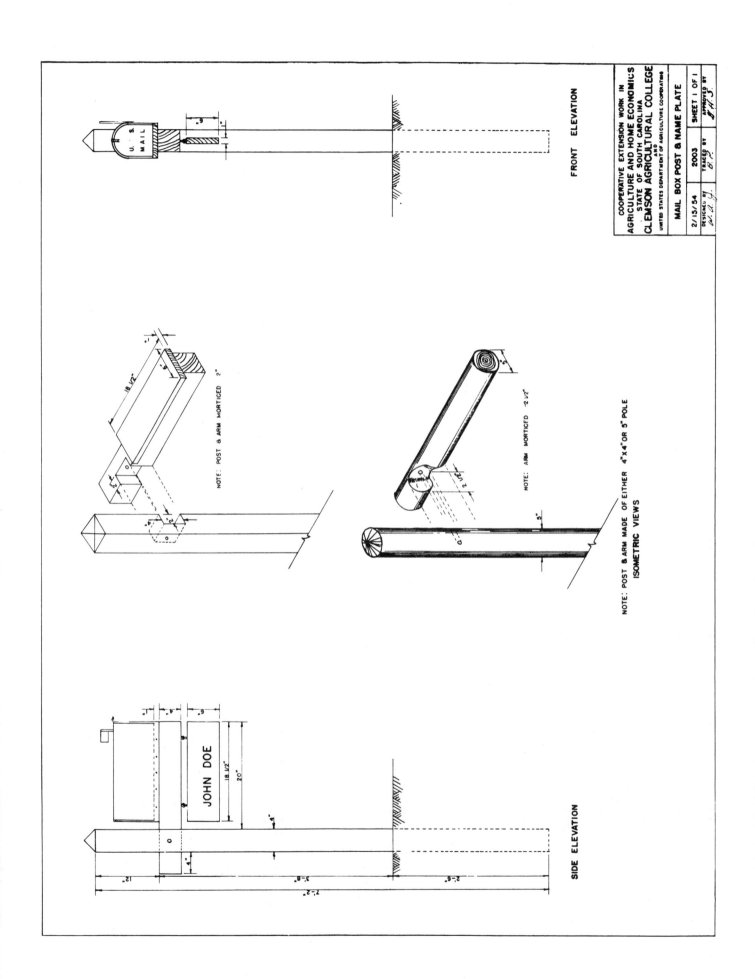

FRONT ELEVATION

SIDE ELEVATION

ISOMETRIC VIEWS

JOHN DOE

U. S. MAIL

NOTE: POST & ARM MORTICED 2"

NOTE: ARM MORTICED 2 1/2"

NOTE: POST & ARM MADE OF EITHER 4"x4" OR 5" POLE

COOPERATIVE EXTENSION WORK IN
AGRICULTURE AND HOME ECONOMICS
STATE OF SOUTH CAROLINA
CLEMSON AGRICULTURAL COLLEGE
AND
UNITED STATES DEPARTMENT OF AGRICULTURE COOPERATING

MAIL BOX POST & NAME PLATE

2/15/54	2003	SHEET 1 OF 1
DESIGNED BY	TRACED BY	APPROVED BY

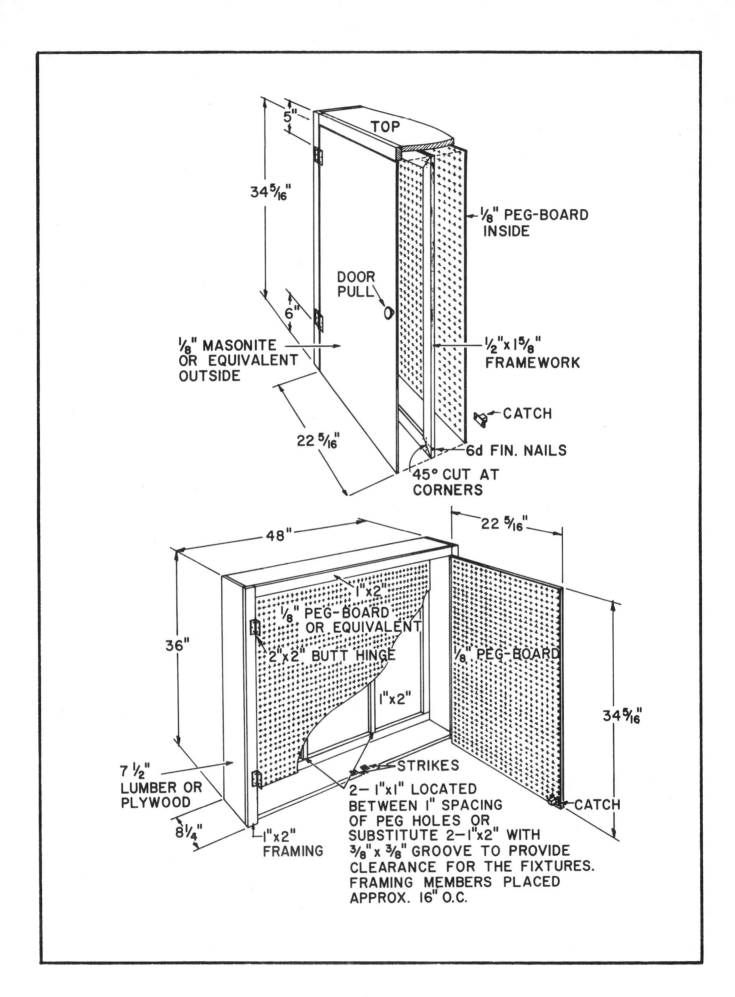

TOP

5"

34 5/16"

6"

1/8" MASONITE
OR EQUIVALENT
OUTSIDE

22 5/16"

DOOR
PULL

1/8" PEG-BOARD
INSIDE

1/2" x 1 5/8"
FRAMEWORK

CATCH

6d FIN. NAILS

45° CUT AT
CORNERS

48"

22 5/16"

1" x 2"

1/8" PEG-BOARD
OR EQUIVALENT

2" x 2" BUTT HINGE

1/8" PEG-BOARD

36"

1" x 2"

34 5/16"

7 1/2"
LUMBER OR
PLYWOOD

8 1/4"

1" x 2"
FRAMING

STRIKES

2 – 1" x 1" LOCATED
BETWEEN 1" SPACING
OF PEG HOLES OR
SUBSTITUTE 2 – 1" x 2" WITH
3/8" x 3/8" GROOVE TO PROVIDE
CLEARANCE FOR THE FIXTURES.
FRAMING MEMBERS PLACED
APPROX. 16" O.C.

CATCH

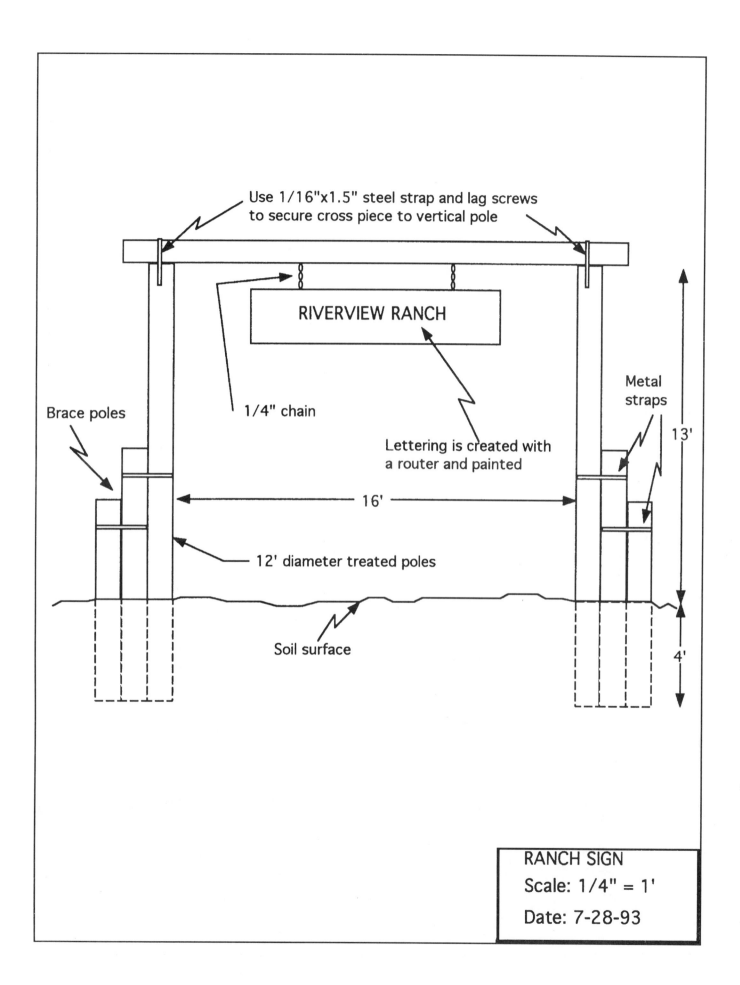

Use 1/16"x1.5" steel strap and lag screws
to secure cross piece to vertical pole

RIVERVIEW RANCH

Brace poles

1/4" chain

Metal
straps

13'

Lettering is created with
a router and painted

16'

12' diameter treated poles

Soil surface

4'

RANCH SIGN
Scale: 1/4" = 1'
Date: 7-28-93

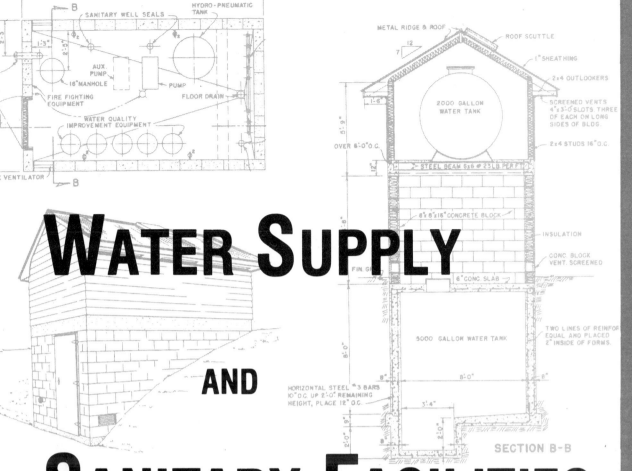

WATER SUPPLY

AND

SANITARY FACILITIES

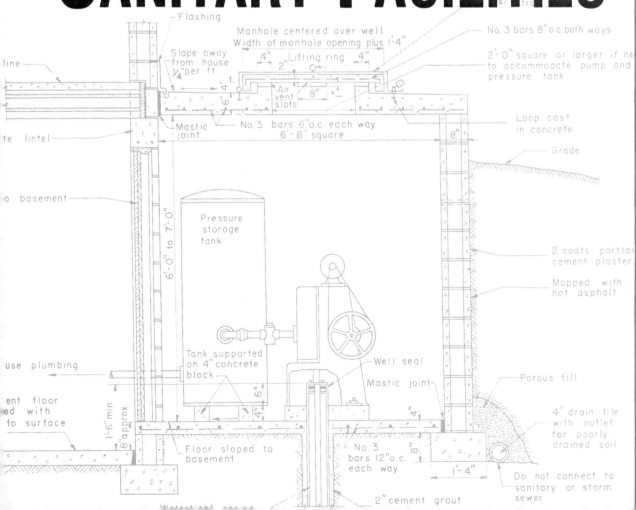

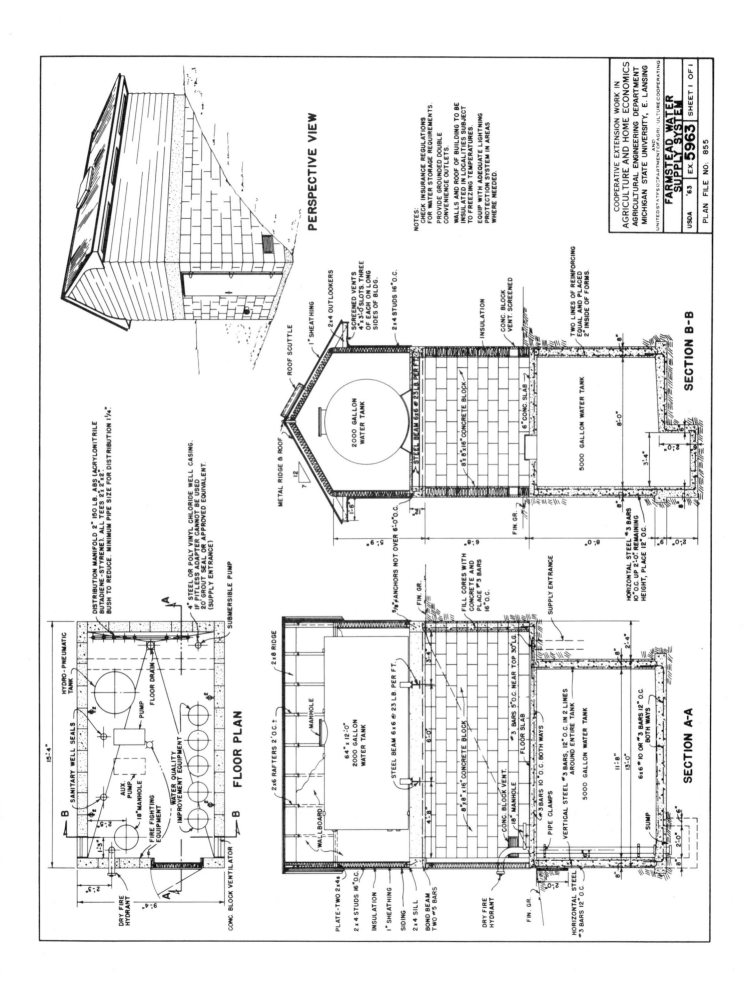

PERSPECTIVE VIEW

NOTES:
CHECK INSURANCE REGULATIONS
FOR WATER STORAGE REQUIREMENTS.
PROVIDE GROUNDED DOUBLE
CONVENIENCE OUTLETS.

WALLS AND ROOF OF BUILDING TO BE
INSULATED IN LOCALITIES SUBJECT
TO FREEZING TEMPERATURES.

EQUIP WITH ADEQUATE LIGHTNING
PROTECTION SYSTEM IN AREAS
WHERE NEEDED.

COOPERATIVE EXTENSION WORK IN
AGRICULTURE AND HOME ECONOMICS
AGRICULTURAL ENGINEERING DEPARTMENT
MICHIGAN STATE UNIVERSITY, E. LANSING
AND
UNITED STATES DEPARTMENT OF AGRICULTURE COOPERATING

FARMSTEAD WATER
SUPPLY SYSTEM

USDA   '63   EX. 5963   SHEET I OF I

PLAN FILE NO. 855

SECTION B-B

ROOF SCUTTLE
1" SHEATHING
2×4 OUTLOOKERS
SCREENED VENTS
4"×3'-0 SLOTS. THREE
OF EACH ON LONG
SIDES OF BLDG.
2×4 STUDS 16" O.C.
METAL RIDGE & ROOF
2000 GALLON
WATER TANK
STEEL BEAM 6×6 @ 23 LB. PER FT.
8"× 8"×16" CONCRETE BLOCK
INSULATION
CONC. BLOCK
VENT. SCREENED
6" CONC. SLAB
TWO LINES OF REINFORCING
EQUAL AND PLACED
2" INSIDE OF FORMS.
5000 GALLON WATER TANK
FIN. GR.
SUPPLY ENTRANCE
HORIZONTAL STEEL #3 BARS
10" O.C. UP 2'-0" REMAINING
HEIGHT, PLACE 12" O.C.

12
7

SECTION A-A

DISTRIBUTION MANIFOLD 2" 150 LB. ABS (ACRYLONITRILE
BUTADIENE-STYRENE). ALL TEES 2"×2"×12".
BUSH TO REDUCE. MINIMUM PIPE SIZE FOR DISTRIBUTION 1¼".

4" STEEL OR POLY VINYL CHLORIDE WELL CASING.
IF PITLESS ADAPTER CANNOT BE USED
20 GROUT SEAL OR APPROVED EQUIVALENT.
(SUPPLY ENTRANCE)

SUBMERSIBLE PUMP

FLOOR PLAN

15'-4"

HYDRO - PNEUMATIC
TANK
SANITARY WELL SEALS
PUMP
FLOOR DRAIN
AUX.
PUMP
18" MANHOLE
FIRE FIGHTING
EQUIPMENT
WATER QUALITY
IMPROVEMENT EQUIPMENT
CONC. BLOCK VENTILATOR
DRY FIRE
HYDRANT

PLATE-TWO 2×4s
2×6 RAFTERS 2' O.C.±
2×8 RIDGE
MANHOLE
64"× 12'-0"
2000 GALLON
WATER TANK
STEEL BEAM 6×6 @ 23 LB. PER FT.
8"× 8"×16" CONCRETE BLOCK
WALLBOARD
CONC. BLOCK VENT.
18" MANHOLE
PIPE CLAMPS
#3 BARS 5"O.C. NEAR TOP 30" LG.
#3 BARS 10" O.C. BOTH WAYS
FLOOR SLAB
VERTICAL STEEL #3 BARS, 12" O.C. IN 2 LINES
AROUND ENTIRE TANK
5000 GALLON WATER TANK
6×6 #10 OR #3 BARS 12" O.C.
BOTH WAYS
SUMP
DRY FIRE
HYDRANT
FIN. GR.
HORIZONTAL STEEL
#3 BARS 12" O.C.
SUPPLY ENTRANCE

2×4 STUDS 16" O.C.
INSULATION
1" SHEATHING
SIDING
SILL
BOND BEAM
TWO #5 BARS

11'-8"
13'-0"
6'-0"
4'-8"
3'-4"
2'-4"
8"
2'-0"
8"
6"

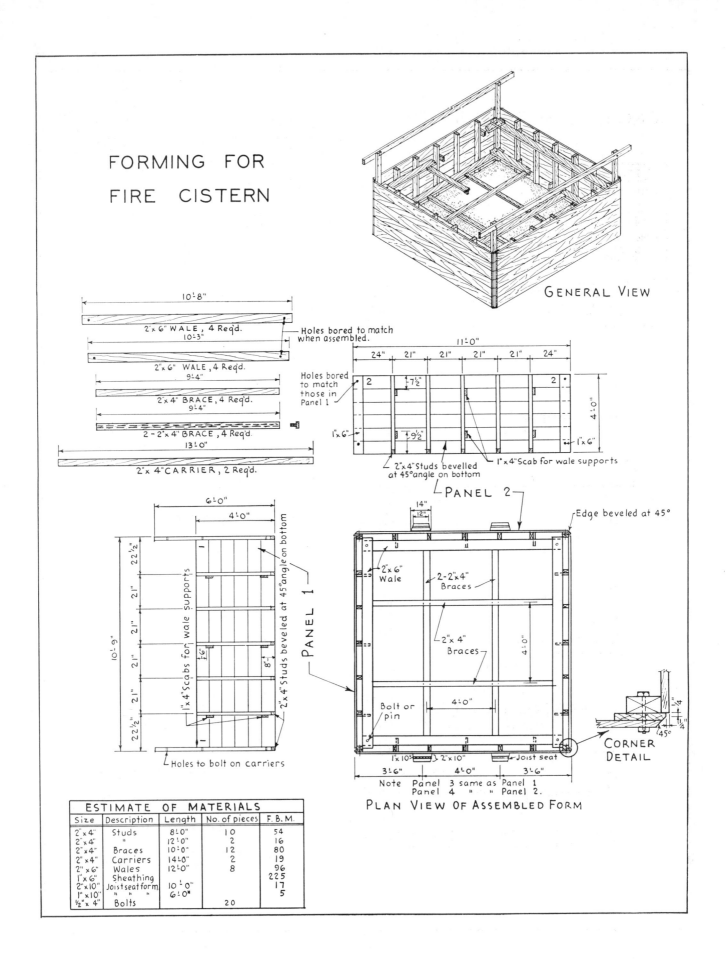

FORMING FOR FIRE CISTERN

GENERAL VIEW

10'-8"
2"x6" WALE, 4 Req'd.

10'-3"
2"x6" WALE, 4 Req'd.

Holes bored to match when assembled.

9'-4"
2"x4" BRACE, 4 Req'd.

9'-4"
2-2"x4" BRACE, 4 Req'd.

13'-0"
2"x4" CARRIER, 2 Req'd.

Holes bored to match those in Panel 1

11'-0"
24" 21" 21" 21" 21" 24"

4'-0"

7½"

9½"

1"x6"

2"x4" Studs bevelled at 45° angle on bottom

1"x4" Scab for wale supports

1"x6"

PANEL 2

6'-0"
4'-0"

22½" 21" 21" 21" 21" 22½"

10'-9"

1"x4" Scabs for wale supports

8'

2"x4" Studs beveled at 45° angle on bottom

Holes to bolt on carriers

PANEL 1

Edge beveled at 45°

14"
12"

2"x6" Wale

2-2"x4" Braces

2"x4" Braces

4'-0"

Bolt or pin

4'-0"

1"x10"   2"x10"   Joist seat

3'-6"   4'-0"   3'-6"

Note Panel 3 same as Panel 1
Panel 4 " " Panel 2.

PLAN VIEW OF ASSEMBLED FORM

CORNER DETAIL

45°

ESTIMATE OF MATERIALS				
Size	Description	Length	No. of pieces	F.B.M.
2"x4"	Studs	8'-0"	10	54
2"x4"	"	12'-0"	2	16
2"x4"	Braces	10'-0"	12	80
2"x4"	Carriers	14'-0"	2	19
2"x6"	Wales	12'-0"	8	96
1"x6"	Sheathing			225
2"x10"	Joist seat form	10'-0"		17
1"x10"	" "	6'-0"		5
½"x4"	Bolts		20	

30

CONCRETE FIRE CISTERN

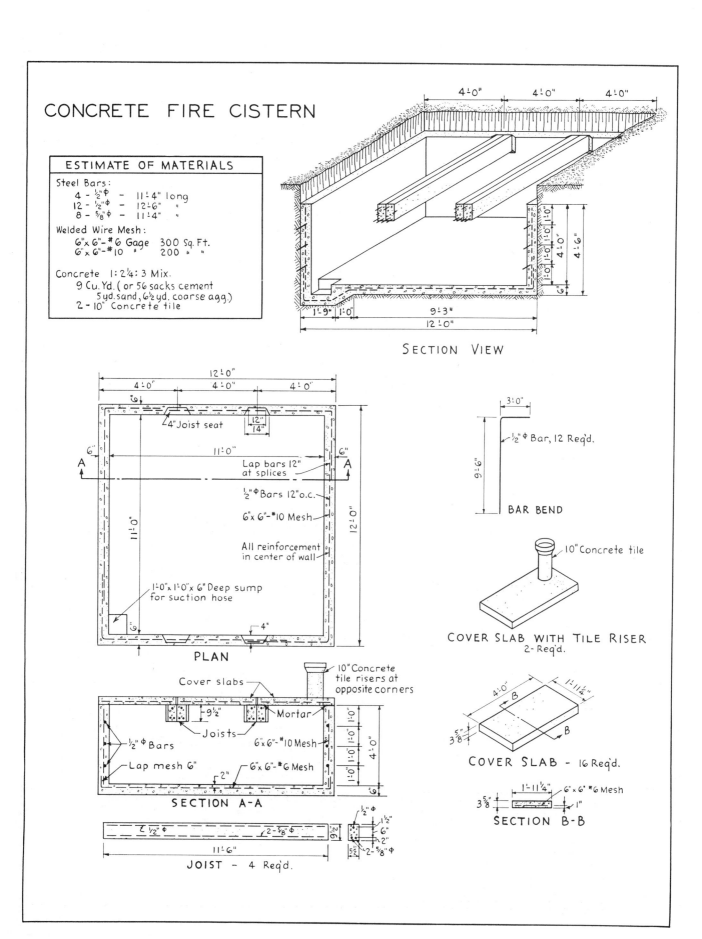

ESTIMATE OF MATERIALS

Steel Bars:
- 4 - ½"∅ – 11'-4" long
- 12 - ½"∅ – 12'-6" "
- 8 - ⅝"∅ – 11'-4" "

Welded Wire Mesh:
- 6"x 6"-#6 Gage   300 Sq. Ft.
- 6"x 6"-#10 "   200 " "

Concrete 1:2¼: 3 Mix.
- 9 Cu. Yd. (or 56 sacks cement
  5 yd. sand, 6½ yd. coarse agg.)
- 2 - 10" Concrete tile

SECTION VIEW

4'-0"   4'-0"   4'-0"

1'-0" 1'-0" 1'-0" 4'-0" 4'-6" 6"

1'-9" 1'-0"   9'-3"   12'-0"

PLAN

12'-0"
4'-0"   4'-0"   4'-0"

6"
4" Joist seat
12"/14"
11'-0"
6"
A — A
Lap bars 12" at splices
½"∅ Bars 12" o.c.
6"x 6"-#10 Mesh
All reinforcement in center of wall
11'-0"
12'-0"
1'-0"x 1'-0"x 6" Deep sump for suction hose
6"
4"

BAR BEND

3'-0"
½"∅ Bar, 12 Req'd.
9'-6"

10" Concrete tile

COVER SLAB WITH TILE RISER
2- Req'd.

SECTION A-A

Cover slabs
10" Concrete tile risers at opposite corners
9½"
Mortar
Joists
6"x 6"-#10 Mesh
½"∅ Bars
Lap mesh 6"
6"x 6"-#6 Mesh
2"
1'-0" 1'-0" 1'-0" 1'-0" 4'-0" 6"

COVER SLAB - 16 Req'd.

4'-0"
B
3⅝"
1'-11¼"
B

SECTION B-B

1'-11¼"   6"x 6"-#6 Mesh
3⅝"   1"

JOIST - 4 Req'd.

½"∅
2-⅝"∅
9½"
11'-6"
½"∅
½"
6"
2"
2"
5½"
2-⅝"∅

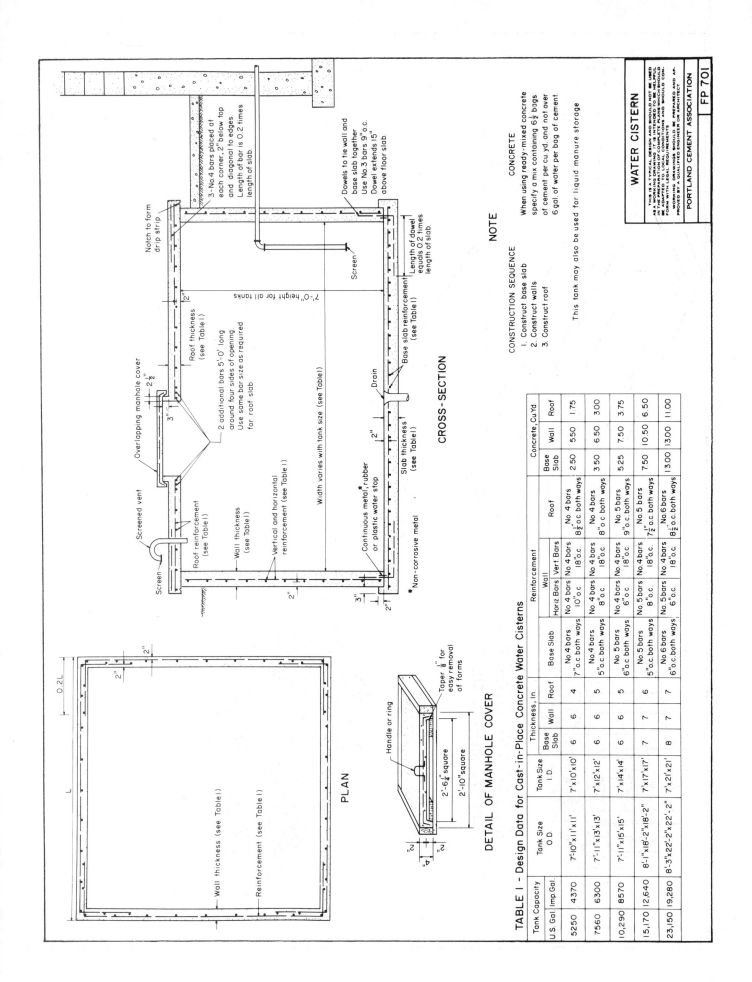

CROSS-SECTION

PLAN

DETAIL OF MANHOLE COVER

Notch to form drip strip

Overlapping manhole cover

Screened vent

Roof reinforcement (see Table I)

Screen

Roof thickness (see Table I)

2 additional bars 5'-0" long around four sides of opening. Use same bar size as required for roof slab

3-No.4 bars placed at each corner, 2" below top and diagonal to edges. Length of bar is 0.2 times length of slab

Screen

Dowels to tie wall and base slab together. Use No.3 bars 9"o.c. Dowel extends 15" above floor slab

7'-0" height for all tanks

Base slab reinforcement (see Table I)

Length of dowel equals 0.2 times length of slab

Wall thickness (see Table I)

Vertical and horizontal reinforcement (see Table I)

Width varies with tank size (see Table I)

Continuous metal, rubber or plastic water stop

Drain

Slab thickness (see Table I)

*Non-corrosive metal

Handle or ring

Taper ⅛" for easy removal of forms

2'-6¼" square

2'-10" square

NOTE

CONSTRUCTION SEQUENCE
1. Construct base slab
2. Construct walls
3. Construct roof

This tank may also be used for liquid manure storage.

CONCRETE

When using ready-mixed concrete specify a mix containing 6½ bags of cement per cu. yd. and not over 6 gal. of water per bag of cement.

WATER CISTERN

PORTLAND CEMENT ASSOCIATION

FP 701

TABLE I - Design Data for Cast-in-Place Concrete Water Cisterns

Tank Capacity U.S. Gal.	Tank Capacity Imp. Gal.	Tank Size O.D.	Tank Size I.D.	Thickness, In. Base Slab	Thickness, In. Wall	Thickness, In. Roof	Reinforcement Base Slab	Reinforcement Wall Horiz. Bars	Reinforcement Wall Vert. Bars	Reinforcement Roof	Concrete, Cu.Yd. Base Slab	Concrete, Cu.Yd. Wall	Concrete, Cu.Yd. Roof
5250	4370	7'-10"x11'x11'	7'x10'x10'	6	6	4	No.4 bars 7"o.c. both ways	No.4 bars 10"o.c.	No.4 bars 18"o.c.	No.4 bars 8½"o.c. both ways	2.50	5.50	1.75
7560	6300	7'-11"x13'x13'	7'x12'x12'	6	6	5	No.4 bars 5"o.c. both ways	No.4 bars 8"o.c.	No.4 bars 18"o.c.	No.4 bars 8"o.c. both ways	3.50	6.50	3.00
10,290	8570	7'-11"x15'x15'	7'x14'x14'	6	6	5	No.5 bars 6"o.c. both ways	No.4 bars 6"o.c.	No.4 bars 18"o.c.	No.5 bars 9"o.c. both ways	5.25	7.50	3.75
15,170	12,640	8'-1"x18'-2"x18'-2"	7'x17'x17'	7	7	6	No.5 bars 5"o.c. both ways	No.5 bars 8"o.c.	No.4 bars 18"o.c.	No.5 bars 7½"o.c. both ways	7.50	10.50	6.50
23,150	19,280	8'-3"x22'-2"x22'-2"	7'x21'x21'	8	7	7	No.6 bars 6"o.c. both ways	No.5 bars 6"o.c.	No.4 bars 18"o.c.	No.6 bars 8½"o.c. both ways	13.00	13.00	11.00

32

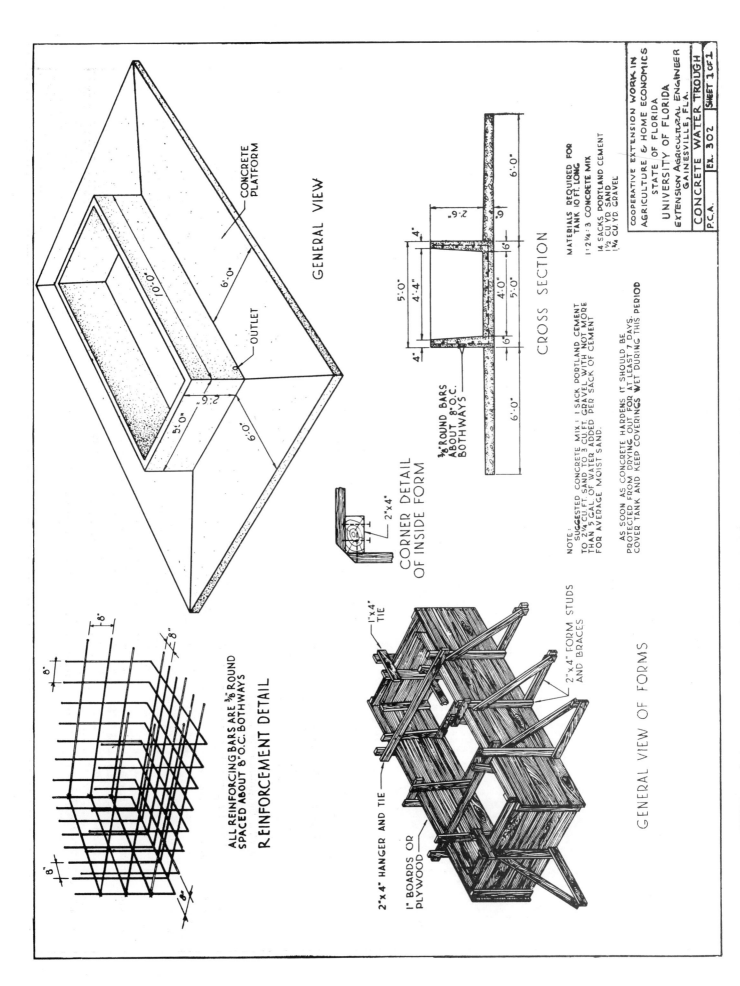

GENERAL VIEW

CONCRETE PLATFORM

OUTLET

10'-0"

6'-0"

5'-0"

6'-0"

2'-6"

CORNER DETAIL OF INSIDE FORM

2"x4"

CROSS SECTION

4"

5'-0"

4'-4"

4'-0"

5'-0"

6'-0"

2'-6"

6"

6"

6"

4"

6'-0"

⅜" ROUND BARS ABOUT 8" O.C. BOTHWAYS

MATERIALS REQUIRED FOR TANK 10 FT. LONG
1:2¼:3 CONCRETE MIX
14 SACKS PORTLAND CEMENT
1½ CU. YD SAND
1¾ CU. YD GRAVEL

NOTE: SUGGESTED CONCRETE MIX: 1 SACK PORTLAND CEMENT TO 2¼ CU. FT. SAND TO 3 CU. FT. GRAVEL WITH NOT MORE THAN 5 GAL. OF WATER ADDED PER SACK OF CEMENT FOR AVERAGE MOIST SAND.

AS SOON AS CONCRETE HARDENS IT SHOULD BE PROTECTED FROM DRYING OUT FOR AT LEAST 7 DAYS. COVER TANK AND KEEP COVERINGS WET DURING THIS PERIOD

8"

8"

8"

8"

8"

ALL REINFORCING BARS ARE ⅜" ROUND SPACED ABOUT 8" O.C. BOTHWAYS

REINFORCEMENT DETAIL

2"x4" HANGER AND TIE

1"x4" TIE

2"x4" FORM STUDS AND BRACES

1" BOARDS OR PLYWOOD

GENERAL VIEW OF FORMS

COOPERATIVE EXTENSION WORK IN AGRICULTURE & HOME ECONOMICS
STATE OF FLORIDA
UNIVERSITY OF FLORIDA
EXTENSION AGRICULTURAL ENGINEER
GAINESVILLE, FLA.
CONCRETE WATER TROUGH
P.C.A. | EX. 302 | SHEET 1 OF 1

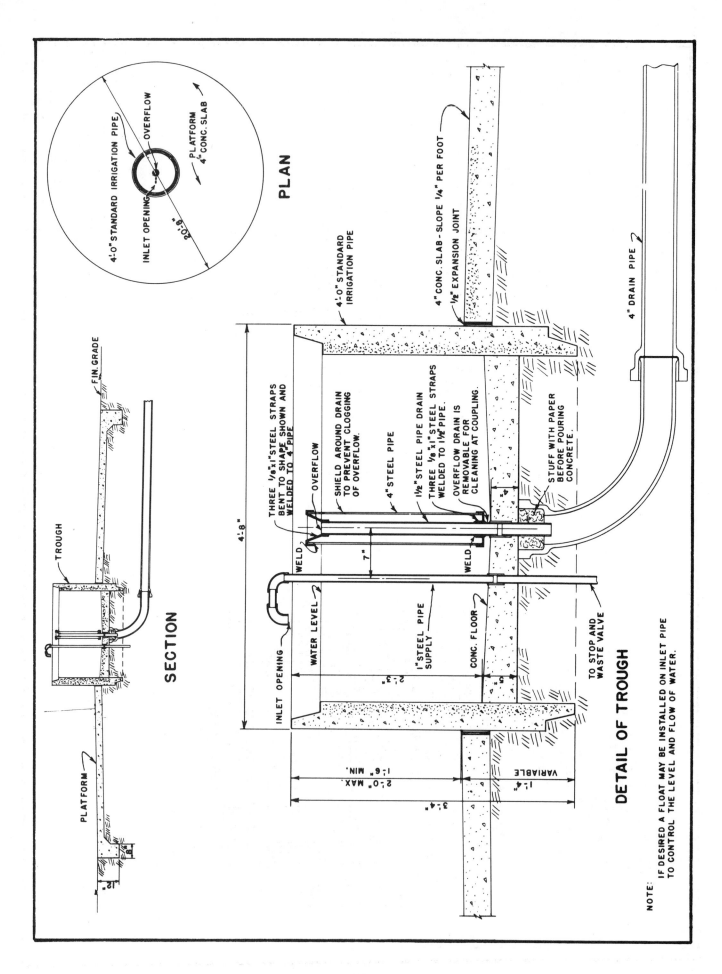

PLAN

4'-0" STANDARD IRRIGATION PIPE

OVERFLOW

INLET OPENING

PLATFORM 4" CONC. SLAB

8'-0"

4'-0" STANDARD IRRIGATION PIPE

4" CONC. SLAB - SLOPE ¼ PER FOOT

½" EXPANSION JOINT

4" DRAIN PIPE

PLATFORM

FIN. GRADE

TROUGH

SECTION

12"

18"

THREE ⅛"x1" STEEL STRAPS BENT TO SHAPE SHOWN AND WELDED TO 4" PIPE

OVERFLOW

SHIELD AROUND DRAIN TO PREVENT CLOGGING OF OVERFLOW.

4" STEEL PIPE

1½" STEEL PIPE DRAIN

THREE ⅛"x1" STEEL STRAPS WELDED TO 1½" PIPE.

OVERFLOW DRAIN IS REMOVABLE FOR CLEANING AT COUPLING.

STUFF WITH PAPER BEFORE POURING CONCRETE.

WELD

WELD

7"

WATER LEVEL

INLET OPENING

1" STEEL PIPE SUPPLY

CONC. FLOOR

2'-3"

4'-8"

3'-4"

2'-0" MAX.
1'-6" MIN.

VARIABLE

1'-4"

TO STOP AND WASTE VALVE

DETAIL OF TROUGH

NOTE:
IF DESIRED A FLOAT MAY BE INSTALLED ON INLET PIPE TO CONTROL THE LEVEL AND FLOW OF WATER.

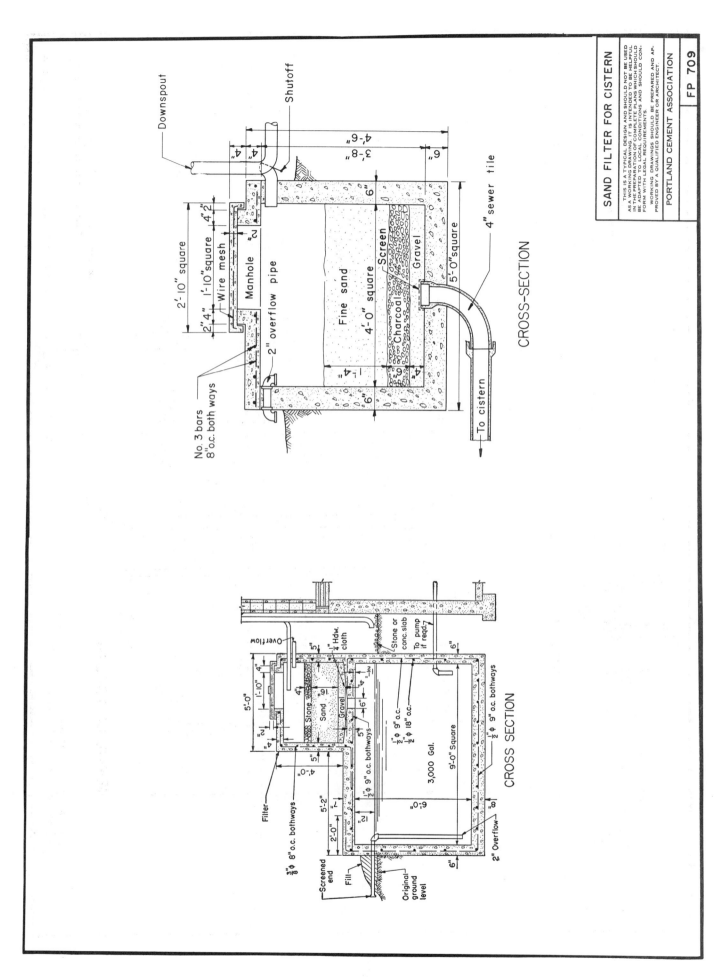

CROSS-SECTION

CROSS SECTION

SAND FILTER FOR CISTERN

THIS IS A TYPICAL DESIGN AND SHOULD NOT BE USED AS A WORKING DRAWING. IT IS INTENDED TO BE HELPFUL IN THE PREPARATION OF COMPLETE PLANS WHICH SHOULD BE ADAPTED TO LOCAL CONDITIONS AND SHOULD CONFORM WITH LEGAL REQUIREMENTS.

WORKING DRAWINGS SHOULD BE PREPARED AND APPROVED BY A QUALIFIED ENGINEER OR ARCHITECT.

PORTLAND CEMENT ASSOCIATION

FP 709

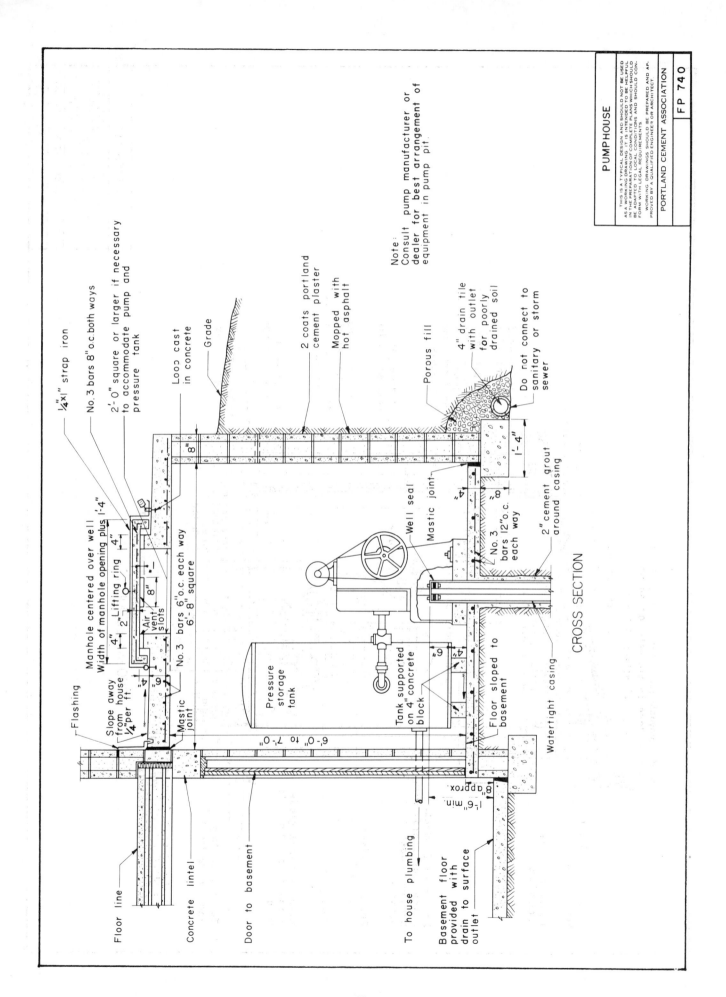

CROSS SECTION

¼"x1" strap iron

No.3 bars 8"o.c. both ways

2'-0" square or larger if necessary to accommodate pump and pressure tank

Loop cast in concrete

Grade

2 coats portland cement plaster

Mopped with hot asphalt

Porous fill

4" drain tile with outlet for poorly drained soil

Do not connect to sanitary or storm sewer

Note:
Consult pump manufacturer or dealer for best arrangement of equipment in pump pit

Manhole centered over well
Width of manhole opening plus 1'-4"

Lifting ring

Air vent slots

No.3 bars 6"o.c. each way 6'-8" square

Well seal

Mastic joint

No.3 bars 12"o.c. each way

2" cement grout around casing

Flashing

Slope away from house ¼" per ft.

Mastic joint

Pressure storage tank

Tank supported on 4" concrete block

Floor sloped to basement

Watertight casing

Floor line

Concrete lintel

Door to basement

To house plumbing

Basement floor provided with drain to surface outlet

6'-0" to 7'-0"

1'-6" min.

8" approx.

PUMPHOUSE

THIS IS A TYPICAL DESIGN AND SHOULD NOT BE USED AS A WORKING DRAWING. IT IS INTENDED TO BE HELPFUL IN THE PREPARATION OF COMPLETE PLANS WHICH SHOULD BE ADAPTED TO LOCAL CONDITIONS AND SHOULD CON-FORM WITH LEGAL REQUIREMENTS.
WORKING DRAWINGS SHOULD BE PREPARED AND AP-PROVED BY A QUALIFIED ENGINEER OR ARCHITECT.

PORTLAND CEMENT ASSOCIATION

FP 740

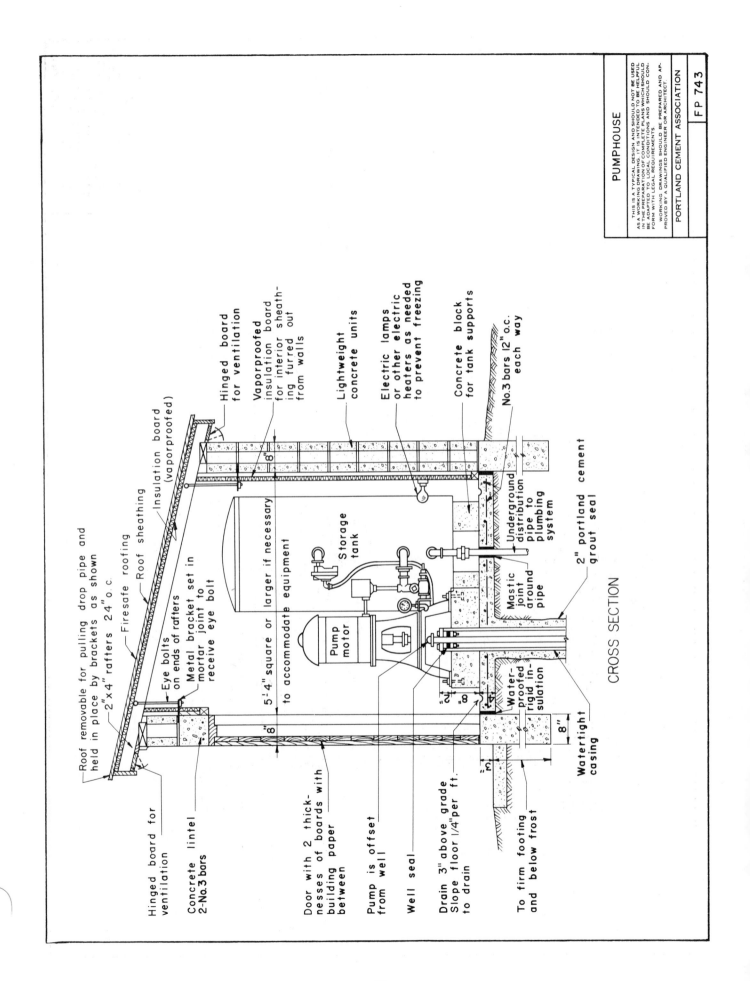

CROSS SECTION

Roof removable for pulling drop pipe and held in place by brackets as shown

2"x4" rafters 24" o.c.

Firesafe roofing

Roof sheathing

Insulation board (vaporproofed)

Hinged board for ventilation

Eye bolts on ends of rafters

Metal bracket set in mortar joint to receive eye bolt

Concrete lintel 2-No.3 bars

Hinged board for ventilation

Door with 2 thicknesses of boards with building paper between

Pump is offset from well

Well seal

Drain 3" above grade Slope floor 1/4" per ft. to drain

To firm footing and below frost

5'-4" square or larger if necessary to accommodate equipment

Storage tank

Pump motor

Vaporproofed insulation board for interior sheathing furred out from walls

Lightweight concrete units

Electric lamps or other electric heaters as needed to prevent freezing

Concrete block for tank supports

No.3 bars 12" o.c. each way

Underground distribution pipe to plumbing system

Mastic joint around pipe

2" portland cement grout seal

Waterproofed rigid insulation

Watertight casing

PUMPHOUSE

FP 743

PORTLAND CEMENT ASSOCIATION

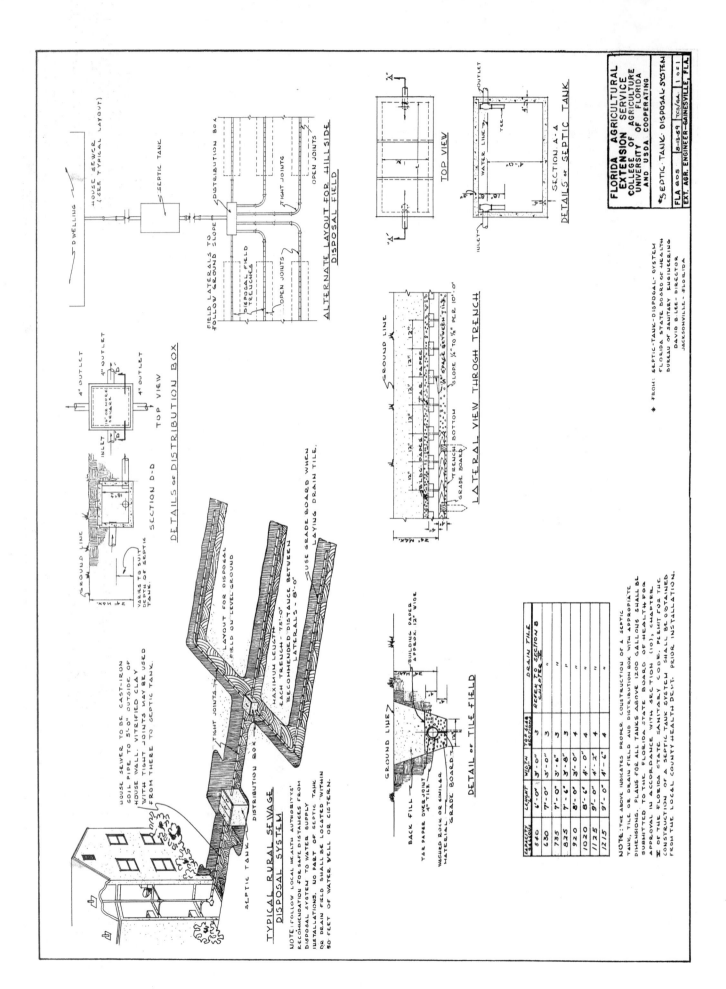

TYPICAL RURAL SEWAGE DISPOSAL SYSTEM

NOTE: FOLLOW LOCAL HEALTH AUTHORITY'S RECOMMENDATION FOR SAFE DISTANCES FROM DISPOSAL SYSTEM TO WATER SUPPLY. NO PART OF SEPTIC TANK OR DRAIN FIELD SHALL BE LOCATED WITHIN 50 FEET OF WATER WELL OR CISTERN.

DETAILS OF DISTRIBUTION BOX

TOP VIEW

SECTION D-D

DETAIL OF TILE FIELD

CAPACITY GALLONS	LENGTH	WIDTH	TOP SLAB SECTION	DRAIN TILE REFER TO SECTION B
540	6'-0"	3'-0"	3	REFER TO CHAPTER IV
630	7'-0"	3'-0"	3	"
735	7'-6"	3'-6"	3	"
825	7'-6"	3'-8"	4	"
920	8'-0"	3'-0"	4	"
1020	8'-6"	4'-0"	4	"
1125	9'-0"	4'-2"	4	"
1215	9'-0"	4'-6"	4	"

NOTE: THE ABOVE INDICATES PROPER CONSTRUCTION OF A SEPTIC TANK, TILE OR DRAIN FIELD AND DISTRIBUTION BOX WITH APPROPRIATE DIMENSIONS. PLANS FOR ALL TANKS ABOVE 1200 GALLONS SHALL BE SUBMITTED TO THE FLORIDA STATE BOARD OF HEALTH FOR APPROVAL IN ACCORDANCE WITH SECTION (10), CHAPTER IV OF THE FLORIDA STATE SANITARY CODE. PERMIT FOR THE CONSTRUCTION OF A SEPTIC TANK SYSTEM SHALL BE OBTAINED FROM THE LOCAL COUNTY HEALTH DEPT. PRIOR INSTALLATION.

ALTERNATE LAYOUT FOR HILLSIDE DISPOSAL FIELD

TOP VIEW

DETAILS OF SEPTIC TANK

SECTION A-A

LATERAL VIEW THROGH TRENCH

* FROM: SEPTIC-TANK-DISPOSAL-SYSTEM FLORIDA STATE BOARD OF HEALTH BUREAU OF SANITARY ENGINEERING DAVID B. LEE- DIRECTOR JACKSONVILLE, FLORIDA

FLORIDA AGRICULTURAL EXTENSION SERVICE COLLEGE OF AGRICULTURE UNIVERSITY OF FLORIDA AND USDA COOPERATING

"SEPTIC TANK" DISPOSAL SYSTEM

FLA 805 8-13-59 TCS/66A 1 OF 1
EXT. AGR. ENGINEER-GAINESVILLE, FLA.

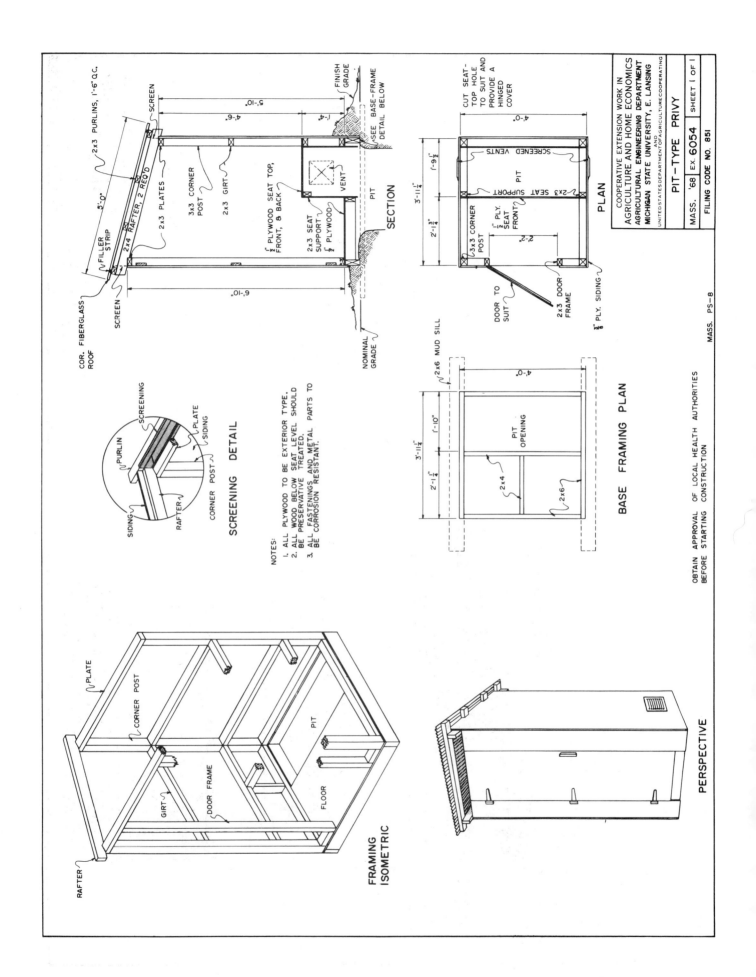

SECTION

SCREENING DETAIL

NOTES:
1. ALL PLYWOOD TO BE EXTERIOR TYPE.
2. ALL WOOD BELOW SEAT LEVEL SHOULD BE PRESERVATIVE TREATED.
3. ALL FASTENINGS AND METAL PARTS TO BE CORROSION RESISTANT.

PLAN

BASE FRAMING PLAN

FRAMING ISOMETRIC

PERSPECTIVE

OBTAIN APPROVAL OF LOCAL HEALTH AUTHORITIES BEFORE STARTING CONSTRUCTION

COOPERATIVE EXTENSION WORK IN
AGRICULTURE AND HOME ECONOMICS
AGRICULTURAL ENGINEERING DEPARTMENT
MICHIGAN STATE UNIVERSITY, E. LANSING
AND
UNITED STATES DEPARTMENT OF AGRICULTURE COOPERATING

PIT-TYPE PRIVY

MASS. '68 | Ex. 6054 | SHEET 1 OF 1
FILING CODE NO. 851

MASS. PS—8

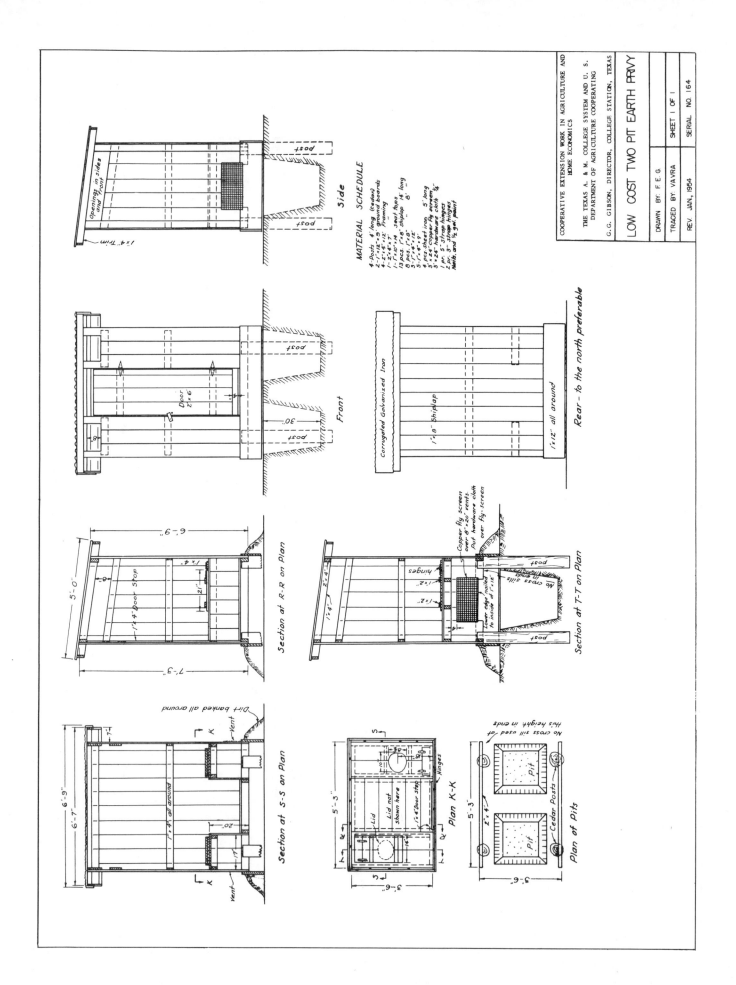

COOPERATIVE EXTENSION WORK IN AGRICULTURE AND HOME ECONOMICS

THE TEXAS A. & M. COLLEGE SYSTEM AND U. S. DEPARTMENT OF AGRICULTURE COOPERATING

G.G. GIBSON, DIRECTOR, COLLEGE STATION, TEXAS

LOW COST TWO PIT EARTH PRIVY

DRAWN BY: F. E. G.

TRACED BY: VAVRA

REV. JAN, 1954

SHEET 1 OF 1

SERIAL NO. 164

Side

Opening in sides and Front

1"x4" Trim

MATERIAL SCHEDULE

4-Posts 4' long (cedar)
2-1"x12"x9' ground boards
4-2"x4"x12' Framing
1-1"x10"x14' Seat tops
13 pcs. 1"x8" shiplap 14' long
8-Post 1"x6" 8'''
3-1"x4"x12'
5-1"x4"x9'
4 pcs. sheet iron 5' long
3'x24' copper fly screen
3'x24' hardware cloth ¼"
2 pr. 5" strap hinges
2 pc. 3" strap hinges
Nails and ½ gal. paint

Front

Door 2"x6"

30"

Rear - to the north preferable

Corrugated Galvanized Iron

1"x8" shiplap

1"x12" all around

Section at R-R on Plan

6'-9"

5'-0"

1"x4" Door Stop

21"

1"x4"

7'-3"

Section at T-T on Plan

Copper fly screen over 8"x20" vents.
Put hardware cloth over fly-screen

2"x4"

1"x4"

hinges

1"x2"

1"x2"

No cross sills in ends

Lower edge nailed to inside of 1"x12"

post

post

Section at S-S on Plan

Dirt banked all around

Vent

6'-9"

6'-7"

7"

1"x4" all around

20"

17"

Vent

K

K

Plan K-K

5'-3"

Lid

Lid not shown here

1"x4" Door Stop

Hinges

3'-6"

S

S

Q

Q

Plan of Pits

No cross sill used at this height in ends

Pit

Pit

Cedar Posts

2"x4"

5'-3"

3'-6"

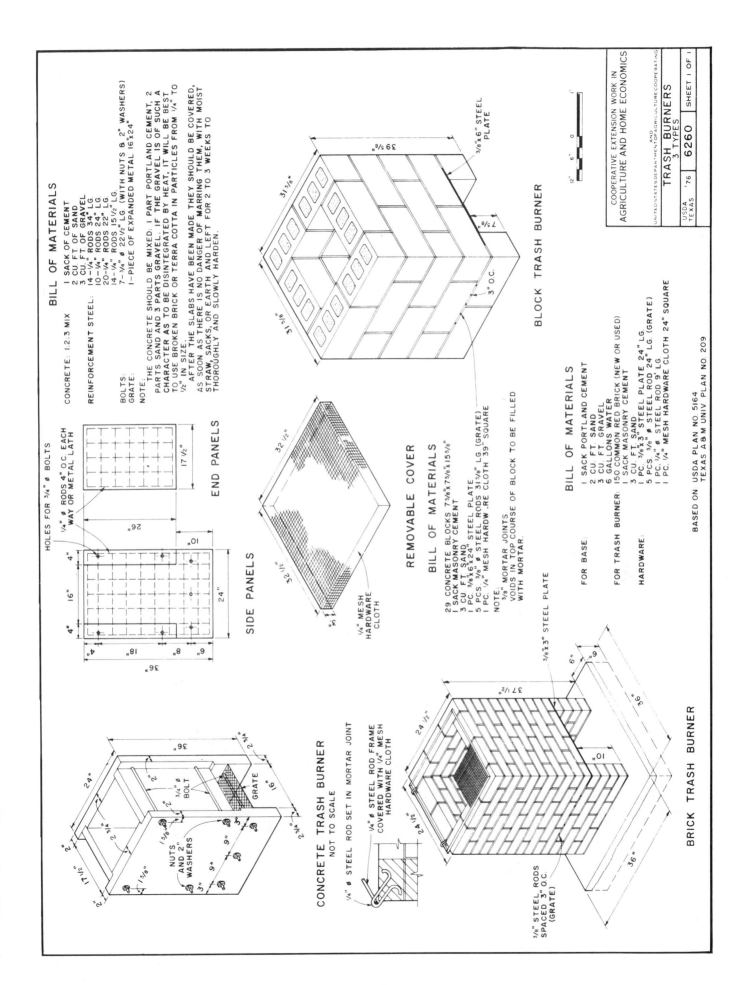

BILL OF MATERIALS

CONCRETE: 1:2:3 MIX
1 SACK OF CEMENT
2 CU. FT. OF SAND
3 CU. FT. OF GRAVEL

REINFORCEMENT STEEL:
14—1/4" RODS 34" LG
10—1/4" RODS 24" LG
20—1/4" RODS 22" LG
14—1/4" RODS 15½" LG

BOLTS:
7—3/4" ø 22½" LG (WITH NUTS & 2" WASHERS)

GRATE:
1—PIECE OF EXPANDED METAL 16"x24"

NOTE:
THE CONCRETE SHOULD BE MIXED: 1 PART PORTLAND CEMENT, 2 PARTS SAND AND 3 PARTS GRAVEL. IF THE GRAVEL IS OF SUCH A CHARACTER AS TO BE DISINTEGRATED BY HEAT, IT WILL BE BEST TO USE BROKEN BRICK OR TERRA COTTA IN PARTICLES FROM 1/4 TO 1/2" IN SIZE.

AFTER THE SLABS HAVE BEEN MADE THEY SHOULD BE COVERED, AS SOON AS THERE IS NO DANGER OF MARRING THEM, WITH MOIST STRAW, SACKS, OR EARTH AND LEFT FOR 2 TO 3 WEEKS TO THOROUGHLY AND SLOWLY HARDEN.

HOLES FOR 3/4" ø BOLTS
1/4" ø RODS 4" O.C. EACH WAY OR METAL LATH

17½"
26"

END PANELS

10"
16"
4"
4"
24"
4"
18"
8"
6"
36"

SIDE PANELS

BLOCK TRASH BURNER

39 5/8"
31 5/8"
31 5/8"
7 5/8"
3/8"x6" STEEL PLATE
3" O.C.

REMOVABLE COVER

32½"
32½"
5"
1/4" MESH HARDWARE CLOTH

BILL OF MATERIALS

29 CONCRETE BLOCKS 7 5/8"x 7 5/8"x 15 5/8"
1 SACK MASONRY CEMENT
3 CU. FT. SAND
1 PC. 3/8"x6"x24" STEEL PLATE
5 PCS. 3/8" ø STEEL RODS 31 5/8" LG. (GRATE)
1 PC. 1/4" MESH HARDW. RE CLOTH 39" SQUARE

NOTE:
3/8" MORTAR JOINTS
VOIDS IN TOP COURSE OF BLOCK TO BE FILLED WITH MORTAR.

BILL OF MATERIALS

FOR BASE:
1 SACK PORTLAND CEMENT
2 CU. FT. SAND
3 CU. FT. GRAVEL
6 GALLONS WATER

FOR TRASH BURNER:
150 COMMON RED BRICK (NEW OR USED)
1 SACK MASONRY CEMENT
3 CU. FT. SAND

HARDWARE:
1 PC. 3/8"x3" STEEL PLATE 24" LG.
5 PCS. 3/8" ø STEEL ROD 24" LG. (GRATE)
1 PC. 1/4" ø STEEL ROD 9' LG
1 PC. 1/4" MESH HARDWARE CLOTH 24" SQUARE

BASED ON USDA PLAN NO.5164
TEXAS A&M UNIV PLAN NO. 209

CONCRETE TRASH BURNER

NOT TO SCALE

36"
24"
2"
2 1/4"
2"
2"
3/4" ø BOLT
GRATE
6"
NUTS AND 2" WASHERS
3"
9"
9"
9"
3"
17½"
1 5/8"
2"

1/4" ø STEEL ROD SET IN MORTAR JOINT

1/4" ø STEEL ROD FRAME COVERED WITH 1/4" MESH HARDWARE CLOTH

BRICK TRASH BURNER

37½"
24½"
6"
9"
10"
36"
36"
24½"

3/8" STEEL RODS SPACED 3" O.C. (GRATE)
3/8"x3" STEEL PLATE

COOPERATIVE EXTENSION WORK IN AGRICULTURE AND HOME ECONOMICS
UNITED STATES DEPARTMENT OF AGRICULTURE COOPERATING

TRASH BURNERS
3 TYPES
SHEET 1 OF 1

USDA
TEXAS '76 6260

GARBAGE CAN MOUNT

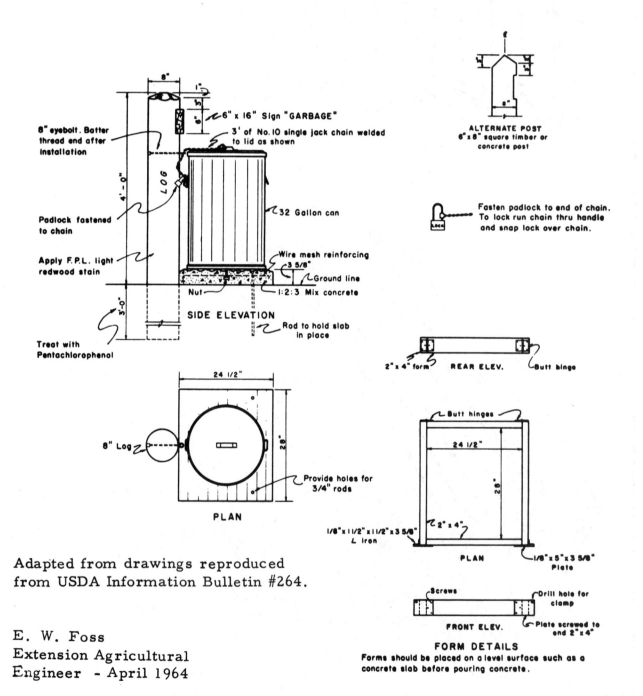

8" eyebolt. Batter thread end after installation

Padlock fastened to chain

Apply F.P.L. light redwood stain

Treat with Pentachlorophenol

6" x 16" Sign "GARBAGE"

3' of No. 10 single jack chain welded to lid as shown

LOG

32 Gallon can

Wire mesh reinforcing

3 5/8"

Ground line

Nut

1:2:3 Mix concrete

Rod to hold slab in place

SIDE ELEVATION

ALTERNATE POST
6" x 8" square timber or concrete post

Fasten padlock to end of chain. To lock run chain thru handle and snap lock over chain.

24 1/2"

8" Log

28"

Provide holes for 3/4" rods

PLAN

2" x 4" form   REAR ELEV.   Butt hinge

Butt hinges

24 1/2"

28"

1/8" x 1 1/2" x 1 1/2" x 3 5/8" L iron

2" x 4"

PLAN

1/8" x 5" x 3 5/8" Plate

Screws   Drill hole for clamp

FRONT ELEV.   Plate screwed to end 2" x 4"

FORM DETAILS
Forms should be placed on a level surface such as a concrete slab before pouring concrete.

Adapted from drawings reproduced from USDA Information Bulletin #264.

E. W. Foss
Extension Agricultural
Engineer - April 1964

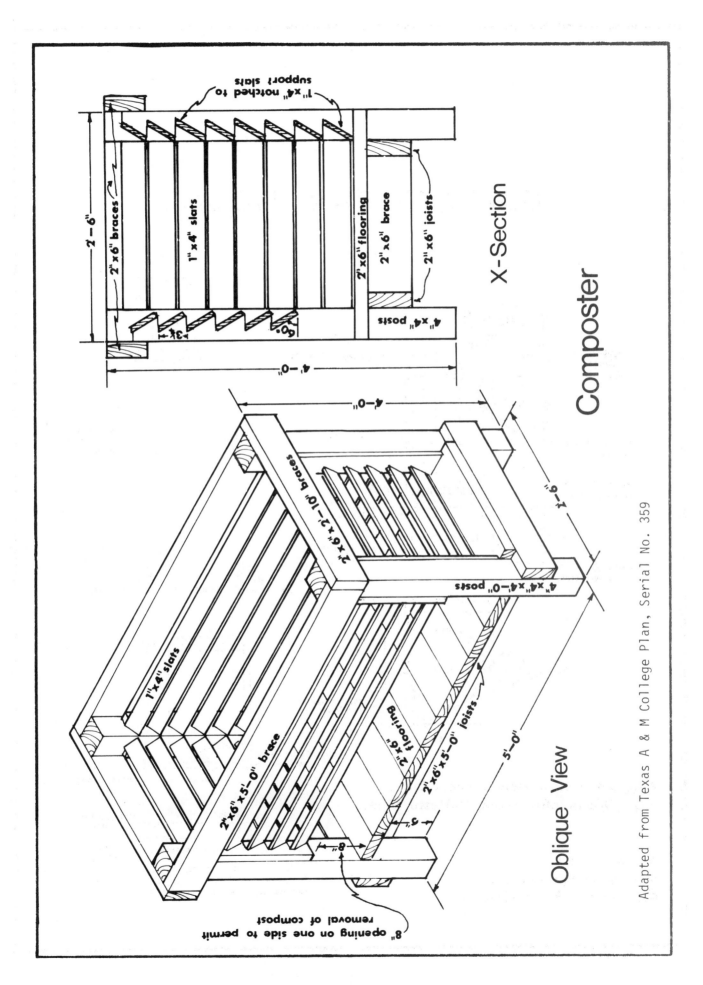

Composter

X-Section

2'-6"

2"x6" braces

1"x4" notched to support slats

1"x4" slats

2"x6" flooring

2"x6" brace

2"x6" joists

4"x4" posts

3½"

60°

4'-0"

Oblique View

4'-0"

2"x6"x2'-10" braces

1"x4" slats

1'-6"

4"x4"x4'-0" posts

2"x6"x5'-0" brace

2"x6" flooring

2"x6"x5'-0" joists

5'-0"

3"

8"

8" opening on one side to permit removal of compost

Adapted from Texas A & M College Plan, Serial No. 359

43

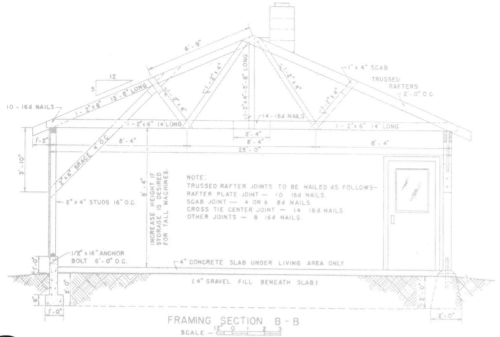

FRAMING SECTION B-B
SCALE — 1½"=0 1 2

NOTE:
TRUSSED RAFTER JOINTS TO BE NAILED AS FOLLOWS—
RAFTER PLATE JOINT — 10 16d NAILS.
SCAB JOINT — 4 OR 6 8d NAILS.
CROSS TIE CENTER JOINT — 14 16d NAILS.
OTHER JOINTS — 8 16d NAILS.

STORAGE SHEDS
AND GARAGES

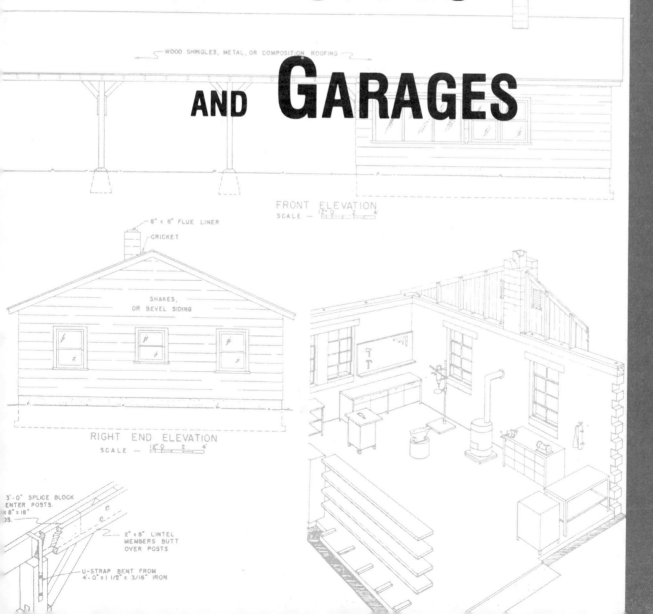

FRONT ELEVATION
SCALE — 1"=0 2 4

RIGHT END ELEVATION
SCALE — 1"=0 2 4

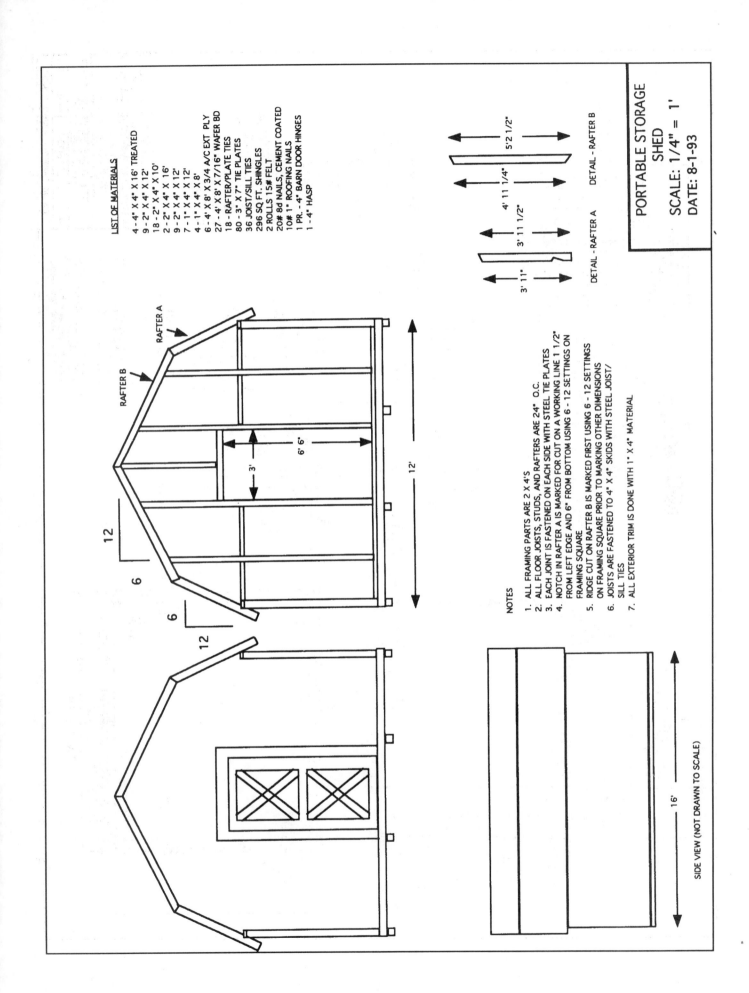

LIST OF MATERIALS

4 - 4" X 4" X 16' TREATED
9 - 2" X 4" X 12'
18 - 2" X 4" X 10'
2 - 2" X 4" X 16'
9 - 2" X 4" X 12'
7 - 1" X 4" X 12'
4 - 1" X 4" X 8'
6 - 4' X 8' X 3/4 A/C EXT PLY
27 - 4' X 8' X 7/16" WAFER BD
18 - RAFTER/PLATE TIES
80 - 3" X 7" TIE PLATES
36 JOIST/SILL TIES
296 SQ FT. SHINGLES
2 ROLLS 15# FELT
20# 8d NAILS, CEMENT COATED
10# 1" ROOFING NAILS
1 PR. - 4" BARN DOOR HINGES
1 - 4" HASP

5'2 1/2"

4' 11 1/4"

DETAIL - RAFTER B

3' 11 1/2"

3' 11"

DETAIL - RAFTER A

RAFTER A

RAFTER B

6' 6"

3'

12

12

6

6

12

12

PORTABLE STORAGE
SHED

SCALE: 1/4" = 1'

DATE: 8-1-93

NOTES

1. ALL FRAMING PARTS ARE 2 X 4'S
2. ALL FLOOR JOISTS, STUDS, AND RAFTERS ARE 24" O.C.
3. EACH JOINT IS FASTENED ON EACH SIDE WITH STEEL TIE PLATES
4. NOTCH IN RAFTER A IS MARKED FOR CUT ON A WORKING LINE 1 1/2" FROM LEFT EDGE AND 6" FROM BOTTOM USING 6 - 12 SETTINGS ON FRAMING SQUARE
5. RIDGE CUT ON RAFTER B IS MARKED FIRST USING 6 - 12 SETTINGS ON FRAMING SQUARE PRIOR TO MARKING OTHER DIMENSIONS
6. JOISTS ARE FASTENED TO 4" X 4" SKIDS WITH STEEL JOIST/ SILL TIES
7. ALL EXTERIOR TRIM IS DONE WITH 1" X 4" MATERIAL

16'

SIDE VIEW (NOT DRAWN TO SCALE)

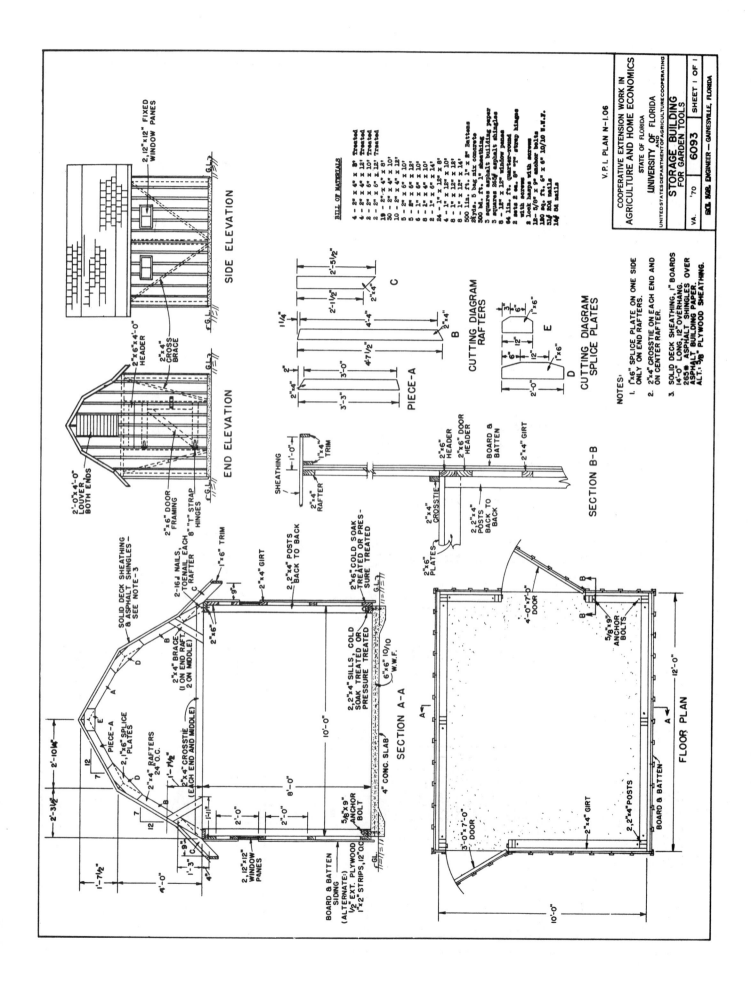

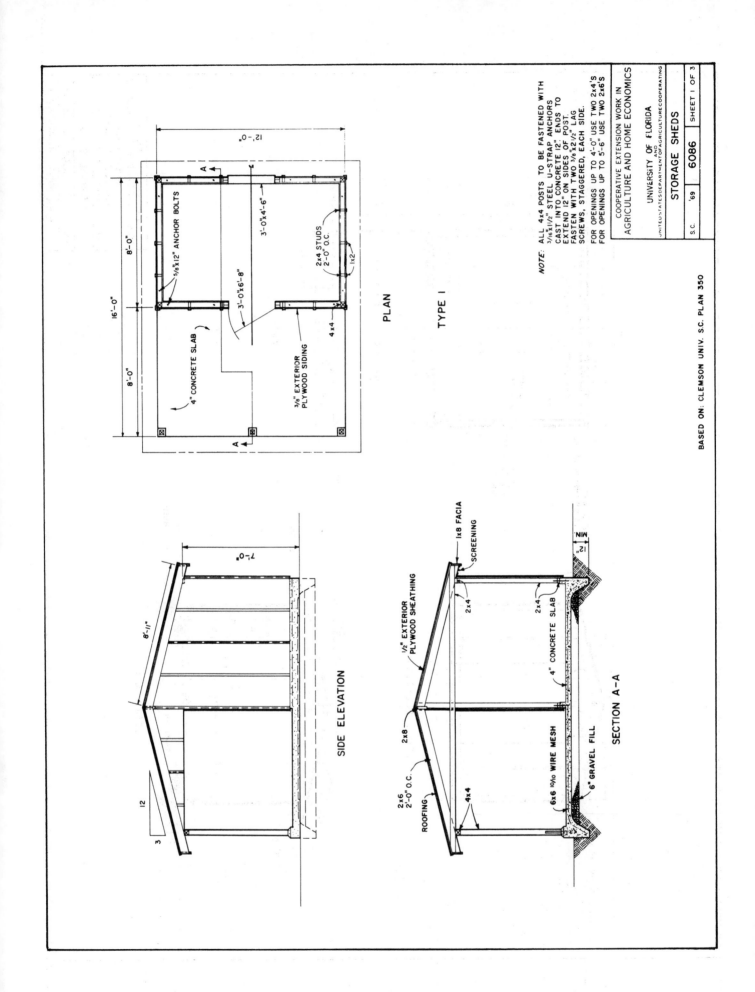

PLAN

12'-0"

16'-0"

8'-0" 8'-0"

5/8"x12" ANCHOR BOLTS

3'-0"x4'-6"

3'-0"x6'-8"

2x4 STUDS 2'-0" O.C.

1x2

4" CONCRETE SLAB

3/8" EXTERIOR PLYWOOD SIDING

4x4

A   A

TYPE I

NOTE: ALL 4x4 POSTS TO BE FASTENED WITH 3/16"x1 1/2" STEEL U-STRAP ANCHORS CAST INTO CONCRETE 12" ENDS TO EXTEND 12" ON SIDES OF POST. FASTEN WITH TWO 3/8"x2 1/2" LAG SCREWS, STAGGERED, EACH SIDE.

FOR OPENINGS UP TO 4'-0" USE TWO 2x4'S
FOR OPENINGS UP TO 5'-6" USE TWO 2x6'S

COOPERATIVE EXTENSION WORK IN
AGRICULTURE AND HOME ECONOMICS

UNIVERSITY OF FLORIDA
AND
UNITED STATES DEPARTMENT OF AGRICULTURE COOPERATING

STORAGE SHEDS

S.C. '69 6086 SHEET 1 OF 3

BASED ON: CLEMSON UNIV. S.C. PLAN 350

SIDE ELEVATION

7'-0"

8'-11"

12
3

SECTION A-A

1x8 FACIA

SCREENING

1/2" EXTERIOR PLYWOOD SHEATHING

2x4

2x4

4" CONCRETE SLAB

12" MIN.

2x8

2x6 2'-0" O.C.

ROOFING

4x4

6x6 10/10 WIRE MESH

6" GRAVEL FILL

48

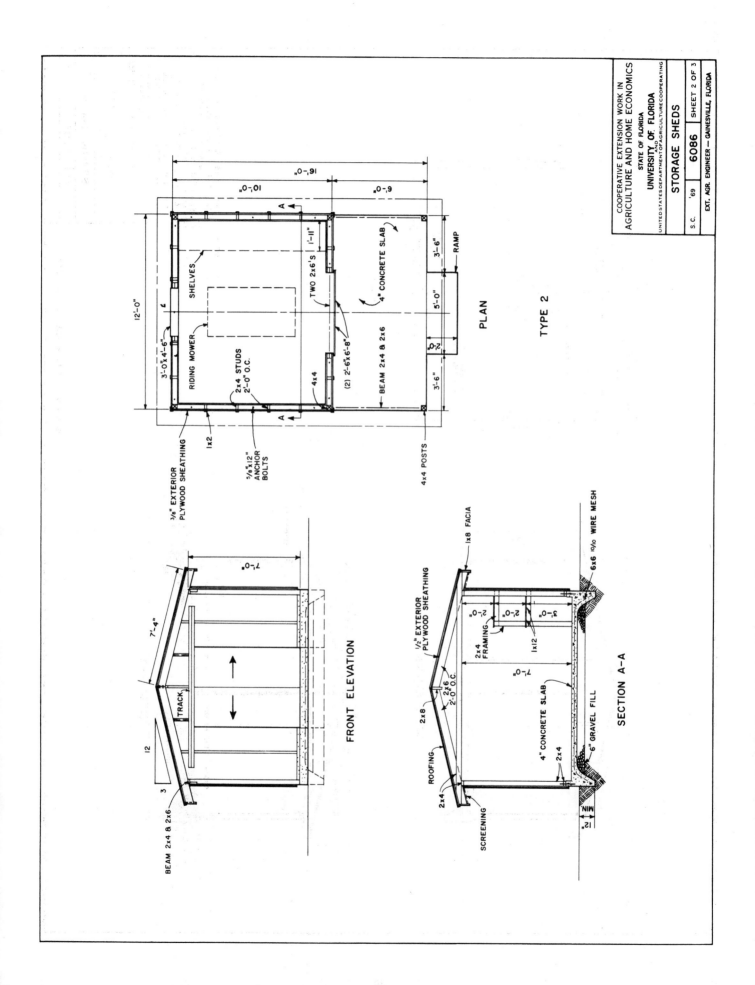

PLAN

TYPE 2

FRONT ELEVATION

SECTION A-A

COOPERATIVE EXTENSION WORK IN
AGRICULTURE AND HOME ECONOMICS
STATE OF FLORIDA
UNIVERSITY OF FLORIDA
AND
UNITED STATES DEPARTMENT OF AGRICULTURE COOPERATING

STORAGE SHEDS

| S.C. | '69 | 6086 | SHEET 2 OF 3 |

EXT. AGR. ENGINEER — GAINESVILLE, FLORIDA

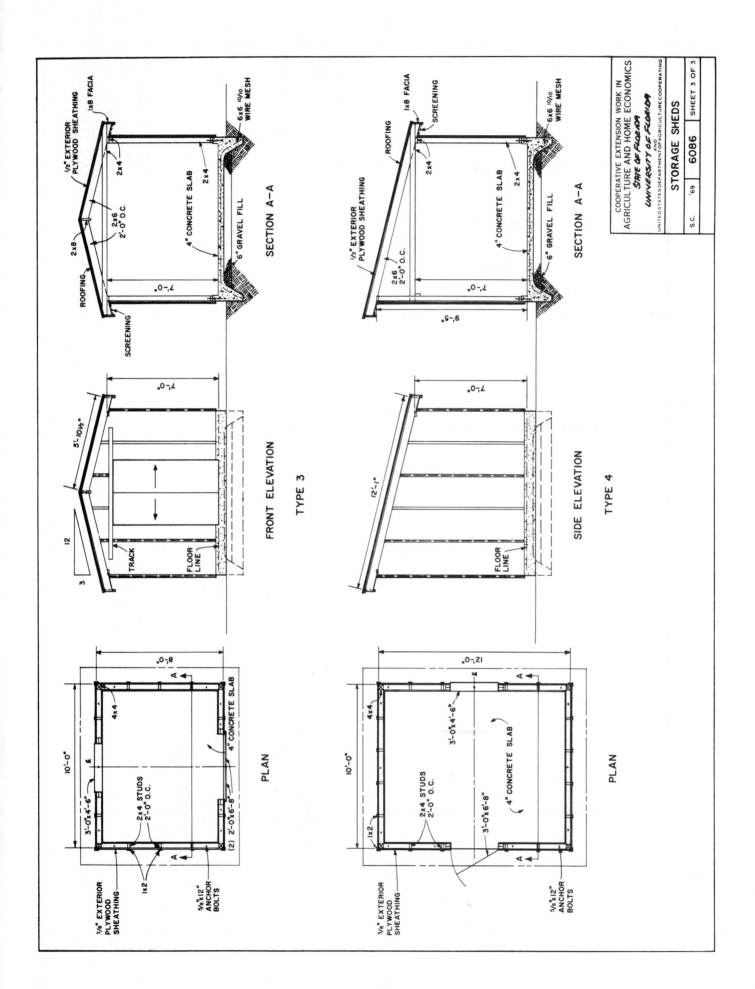

SECTION A-A

1x8 FACIA
½" EXTERIOR PLYWOOD SHEATHING
2x4
2x6 2'-0" O.C.
2x8
ROOFING
SCREENING
2x4
4" CONCRETE SLAB
6x6 10/10 WIRE MESH
6" GRAVEL FILL
7'-0"

FRONT ELEVATION

TYPE 3

5'-10½"
7'-0"
12
3
TRACK
FLOOR LINE

PLAN

8'-0"
10'-0"
4x4
4" CONCRETE SLAB
3'-0"x4'-6"
2x4 STUDS 2'-0" O.C.
(2) 2'-0"x6'-8"
1x2
⅜" EXTERIOR PLYWOOD SHEATHING
⅝"x12" ANCHOR BOLTS

SECTION A-A

1x8 FACIA
SCREENING
ROOFING
2x4
½" EXTERIOR PLYWOOD SHEATHING
2x6 2'-0" O.C.
2x4
4" CONCRETE SLAB
6x6 10/10 WIRE MESH
6" GRAVEL FILL
7'-0"
9'-5"

SIDE ELEVATION

TYPE 4

7'-0"
12'-1"
FLOOR LINE

PLAN

12'-0"
10'-0"
4x4
3'-0"x4'-6"
4" CONCRETE SLAB
2x4 STUDS 2'-0" O.C.
1x2
3'-0"x6'-8"
⅜" EXTERIOR PLYWOOD SHEATHING
⅝"x12" ANCHOR BOLTS
A

COOPERATIVE EXTENSION WORK IN AGRICULTURE AND HOME ECONOMICS
STATE OF FLORIDA
UNIVERSITY OF FLORIDA
AND
UNITED STATES DEPARTMENT OF AGRICULTURE COOPERATING

STORAGE SHEDS

S.C.   '69   6086   SHEET 3 OF 3

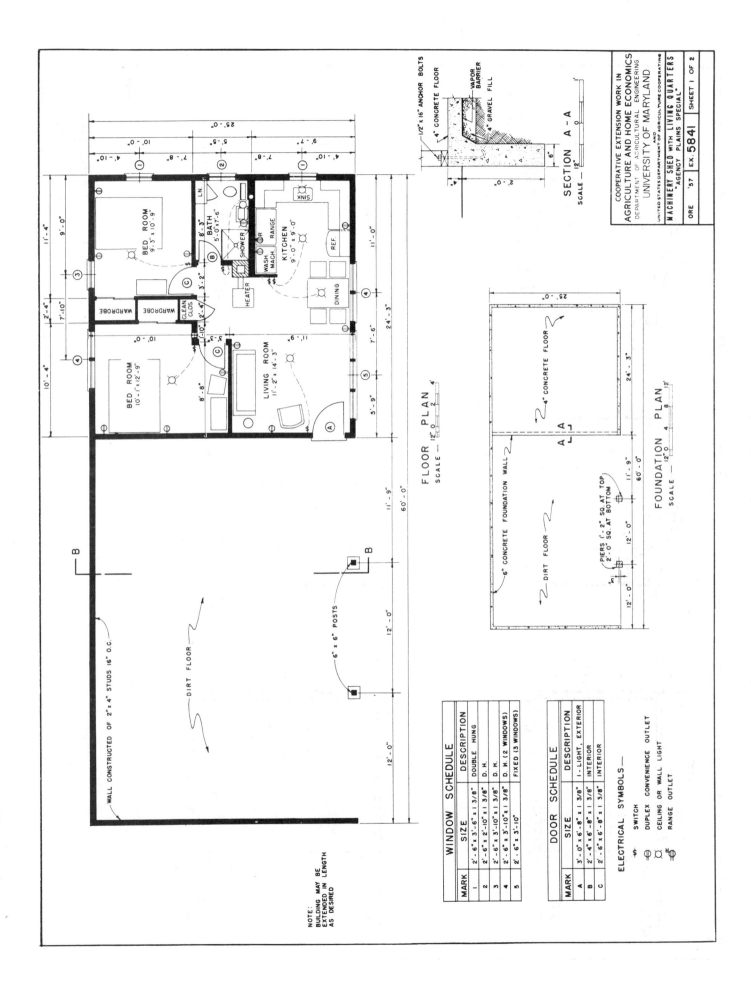

FLOOR PLAN
SCALE — 12"

BED ROOM
9'-3" x 10'-9"

BATH
5'-0" x 7'-6"

KITCHEN
9'-0" x 9'-0"

SINK
RANGE
REF.
WASH MACH.
SHOWER
HEATER
DINING
LN
CLEAN CLOS.
WARDROBE
WARDROBE

BED ROOM
10'-1" x 12'-9"

LIVING ROOM
11'-2" x 14'-3"

DIRT FLOOR

WALL CONSTRUCTED OF 2" x 4" STUDS 16" O.C.

6" x 6" POSTS

NOTE:
BUILDING MAY BE
EXTENDED IN LENGTH
AS DESIRED

SECTION A - A
SCALE — 12"

1/2" x 16" ANCHOR BOLTS
4" CONCRETE FLOOR
VAPOR BARRIER
GRAVEL FILL

FOUNDATION PLAN
SCALE — 12"

4" CONCRETE FLOOR
6" CONCRETE FOUNDATION WALL
DIRT FLOOR
PIERS 1'-2" SQ. AT TOP
2'-0" SQ. AT BOTTOM

WINDOW SCHEDULE

MARK	SIZE	DESCRIPTION
1	2'-6" x 3'-6" x 1 3/8"	DOUBLE HUNG
2	2'-6" x 2'-10" x 1 3/8"	D. H.
3	2'-6" x 3'-10" x 1 3/8"	D. H.
4	2'-6" x 3'-10" x 1 3/8"	D. H. (2 WINDOWS)
5	2'-6" x 3'-10"	FIXED (3 WINDOWS)

DOOR SCHEDULE

MARK	SIZE	DESCRIPTION
A	3'-0" x 6'-8" x 1 3/8"	1 - LIGHT, EXTERIOR
B	2'-4" x 6'-8" x 1 3/8"	INTERIOR
C	2'-6" x 6'-8" x 1 3/8"	INTERIOR

ELECTRICAL SYMBOLS—

$ SWITCH
DUPLEX CONVENIENCE OUTLET
CEILING OR WALL LIGHT
RANGE OUTLET

COOPERATIVE EXTENSION WORK IN
AGRICULTURE AND HOME ECONOMICS
DEPARTMENT OF AGRICULTURAL ENGINEERING
UNIVERSITY OF MARYLAND
AND
UNITED STATES DEPARTMENT OF AGRICULTURE COOPERATING
MACHINERY SHED WITH LIVING QUARTERS
"AGENCY PLAINS SPECIAL"

| ORE. '57 | EX. 5841 | SHEET 1 OF 2 |

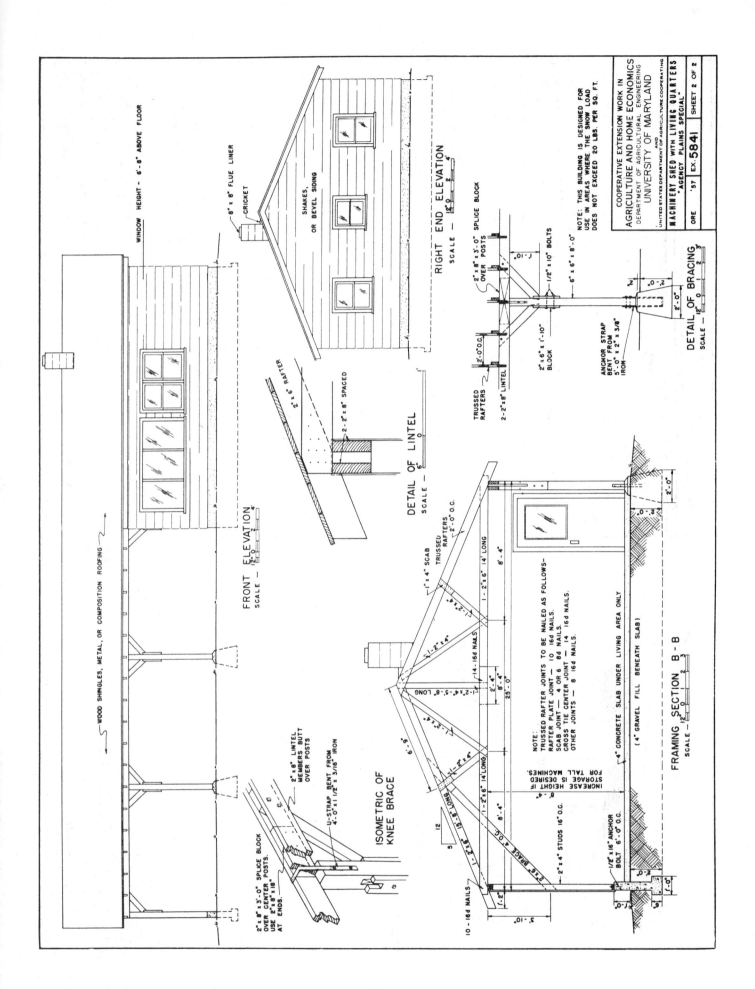

FRONT ELEVATION
SCALE — 12' = 0"

WOOD SHINGLES, METAL, OR COMPOSITION ROOFING

WINDOW HEIGHT - 6'-8" ABOVE FLOOR

8" x 8" FLUE LINER
CRICKET

SHAKES, OR BEVEL SIDING

RIGHT END ELEVATION
SCALE — 12' = 0"

2" x 6" RAFTER

2 - 2" x 8" SPACED

DETAIL OF LINTEL
SCALE — 6" = 0"

2" x 8" x 3'-0" SPLICE BLOCK OVER CENTER POSTS. USE 2" x 8" x 18" AT ENDS.

2" x 8" LINTEL MEMBERS BUTT OVER POSTS

U-STRAP BENT FROM 4'-0" x 1½" x 3/16" IRON

ISOMETRIC OF KNEE BRACE

2" x 8" x 3'-0" SPLICE BLOCK OVER POSTS

2 - 2" x 8" LINTEL

TRUSSED RAFTERS

2' - 0" O.C.

1/2" x 10" BOLTS

2" x 6" x 1'-10" BLOCK

6" x 6" x 8'-0"

ANCHOR STRAP BENT FROM 5'-0" x 2" x 3/8" IRON

DETAIL OF BRACING
SCALE — 12' = 0"

NOTE: THIS BUILDING IS DESIGNED FOR USE IN AREAS WHERE THE SNOW LOAD DOES NOT EXCEED 20 LBS. PER SQ. FT.

1" x 4" SCAB

TRUSSED RAFTERS 2'-0" O.C.

1 - 2" x 6" 14' LONG

8' - 4"

1 - 2" x 4"

14 - 16d NAILS

1 - 2" x 4"

2' - 4"

25' - 0"

1 - 2" x 4" - 5'-8" LONG

1 - 2" x 4"

1 - 2" x 4"

6' - 9"

12

5

2" x 8" BRACE 4'-0"

2" x 8" 15'-8" LONG

1 - 2" x 6" 14' LONG

8' - 4"

8' - 4"

10 - 16d NAILS

2" x 4" STUDS 16" O.C.

1/2" x 16" ANCHOR BOLT 6'-0" O.C.

4" CONCRETE SLAB UNDER LIVING AREA ONLY

(4" GRAVEL FILL BENEATH SLAB)

2' - 0"

NOTE:
TRUSSED RAFTER JOINTS TO BE NAILED AS FOLLOWS—
RAFTER PLATE JOINT — 10 16d NAILS.
SCAB JOINT — 4 OR 6 8d NAILS.
CROSS TIE CENTER JOINT — 14 16d NAILS.
OTHER JOINTS — 8 16d NAILS.

INCREASE HEIGHT IF STORAGE IS DESIRED FOR TALL MACHINES.

FRAMING SECTION B - B
SCALE — 12' = 0"

3' - 10"

COOPERATIVE EXTENSION WORK IN
AGRICULTURE AND HOME ECONOMICS
DEPARTMENT OF AGRICULTURAL ENGINEERING
UNIVERSITY OF MARYLAND
UNITED STATES DEPARTMENT OF AGRICULTURE COOPERATING
MACHINERY SHED WITH LIVING QUARTERS
"AGENCY PLAINS SPECIAL"
ORE   '57 EX. 5841 SHEET 2 OF 2

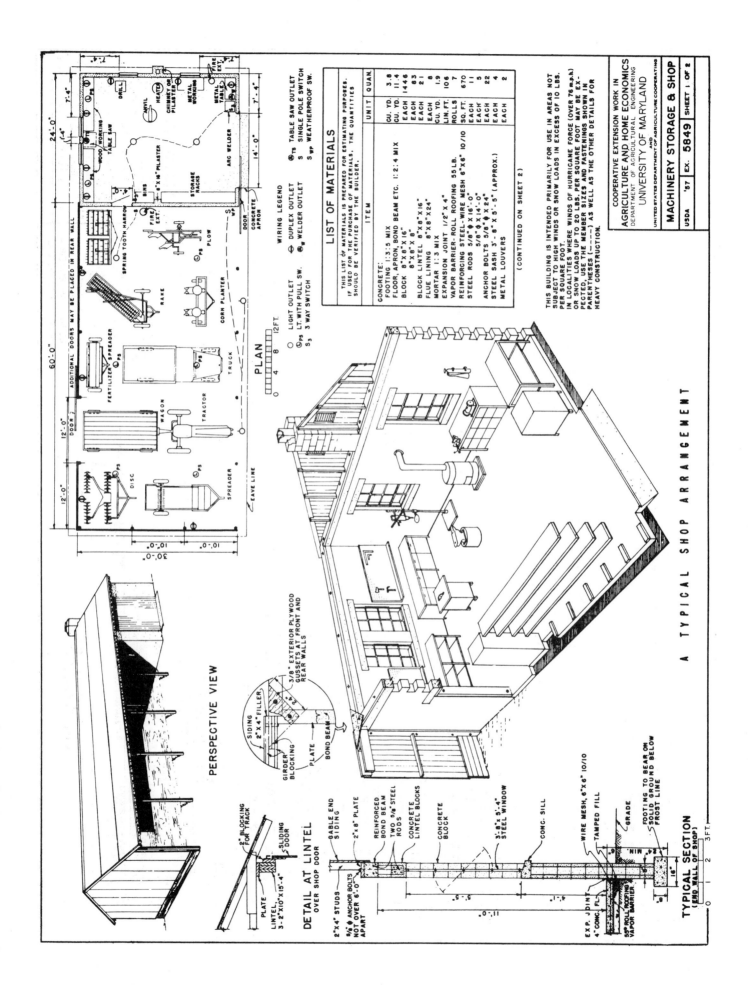

PLAN

PERSPECTIVE VIEW

DETAIL AT LINTEL
OVER SHOP DOOR

TYPICAL SECTION
(END WALL OF SHOP)

A TYPICAL SHOP ARRANGEMENT

WIRING LEGEND
⊕ DUPLEX OUTLET
⊕w WELDER OUTLET
○ LIGHT OUTLET
○Ps LT. WITH PULL SW.
S₃ 3 WAY SWITCH
⊕TS TABLE SAW OUTLET
S SINGLE POLE SWITCH
S WP WEATHERPROOF SW.

LIST OF MATERIALS

THIS LIST OF MATERIALS IS PREPARED FOR ESTIMATING PURPOSES.
IF USED FOR THE PURCHASE OF MATERIALS, THE QUANTITIES
SHOULD BE VERIFIED BY THE BUILDER.

ITEM	UNIT	QUAN.
CONCRETE:		
FOOTING 1:3:5 MIX	CU. YD.	3.8
FLOOR, APRON, BOND BEAM ETC. 1:2:4 MIX	CU. YD.	11.4
BLOCK 8"x8"x16"	EACH	1446
8"x6"x16"	EACH	83
8"x8"x 8"	EACH	21
BLOCK LINTEL 8"x8"x16"	EACH	8
FLUE LINING 8"x8"x24"	EACH	1.9
MORTAR 1:3 MIX	CU. YD.	106
EXPANSION JOINT 1/2"x 4"	LIN. FT.	7
VAPOR BARRIER-ROLL ROOFING 55 LB.	ROLLS	670
REINFORCING STEEL-WIRE MESH 6"x6" 10/10	SQ. FT.	11
STEEL RODS 5/8"⌀ x16'-0"	EACH	5
5/8"⌀ x14'-0"	EACH	22
ANCHOR BOLTS 5/8"⌀ x 24"	EACH	4
STEEL SASH 3'- 8"x 5'-5" (APPROX.)	EACH	2
METAL LOUVERS	EACH	

(CONTINUED ON SHEET 2)

THIS BUILDING IS INTENDED PRIMARILY FOR USE IN AREAS NOT
SUBJECT TO HIGH WINDS OR SNOW LOADS IN EXCESS OF 10 LBS.
PER SQUARE FOOT.
IN LOCALITIES WHERE WINDS OF HURRICANE FORCE (OVER 76 m.p.h.)
OR SNOW LOADS UP TO 20 LBS. PER SQUARE FOOT MAY BE EX-
PECTED, USE THE MEMBER SIZES AND FASTENINGS SHOWN IN
PARENTHESES (----) AS WELL AS THE OTHER DETAILS FOR
HEAVY CONSTRUCTION.

COOPERATIVE EXTENSION WORK IN
AGRICULTURE AND HOME ECONOMICS
DEPARTMENT OF AGRICULTURAL ENGINEERING
UNIVERSITY OF MARYLAND
UNITED STATES DEPARTMENT OF AGRICULTURE COOPERATING

MACHINERY STORAGE & SHOP

| USDA | '57 | EX. 5849 | SHEET 1 OF 2 |

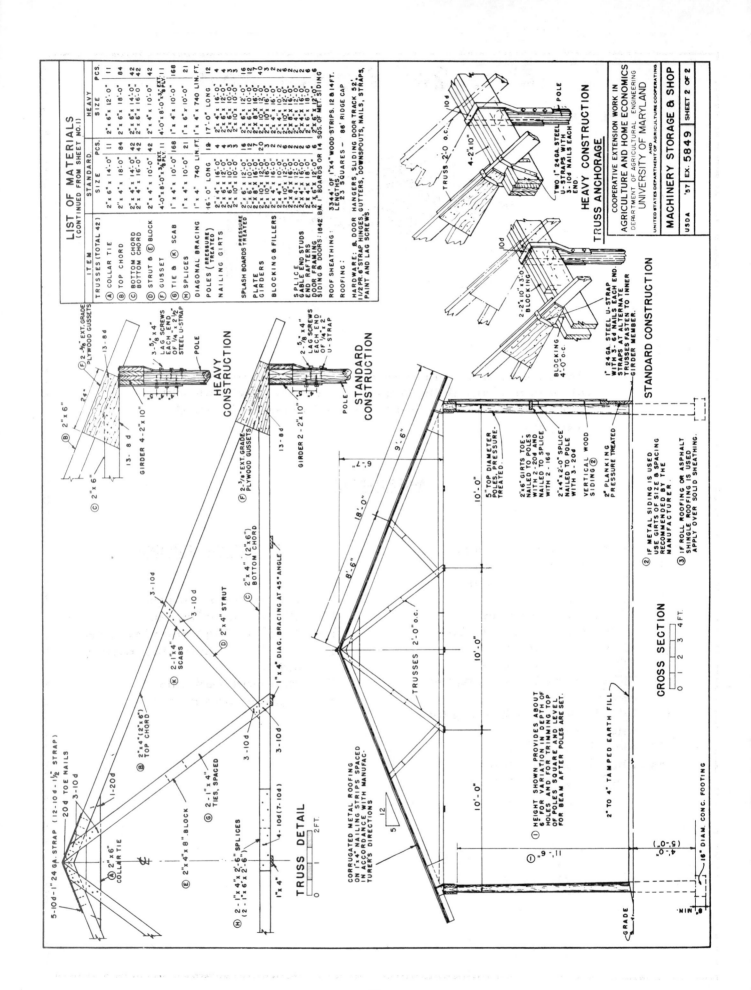

14' x 24' Tractor Port

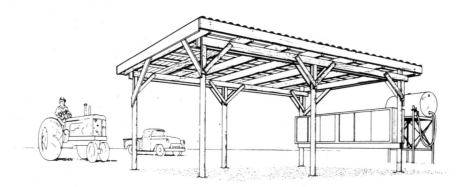

This is a plan of a pole-type tractor port which can be built near the house and serves as a handy shelter for frequently used tractors and trucks. Storage cabinets can be hung between the poles and used for small tools, oil, grease, etc.

MATERIALS LIST

* 3 - 16', 4'' top penta-treated poles.
* 3 - 15', 4'' top penta-treated poles.
  8 - 2'' x 8'' x 12' rafter supports.
  7 - 2'' x 10'' x 16' rafters.
  2 - 1'' x 12'' x 16' trim sides.
  4 - 1'' x 10'' x 14' trim, front & back.
  4 - 2'' x 6'' x 12' braces.
18 - 2'' x 4'' x 14' roof purlins.
13 - 26'' x 9' sheets, 2-1/2'' corrugated
     metal roofing.
13 - 26'' x 8' sheets, 2-1/2'' corrugated
     metal roofing.
5#, 40d. deformed shank nails.
5#, 20d. deformed shank nails.
3#, 2-1/2'' ring shank roofing nails

TO ENCLOSE ONE END

* 1 - 10', 4'' top penta-treated pole.
  1 - 2'' x 6'' x 14' nailing girt.
* 3 - 2'' x 6'' x 14' penta-treated sill boards.
36 - 1'' x 6'' x 12' #3 dressed & matched
     boards.
5#, 20d. deformed shank nails.
10#, 8d. galv. or aluminum nails.

12' X 24' POLE TYPE SINGLE CARPORT

24'-0"

12'-0"

2 - 2x8

7'-0"

11'0"

4" TOP 10' LONG POLE

36"

PLANTERS BETWEEN POLES

CARPORT ATTACHED TO HOME

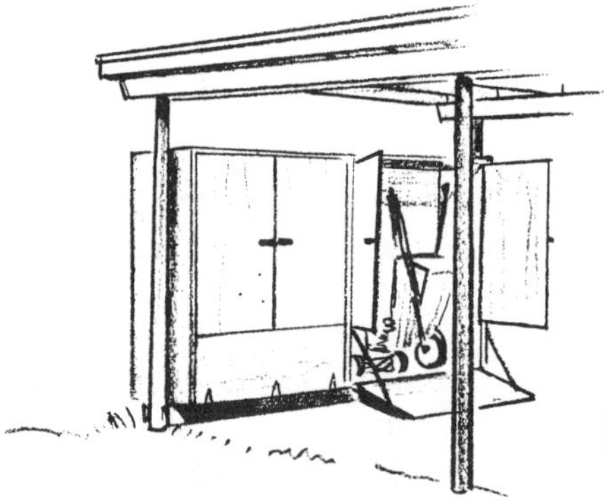

STORAGE UNITS BETWEEN
END POLES

DAVE SWARTWOUT ASSOCIATES

Homeowners can protect their cars from the sun and rain in summer and from frost and snow in winter with this economical, easy-to-build carport. This 12-foot by 24-foot free-standing single carport can be modified for attachment to the house by resting the joist ends on a 2'' x 4'' ledger lag screwed to the house studs.

MATERIALS LIST

* 8 - 10' x 4'' tops, penta-treated poles.	100 lin. ft. - 1'' x 2'' roof trim.	3 sqs. - roll roofing
4 - 2'' x 8'' x 24' beams.	2 - 1'' x 6'' x 24' fascia.	8 - ½'' x 9'' bolts and nuts.
2 - 2'' x 4'' x 14' braces and ties.	288 sq. ft. - 1'' x 6'' T & G roof sheathing.	Washers, roofing cement, nails, etc.,
13 - 2'' x 6'' x 12' roof joists.	3 sqs. - 15# asphalt felt.	as needed.

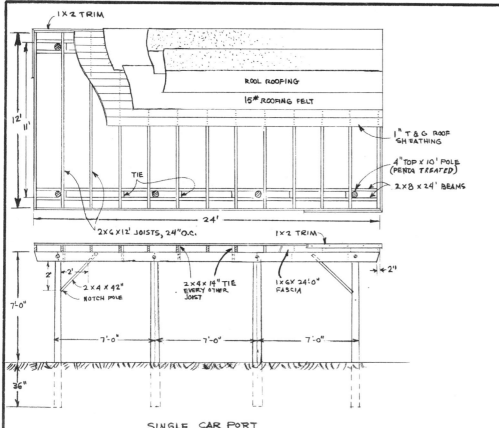

SINGLE CAR PORT

Labels on diagram:
- 1 X 2 TRIM
- ROOL ROOFING
- 15# ROOFING FELT
- 1" T & G ROOF SHEATHING
- 4" TOP X 10' POLE (PENTA TREATED)
- 2 X 8 X 24' BEAMS
- TIE
- 12'
- 11'
- 24'
- 2 X 6 X 12' JOISTS, 24" O.C.
- 1 X 2 TRIM
- 2'
- 2 X 4 X 42" NOTCH POLE
- 2 X 4 X 14" TIE EVERY OTHER JOIST
- 1 X 6 X 24'-0" FASCIA
- 2"
- 7'-0"
- 7'-0"
- 7'-0"
- 7'-0"
- 36"

CONSTRUCTION STEPS

1. Lay out an 11 x 21-foot rectangle on the ground where carport will be situated. Square corners of the area by using a 6 x 8 x 10-foot triangle at the corners.

2. Locate and dig the holes 3-feet deep for the penta-treated poles.

3. Pick the four straightest poles for the corner holes. Backfill just enough to keep poles upright. Check the distance between them and temporarily brace them with sheathing boards nailed diagonally between each pair of end poles.

4. Locate and nail the two outside 2'' x 8'' x 24' beams to the poles. Use ring-shanked nails for better gripping power in the poles.

5. Put in other four poles and nail the beams to them. Add the 2'' x 6'' x 12' roof joists over the end poles and square and plumb the entire structure. Use sheathing material for temporary braces.

6. Add the inside beams and short diagonal braces. Notch the lower ends of the braces into the poles. Drill beams and poles for one-half inch bolts, one at each joint.

7. Add the rest of the joists, toe nailing to the beams. Add short tie pieces at every other joist.

8. Nail the fascia and sheathing in place. Also nail up the 1'' x 2'' trim to cover the edge of the sheathing.

9. Cover the sheathing with a layer of 15# asphalt felt followed by roll roofing set in roofing cement.

10. For the storage unit, add two 2'' x 6'' penta-treated beams between the poles. Build the unit from 3/4-inch exterior plywood.

11. The flower boxes are also built on a 2'' x 6'' penta-treated beam between poles. Make the ends from 1'' x 12'' lumber and the sides from grooved exterior plywood.

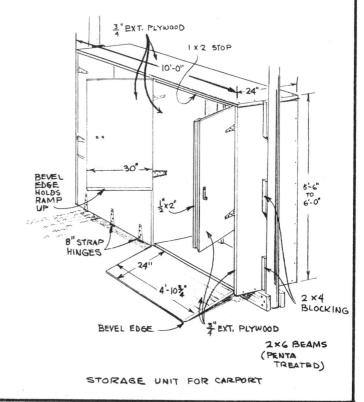

Labels on diagram:
- 3/4" EXT. PLYWOOD
- 1 X 2 STOP
- 10'-0"
- 24"
- BEVEL EDGE HOLDS RAMP UP
- 30"
- 1/2" X 2"
- 5'-6" TO 6'-0"
- 8" STRAP HINGES
- 24"
- 2 X 4 BLOCKING
- BEVEL EDGE
- 3/4" EXT. PLYWOOD
- 4'-10 3/4"
- 2 X 6 BEAMS (PENTA TREATED)

STORAGE UNIT FOR CARPORT

57

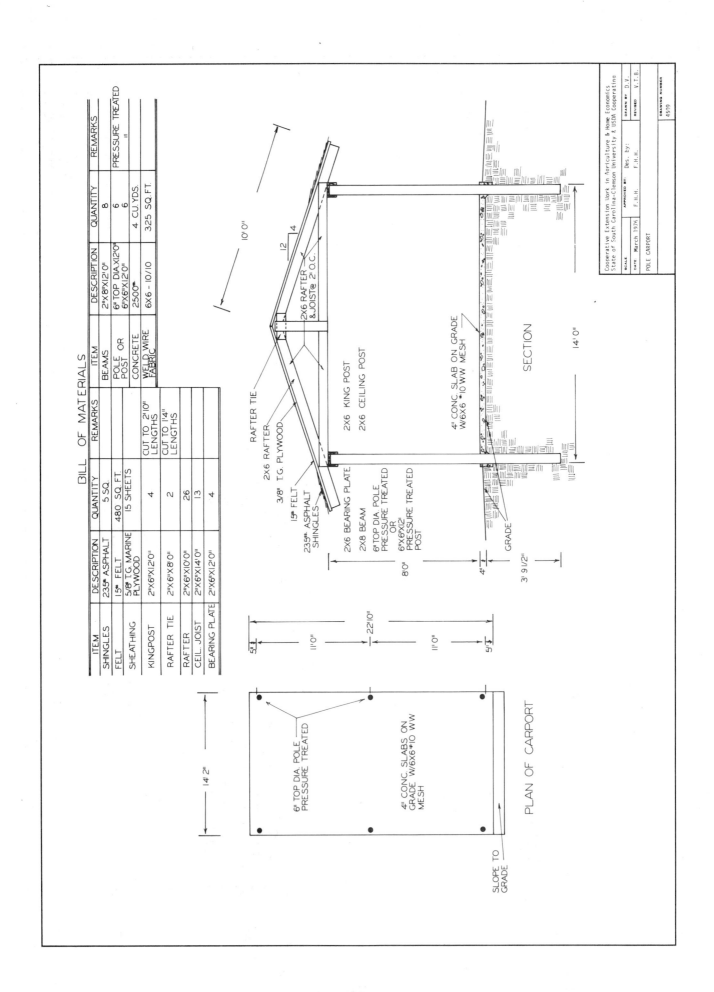

BILL OF MATERIALS

ITEM	DESCRIPTION	QUANTITY	REMARKS
SHINGLES	235# ASPHALT	5 SQ.	
FELT	15# FELT	480 SQ. FT.	
SHEATHING	5/8" T.G. MARINE PLYWOOD	15 SHEETS	
KINGPOST	2"X6"X12'0"	4	CUT TO 2'10" LENGTHS
RAFTER TIE	2"X6"X8'0"	2	CUT TO 14'1" LENGTHS
RAFTER	2"X6"X10'0"	26	
CEIL. JOIST	2"X6"X14'0"	13	
BEARING PLATE	2"X6"X12'0"	4	

ITEM	DESCRIPTION	QUANTITY	REMARKS
BEAMS	2"X8"X12'0"	8	
POLE OR POST	6" TOP DIA X12'0" 6"X6"X12'0"	6 6	PRESSURE TREATED "
CONCRETE	2500#	4 CU.YDS.	
WELD WIRE FABRIC	6x6 - 10/10	325 SQ.FT.	

RAFTER TIE

2X6 RAFTER

3/8" T.G. PLYWOOD

15# FELT

235# ASPHALT SHINGLES

2X6 BEARING PLATE

2X8 BEAM

6" TOP DIA. POLE PRESSURE TREATED OR 6"X6"X12' PRESSURE TREATED POST

2X6 RAFTER &JOIST@ 2' O.C.

2X6 KING POST

2X6 CEILING POST

4" CONC. SLAB ON GRADE W/6X6 #-10 WW MESH

GRADE

10'0"

12
4

SECTION

14'0"

8'0"

4"

3' 9 1/2"

14' 2"

5"

11'0"

22'10"

11'0"

5"

6" TOP DIA POLE PRESSURE TREATED

4" CONC. SLABS ON GRADE W/6X6#-10 WW MESH

SLOPE TO GRADE

PLAN OF CARPORT

Cooperative Extension Work in Agriculture & Home Economics
State of South Carolina-Clemson University & USDA Cooperating

POLE CARPORT

SCALE	APPROVED BY	DRAWN BY D.V.
DATE March 1976	F.H.H. Des. by:	REVISED V.T.B.
	F.H.H.	

DRAWING NUMBER 4509

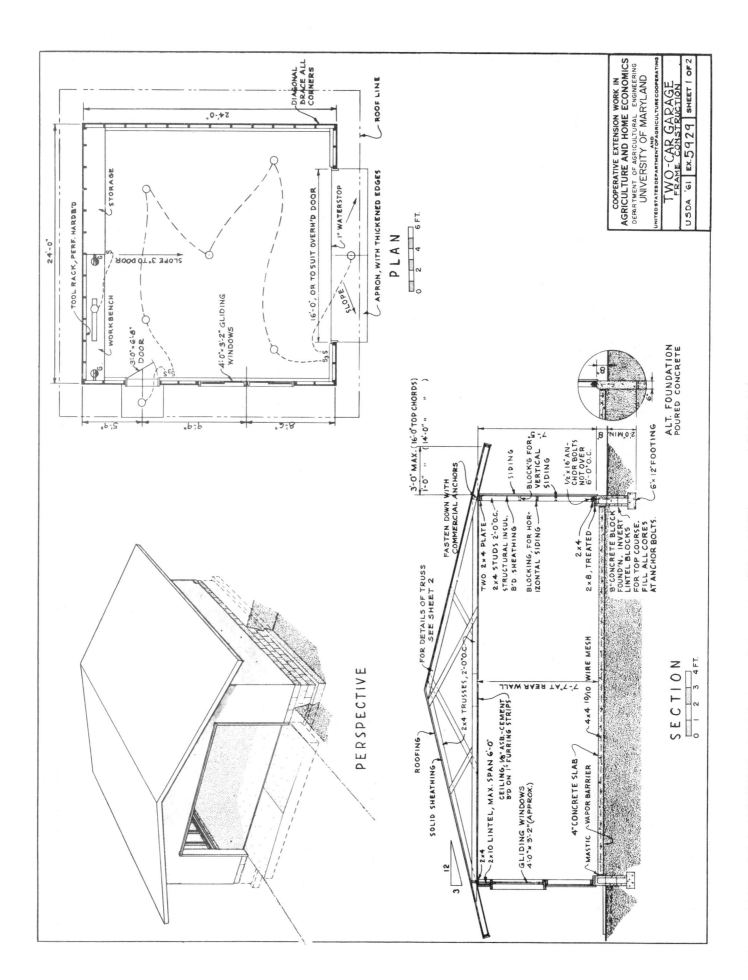

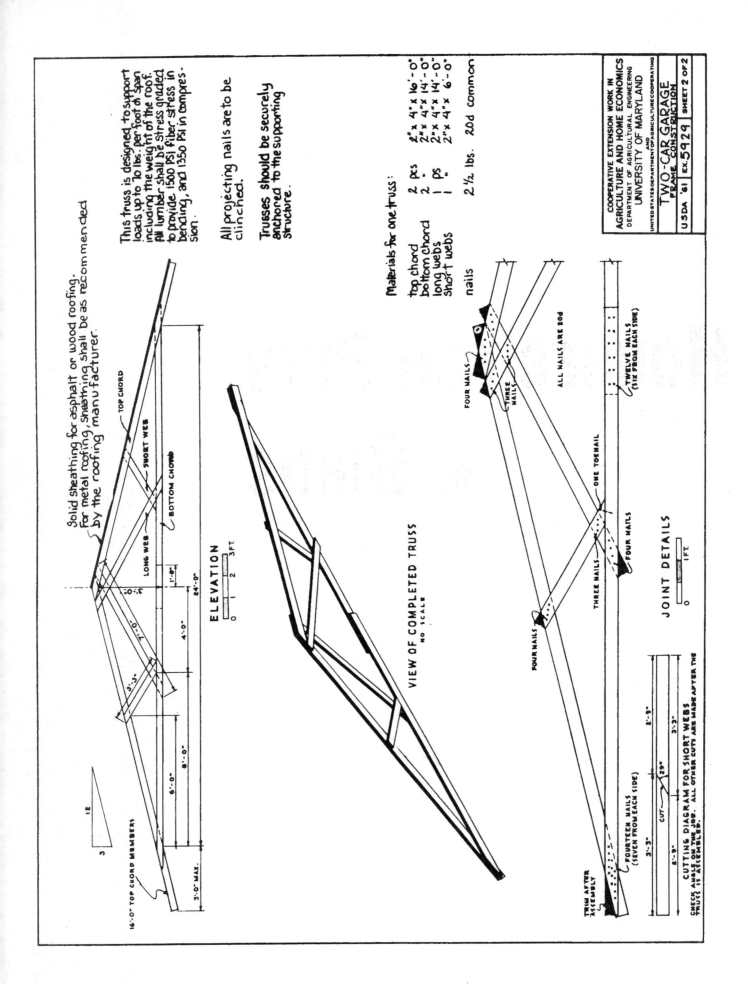

Solid sheathing for asphalt or wood roofing. For metal roofing, sheathing shall be as recommended by the roofing manufacturer.

This truss is designed to support loads up to 70 lbs. per foot of span including the weight of the roof. All lumber shall be stress graded to provide 1500 PSI fiber stress in bending, and 1350 PSI in compression.

All projecting nails are to be clinched.

Trusses should be securely anchored to the supporting structure.

Materials for one truss:

top chord	2 pcs.	2"x 4"x 16'-0"
bottom chord	2 "	2"x 4"x 14'-0"
long webs	1 pc.	2"x 4"x 14'-0"
short webs	1 "	2"x 4"x 6'-0"
nails	2½ lbs.	20d common

TOP CHORD

SHORT WEB

BOTTOM CHORD

LONG WEB

1'-0"

4'-0"

24'-0"

7'-0"

3'-3"

8'-0"

6'-0"

3'-0" MAX.

16'-0" TOP CHORD MEMBERS

12
3

ELEVATION

0   1   2   3 FT.

VIEW OF COMPLETED TRUSS
NO SCALE

FOUR NAILS

THREE NAILS

ALL NAILS ARE 20d

TWELVE NAILS
(SIX FROM EACH SIDE)

ONE TOENAIL

FOUR NAILS

THREE NAILS

FOUR NAILS

JOINT DETAILS

0   1 FT

TRIM AFTER ASSEMBLY

FOURTEEN NAILS
(SEVEN FROM EACH SIDE)

3'-3"

2'-9"

3'-3"

2'-9"

CUT   29°

CUTTING DIAGRAM FOR SHORT WEBS
CHECK ANGLE CUT ON THE JOB. ALL OTHER CUTS ARE MADE AFTER THE TRUSS IS ASSEMBLED.

COOPERATIVE EXTENSION WORK IN AGRICULTURE AND HOME ECONOMICS
DEPARTMENT OF AGRICULTURAL ENGINEERING
UNIVERSITY OF MARYLAND
AND
UNITED STATES DEPARTMENT OF AGRICULTURE COOPERATING

TWO-CAR GARAGE
FRAME CONSTRUCTION

USDA '61 | Ex. 5929 | SHEET 2 OF 2

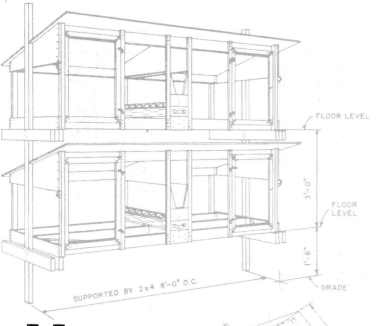

FLOOR LEVEL

FLOOR LEVEL

3'-0"

1'-6"

GRADE

SUPPORTED BY 2x4 8'-0" O.C.

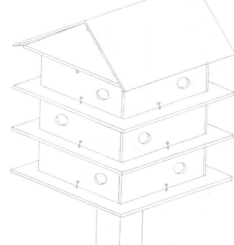

PERSPECTIVE

HOUSES FOR PETS AND BIRDS

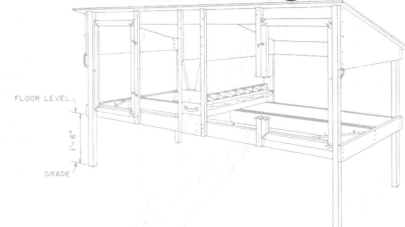

12"

20"

FLOOR LEVEL

1'-6"

GRADE

PERSPECTIVE OF SINGLE DECK
HUTCHES WITH 2x2 LEGS

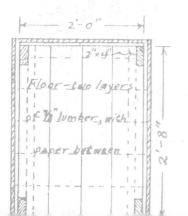

2'-0"

2"x4

Floor—two layers
of ½" lumber, with
paper between

2'-8"

SECTION

Top may be made removable, if desired.

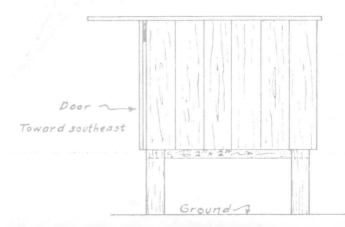

Door

Toward southeast

2"x2"

Ground

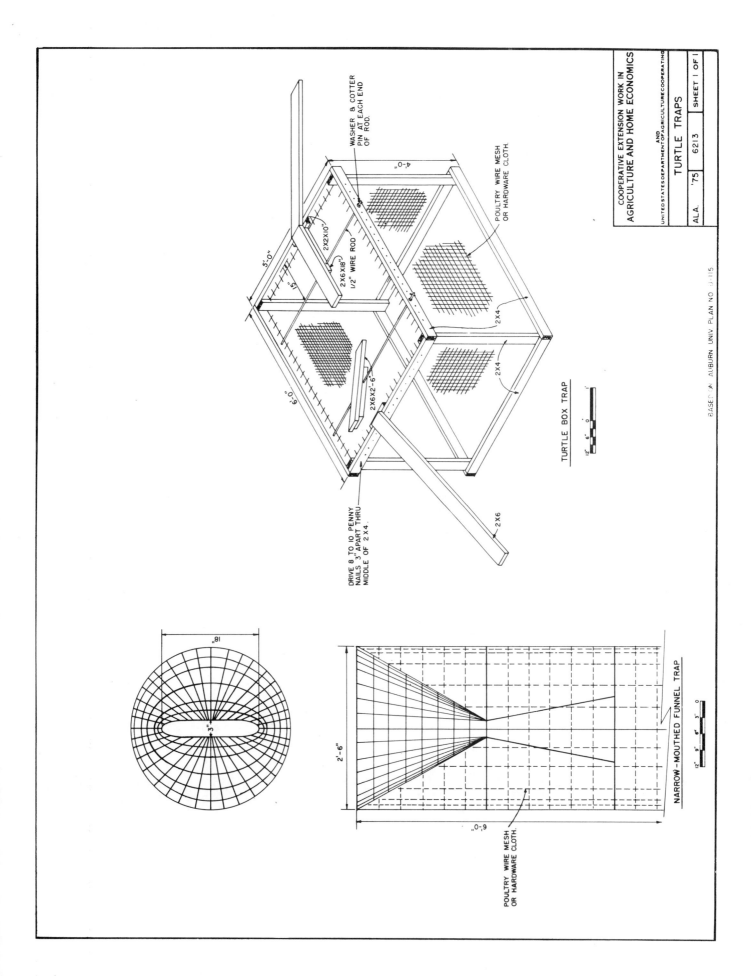

TURTLE BOX TRAP

WASHER & COTTER
PIN AT EACH END
OF ROD.

POULTRY WIRE MESH
OR HARDWARE CLOTH.

2X2X10"

2X6X18"
1/2" WIRE ROD

2X4

2X4

2X6X2'-6"

DRIVE 8 TO 10 PENNY
NAILS 3" APART THRU
MIDDLE OF 2X4.

2X6

5'-0"

4'-0"

5"

6'-0"

COOPERATIVE EXTENSION WORK IN
AGRICULTURE AND HOME ECONOMICS

AND
UNITED STATES DEPARTMENT OF AGRICULTURE COOPERATING

TURTLE TRAPS

ALA.   '75   6213   SHEET 1 OF 1

BASED ON AUBURN UNIV PLAN NO G-115

NARROW-MOUTHED FUNNEL TRAP

POULTRY WIRE MESH
OR HARDWARE CLOTH.

18"

3"

2'-6"

6'-0"

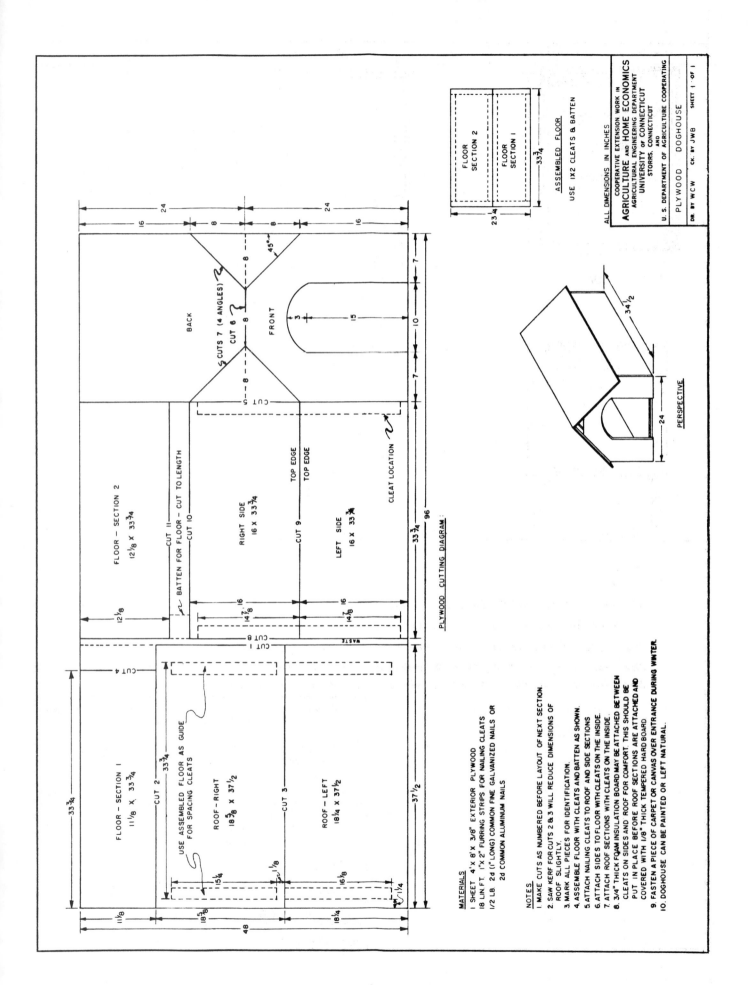

MATERIALS

1 SHEET 4' x 8' x 3/8" EXTERIOR PLYWOOD
18 LIN. FT. 1"x 2" FURRING STRIPS FOR NAILING CLEATS
1/2 LB. 2d (1" LONG) COMMON FINE GALVANIZED NAILS OR
   2d COMMON ALUMINUM NAILS

NOTES

1. MAKE CUTS AS NUMBERED BEFORE LAYOUT OF NEXT SECTION.
2. SAW KERF FOR CUTS 2 & 3 WILL REDUCE DIMENSIONS OF
   ROOF SLIGHTLY.
3. MARK ALL PIECES FOR IDENTIFICATION.
4. ASSEMBLE FLOOR WITH CLEATS AND BATTEN AS SHOWN.
5. ATTACH NAILING CLEATS TO ROOF AND SIDE SECTIONS
6. ATTACH SIDES TO FLOOR WITH CLEATS ON THE INSIDE.
7. ATTACH ROOF SECTIONS WITH CLEATS ON THE INSIDE.
8. 3/4" THICK FOAM INSULATION BOARD MAY BE ATTACHED BETWEEN
   CLEATS ON SIDES AND ROOF FOR COMFORT. THIS SHOULD BE
   PUT IN PLACE BEFORE ROOF SECTIONS ARE ATTACHED AND
   COVERED WITH 1/8" THICK TEMPERED HARD BOARD.
9. FASTEN A PIECE OF CARPET OR CANVAS OVER ENTRANCE DURING WINTER.
10. DOGHOUSE CAN BE PAINTED OR LEFT NATURAL.

PLYWOOD CUTTING DIAGRAM:

FLOOR – SECTION 2
12 1/8 X, 33 3/4

BATTEN FOR FLOOR – CUT TO LENGTH

RIGHT SIDE
16 x 33 3/4

LEFT SIDE
16 x 33 3/4

CLEAT LOCATION

FLOOR – SECTION 1
11 1/8 X, 33 3/4

USE ASSEMBLED FLOOR AS GUIDE
FOR SPACING CLEATS

ROOF – RIGHT
18 3/8 x 37 1/2

ROOF – LEFT
18 1/4 x 37 1/2

BACK

FRONT

CUTS 7 (4 ANGLES)
CUT 6

ASSEMBLED FLOOR

FLOOR
SECTION 2

FLOOR
SECTION 1

33 3/4

USE 1x2 CLEATS & BATTEN

PERSPECTIVE

ALL DIMENSIONS IN INCHES

COOPERATIVE EXTENSION WORK IN
AGRICULTURE AND HOME ECONOMICS
AGRICULTURAL ENGINEERING DEPARTMENT
UNIVERSITY OF CONNECTICUT
STORRS, CONNECTICUT
AND
U.S. DEPARTMENT OF AGRICULTURE COOPERATING

PLYWOOD DOGHOUSE

DR. BY W.C.W   CK. BY J.W.B   SHEET 1 OF 1

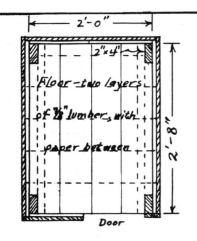

FLOOR PLAN

2'-0"

2"x4"

Floor—two layers of ⅞" lumber, with paper between

2'-8"

Door

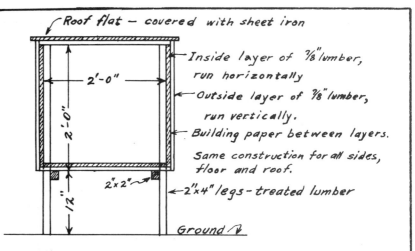

Roof flat — covered with sheet iron

2'-0"

2'-0"

12"

2"x2"

Inside layer of ⅞" lumber, run horizontally

Outside layer of ⅞" lumber, run vertically.

Building paper between layers.

Same construction for all sides, floor and roof.

2"x4" legs—treated lumber

Ground

SECTION

Top may be made removable, if desired.

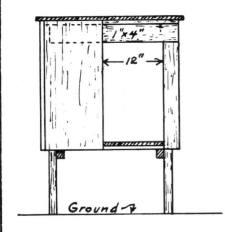

1"x4"

12"

Ground

FRONT

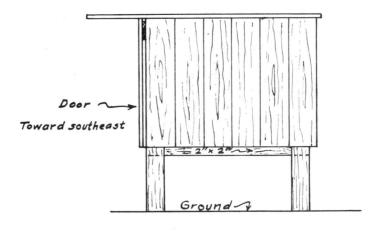

Door

Toward southeast

2"x2"

Ground

SIDE VIEW

THREE STORY DOG HOUSE.   Dog may get in the house, under it, or on the roof.

Size of house, according to size of dog.

The sides of the house may be made of one layer of ⅜" weather-proof plywood.

The roof may be one piece of weather-proof plywood, stiffened with cleats.

Sheet iron may be omitted from a plywood roof, if plywood is kept painted.

COOPERATIVE EXTENSION WORK IN AGRICULTURE AND HOME ECONOMICS

THE TEXAS A. & M. COLLEGE SYSTEM AND U. S. DEPARTMENT OF AGRICULTURE COOPERATING

G.G. GIBSON, DIRECTOR, COLLEGE STATION, TEXAS

DOG HOUSE

DRAWN BY: M. R. B.	SCALE AS SHOWN
TRACED BY: M. R. B.	SHEET 1 OF 1
REV. JUNE, 1954	SERIAL NO. 315

MATERIAL: 3/8" OR 1/2" EXTERIOR GRADE PLYWOOD.

NOTE:

ROOF TO BE ATTACHED WITH EYE SCREW.

Bluebirds like open areas away from trees, such as pastures, meadows, and large lawns. Bluebirds seem to prefer houses that open toward the south, and if utility lines or a wire fence is nearby, so much the better. Houses should be placed to have some afternoon shade to reduce the danger of overheating. Space houses 200 feet, or more, apart.

Assemble the bluebird house with coated box nails or screws. Wood used in construction should be stained green or brown. Copper naphthanate works very well.

The Bluebird house should be mounted on a pipe, a pole, or tree trunk 4 to 6 feet from the ground. A piece of sheet metal fastened below the house and around the pole or tree, tends to keep out predatory snakes.

Bluebirds do not need a perch by the entrance. A perch would tend to attract English sparrows and other undesirable species.

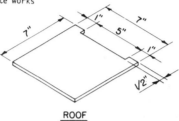

ROOF

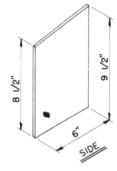

SIDE

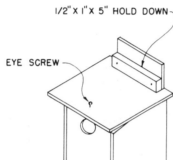

1/2" X 1" X 5" HOLD DOWN

EYE SCREW

FLOOR TO BE RECESSED 1/4"

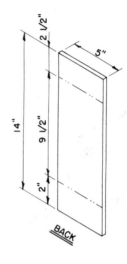

BACK

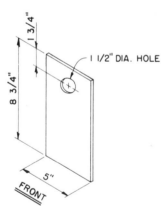

1 1/2" DIA. HOLE

FRONT

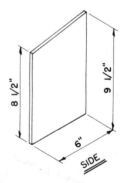

SIDE

1/4" X 45° - EACH CORNER

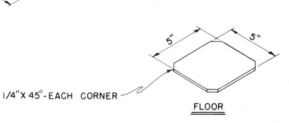

FLOOR

DUNCAN BLUEBIRD HOUSE

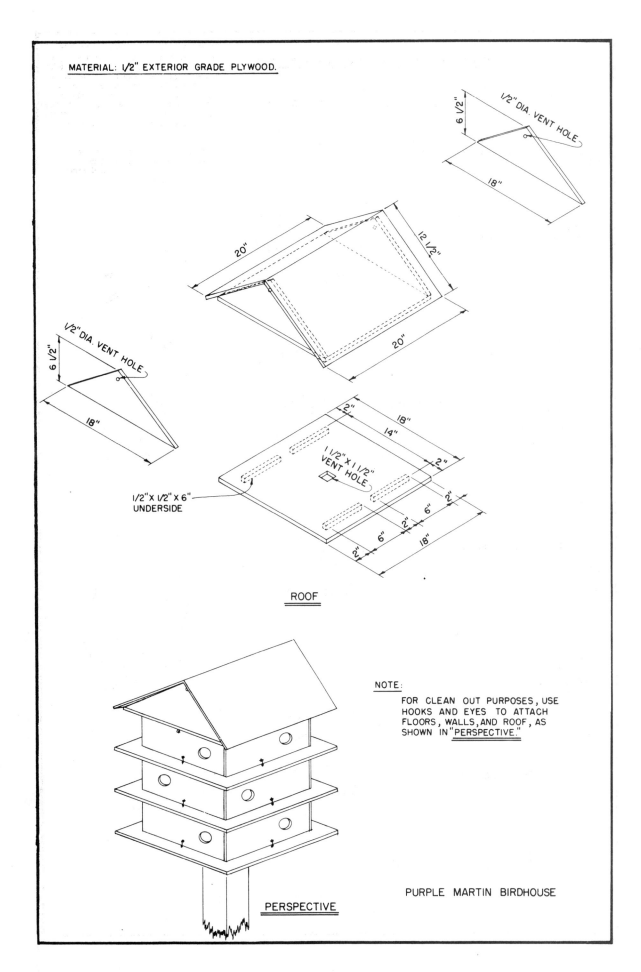

MATERIAL: 1/2" EXTERIOR GRADE PLYWOOD.

1/2" DIA. VENT HOLE

6 1/2"

18"

20"

12 1/2"

20"

1/2" DIA. VENT HOLE

6 1/2"

18"

1/2" X 1/2" X 6"
UNDERSIDE

2"

18"

14"

1 1/2" X 1 1/2"
VENT HOLE

2"

2"

6"

2"

6"

18"

2"

ROOF

NOTE:

FOR CLEAN OUT PURPOSES, USE
HOOKS AND EYES TO ATTACH
FLOORS, WALLS, AND ROOF, AS
SHOWN IN "PERSPECTIVE."

PERSPECTIVE

PURPLE MARTIN BIRDHOUSE

67

MATERIAL: 3/8" OR 1/2" EXTERIOR GRADE PLYWOOD.

NOTE:
ROOF TO BE ATTACHED WITH EYE SCREW.

Assemble Wood Duck House with coated box nails or screws. A good coat of paint or copper naphthanate will prolong the life of the house. Place 6 to 10 inches of shavings in bottom for nest.

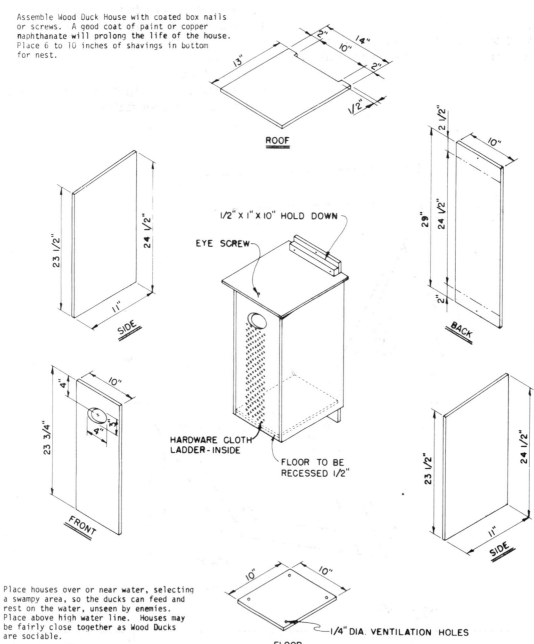

ROOF

1/2" X 1" X 10" HOLD DOWN

EYE SCREW

BACK

SIDE

HARDWARE CLOTH LADDER-INSIDE

FLOOR TO BE RECESSED 1/2"

FRONT

SIDE

1/4" DIA. VENTILATION HOLES

FLOOR

Place houses over or near water, selecting a swampy area, so the ducks can feed and rest on the water, unseen by enemies. Place above high water line. Houses may be fairly close together as Wood Ducks are sociable.

If the house is placed on a pipe, the pipe can be greased with axle grease, water pump grease, or any durable grease. If the house is placed on a pole, a piece of sheet metal fastened below the house and around the pole will keep raccoons from getting to the ducks' eggs.

Do not place houses in a straight line. Do not place houses so that limbs or tree branches droop in front of the entrance. Do not place the entrance within jumping distance of raccoons or squirrels.

WOOD DUCK HOUSE

Wren House

MATERIALS:

1 piece 1" x 6" x 24" (actual size about 3/4" x 5 1/2")

1 piece 1" x 4" x 12" (actual size about 3/4" x 3 1/2" x 12")

Use box lumber, bevel siding, exterior plywood, heavy asphalt roofing or tin for roof

4 - roundhead wood screws to attach one side of roof

9 - 2" nails

8 - 1 1/2" nails

Water repellent wood preservative or penetrating exterior stain for finish

NOTE: Attach one side of roof with wood screws, so it can be removed for annual house cleaning.

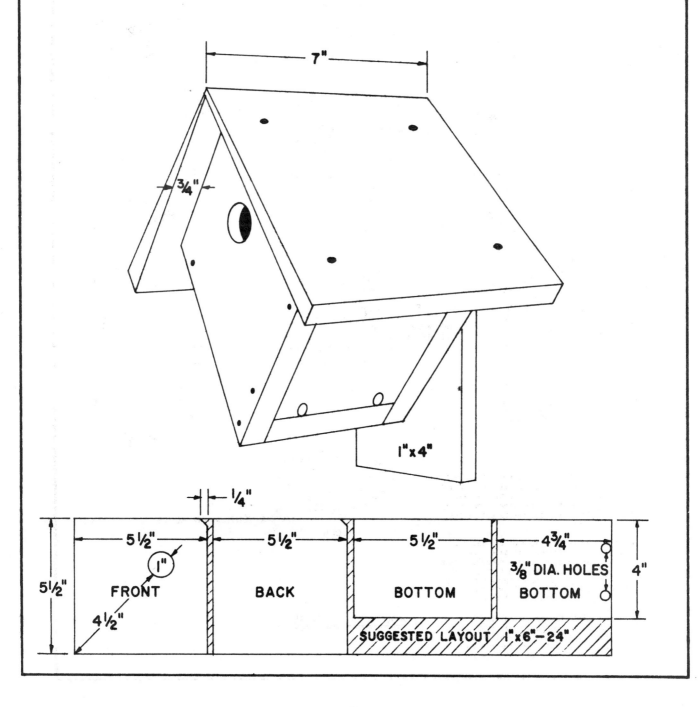

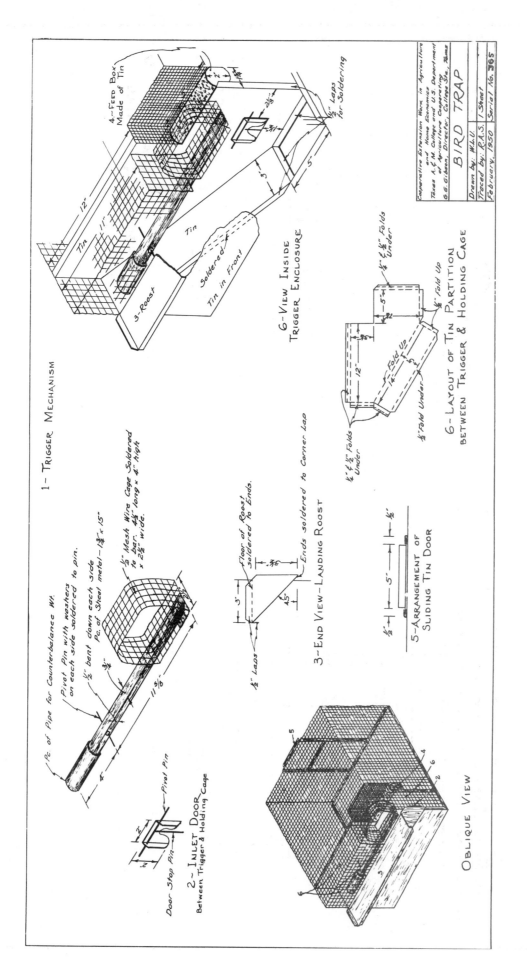

BIRD TRAP

Cooperative Extension Work in Agriculture and Home Economics
Texas A. & M. College and U. S. Department of Agriculture Cooperating.
G. G. Gibson, Director, College Sta., Texas

Drawn by: W.&.U.	1 Sheet
Traced by: R.A.S.	Serial No. 365
February, 1950	

1 – TRIGGER MECHANISM

6 – VIEW INSIDE TRIGGER ENCLOSURE

6 – LAYOUT OF TIN PARTITION
between Trigger & Holding Cage

2 – INLET DOOR
Between Trigger & Holding Cage

3 – END VIEW – LANDING ROOST

5 – ARRANGEMENT OF SLIDING TIN DOOR

OBLIQUE VIEW

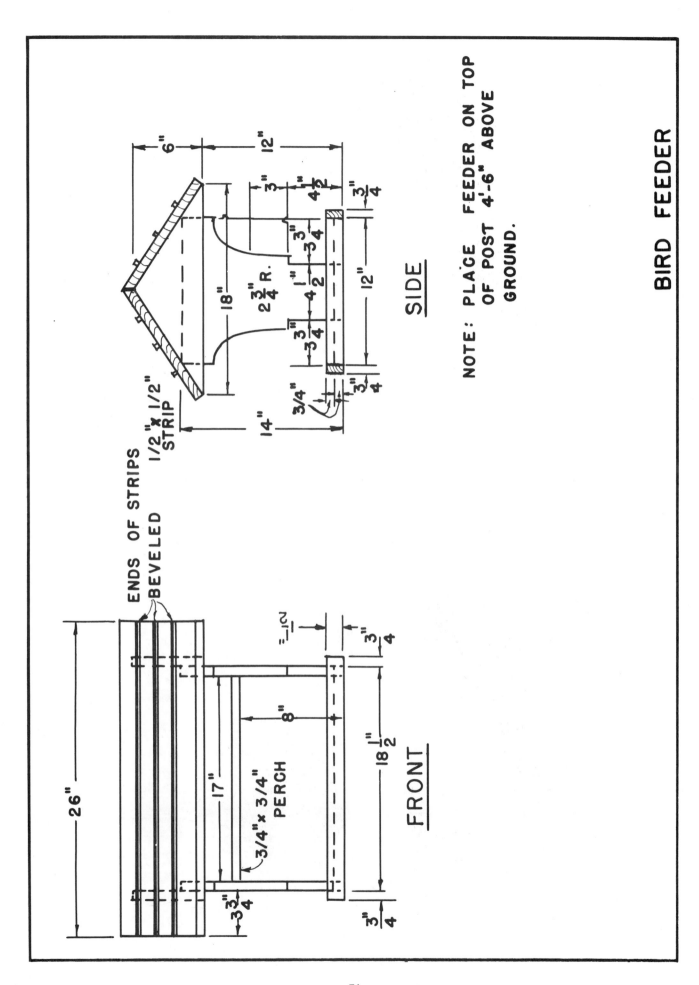

SIDE

FRONT

NOTE: PLACE FEEDER ON TOP
OF POST 4'-6" ABOVE
GROUND.

ENDS OF STRIPS
BEVELED

1/2" x 1/2"
STRIP

3/4" x 3/4"
PERCH

BIRD FEEDER

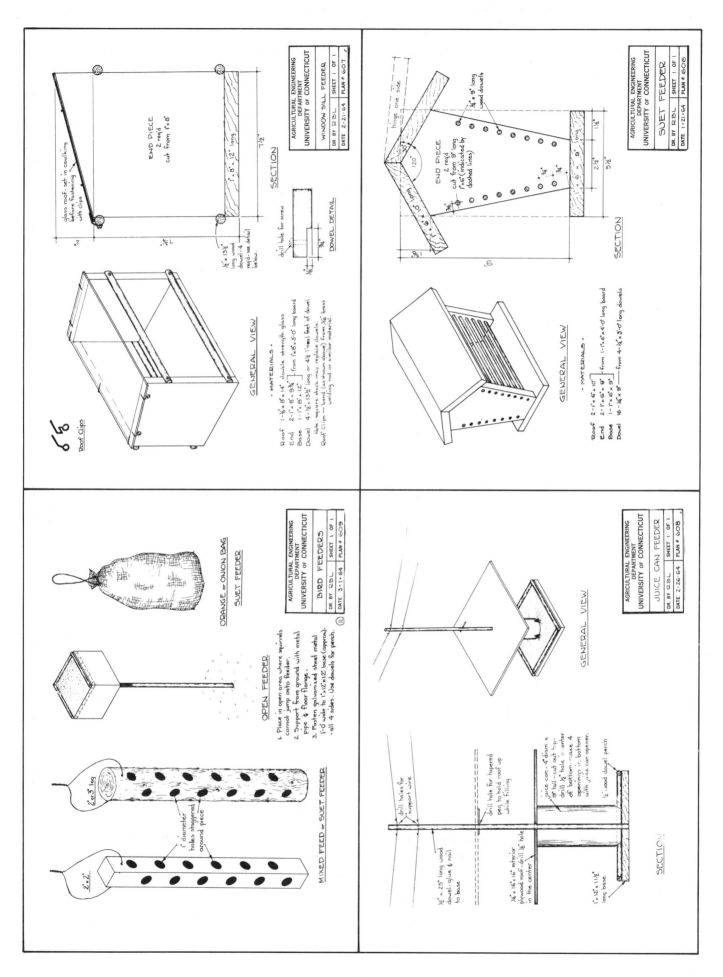

SECTION

END PIECE
2 req'd
cut from 1"x8"

glass roof set in caulking
before fastening with clips

¼" x 13½" long wood
dowel-see detail below

drill hole for screw

DOWEL DETAIL

GENERAL VIEW

Roof Clips

• MATERIALS •

Roof   1-⅛ x 8 x 14" double strength glass
End   2-1" x 8" x 9¾" ⎱ from 1"x 8"x 3'-0" long board
Base   1-1" x 8" x 12" ⎰
Dowel   4-¼" x 13½" long or 4½ lineal feet of dowel
Note: square stock may replace dowels.
Roof Clips-bend (as shown above) from 1/16 brass
welding rod or similar material.

AGRICULTURAL ENGINEERING
DEPARTMENT
UNIVERSITY of CONNECTICUT
WINDOW SILL FEEDER
DR BY R.B.L.   SHEET 1 OF 1
DATE 2-21-64 PLAN # 607

SECTION

END PIECE
2 req'd
cut from 9" long
1"x6" (indicated by
dashed lines)

hinge one side

¼" x 9" long
wood dowels

120°
30°

GENERAL VIEW

• MATERIALS •

Roof   2-1" x 6" x 10" ⎱
End   2-1" x 6" x 9"   ⎰ from 1-1"x 6"x 4'-0" long board
Base   1-1" x 6" x 9"
Dowel   16-¼" x 9" from 4-¼" x 3'-0" long dowels

AGRICULTURAL ENGINEERING
DEPARTMENT
UNIVERSITY of CONNECTICUT
SUET FEEDER
DR BY R.B.L.   SHEET 1 OF 1
DATE 1-21-64 PLAN # 606

ORANGE or ONION BAG
SUET FEEDER

OPEN FEEDER

1. Place in open area where squirrels
   cannot jump onto feeder.
2. Support from ground with metal
   pipe & floor flange.
3. Fasten galvanized sheet metal
   1'-0" wide to 1"x12"x12" base (approx.)
   -all 4 sides. Use dowels for perch.

1" diameter
holes staggered
around piece

2' or 3' log

2" x 2"

MIXED FEED or SUET FEEDER

AGRICULTURAL ENGINEERING
DEPARTMENT
UNIVERSITY of CONNECTICUT
BIRD FEEDERS
DR BY R.B.L.   SHEET 1 OF 1
DATE 3-1-64 PLAN # 609

GENERAL VIEW

drill holes for
support wire

drill hole for tapered
peg to hold roof up
while filling

juice can - 4" diam. x
9" tall - cut out top-
drill ½" hole in center
of bottom- raise 4
openings in bottom
with juice can opener.

¼" x 16 x 16" exterior
plywood roof drill ½" hole
in the center

½" x 25" long wood
dowel-glue & nail
to base

½" wood dowel perch

1" x 12" x 11½"
long base

SECTION

AGRICULTURAL ENGINEERING
DEPARTMENT
UNIVERSITY of CONNECTICUT
JUICE CAN FEEDER
DR BY R.B.L.   SHEET 1 OF 1
DATE 2-26-64 PLAN # 608

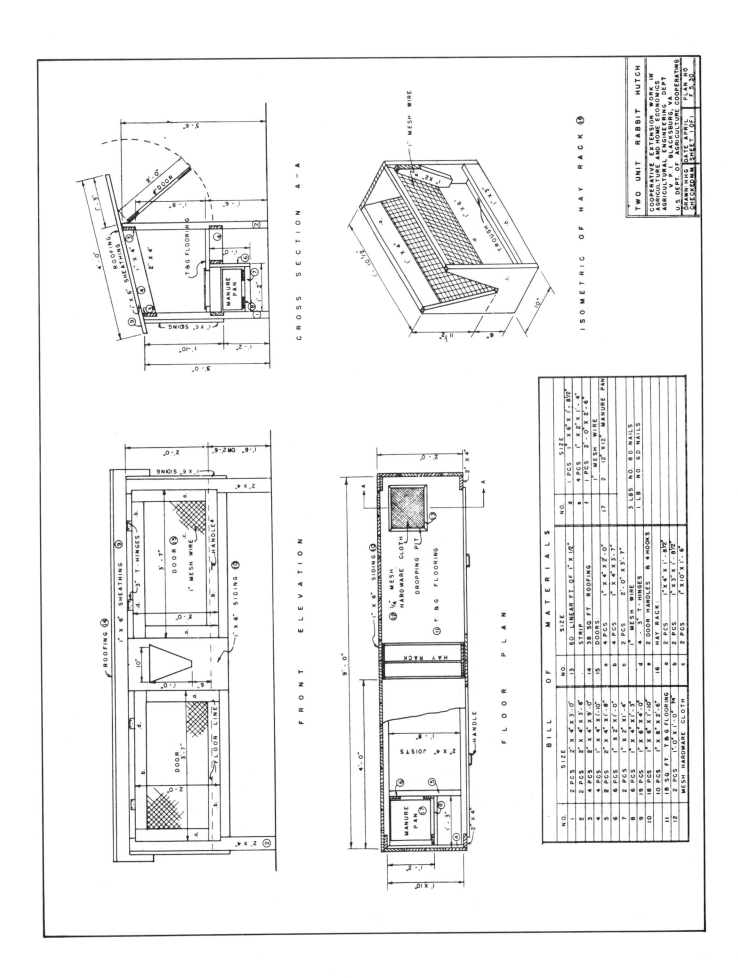

CROSS SECTION A-A

ISOMETRIC OF HAY RACK ⑬

FRONT ELEVATION

FLOOR PLAN

	BILL	OF	MATERIALS	
NO.		SIZE	NO.	SIZE
1	2 PCS	2"x 4"x 3'-0"	13	60 LINEAR FT OF 1"x 1/2" STRIP
2	2 PCS	2"x 4"x 3'-6"	14	38 SQ. FT ROOFING
3	4 PCS	2"x 4"x 9'-0"	15	DOORS:
4	4 PCS	1"x 4"x 1'-8"	a	4 PCS 1"x 4"x 2'-0"
5	2 PCS	2"x 4"x 1'-0"	b	4 PCS 1"x 4"x 3'-7"
6	6 PCS	1"x 2"x 1'-4"	c	2 PCS 2'-0" x 3'-7" MESH WIRE
7	6 PCS	1"x 4"x 1'-3"	d	4 - 3" T-HINGES
8	6 PCS	1"x 2"x 1'-4"	e	2 DOOR HANDLES & 4 HOOKS
9	19 PCS	1"x 6"x 4'-0"	16	HAY RACK:
10	18 PCS	1"x 6"x 2'-6"	a	2 PCS 1"x 4"x 1'-81/2"
11	18 SQ. FT. T&G FLOORING		b	2 PCS 1"x 3"x 1'-81/2"
12	2 PCS 1'-0"x 1'-0" 1/4" MESH HARDWARE CLOTH		c	2 PCS 1"x10"x 1'-6"

NO.		SIZE
d	1 PCS	1"x 6"x 1'-81/2"
e	4 PCS	1"x 2"x 1'-4"
f	1 PCS	2'-0 x 2'-6" MESH WIRE
17	2	12"x 12" MANURE PAN
	3 LBS NO. 8 D NAILS	
	1 LB NO. 6 D NAILS	

TWO UNIT RABBIT HUTCH

COOPERATIVE EXTENSION WORK IN
AGRICULTURE AND HOME ECONOMICS
AGRICULTURAL ENGINEERING DEPT.
V.P.I. BLACKSBURG, VA.
U.S. DEPT. OF AGRICULTURE COOPERATING

DRAWN: MHG   DATE APRIL   PLAN NO.
CHECKED M.M.   SHEET 1 OF 1   F 5.30

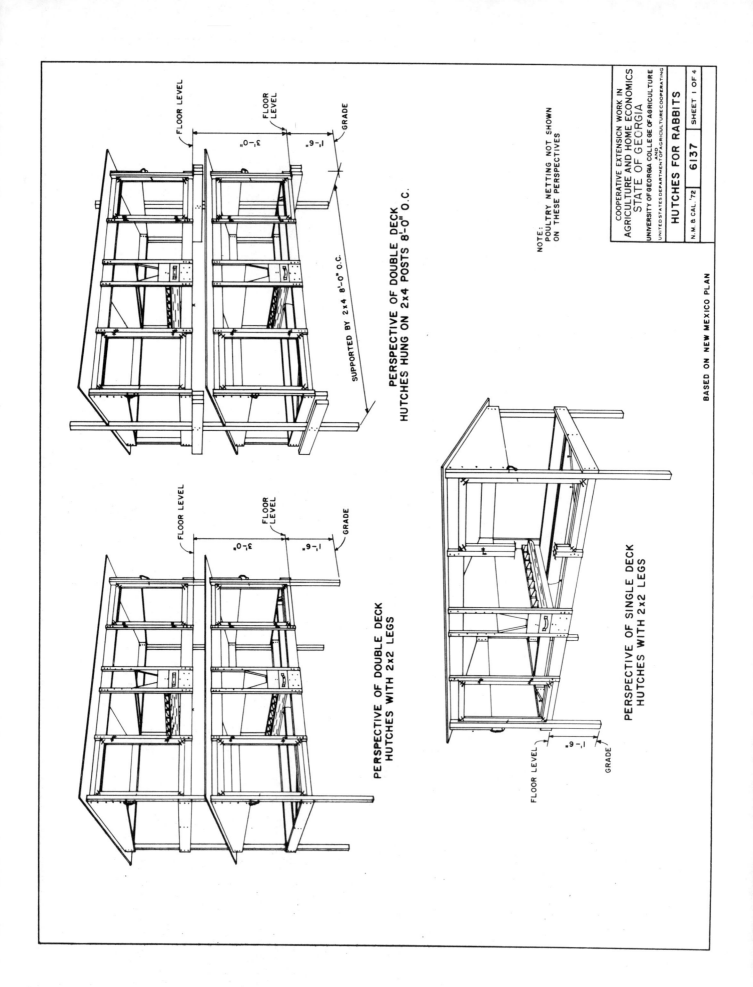

PERSPECTIVE OF DOUBLE DECK
HUTCHES HUNG ON 2x4 POSTS 8'-0" O.C.

PERSPECTIVE OF DOUBLE DECK
HUTCHES WITH 2x2 LEGS

PERSPECTIVE OF SINGLE DECK
HUTCHES WITH 2x2 LEGS

NOTE::
POULTRY NETTING NOT SHOWN
ON THESE PERSPECTIVES

COOPERATIVE EXTENSION WORK IN
AGRICULTURE AND HOME ECONOMICS
STATE OF GEORGIA
UNIVERSITY OF GEORGIA COLLEGE OF AGRICULTURE
AND
UNITED STATES DEPARTMENT OF AGRICULTURE COOPERATING

HUTCHES FOR RABBITS

| N.M. 8 CAL. '72 | 6137 | SHEET 1 OF 4 |

BASED ON NEW MEXICO PLAN

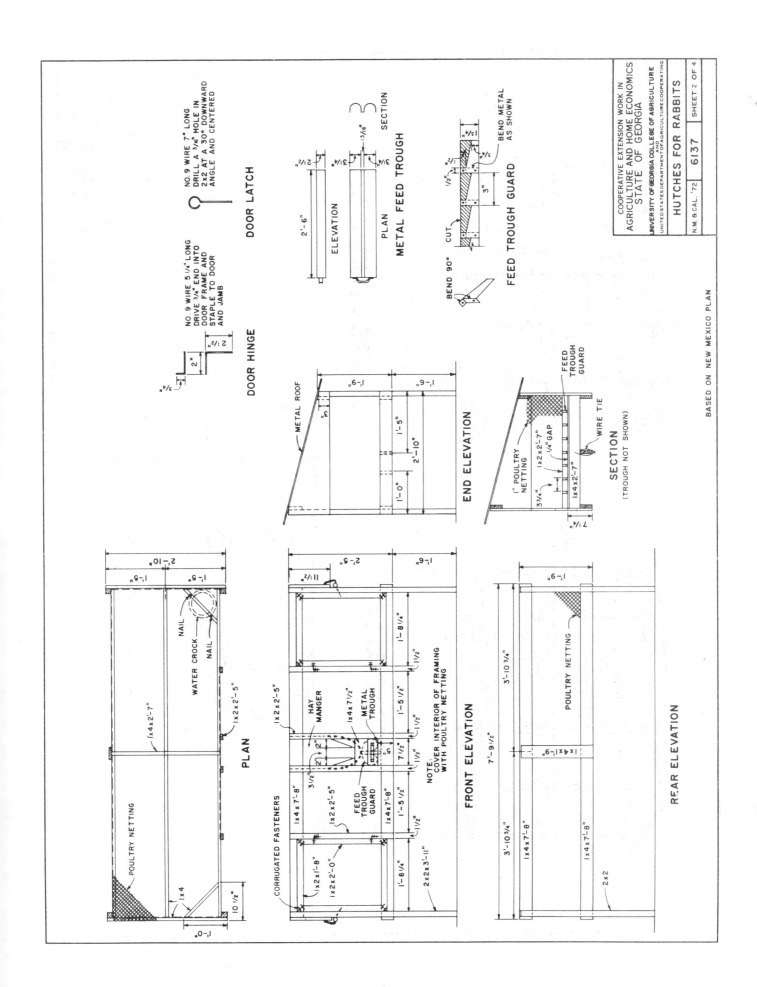

DOOR LATCH

NO. 9 WIRE 7" LONG
DRILL A 3/16" HOLE IN
2x2 AT A 30° DOWNWARD
ANGLE AND CENTERED

DOOR HINGE

NO. 9 WIRE 5 1/4" LONG
DRIVE 3/4" END INTO
DOOR FRAME AND
STAPLE TO DOOR
AND JAMB

METAL FEED TROUGH

ELEVATION

PLAN

SECTION

FEED TROUGH GUARD

BEND METAL
AS SHOWN

CUT

BEND 90°

END ELEVATION

METAL ROOF

SECTION
(TROUGH NOT SHOWN)

1" POULTRY
NETTING

FEED
TROUGH
GUARD

WIRE TIE

PLAN

POULTRY NETTING

NAIL
WATER CROCK
NAIL

FRONT ELEVATION

CORRUGATED FASTENERS

HAY MANGER

METAL TROUGH

FEED
TROUGH
GUARD

NOTE:
COVER INTERIOR OF FRAMING
WITH POULTRY NETTING

REAR ELEVATION

POULTRY NETTING

COOPERATIVE EXTENSION WORK IN
AGRICULTURE AND HOME ECONOMICS
STATE OF GEORGIA
UNIVERSITY OF GEORGIA COLLEGE OF AGRICULTURE
AND
UNITED STATES DEPARTMENT OF AGRICULTURE COOPERATING

HUTCHES FOR RABBITS

N.M. & CAL. '72 | 6137 | SHEET 2 OF 4

BASED ON NEW MEXICO PLAN

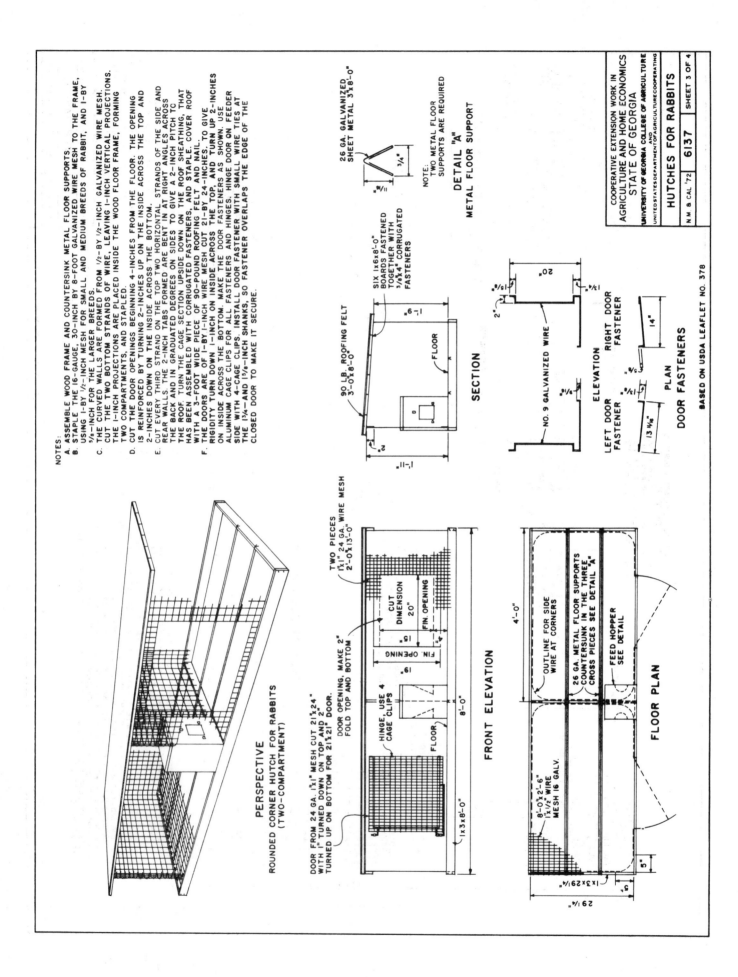

NOTES:

A. ASSEMBLE WOOD FRAME AND COUNTERSINK METAL FLOOR SUPPORTS.

B. STAPLE THE 16-GAUGE, 30-INCH BY 8-FOOT GALVANIZED WIRE MESH TO THE FRAME, USING 1-BY 1/2-INCH MESH FOR SMALL AND MEDIUM BREEDS OF RABBIT, AND 1-BY 5/8-INCH FOR THE LARGER BREEDS.

C. THE CURVED WALLS ARE FORMED FROM 1/2- BY 1/2-INCH GALVANIZED WIRE MESH. CUT THE TWO BOTTOM STRANDS OF WIRE, LEAVING 1-INCH VERTICAL PROJECTIONS. THE 1-INCH PROJECTIONS ARE PLACED INSIDE THE WOOD FLOOR FRAME, FORMING TWO COMPARTMENTS, AND STAPLED.

D. CUT THE DOOR OPENINGS BEGINNING 4-INCHES FROM THE FLOOR. THE OPENING IS REINFORCED BY TURNING 2-INCHES UP ON THE INSIDE ACROSS THE TOP AND 2-INCHES DOWN ON THE INSIDE ACROSS THE BOTTOM.

E. CUT EVERY THIRD STRAND ON THE TOP TWO HORIZONTAL STRANDS OF THE SIDE AND REAR WALLS. THE 2-INCH TABS FORMED ARE BENT IN AT RIGHT ANGLES ACROSS THE BACK AND IN GRADUATED DEGREES ON SIDES TO GIVE A 2-INCH PITCH TO THE ROOF. TURN THE CAGE SECTION UPSIDE DOWN ON THE ROOF SHEATHING, THAT HAS BEEN ASSEMBLED WITH CORRUGATED FASTENERS, AND STAPLE. COVER ROOF WITH A 3-FOOT WIDE PIECE OF 90-POUND ROOFING FELT AND NAIL.

F. THE DOORS ARE OF 1-BY 1-INCH WIRE MESH CUT 21- BY 24-INCHES. TO GIVE RIGIDITY TURN DOWN 1-INCH ON INSIDE ACROSS THE TOP, AND TURN UP 2-INCHES ON INSIDE ACROSS THE BOTTOM. MAKE THE DOOR FASTENERS AS SHOWN. USE ALUMINUM CAGE CLIPS FOR ALL FASTENERS AND HINGES. HINGE DOOR ON FEEDER SIDE WITH 4-CAGE CLIPS. INSTALL DOOR FASTENER WITH SMALL WIRE TIES AT THE 1 3/4—AND 1 5/8-INCH SHANKS, SO FASTENER OVERLAPS THE EDGE OF THE CLOSED DOOR TO MAKE IT SECURE.

PERSPECTIVE

ROUNDED CORNER HUTCH FOR RABBITS
(TWO-COMPARTMENT)

DOOR FROM 24 GA. 1"x1" MESH CUT 21½"x24"
WITH 1" TURNED DOWN ON TOP AND 2"
TURNED UP ON BOTTOM FOR 21½x21" DOOR.

TWO PIECES
1"x1" 24 GA. WIRE MESH
2'-0"x13'-0"

CUT DIMENSION 20"

FIN. OPENING 15"

FIN. OPENING 19"

DOOR OPENING, MAKE 2"
FOLD TOP AND BOTTOM

HINGE, USE 4
CAGE CLIPS

FLOOR

8'-0"

1x3x8'-0"

FRONT ELEVATION

8'-0"x 2'-6"
1"x½" WIRE
MESH 16 GALV.

OUTLINE FOR SIDE
WIRE AT CORNERS

26 GA. METAL FLOOR SUPPORTS
COUNTERSUNK IN THE THREE
CROSS PIECES SEE DETAIL "A"

FEED HOPPER
SEE DETAIL

4'-0"

1x3x29¼"

5"

5"

29¼"

FLOOR PLAN

90 LB. ROOFING FELT
3'-0"x8'-0"

SIX 1x6x8'-0"
BOARDS FASTENED
TOGETHER WITH
3/8"x¼" CORRUGATED
FASTENERS

1'-9"

FLOOR

2"

1'-11"

SECTION

26 GA. GALVANIZED
SHEET METAL 3"x8'-0"

11/16"

¾"

NOTE:
TWO METAL FLOOR
SUPPORTS ARE REQUIRED

DETAIL "A"
METAL FLOOR SUPPORT

20"

2"

1¾"

1½"

NO. 9 GALVANIZED WIRE

ELEVATION

LEFT DOOR
FASTENER

13 9/16"

RIGHT DOOR
FASTENER

14"

PLAN

DOOR FASTENERS

BASED ON USDA LEAFLET NO. 378

COOPERATIVE EXTENSION WORK IN
AGRICULTURE AND HOME ECONOMICS
STATE OF GEORGIA
UNIVERSITY OF GEORGIA COLLEGE OF AGRICULTURE
AND
UNITED STATES DEPARTMENT OF AGRICULTURE COOPERATING

HUTCHES FOR RABBITS

N.M. & CAL. '72 | 6137 | SHEET 3 OF 4

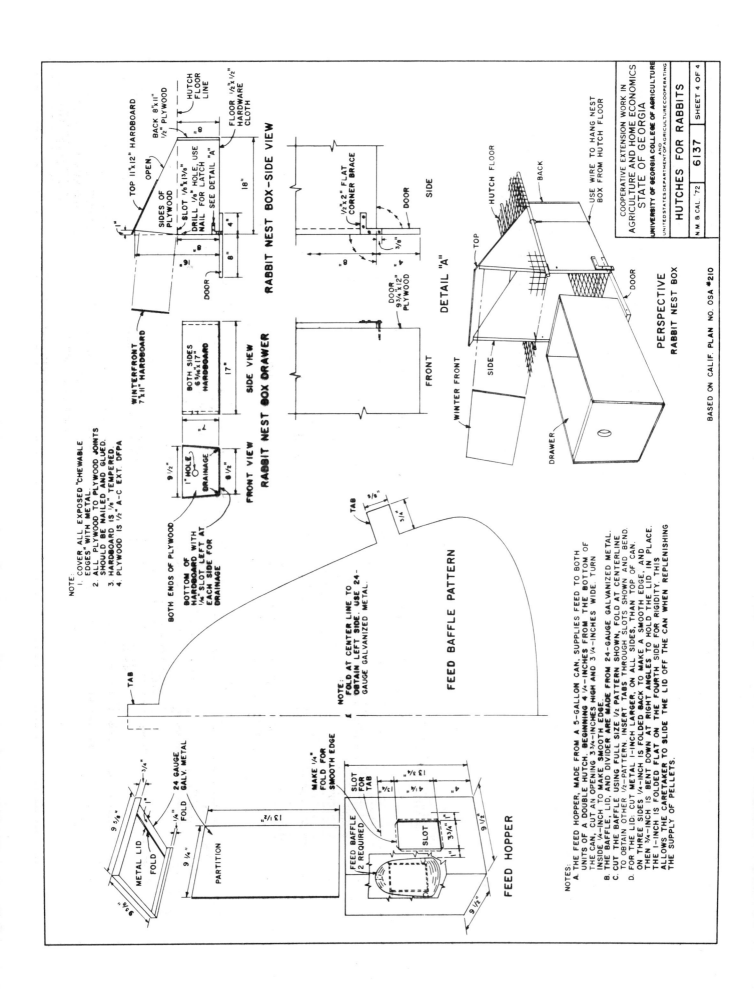

GREENHOUSES

FRAMING MEASUREMENTS

11 5/8" 4'-0 3/8"
4'-6"
2'-4 3/16"
10 1/2"
HEAD
18"
(12) 4d NAILS EACH SIDE
3/8" PLYWOOD GUSSETS
10 1/2"
EAVE
(12) 4d NAILS EACH SIDE
5'-1 13/16"
5'-3"

ISOMETRIC VIEW

5/4 x 4 PURLINS
BENCH & BENCH SUPPORTS NOT SHOWN IN THIS VIEW
2 x 4 FRAMES
SEE NOTE #1
3/8" GUSSET PLATES
2 x 4
4'-0"±
4'-0"±
4'-0"±
6'-3"
2 x 4 SILL P.T WITH COPPER NAPHTHENATE
2'-6"
1 x 12 REDWOOD BOARD
6'-0"±
6'-0"±
5'-0"
5'-0"
ALTERNATE: FLAT FIBERGLASS PANELS AT END

DETAIL "A"

COMMERCIAL OR HOME BUILT BENCH
1 1/4" PIPE OVER SUPPORTS
1/4" x 4" BOLTS
2 x 4
2'-0"
BRICK OR BLOCKS UNDER SUPPORTS
3'-9"

END VIEW

GUSSET "A"
SEE DOOR DETAIL
10'-0"
2" x 3" RAFTER
6'-2"
GUSSET "B"
2'-0" 1'-8" 2'-6"
10'-0"
SEE BASE DETAIL

CROSS SECTION

11 5/8" 4'-0 3/8"
RIDGE ROLL
CORRUGATED FIBERGLASS PANELS
12
7
5/4 x 4 PURLINS (3) EACH SIDE
25
3/8" PLYWOOD GUSSETS
DOOR ONE END
CORRUGATED FIBERGLASS PANELS
5/4 x 4 DOOR FRAME
BENCH SUPPORTS SEE DETAIL "A"
3" GRAVEL FILL
1 x 12 REDWOOD BOARD
GRADE
10'-0"
4 x 4 x 4'-0" POST AT CORNERS AND CENTERS PRESSURE-TREATED WITH COPPER NAPHTHENATE

12'-0"
4'-0" 4'-0" 4'-0"
3'-9"
BENCH SUPPORTS
BENCH
END SUPPORT
10'-0"
2'-6"
DOOR ONE END
3'-9"

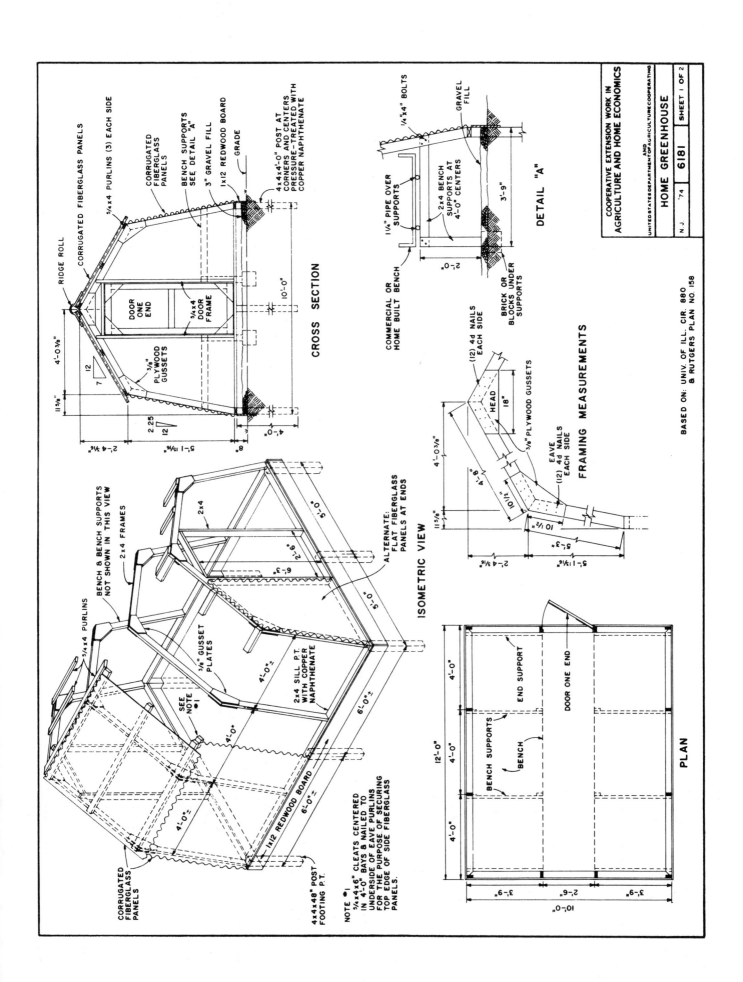

CROSS SECTION

DETAIL "A"

ISOMETRIC VIEW

FRAMING MEASUREMENTS

PLAN

COOPERATIVE EXTENSION WORK IN
AGRICULTURE AND HOME ECONOMICS
AND
UNITED STATES DEPARTMENT OF AGRICULTURE COOPERATING

HOME GREENHOUSE

N.J. | '74 | 6181 | SHEET 1 OF 2

BASED ON: UNIV. OF ILL. CIR. 880
& RUTGERS PLAN NO. 158

NOTE #1
5/4 x 4 x 6" CLEATS CENTERED
IN 4'-0" BAYS 8 NAILED TO
UNDERSIDE OF EAVE PURLINS
FOR THE PURPOSE OF SECURING
TOP EDGE OF SIDE FIBERGLASS
PANELS.

81

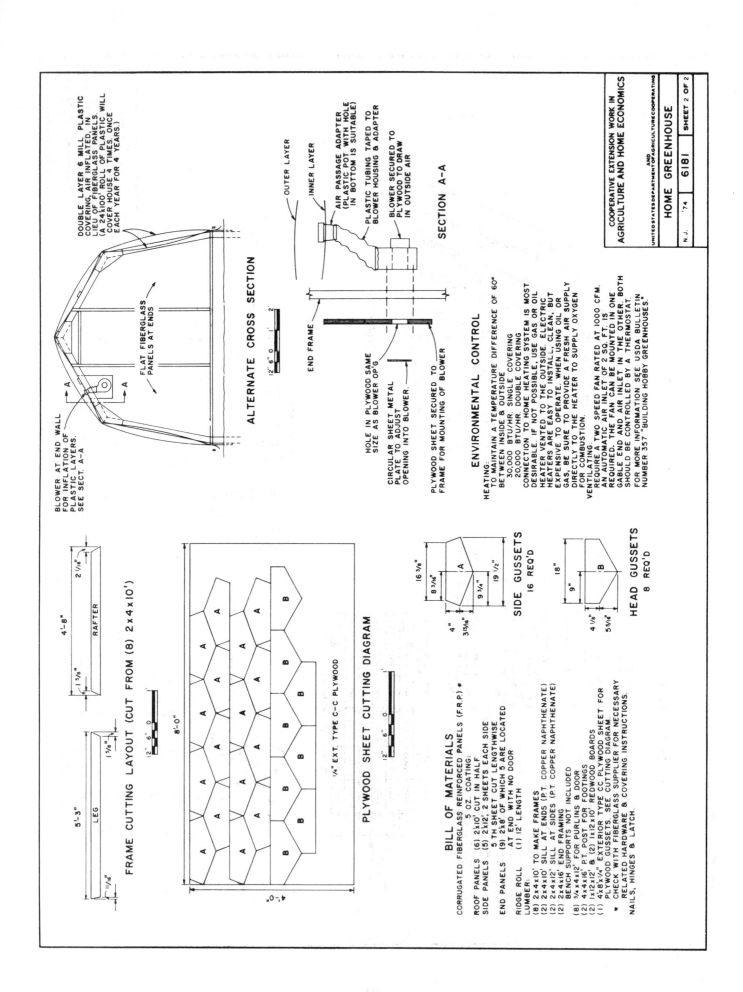

DOUBLE LAYER 6 MILL PLASTIC COVERING, AIR INFLATED, IN LIEU OF FIBERGLASS PANELS. (A 24x100' ROLL OF PLASTIC WILL COVER HOUSE 4 TIMES. ONCE EACH YEAR FOR 4 YEARS.)

BLOWER AT END WALL FOR INFLATION OF PLASTIC LAYERS. SEE SECT. A-A

FLAT FIBERGLASS PANELS AT ENDS

ALTERNATE CROSS SECTION

OUTER LAYER

INNER LAYER

AIR PASSAGE ADAPTER (PLASTIC POT WITH HOLE IN BOTTOM IS SUITABLE)

PLASTIC TUBING TAPED TO BLOWER HOUSING & ADAPTER

BLOWER SECURED TO PLYWOOD TO DRAW IN OUTSIDE AIR

SECTION A-A

END FRAME

HOLE IN PLYWOOD SAME SIZE AS BLOWER OP'G

CIRCULAR SHEET METAL PLATE TO ADJUST OPENING INTO BLOWER.

PLYWOOD SHEET SECURED TO FRAME FOR MOUNTING OF BLOWER.

ENVIRONMENTAL CONTROL

HEATING:
TO MAINTAIN A TEMPERATURE DIFFERENCE OF 60° BETWEEN INSIDE & OUTSIDE
30,000 BTU/HR. SINGLE COVERING
20,000 BTU/HR. DOUBLE COVERING
CONNECTION TO HOME HEATING SYSTEM IS MOST DESIRABLE. IF NOT POSSIBLE, USE GAS OR OIL HEATER VENTED TO THE OUTSIDE. ELECTRIC HEATERS ARE EASY TO INSTALL, CLEAN, BUT EXPENSIVE TO OPERATE. WHEN USING OIL OR GAS, BE SURE TO PROVIDE A FRESH AIR SUPPLY DIRECTLY TO THE HEATER TO SUPPLY OXYGEN FOR COMBUSTION.

VENTILATING:
REQUIRE A TWO SPEED FAN RATED AT 1000 CFM. AN AUTOMATIC AIR INLET OF 2 SQ. FT. IS REQUIRED. THE FAN CAN BE MOUNTED IN ONE GABLE END AND AIR INLET IN THE OTHER. BOTH SHOULD BE CONTROLLED BY A THERMOSTAT.
FOR MORE INFORMATION SEE USDA BULLETIN NUMBER 357 "BUILDING HOBBY GREENHOUSES."

FRAME CUTTING LAYOUT (CUT FROM (8) 2x4x10')

5'-3"
LEG
1 5/8"
11/16"

4'-8"
2 1/8"
RAFTER
1 5/8"

PLYWOOD SHEET CUTTING DIAGRAM

8'-0"
4'-0"

A A A A
A A A A
A A A A A
B B B
B B B
B B B
B B B

1/4" EXT. TYPE C-C PLYWOOD

SIDE GUSSETS
16 REQ'D

16 3/16"
8 3/16"
19 1/2"
9 3/4"
4"
3 13/16"
A

HEAD GUSSETS
8 REQ'D

18"
9"
4 1/8"
5 5/16"
B

BILL OF MATERIALS

CORRUGATED FIBERGLASS REINFORCED PANELS (F.R.P.) *
5 OZ. COATING:

ROOF PANELS (6) 2x10' CUT IN HALF
SIDE PANELS (5) 2x12', 2 SHEETS EACH SIDE
5 TH SHEET CUT LENGTHWISE
END PANELS (9) 2x8' OF WHICH 5 ARE LOCATED
AT END WITH NO DOOR
RIDGE ROLL (1) 12' LENGTH

LUMBER:
(8) 2x4x10' TO MAKE FRAMES
(2) 2x4x10' SILL AT ENDS (P.T. COPPER NAPHTHENATE)
(2) 2x4x12' SILL AT SIDES (P.T. COPPER NAPHTHENATE)
(2) 2x4x16' END FRAMING
5/4x4x12' FOR PURLINS & DOOR
BENCH SUPPORTS NOT INCLUDED
(8) 4x4x16' P.T. POST FOR FOOTINGS
(2) 1x12x12' & (2) 1x12x10' REDWOOD BOARDS
(1) 4'x8'x1/4" EXTERIOR TYPE CC PLYWOOD SHEET FOR PLYWOOD GUSSETS. SEE CUTTING DIAGRAM.

* CHECK WITH FIBERGLASS SUPPLIER FOR NECESSARY RELATED HARDWARE & COVERING INSTRUCTIONS.
NAILS, HINGES & LATCH.

COOPERATIVE EXTENSION WORK IN
AGRICULTURE AND HOME ECONOMICS
AND
UNITED STATES DEPARTMENT OF AGRICULTURE COOPERATING

HOME GREENHOUSE

N.J. '74   6181   SHEET 2 OF 2

COOPERATIVE EXTENSION WORK IN
AGRICULTURE AND HOME ECONOMICS
AGRICULTURAL ENGINEERING DEPARTMENT
UNIVERSITY OF CONNECTICUT
STORRS, CONNECTICUT
AND
U.S. DEPARTMENT OF AGRICULTURE COOPERATING

"A" FRAME HOME GRENHOUSE

DR BY JWB	CK BY REP	SHEET 1 OF 2
	DATE 7-3-67	PLAN # 238

CONSTRUCTION NOTES

GENERAL

SELECT A LEVEL, WELL DRAINED SITE NEAR WATER AND ELECTRICITY.

TREAT BASE WITH TWO COATS OF A COPPER NAPHTHENATE WOOD PRESERVATIVE. SCREW ANCHORS INTO GROUND, SLOT BASE AND TIGHTEN ANCHOR TO BASE.

FRAME

USE CONSTRUCTION GRADE FIR.

PAINT FRAME WITH AN EXTERIOR WHITE PAINT. DOORS CAN BE PLACED IN ONE OR BOTH END WALLS.

COVERING

FOR YEAR AROUND USE, TWO LAYERS OF PLASTIC SHOULD BE USED.

FOR SPRING AND FALL USE, SINGLE LAYER IS SUFFICIENT.

TO REDUCE LABOR OF REPLACING PLASTIC, A 4-5 YEAR ULTRA-VIOLET RESISTANT VINYL PLASTIC SHOULD BE USED ON THE OUTSIDE. INNER LAYER CAN BE POLYETHYLENE AND CAN BE ATTACHED WITH EITHER BATTEN STRIPS OR

3/8" STAPLES OVER HEAVY TWINE.

WALKS AND BENCHES

A CENTER WALK OF STONES OR BRICKS LAID IN SAND CAN BE ADDED AFTER THE GREENHOUSE IS BUILT.

BENCHES 30-32 INCHES HIGH AND TREATED WITH A COPPER NAPHTHENATE WOOD PRESERVATIVE CAN BE ADDED FOR CONVENIENCE.

VENTILATION

A 10 INCH DIAMETER FAN WITH AUTOMATIC LOUVER AND THERMOSTAT SHOULD BE PLACED ABOVE DOOR ON ONE END WALL.

LOCATE A 10 OR 12 INCH INTAKE LOUVER ABOVE DOOR ON OPPOSITE END WALL.

PLACE THERMOSTAT ALONG SIDEWALL NEAR PLANT LEVEL.

HEAT

HEAT MAY BE SUPPLIED FROM THE HOME HEATING SYSTEM OR FROM A SEPARATE HEATER. OUTPUT REQUIRED CAN BE OBTAINED FROM THE FOLLOW- ING TABLE.

MINIMUM OUTSIDE TEMPERATURE	SINGLE LAYER PLASTIC BTU/HR.				DOUBLE LAYER PLASTIC BTU/HR			
30°	6800	10200	13600		3800	5700	7600
20°	10200	13600	17000		5700	7600	9500
10°	13600	17000	20400		7600	9500	11400
0°	17000	20400	23800		9500	11400	13300
-10°	20400	23800	27100		11400	13300	15200
	50°	60°	70°		50°	60°	70°

MINIMUM INSIDE TEMPERATURE

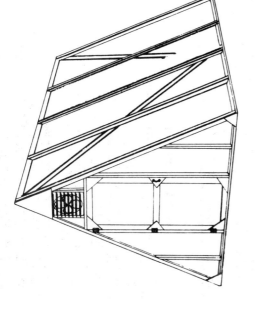

PERSPECTIVE

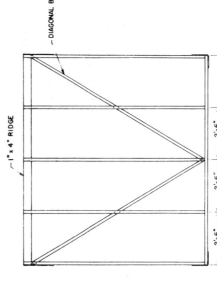

— DIAGONAL BRACE (1" x 3" x 12')

— 1" x 4" RIDGE

2'-6" 2'-6" 10'-0" 2'-6" 2'-6"

SIDE VIEW

GUSSET "A"

SEE DOOR DETAIL

2" x 3" RAFTER

10'-0"

10'-0"

GUSSET "B"

SEE BASE DETAIL

2'-0" 1'-8" 2'-6"

6'-2"

END VIEW

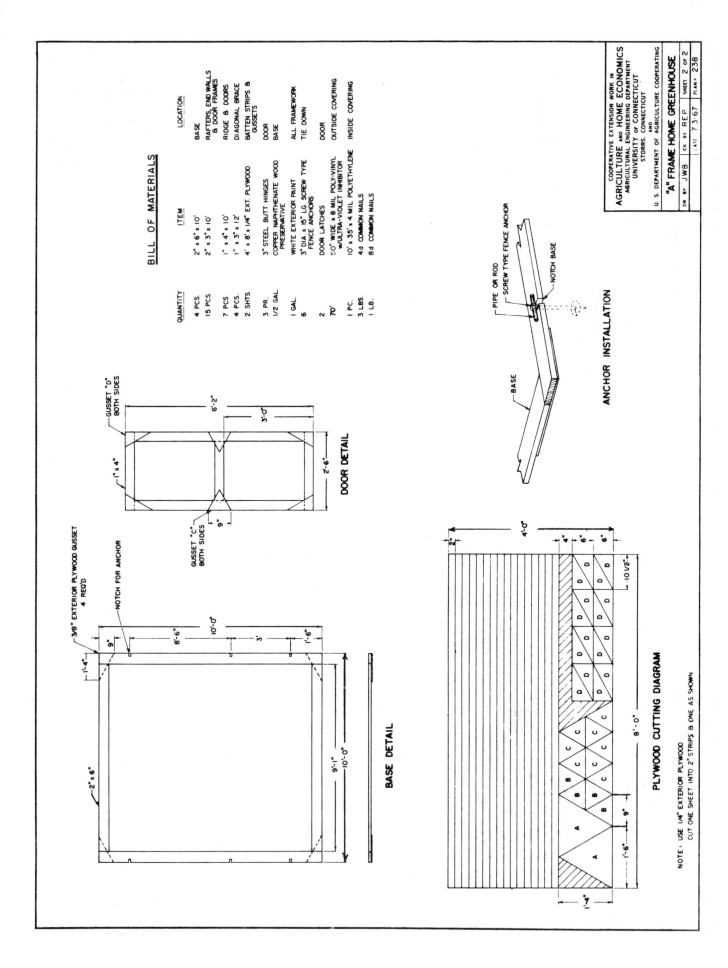

BILL OF MATERIALS

QUANTITY	ITEM	LOCATION
4 PCS.	2" x 6" x 10'	BASE
15 PCS.	2" x 3" x 10'	RAFTERS, END WALLS & DOOR FRAMES
7 PCS	1" x 4" x 10'	RIDGE & DOORS
4 PCS.	1" x 3" x 12'	DIAGONAL BRACE
2 SHTS.	4' x 8' x 1/4" EXT. PLYWOOD	BATTEN STRIPS & GUSSETS
3 PR.	3" STEEL BUTT HINGES	DOOR
1/2 GAL.	COPPER NAPHTHENATE WOOD PRESERVATIVE	BASE
1 GAL.	WHITE EXTERIOR PAINT	ALL FRAMEWORK
6	3" DIA. x 15" LG. SCREW TYPE FENCE ANCHORS	TIE DOWN
2	DOOR LATCHES	DOOR
70'	50" WIDE x 8 MIL POLY-VINYL w/ULTRA-VIOLET INHIBITOR	OUTSIDE COVERING
1 PC.	10' x 35' x 4 MIL POLYETHYLENE	INSIDE COVERING
3 LBS.	4d COMMON NAILS	
1 LB.	8d COMMON NAILS	

ANCHOR INSTALLATION

PIPE OR ROD
SCREW TYPE FENCE ANCHOR
NOTCH BASE
BASE

DOOR DETAIL

GUSSET "D" BOTH SIDES
1" x 4"
6'-2"
3'-0"
2'-6"
GUSSET "C" BOTH SIDES
9"

BASE DETAIL

3/8" EXTERIOR PLYWOOD GUSSET 4 REQ'D
NOTCH FOR ANCHOR
2" x 6"
1'-4"
9"
8'-6"
10'-0"
3'
1'-6"
9'-1"
10'-0"

PLYWOOD CUTTING DIAGRAM

4'-0"
2"
4"
6"
6"
10 1/2"
8'-0"
9"
1'-6"

NOTE: USE 1/4" EXTERIOR PLYWOOD
CUT ONE SHEET INTO 2' STRIPS & ONE AS SHOWN

COOPERATIVE EXTENSION WORK IN
AGRICULTURE AND HOME ECONOMICS
AGRICULTURAL ENGINEERING DEPARTMENT
UNIVERSITY OF CONNECTICUT
STORRS, CONNECTICUT
AND
U. S. DEPARTMENT OF AGRICULTURE COOPERATING

"A" FRAME HOME GREENHOUSE
SHEET 2 OF 2
DR BY JWB   CK BY REP   DATE 7-3-67   PLAN 238

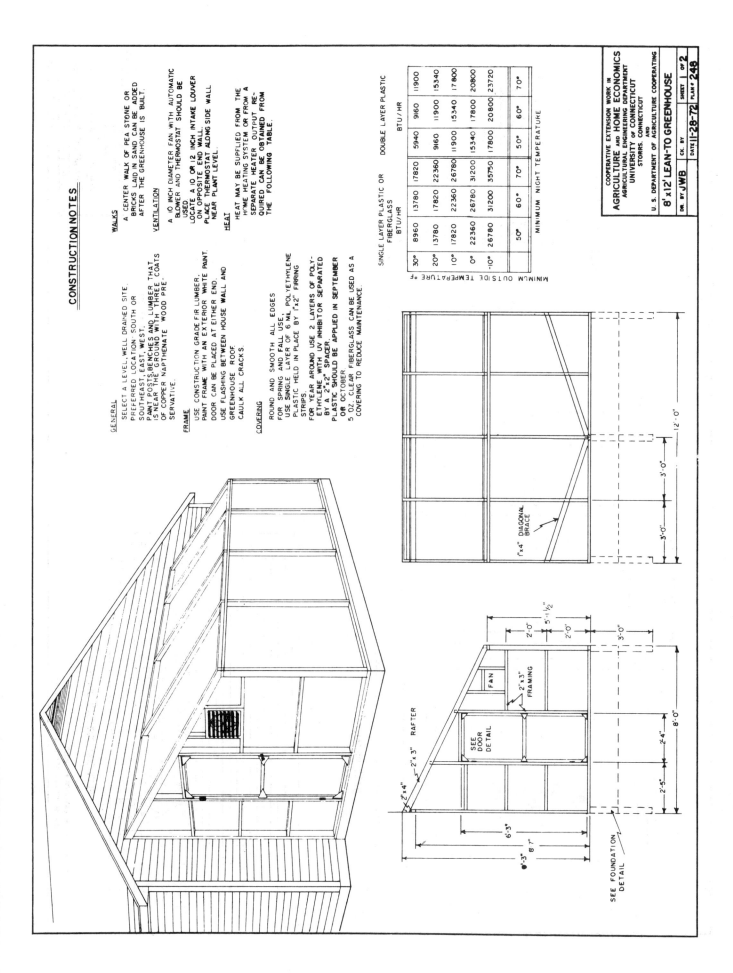

CONSTRUCTION NOTES

GENERAL
SELECT A LEVEL, WELL DRAINED SITE. PREFERRED LOCATION: SOUTH OR SOUTHEAST, EAST, WEST. PAINT POSTS, BENCHES AND LUMBER THAT IS NEAR THE GROUND WITH THREE COATS OF COPPER NAPTHENATE WOOD PRESERVATIVE.

FRAME
USE CONSTRUCTION GRADE FIR LUMBER. PAINT FRAME WITH AN EXTERIOR WHITE PAINT. DOOR CAN BE PLACED AT EITHER END. USE FLASHING BETWEEN HOUSE WALL AND GREENHOUSE ROOF. CAULK ALL CRACKS.

COVERING
ROUND AND SMOOTH ALL EDGES FOR SPRING AND FALL USE, USE SINGLE LAYER OF 6 MIL. POLYETHYLENE PLASTIC HELD IN PLACE BY 1"x2" FIRRING STRIPS.
FOR YEAR AROUND USE 2 LAYERS OF POLYETHYLENE WITH UV INHIBITOR SEPARATED BY A 2"x2" SPACER. PLASTIC SHOULD BE APPLIED IN SEPTEMBER OR OCTOBER.
5 OZ. CLEAR FIBERGLASS CAN BE USED AS A COVERING TO REDUCE MAINTENANCE.

WALKS
A CENTER WALK OF PEA STONE OR BRICKS LAID IN SAND CAN BE ADDED AFTER THE GREENHOUSE IS BUILT.

VENTILATION
A 10 INCH DIAMETER FAN WITH AUTOMATIC BLOWER AND THERMOSTAT SHOULD BE USED.
LOCATE A 10 OR 12 INCH INTAKE LOUVER ON OPPOSITE END WALL. PLACE THERMOSTAT ALONG SIDE WALL NEAR PLANT LEVEL.

HEAT
HEAT MAY BE SUPPLIED FROM THE HOME HEATING SYSTEM OR FROM A SEPARATE HEATER OUTPUT REQUIRED CAN BE OBTAINED FROM THE FOLLOWING TABLE.

MINIMUM OUTSIDE TEMPERATURE °F	SINGLE LAYER PLASTIC OR FIBERGLASS BTU/HR		DOUBLE LAYER PLASTIC BTU/HR	
	50°	60° 70°	50° 60°	70°
30°	8960	13780 17820	5940 9160	11900
20°	13780	17820 22360	9160 11900	15340
10°	17820	22360 26780	11900 15340	17800
0°	22360	26780 31200	15340 17800	20800
-10°	26780	31200 35750	17800 20800	23720

MINIMUM NIGHT TEMPERATURE

1"x4" DIAGONAL BRACE

12'-0"
3'-0"
3'-0"

RAFTER
2"x3"
2"x4"
2"x3" FRAMING
FAN
SEE DOOR DETAIL
SEE FOUNDATION DETAIL

5'-1½"
2'-0"
2'-0"
3'-0"
8'-0"
2'-4"
2'-5"
6'-3"
8'-7"
8'-3"

COOPERATIVE EXTENSION WORK IN
AGRICULTURE AND HOME ECONOMICS
AGRICULTURAL ENGINEERING DEPARTMENT
UNIVERSITY OF CONNECTICUT
STORRS, CONNECTICUT
AND
U. S. DEPARTMENT OF AGRICULTURE COOPERATING

8'x12' LEAN-TO GREENHOUSE
DR. BY JWB   CK. BY   SHEET 1 OF 2
DATE 11-28-72   PLAN # 248

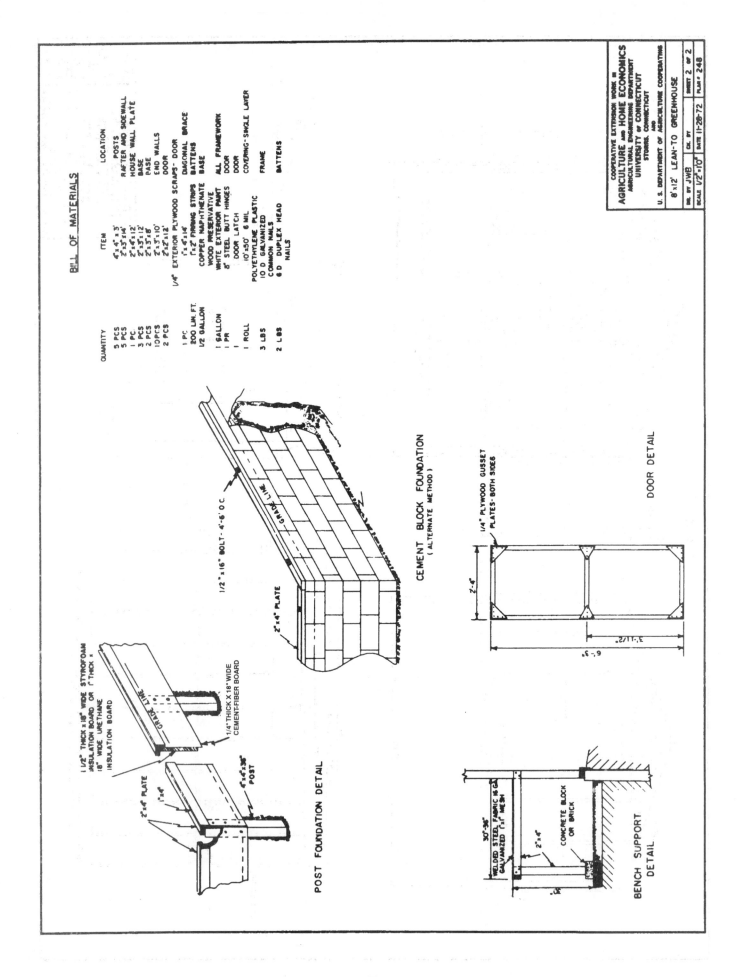

BILL OF MATERIALS

QUANTITY	ITEM	LOCATION
5 PCS	4"x4"x3'	POSTS
5 PCS	2"x3"x14'	RAFTER AND SIDEWALL
1 PC.	2"x4"x12'	HOUSE WALL PLATE
3 PCS	2"x3"x12'	BASE
10 PCS	2"x3"x10'	END WALLS
2 PCS	2"x2"x12'	DOOR
	1/4" EXTERIOR PLYWOOD SCRAPS- DOOR	DIAGONAL BRACE
1 PC	1"x4"x14'	BATTENS
200 LIN. FT.	1"x 2" FURRING STRIPS	BASE
1/2 GALLON	COPPER NAPHTHENATE WOOD PRESERVATIVE	ALL FRAMEWORK
1 GALLON	WHITE EXTERIOR PAINT	DOOR
1 PR	8" STEEL BUTT HINGES	DOOR
	DOOR LATCH	
1 ROLL	POLYETHYLENE PLASTIC 10'x50' 6 MIL	COVERING- SINGLE LAYER
3 LBS	10 D GALVANIZED COMMON NAILS	FRAME
2 LBS	6 D DUPLEX HEAD NAILS	BATTENS

CEMENT BLOCK FOUNDATION
(ALTERNATE METHOD)

1/2" x 16" BOLT- 4'-6' O.C.

GRADE LINE

2"x4" PLATE

POST FOUNDATION DETAIL

1 1/2" THICK x 18" WIDE STYROFOAM INSULATION BOARD OR 1" THICK x 18" WIDE URETHANE INSULATION BOARD

2"x4" PLATE

1"x4"

4"x4"x36" POST

1/4"THICK X 18"WIDE CEMENT-FIBER BOARD

GRADE LINE

DOOR DETAIL

1/4" PLYWOOD GUSSET PLATES- BOTH SIDES

2'-6"

3'-11 1/2"

6'-3"

BENCH SUPPORT DETAIL

30"-36" WELDED STEEL FABRIC 16 GA. GALVANIZED 1"x1" MESH

2"x4"

CONCRETE BLOCK OR BRICK

COOPERATIVE EXTENSION WORK IN
AGRICULTURE AND HOME ECONOMICS
AGRICULTURAL ENGINEERING DEPARTMENT
UNIVERSITY OF CONNECTICUT
STORRS, CONNECTICUT
AND
U. S. DEPARTMENT OF AGRICULTURE COOPERATING

8'x12' LEAN-TO GREENHOUSE

| DR. BY JWB | CK. BY | SHEET 2 OF 2 |
| SCALE 1/2"=1'-0" | DATE 11-28-72 | PLAN # 248 |

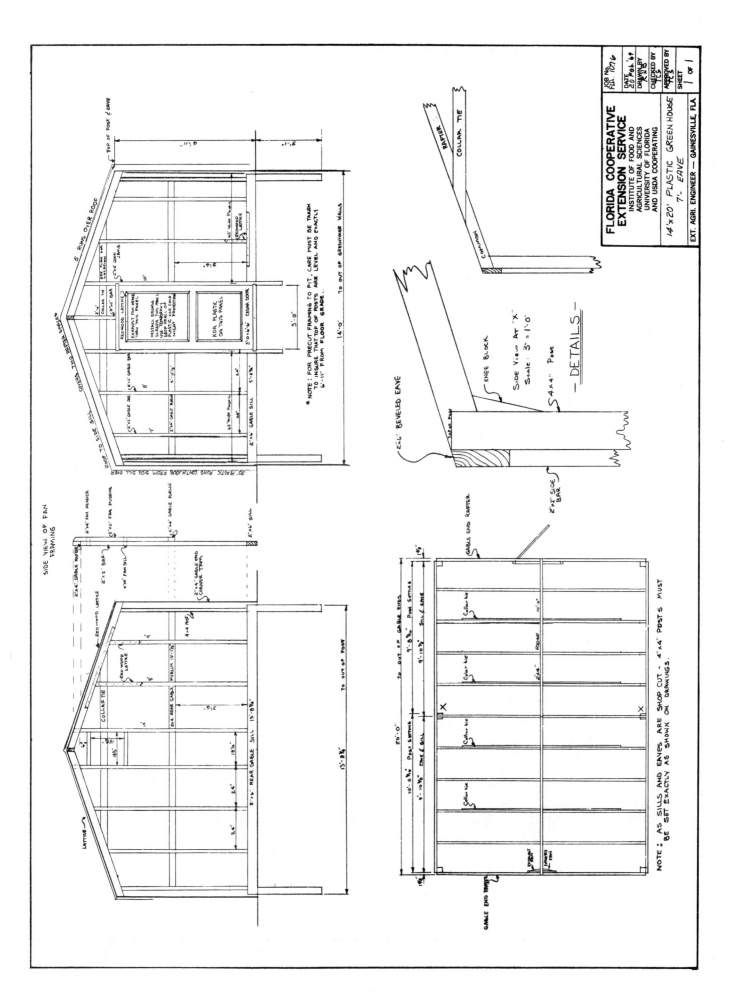

FLORIDA COOPERATIVE
EXTENSION SERVICE
INSTITUTE OF FOOD AND
AGRICULTURAL SCIENCES
UNIVERSITY OF FLORIDA
AND USDA COOPERATING

14' x 20' PLASTIC GREEN HOUSE
7'- EAVE

EXT. AGRI. ENGINEER — GAINESVILLE, FLA.

JOB No. FLA. 1076
DATE 20 Feb '69
DRAWN BY
CHECKED BY
APPROVED BY
SHEET 1 OF 1

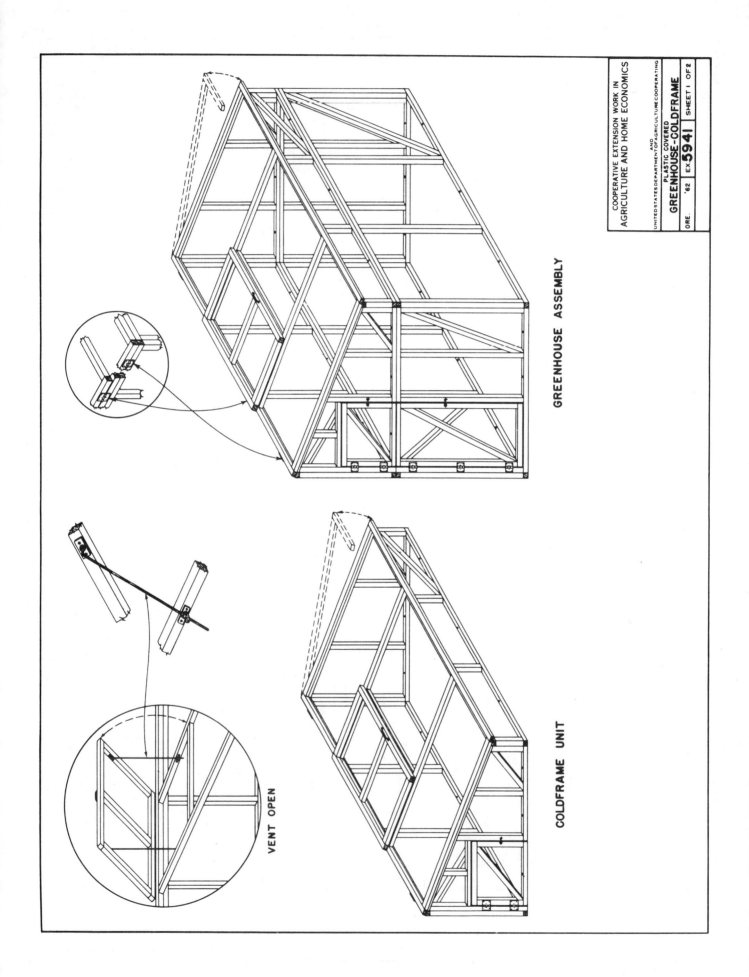

GREENHOUSE ASSEMBLY

COLDFRAME UNIT

VENT OPEN

COOPERATIVE EXTENSION WORK IN
AGRICULTURE AND HOME ECONOMICS
AND
UNITED STATES DEPARTMENT OF AGRICULTURE COOPERATING
PLASTIC COVERED
GREENHOUSE-COLDFRAME
ORE. '62 EX 5941 SHEET I OF 2

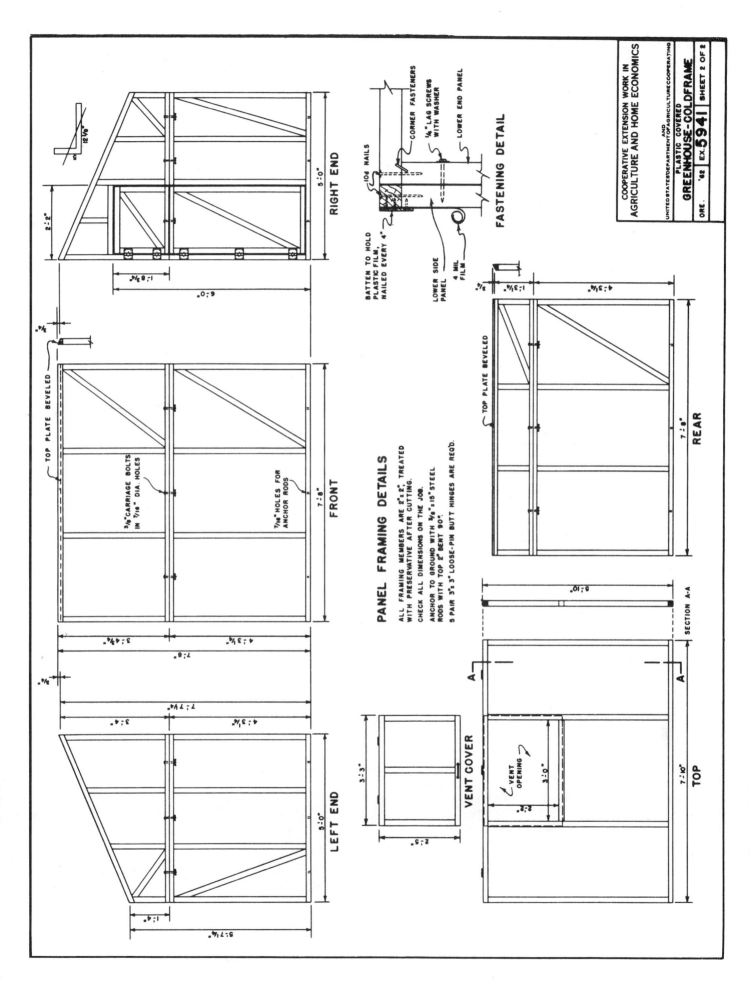

RIGHT END

FASTENING DETAIL

CORNER FASTENERS

¼" LAG SCREWS WITH WASHER

LOWER END PANEL

10d NAILS

BATTEN TO HOLD PLASTIC FILM, NAILED EVERY 4"

LOWER SIDE PANEL

4 MIL FILM

TOP PLATE BEVELED

FRONT

⅜" CARRIAGE BOLTS IN 7/16" DIA. HOLES

7/16" HOLES FOR ANCHOR RODS

TOP PLATE BEVELED

REAR

PANEL FRAMING DETAILS

ALL FRAMING MEMBERS ARE 2"x2", TREATED WITH PRESERVATIVE AFTER CUTTING.

CHECK ALL DIMENSIONS ON THE JOB.

ANCHOR TO GROUND WITH ⅜"x15"STEEL RODS WITH TOP 2" BENT 90°.

5 PAIR 3"x 3" LOOSE-PIN BUTT HINGES ARE REQ'D.

LEFT END

VENT COVER

VENT OPENING

SECTION A-A

TOP

COOPERATIVE EXTENSION WORK IN AGRICULTURE AND HOME ECONOMICS

AND

UNITED STATES DEPARTMENT OF AGRICULTURE COOPERATING

PLASTIC COVERED

GREENHOUSE-COLDFRAME

ORE.   '62   EX.594| SHEET 2 OF 2

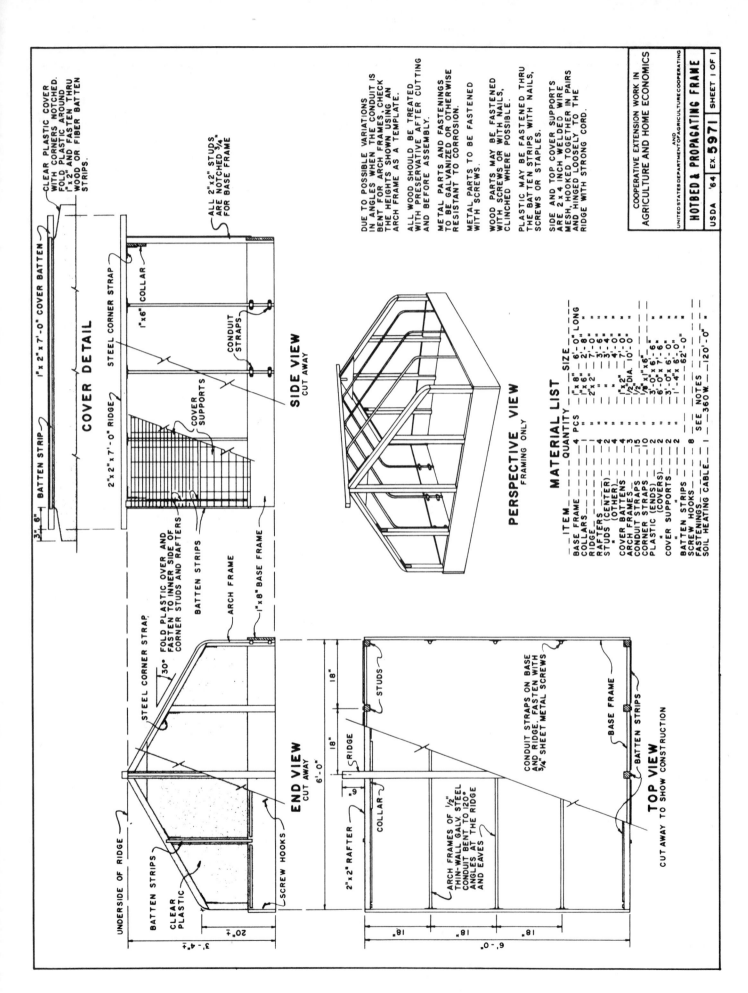

COVER DETAIL

CLEAR PLASTIC COVER WITH CORNERS NOTCHED. FOLD PLASTIC AROUND 1"x2" AND FASTEN THRU WOOD OR FIBER BATTEN STRIPS.

1"x 2"x 7'- 0" COVER BATTEN

BATTEN STRIP

3" 6"

2"x 2"x 7'-0" RIDGE

STEEL CORNER STRAP

1"x 6" COLLAR

CONDUIT STRAPS

ALL 2"x2" STUDS ARE NOTCHED 3/4" FOR BASE FRAME

COVER SUPPORTS

SIDE VIEW
CUT AWAY

FOLD PLASTIC OVER AND FASTEN TO INNER SIDE OF CORNER STUDS AND RAFTERS

BATTEN STRIPS

ARCH FRAME

1"x 8" BASE FRAME

STEEL CORNER STRAP

30°

UNDERSIDE OF RIDGE

BATTEN STRIPS

CLEAR PLASTIC

SCREW HOOKS

END VIEW
CUT AWAY

20"±

3'- 4"±

RIDGE

COLLAR

2"x 2" RAFTER

STUDS

18"

18"

18"

6"

6'- 0"

CONDUIT STRAPS ON BASE AND RIDGE. FASTEN WITH 3/4" SHEET METAL SCREWS

ARCH FRAMES OF 1/2" THIN-WALL GALV. STEEL CONDUIT BENT TO 120° ANGLES AT THE RIDGE AND EAVES

BASE FRAME

BATTEN STRIPS

TOP VIEW
CUT AWAY TO SHOW CONSTRUCTION

18"

18"

18"

6'- 0"

DUE TO POSSIBLE VARIATIONS IN ANGLES WHEN THE CONDUIT IS BENT FOR ARCH FRAMES, CHECK THE HEIGHTS SHOWN USING AN ARCH FRAME AS A TEMPLATE.

ALL WOOD SHOULD BE TREATED WITH PRESERVATIVE AFTER CUTTING AND BEFORE ASSEMBLY.

METAL PARTS AND FASTENINGS TO BE GALVANIZED OR OTHERWISE RESISTANT TO CORROSION.

METAL PARTS TO BE FASTENED WITH SCREWS.

WOOD PARTS MAY BE FASTENED WITH SCREWS OR WITH NAILS, CLINCHED WHERE POSSIBLE.

PLASTIC MAY BE FASTENED THRU THE BATTEN STRIPS WITH NAILS, SCREWS OR STAPLES.

SIDE AND TOP COVER SUPPORTS ARE 2x 4 INCH WELDED WIRE MESH, HOOKED TOGETHER IN PAIRS AND HINGED LOOSELY TO THE RIDGE WITH STRONG CORD.

PERSPECTIVE VIEW
FRAMING ONLY

MATERIAL LIST

ITEM	QUANTITY	SIZE
BASE FRAME	4 PCS	1"x 8" — 6'- 0" LONG
COLLARS	4 "	1"x 6" — 2'- 8"
RIDGE	1 "	2"x 2" — 7'- 0"
RAFTERS	4 "	" — 3'- 4"
STUDS (CENTER)	2 "	" — 4'- 0"
STUDS (OTHER)	4 "	1"x 2" — 4'- 0"
COVER BATTENS	4 "	1"x 2" — 7'- 0"
ARCH FRAMES	3 "	1/2" DIA. 10'- 0"
CONDUIT STRAPS	15 "	1/2" x 1"x 6"
CORNER STRAPS	10 "	3'- 0" x 6"
PLASTIC (ENDS)	2 "	5'- 0" x 7'- 6"
" (COVERS)	2 "	3'- 0" x 6'- 0"
COVER SUPPORTS	2 "	1'- 4" x 6'- 0"
BATTEN STRIPS	2 "	— 62'- 0"
SCREW HOOKS	8 "	SEE NOTES
SOIL HEATING CABLE	1 "	360 W. — 120'- 0"

COOPERATIVE EXTENSION WORK IN AGRICULTURE AND HOME ECONOMICS

AND UNITED STATES DEPARTMENT OF AGRICULTURE COOPERATING

HOTBED & PROPAGATING FRAME

USDA '64 EX. 5971 SHEET 1 OF 1

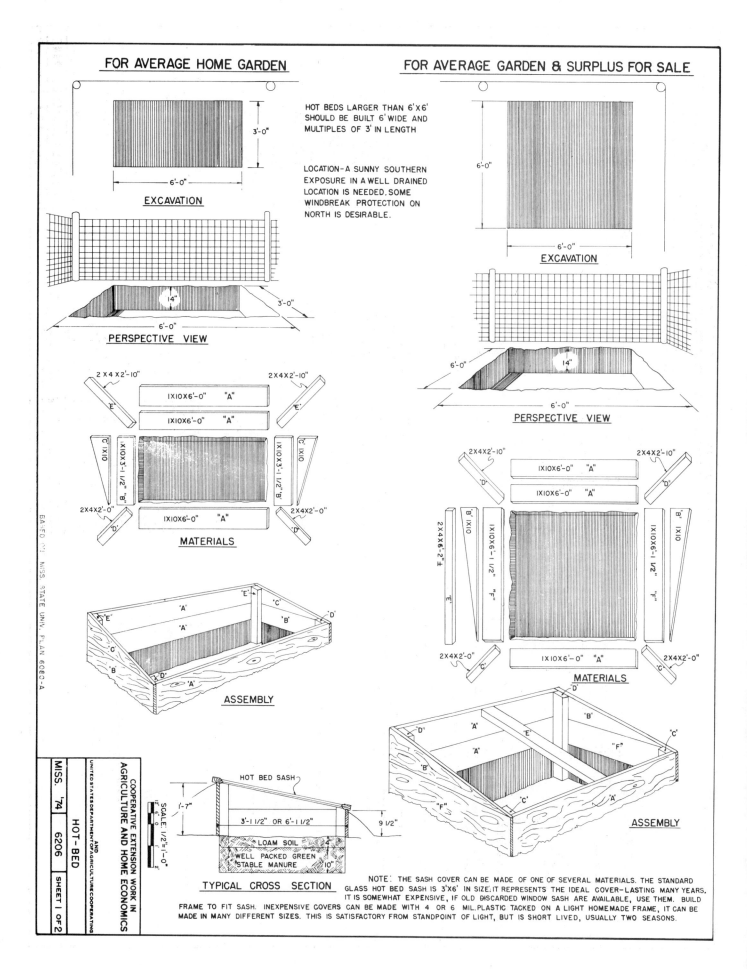

FOR AVERAGE HOME GARDEN

EXCAVATION

3'-0"
6'-0"

PERSPECTIVE VIEW

14"
3'-0"
6'-0"

HOT BEDS LARGER THAN 6'X6'
SHOULD BE BUILT 6' WIDE AND
MULTIPLES OF 3' IN LENGTH

LOCATION-A SUNNY SOUTHERN
EXPOSURE IN A WELL DRAINED
LOCATION IS NEEDED. SOME
WINDBREAK PROTECTION ON
NORTH IS DESIRABLE.

FOR AVERAGE GARDEN & SURPLUS FOR SALE

EXCAVATION

6'-0"
6'-0"

PERSPECTIVE VIEW

6'-0"
14"
6'-0"

MATERIALS

2 X 4 X 2'-10" "E"
1X10X6'-0" "A"
1X10X6'-0" "A"
2X4X2'-10" "E"
"C" 1X10
1X10X3'-1 1/2" "B"
"C" 1X10
1X10X3'-1 1/2" "B"
2X4X2'-0" "D"
1X10X6'-0" "A"
2X4X2'-0" "D"

MATERIALS

2X4X2'-10" "D"
1X10X6'-0" "A"
1X10X6'-0" "A"
2X4X2'-10" "D"
"B" 1X10
1X10X6'-1 1/2" "F"
"B" 1X10
1X10X6'-1 1/2" "F"
2X4X6'-2"± "E"
2X4X2'-0" "C"
1X10X6'-0" "A"
2X4X2'-0" "C"

ASSEMBLY

"E" "A" "C"
"E" "B" "D"
"A"
"C"
"B" "D"
"A"

ASSEMBLY

"D" "B"
"D" "A" "E" "C"
"A" "F"
"B" "C"
"F" "A"

MISS. '74 6206 SHEET 1 OF 2
HOT-BED
COOPERATIVE EXTENSION WORK IN
AGRICULTURE AND HOME ECONOMICS
UNITED STATES DEPARTMENT OF AGRICULTURE COOPERATING
AND
BASED ON MISS. STATE UNIV. PLAN 6080-A

TYPICAL CROSS SECTION

HOT BED SASH
SCALE: 1/2"=1'-0"
1'-7"
3'-1 1/2" OR 6'-1 1/2"
9 1/2"
LOAM SOIL 4"
WELL PACKED GREEN
STABLE MANURE 10"

NOTE: THE SASH COVER CAN BE MADE OF ONE OF SEVERAL MATERIALS. THE STANDARD
GLASS HOT BED SASH IS 3'X6' IN SIZE. IT REPRESENTS THE IDEAL COVER-LASTING MANY YEARS.
IT IS SOMEWHAT EXPENSIVE. IF OLD DISCARDED WINDOW SASH ARE AVAILABLE, USE THEM. BUILD
FRAME TO FIT SASH. INEXPENSIVE COVERS CAN BE MADE WITH 4 OR 6 MIL. PLASTIC TACKED ON A LIGHT HOMEMADE FRAME, IT CAN BE
MADE IN MANY DIFFERENT SIZES. THIS IS SATISFACTORY FROM STANDPOINT OF LIGHT, BUT IS SHORT LIVED, USUALLY TWO SEASONS.

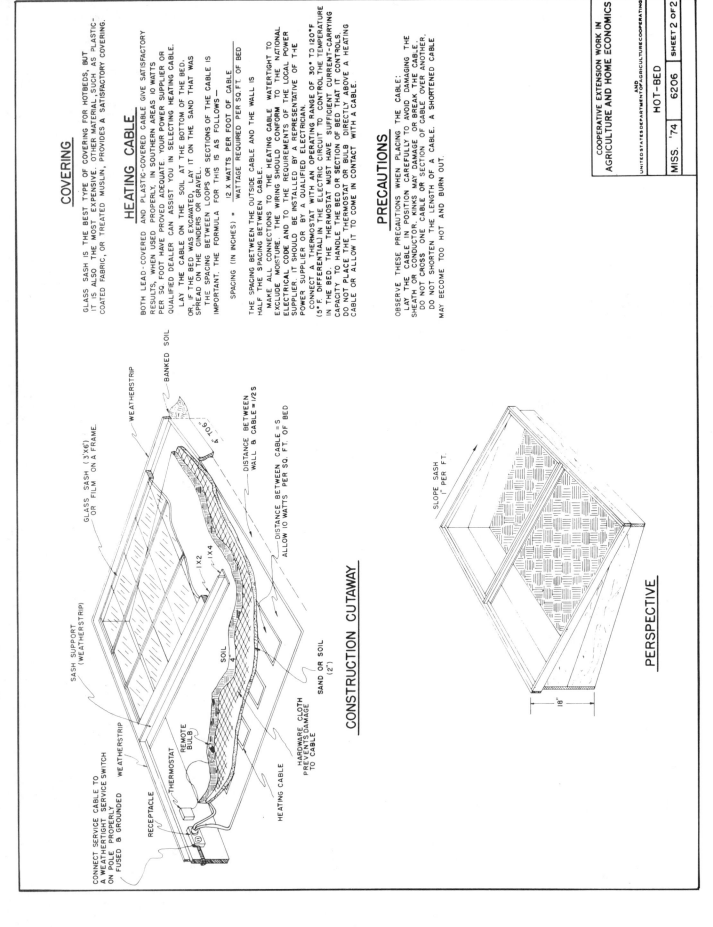

COVERING

GLASS SASH IS THE BEST TYPE OF COVERING FOR HOTBEDS, BUT IT IS ALSO THE MOST EXPENSIVE. OTHER MATERIAL, SUCH AS PLASTIC-COATED FABRIC, OR TREATED MUSLIN, PROVIDES A SATISFACTORY COVERING.

HEATING CABLE

BOTH LEAD-COVERED AND PLASTIC-COVERED CABLE GIVE SATISFACTORY RESULTS, WHEN USED PROPERLY, IN SOUTHERN AREAS 10 WATTS PER SQ. FOOT HAVE PROVED ADEQUATE. YOUR POWER SUPPLIER OR QUALIFIED DEALER CAN ASSIST YOU IN SELECTING HEATING CABLE.

LAY THE CABLE ON THE SOIL AT THE BOTTOM OF THE BED, OR, IF THE BED WAS EXCAVATED, LAY IT ON THE SAND THAT WAS SPREAD ON THE CINDERS OR GRAVEL.

THE SPACING BETWEEN LOOPS OR SECTIONS OF THE CABLE IS IMPORTANT. THE FORMULA FOR THIS IS AS FOLLOWS —

SPACING (IN INCHES) = $\dfrac{12 \times \text{WATTS PER FOOT OF CABLE}}{\text{WATTAGE REQUIRED PER SQ.FT. OF BED}}$

THE SPACING BETWEEN THE OUTSIDE CABLE AND THE WALL IS HALF THE SPACING BETWEEN CABLE.

MAKE ALL CONNECTIONS TO THE HEATING CABLE WATERTIGHT TO EXCLUDE MOISTURE. THE WIRING SHOULD CONFORM TO THE NATIONAL ELECTRICAL CODE AND TO THE REQUIREMENTS OF THE LOCAL POWER SUPPLIER. IT SHOULD BE INSTALLED BY A REPRESENTATIVE OF THE POWER SUPPLIER OR BY A QUALIFIED ELECTRICIAN.

CONNECT A THERMOSTAT WITH AN OPERATING RANGE OF 30° TO 120°F (5°F. DIFFERENTIAL) IN THE ELECTRIC CIRCUIT TO CONTROL THE TEMPERATURE IN THE BED. THE THERMOSTAT MUST HAVE SUFFICIENT CURRENT-CARRYING CAPACITY TO HANDLE THE BED OR SECTION OF BED THAT IT CONTROLS. DO NOT PLACE THE THERMOSTAT OR BULB DIRECTLY ABOVE A HEATING CABLE OR ALLOW IT TO COME IN CONTACT WITH A CABLE.

PRECAUTIONS

OBSERVE THESE PRECAUTIONS WHEN PLACING THE CABLE:
LAY THE CABLE IN POSITION CAREFULLY TO AVOID DAMAGING THE SHEATH OR CONDUCTOR. KINKS MAY DAMAGE OR BREAK THE CABLE.
DO NOT CROSS ONE CABLE OR SECTION OF CABLE OVER ANOTHER.
DO NOT SHORTEN THE LENGTH OF A CABLE. A SHORTENED CABLE MAY BECOME TOO HOT AND BURN OUT.

CONSTRUCTION CUTAWAY

CONNECT SERVICE CABLE TO A WEATHERTIGHT SERVICE SWITCH ON POLE PROPERLY FUSED & GROUNDED

WEATHERSTRIP

SASH SUPPORT (WEATHERSTRIP)

GLASS SASH (3'X6') OR FILM ON A FRAME.

WEATHERSTRIP

BANKED SOIL

DISTANCE BETWEEN WALL & CABLE = 1/2 S

DISTANCE BETWEEN CABLE = S
ALLOW 10 WATTS PER SQ. FT. OF BED

1 X 2

1 X 4

SOIL 4"

SAND OR SOIL (2")

HARDWARE CLOTH PREVENTS DAMAGE TO CABLE

HEATING CABLE

REMOTE BULB

THERMOSTAT

RECEPTACLE

PERSPECTIVE

SLOPE SASH 1" PER FT.

18"

COOPERATIVE EXTENSION WORK IN
AGRICULTURE AND HOME ECONOMICS
AND
UNITED STATES DEPARTMENT OF AGRICULTURE COOPERATING

HOT-BED

MISS. '74   6206   SHEET 2 OF 2

PICNIC & RECREATION EQUIPMENT

SIX 20d COMMON NAILS (EACH SIDE)
2 x 6 PURLINS 2'-0" o.c.
2 x 8 PURLIN TIES
2 1/2 CORRUGATED METAL ROOF

SIX 20d COMMON NAILS

2 x 8 x 2-6

2 x 4 STRUT
20d COMMON NAILS

TWO 2 x 8 x 10-0" RAFTERS
SIX 20d COMMON NAILS

ONE 5/8 x 14" GALV.
BOLT

2 x 4
ONE 5/8 x 9" GALV.
BOLT

TWO 2 x 8 x 16-0" CROSS BEAM

ONE 5/8 x 9" GALV. BOLT

5/8 x 10" GALV. BOLT, WASHERS, AND NUT.
6" TOP DIAMETER OF 20 POLES (PRESSURE-TREATED)
POLES FLATTENED ON TWO SIDES AT TOP
TO RECEIVE CROSS BEAMS

19"

5'-4"

9-0"

2 x 8 BLOCKING

"D"

4 x 4 x 8-0"
HANDRAIL

2 x 6

2 x 6 BRACES PRESSURE-TREATED

1/8" CABLE

2 x 4

WINCH

1 1/2" PIPE SEPARATOR WITH 5/8 x 12" GALV.
BOLT, WASHERS, AND NUT.

EAT AND STORAGE
EE DETAIL

2 x 8

2 x 8 FRAMING

5/8 x 12" GALV. BOLT,
WASHERS, AND NUT.

WATER LINE

RIVER BOTTOM

SECTION C-C

8'-0"

50'-0"

STAKE IS 1" ROUND BAR
3'-0" LONG. HEIGHT ABOVE
GROUND IS 10".

40'-0"

HORSE SHOE

10'-0"

2'-0"

5'-6"

5'-0"

9'-0"

6"

3/4"

52'-0"

6'-6"   1'-6" 3'-0" 3'-0" 3'-0" 3'-0"   12'-0"   3'-0" 3'-0" 3'-0" 3'-0" 1'-6"   6'-6"

3'-0"

DEAD LINES

3'-0"

10 OFF 7 8 10

LINES
3/4" WIDE
PAINTED BLACK

10 8 7 OFF

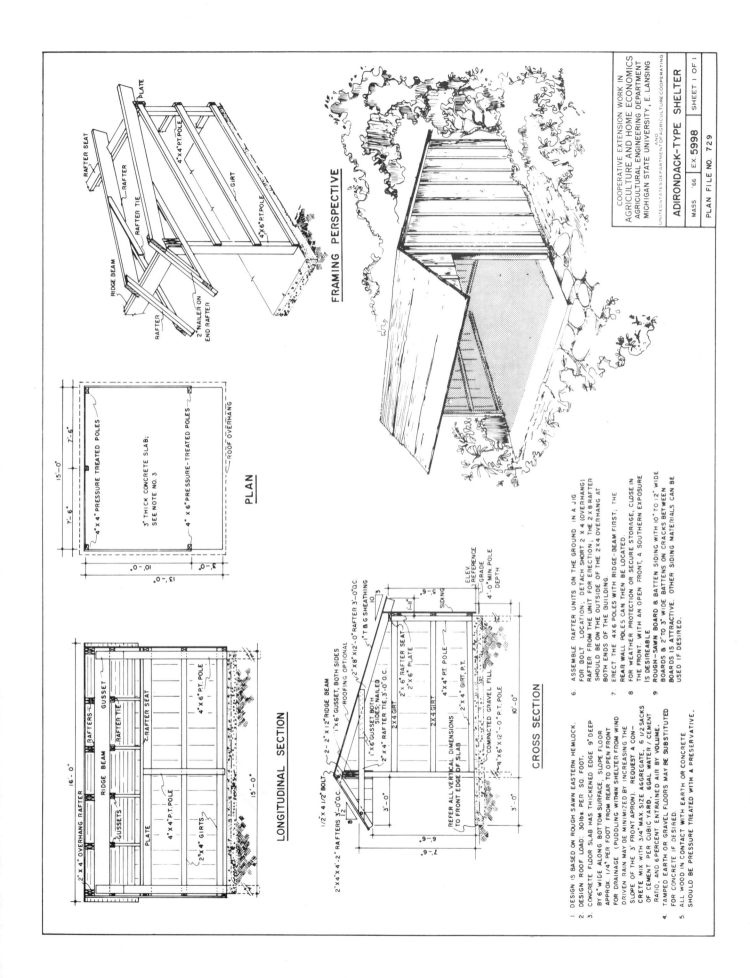

FRAMING PERSPECTIVE

RAFTER SEAT
PLATE
RAFTER
RAFTER TIE
RIDGE BEAM
4"X4"P.T.POLE
RAFTER
GIRT
2" NAILER ON END RAFTER
4"X 6"P.T.POLE

COOPERATIVE EXTENSION WORK IN
AGRICULTURE AND HOME ECONOMICS
AGRICULTURAL ENGINEERING DEPARTMENT
MICHIGAN STATE UNIVERSITY, E. LANSING
AND
UNITED STATES DEPARTMENT OF AGRICULTURE, COOPERATING

ADIRONDACK-TYPE SHELTER

MASS '66 | EX. 5998 | SHEET 1 OF 1

PLAN FILE NO. 729

PLAN

15'-0"
7'-6"   7'-6"
4"X 4" PRESSURE TREATED POLES
3" THICK CONCRETE SLAB;
SEE NOTE NO. 3
4" X 6" PRESSURE-TREATED POLES
ROOF OVERHANG
10'-0"
3'-0"
13'-0"

LONGITUDINAL SECTION

2"X 4" OVERHANG RAFTER
16'-0"
RAFTERS
GUSSET
RIDGE BEAM
RAFTER TIE
RAFTER SEAT
GUSSETS
PLATE
4"X 4" P.T. POLE
4"X 6" P.T. POLE
2"X 4" GIRTS
15'-0"

CROSS SECTION

2'X4'X4'-2" RAFTERS 3'-0"O.C.
1/2"X 4 1/2" BOLT
2- 2"X 1 2" RIDGE BEAM
1"X 6" GUSSET, BOTH SIDES
ROOFING OPTIONAL
2"X 8"X 12'-0" RAFTER 3'-0" O.C.
1"X 6" GUSSET BOTH SIDES; NAILED
2"X 4" RAFTER TIE, 3'-0" O.C.
1" T & G SHEATHING
10
3
2'-6"
ELEV REFERENCE GRADE
1'-11"
SIDING
4'-0" MIN. POLE DEPTH
2"X 6" RAFTER SEAT
2"X 6" PLATE
2X4 GIRT
2X4 GIRT
4"X 4" P.T. POLE
2"X 4" GIRT, P.T.
COMPACTED GRAVEL FILL
4"X6"X12'-0" P.T. POLE
REFER ALL VERTICAL DIMENSIONS TO FRONT EDGE OF SLAB
10'-0"
3'-0"
9'-6"
7'-6"

1. DESIGN IS BASED ON ROUGH SAWN EASTERN HEMLOCK.
2. DESIGN ROOF LOAD: 30 lbs PER SQ. FOOT.
3. CONCRETE FLOOR SLAB HAS THICKENED EDGE 9" DEEP BY 6" WIDE ALONG BOTTOM SURFACE. SLOPE FLOOR APPROX. 1/4" PER FOOT FROM REAR TO OPEN FRONT FOR DRAINAGE. (PUDDLING WITHIN SHELTER FROM WIND DRIVEN RAIN MAY BE MINIMIZED BY INCREASING THE SLOPE OF THE 3' FRONT APRON). REQUEST A CON- CRETE MIX WITH 3/4" MAX SIZE AGGREGATE, 6 1/2 SACKS OF CEMENT PER CUBIC YARD, 6 GAL WATER / CEMENT RATIO, AND 6 PERCENT ENTRAINED AIR BY VOLUME.
4. TAMPED EARTH OR GRAVEL FLOORS MAY BE SUBSTITUTED FOR CONCRETE IF DESIRED.
5. ALL WOOD IN CONTACT WITH EARTH OR CONCRETE SHOULD BE PRESSURE TREATED WITH A PRESERVATIVE.

6. ASSEMBLE RAFTER UNITS ON THE GROUND IN A JIG FOR BOLT LOCATION; DETACH SHORT 2 X 4 (OVERHANG) RAFTER FROM THE UNIT FOR ERECTION; THE 2 X 8 RAFTER SHOULD BE ON THE OUTSIDE OF THE 2X4 OVERHANG AT BOTH ENDS OF THE BUILDING.
7. ERECT THE 4X6 POLES WITH RIDGE-BEAM FIRST; THE REAR WALL POLES CAN THEN BE LOCATED.
8. FOR WEATHER PROTECTION OR SECURE STORAGE, CLOSE IN THE FRONT. WITH AN OPEN FRONT, A SOUTHERN EXPOSURE IS DESIRABLE
9. ROUGH-SAWN BOARD & BATTEN SIDING WITH 10" TO 12" WIDE BOARDS & 2"TO 3" WIDE BATTENS ON CRACKS BETWEEN BOARDS IS ATTRACTIVE. OTHER SIDING MATERIALS CAN BE USED IF DESIRED.

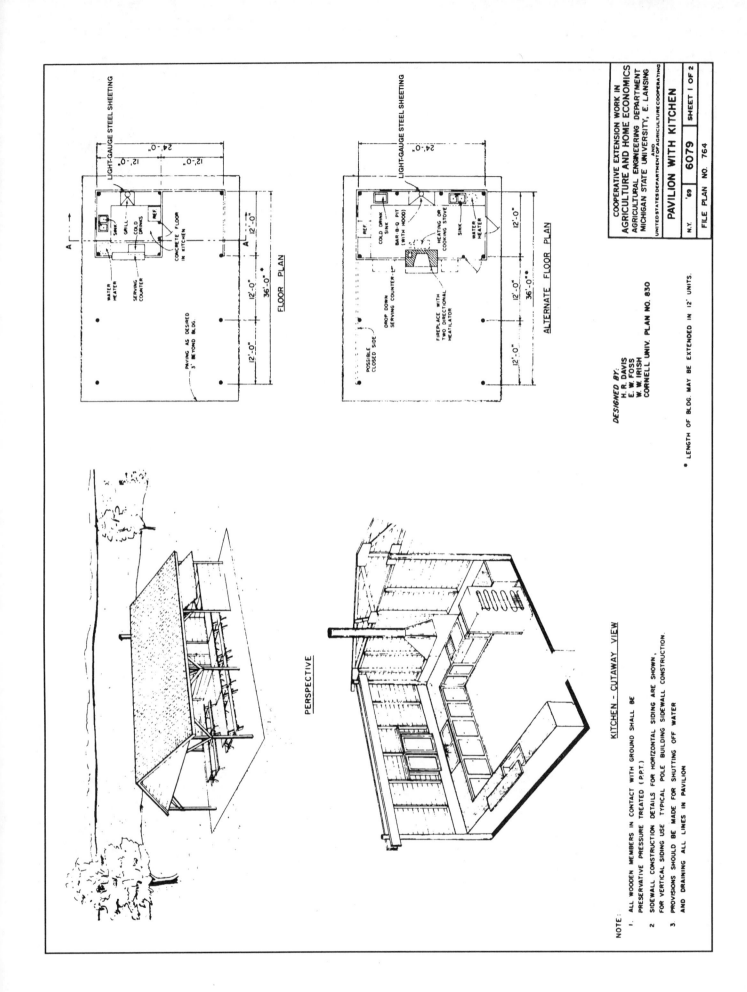

LIGHT-GAUGE STEEL SHEETING

24'-0"
12'-0" 12'-0"

WATER HEATER
SINK
GRILL
COLD DRINKS
SERVING COUNTER
REF

CONCRETE FLOOR IN KITCHEN

A

A

12'-0" 12'-0" 12'-0"
36'-0"*

PAVING AS DESIRED 3' BEYOND BLDG.

FLOOR PLAN

LIGHT-GAUGE STEEL SHEETING

24'-0"

REF
COLD DRINK SINK
BAR-B-Q PIT (WITH HOOD)
HEATING OR COOKING STOVE
SINK
WATER HEATER

POSSIBLE CLOSED SIDE

DROP DOWN SERVING COUNTER

FIREPLACE WITH TWO DIRECTIONAL HEATILATOR

12'-0" 12'-0" 12'-0"
36'-0"*

ALTERNATE FLOOR PLAN

KITCHEN - CUTAWAY VIEW

PERSPECTIVE

NOTE:
1. ALL WOODEN MEMBERS IN CONTACT WITH GROUND SHALL BE PRESERVATIVE PRESSURE TREATED (P.P.T.)

2. SIDEWALL CONSTRUCTION DETAILS FOR HORIZONTAL SIDING ARE SHOWN. FOR VERTICAL SIDING USE TYPICAL POLE BUILDING SIDEWALL CONSTRUCTION.

3. PROVISIONS SHOULD BE MADE FOR SHUTTING OFF WATER AND DRAINING ALL LINES IN PAVILION

DESIGNED BY:
H. R. DAVIS
E. W. FOSS
W. W. IRISH
CORNELL UNIV. PLAN NO. 830

COOPERATIVE EXTENSION WORK IN
AGRICULTURE AND HOME ECONOMICS
AGRICULTURAL ENGINEERING DEPARTMENT
MICHIGAN STATE UNIVERSITY, E. LANSING
AND
UNITED STATES DEPARTMENT OF AGRICULTURE COOPERATING

PAVILION WITH KITCHEN

N.Y.   '69   6079   SHEET 1 OF 2

FILE PLAN NO. 764

* LENGTH OF BLDG. MAY BE EXTENDED IN 12' UNITS.

96

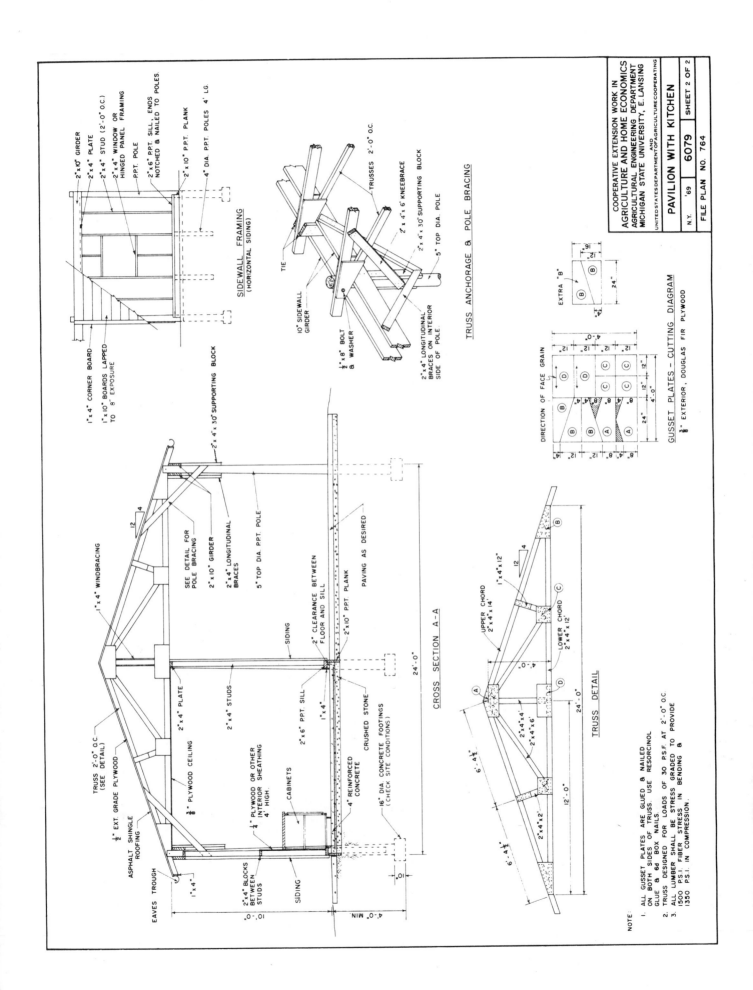

SIDEWALL FRAMING
(HORIZONTAL SIDING)

TRUSS ANCHORAGE & POLE BRACING

CROSS SECTION A-A

TRUSS DETAIL

GUSSET PLATES – CUTTING DIAGRAM
3/8" EXTERIOR, DOUGLAS FIR PLYWOOD

COOPERATIVE EXTENSION WORK IN
AGRICULTURE AND HOME ECONOMICS
AGRICULTURAL ENGINEERING DEPARTMENT
MICHIGAN STATE UNIVERSITY, E. LANSING
UNITED STATES DEPARTMENT OF AGRICULTURE COOPERATING

PAVILION WITH KITCHEN

N.Y. '69   6079   SHEET 2 OF 2

FILE PLAN NO. 764

NOTE:
1. ALL GUSSET PLATES ARE GLUED & NAILED ON BOTH SIDES OF TRUSS. USE RESORCINOL GLUE & 6d BOX NAILS.
2. TRUSS DESIGNED FOR LOADS OF 30 P.S.F. AT 2'-0" O.C.
3. ALL LUMBER SHALL BE STRESS GRADED TO PROVIDE 1500 P.S.I. FIBER STRESS IN BENDING & 1350 P.S.I. IN COMPRESSION.

A practical solution to the problem of providing economical changing facilities for bathers. Note that the toilet areas are under cover, while the changing areas are left open to be dried by sunlight. A course of precast concrete louvre blocks along the bottom on both sides will further aid in keeping air circulating inside. The over-all architectural lines are pleasing, and the building lends itself to placement at pools as well as at natural-type bathing areas.

SIDE ELEVATION

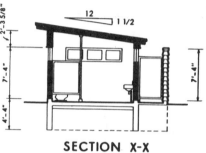

SECTION X-X

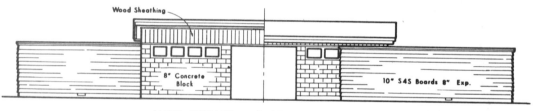

HALF FRONT and REAR ELEVATION

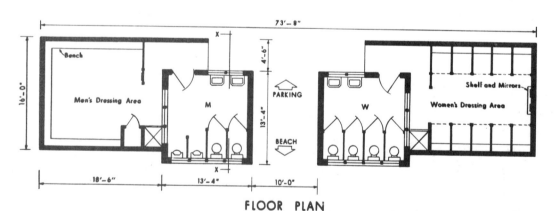

FLOOR PLAN

SCS - 905 7-63	U. S. DEPARTMENT OF AGRICULTURE SOIL CONSERVATION SERVICE

BATH HOUSE
TWO ROOMS WITH TOILETS

FROM DESIGN VOLUMES OF THE PARK PRACTICE PROGRAM
NATIONAL CONFERENCE ON STATE PARKS
DESIGN SHEET NO. R-4700

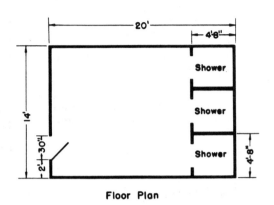

Floor Plan

20'

4'8"

Shower

Shower

Shower

14'

2'

30"

4'8"

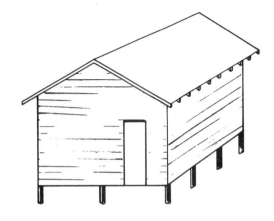

NOTE: Space Joists, Studding and
Rafters 30" on Centers.

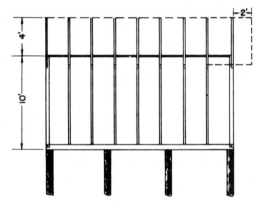

Side Elevation

4'

2'

10'

End Elevation

10'

7'

Foundation Plan

7'

14'

30"

6'-8"

20'

BILL OF MATERIALS

12	8" x 8'	Cypress Piles
6	2" x 6" x 20'	Sills
12	2" x 6" x 14'	Cross Beams
4	4" x 4" x 10'	Studding
22	2" x 4" x 10'	Studding
2	2" x 4" x 20'	Plates
2	2" x 4" x 14'	Plates
18	2" x 4" x 10'	Rafters
500	Square Feet	Roof Sheathing
900	Square Feet	8" Siding
100	Square Feet	1½" x 2½" x 10' Strips
300	Square Feet	1" Flooring
400	Square Feet	Roofing
	Nails	

Note: Shower fixtures not shown.

SCS-904	U. S. DEPARTMENT OF AGRICULTURE
7-63	SOIL CONSERVATION SERVICE

BATH HOUSE
SINGLE ROOM WITH SHOWERS

FROM ORIGINAL DESIGN BY
NORTH CAROLINA
DEPARTMENT OF CONSERVATION AND DEVELOPMENT

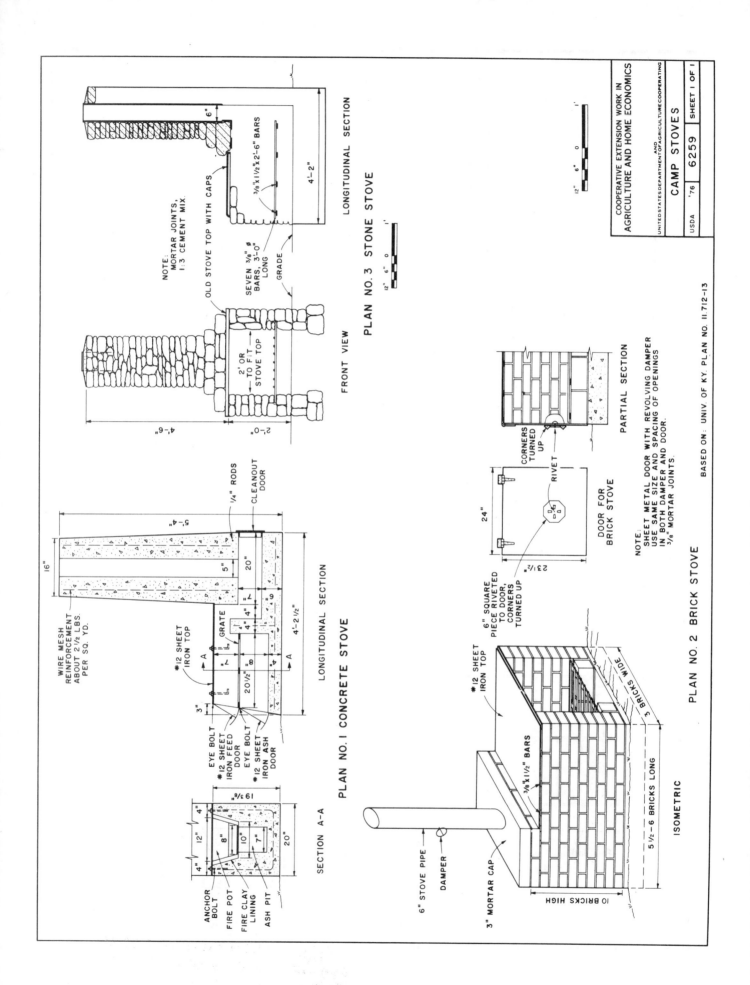

PLAN NO.3 STONE STOVE

FRONT VIEW

LONGITUDINAL SECTION

NOTE:
MORTAR JOINTS,
1:3 CEMENT MIX

OLD STOVE TOP WITH CAPS

SEVEN 3/8" ⌀ BARS, 3'-0" LONG

GRADE

3/8"x1 1/2"x2'-6" BARS

2' OR TO FIT STOVE TOP

4'-6"

2'-0"

4'-2"

6"

12" 6" 0   1'

PLAN NO. I CONCRETE STOVE

LONGITUDINAL SECTION

SECTION A-A

WIRE MESH REINFORCEMENT ABOUT 2 1/2 LBS. PER SQ. YD.

1/4" RODS

CLEANOUT DOOR

#12 SHEET IRON TOP

GRATE

EYE BOLT

#12 SHEET IRON FEED DOOR

EYE BOLT

#12 SHEET IRON ASH DOOR

ANCHOR BOLT

FIRE POT

FIRE CLAY LINING

ASH PIT

16"

5'-4"

20"

5"

7"

4" 4"

6

20 1/2"

8

7

3"

4'-2 1/2"

4" 12" 4"

8" 10" 7"

20"

19 3/8"

PLAN NO. 2 BRICK STOVE

ISOMETRIC

DOOR FOR BRICK STOVE

PARTIAL SECTION

NOTE:
SHEET METAL DOOR WITH REVOLVING DAMPER
USE SAME SIZE AND SPACING OF OPENINGS
IN BOTH DAMPER AND DOOR.
3/8" MORTAR JOINTS.

CORNERS TURNED UP

RIVET

24"

23 1/2"

6" SQUARE PIECE RIVETED TO DOOR, CORNERS TURNED UP

#12 SHEET IRON TOP

3/8"x1 1/2" BARS

3 BRICKS WIDE

5 1/2 - 6 BRICKS LONG

10 BRICKS HIGH

6" STOVE PIPE

DAMPER

3" MORTAR CAP

COOPERATIVE EXTENSION WORK IN
AGRICULTURE AND HOME ECONOMICS
AND
UNITED STATES DEPARTMENT OF AGRICULTURE COOPERATING

CAMP STOVES

USDA '76 6259 SHEET 1 OF 1

BASED ON: UNIV. OF KY. PLAN NO. II.712-13

12" 6" 0   1'

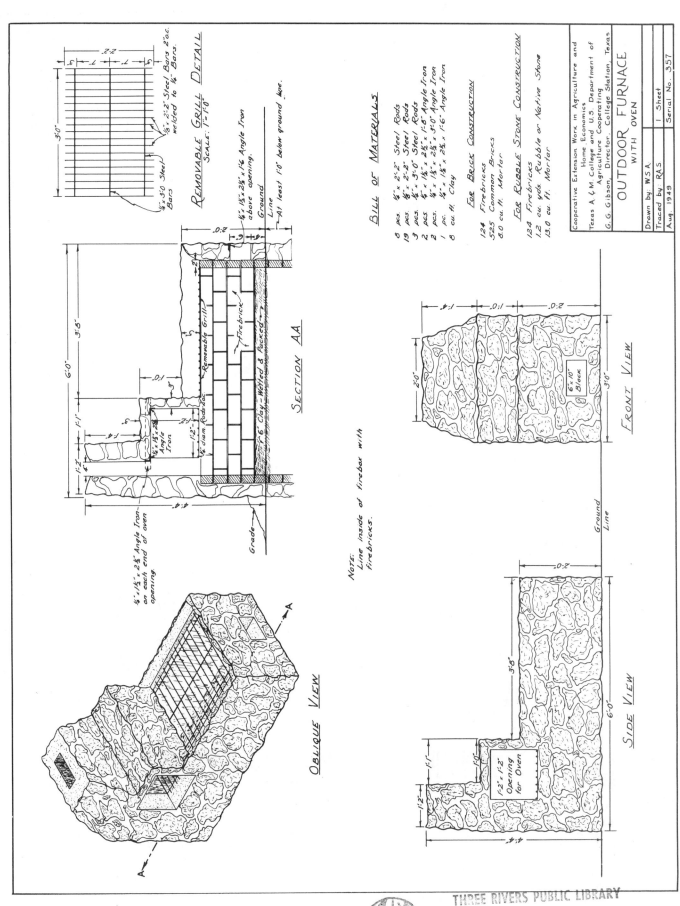

REMOVABLE GRILL DETAIL
SCALE: 1" = 1'-0"

⅛" x 2'-2" Steel Bars 2" o.c. welded to ¼" Bars.

¼" x 3'-0" Steel Bars

SECTION AA

¼" x 1⅜" x 2⅝" Angle Iron above opening.

Ground Line

At least 1'-0" below ground line.

Removable Grill

Firebrick

6" Clay - Wetted & Packed

Grade

¼" x 1⅜" x 2⅝" Angle Iron on each end of oven opening

¼" x 1⅜" x 2⅝" Angle Iron

⅜" diam. Rods 2" o.c.

NOTE:
Line inside of firebox with firebricks.

OBLIQUE VIEW

FRONT VIEW

6"x10" Block

Ground Line

SIDE VIEW

6'-0"
3'-8"
1'-1"
1'-2"
4'-4"

1'-2" x 1'-2" Opening for Oven

BILL OF MATERIALS

8 pcs.   ¼" x 2'-2"   Steel Rods
19 pcs. ⅜" x 2'-2"   Steel Rods
3 pcs.   ¼" x 3'-0"   Steel Rods
2 pcs.   ¼" x 1⅜" x 2⅝" x 1'-5" Angle Iron
2 pcs.   ¼" x 1⅜" x 2⅝" x 3'-0" Angle Iron
1 pc.   ¼" x 1⅜" x 2⅝" 1'-6" Angle Iron
8 cu. ft. Clay

For Brick Construction
124 Firebricks
525 Common Bricks
8.0 cu. ft. Mortar

For Rubble Stone Construction
124 Firebricks
1.2 cu. yds Rubble or Native Stone
13.0 cu. ft. Mortar

Cooperative Extension Work in Agriculture and Home Economics
Texas A. & M. College and U.S. Department of Agriculture Cooperating
G. G. Gibson, Director, College Station, Texas.

OUTDOOR FURNACE
WITH OVEN

Drawn by: W.S.A.   1 Sheet
Traced by: R.A.S.   Serial No. 357
Aug. 1949

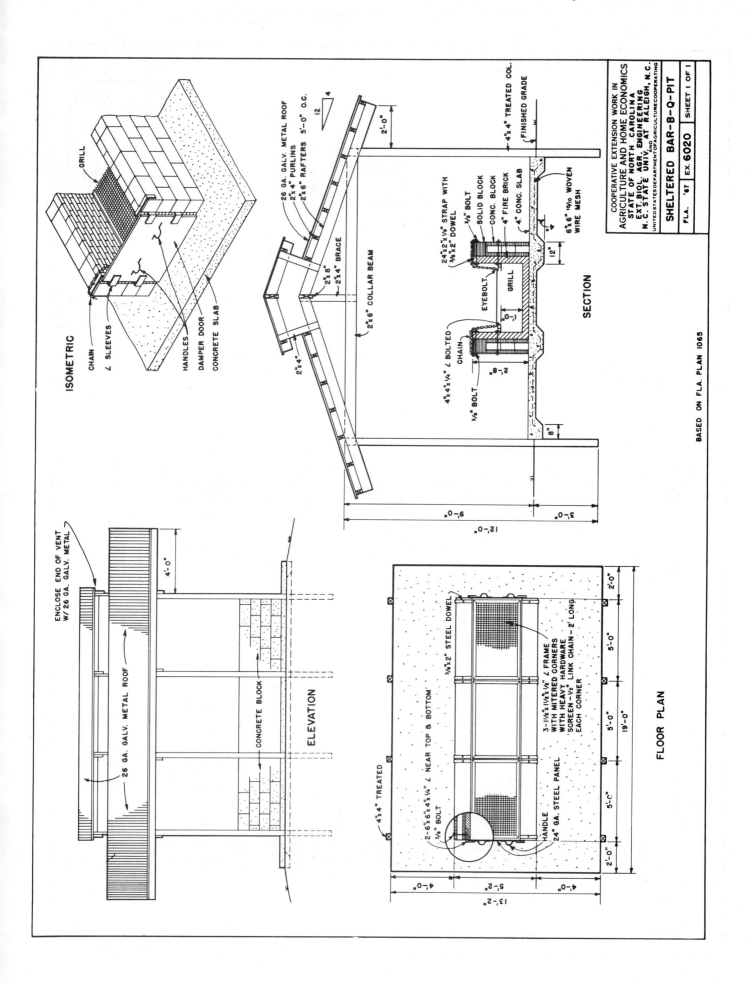

ISOMETRIC

GRILL
CHAIN
∠ SLEEVES
HANDLES
DAMPER DOOR
CONCRETE SLAB

26 GA. GALV. METAL ROOF
2"x4" PURLINS
2"x6" RAFTERS 5'-0" O.C.
12
4

2"x8"
2"x4" BRACE
2"x6" COLLAR BEAM
2"x4"

2'-0"

4"x4" TREATED COL.
FINISHED GRADE

24"x2"x⅛" STRAP WITH ⅜"x12" DOWEL
¾" BOLT
SOLID BLOCK
CONC. BLOCK
4" FIRE BRICK
4" CONC. SLAB
6"x6" ¹⁰⁄₁₀ WOVEN WIRE MESH

EYEBOLT
GRILL
1'-0"
12"

4"x4"x¼" ∠ BOLTED
CHAIN
4"x4"x¼" ∠
¾" BOLT
2'-8"

8"

SECTION

3'-0"
9'-0"
12'-0"

ENCLOSE END OF VENT W/ 26 GA. GALV. METAL

26 GA. GALV. METAL ROOF

CONCRETE BLOCK

4'-0"

ELEVATION

4"x4" TREATED

⅜"x12" STEEL DOWEL

3-1½"x1¼"x¼" ∠ FRAME WITH MITERED CORNERS WITH HEAVY HARDWARE
SCREEN -½" LINK CHAIN - 2' LONG EACH CORNER

2-6"x6"x4"x¼" ∠ NEAR TOP & BOTTOM
¾" BOLT
HANDLE
24" GA. STEEL PANEL

2'-0"
5'-0"
5'-0"
2'-0"
19'-0"

4'-0"
5'-2"
4'-0"
13'-2"

FLOOR PLAN

COOPERATIVE EXTENSION WORK IN AGRICULTURE AND HOME ECONOMICS
STATE OF NORTH CAROLINA
EXT. BIOL. AGR. ENGINEERING,
N.C. STATE UNIV. AT RALEIGH, N.C.
UNITED STATES DEPARTMENT OF AGRICULTURE COOPERATING

SHELTERED BAR-B-Q-PIT

FLA. '67 | EX. 6020 | SHEET 1 OF 1

BASED ON FLA. PLAN 1065

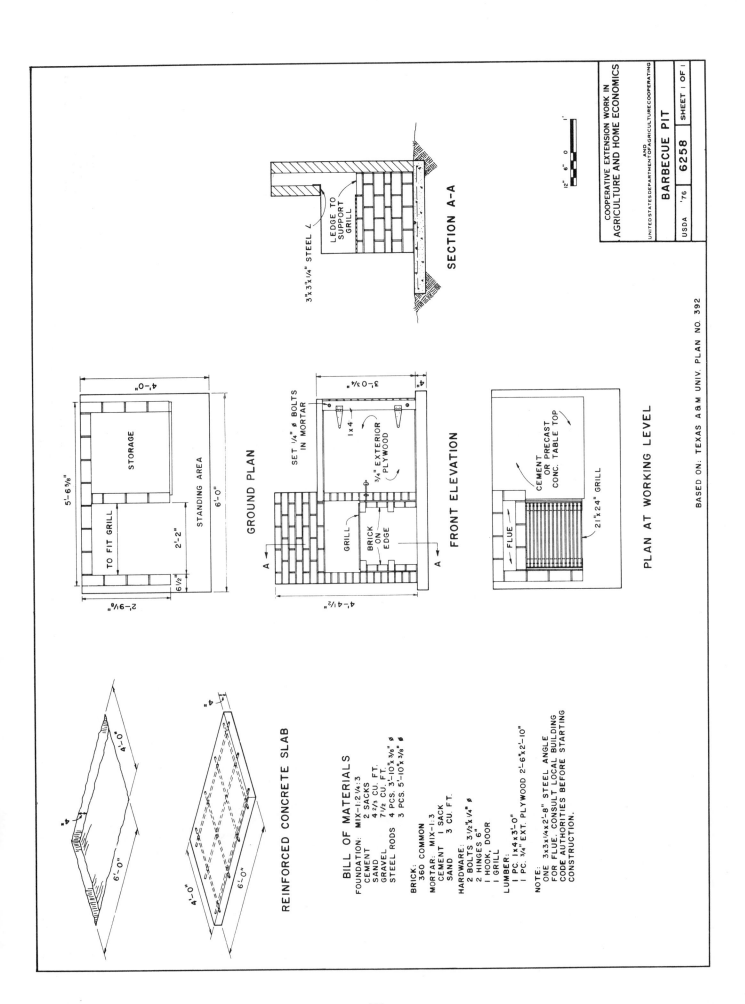

SECTION A-A

3"x3"x1/4" STEEL ∟

LEDGE TO SUPPORT GRILL

COOPERATIVE EXTENSION WORK IN
AGRICULTURE AND HOME ECONOMICS
AND
UNITEDSTATESDEPARTMENTOFAGRICULTURECOOPERATING

BARBECUE PIT

USDA '76 | 6258 | SHEET I OF I

12" 6" 0 1'

GROUND PLAN

4'-0"
5'-6 5/8"
STORAGE
STANDING AREA
2'-2"
6 1/2"
TO FIT GRILL
2'-9 1/8"

FRONT ELEVATION

3'-0 3/4"
4"
SET 1/4" ø BOLTS IN MORTAR
1x4
3/4" EXTERIOR PLYWOOD
GRILL
BRICK ON EDGE
4'-4 1/2"
A A

PLAN AT WORKING LEVEL

CEMENT OR PRECAST CONC. TABLE TOP
FLUE
21"x24" GRILL

BASED ON: TEXAS A&M UNIV. PLAN NO. 392

REINFORCED CONCRETE SLAB

4'-0"
6'-0"
4"
4'-0"
6'-0"
4"

BILL OF MATERIALS

FOUNDATION: MIX—1:2 1/4:3
CEMENT   2 SACKS
SAND   4 2/3 CU. FT.
GRAVEL   7 1/2 CU. FT.
STEEL RODS 4 PCS. 3'-10"x 3/8" ø
            3 PCS. 5'-10"x 3/8" ø

BRICK: 360 COMMON

MORTAR: MIX—1:3
CEMENT   1 SACK
SAND   3 CU. FT.

HARDWARE:
2 BOLTS 3 1/2"x 1/4" ø
2 HINGES 6"
1 HOOK, DOOR
1 GRILL

LUMBER:
1 PC. 1x4x3'-0"
1 PC. 3/4" EXT. PLYWOOD 2'-6"x2'-10"

NOTE:
ONE 3x3x1/4x2'-8" STEEL ANGLE
FOR FLUE. CONSULT LOCAL BUILDING
CODE AUTHORITIES BEFORE STARTING
CONSTRUCTION.

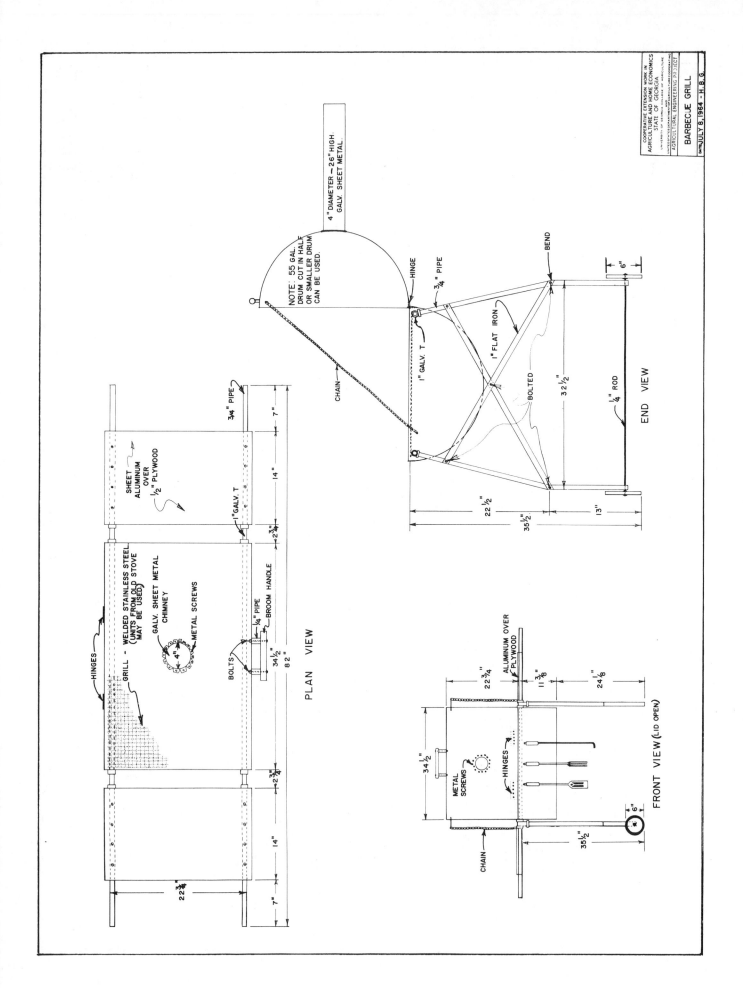

COOPERATIVE EXTENSION WORK IN
AGRICULTURE AND HOME ECONOMICS
STATE OF GEORGIA
UNIVERSITY OF GEORGIA COLLEGE OF AGRICULTURE
AND
UNITED STATES DEPARTMENT OF AGRICULTURE COOPERATING
AGRICULTURAL ENGINEERING PROJECT
BARBECUE GRILL
DATE JULY 8, 1964 - H. B. G.

END VIEW

4" DIAMETER – 26" HIGH.
GALV. SHEET METAL.

NOTE: 55 GAL.
DRUM CUT IN HALF
OR SMALLER DRUM
CAN BE USED.

HINGE

¾" PIPE

BEND

1" GALV. T

1" FLAT IRON

BOLTED

CHAIN

32½"

¼" ROD

6"

22½"

13"

35½"

PLAN VIEW

¾" PIPE

7"

SHEET
ALUMINUM
OVER
½" PLYWOOD

14"

1" GALV. T

2 ¾"

HINGES

GRILL – WELDED STAINLESS STEEL
(UNITS FROM OLD STOVE
MAY BE USED)

GALV. SHEET METAL
CHIMNEY

METAL SCREWS

4"

BOLTS

¼" PIPE

BROOM HANDLE

34½"

82"

2 ¾"

14"

7"

22 ¾"

FRONT VIEW (LID OPEN)

22 ¾"

ALUMINUM OVER
PLYWOOD

11 ⅜"

24 ⅛"

34½"

METAL
SCREWS

HINGES

CHAIN

35½"

6"

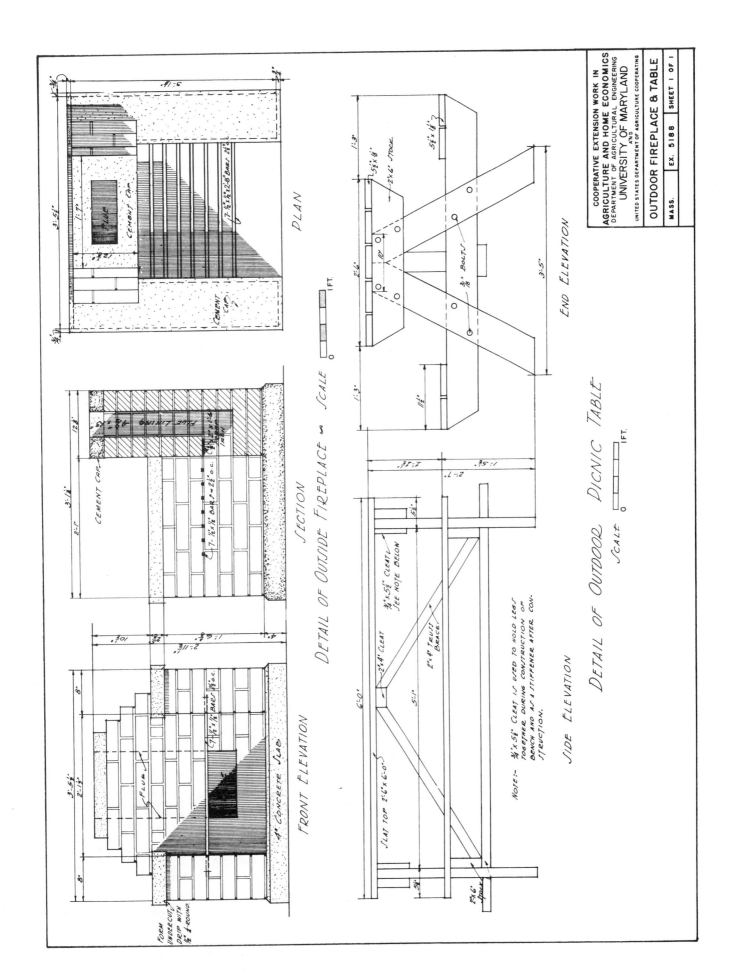

PLAN

DETAIL OF OUTSIDE FIREPLACE & SCALE

SECTION

FRONT ELEVATION

END ELEVATION

SIDE ELEVATION

DETAIL OF OUTDOOR PICNIC TABLE

SCALE

NOTE:- ¾"x 5½" CLEAT IS USED TO HOLD LEGS
TOGETHER DURING CONSTRUCTION OF
BENCH AND AS A STIFFENER AFTER CON-
STRUCTION.

COOPERATIVE EXTENSION WORK IN
AGRICULTURE AND HOME ECONOMICS
DEPARTMENT OF AGRICULTURAL ENGINEERING
UNIVERSITY OF MARYLAND
AND
UNITED STATES DEPARTMENT OF AGRICULTURE COOPERATING

OUTDOOR FIREPLACE & TABLE

MASS. | EX. 5188 | SHEET 1 OF 1

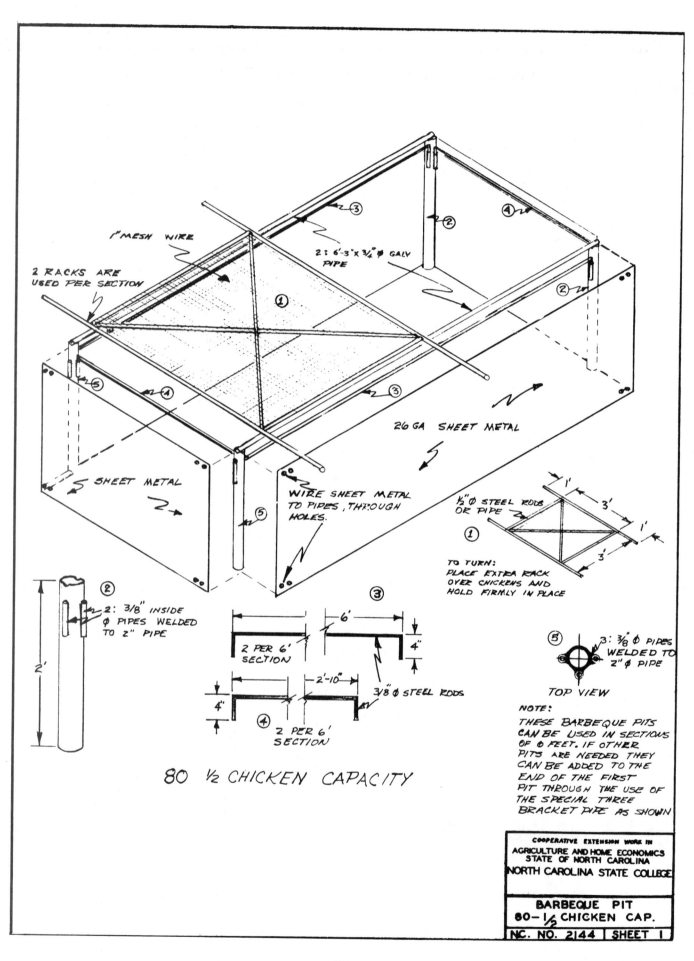

1" MESH WIRE

2 RACKS ARE USED PER SECTION

2: 6'-3" x ¾" Ø GALV PIPE

26 GA SHEET METAL

SHEET METAL

WIRE SHEET METAL TO PIPES, THROUGH HOLES.

②
2: 3/8" INSIDE Ø PIPES WELDED TO 2" PIPE
2'

③
2 PER 6' SECTION
6'
4"

④
4'
2'-10"
2 PER 6' SECTION
3/8" Ø STEEL RODS

① ½" Ø STEEL RODS OR PIPE
1'
3'
1'
3'

TO TURN:
PLACE EXTRA RACK OVER CHICKENS AND HOLD FIRMLY IN PLACE

⑤ 3: 3/8" Ø PIPES WELDED TO 2" Ø PIPE

TOP VIEW

NOTE:
THESE BARBEQUE PITS CAN BE USED IN SECTIONS OF 6 FEET. IF OTHER PITS ARE NEEDED THEY CAN BE ADDED TO THE END OF THE FIRST PIT THROUGH THE USE OF THE SPECIAL THREE BRACKET PIPE AS SHOWN

80 ½ CHICKEN CAPACITY

COOPERATIVE EXTENSION WORK IN
AGRICULTURE AND HOME ECONOMICS
STATE OF NORTH CAROLINA
NORTH CAROLINA STATE COLLEGE

BARBEQUE PIT
80-½ CHICKEN CAP.
NC. NO. 2144   SHEET 1

COMBINATION PICNIC TABLE AND BENCH

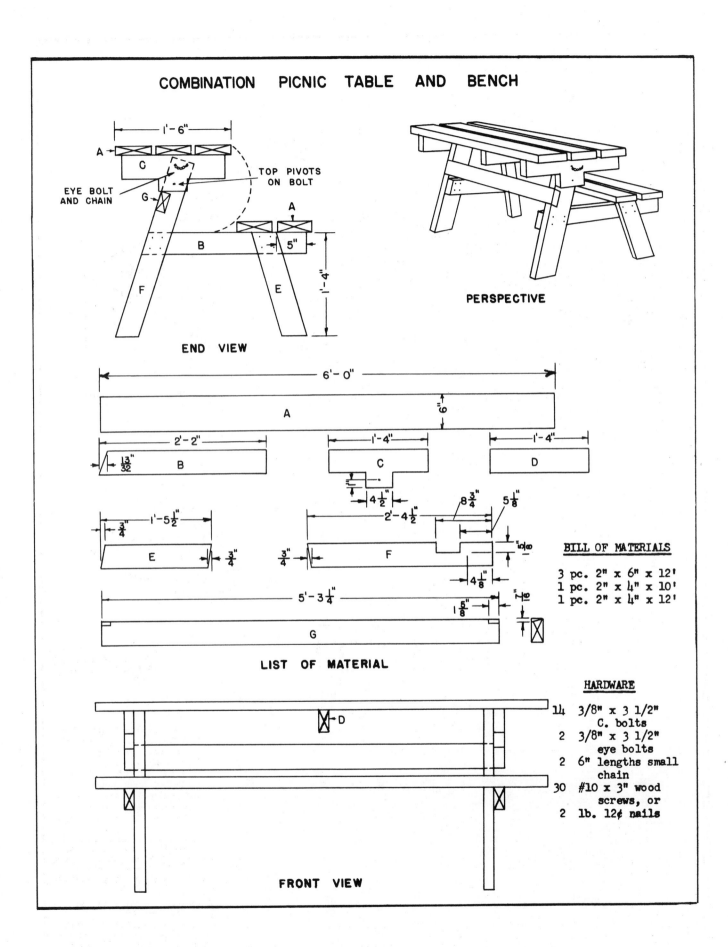

1'-6"

A

C

EYE BOLT
AND CHAIN

G

TOP PIVOTS
ON BOLT

A

B

5"

F

E

1'-4"

END VIEW

PERSPECTIVE

6'-0"

A

6"

2'-2"

1 3/32" B

1'-4"

C

4 1/2"

1'-4"

D

1'-5 1/2"

3/4"

E

3/4"

2'-4 1/2"

3/4"

F

8 3/4"

5 1/8"

5/8"

4 1/8"

BILL OF MATERIALS

3 pc. 2" x 6" x 12'
1 pc. 2" x 4" x 10'
1 pc. 2" x 4" x 12'

5'-3 1/4"

1 5/8"

7/16"

G

LIST OF MATERIAL

HARDWARE

14   3/8" x 3 1/2"
       C. bolts
2   3/8" x 3 1/2"
       eye bolts
2   6" lengths small
       chain
30   #10 x 3" wood
       screws, or
2 lb. 12¢ nails

D

FRONT VIEW

107

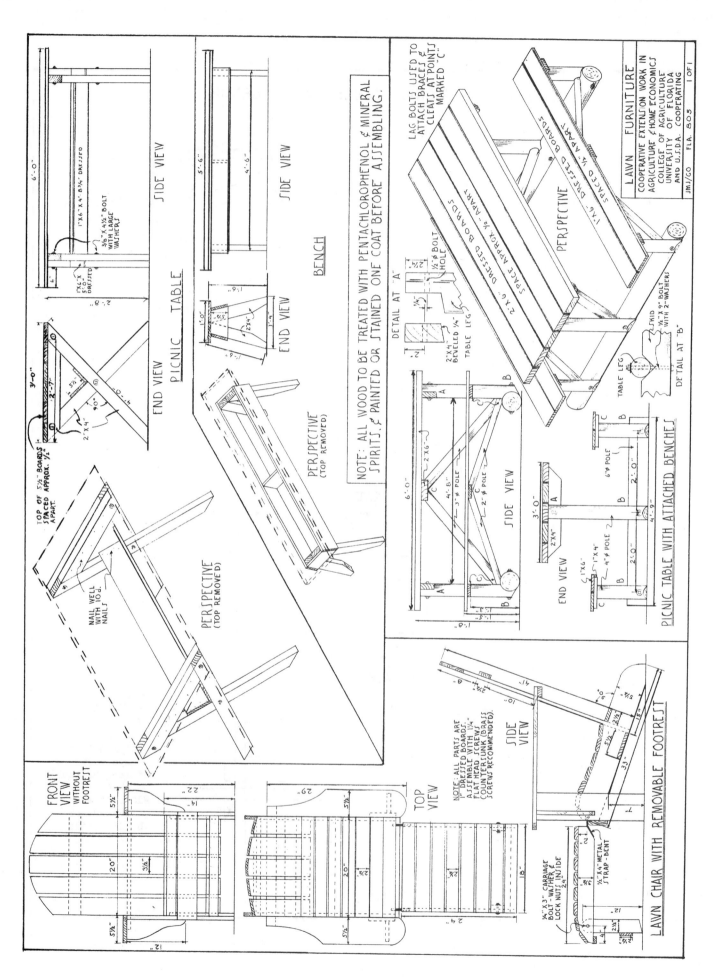

NOTE: ALL WOOD TO BE TREATED WITH PENTACHLOROPHENOL & MINERAL SPIRITS, & PAINTED OR STAINED ONE COAT BEFORE ASSEMBLING.

LAWN FURNITURE

Cooperative Extension Work in Agriculture & Home Economics
College of Agriculture
University of Florida
and U.S.D.A. Cooperating

JMI/GO   FLA. 805   1 OF 1

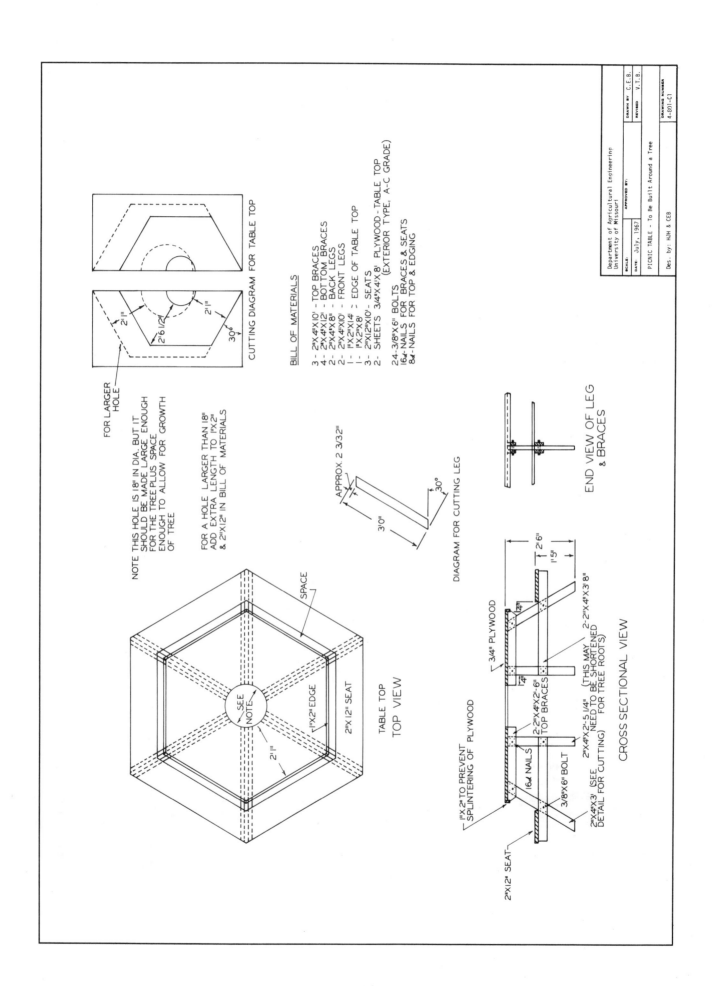

CUTTING DIAGRAM FOR TABLE TOP

FOR LARGER HOLE

NOTE THIS HOLE IS 18" IN DIA. BUT IT SHOULD BE MADE LARGE ENOUGH FOR THE TREE PLUS SPACE ENOUGH TO ALLOW FOR GROWTH OF TREE

FOR A HOLE LARGER THAN 18" ADD EXTRA LENGTH TO 1"X2" & 2"X12" IN BILL OF MATERIALS

2'1"
2'6 1/2"
2'1"
30°

BILL OF MATERIALS

3 - 2"X4"X10' - TOP BRACES
4 - 2"X4"X12' - BOTTOM BRACES
2 - 2"X4"X8" - BACK LEGS
2 - 2"X4"X10' - FRONT LEGS
1 - 1"X2"X14' - EDGE OF TABLE TOP
1 - 1"X2"X8' -
3 - 2"X12"X10' - SEATS
2 - SHEETS 3/4"X4'X8' PLYWOOD - TABLE TOP
        (EXTERIOR TYPE, A-C GRADE)

24 - 3/8"X6" BOLTS
16d - NAILS FOR BRACES & SEATS
8d - NAILS FOR TOP & EDGING

APPROX 2 3/32"
3'0"
30°

DIAGRAM FOR CUTTING LEG

END VIEW OF LEG & BRACES

TABLE TOP
TOP VIEW

SPACE
SEE NOTE
1"X2" EDGE
2'1"
2"X 12" SEAT

2'6"
1'5"
3/4" PLYWOOD
2-2"X4"X2'-6" TOP BRACES
1"X2" TO PREVENT SPLINTERING OF PLYWOOD
16d NAILS
3/8"X6" BOLT
2"X4"X3' (SEE DETAIL FOR CUTTING)
2"X4"X2'-5 1/4" (THIS MAY NEED TO BE SHORTENED FOR TREE ROOTS)
2-2"X4"X3'3'8"
2"X12" SEAT

CROSS SECTIONAL VIEW

Department of Agricultural Engineering
University of Missouri

SCALE:
DATE: July, 1967

PICNIC TABLE - To Be Built Around a Tree

Des. by: HJH & CEB

DRAWN BY: C.E.B.
REVISED: V.T.B.
APPROVED BY:

DRAWING NUMBER
4-001-C1

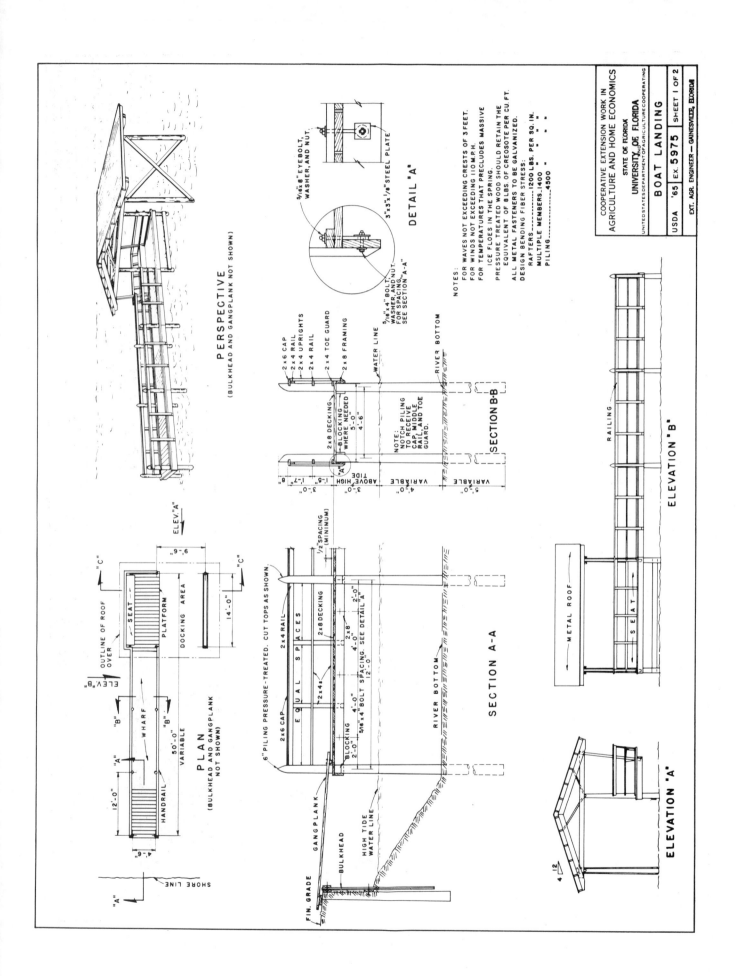

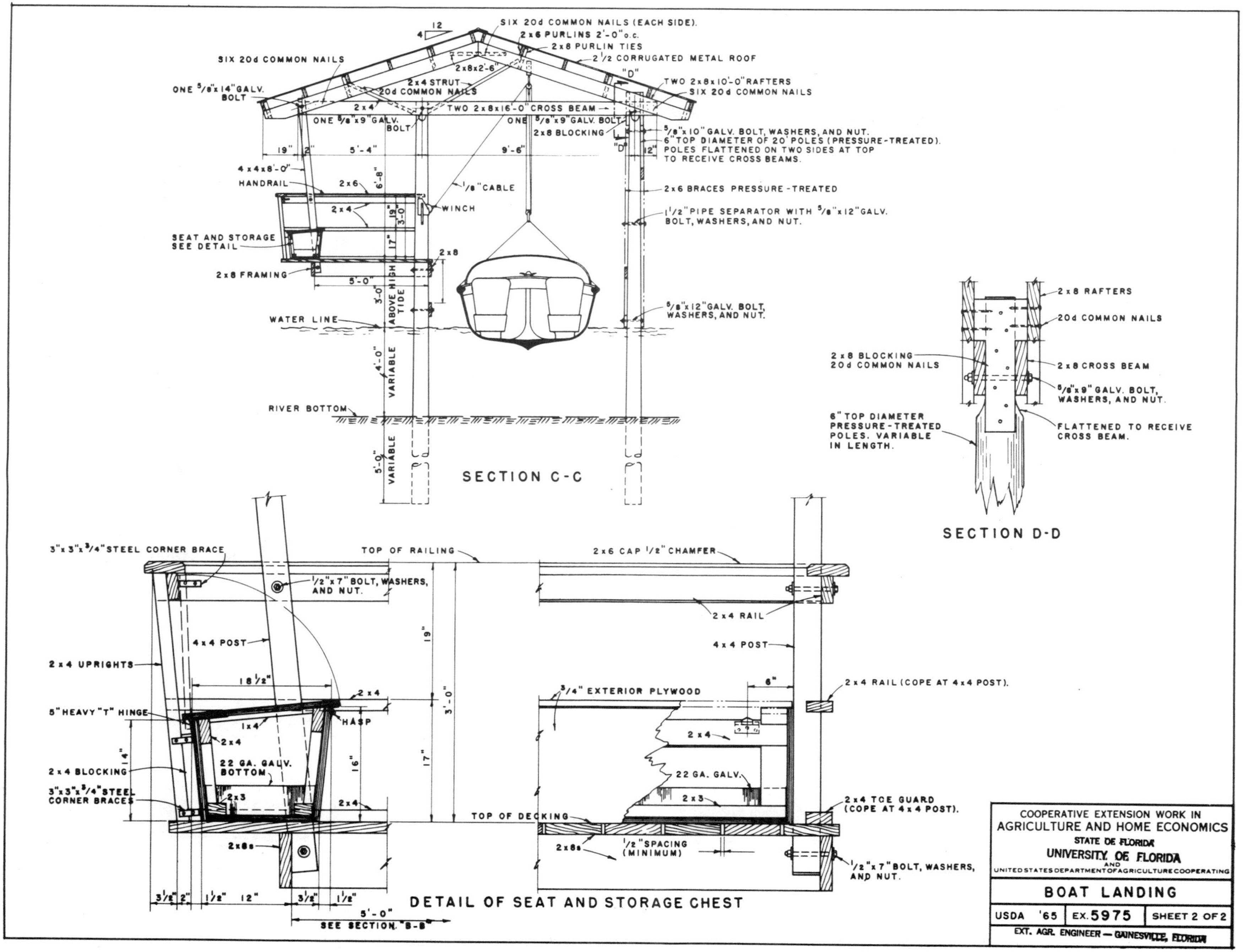
SIX 20d COMMON NAILS (EACH SIDE).
2 x 6 PURLINS 2'-0" o.c.
2 x 8 PURLIN TIES
2 1/2 CORRUGATED METAL ROOF
SIX 20d COMMON NAILS
ONE 5/8"x 14" GALV. BOLT
2 x 8 x 2'-6"
2 x 4 STRUT
20d COMMON NAILS
"D"
TWO 2 x 8 x 10'-0" RAFTERS
SIX 20d COMMON NAILS
2 x 4
TWO 2 x 8 x 16'-0" CROSS BEAM
ONE 5/8"x 9" GALV. BOLT
ONE 5/8"x 9" GALV. BOLT
2 x 8 BLOCKING
5/8"x 10" GALV. BOLT, WASHERS, AND NUT.
6" TOP DIAMETER OF 20' POLES (PRESSURE-TREATED). POLES FLATTENED ON TWO SIDES AT TOP TO RECEIVE CROSS BEAMS.
19"
2"
5'-4"
9'-6"
12"
4 x 4 x 8'-0"
HANDRAIL
2 x 6
6'-8"
1/8" CABLE
2 x 6 BRACES PRESSURE-TREATED
2 x 4
19"
3'-0"
WINCH
1 1/2" PIPE SEPARATOR WITH 5/8"x 12" GALV. BOLT, WASHERS, AND NUT.
SEAT AND STORAGE SEE DETAIL
17"
2 x 8
2 x 8 FRAMING
5'-0"
3'-0"
ABOVE HIGH TIDE
5/8"x 12" GALV. BOLT, WASHERS, AND NUT.
WATER LINE
4'-0"
VARIABLE
RIVER BOTTOM
5'-0"
VARIABLE
SECTION C-C
2 x 8 RAFTERS
20d COMMON NAILS
2 x 8 BLOCKING
20d COMMON NAILS
2 x 8 CROSS BEAM
5/8"x 9" GALV. BOLT, WASHERS, AND NUT.
6" TOP DIAMETER PRESSURE-TREATED POLES. VARIABLE IN LENGTH.
FLATTENED TO RECEIVE CROSS BEAM.
SECTION D-D
3"x 3"x 3/4" STEEL CORNER BRACE
TOP OF RAILING
2 x 6 CAP 1/2" CHAMFER
1/2"x 7" BOLT, WASHERS, AND NUT.
2 x 4 RAIL
4 x 4 POST
19"
4 x 4 POST
2 x 4 UPRIGHTS
18 1/2"
3'-0"
6"
2 x 4 RAIL (COPE AT 4 x 4 POST).
2 x 4
3/4" EXTERIOR PLYWOOD
5" HEAVY "T" HINGE
1 x 4
HASP
2 x 4
2 x 4
14"
16"
17"
22 GA. GALV. BOTTOM
22 GA. GALV.
2 x 4 BLOCKING
3"x 3"x 3/4" STEEL CORNER BRACES
2 x 3
2 x 3
2 x 4
TOP OF DECKING
2 x 4 TOE GUARD (COPE AT 4 x 4 POST).
2 x 8s
2 x 8s
1/2" SPACING (MINIMUM)
1/2"x 7" BOLT, WASHERS, AND NUT.
3 1/2"
2"
1 1/2"
12"
3 1/2"
1 1/2"
5'-0"
SEE SECTION "B-B"
DETAIL OF SEAT AND STORAGE CHEST
COOPERATIVE EXTENSION WORK IN
AGRICULTURE AND HOME ECONOMICS
STATE OF FLORIDA
UNIVERSITY OF FLORIDA
AND
UNITED STATES DEPARTMENT OF AGRICULTURE COOPERATING
BOAT LANDING
USDA '65
EX. 5975
SHEET 2 OF 2
EXT. AGR. ENGINEER — GAINESVILLE, FLORIDA

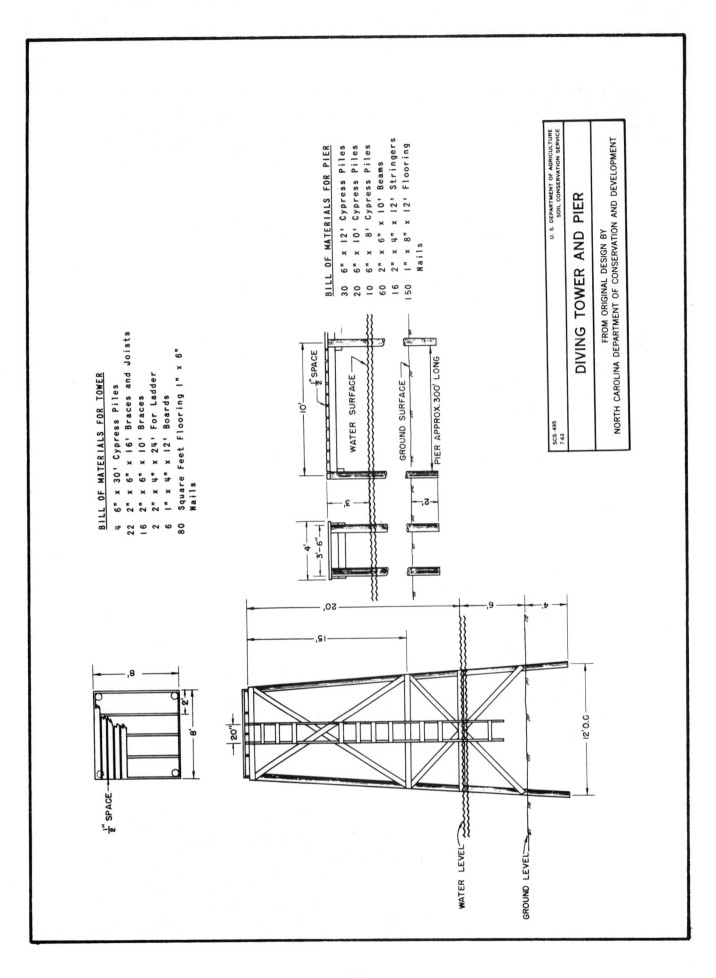

BILL OF MATERIALS FOR TOWER

4 6" x 30' Cypress Piles
22 2" x 6" x 16' Braces and Joists
16 2" x 6" x 10' Braces
2 2" x 4" x 24' For Ladder
6 1" x 4" x 12' Boards
80 Square Feet Flooring 1" x 6"
   Nails

BILL OF MATERIALS FOR PIER

30 6" x 12' Cypress Piles
20 6" x 10' Cypress Piles
10 6" x 8' Cypress Piles
60 2" x 6" x 10' Beams
16 2" x 4" x 12' Stringers
150 1" x 8" x 12' Flooring
    Nails

WATER SURFACE

GROUND SURFACE

PIER APPROX. 300' LONG

1/2" SPACE

10'

4'

3'-6"

3'

2'

20'

15'

20"

8'

2'

8'

1/2" SPACE

12' O.C.

6'

4'

WATER LEVEL

GROUND LEVEL

U. S. DEPARTMENT OF AGRICULTURE
SOIL CONSERVATION SERVICE

DIVING TOWER AND PIER

FROM ORIGINAL DESIGN BY
NORTH CAROLINA DEPARTMENT OF CONSERVATION AND DEVELOPMENT

SCS-495
7-63

In recent years the word "flotation" has come to mean considerably more than lashing watertight drums beneath the object to be floated. With the advances in chemical technology has come unicellular expanded polystyrene bearing the name Styrofoam.

Douglas fir and redwood are recommended for decking, stringers and bracing; white oak for steps; maple for dowels. All wood should be treated with cuprinol before assembly. If creosote is used on the submerged redwood, 22 gauge galvanized sheet metal is recommended as a shield for the Styrofoam. Ladder might be painted white. All metal parts, including nails, should be hot dip galvanized.

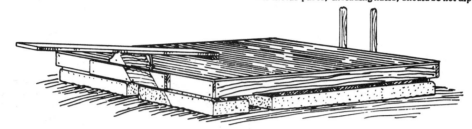

DIVING RAFT

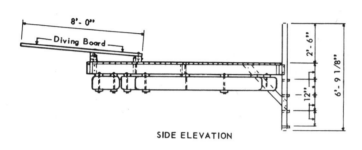

SIDE ELEVATION

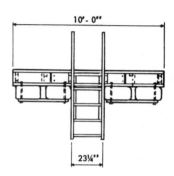

REAR ELEVATION

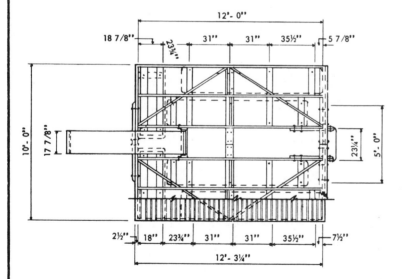

PLAN

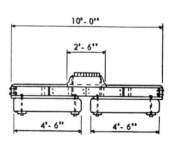

FRONT ELEVATION

SCS-496 6-63	U. S. DEPARTMENT OF AGRICULTURE SOIL CONSERVATION SERVICE

DIVING RAFT-STYROFOAM

FROM DESIGN VOLUMES OF THE PARK PRACTICE PROGRAM
NATIONAL CONFERENCE ON STATE PARKS
DESIGN SHEET NO. R-4904

HORSESHOES, SHUFFLEBOARD
AND TABLE TENNIS

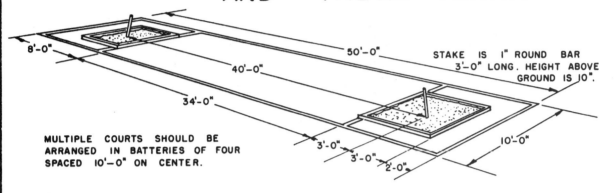

50'-0"

STAKE IS 1" ROUND BAR
3'-0" LONG. HEIGHT ABOVE
GROUND IS 10".

8'-0"

40'-0"

34'-0"

MULTIPLE COURTS SHOULD BE
ARRANGED IN BATTERIES OF FOUR
SPACED 10'-0" ON CENTER.

3'-0"

3'-0"

2'-0"

10'-0"

HORSESHOES

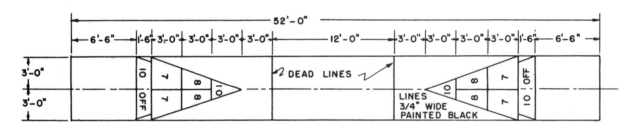

52'-0"

6'-6" 1'-6" 3'-0" 3'-0" 3'-0" 3'-0"   12'-0"   3'-0" 3'-0" 3'-0" 3'-0" 1'-6" 6'-6"

3'-0"

3'-0"

10 7 8   DEAD LINES   8 7 10
OFF 7 8 10   10 8 7 OFF

LINES
3/4" WIDE
PAINTED BLACK

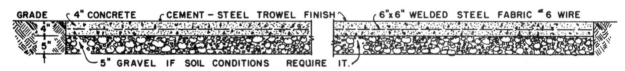

GRADE   4" CONCRETE   CEMENT — STEEL TROWEL FINISH   6"x6" WELDED STEEL FABRIC 6 WIRE

4"

5"

5" GRAVEL IF SOIL CONDITIONS REQUIRE IT.

SHUFFLEBOARD

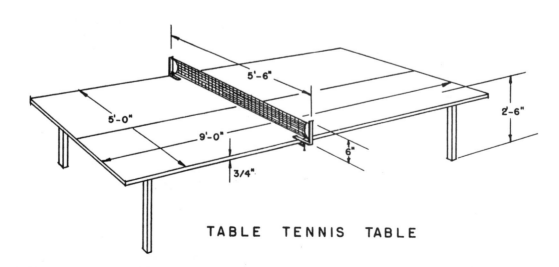

5'-6"

5'-0"

9'-0"

2'-6"

6"

3/4"

TABLE TENNIS TABLE

TRACK AND FIELD

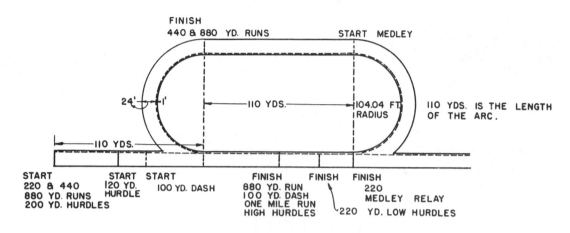

FINISH
440 & 880 YD. RUNS   START MEDLEY

24'←1'   ←110 YDS.→   104.04 FT   110 YDS. IS THE LENGTH
                        RADIUS   OF THE ARC.

←110 YDS.→

START   START   START
220 & 440   120 YD. 100 YD. DASH   FINISH   FINISH   FINISH
880 YD. RUNS   HURDLE   880 YD. RUN   220
200 YD. HURDLES   100 YD. DASH   MEDLEY RELAY
                                        ONE MILE RUN   220 YD. LOW HURDLES
                                        HIGH HURDLES

QUARTER-MILE RUNNING TRACK

←RUNWAY→   MAX. THROW = 250' ±
80' MIN. FOR A.A.U.   ←SCRATCH LINE
CHAMPIONSHIP   FLUSH BOARD   12'-0" LONG , 2 3/4" WIDE, 8" DEEP

JAVELIN THROW

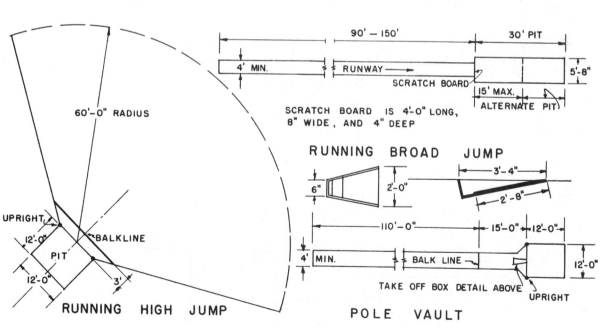

60'-0" RADIUS

                    90' — 150'   30' PIT
4' MIN.   ←RUNWAY→   5'-8"
             SCRATCH BOARD
                                    15' MAX.
                                    ALTERNATE PIT

SCRATCH BOARD IS 4'-0" LONG,
8" WIDE, AND 4" DEEP

RUNNING BROAD JUMP

6"   2'-0"   ←3'-4"→
                  ←2'-8"→

UPRIGHT   ←110'-0"→   ←15'-0"→←12'-0"→
12'-0"   4' MIN.   ←BALK LINE→   12'-0"
    BALKLINE
PIT   TAKE OFF BOX DETAIL ABOVE
12'-0"   UPRIGHT
     3'

RUNNING HIGH JUMP   POLE VAULT

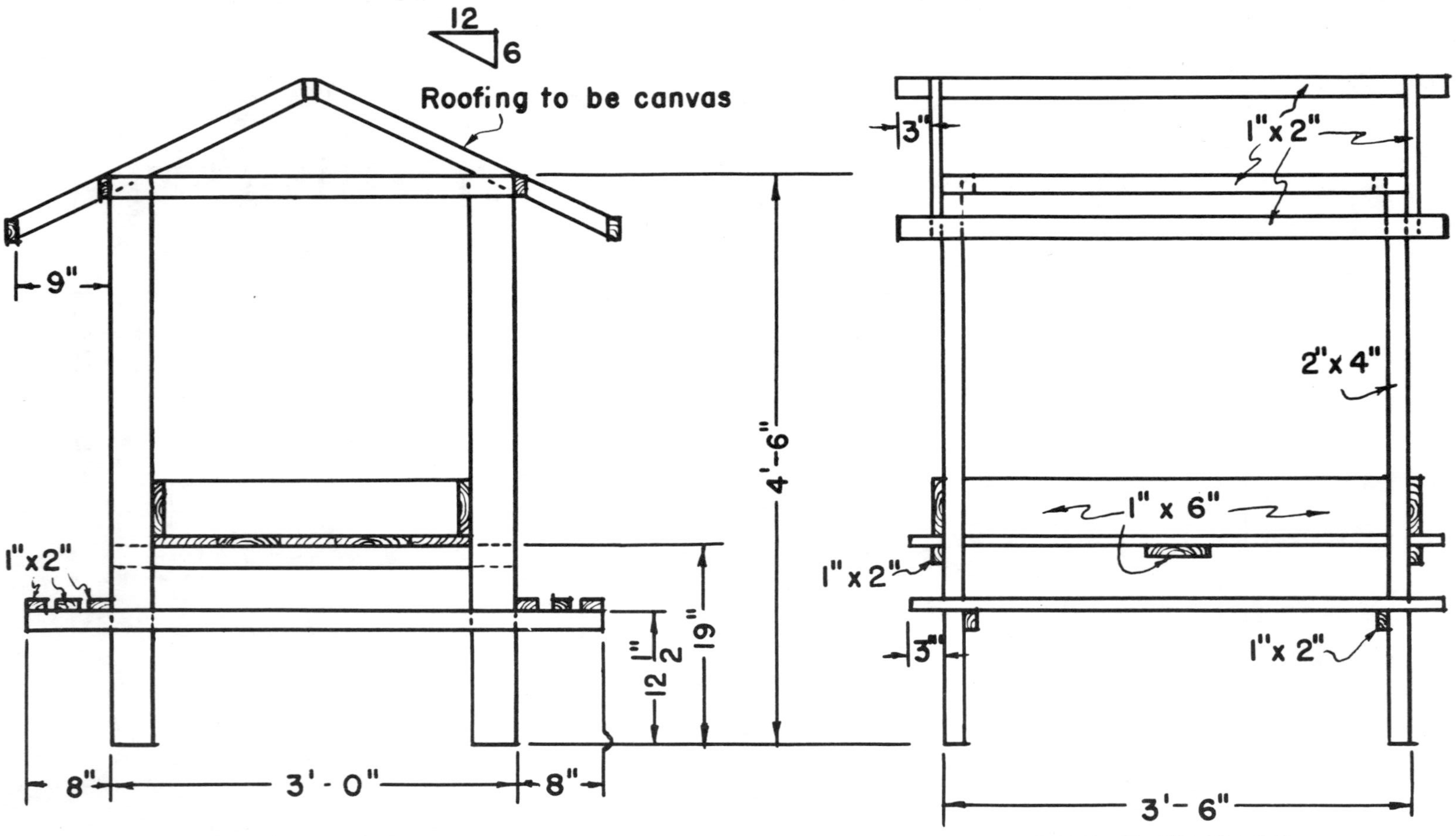

SAND BOX

1" x 2"

2" x 4"

1" x 6"

1" x 2"

3'-6"

3"

3"

1" x 2"

SIDE ELEVATION

4'-6"

19"

12
2

1"

8"

Roofing to be canvas

12
6

9"

3'-0"

8"

1" x 2"

CROSS SECTION

116

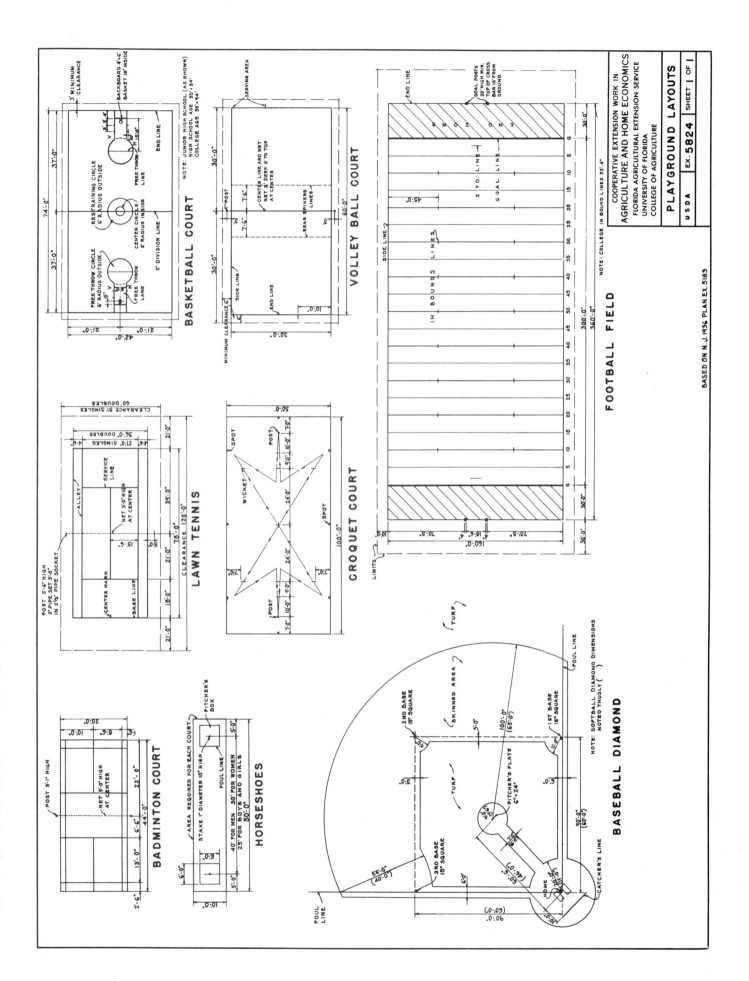

BASKETBALL COURT

VOLLEY BALL COURT

FOOTBALL FIELD

NOTE: COLLEGE IN BOUND LINES 53'-4"

LAWN TENNIS

CROQUET COURT

BADMINTON COURT

HORSESHOES

BASEBALL DIAMOND

NOTE: SOFTBALL DIAMOND DIMENSIONS NOTED THUSLY ( )

PLAYGROUND LAYOUTS

COOPERATIVE EXTENSION WORK IN
AGRICULTURE AND HOME ECONOMICS
FLORIDA AGRICULTURAL EXTENSION SERVICE
UNIVERSITY OF FLORIDA
COLLEGE OF AGRICULTURE

USDA   EX. 5824   SHEET 1 OF 1

BASED ON N.J. 1936 PLAN EX. 5183

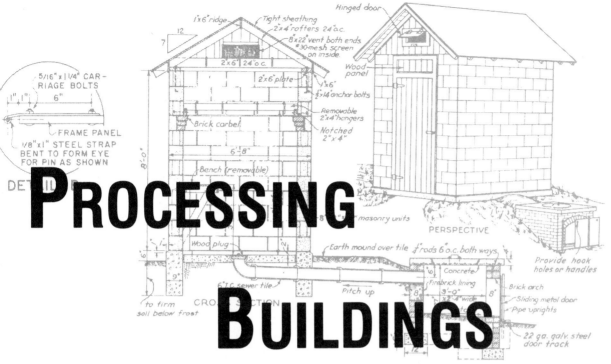

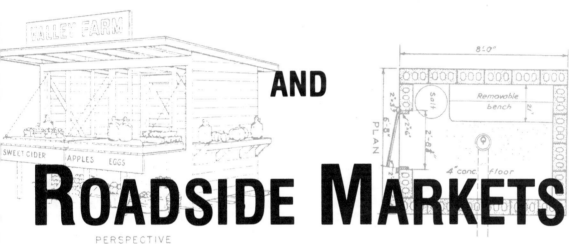

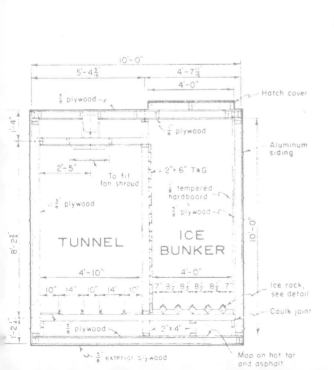

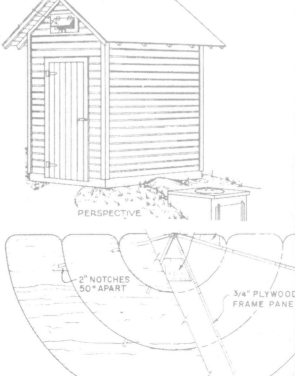

PROCESSING BUILDINGS AND ROADSIDE MARKETS

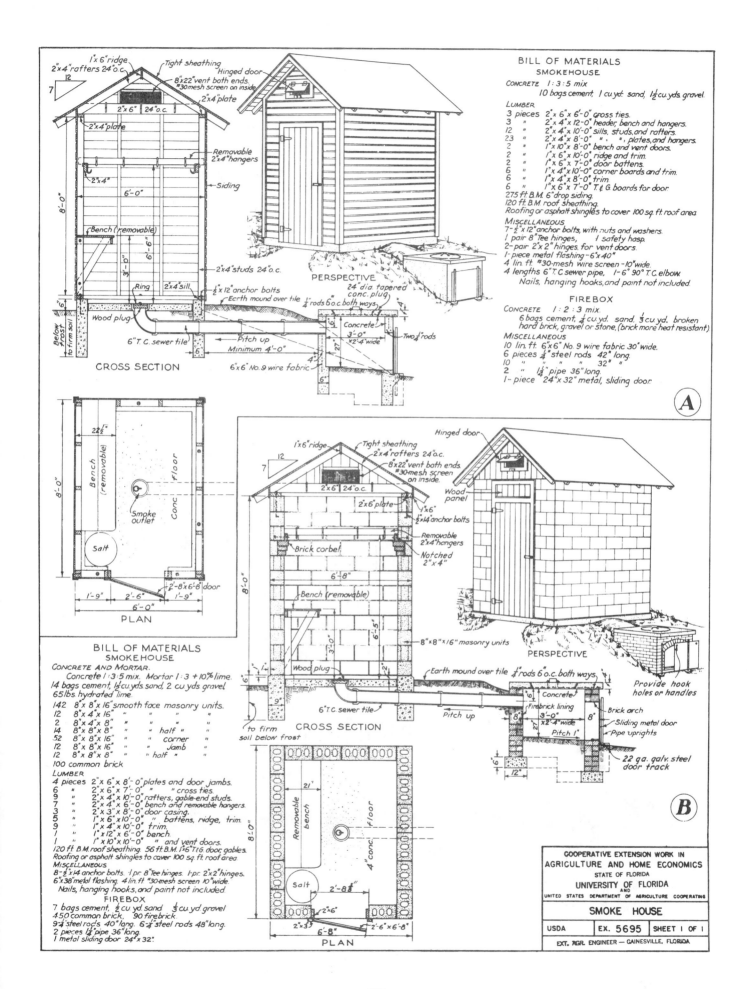

BILL OF MATERIALS
SMOKEHOUSE

CONCRETE 1 : 3 : 5 mix
   10 bags cement, 1 cu. yd. sand, 1½ cu. yds. gravel.

LUMBER
3 pieces 2" x 6" x 6'-0" cross ties.
3 "   2" x 4" x 12'-0" header, bench and hangers.
12 " 2" x 4" x 10'-0" sills, studs, and rafters.
23 " 2" x 4" x 8'-0" " ", plates, and hangers.
2 "   1" x 10" x 8'-0" bench and vent doors.
2 "   1" x 6" x 10'-0" ridge and trim.
2 "   1" x 6" x 7'-0" door battens.
6 "   1" x 4" x 10'-0" corner boards and trim.
6 "   1" x 4" x 8'-0" trim.
6 "   1" x 6" x 7'-0" T. & G. boards for door.
275 ft. B.M. 6" drop siding.
120 ft. B.M. roof sheathing.
Roofing or asphalt shingles to cover 100 sq. ft. roof area.

MISCELLANEOUS
7 - ½" x 12" anchor bolts, with nuts and washers.
1 pair 8" Tee hinges,   1 safety hasp.
2 - pair 2" x 2" hinges, for vent doors.
1 - piece metal flashing - 6" x 40".
4 lin. ft. #30-mesh wire screen - 10" wide.
4 lengths 6" T.C. sewer pipe, 1 - 6" 90° T.C. elbow.
   Nails, hanging hooks, and paint not included.

FIREBOX

CONCRETE 1 : 2 : 3 mix.
  6 bags cement, ½ cu. yd. sand, ⅓ cu. yd. broken
  hard brick, gravel or stone, (brick more heat resistant).

MISCELLANEOUS
10 lin. ft. 6" x 6" No. 9 wire fabric 30" wide.
6 pieces ¼" steel rods 42" long.
10 "   "   "   32" "
2 " 1¼" pipe 36" long.
1 - piece 24" x 32" metal, sliding door.

(A)

BILL OF MATERIALS
SMOKEHOUSE

CONCRETE AND MORTAR.
  Concrete 1 : 3 : 5 mix. Mortar 1 : 3 + 10% lime.
14 bags cement, 1½ cu. yds. sand, 2 cu. yds. gravel.
65 lbs. hydrated lime.

142 8" x 8" x 16" smooth face masonry units.
12   8" x 4" x 16" "   "   "   "
2   8" x 4" x 8"   "   "   half   "
14   8" x 8" x 8"   "   " half   "
52   8" x 8" x 16" "   " corner "
12   8" x 8" x 16" "   " jamb   "
12   8" x 8" x 8"   "   " half   "
100 common brick

LUMBER
4 pieces 2" x 6" x 8'-0" plates and door jambs.
6 "   2" x 6" x 7'-0" "   cross ties.
9 "   2" x 4" x 10'-0" rafters, gable-end studs.
7 "   2" x 4" x 6'-0" bench and removable hangers.
3 "   2" x 3" x 8'-0" door casing.
5 "   1" x 6" x 10'-0" " battens, ridge, trim.
9 "   1" x 4" x 10'-0" trim.
1 "   1" x 12" x 6'-0" bench.
1 "   1" x 10" x 10'-0" " and vent doors.
120 ft. B.M. roof sheathing. 56 ft. B.M. 1"x6" T&G door; gables.
Roofing or asphalt shingles to cover 100 sq. ft. roof area.

MISCELLANEOUS
8 - ½" x 14" anchor bolts. 1 pr. 8" Tee hinges. 1-pr. 2" x 2" hinges.
6" x 38" metal flashing. 4 lin. ft. #30-mesh screen 10" wide.
  Nails, hanging hooks, and paint not included.

FIREBOX
7 bags cement, ½ cu. yd. sand, ⅓ cu. yd. gravel.
450 common brick, 90 firebrick.
9-¼" steel rods 40" long. 6-¼" steel rods 48" long.
2 pieces 1¼" pipe 36" long.
1 metal sliding door 24" x 32".

(B)

COOPERATIVE EXTENSION WORK IN
AGRICULTURE AND HOME ECONOMICS
STATE OF FLORIDA
UNIVERSITY OF FLORIDA and
UNITED STATES DEPARTMENT OF AGRICULTURE COOPERATING

SMOKE HOUSE

| USDA | EX. 5695 | SHEET 1 OF 1 |

EXT. AGR. ENGINEER — GAINESVILLE, FLORIDA

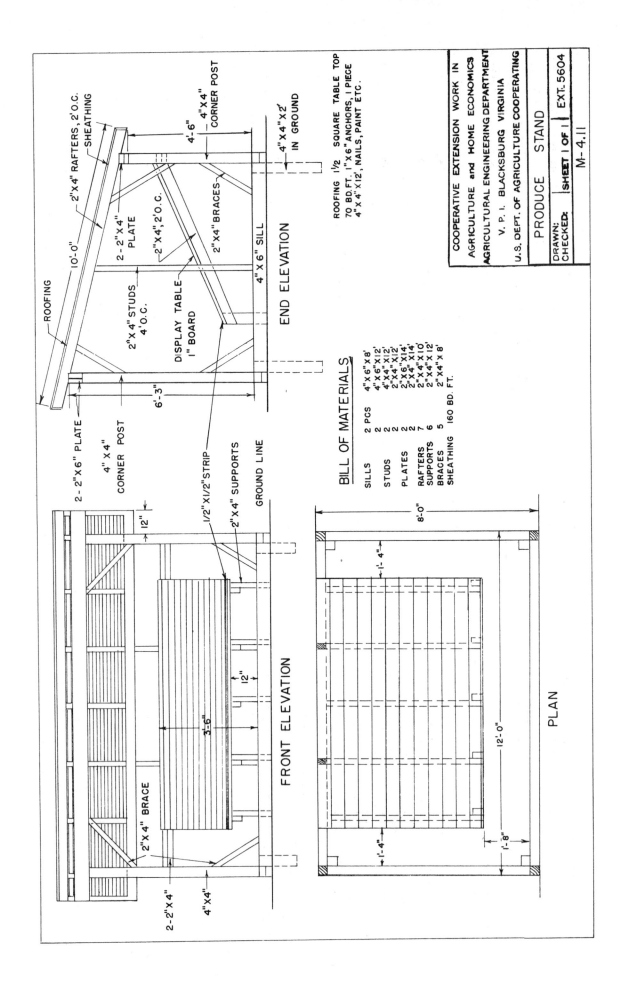

END ELEVATION

2"X4" RAFTERS, 2' O.C.
SHEATHING
4"X4" CORNER POST
4'-6"
ROOFING
10'-0"
2-2"X4" PLATE
2"X4", 2' O.C.
2"X4" STUDS 4' O.C.
2"X4" BRACES
DISPLAY TABLE 1" BOARD
4"X6" SILL
4"X4"X2' IN GROUND
6'-3"

ROOFING 1½ SQUARE TABLE TOP
70 BD. FT. 1"X6" ANCHORS, 1 PIECE
4"X4"X12, NAILS, PAINT ETC.

FRONT ELEVATION

2-2"X6" PLATE
4"X4" CORNER POST
½"X½" STRIP
2"X4" SUPPORTS
GROUND LINE
12"
12"
3'-6"
2"X4" BRACE
2-2"X4"
4"X4"

BILL OF MATERIALS

SILLS	2 PCS	4"X6"X8'
	2	4"X6"X12'
STUDS	2	4"X4"X12'
	2	2"X4"X12'
PLATES	2	2"X6"X14'
RAFTERS	7	2"X4"X14'
SUPPORTS	6	2"X4"X10'
BRACES	5	2"X4"X12'
SHEATHING	160 BD. FT.	2"X4"X8'

PLAN

8'-0"
1'-4"
1'-4"
12'-0"
1'-8"
4"

COOPERATIVE EXTENSION WORK IN
AGRICULTURE and HOME ECONOMICS
AGRICULTURAL ENGINEERING DEPARTMENT
V. P. I. BLACKSBURG VIRGINIA
U.S. DEPT. OF AGRICULTURE COOPERATING

PRODUCE STAND

DRAWN:
CHECKED: | SHEET 1 OF 1 | EXT. 5604
M- 4.11

122

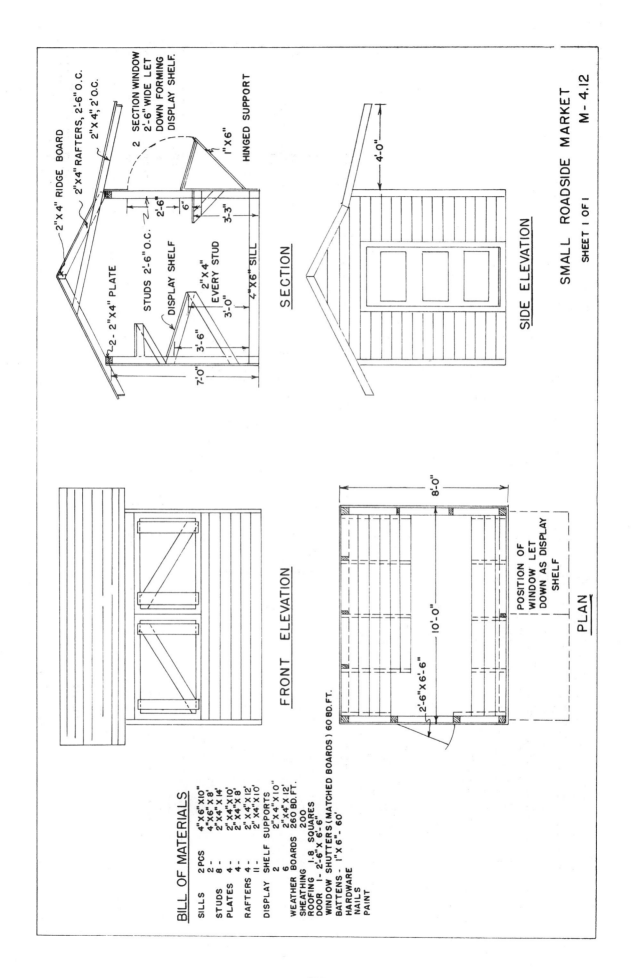

SECTION

2"X4" RIDGE BOARD

2"X4" RAFTERS, 2'-6" O.C.

2"X4", 2' O.C.

2 SECTION WINDOW 2'-6" WIDE LET DOWN FORMING DISPLAY SHELF.

1"X6"

HINGED SUPPORT

2-2"X4" PLATE

STUDS 2'-6" O.C.

DISPLAY SHELF

2"X4" EVERY STUD

4"X6" SILL

2'-6"

6"

3'-3"

3'-0"

3'-6"

7'-0"

SIDE ELEVATION

4'-0"

FRONT ELEVATION

PLAN

8'-0"

10'-0"

POSITION OF WINDOW LET DOWN AS DISPLAY SHELF

2'-6"X 6'-6"

BILL OF MATERIALS

SILLS   2 PCS   4"X6"X10"

STUDS   2 -   4"X6"X8'
         8 -   2"X4"X14'

PLATES   4 -   2"X4"X10'
         4 -   2"X4"X8'

RAFTERS   4 -   2"X4"X12'
         11 -   2"X4"X10'

DISPLAY SHELF SUPPORTS
         2   2"X4"X10"
         6   2"X4"X12'

WEATHER BOARDS   260 BD. FT.

SHEATHING   200

ROOFING   1.8 SQUARES

DOOR   1 - 2'-6"X 6'-6"

WINDOW SHUTTERS (MATCHED BOARDS) 60 BD. FT.

BATTENS - 1"X 6"- 60'

HARDWARE

NAILS

PAINT

SMALL ROADSIDE MARKET

M-4.12

SHEET 1 OF 1

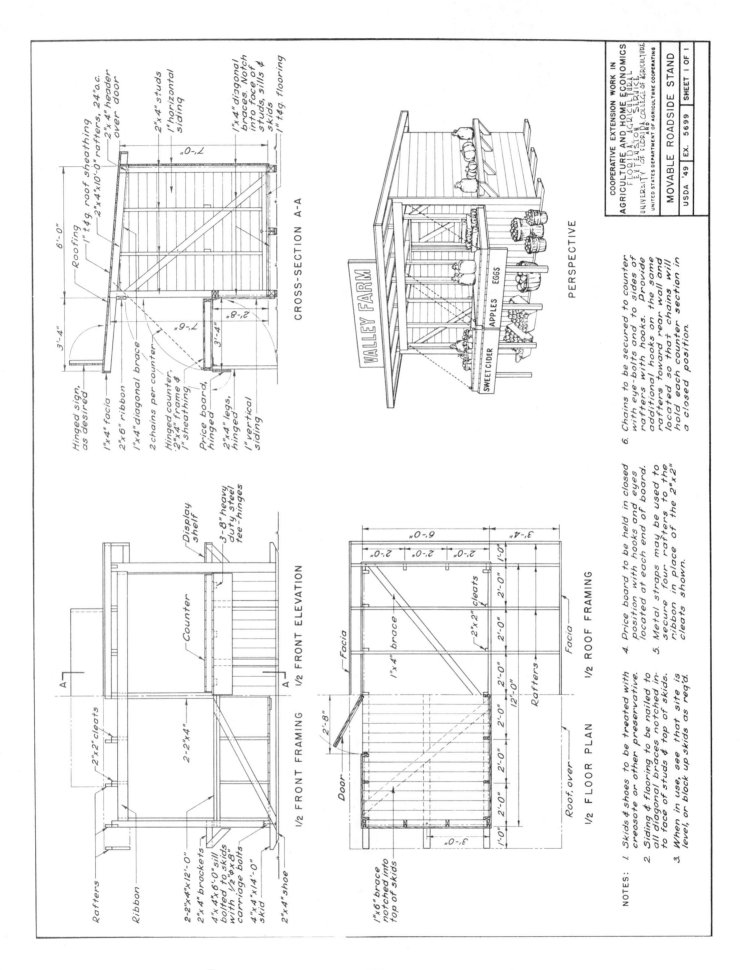

CROSS-SECTION A-A

7'-0"

6'-0"

3'-4"

2'-8"

3'-4"

Roofing

Hinged sign, as desired

1"x4" facia

2"x6" ribbon

1"x4" diagonal brace

2 chains per counter

Hinged counter, 2"x4" frame & 1" sheathing

Price board, hinged

2"x4" legs, hinged

1" vertical siding

1"x4" diagonal braces. Notch into face of studs, sills & skids

1" t&g flooring

1" horizontal siding

2"x4" studs

2"x4" header over door

1" t&g roof sheathing

2"x4"x10'-0" rafters, 24"o.c.

PERSPECTIVE

VALLEY FARM

SWEET CIDER   APPLES   EGGS

1/2 FRONT ELEVATION

1/2 FRONT FRAMING

A

A

Rafters

Ribbon

2"x2" cleats

2-2"x4"

2-2"x4"x12'-0" sill bolted to skids with 1/2"Øx8" carriage bolts

4"x4"x14'-0" skid

2"x4" shoe

2"x4" brackets

Display shelf

3-8" heavy steel tee-hinges

Counter

1/2 FLOOR PLAN

1/2 ROOF FRAMING

Facia

Facia

Door

2'-8"

1'-6" brace notched into top of skids

1"x4" brace

2"x2" cleats

Rafters

Roof, over

3'-0"

1'-0" 2'-0" 2'-0" 2'-0" 2'-0" 2'-0" 12'-0"

6'-0"

2'-0" 2'-0" 2'-0" 1'-0"

3'-4"

NOTES: 1. Skids & shoes to be treated with creosote or other preservative.
2. Siding & flooring to be nailed to all diagonal braces notched into face of studs & top of skids.
3. When in use, see that site is level, or block up skids as req'd.

4. Price board to be held in closed position with hooks and eyes located at each end of board.
5. Metal straps may be used to secure four rafters to the ribbon in place of the 2"x2" cleats shown.

6. Chains to be secured to counter with eye-bolts and to sides of rafters with hooks. Provide additional hooks on the same rafters toward rear wall and located so that chains will hold each counter section in a closed position.

COOPERATIVE EXTENSION WORK IN AGRICULTURE AND HOME ECONOMICS
FLORIDA AGRICULTURAL EXTENSION SERVICE
UNIVERSITY OF FLORIDA, COLLEGE OF AGRICULTURE
AND UNITED STATES DEPARTMENT OF AGRICULTURE COOPERATING

MOVABLE ROADSIDE STAND

USDA '49 EX. 5699 SHEET 1 OF 1

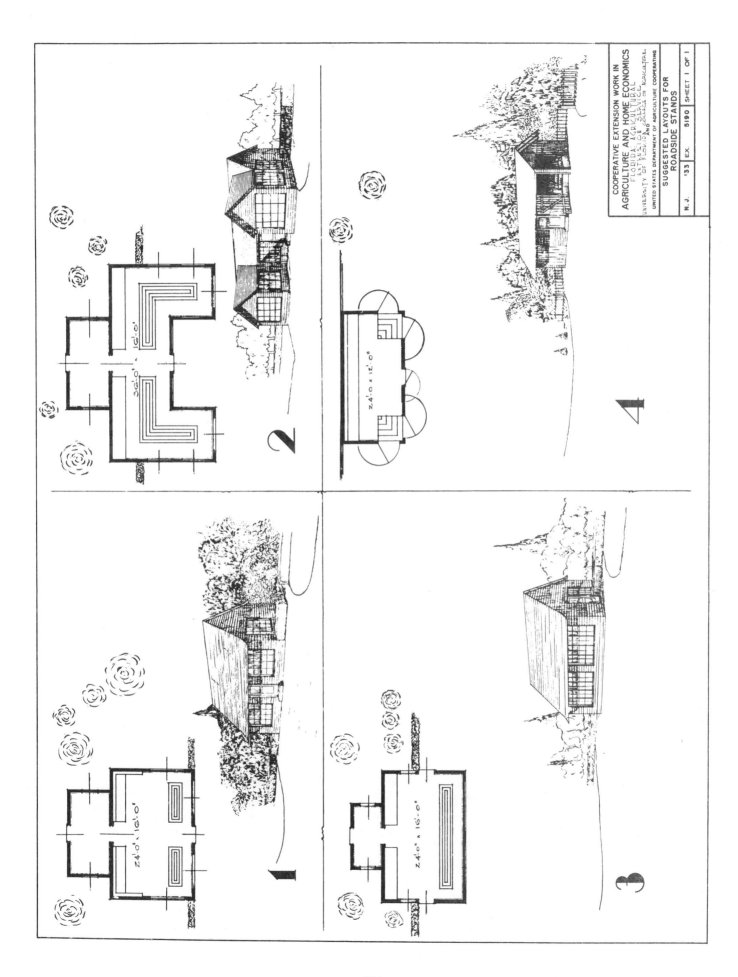

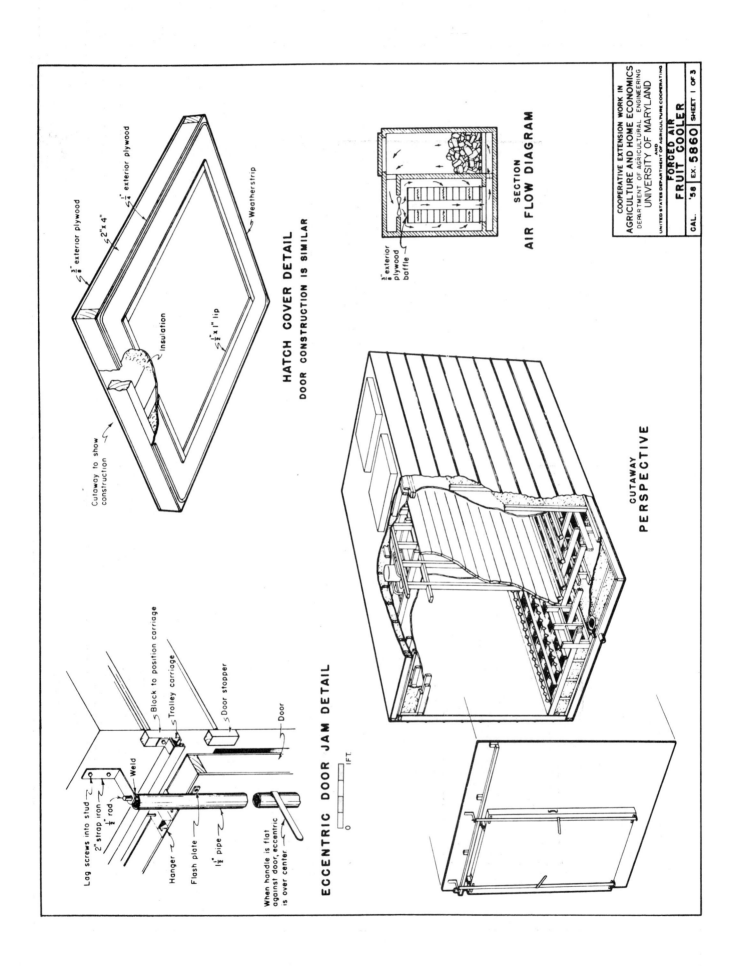

HATCH COVER DETAIL
DOOR CONSTRUCTION IS SIMILAR

- $\frac{3}{8}''$ exterior plywood
- $\frac{1}{4}''$ exterior plywood
- 2"x4"
- Weatherstrip
- Insulation
- $\frac{1}{2}'' \times 1''$ lip
- Cutaway to show construction

SECTION
AIR FLOW DIAGRAM

- $\frac{3}{8}''$ exterior plywood baffle

CUTAWAY
PERSPECTIVE

ECCENTRIC DOOR JAM DETAIL

- Block to position carriage
- Trolley carriage
- Door stopper
- Door
- Lag screws into stud
- 2" strap iron
- $\frac{1}{2}''$ rod
- Weld
- Hanger
- Flash plate
- $1\frac{1}{2}''$ pipe
- When handle is flat against door, eccentric is over center.

1 FT.
0

COOPERATIVE EXTENSION WORK IN
AGRICULTURE AND HOME ECONOMICS
DEPARTMENT OF AGRICULTURAL ENGINEERING
UNIVERSITY OF MARYLAND
UNITED STATES DEPARTMENT OF AGRICULTURE COOPERATING

FORCED AIR
FRUIT COOLER
CAL. '58 | EX. 5860 | SHEET 1 OF 3

126

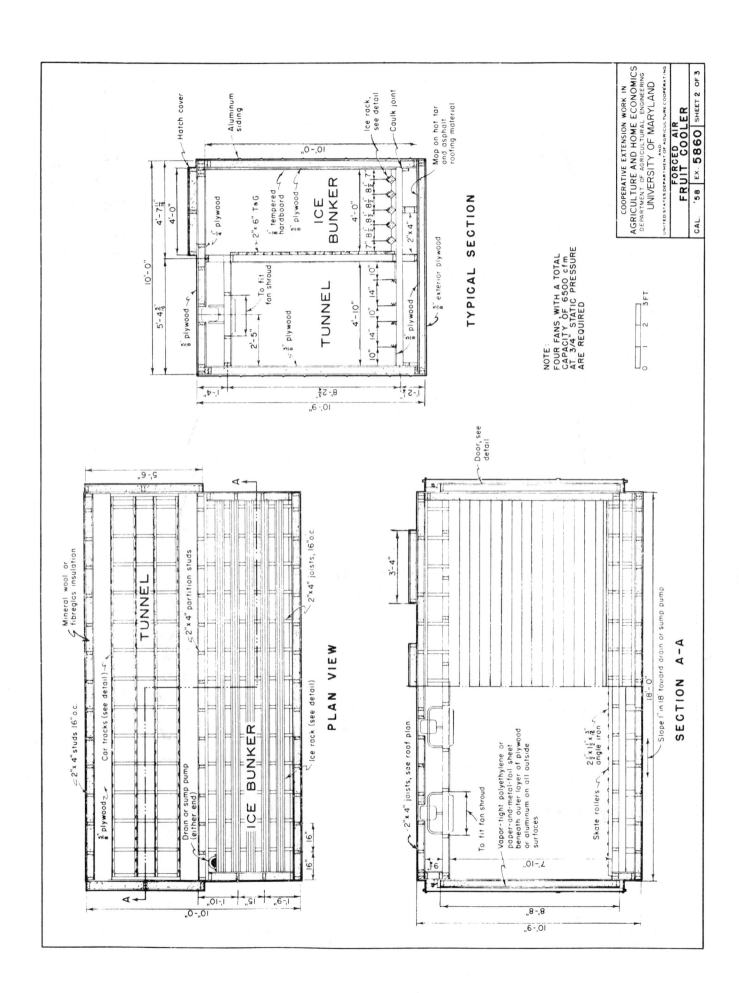

NOTE:
FOUR FANS, WITH A TOTAL
CAPACITY OF 6500 cfm
AT 3/4" STATIC PRESSURE
ARE REQUIRED

TYPICAL SECTION

Hatch cover
Aluminum siding
Ice rack, see detail
Caulk joint
Mop on hot tar and asphalt roofing material

1/4" plywood
2"x6" T&G
1/8" tempered hardboard
3/8" plywood
ICE BUNKER
2"x4"
5/8" exterior plywood

3/8" plywood
To fit fan shroud
TUNNEL
3/8" plywood
5/8" plywood

10'-0"
4'-7 11/16"
4'-0"
5'-4 5/16"
2'-5"
4'-10"
4'-0"
10" 14" 10" 14" 10"
7" 8 1/2" 8 1/2" 8 1/2" 8 1/2" 7"
1'-4"
8'-2 1/4"
1'-2 1/4"
10'-9"

PLAN VIEW

Mineral wool or fibreglas insulation
2"x4" studs 16" o.c.
Car tracks (see detail)
2"x4" partition studs
2"x4" joists, 16" o.c.
TUNNEL
3/8" plywood
ICE BUNKER
Drain or sump pump (either end)
Ice rack (see detail)

5'-6"
16" 16" 16"
1'-10" 15" 1'-9"
10'-0"
A   A

SECTION A-A

Door, see detail
2"x4" joists, see roof plan
To fit fan shroud
Vapor-tight polyethylene or paper-and-metal-foil sheet beneath outer layer of plywood or aluminum on all outside surfaces
Skate rollers
2 1/2"x1 1/2"x 3/16" angle iron
Slope 1" in 18' toward drain or sump pump

3'-4"
18'-0"
7'-10"
1/16"
8'-8"
10'-9"

COOPERATIVE EXTENSION WORK IN
AGRICULTURE AND HOME ECONOMICS
DEPARTMENT OF AGRICULTURAL ENGINEERING
UNIVERSITY OF MARYLAND
AND
UNITED STATES DEPARTMENT OF AGRICULTURE COOPERATING

FORCED AIR
FRUIT COOLER
CAL. '58 EX. 5860 SHEET 2 OF 3

0 1 2 3 FT

127

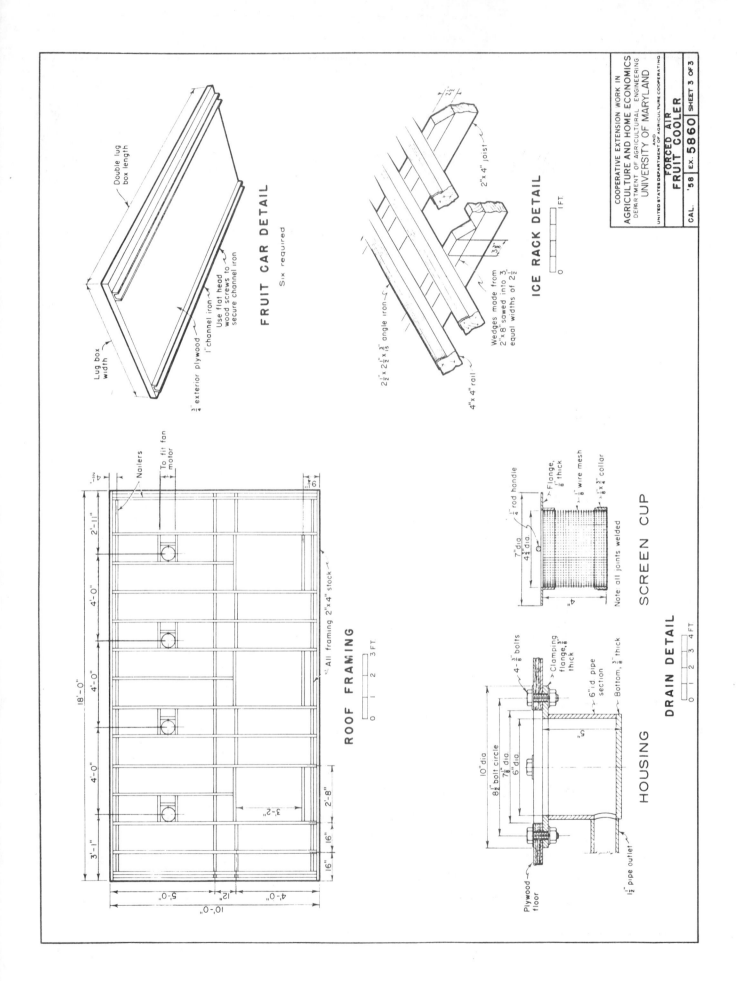

FRUIT CAR DETAIL

Six required

Double lug box length

Lug box width

1" channel iron

Use flat head wood screws to secure channel iron

3/4 exterior plywood

ICE RACK DETAIL

2" x 4" Joist

3 1/2"

Wedges made from 2" x 8" sawed into 3 equal widths of 2 1/2

2 1/2" x 2 1/2" x 3/16" angle iron

4" x 4" rail

0   1 FT

ROOF FRAMING

Nailers

To fit fan motor

2'-11"

4'-0"

4'-0"

18'-0"

4'-0"

2'-8"

3'-1"   16"   16"   16"

12"

3'-2"

4'-0"

5'-0"

10'-0"

All framing 2" x 4" stock

0   1   2   3 FT

SCREEN CUP

Flange, 1/8" thick

1/4" rod handle

1" wire mesh

1" x 3/4" collar

7" dia

4 1/4" dia

4"

Note all joints welded

DRAIN DETAIL

4 - 3/8" bolts

Clamping flange, 3/8" thick

6" id pipe section

Bottom, 3" thick

10" dia

8 1/2" bolt circle

7 1/8" dia

6" dia

5"

Plywood floor

1 1/2" pipe outlet

HOUSING

0   1   2   3   4 FT

COOPERATIVE EXTENSION WORK IN
AGRICULTURE AND HOME ECONOMICS
DEPARTMENT OF AGRICULTURAL ENGINEERING
UNIVERSITY OF MARYLAND
AND
UNITED STATES DEPARTMENT OF AGRICULTURE COOPERATING

FORCED AIR
FRUIT COOLER

CAL. '58 EX. 5860 SHEET 3 OF 3

128

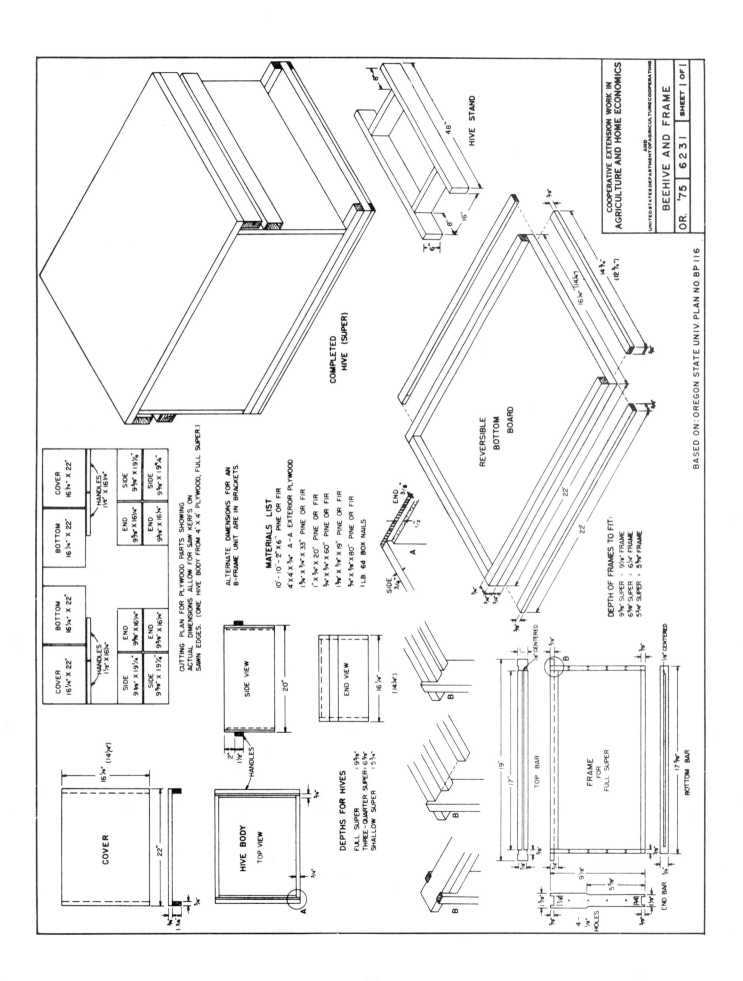

BEEHIVE AND FRAME

COOPERATIVE EXTENSION WORK IN AGRICULTURE AND HOME ECONOMICS
AND
UNITED STATES DEPARTMENT OF AGRICULTURE COOPERATING

OR. '75   6231   SHEET 1 OF 1

BASED ON: OREGON STATE UNIV PLAN NO. BP 116

HIVE STAND

COMPLETED HIVE (SUPER)

REVERSIBLE BOTTOM BOARD

MATERIALS LIST

10' - 10" - 2" X 6" PINE OR FIR
4 X 4 X 3/4" A-A EXTERIOR PLYWOOD
1 3/8" X 3/4" X 33" PINE OR FIR
1" X 3/4" X 20" PINE OR FIR
3/4" X 3/4" X 60" PINE OR FIR
1 3/8" X 3/8" X 19" PINE OR FIR
3/4" X 3/8" X 80" PINE OR FIR
1 LB 6d BOX NAILS

ALTERNATE DIMENSIONS FOR AN
8-FRAME UNIT ARE IN BRACKETS.

CUTTING PLAN FOR PLYWOOD PARTS SHOWING
ACTUAL DIMENSIONS ALLOW FOR SAW KERFS ON
SAWN EDGES. (ONE HIVE BODY FROM 4' X 4' PLYWOOD, FULL SUPER)

COVER 16 1/4" X 22"	BOTTOM 16 1/4" X 22"	COVER 16 1/4" X 22"
HANDLES 1 1/8" X 16 1/4"		HANDLES 1 1/8" X 16 1/4"
SIDE 9 5/8" X 19 7/8"	END 9 5/8" X 16 1/4"	SIDE 9 5/8" X 19 7/8"
SIDE 9 5/8" X 19 7/8"	END 9 5/8" X 16 1/4"	SIDE 9 5/8" X 19 7/8"

COVER 16 1/4" X 22"	BOTTOM 16 1/4" X 22"
HANDLES 1 1/8" X 16 1/4"	
SIDE 9 5/8" X 19 7/8"	END 9 5/8" X 16 1/4"
SIDE 9 5/8" X 19 7/8"	END 9 5/8" X 16 1/4"

SIDE VIEW

END VIEW

COVER

HIVE BODY TOP VIEW

HANDLES

DEPTHS FOR HIVES

FULL SUPER : 9 5/8"
THREE-QUARTER SUPER : 6 5/8"
SHALLOW SUPER : 5 3/4"

DEPTH OF FRAMES TO FIT:

9 1/8" SUPER : 9 1/8" FRAME
6 1/4" SUPER : 6 1/4" FRAME
5 3/8" SUPER : 5 3/8" FRAME

TOP BAR

FRAME FOR FULL SUPER

BOTTOM BAR

END BAR

129

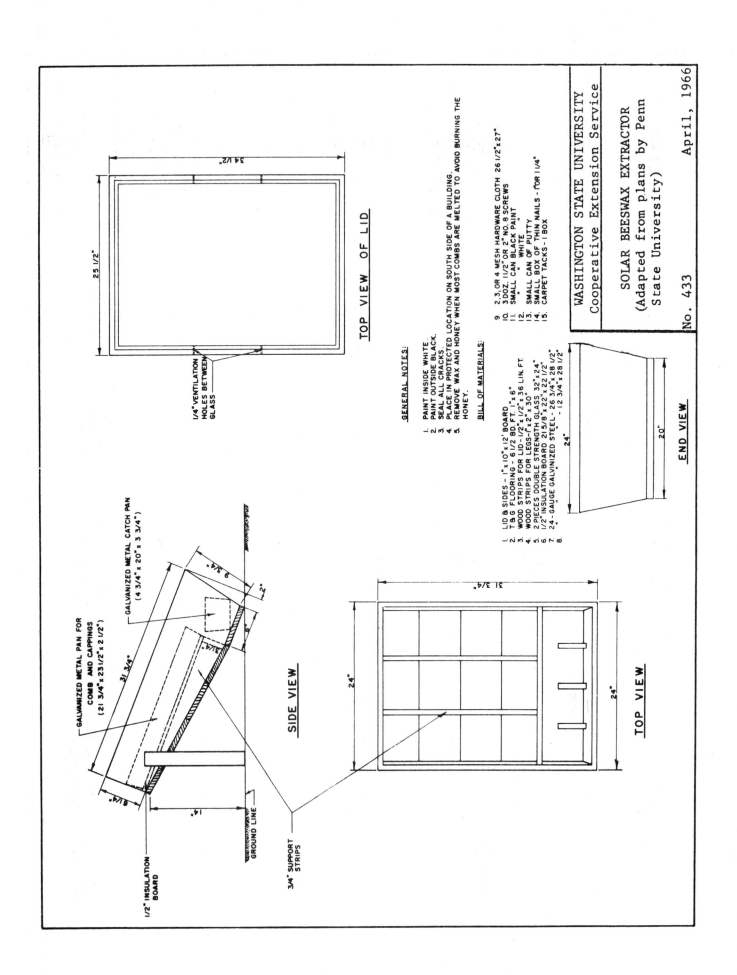

TOP VIEW OF LID

34 1/2"

25 1/2"

1/4" VENTILATION HOLES BETWEEN GLASS

GENERAL NOTES:

1. PAINT INSIDE WHITE.
2. PAINT OUTSIDE BLACK.
3. SEAL ALL CRACKS.
4. PLACE IN PROTECTED LOCATION ON SOUTH SIDE OF A BUILDING.
5. REMOVE WAX AND HONEY WHEN MOST COMBS ARE MELTED TO AVOID BURNING THE HONEY.

BILL OF MATERIALS:

1. LID & SIDES - 1"x 10"x 12' BOARD
2. T&G FLOORING - 6 1/2 BD. FT. 1"x 6"
3. WOOD STRIPS FOR LID - 1/2"x 1/2"x 36 LIN. FT.
4. WOOD STRIPS FOR LEGS - 1"x 2"x 30"
5. 2 PIECES DOUBLE STRENGTH GLASS 32"x 24"
6. 1/2" INSULATION BOARD 21 5/8 x 22 x 22 1/2
7. 24 "INSULATION BOARD 26 3/4"x 28 1/2"
8. 24 - GAUGE GALVANIZED STEEL - 26 3/4"x 28 1/2"
   - 12 3/4"x 28 1/2"

9. 2, 3, OR 4 MESH HARDWARE CLOTH 26 1/2"x 27"
10. 3 DOZ. 1 1/2" OR 2" NO. 8 SCREWS
11. SMALL CAN BLACK PAINT
12. "   "   WHITE
13. SMALL CAN OF PUTTY
14. SMALL BOX OF THIN NAILS - FOR 1/4"
15. CARPET TACKS - 1 BOX

WASHINGTON STATE UNIVERSITY
Cooperative Extension Service

SOLAR BEESWAX EXTRACTOR
(Adapted from plans by Penn State University)

No. 433   April, 1966

END VIEW

20"

24"

SIDE VIEW

GALVANIZED METAL PAN FOR COMB AND CAPPINGS (21 3/4"x 23 1/2" x 2 1/2")

GALVANIZED METAL CATCH PAN (4 3/4"x 20"x 3 3/4")

31 3/4"

9 3/4"

2"

6"

3/4"

6 3/4"

4"

1/2" INSULATION BOARD

GROUND LINE

3/4" SUPPORT STRIPS

TOP VIEW

31 3/4"

24"

24"

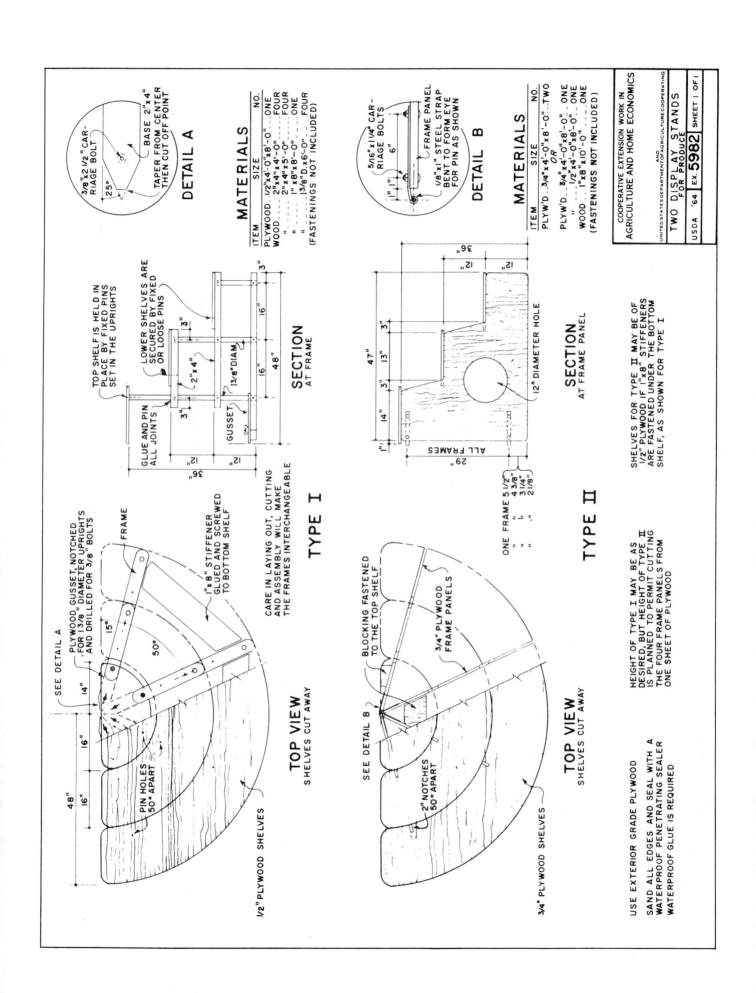

DETAIL A

3/8"x2 1/2" CAR-RIAGE BOLT
BASE 2"x4"
TAPER FROM CENTER THEN CUT OFF POINT
25°

MATERIALS

ITEM	SIZE	NO.
PLYWOOD	1/2"x4'-0"x8'-0"	ONE
WOOD	2"x4"x4'-0"	FOUR
"	2"x4"x5'-0"	ONE
"	1"x8"x8'-0"	FOUR
"	13/8"D.x6'-0"	ONE
(FASTENINGS NOT INCLUDED)		

DETAIL B

5/16"x1 1/4" CAR-RIAGE BOLTS
6"
FRAME PANEL
1/8"x1" STEEL STRAP BENT TO FORM EYE FOR PIN AS SHOWN

MATERIALS

ITEM	SIZE	NO.
PLYW'D	3/4"x4'-0"x8'-0"	TWO
	OR	
PLYW'D	3/4"x4'-0"x8'-0"	ONE
"	1/2"x4'-0"x8'-0"	ONE
WOOD	1"x8"x10'-0"	ONE
(FASTENINGS NOT INCLUDED)		

COOPERATIVE EXTENSION WORK IN AGRICULTURE AND HOME ECONOMICS
UNITED STATES DEPARTMENT OF AGRICULTURE COOPERATING

TWO DISPLAY STANDS FOR PRODUCE

USDA '64 | EX. **5982** | SHEET 1 OF 1

SECTION AT FRAME

TOP SHELF IS HELD IN PLACE BY FIXED PINS SET IN THE UPRIGHTS
LOWER SHELVES ARE SECURED BY FIXED OR LOOSE PINS
GLUE AND PIN ALL JOINTS
2"x4"
13/8"DIAM.
GUSSET
3"
3"
3"
16"
16"
16"
48"
12"
12"
36"

SECTION AT FRAME PANEL

36"
12"
12"
3"
3"
13"
3"
47"
14"
ALL FRAMES
12" DIAMETER HOLE
29"

ONE FRAME 5 1/2"
" " 4 3/8"
" " 3 1/4"
" " 2 1/8"

TYPE I

PLYWOOD GUSSET, NOTCHED FOR 13/8" DIAMETER UPRIGHTS AND DRILLED FOR 3/8" BOLTS
FRAME
1"x8" STIFFENER GLUED AND SCREWED TO BOTTOM SHELF
SEE DETAIL A
15°
50°
14"
CARE IN LAYING OUT, CUTTING AND ASSEMBLY WILL MAKE THE FRAMES INTERCHANGEABLE
PIN HOLES 50° APART
48"
16"
16"

TOP VIEW SHELVES CUT AWAY

1/2" PLYWOOD SHELVES

TYPE II

BLOCKING FASTENED TO THE TOP SHELF
3/4" PLYWOOD FRAME PANELS
SEE DETAIL B
2" NOTCHES 50° APART

TOP VIEW SHELVES CUT AWAY

3/4" PLYWOOD SHELVES

SHELVES FOR TYPE II MAY BE OF 1/2" PLYWOOD IF 1"x8" STIFFENERS ARE FASTENED UNDER THE BOTTOM SHELF, AS SHOWN FOR TYPE I

HEIGHT OF TYPE I MAY BE AS DESIRED, BUT HEIGHT OF TYPE II IS PLANNED TO PERMIT CUTTING THE FOUR FRAME PANELS FROM ONE SHEET OF PLYWOOD

USE EXTERIOR GRADE PLYWOOD
SAND ALL EDGES AND SEAL WITH A WATERPROOF PENETRATING SEALER
WATERPROOF GLUE IS REQUIRED

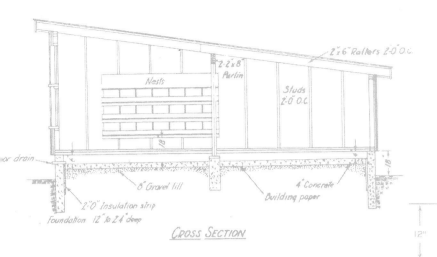

Nests

2-2"x8"
Purlin

2"x6" Rafters 2'-0" O.C.

Studs
2'-0" O.C.

18"

18"

or drain

6" Gravel fill

4" Concrete

Building paper

2'-0" Insulation strip

Foundation 12" to 24" deep

CROSS SECTION

1"X 3"

1"X 2"

12"

4"

6 1/4"

1"X 6"

1"X 12"

1"X 3" PERCH

POULTRY HOUSES

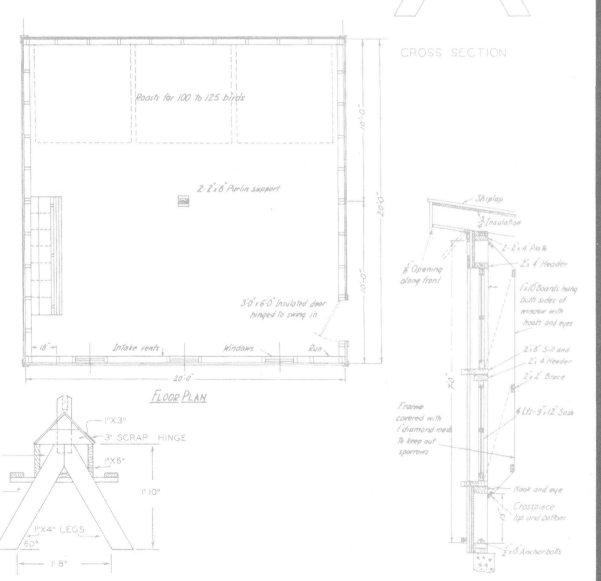

CROSS SECTION

Roosts for 100 to 125 birds

10'-0"

2-2"x8" Purlin support

20'-0"

10'-0"

3'-0"x6'-0" Insulated door
hinged to swing in

18"

Intake vents

Windows

Run

20'-0"

FLOOR PLAN

1"X 3"

3" Scrap Hinge

1"X 6"

1"X 6"

1"X 3"

1' 10"

1"X 4" LEGS
60°

1' 8"

Shiplap

Insulation

2-2"x4" Plate

2"x 4" Header

1"x 10" Boards hung
both sides of
window with
hooks and eyes

1" Opening
along front

2"x8" Sill and
2"x 4" Header

2"x 2" Brace

4 Lts-9"x12" Sash

Frame
covered with
1" diamond mesh
to keep out
sparrows

7'-0"

Hook and eye

Crosspiece
top and bottom

2"x8" Anchorbolts

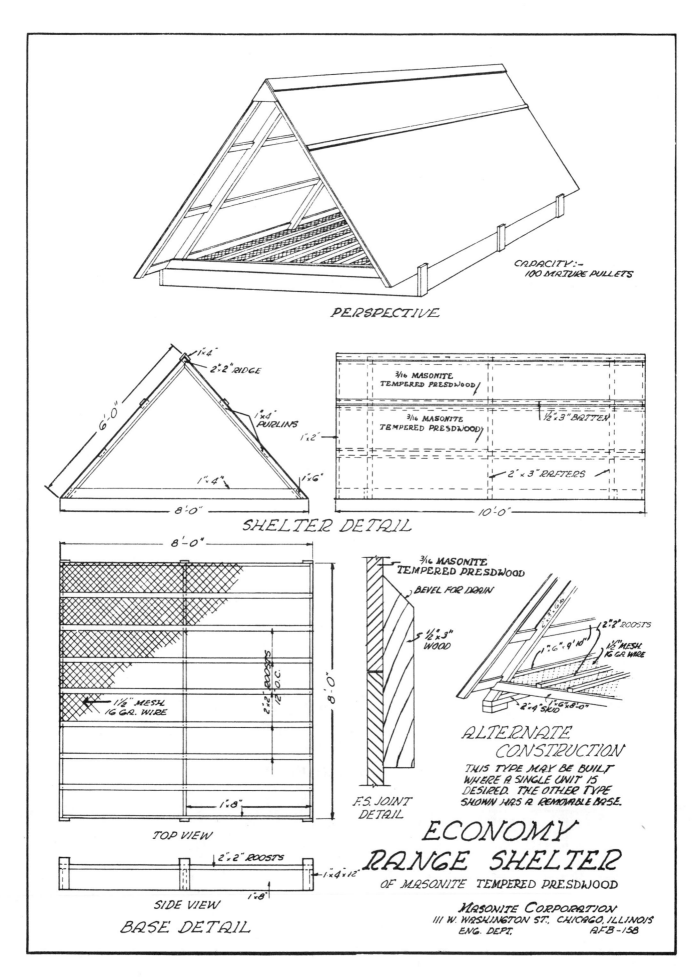

9

PERSPECTIVE

CAPACITY:-
100 MATURE PULLETS

SHELTER DETAIL

F.S. JOINT
DETAIL

ALTERNATE
CONSTRUCTION

THIS TYPE MAY BE BUILT
WHERE A SINGLE UNIT IS
DESIRED. THE OTHER TYPE
SHOWN HAS A REMOVABLE BASE.

TOP VIEW

SIDE VIEW

BASE DETAIL

ECONOMY
RANGE SHELTER
OF MASONITE TEMPERED PRESDWOOD

MASONITE CORPORATION
111 W. WASHINGTON ST., CHICAGO, ILLINOIS
ENG. DEPT.   AFB-158

Plan View of Sled, Barrel and Trough

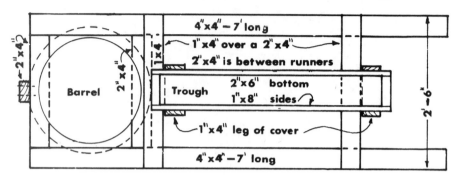

4"x4" – 7' long

1"x4" over a 2"x4"

2"x4" is between runners

2"x4"

Barrel

2"x4"

1"x4"

Trough 2"x6" bottom
1"x8" sides

1"x4" leg of cover

4"x4" – 7' long

2'-6"

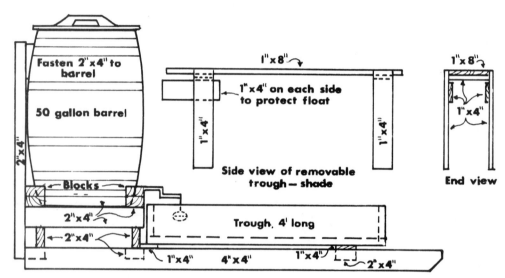

Fasten 2"x4" to barrel

50 gallon barrel

2"x4"

Blocks

2"x4"

2"x4"

1"x4"

4"x4"

1"x4"

2"x4"

Trough, 4' long

1"x8"

1"x4" on each side to protect float

1"x4"

1"x4"

Side view of removable trough — shade

1"x8"

1"x4"

End view

Side view

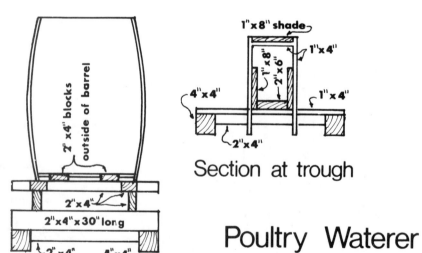

2"x4" blocks outside of barrel

2"x4"

2"x4"x30" long

2"x4"

4"x4"

Section at barrel

1"x8" shade

1"x8"

2"x6"

1"x4"

4"x4"

1"x4"

2"x4"

Section at trough

Poultry Waterer

Adapted from Texas A & M College Plan, Serial No. 327.

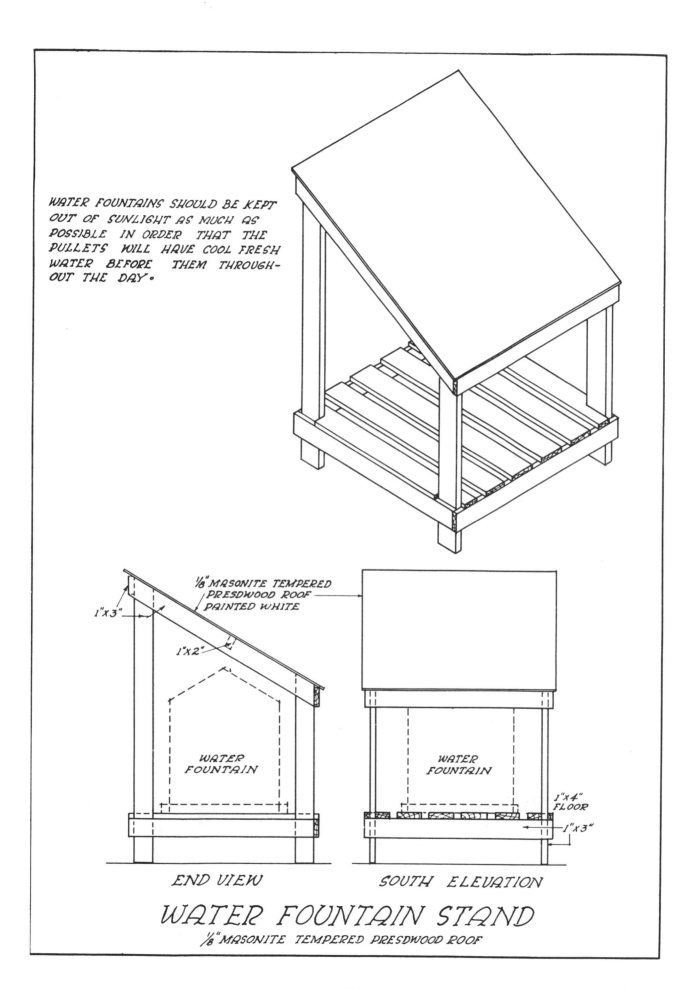

WATER FOUNTAINS SHOULD BE KEPT
OUT OF SUNLIGHT AS MUCH AS
POSSIBLE IN ORDER THAT THE
PULLETS WILL HAVE COOL FRESH
WATER BEFORE THEM THROUGH-
OUT THE DAY.

⅛" MASONITE TEMPERED
PRESDWOOD ROOF
PAINTED WHITE

1"x3"

1"x2"

WATER
FOUNTAIN

WATER
FOUNTAIN

1"x4"
FLOOR

1"x3"

END VIEW

SOUTH ELEVATION

WATER FOUNTAIN STAND
⅛" MASONITE TEMPERED PRESDWOOD ROOF

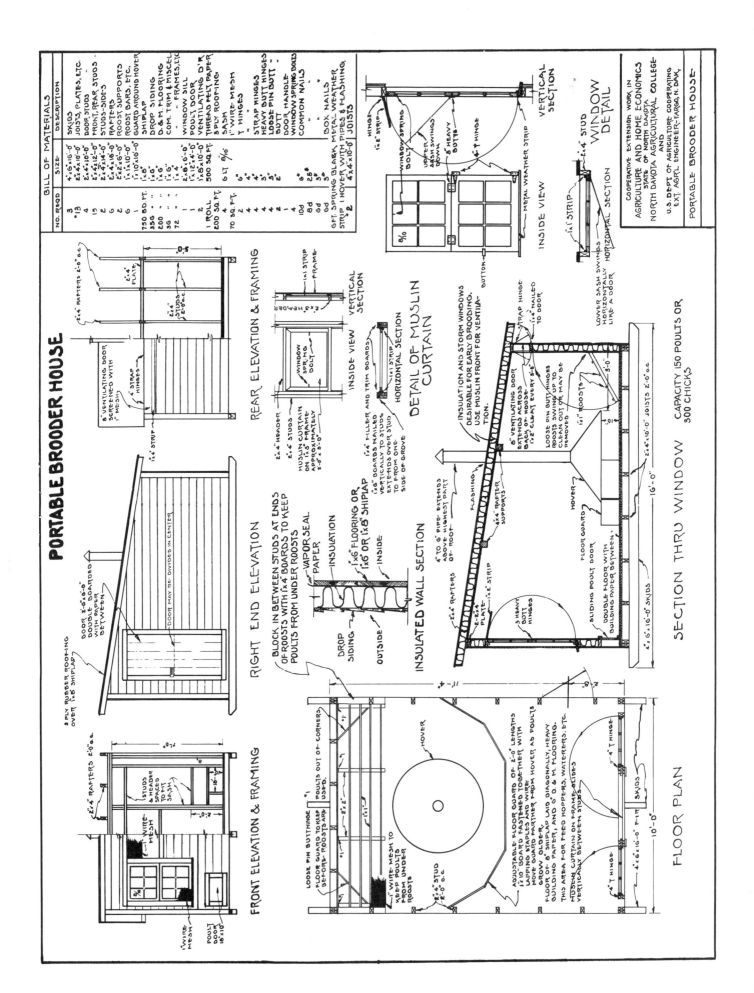

PORTABLE BROODER HOUSE

BILL OF MATERIALS

NO. REQ'D	SIZE	DESCRIPTION
3	4"x16'-0"	SKIDS
*13	2"x4"x10'-0"	JOISTS, PLATES, ETC.
4	2"x4"x10'-0"	DOOR STUD
15	2"x4"x12'-0"	FRONT, REAR STUDS
2	2"x4"x14'-0"	STUDS—SIDE S
6	2"x4"x16'-0"	RAFTERS
6	2"x2"x6'-0"	ROOST SUPPORTS
6	1"x1"x10'-0"	ROOST BARS, ETC.
	1"x6"x10'-0"	GUARD AROUND HOVER
750 SQ. FT.		SHIPLAP
350	1"x6"	DROP SIDING
200	1"x6"	D.& M. FLOORING
30	1"x6"	COM. TRIM MISCEL.
72	1"x4"	" FRAMES,ETC.
	2'-6"x6'-0"	WINDOW SILL
1 ROLL		POULT DOOR
200 SQ.FT.	1"x12'x4'-0"	VENTILATING D'R
	1"x6"x10'-0"	THREAD FELT PAPER
70 SQ.FT.	500 SQ.FT.	3 PLY ROOFING
2		SASH
	6'LT 8/10	1" WIRE MESH
4	4"	STRAP HINGES
4	4"	HEAVY BUTT HINGES
4	3"	LOOSE PIN BUTT "
2	2"	BUTT
4		DOOR HANDLE
4	6"	WINDOW SPRING BOLTS
	8d	COMMON NAILS
	10d	BOX NAILS
	6d	
	2.5*	
	6d	
	3*	
	5*	

GFT. SPRING BLACK METAL WEATHER
STRIP 1 HOVER WITH PIPES & FLASHING,
2 4"x4"x10'-0" JOISTS

WINDOW DETAIL

VERTICAL SECTION

INSIDE VIEW

WINDOW SPRING BOLT
UPPER SASH SWINGS DOWN
8" HEAVY BUTTS
4" T HINGE
METAL WEATHER STRIP
1"x1" STRIP
2"x4" STUD
HORIZONTAL SECTION

COOPERATIVE EXTENSION WORK IN
AGRICULTURE AND HOME ECONOMICS
STATE OF NORTH DAKOTA
NORTH DAKOTA AGRICULTURAL COLLEGE
AND
U.S. DEPT. OF AGRICULTURE COOPERATING
EXT. AGRIL ENGINEER—FARGO, N. DAK.

PORTABLE BROODER HOUSE

REAR ELEVATION & FRAMING

2"x4" RAFTERS 2'-0" o.c.
2"x4" PLATE
2"x4" STUDS 2'-0"o.c.
6'-0
6" VENTILATING DOOR SCREENED WITH 1" MESH
4" STRAP HINGES
1"x4" STRIP

VERTICAL SECTION
1"x1" STRIP
FRAME
2"x6" HEADER

INSIDE VIEW
WINDOW SPRING BOLT
2"x4" HEADER
2"x4" STUDS
MUSLIN CURTAIN ON 1"x3" FRAME APPROXIMATELY 2'-6"x6'-0"

DETAIL OF MUSLIN CURTAIN
HORIZONTAL SECTION
1"x1" STRIP
1"x6" FILLER AND TRIM BOARDS
1"x6" BOARDS NAILED VERTICALLY TO STUDS EXTEND-ENDS OVER STUD TO FORM ONE SIDE OF GROVE

RIGHT END ELEVATION
3 PLY RUBBER ROOFING OVER 1"x8 SHIPLAP
DOOR 2'-6"x6'-0" DOUBLE BOARDED WITH PAPER BETWEEN
DOOR MAY BE DIVIDED IN CENTER

BLOCK IN BETWEEN STUDS AT ENDS OF ROOSTS WITH 1x4 BOARDS TO KEEP POULTS FROM UNDER ROOSTS

INSULATED WALL SECTION
VAPOR SEAL PAPER
INSULATION
1"x6" FLOORING OR 1"x6 OR 1"x8" SHIPLAP
INSIDE
DROP SIDING
OUTSIDE

SECTION THRU WINDOW   CAPACITY 150 POULTS OR 300 CHICKS

INSULATION AND STORM WINDOWS DESIRABLE FOR EARLY BROODING, USE MUSLIN FRONT FOR VENTILA-TION.
STRAP HINGE
1"x4" NAILED TO DOOR
6" VENTILATING DOOR EXTENDS ACROSS BACK OF HOUSE
1"x2" CLEAT EVERY 2'-0"
LOOSE PIN BUTT HINGES, ROOSTS SWING UP TO CLEAN OUT OR MAY BE REMOVED
1"x1" ROOSTS
4" TO 6" PIPE EXTENDS ABOVE HIGHEST PART OF ROOF
FLASHING
4"x4" RAFTER SUPPORTS
2"x4" RAFTERS
2-2"x4" PLATE
3" HEAVY BUTT HINGES
FLOOR GUARD
HOVER
SLIDING POULT DOOR
DOUBLE FLOOR WITH BUILDING PAPER BETWEEN
4", 6", 16'-0" SKIDS
2"x4"x16'-0" JOISTS 2'-0" o.c.
3'-0
16'-0"
LOWER SASH SWINGS HORIZONTALLY LIKE A DOOR

FRONT ELEVATION & FRAMING
2"x4" RAFTERS 2'-0"o.c.
STUDS & HEADER TO FIT SASH
WIRE MESH
1" WIRE MESH TO KEEP POULTS FROM UNDER
POULT DOOR 18"x10"

FLOOR PLAN
11'-4"
10'-0"
LOOSE PIN BUTT HINGE
1"x10" BOARD FASTENED TOGETHER WITH LAPPING STAPLES AND WIRE
POULTS OUT OF CORNERS WHEN POULTS ARE USED.
HOVER
ADJUSTABLE FLOOR GUARD OF 2'-0" LENGTHS 1"x10" BOARD FASTENED TOGETHER WITH LAPPING STAPLES AND WIRE MOVE GUARD FARTHER FROM HOVER AS POULTS GROW OLDER.
FLOOR OF 6" SHIPLAP LAID DIAGONALLY, HEAVY BUILDING PAPER, AND 6" D. & M. FLOORING.
THIS AREA FOR FEED HOPPERS, WATERERS, ETC.
MUSLIN CURTAIN ON FRAME SLIDES VERTICALLY BETWEEN STUDS
2"x4" STUD 2'-0" o.c.
4"x6"x16'-0" FIR SKIDS
4" HINGE

138

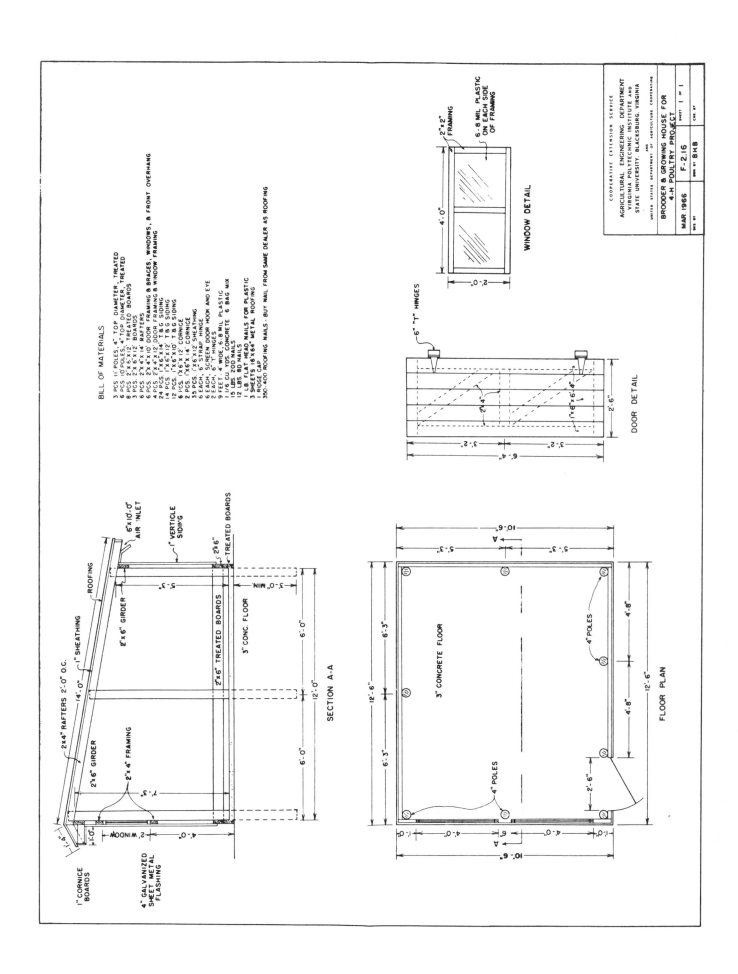

BILL OF MATERIALS

3 PCS 11 POLES, 4" TOP DIAMETER, TREATED
6 PCS 10 POLES, 4" TOP DIAMETER, TREATED
8 PCS 2"x6"x12' TREATED BOARDS
3 PCS 2"x6"x12' BOARDS
6 PCS 2"x4"x14' RAFTERS
6 PCS 2"x4"x10' DOOR FRAMING & BRACES, WINDOWS, & FRONT OVERHANG
4 PCS 2"x4"x12' DOOR FRAMING & WINDOW FRAMING
24 PCS 1"x6"x14' T & G SIDING
14 PCS 1"x6"x12' T & G SIDING
12 PCS 1"x6"x10' T & G SIDING
6 PCS 1"x6"x12' CORNICE
2 PCS 1"x6"x14' CORNICE
35 PCS 1"x6"x12' SHEATHING
6 EACH, 6' STRAP HINGE
6 EACH, SCREEN DOOR HOOK AND EYE
2 EACH, 6" T HINGES
9 FEET, 4' WIDE, 6-8 MIL PLASTIC
1 1/6 CU. YDS. CONCRETE   6 BAG MIX
1 LB FLAT HEAD NAILS FOR PLASTIC
15 LBS 200 NAILS
12 LBS 80 NAILS
3 SHEETS 16"x64" METAL ROOFING
1 RIDGE CAP
350-400 ROOFING NAILS - BUY NAIL FROM SAME DEALER AS ROOFING

WINDOW DETAIL

2"x2" FRAMING

6-8 MIL PLASTIC ON EACH SIDE OF FRAMING

4'-0"

2'-0"

DOOR DETAIL

6" "T" HINGES

2'-6"

3'-2"   3'-2"

6'-4"

2'-4"

1"x6"x6'-4"

SECTION A-A

2"x4" RAFTERS 2'-0" O.C.

1" SHEATHING

ROOFING

6"x10'-0" AIR INLET

1" VERTICLE SIDING

2"x6"

TREATED BOARDS

2"x6" GIRDER

2"x6" TREATED BOARDS

3" CONC. FLOOR

3'-0" MIN.

5'-3"

6'-0"

12'-0"

6'-0"

14'-0"

2"x6" GIRDER

2"x4" FRAMING

7'-3"

1" CORNICE BOARDS

4" GALVANIZED SHEET METAL FLASHING

1'-0"

2' WINDOW

4'-0"

FLOOR PLAN

10'-6"

5'-3"   5'-3"

A

3" CONCRETE FLOOR

4" POLES

4" POLES

12'-6"

6'-3"   6'-3"

4'-8"   4'-8"

2'-6"

1'-0"   4'-0"   6"   4'-0"   1'-0"

10'-6"

A

COOPERATIVE EXTENSION SERVICE
AGRICULTURAL ENGINEERING DEPARTMENT
VIRGINIA POLYTECHNIC INSTITUTE AND
STATE UNIVERSITY, BLACKSBURG, VIRGINIA
AND
UNITED STATES DEPARTMENT OF AGRICULTURE COOPERATING

BROODER & GROWING HOUSE FOR
4-H POULTRY PROJECT

F-2.16   SHEET: 1 OF 1

MAR. 1966   DES BY   DRN BY BHB   CHK BY

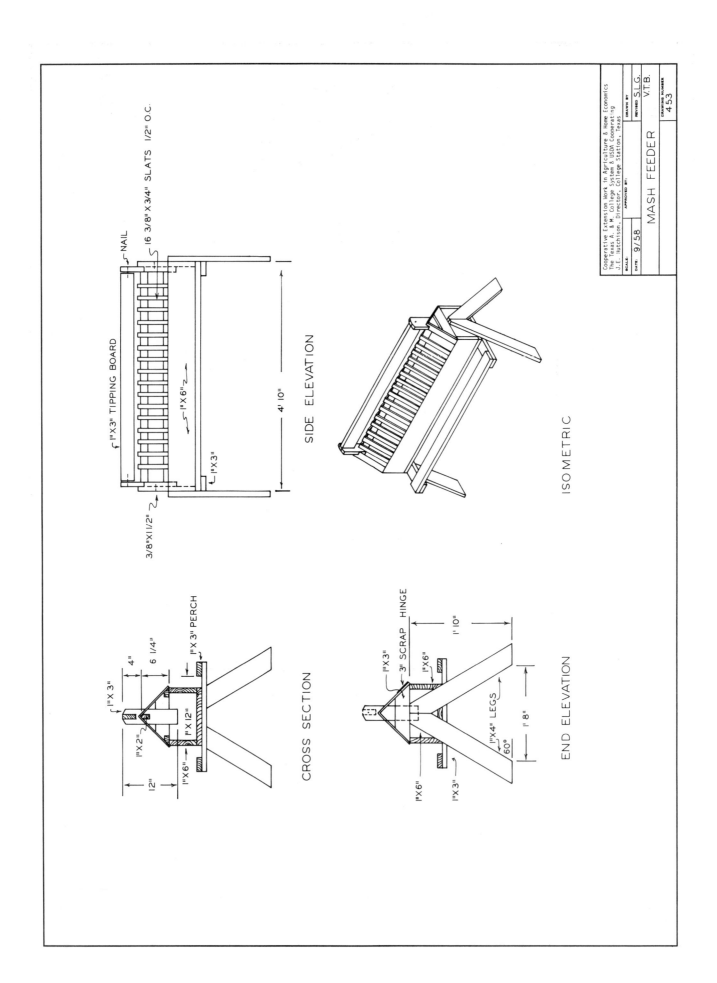

16 3/8" X 3/4" SLATS 1/2" O.C.

NAIL

1"X 3" TIPPING BOARD

1"X 6"

4' 10"

3/8"X I 1/2"

1"X 3"

SIDE ELEVATION

ISOMETRIC

CROSS SECTION

4"

6 1/4"

1"X 3"

1"X 3" PERCH

1"X 2"

1"X 12"

12"

1"X 6"

END ELEVATION

3" SCRAP HINGE

1"X 3"

1' 10"

1"X6"

1"X4" LEGS

1' 8"

60°

1"X 6"

1"X 3"

Cooperative Extension Work in Agriculture & Home Economics
The Texas A. & M. College System & USDA Cooperating
J.E. Hutchison, Director, College Station, Texas

SCALE:

DATE: 9/58

APPROVED BY:

DRAWN BY:

REVISED S.L.G.
V.T.B.

MASH FEEDER

DRAWING NUMBER
453

140

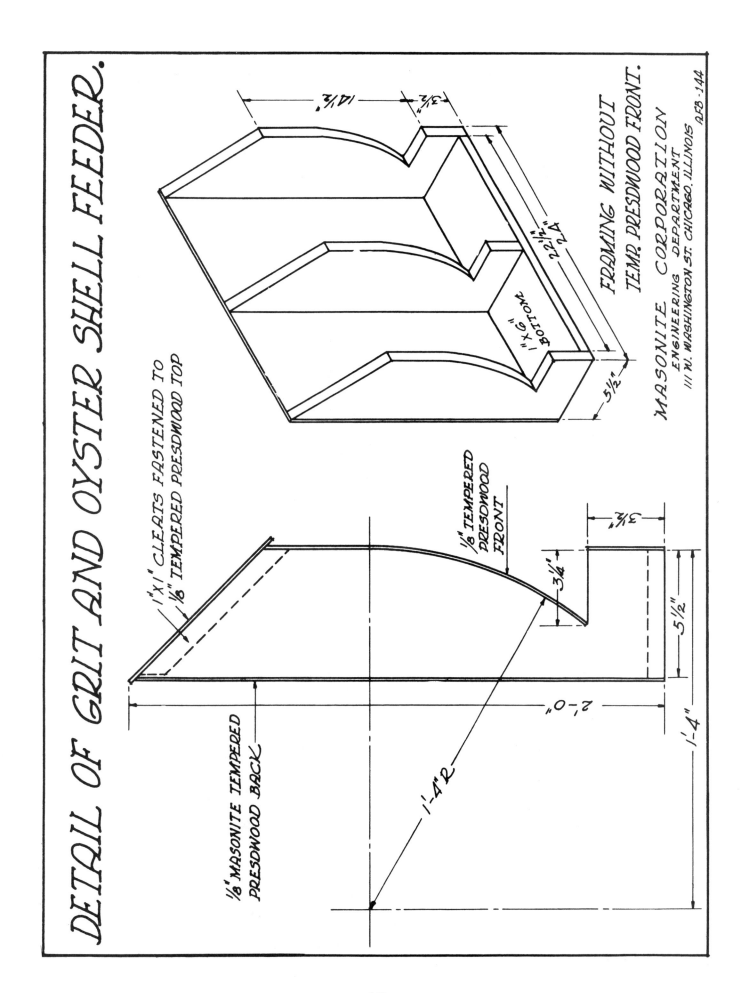

DETAIL OF GRIT AND OYSTER SHELL FEEDER.

FRAMING WITHOUT
TEMP. PRESDWOOD FRONT.

MASONITE CORPORATION
ENGINEERING DEPARTMENT
111 W. WASHINGTON ST. CHICAGO. ILLINOIS

AFB-144

1"×1" CLEATS FASTENED TO
⅛" TEMPERED PRESDWOOD TOP

1"×6" BOTTOM

10½"

3½"

22½"
24

5½"

⅛" MASONITE TEMPERED
PRESDWOOD BACK

⅛" TEMPERED PRESDWOOD
FRONT

3¼"

3½"

5½"

2'-0"

1'-4"

1'-4" R

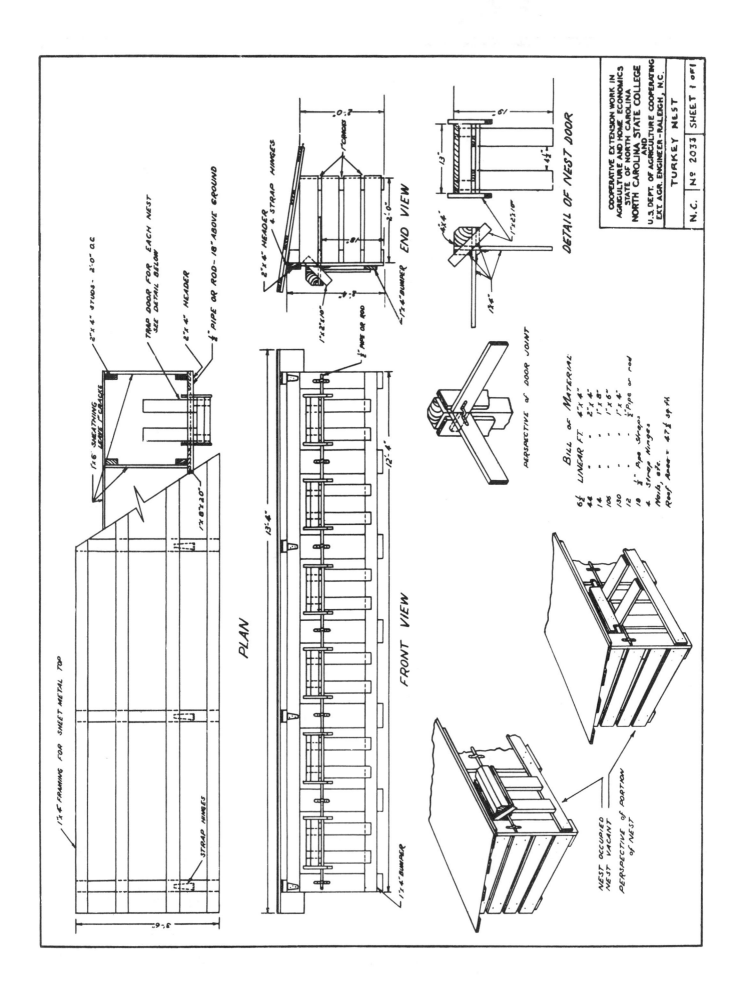

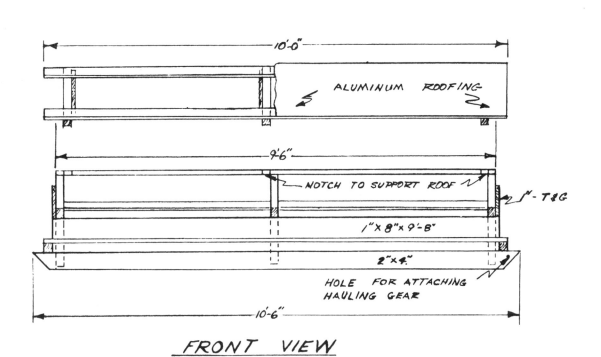

10'-0"

ALUMINUM ROOFING

9'-6"

NOTCH TO SUPPORT ROOF

1"-T&G

1"X 8"X 9'-8"

2"X 4"

HOLE FOR ATTACHING
HAULING GEAR

10'-6"

FRONT VIEW

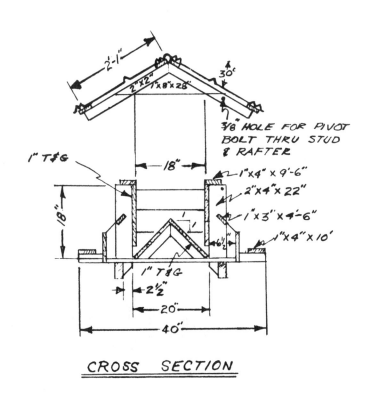

2'-1"

30°

2"X2"   1"X 8"X 28"

3/8" HOLE FOR PIVOT
BOLT THRU STUD
& RAFTER

18"

1" T&G

1"X4" X 9'-6"

2"X 4"X 22"

1"X 3"X 4'-6"

18"

1"

6½"

1"X 4"X 10'

1" T&G

2½"

20"

40"

CROSS SECTION

BILL OF MATERIALS

LUMBER :

3 PCS	2"X4"X12'	
3 PCS	2"X 2"X12'	
8 PCS.	1"X 4"X 10'	
2 PCS	1"X 3"X10'	
3 PCS.	1"X 8"X 10'	
100 BD FT.	1" T&G.	

ROOFING :

2 PCS. 26"X10' ALUMINUM

COOPERATIVE EXTENSION WORK IN
AGRICULTURE & HOME ECONOMICS
STATE OF NORTH CAROLINA
NORTH CAROLINA STATE COLLEGE
AND
U.S. DEPT. OF AGRICULTURE COOPERATING
EXT. AGRI. ENGINEER - RALEIGH, N.C.

TURKEY RANGE SELF FEEDER

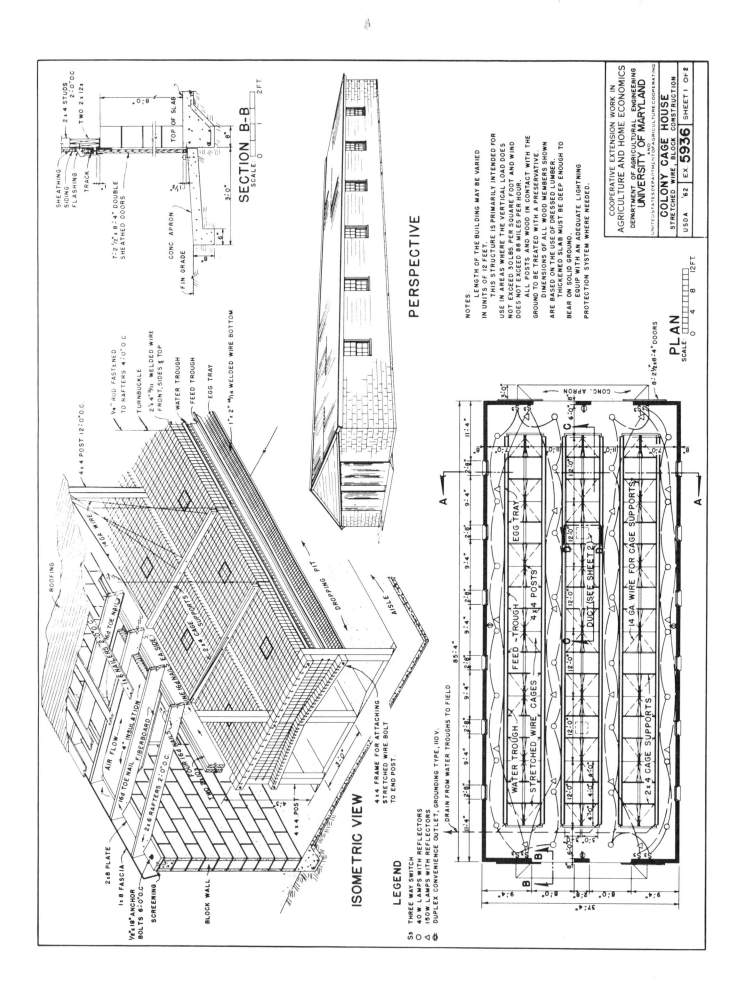

SECTION B-B
SCALE

2 X 4 STUDS 2'-0" O.C.
TWO 2 X 12s
8'-0"
TOP OF SLAB
SHEATHING
SIDING
FLASHING
TRACK
7'-2½" X 8'-4" DOUBLE SHEATHED DOORS
8"
CONC. APRON
FIN GRADE
3'-0"
6"
6"
8"
2FT

PERSPECTIVE

ISOMETRIC VIEW

ROOFING
¼" ROD FASTENED TO RAFTERS 4'-0" O.C.
TURNBUCKLE
2" X 4" ⁹⁄₁₄ WELDED WIRE FRONT, SIDES & TOP
WATER TROUGH
FEED TROUGH
EGG TRAY
1" X 2" ¹⁴⁄₁₄ WELDED WIRE BOTTOM
4 X 4 POST 12'-0" O.C.
14 GA WIRE
2 X 4 CAGE SUPPORTS
DROPPING PIT
AISLE
4 X 4 FRAME FOR ATTACHING STRETCHED WIRE BOLT TO END POST.
1 X 8 NAILERS 2'-0" O.C.
16d TOE NAIL
9 16d NAILS
NINE 16d NAILS
AIR FLOW
INSULATION
FIBERBOARD
16d TOE NAIL
FOUR 16d NAILS
2 X 6 RAFTERS 2'-0" O.C.
TWO 2 X 10s
4 X 4 POST
3'-0"
EASIDE
2 X 8 PLATE
1 X 8 FASCIA
½" X 18" ANCHOR BOLTS 6'-0" O.C.
SCREENING
BLOCK WALL

LEGEND
S₃ THREE WAY SWITCH
○ 40 W LAMPS WITH REFLECTORS
△ 150 W LAMPS WITH REFLECTORS
⌼ DUPLEX CONVENIENCE OUTLET, GROUNDING TYPE, 110V.

NOTES:
LENGTH OF THE BUILDING MAY BE VARIED IN UNITS OF 12 FEET.
THIS STRUCTURE IS PRIMARILY INTENDED FOR USE IN AREAS WHERE THE VERTICAL LOAD DOES NOT EXCEED 30 LBS PER SQUARE FOOT AND WIND DOES NOT EXCEED 88 MILES PER HOUR.
ALL POSTS AND WOOD IN CONTACT WITH THE GROUND TO BE TREATED WITH A PRESERVATIVE.
DIMENSIONS OF ALL WOOD MEMBERS SHOWN ARE BASED ON THE USE OF DRESSED LUMBER.
THICKENED SLAB MUST BE DEEP ENOUGH TO BEAR ON SOLID GROUND.
EQUIP WITH AN ADEQUATE LIGHTNING PROTECTION SYSTEM WHERE NEEDED.

PLAN
SCALE
0 4 8 12FT.

CONC. APRON
3'-0"
8'-2½" X 8'-4" DOORS
EGG TRAY
FEED TROUGH
4 X 4 POSTS
DUCT (SEE SHEET 2)
14 GA WIRE FOR CAGE SUPPORTS
WATER TROUGH
STRETCHED WIRE CAGES
2 X 4 CAGE SUPPORTS
DRAIN FROM WATER TROUGHS TO FIELD
85'-4"
37'-4"
11'-4"
12'-0"
12'-0"
9'-4"
6'-4"
8'-0"
2'-8"

COOPERATIVE EXTENSION WORK IN AGRICULTURE AND HOME ECONOMICS
DEPARTMENT OF AGRICULTURAL ENGINEERING
UNIVERSITY OF MARYLAND
UNITEDSTATESDEPARTMENTOFAGRICULTURECOOPERATING

COLONY CAGE HOUSE
STRETCHED WIRE, BLOCK CONSTRUCTION
USDA '62 EX. 5936 SHEET 1 OF 2

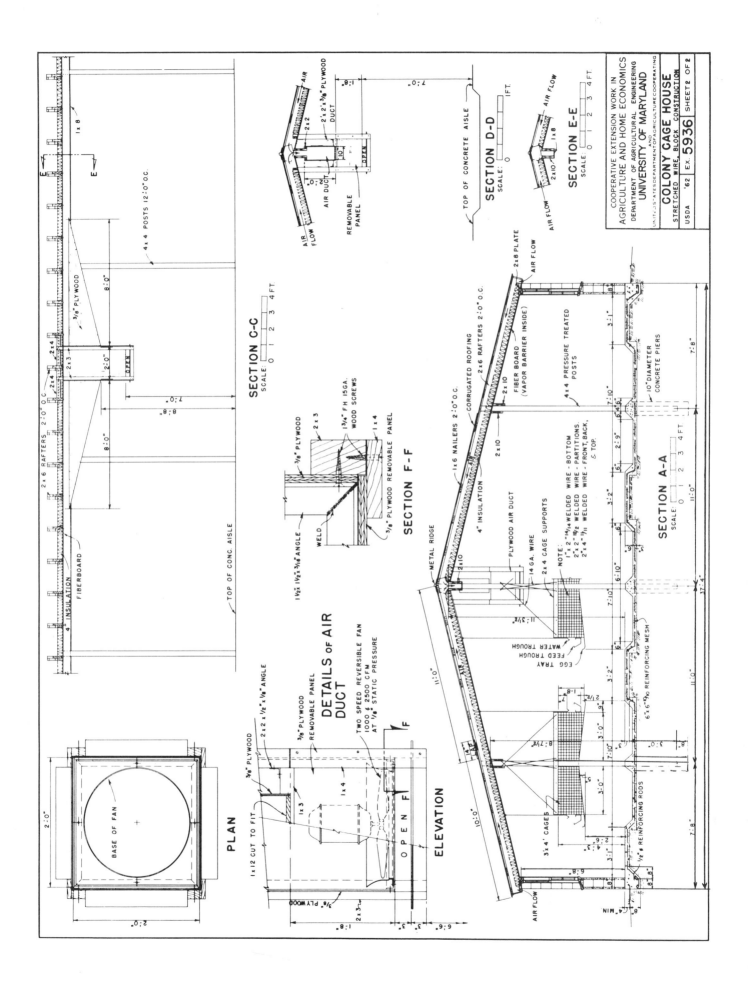

PLAN

2'-0"

BASE OF FAN

2'-0"

DETAILS of AIR DUCT

3/8" PLYWOOD
REMOVABLE PANEL
2 x 2 x 1/2 x 1/8" ANGLE
1 x 12 CUT TO FIT

TWO SPEED REVERSIBLE FAN
1000 & 2500 CFM
AT 1/8" STATIC PRESSURE

1 x 3

1 x 4

OPEN F

3/8" PLYWOOD

2 x 3

ELEVATION

SECTION C-C
SCALE: 0 1 2 3 4 FT

3/8" PLYWOOD

2 x 3

1 3/4" FH 15 GA.
WOOD SCREWS

1 x 4

WELD

1 1/2 x 1 1/2 x 3/16" ANGLE

3/8" PLYWOOD REMOVABLE PANEL

SECTION F-F

AIR FLOW

2 x 2

2 1/2 x 3/8 PLYWOOD DUCT

REMOVABLE PANEL

AIR DUCT

OPEN

SECTION D-D
SCALE: 0 1 FT.

TOP OF CONCRETE AISLE

AIR FLOW

2 x 2

1 x 8

2 x 10

SECTION E-E
SCALE: 0 1 2 3 4 FT

AIR FLOW

1 x 8

4 x 4 POSTS 12'-0" O.C.

3/8" PLYWOOD

2 x 4

2 x 3

2 x 4

2 x 6 RAFTERS 2'-0" O.C.

4" INSULATION

FIBERBOARD

TOP OF CONC. AISLE

2 x 8 PLATE
AIR FLOW

CORRUGATED ROOFING

2 x 6 RAFTERS 2'-0" O.C.

FIBER BOARD
(VAPOR BARRIER INSIDE)

4 x 4 PRESSURE TREATED
POSTS

10" DIAMETER
CONCRETE PIERS

1 x 6 NAILERS 2'-0" O.C.

4" INSULATION

PLYWOOD AIR DUCT

14 GA. WIRE

2 x 4 CAGE SUPPORTS

NOTE:
1 x 2 "14/14 WELDED WIRE - BOTTOM
2 x 2 "9/2 WELDED WIRE - PARTITIONS.
2 x 4 "9/11 WELDED WIRE - FRONT, BACK,
& TOP.

METAL RIDGE

2 x 10

EGG TRAY
FEED TROUGH
WATER TROUGH

3 x 4 CAGES

1/2 "ø "l REINFORCING RODS

6 x 6 "9/10 REINFORCING MESH

4" MIN

AIR FLOW

SECTION A-A
SCALE: 0 1 2 3 4 FT

COOPERATIVE EXTENSION WORK IN
AGRICULTURE AND HOME ECONOMICS
DEPARTMENT OF AGRICULTURAL ENGINEERING
UNIVERSITY OF MARYLAND
AND
UNITED STATES DEPARTMENT OF AGRICULTURE COOPERATING

COLONY CAGE HOUSE
STRETCHED WIRE, BLOCK CONSTRUCTION

USDA '62 EX. 5936 SHEET 2 OF 2

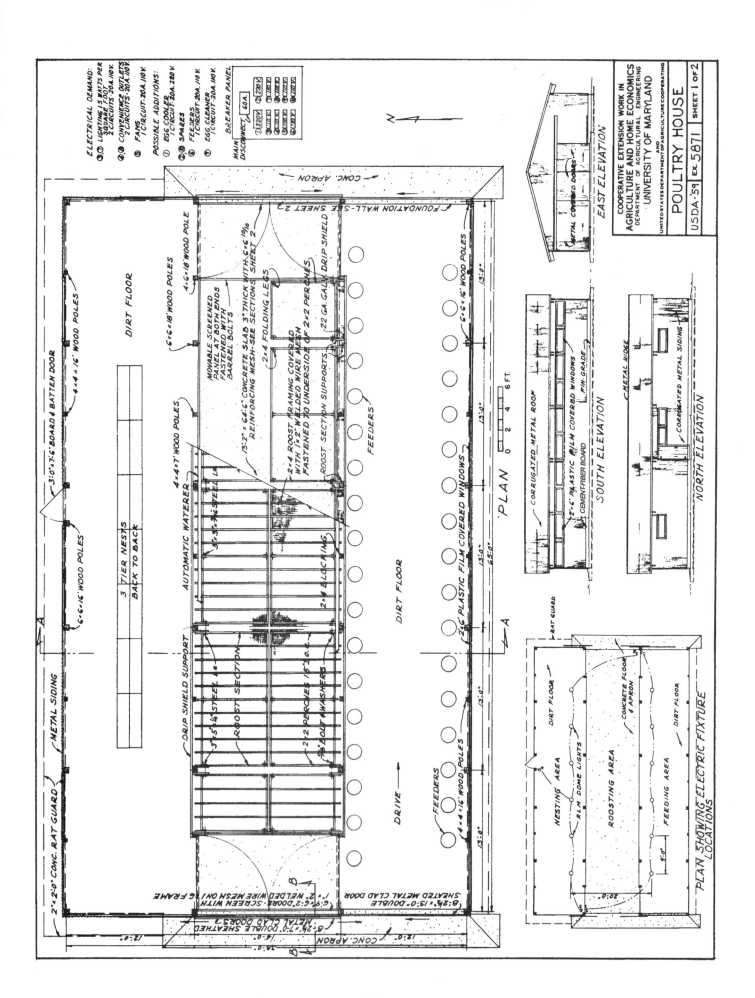

PLAN

POULTRY HOUSE

COOPERATIVE EXTENSION WORK IN
AGRICULTURE AND HOME ECONOMICS
DEPARTMENT OF AGRICULTURAL ENGINEERING
UNIVERSITY OF MARYLAND
AND
UNITED STATES DEPARTMENT OF AGRICULTURE COOPERATING

USDA-'59 | ex. 5,871 | SHEET 1 of 2

EAST ELEVATION

SOUTH ELEVATION

NORTH ELEVATION

PLAN SHOWING ELECTRIC FIXTURE
LOCATIONS

ELECTRICAL DEMAND:
LIGHTING 1.5 WATTS PER SQUARE FOOT. 2 CIRCUITS 20A.110V.
CONVENIENCE OUTLETS 2 CIRCUITS-20A.110V.
FANS 1 CIRCUIT-20A.110V.
POSSIBLE ADDITIONS:
EGG COOLER 1 CIRCUIT-20A.220V.
SPARES
FEEDERS 1 CIRCUIT-20A.110V.
EGG CLEANER 1 CIRCUIT-20A.110V.
BREAKER PANEL
MAIN DISCONNECT 60A.

146

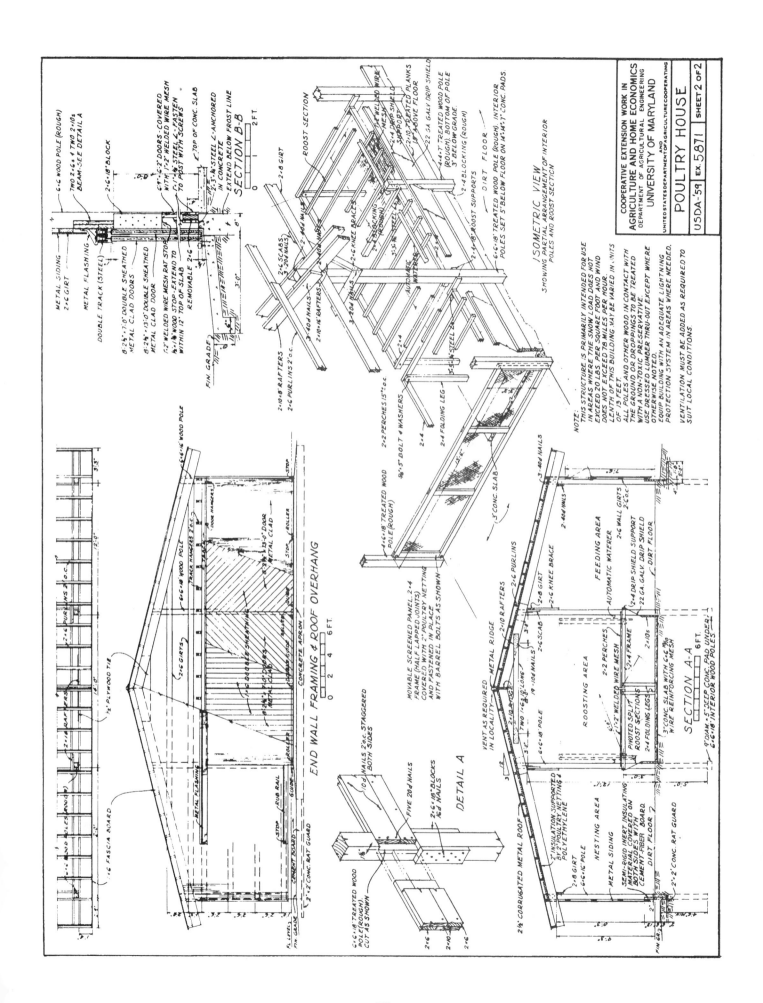

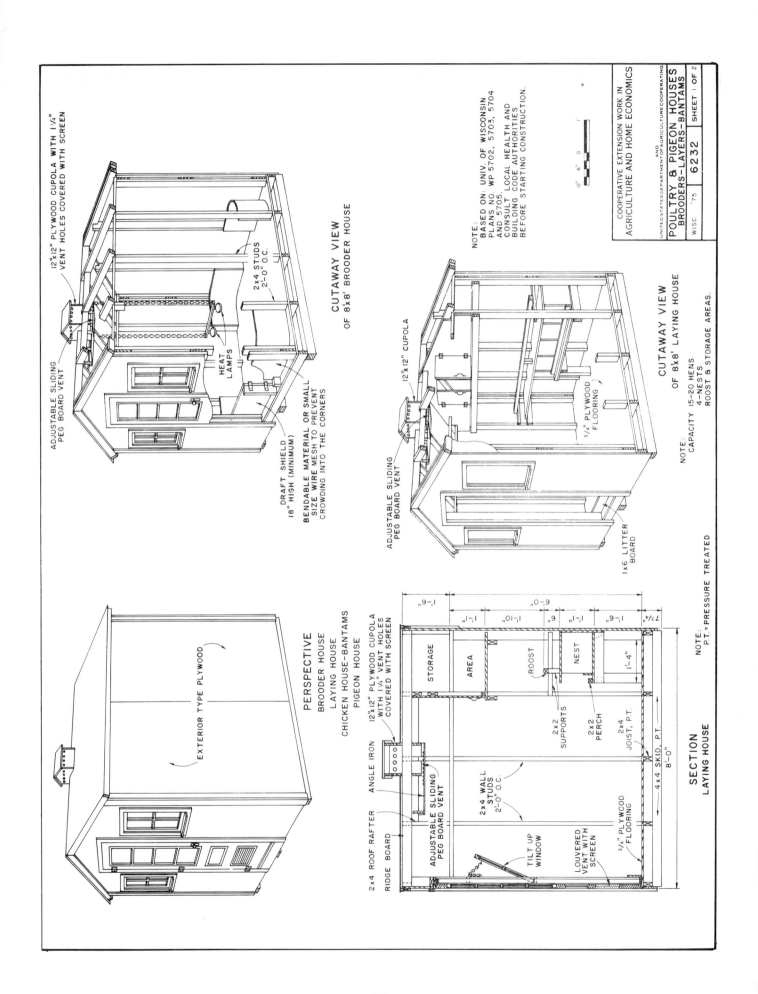

CUTAWAY VIEW
OF 8'x8' BROODER HOUSE

12"x12" PLYWOOD CUPOLA WITH 1¼" VENT HOLES COVERED WITH SCREEN

ADJUSTABLE SLIDING PEG BOARD VENT

2x4 STUDS 2'-0" O.C.

HEAT LAMPS

DRAFT SHIELD 18" HIGH (MINIMUM)

BENDABLE MATERIAL OR SMALL SIZE WIRE MESH TO PREVENT CROWDING INTO THE CORNERS

CUTAWAY VIEW
OF 8'x8' LAYING HOUSE

12"x12" CUPOLA

ADJUSTABLE SLIDING PEG BOARD VENT

¾" PLYWOOD FLOORING

NOTE:
CAPACITY 15-20 HENS
4-NESTS
ROOST & STORAGE AREAS.

1x6 LITTER BOARD

NOTE:
BASED ON: UNIV. OF WISCONSIN
PLANS NO. WP 5702, 5703, 5704
AND 5705.
CONSULT LOCAL HEALTH AND
BUILDING CODE AUTHORITIES
BEFORE STARTING CONSTRUCTION.

COOPERATIVE EXTENSION WORK IN
AGRICULTURE AND HOME ECONOMICS
AND
UNITED STATES DEPARTMENT OF AGRICULTURE COOPERATING

POULTRY & PIGEON HOUSES
BROODERS-LAYERS-BANTAMS

WISC. '75 | 6232 | SHEET I OF 2

12" 6" 0 1'

PERSPECTIVE
BROODER HOUSE
LAYING HOUSE
CHICKEN HOUSE-BANTAMS
PIGEON HOUSE

EXTERIOR TYPE PLYWOOD

SECTION
LAYING HOUSE

12"x12" PLYWOOD CUPOLA
WITH 1¼" VENT HOLES
COVERED WITH SCREEN

2x4 ROOF RAFTER

RIDGE BOARD

ANGLE IRON

ADJUSTABLE SLIDING PEG BOARD VENT

2x4 WALL STUDS 2'-0" O.C.

TILT UP WINDOW

¾" PLYWOOD FLOORING

LOUVERED VENT WITH SCREEN

STORAGE

AREA

ROOST

NEST

2x2 SUPPORTS

2x2 PERCH

2x4 JOIST, P.T.

4x4 SKID, P.T.

8'-0"

1'-6"

1'-1"

1'-10"

6"

1'-1"

1'-6"

7 3/4"

1'-4"

NOTE:
P.T.= PRESSURE TREATED

148

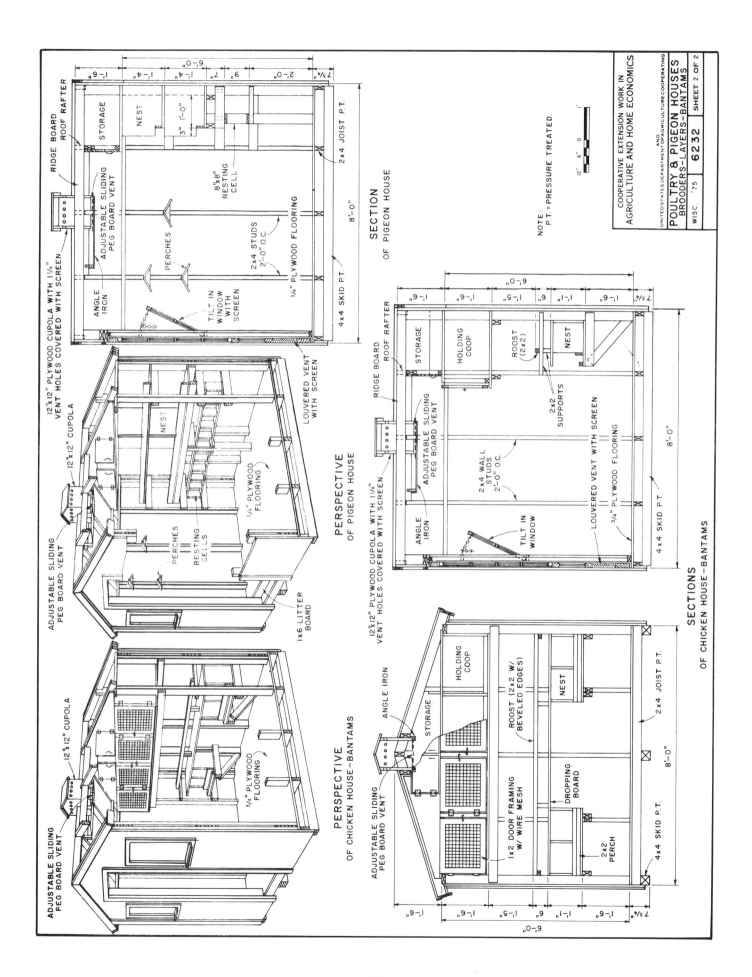

RIDGE BOARD
ROOF RAFTER
STORAGE
NEST
12"x12" PLYWOOD CUPOLA WITH 1¼"
VENT HOLES COVERED WITH SCREEN
ADJUSTABLE SLIDING
PEG BOARD VENT
ANGLE
IRON
8¼"x8" RESTING CELL
PERCHES
2 x 4 STUDS
2'-0" O.C.
TILT IN
WINDOW
WITH SCREEN
¾" PLYWOOD FLOORING
2 x 4 JOIST P.T.
8'-0"
4 x 4 SKID P.T.
LOUVERED VENT
WITH SCREEN

SECTION
OF PIGEON HOUSE

12"x12" PLYWOOD CUPOLA
12"x12" CUPOLA
NEST
ADJUSTABLE
SLIDING
PEG BOARD VENT
¾" PLYWOOD
FLOORING
PERCHES
RESTING
CELLS
1x6 LITTER
BOARD

PERSPECTIVE
OF PIGEON HOUSE

RIDGE BOARD
ROOF RAFTER
STORAGE
HOLDING
COOP
ROOST
(2x2)
2 x 2
SUPPORTS
NEST
ADJUSTABLE SLIDING
PEG BOARD VENT
ANGLE
IRON
2 x 4 WALL
STUDS
2'-0" O.C.
TILT IN
WINDOW
LOUVERED VENT WITH SCREEN
¾" PLYWOOD FLOORING
4 x 4 SKID P.T.
8'-0"

SECTIONS
OF CHICKEN HOUSE—BANTAMS

12"x12" PLYWOOD CUPOLA WITH 1¼"
VENT HOLES COVERED WITH SCREEN
12"x12" CUPOLA
ADJUSTABLE SLIDING
PEG BOARD VENT
¾" PLYWOOD FLOORING

PERSPECTIVE
OF CHICKEN HOUSE—BANTAMS

ANGLE IRON
HOLDING
COOP
STORAGE
ROOST (2x2 W/
BEVELED EDGES)
NEST
2 x 4 JOIST P.T.
ADJUSTABLE SLIDING
PEG BOARD VENT
1x2 DOOR FRAMING
W/ WIRE MESH
DROPPING
BOARD
2x2
PERCH
4 x 4 SKID P.T.
8'-0"

COOPERATIVE EXTENSION WORK IN
AGRICULTURE AND HOME ECONOMICS
AND
UNITEDSTATESDEPARTMENTOFAGRICULTURECOOPERATING
POULTRY & PIGEON HOUSES
BROODERS—LAYERS—BANTAMS
WISC. '75   6232   SHEET 2 OF 2

NOTE:
P.T. = PRESSURE TREATED.

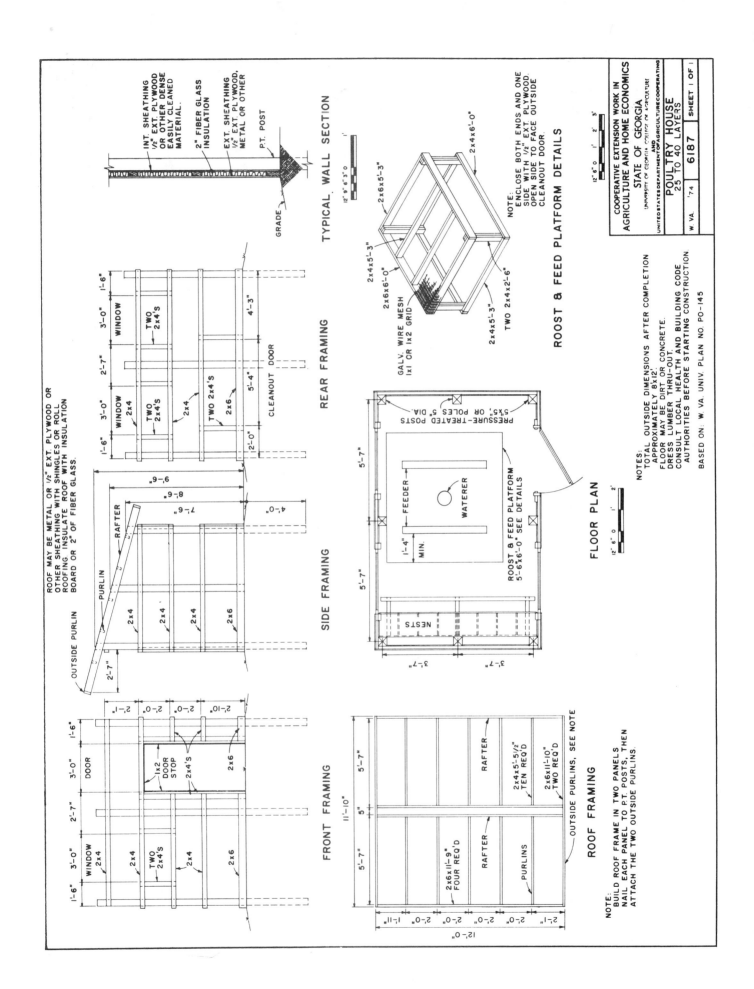

TYPICAL WALL SECTION

INT. SHEATHING 1/2" EXT. PLYWOOD OR OTHER DENSE EASILY CLEANED MATERIAL.

2" FIBER GLASS INSULATION

EXT. SHEATHING 1/2" EXT. PLYWOOD, METAL OR OTHER

P.T. POST

GRADE

12" 9" 6" 3" 0   1'

ROOST & FEED PLATFORM DETAILS

NOTE:
ENCLOSE BOTH ENDS AND ONE SIDE WITH 1/2" EXT PLYWOOD. OPEN SIDE TO FACE OUTSIDE CLEANOUT DOOR.

2x4x6'-0"
2x6x5'-3"
2x4x5'-3"
2x6x6'-0"
GALV. WIRE MESH 1x1 OR 1x2 GRID
2x4x5'-3"
2x4x6'-0"
TWO 2x4x2'-6"

12" 6" 0   1'   2'   3'

REAR FRAMING

1'-6"   3'-0"   2'-7"   3'-0"   1'-6"
WINDOW   WINDOW
2x4   TWO 2x4'S   TWO 2x4'S
2x4   TWO 2x4'S
5'-4"   2x6
CLEANOUT DOOR
2'-0"
4'-3"

SIDE FRAMING

9'-6"
8'-6"
7'-6"
4'-0"
OUTSIDE PURLIN
PURLIN
RAFTER
2x4   2x4   2x4   2x6
2'-7"

ROOF MAY BE METAL OR 1/2" EXT. PLYWOOD OR OTHER SHEATHING WITH SHINGLES OR ROLL ROOFING. INSULATE ROOF WITH INSULATION BOARD OR 2" OF FIBER GLASS.

FLOOR PLAN

5'-7"   5'-7"
PRESSURE-TREATED POSTS 5"x5", OR POLES 5" DIA.
FEEDER
1'-4" MIN.
WATERER
NESTS
ROOST & FEED PLATFORM 5'-6"x6'-0" SEE DETAILS
3'-7"   3'-7"

12" 6" 0   1'   2'

NOTES:
TOTAL OUTSIDE DIMENSIONS AFTER COMPLETION APPROXIMATELY 8x12.
FLOOR MAY BE DIRT OR CONCRETE.
DRESS LUMBER THRU-OUT.
CONSULT LOCAL HEALTH AND BUILDING CODE AUTHORITIES BEFORE STARTING CONSTRUCTION.

BASED ON: W. VA. UNIV. PLAN NO. PO-145

FRONT FRAMING

2'-1"   2'-0"   2'-0"   2'-10"
1'-6"   3'-0"   2'-7"   3'-0"   1'-6"
WINDOW   DOOR   WINDOW
2x4   TWO 2x4'S   2x4
1x2 DOOR STOP
2x4'S
2x6   2x6

NOTE:
BUILD ROOF FRAME IN TWO PANELS NAIL EACH PANEL TO P.T. POSTS, THEN ATTACH THE TWO OUTSIDE PURLINS.

ROOF FRAMING

5'-7"   5'-7"
11'-10"
5"   5"
1'-11"
OUTSIDE PURLINS, SEE NOTE
2x6x11'-9" FOUR REQ'D
2x4x5-5/2" TEN REQ'D
2x6x11'-10" TWO REQ'D
RAFTER   RAFTER
PURLINS
2'-1"   2'-0"   2'-0"   2'-0"   2'-0"   1'-11"
12'-0"

COOPERATIVE EXTENSION WORK IN
AGRICULTURE AND HOME ECONOMICS
STATE OF GEORGIA
UNIVERSITY OF GEORGIA COLLEGE OF AGRICULTURE
AND
UNITED STATES DEPARTMENT OF AGRICULTURE COOPERATING

POULTRY HOUSE
25 TO 40 LAYERS

W. VA.   '74   6187   SHEET 1 OF 1

12" 9" 6" 3" 0   1'   2'   3'

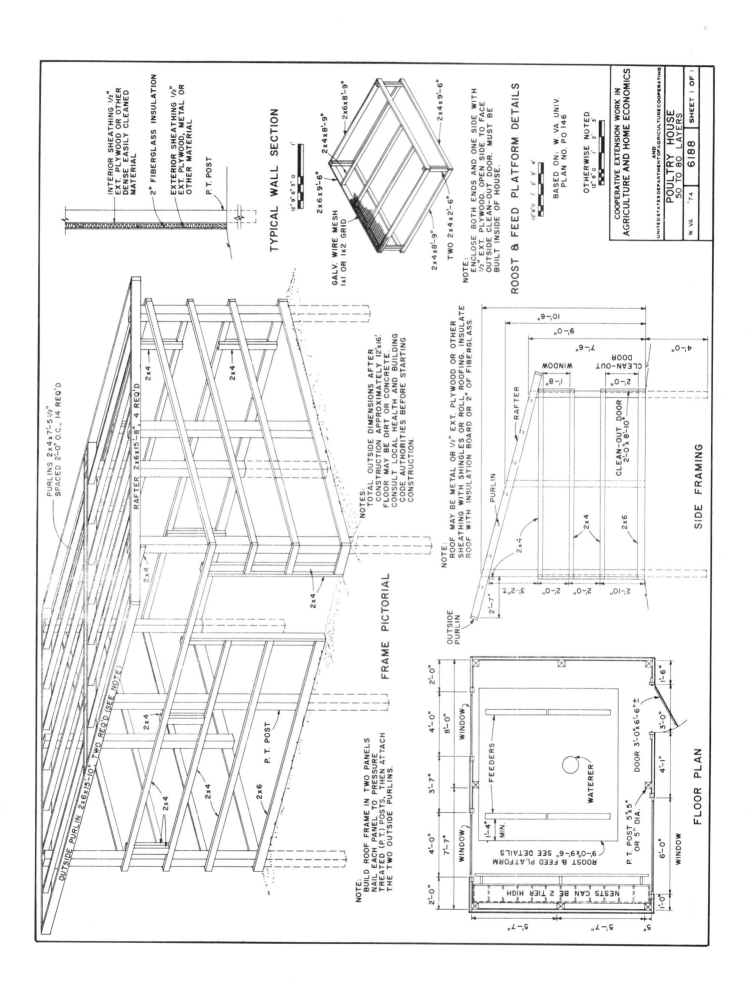

TYPICAL WALL SECTION

INTERIOR SHEATHING 1/2"
EXT. PLYWOOD OR OTHER
DENSE EASILY CLEANED
MATERIAL

2" FIBERGLASS INSULATION

EXTERIOR SHEATHING 1/2"
EXT. PLYWOOD, METAL OR
OTHER MATERIAL

P.T. POST

12"9"6"3"0   1'

2x4x8'-9"
2x6x8'-9"

2x4x9'-6"

2x6x9'-6"
GALV. WIRE MESH
1x1 OR 1x2 GRID

2x4x8'-9"

TWO 2x4x2'-6"

NOTE:
ENCLOSE BOTH ENDS AND ONE SIDE WITH
1/2" EXT. PLYWOOD. OPEN SIDE TO FACE
OUTSIDE CLEAN-OUT DOOR. MUST BE
BUILT INSIDE OF HOUSE.

ROOST & FEED PLATFORM DETAILS
12'6"0   1' 2' 3' 4'

BASED ON: W. VA. UNIV.
PLAN NO. PO 146

OTHERWISE NOTED
12'6"0   1' 2' 3'

COOPERATIVE EXTENSION WORK IN
AGRICULTURE AND HOME ECONOMICS
AND
UNITED STATES DEPARTMENT OF AGRICULTURE COOPERATING

POULTRY HOUSE
50 TO 80 LAYERS

W. VA. '74   6188   SHEET 1 OF 1

PURLINS 2x4x7'-5 1/2"
SPACED 2'-0" O.C., 14 REQ'D

RAFTER 2x6x15'-8", 4 REQ'D

2x4

2x4

2x4

2x4

2x4

OUTSIDE PURLIN 2x6x15'-10", TWO REQ'D (SEE NOTE)

2x4

2x4

2x4

2x6

P.T. POST

NOTES:
TOTAL OUTSIDE DIMENSIONS AFTER
CONSTRUCTION APPROXIMATELY 12'x16'.
FLOOR MAY BE DIRT OR CONCRETE.
CONSULT LOCAL HEALTH AND BUILDING
CODE AUTHORITIES BEFORE STARTING
CONSTRUCTION.

FRAME PICTORIAL

NOTE:
BUILD ROOF FRAME IN TWO PANELS.
NAIL EACH PANEL TO PRESSURE
TREATED (P.T.) POSTS, THEN ATTACH
THE TWO OUTSIDE PURLINS.

NOTE:
ROOF MAY BE METAL OR 1/2" EXT. PLYWOOD OR OTHER
SHEATHING WITH SHINGLES OR ROLL ROOFING. INSULATE
ROOF WITH INSULATION BOARD OR 2" OF FIBERGLASS.

10'-6"
9'-0"
7'-6"
4'-0"

RAFTER

PURLIN

WINDOW
1'-8"

CLEAN-OUT
DOOR
2'-0"

2x4

2x6

CLEAN-OUT DOOR
2'-0"x 8'-10"

OUTSIDE
PURLIN

2'-7"

3'-2 1/4"   2'-0"   2'-0"   2'-10"

SIDE FRAMING

2'-0"   4'-0"   3'-7"   4'-0"   7'-7"   4'-0"   2'-0"
8'-0"

WINDOW

WINDOW

FEEDERS

1'-4"
MIN.

WATERER

ROOST & FEED PLATFORM
9'-0"x 9'-6", SEE DETAILS

P.T. POST 5"x 5"
OR 5" DIA.

NESTS CAN BE 2 TIER HIGH

DOOR 3'-0"x 6'-6" ±

1'-6"

3'-0"

4'-1"

6'-0"

WINDOW

1'-0"

5"   5'-7"   5'-7"

FLOOR PLAN

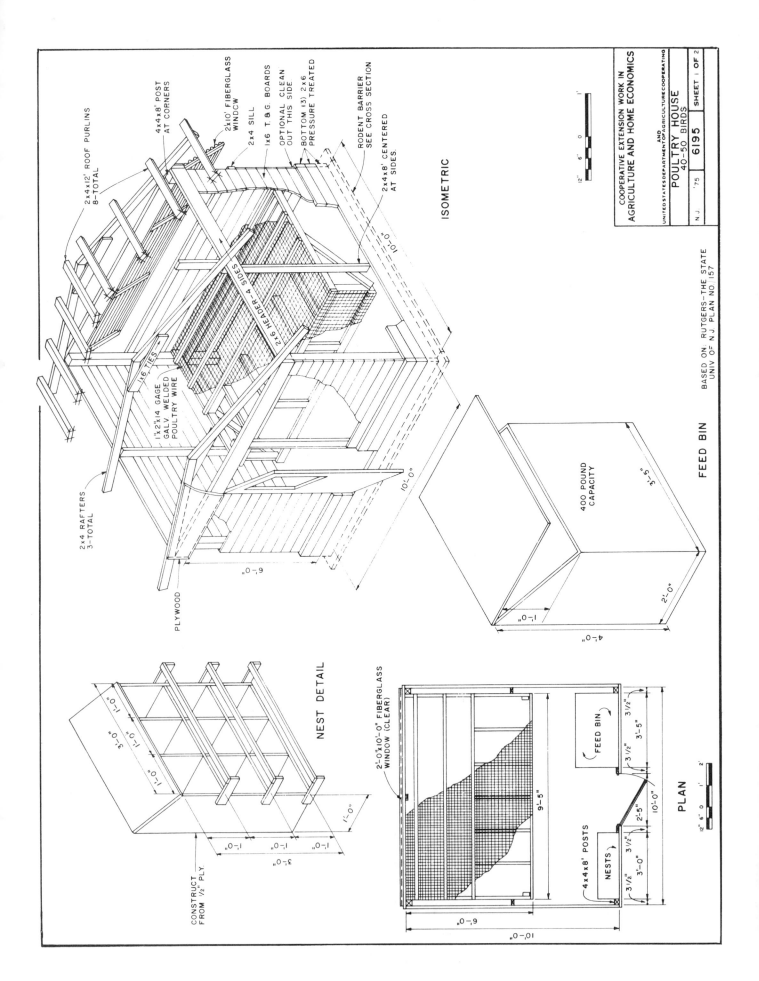

ISOMETRIC

2x4x12' ROOF PURLINS
8-TOTAL

4x4x8' POST
AT CORNERS

2½x10' FIBERGLASS
WINDOW

2x4 SILL

1x6 T.& G. BOARDS

OPTIONAL CLEAN
OUT THIS SIDE

BOTTOM (3) 2x6
PRESSURE TREATED

RODENT BARRIER
SEE CROSS SECTION

2x4x8' CENTERED
AT SIDES.

2x6 HEADER-4 SIDES

1x6 TIES

1"x2"x14 GAGE
GALV WELDED
POULTRY WIRE

10'-0"

2x4 RAFTERS
3-TOTAL

PLYWOOD

9'-0"

COOPERATIVE EXTENSION WORK IN
AGRICULTURE AND HOME ECONOMICS
AND
UNITED STATES DEPARTMENT OF AGRICULTURE COOPERATING

POULTRY HOUSE
40-50 BIRDS

N.J.   '75   6195   SHEET 1 OF 2

BASED ON: RUTGERS—THE STATE
UNIV OF N.J PLAN NO.1157

12" 6" 0   1'

FEED BIN

400 POUND
CAPACITY

3'-5"

1'-0"

2'-0"

4'-0"

NEST DETAIL

CONSTRUCT
FROM ½" PLY.

1'-0"
3'-0"
1'-0"

1'-0"

1'-0" 1'-0" 1'-0"
3'-0"

2'-0"x10'-0" FIBERGLASS
WINDOW (CLEAR)

9'-5"

FEED BIN

3½"
3-5"
3½"

10'-0"

2'-5"

NESTS

3½"
3'-0"
3½"

4x4x8' POSTS

PLAN

9'-0"

10'-0"

12" 6" 0   1'   2'

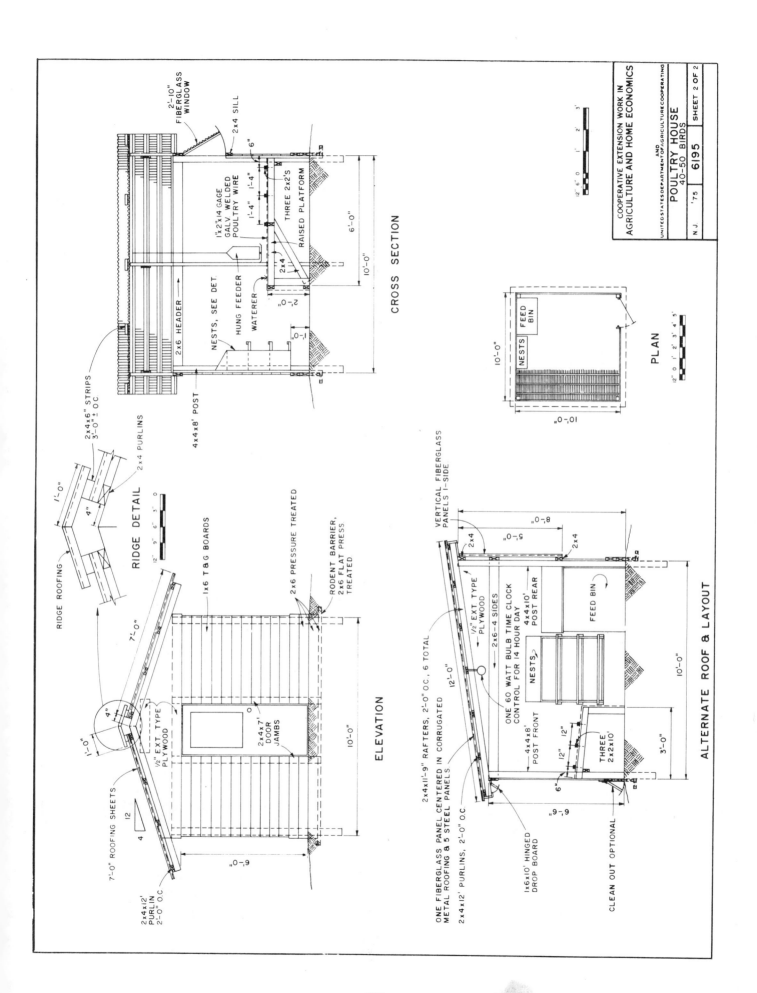

CROSS SECTION

2'-10" FIBERGLASS WINDOW
2x4 SILL
6"
1"x2"x14 GAGE GALV WELDED POULTRY WIRE
1'-4" 1'-4"
1'-4"
THREE 2x2'S
RAISED PLATFORM
2x4
2'-0"
6'-0"
10'-0"
NESTS, SEE DET.
HUNG FEEDER
WATERER
2x6 HEADER
2x4x6" STRIPS 3'-0" ± OC
2x4 PURLINS
4x4x8' POST
1'-0"

RIDGE DETAIL

1'-0"
4"
RIDGE ROOFING

PLAN

FEED BIN
NESTS
10'-0"
10'-0"

ELEVATION

7'-0"
1x6 T&G BOARDS
2x6 PRESSURE TREATED
RODENT BARRIER, 2x6 FLAT PRESS TREATED
4"
1'-0"
1/2" EXT TYPE PLYWOOD
2x4x7' DOOR JAMBS
10'-0"
7'-0" ROOFING SHEETS
12
4
9'-0"
2x4x12' PURLIN 2'-0" O.C.

ALTERNATE ROOF & LAYOUT

VERTICAL FIBERGLASS PANELS 1-SIDE
2x4
8'-0"
5'-0"
2x4
ONE FIBERGLASS PANEL CENTERED IN CORRUGATED METAL ROOFING & 5 STEEL PANELS
2x4x11'-9" RAFTERS, 2'-0" OC, 6 TOTAL
2x4x12' PURLINS, 2'-0" O.C.
1/2" EXT TYPE PLYWOOD
2x6-4 SIDES
4x4x10' POST REAR
FEED BIN
ONE 60 WATT BULB TIME CLOCK CONTROL FOR 14 HOUR DAY
NESTS
4x4x8' POST FRONT
12" 12"
THREE 2x2x10'
6"
3'-0"
10'-0"
1x6x10' HINGED DROP BOARD
9'-0"
CLEAN OUT OPTIONAL

COOPERATIVE EXTENSION WORK IN AGRICULTURE AND HOME ECONOMICS
AND
UNITED STATES DEPARTMENT OF AGRICULTURE COOPERATING
POULTRY HOUSE
40-50 BIRDS
N.J. '75   6195   SHEET 2 OF 2

153

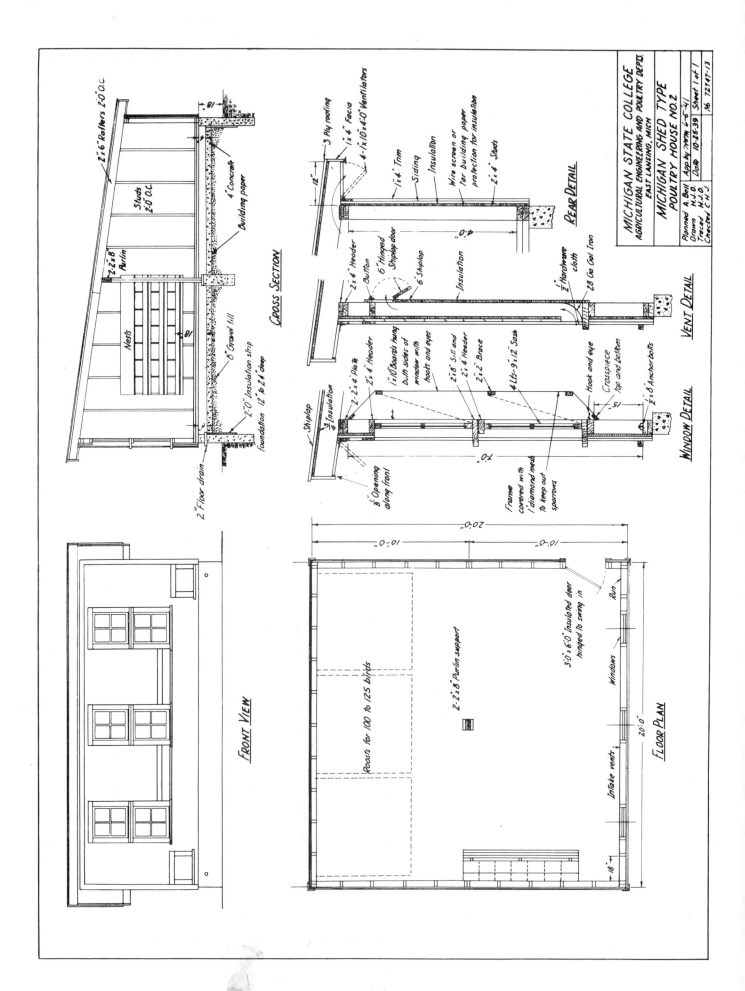

CROSS SECTION

2"x6"Rafters 2'0 O.C.

Studs
2'-0 O.C.

2-2"x8
Purlin

4"Concrete

Building paper

8"Gravel fill

Nests

2'-0" Insulation strip
Foundation 12" to 24" deep

2" Floor drain

3 Ply roofing
1"x 4" Facia
4-1"x10"x4'-0" Ventilators

1"x 4" Trim
Siding
Insulation
Wire screen or
tar building paper
protection for insulation
2"x 4" Studs

REAR DETAIL

2"x 4" Header
Button
6" Hinged
Shiplap door
6" Shiplap
Insulation

VENT DETAIL

1" Hardware
cloth
28 Ga. Gal. Iron

2"x 4" Plate
2"x 4" Header
1"x10"boards hung
both sides of
window with
hooks and eyes
2"x 8" Sill and
2"x 4" Header
2"x 2" Brace
4 Lt.-9"x12" Sash
Shiplap
½" Insulation
Hook and eye
Crosspiece
top and bottom
2"x 8" Anchor bolts

WINDOW DETAIL

Frame
covered with
1" diamond mesh
to keep out
sparrows

½" Opening
along front

MICHIGAN STATE COLLEGE
AGRICULTURAL ENGINEERING AND POULTRY DEPTS.
EAST LANSING, MICH

MICHIGAN SHED TYPE
POULTRY HOUSE NO.2

Planned A. Bell	App by MPM 6-6-41
Drawn H.J.O.	Date 10-25-39	Sheet 1 of 1
Traced H.J.O.	
Checked C.H.J.	No 72747-13

FRONT VIEW

FLOOR PLAN

20'-0"
10'-0"
10'-0"

Roosts for 100 to 125 birds

2-2"x8" Purlin support

3'-0"x6'-0" Insulated door
hinged to swing in

Run

Windows

20'-0"

Intake vents

18"

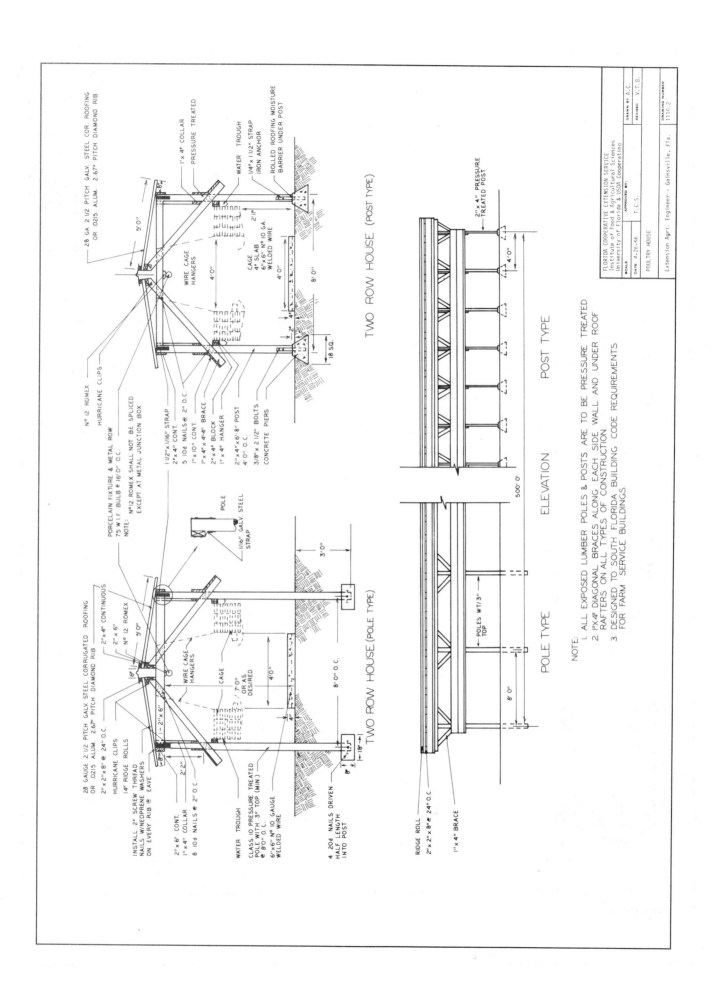

28 GA 2 1/2 PITCH GALV. STEEL COR. ROOFING
OR .0215 ALUM. 2.67" PITCH DIAMOND RIB

1" x 4" COLLAR
PRESSURE TREATED

WATER TROUGH

1/4" x 1 1/2" STRAP
IRON ANCHOR

ROLLED ROOFING MOISTURE
BARRIER UNDER POST

WIRE CAGE
HANGERS

2 1/2"

CAGE
4" SLAB
6"x 6" N° 10 GA.
WELDED WIRE

18 SQ.

TWO ROW HOUSE (POST TYPE)

N° 12 ROMEX

HURRICANE CLIPS

PORCELAIN FIXTURE & METAL ROW
75 W I.F. BULB @ 16'-0" O.C.
NOTE: N°12 ROMEX SHALL NOT BE SPLICED
EXCEPT AT METAL JUNCTION BOX

1 1/2"x 1/16" STRAP
2"x 4" CONT.
5 10d NAILS @ 2" O.C.
1"x 4" x 4-4" BRACE
2"x 4" BLOCK
1"x 4" HANGER

2"x 4"x 6'-8" POST
4'-0" O.C.

3/8"x 2 1/2" BOLTS
CONCRETE PIERS

POLE
1/16" GALV. STEEL
STRAP

28 GAUGE 2 1/2 PITCH GALV STEEL CORRUGATED ROOFING
OR .0215 ALUM. 2.67" PITCH DIAMOND RIB
2" x 2" x 8" @ 24" O.C.

HURRICANE CLIPS

1/4" RIDGE ROLLS

2"x 4" CONTINUOUS
2"x 6"
N° 12 ROMEX

WIRE CAGE
HANGERS

CAGE
7'-0" OR AS DESIRED

1-2"x 6"

INSTALL 2" SCREW THREAD
NAILS W/NEOPRENE WASHERS
ON EVERY RIB @ EAVE

2"x 6" CONT.
1"x 4" COLLAR
8 10d NAILS @ 2" O.C.

WATER TROUGH

CLASS 10 PRESSURE TREATED
POLE WITH 3" TOP (MIN.)
@ 8'0" O.C.
6"x 6" N° 10 GAUGE
WELDED WIRE

4 20d NAILS DRIVEN
HALF LENGTH
INTO POST

8'-0" O.C.

3'-0"

18"

TWO ROW HOUSE (POLE TYPE)

RIDGE ROLL
2"x 2" x 8" @ 24" O.C.
1"x 4" BRACE

POLE TYPE

POLES WT/3"
TOP

8'-0"

500'-0"

2"x 4" PRESSURE
TREATED POST

4'-0"

8'-0"

POST TYPE

ELEVATION

NOTE:
1. ALL EXPOSED LUMBER POLES & POSTS ARE TO BE PRESSURE TREATED
2. 1"x 4" DIAGONAL BRACES ALONG EACH SIDE WALL AND UNDER ROOF
   RAFTERS ON ALL TYPES OF CONSTRUCTION.
3. DESIGNED TO SOUTH FLORIDA BUILDING CODE REQUIREMENTS
   FOR FARM SERVICE BUILDINGS.

FLORIDA COOPERATIVE EXTENSION SERVICE
Institute of Food & Agricultural Sciences
University of Florida & USDA Cooperating

DRAWN BY: A.C.
REVISED: V.T.B.
SCALE:
DATE: 6-26-66
APPROVED BY:
T.C.S.
DRAWING NUMBER: 1110.2

POULTRY HOUSE
Extension Agri. Engineer - Gainsville, Fla.

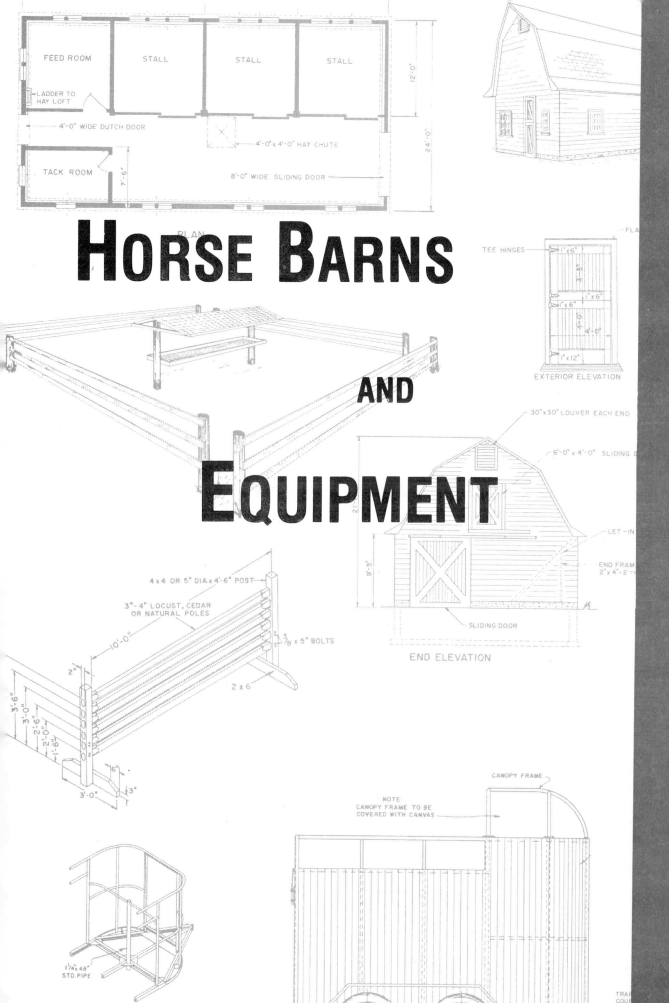

FEED ROOM   STALL   STALL   STALL

12'-0"

24'-0"

LADDER TO HAY LOFT

4'-0" WIDE DUTCH DOOR

4'-0" x 4'-0" HAY CHUTE

TACK ROOM

7'-6"

8'-0" WIDE SLIDING DOOR

PLAN

HORSE BARNS

AND

EQUIPMENT

TEE HINGES

1" x 6"

1" x 6"

4'-0"

1" x 12"

EXTERIOR ELEVATION

30" x 30" LOUVER EACH END

6'-0" x 4'-0" SLIDING D

LET-IN

END FRAM 2" x 4"-2'-

9'-5"

SLIDING DOOR

END ELEVATION

4 x 4 OR 5" DIA x 4'-6" POST

3"- 4" LOCUST, CEDAR OR NATURAL POLES

10'-0"

2"

3'-6"
3'-0"
2'-6"
2'-0"
1'-6"

3/8 x 5" BOLTS

2 x 6

6"

3"

3'-0"

CANOPY FRAME

NOTE: CANOPY FRAME TO BE COVERED WITH CANVAS

1 1/4 x 48" STD. PIPE

TRAI COU

10

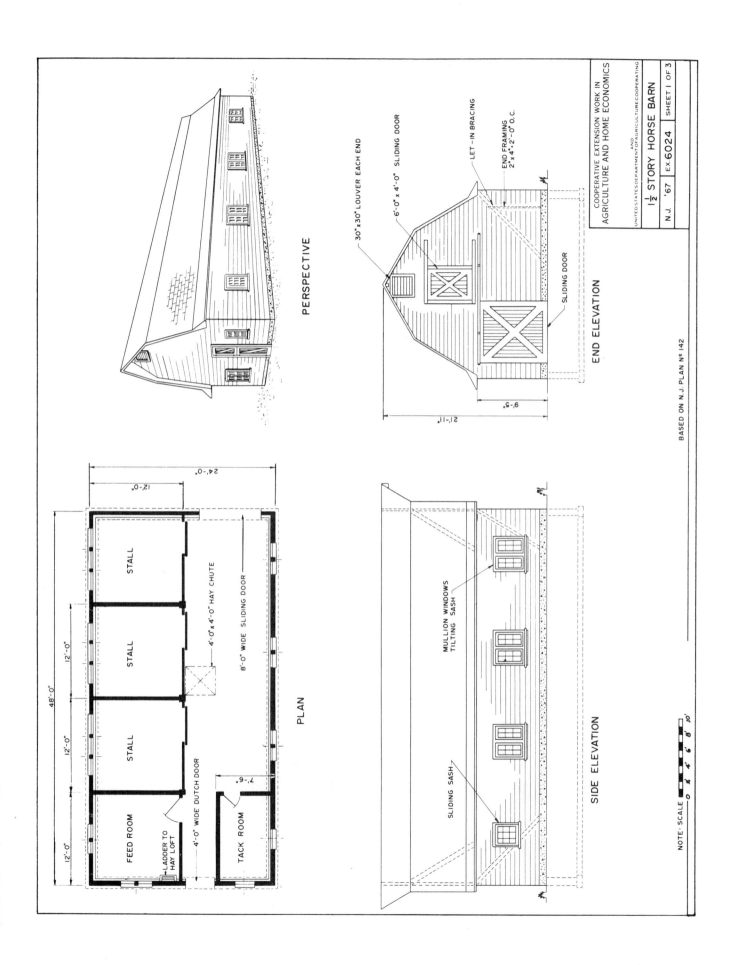

PERSPECTIVE

30" x 30" LOUVER EACH END

6'-0" x 4'-0" SLIDING DOOR

LET - IN BRACING

END FRAMING
2" x 4" - 2' - 0" O.C.

SLIDING DOOR

END ELEVATION

9'-5"

21'-11"

COOPERATIVE EXTENSION WORK IN
AGRICULTURE AND HOME ECONOMICS
AND
UNITED STATES DEPARTMENT OF AGRICULTURE COOPERATING

1½ STORY HORSE BARN

N.J. '67 EX. 6024 SHEET 1 OF 3

BASED ON N.J. PLAN Nº 142

24'-0"

12'-0"

STALL

STALL

STALL

FEED ROOM

4'-0" x 4'-0" HAY CHUTE

8'-0" WIDE SLIDING DOOR

LADDER TO HAY LOFT

4'-0" WIDE DUTCH DOOR

TACK ROOM

7'-6"

48'-0"

12'-0"

12'-0"

12'-0"

12'-0"

PLAN

MULLION WINDOWS
TILTING SASH

SLIDING SASH

SIDE ELEVATION

NOTE: SCALE 0 2' 4' 6' 8' 10'

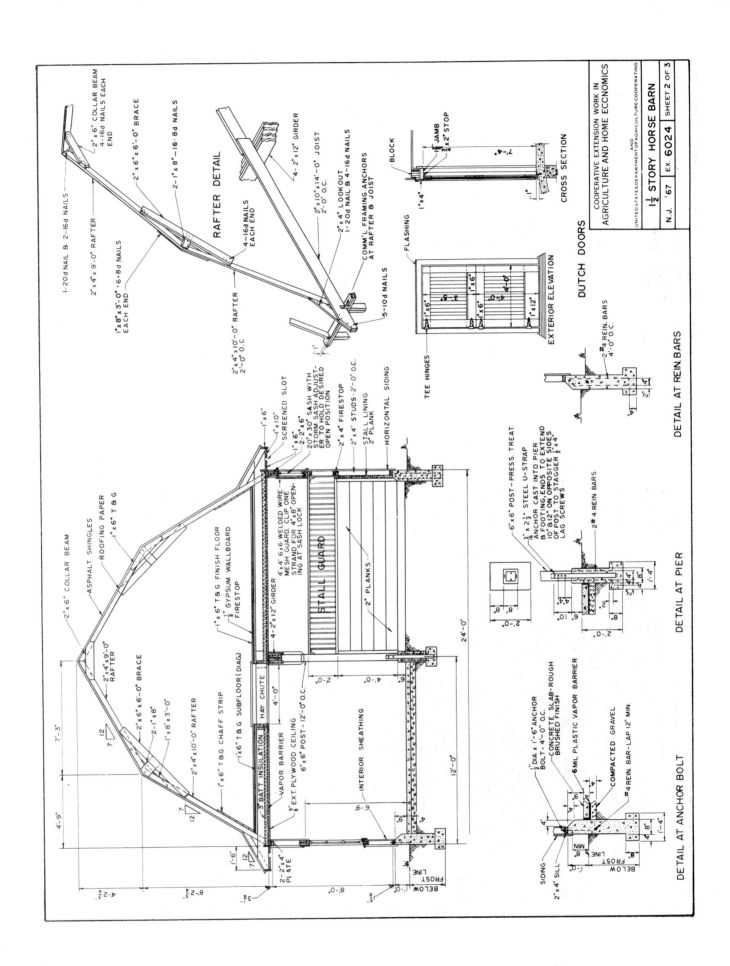

RAFTER DETAIL

CROSS SECTION

DUTCH DOORS

EXTERIOR ELEVATION

DETAIL AT REIN. BARS

DETAIL AT PIER

STALL GUARD

DETAIL AT ANCHOR BOLT

COOPERATIVE EXTENSION WORK IN
AGRICULTURE AND HOME ECONOMICS
AND
UNITED STATES DEPARTMENT OF AGRICULTURE COOPERATING

1½ STORY HORSE BARN

N.J. '67   EX. 6024   SHEET 2 OF 3

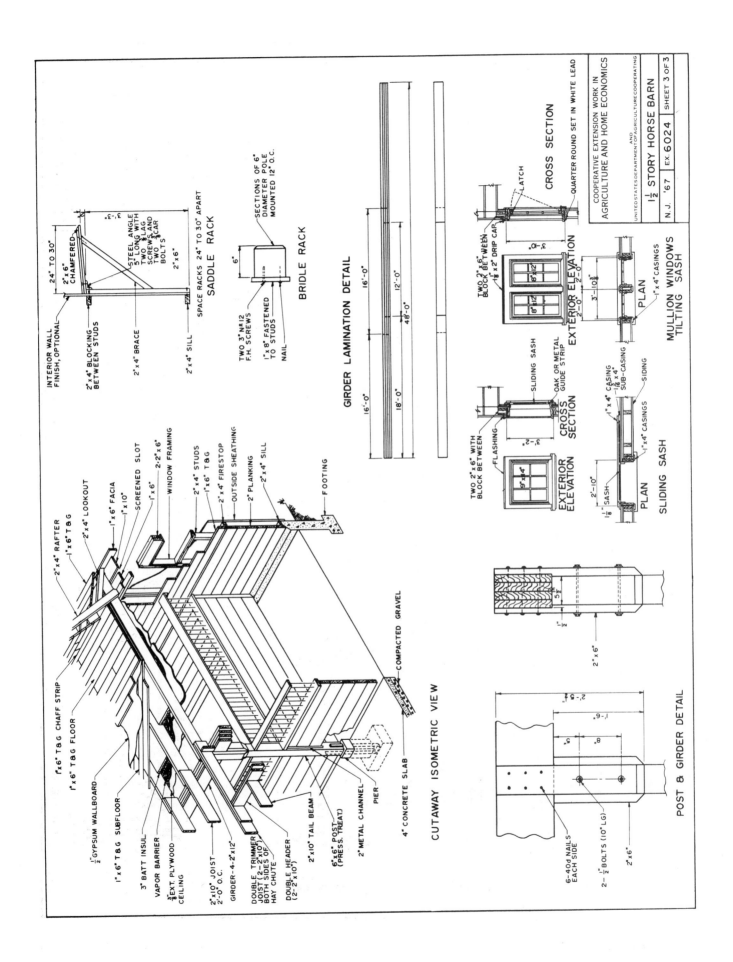

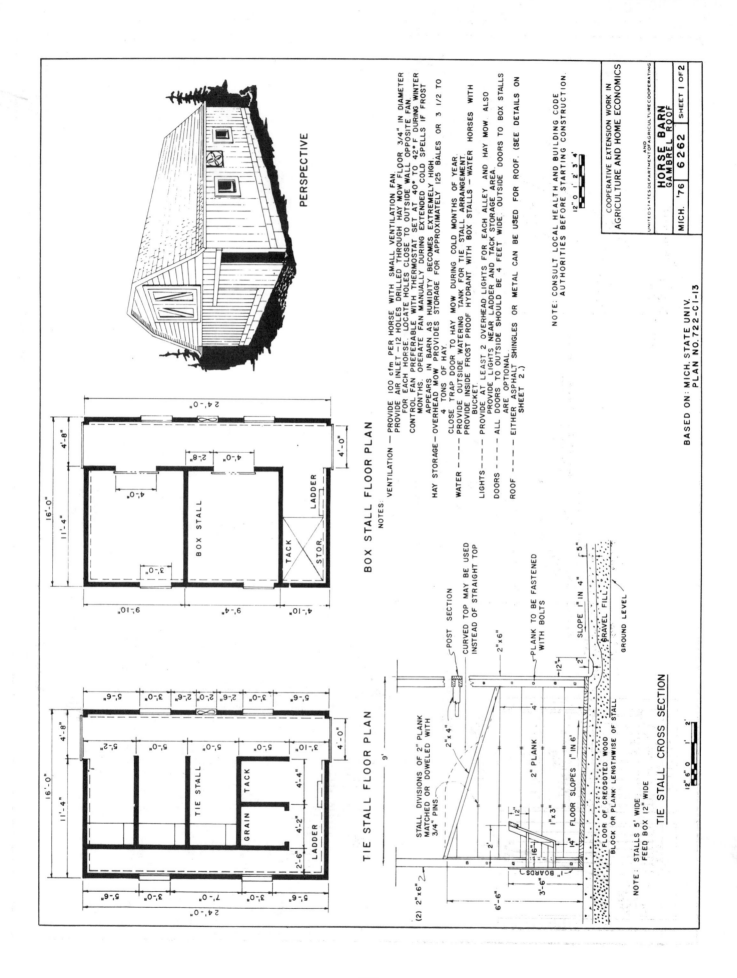

PERSPECTIVE

BOX STALL FLOOR PLAN

BOX STALL

TACK

STOR.

LADDER

TIE STALL FLOOR PLAN

TIE STALL

GRAIN TACK

LADDER

NOTES:

VENTILATION — PROVIDE 100 cfm PER HORSE WITH SMALL VENTILATION FAN. PROVIDE AIR INLET — 12 HOLES DRILLED THROUGH HAY MOW FLOOR 3/4" IN DIAMETER FOR EACH HORSE. LOCATE HOLES CLOSE TO OUTSIDE WALL OPPOSITE FAN. CONTROL FAN PREFERABLE WITH THERMOSTAT SET AT 40° TO 42° F DURING WINTER MONTHS. OPERATE FAN MANUALLY DURING EXTENDED COLD SPELLS IF FROST APPEARS IN BARN AS HUMIDITY BECOMES EXTREMELY HIGH.

HAY STORAGE—OVERHEAD MOW PROVIDES STORAGE FOR APPROXIMATELY 125 BALES OR 3 1/2 TO 4 TONS OF HAY.
CLOSE TRAP DOOR TO HAY MOW DURING COLD MONTHS OF YEAR.

WATER — — — — PROVIDE OUTSIDE WATERING TANK FOR TIE STALL ARRANGEMENT. PROVIDE INSIDE FROST PROOF HYDRANT WITH BOX STALLS — WATER HORSES WITH BUCKET.

LIGHTS — — — PROVIDE AT LEAST 2 OVERHEAD LIGHTS FOR EACH ALLEY AND HAY MOW ALSO PROVIDE LIGHTS NEAR LADDER AND TACK STORAGE AREA.

DOORS — — — ALL DOORS TO OUTSIDE SHOULD BE 4 FEET WIDE. OUTSIDE DOORS TO BOX STALLS ARE OPTIONAL.

ROOF — — — EITHER ASPHALT SHINGLES OR METAL CAN BE USED FOR ROOF. (SEE DETAILS ON SHEET 2.)

NOTE: CONSULT LOCAL HEALTH AND BUILDING CODE AUTHORITIES BEFORE STARTING CONSTRUCTION.

POST SECTION

CURVED TOP MAY BE USED INSTEAD OF STRAIGHT TOP

STALL DIVISIONS OF 2" PLANK MATCHED OR DOWELED WITH 3/4" PINS

(2) 2"x 6"

2"x 4"

2"x 6"

PLANK TO BE FASTENED WITH BOLTS

SLOPE 1" IN 4"

12"

2"

4'

2" PLANK

1" x 3"

FLOOR SLOPES 1" IN 6'

2'

12"

16"

6'-6"

3'-6"

1" BOARDS

4"

5"

GRAVEL FILL

GROUND LEVEL

FLOOR OF CREOSOTED WOOD
BLOCK OR PLANK LENGTHWISE OF STALL

NOTE: STALLS 5' WIDE
FEED BOX 12" WIDE

TIE STALL CROSS SECTION

COOPERATIVE EXTENSION WORK IN
AGRICULTURE AND HOME ECONOMICS
AND
UNITED STATES DEPARTMENT OF AGRICULTURE COOPERATING

HORSE BARN
GAMBREL ROOF

MICH. '76 6262 SHEET 1 OF 2

BASED ON: MICH. STATE UNIV.
PLAN NO. 722-C1-13

162

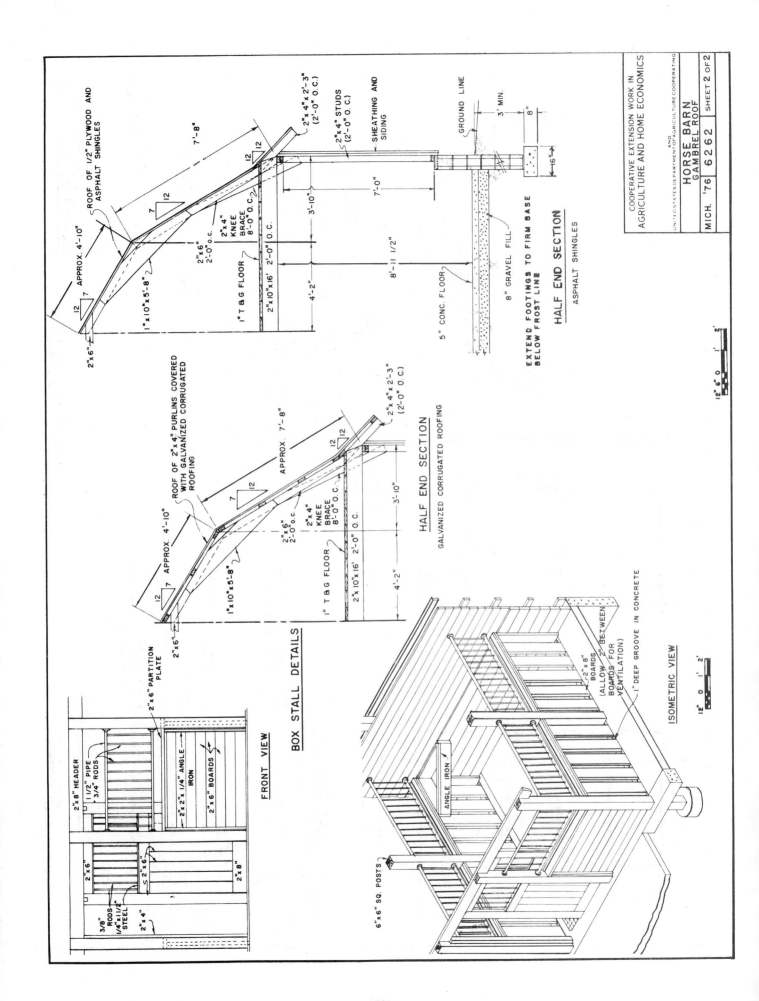

ROOF OF 1/2" PLYWOOD AND ASPHALT SHINGLES

7'-8"

2"x 4" x 2'-3" (2'-0" O.C.)

2"x 4" STUDS (2'-0" O.C.)

SHEATHING AND SIDING

APPROX. 4'-10"

2"x 4" KNEE BRACE 8'-0" O.C.

2"x 6" 2'-0" o.c.

3'-10"

7'-0"

GROUND LINE

3' MIN.

8"

16"

2"x 6"

1"x10"x5'-8"

1" T & G FLOOR

2"x10"x16' 2'-0" O.C.

4'-2"

8'-11 1/2"

5" CONC. FLOOR

8" GRAVEL FILL

EXTEND FOOTINGS TO FIRM BASE BELOW FROST LINE

HALF END SECTION

ASPHALT SHINGLES

COOPERATIVE EXTENSION WORK IN
AGRICULTURE AND HOME ECONOMICS
AND
UNITED STATES DEPARTMENT OF AGRICULTURE COOPERATING

HORSE BARN
GAMBREL ROOF

| MICH. | '76 | 6262 | SHEET 2 OF 2 |

12' 6" 0   1'   2'

ROOF OF 2"x 4" PURLINS COVERED WITH GALVANIZED CORRUGATED ROOFING

APPROX. 7'-8"

2"x 4" x 2'-3" (2'-0" O.C.)

APPROX. 4'-10"

2"x 6" 2'-0" o.c.

2"x 4" KNEE BRACE 8'-0" O.C.

3'-10"

1"x10"x5'-8"

1" T & G FLOOR

2"x10"16' 2'-0" O.C.

4'-2"

HALF END SECTION

GALVANIZED CORRUGATED ROOFING

2"x 6"

BOX STALL DETAILS

2"x 6" PARTITION PLATE

FRONT VIEW

2"x 8" HEADER

1 1/2" PIPE

3/4" RODS

2"x 2"x 1/4" ANGLE IRON

2"x 6" BOARDS

2"x 6"

2"x 6"

2"x 8"

2"x 4"

3/8" RODS 1/4"x11/2" STEEL

2"x 4"

12" DEEP GROOVE IN CONCRETE

2"x 8" BOARDS (ALLOW 2" BETWEEN BOARDS FOR VENTILATION)

ANGLE IRON

6"x 6" SQ. POSTS

ISOMETRIC VIEW

12" 0   1'   2'

163

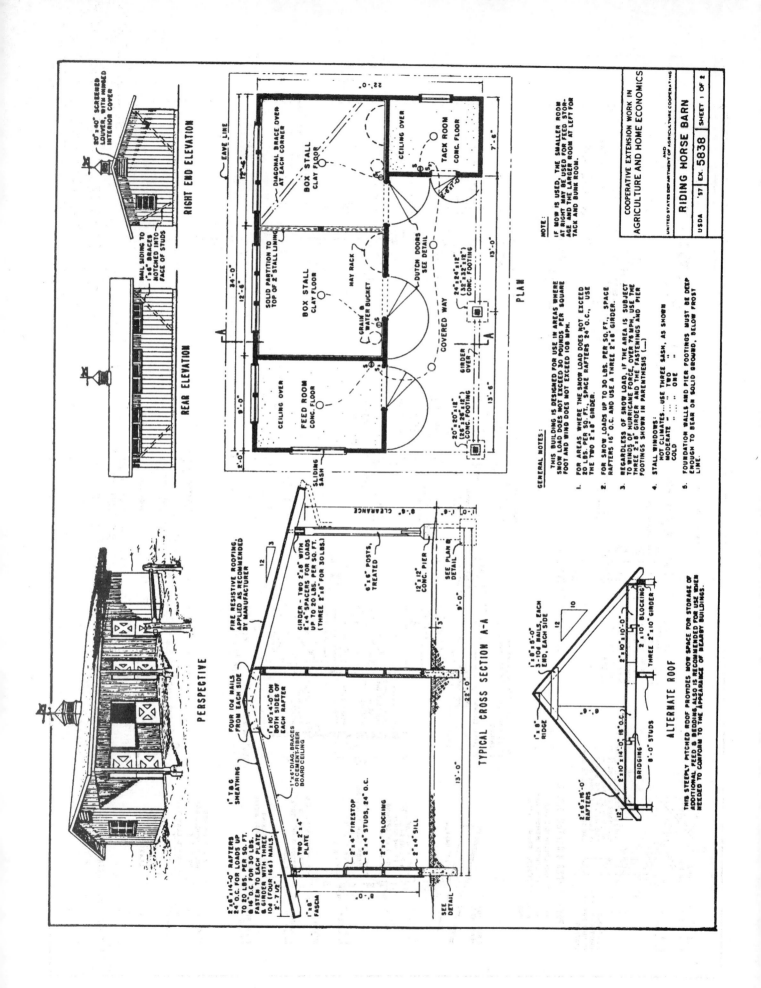

PERSPECTIVE

REAR ELEVATION

RIGHT END ELEVATION

PLAN

TYPICAL CROSS SECTION A-A

ALTERNATE ROOF

This steeply pitched roof provides mow space for storage of additional feed & bedding. Also is recommended for use when needed to conform to the appearance of nearby buildings.

NOTE:
IF MOW IS USED, THE SMALLER ROOM AT RIGHT MAY BE USED FOR FEED STORAGE AND THE LARGER ROOM AT LEFT FOR TACK AND BUNK ROOM.

GENERAL NOTES:
THIS BUILDING IS DESIGNED FOR USE IN AREAS WHERE SNOW LOAD DOES NOT EXCEED 30 POUNDS PER SQUARE FOOT AND WIND DOES NOT EXCEED 100 MPH.

1. FOR AREAS WHERE THE SNOW LOAD DOES NOT EXCEED 20 LBS. PER SQ. FT., SPACE RAFTERS 24" O.C., USE THE TWO 2"x8" GIRDER.

2. FOR SNOW LOADS UP TO 30 LBS. PER SQ. FT., SPACE RAFTERS 16" O.C. AND USE A THREE 2"x8" GIRDER.

3. REGARDLESS OF SNOW LOAD, IF THE AREA IS SUBJECT TO WINDS OF HURRICANE FORCE, OVER 75 MPH, USE THE THREE 2"x8" GIRDER AND THE FASTENINGS AND PIER FOOTINGS SHOWN IN PARENTHESIS (   ).

4. STALL WINDOWS....USE THREE SASH, AS SHOWN
   HOT CLIMATES.......TWO
   MODERATE.......TWO
   COLD.......ONE

6. FOUNDATION WALLS AND PIER FOOTINGS MUST BE DEEP ENOUGH TO BEAR ON SOLID GROUND, BELOW FROST LINE.

COOPERATIVE EXTENSION WORK IN AGRICULTURE AND HOME ECONOMICS
AND
UNITED STATES DEPARTMENT OF AGRICULTURE COOPERATING

RIDING HORSE BARN

USDA | '57 | EX. 5838 | SHEET 1 OF 2

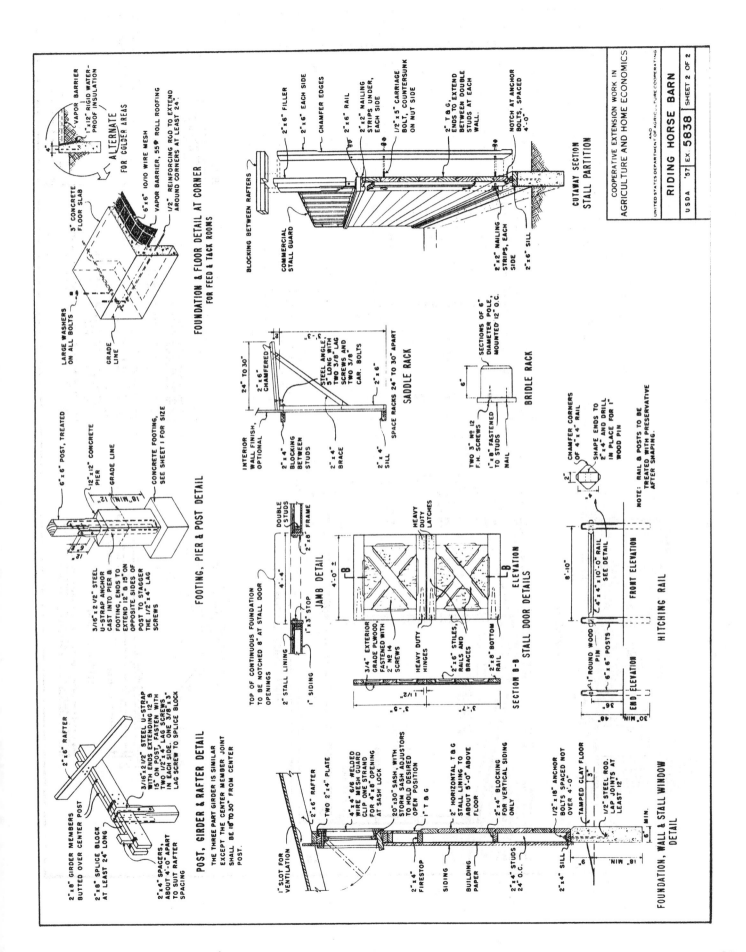

ALTERNATE
for colder areas

VAPOR BARRIER
1"x12" RIGID WATER-
PROOF INSULATION

3" CONCRETE
FLOOR SLAB

6"x6" 10/10 WIRE MESH
VAPOR BARRIER, 55# ROLL ROOFING
1/2" REINFORCING ROD TO EXTEND
AROUND CORNERS AT LEAST 24"

LARGE WASHERS
ON ALL BOLTS

GRADE
LINE

FOUNDATION & FLOOR DETAIL AT CORNER
FOR FEED & TACK ROOMS

BLOCKING BETWEEN RAFTERS

2"x6" FILLER
2"x6" EACH SIDE
CHAMFER EDGES
2"x6" RAIL
2"x2" NAILING
STRIPS UNDER,
EACH SIDE
1/2"x5" CARRIAGE
BOLT, COUNTERSUNK
ON NUT SIDE
2" T&G,
ENDS TO EXTEND
BETWEEN DOUBLE
STUDS AT EACH
WALL.
NOTCH AT ANCHOR
BOLTS, SPACED
4'-0"

COMMERCIAL
STALL GUARD

2"x2" NAILING
STRIPS, EACH
SIDE
2"x6" SILL

CUTAWAY SECTION
STALL PARTITION

6"x6" POST, TREATED

3/16"x2 1/2" STEEL
U-STRAP ANCHOR
CAST INTO PIER &
FOOTING, ENDS TO
EXTEND 12" & 15" ON
OPPOSITE SIDES OF
POST TO STAGGER
THE 1/2"x4" LAG
SCREWS

12"x12" CONCRETE
PIER
GRADE LINE

CONCRETE FOOTING,
SEE SHEET I FOR SIZE

FOOTING, PIER & POST DETAIL

INTERIOR
WALL FINISH,
OPTIONAL

24" TO 30"

2"x6"
CHAMFERED

STEEL ANGLE
5" LONG WITH
TWO 3/8" LAG
SCREWS AND
TWO 3/8"
CAR. BOLTS

2"x6"

2"x4"
BLOCKING
BETWEEN
STUDS

2"x4"
BRACE

2"x4" SILL

SADDLE RACK
SPACE RACKS 24" TO 30" APART

SECTIONS OF 6"
DIAMETER POLE,
MOUNTED 12" O.C.

6"

TWO 3" No 12
F.H. SCREWS
1"x8" FASTENED
TO STUDS
NAIL

BRIDLE RACK

2"x6" RAFTER
2"x8" GIRDER MEMBERS
BUTTED OVER CENTER POST
2"x8" SPLICE BLOCK
AT LEAST 24" LONG
2"x4" SPACERS,
ABOUT 4'-0" APART
TO SUIT RAFTER
SPACING

3/16"x2 1/2" STEEL U-STRAP
WITH ENDS EXTENDING 12" &
15" ON POST, FASTEN WITH
TWO 1/2"x4" LAG SCREWS
IN EACH SIDE. USE 3/8"x3"
LAG SCREW TO SPLICE BLOCK

POST, GIRDER & RAFTER DETAIL

THE THREE PART GIRDER IS SIMILAR
EXCEPT THE CENTER MEMBER JOINT
SHALL BE 18"TO 30" FROM CENTER
POST.

TOP OF CONTINUOUS FOUNDATION
TO BE NOTCHED 8" AT STALL DOOR
OPENINGS

DOUBLE
STUDS
2"x8" FRAME

2" STALL LINING
1" SIDING
1"x3" STOP

JAMB DETAIL

4'-4"

4'-0" ±

3/4" EXTERIOR
GRADE PLYWOOD,
FASTENED WITH
2" No 14
SCREWS

HEAVY DUTY
HINGES

HEAVY
DUTY
LATCHES

2"x6" STILES,
RAILS AND
BRACES
2"x8" BOTTOM
RAIL

ELEVATION

3'-8"

3'-7"

1 1/2"

SECTION B-B

STALL DOOR DETAILS

8'-10"

1" ROUND WOOD
PIN
4"x4" x10'-0" RAIL
SEE DETAIL

6"x6" POSTS

FRONT ELEVATION

END ELEVATION

30" MIN.

48"

36"

CHAMFER CORNERS
OF 4"x4" RAIL

SHAPE ENDS TO
2"x4" AND DRILL
FOR 1"
WOOD PIN

2"

NOTE: RAIL & POSTS TO BE
TREATED WITH PRESERVATIVE
AFTER SHAPING.

HITCHING RAIL

1" SLOT FOR
VENTILATION

2"x6" RAFTER
TWO 2"x4" PLATE

4"x4" 6/6 WELDED
WIRE MESH GUARD
CLIP ONE STRAND
FOR 4"x8" OPENING
AT SASH LOCK

20"x30" SASH, WITH
STORM SASH ADJUSTORS
TO HOLD DESIRED
OPEN POSITION

2" HORIZONTAL T&G
STALL LINING TO
ABOUT 5'-0" ABOVE
FLOOR
1" T&G

2"x4" BLOCKING
FOR VERTICAL SIDING
ONLY

1/2"x18" ANCHOR
BOLTS SPACED NOT
OVER 4'-0"

TAMPED CLAY FLOOR
1/2" STEEL ROD,
LAP JOINTS AT
LEAST 12"

2"x4"
FIRESTOP
SIDING
BUILDING
PAPER
2"x4" STUDS
24" O.C.
2"x4" SILL

6" MIN.

3"

6"

18" MIN.

FOUNDATION, WALL & STALL WINDOW
DETAIL

COOPERATIVE EXTENSION WORK IN
AGRICULTURE AND HOME ECONOMICS
AND
UNITED STATES DEPARTMENT OF AGRIC__TURE COOPERATING

RIDING HORSE BARN   SHEET 2 OF 2

USDA '57 EX. 5838

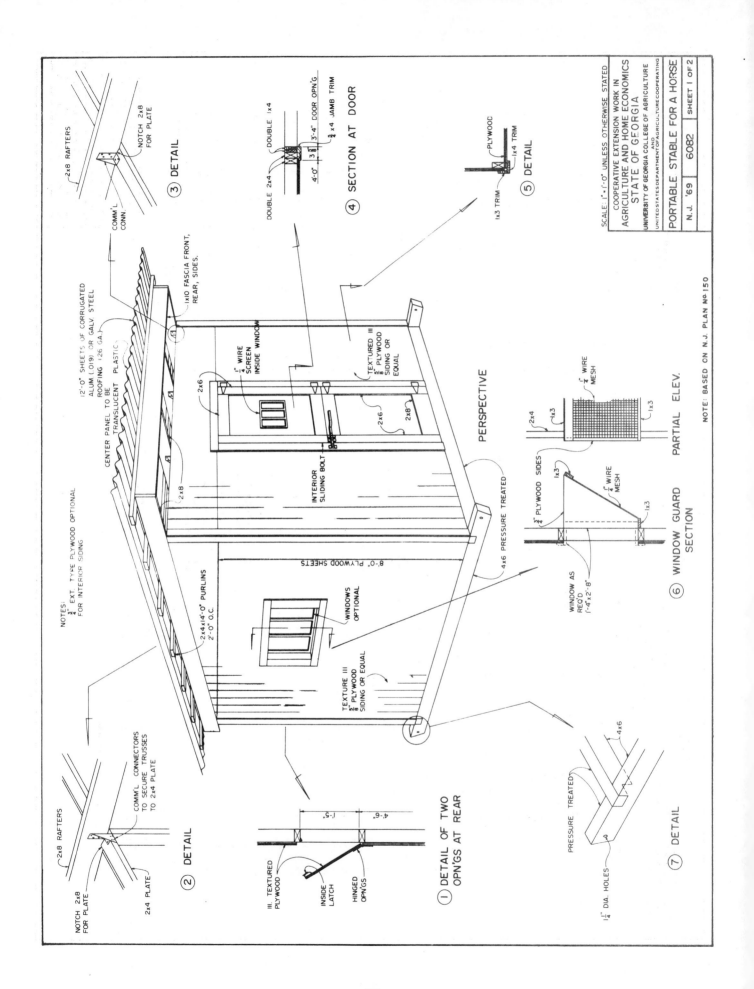

NOTES:
2½" EXT TYPE PLYWOOD OPTIONAL
½" FOR INTERIOR SIDING

12'-0" SHEETS OF CORRUGATED
ALUM (.019) OR GALV. STEEL
ROOFING (.26 GA.)
CENTER PANEL TO BE
TRANSLUCENT PLASTIC

NOTCH 2x8
FOR PLATE

2x8 RAFTERS

COMM'L
CONN.

③ DETAIL

DOUBLE 1x4
DOUBLE 2x4
3'-4" DOOR OPN'G
2 x 4 JAMB TRIM
4'-0"
3'-8"

④ SECTION AT DOOR

1x3 TRIM
PLYWOOD
1x4 TRIM

⑤ DETAIL

1x10 FASCIA FRONT,
REAR, SIDES.

2x6

1" WIRE
4 SCREEN
INSIDE WINDOW

TEXTURED III
5" PLYWOOD
8 SIDING OR
EQUAL

2x6

2x8

INTERIOR
SLIDING BOLT

2x8

PERSPECTIVE

2x4x14'-0" PURLINS
2'-0" O.C.

8'-0" PLYWOOD SHEETS

WINDOWS
OPTIONAL

TEXTURE III
5" PLYWOOD
8 SIDING OR EQUAL

4x6 PRESSURE TREATED

1" WIRE
4 MESH

2x4   1x3   1x3

PARTIAL ELEV.

5" PLYWOOD SIDES
8

1x3

1" WIRE
4 MESH

1x3

WINDOW AS
REQ'D
1'-4"x2'-8"

⑥ WINDOW GUARD
SECTION

NOTE: BASED ON N.J. PLAN N⁰ 150

2x8 RAFTERS

NOTCH 2x8
FOR PLATE

2x4 PLATE

COMM'L CONNECTORS
TO SECURE TRUSSES
TO 2x4 PLATE

② DETAIL

1'-5"
4'-6"

III. TEXTURED
PLYWOOD

INSIDE
LATCH

HINGED
OPN'GS

① DETAIL OF TWO
OPN'GS AT REAR

PRESSURE TREATED

4x6

1¼" DIA. HOLES

⑦ DETAIL

SCALE: 1"=1'-0" UNLESS OTHERWISE STATED
COOPERATIVE EXTENSION WORK IN
AGRICULTURE AND HOME ECONOMICS
STATE OF GEORGIA
UNIVERSITY OF GEORGIA COLLEGE OF AGRICULTURE
AND
UNITED STATES DEPARTMENT OF AGRICULTURE COOPERATING

PORTABLE STABLE FOR A HORSE
N.J.   '69   6082   SHEET 1 OF 2

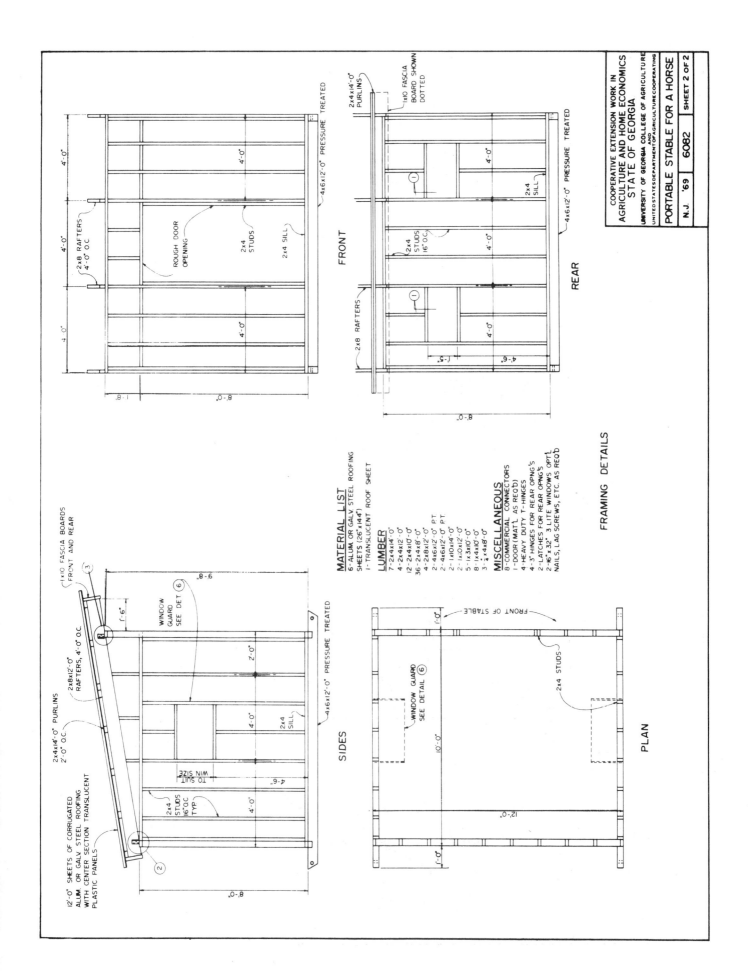

FRONT

REAR

SIDES

PLAN

FRAMING DETAILS

MATERIAL LIST

6 - ALUM OR GALV STEEL ROOFING SHEETS (26"×144")
1 - TRANSLUCENT ROOF SHEET

LUMBER
7 - 2×4×14'-0"
4 - 2×4×12'-0"
12 - 2×4×10'-0"
36 - 2×4×8'-0"
4 - 2×8×12'-0"
2 - 4×6×12'-0" PT
2 - 4×6×12'-0" PT
2 - 1×10×14'-0"
5 - 1×3×10'-0"
8 - 1×4×10'-0"
3 - ¾×4×8'-0"

MISCELLANEOUS
8 - COMMERCIAL CONNECTORS
1 - DOOR (MAT'L AS REQ'D)
4 - HEAVY DUTY T-HINGES
4 - 3" HINGES FOR REAR OPNG'S
2 - LATCHES FOR REAR OPNG'S
2 - 16"×32" 3 LITE WINDOWS OPT'L
NAILS, LAG SCREWS, ETC. AS REQ'D

COOPERATIVE EXTENSION WORK IN
AGRICULTURE AND HOME ECONOMICS
STATE OF GEORGIA
UNIVERSITY OF GEORGIA COLLEGE OF AGRICULTURE
AND
UNITED STATES DEPARTMENT OF AGRICULTURE COOPERATING

PORTABLE STABLE FOR A HORSE
N.J. '69 | 6082 | SHEET 2 of 2

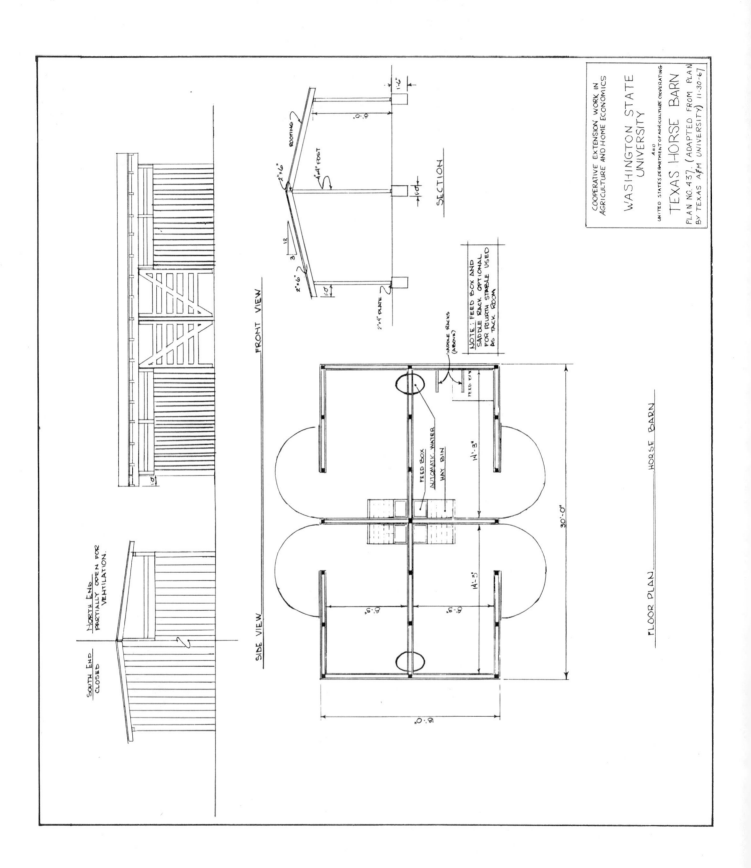

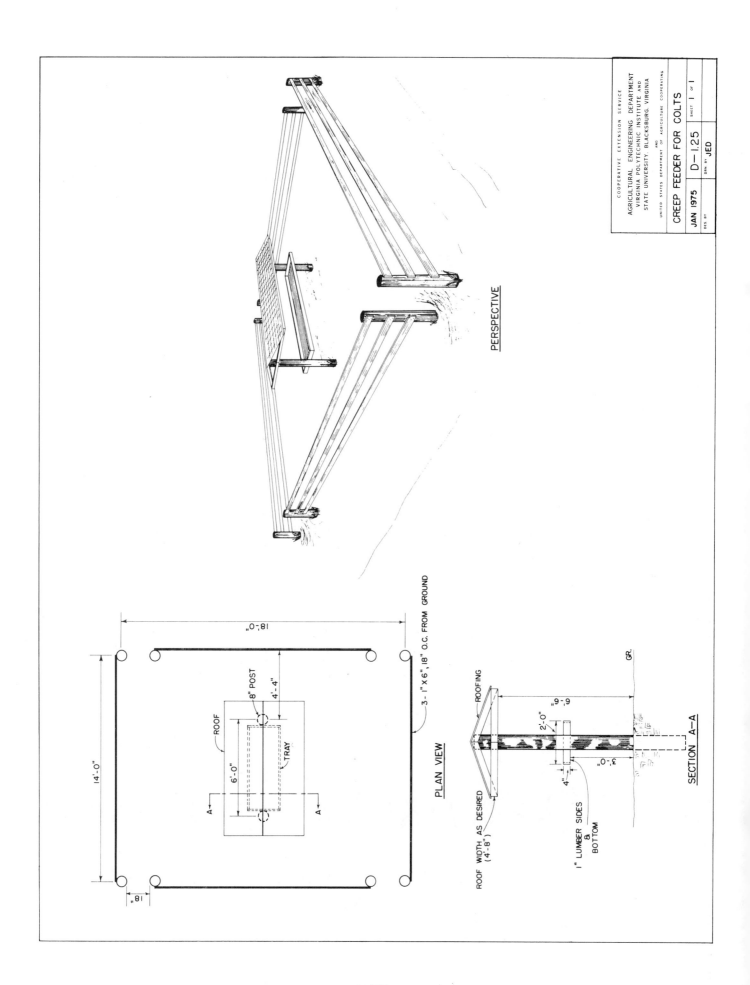

PERSPECTIVE

COOPERATIVE EXTENSION SERVICE

AGRICULTURAL ENGINEERING DEPARTMENT
VIRGINIA POLYTECHNIC INSTITUTE AND
STATE UNIVERSITY, BLACKSBURG, VIRGINIA
AND
UNITED STATES DEPARTMENT OF AGRICULTURE COOPERATING

CREEP FEEDER FOR COLTS | D—1.25 | SHEET 1 OF 1

JAN 1975 | DRN BY JED

DES BY

18'-0"

14'-0"

18"

ROOF

8" POST

4'-4"

6'-0"

TRAY

A   A

PLAN VIEW

3- 1"x6", 18" O.C. FROM GROUND

ROOFING

ROOF WIDTH AS DESIRED
(4'-8")

GR.

9'-6"

2'-0"

4"

3'-0"

1" LUMBER SIDES
&
BOTTOM

SECTION A-A

169

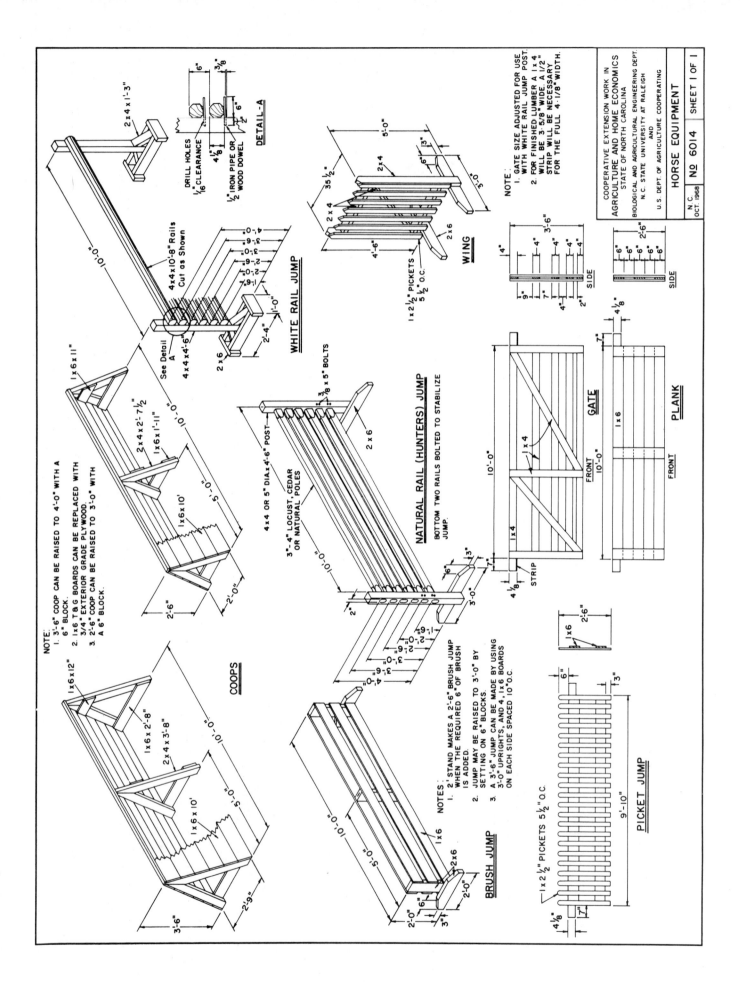

DETAIL-A

DRILL HOLES
1/16 CLEARANCE
1/2" IRON PIPE OR
1/2 WOOD DOWEL

WHITE RAIL JUMP

4x4x10'-8"Rails
Cut as Shown

See Detail A

4x4x4'-6"

2x4x1'-3"

WING

2x4

2x4

2x6

1x2 1/2 PICKETS
5 1/2" O.C.

NOTE:
1. GATE SIZE ADJUSTED FOR USE
WITH WHITE RAIL JUMP POST.
2. FOR FINISHED LUMBER A 1x4
WILL BE 3-5/8" WIDE. A 1/2"
STRIP WILL BE NECESSARY
FOR THE FULL 4-1/8" WIDTH.

SIDE

SIDE

COOPERATIVE EXTENSION WORK IN
AGRICULTURE AND HOME ECONOMICS
STATE OF NORTH CAROLINA
BIOLOGICAL AND AGRICULTURAL ENGINEERING DEPT.
N.C. STATE UNIVERSITY AT RALEIGH
AND
U.S. DEPT. OF AGRICULTURE COOPERATING

HORSE EQUIPMENT

N.C.
OCT. 1968   No 6014   SHEET 1 OF 1

COOPS

NOTE:
1. 3'-6" COOP CAN BE RAISED TO 4'-0" WITH A
6" BLOCK.
2. 1x6 T&G BOARDS CAN BE REPLACED WITH
3/4" EXTERIOR GRADE PLYWOOD.
3. 2'-6" COOP CAN BE RAISED TO 3'-0" WITH
A 6" BLOCK.

1x6x11"

2x4x2'-7 1/2"

1x6x1'-11"

1x6x10'

1x6x12"

1x6x2'-8"

2x4x3'-8"

1x6x10'

NATURAL RAIL (HUNTERS) JUMP

BOTTOM TWO RAILS BOLTED TO STABILIZE
JUMP.

3/8 x 5" BOLTS

2x6

3"-4" LOCUST, CEDAR
OR NATURAL POLES

4x4 OR 5" DIA.x4'-6" POST

2x6

GATE

FRONT

1x4

1x4

STRIP

PLANK

FRONT

1x6

BRUSH JUMP

NOTES:
1. 2' STAND MAKES A 2'-6" BRUSH JUMP
WHEN THE REQUIRED 6" OF BRUSH
IS ADDED.
2. JUMP MAY BE RAISED TO 3'-0" BY
SETTING ON 6" BLOCKS.
3. A 3'-6" JUMP CAN BE MADE BY USING
3'-0" UPRIGHTS, AND 4, 1x6 BOARDS
ON EACH SIDE SPACED 10"O.C.

1x6

2x6

PICKET JUMP

1x2 1/2" PICKETS 5 1/2" O.C.

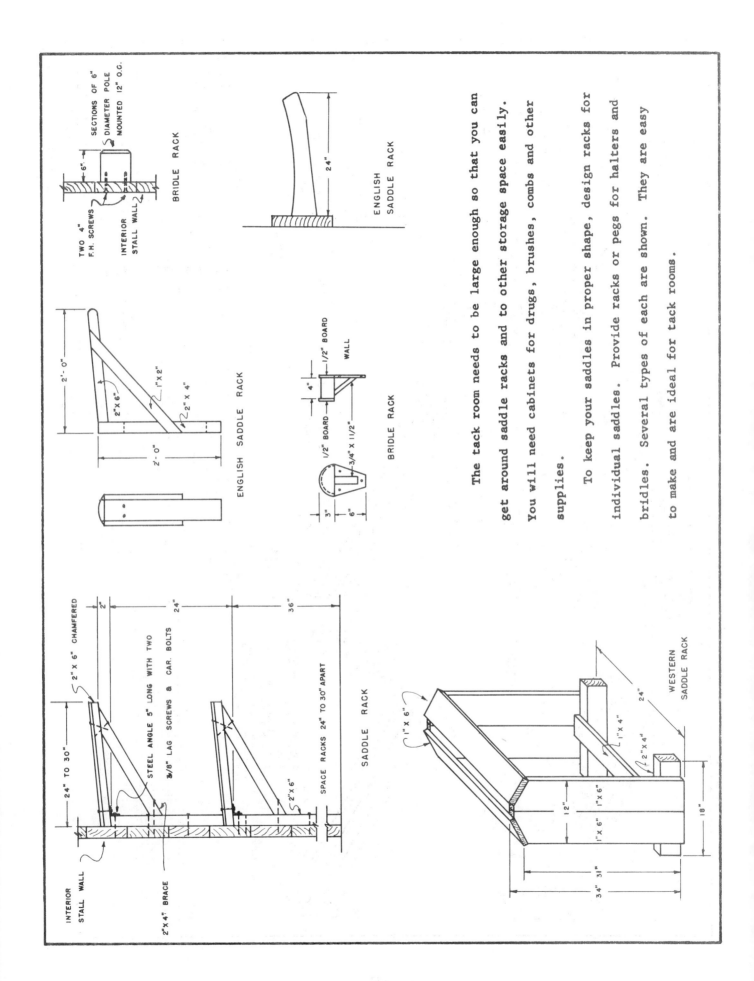

The tack room needs to be large enough so that you can get around saddle racks and to other storage space easily. You will need cabinets for drugs, brushes, combs and other supplies.

To keep your saddles in proper shape, design racks for individual saddles. Provide racks or pegs for halters and bridles. Several types of each are shown. They are easy to make and are ideal for tack rooms.

SECTIONS OF 6"
DIAMETER POLE
MOUNTED 12" O.C.

TWO 4"
F.H. SCREWS

INTERIOR
STALL WALL

BRIDLE RACK

ENGLISH
SADDLE RACK

24"

2'- 0"

2" X 6"

1" X 2"

2" X 4"

2'- 0"

ENGLISH SADDLE RACK

1/2" BOARD

WALL

4"

1/2" BOARD

3/4" X 11/2"

3"

6"

BRIDLE RACK

INTERIOR
STALL WALL

2" X 4" BRACE

2" X 6" CHAMFERED

2"

STEEL ANGLE 5" LONG WITH TWO
3/8" LAG SCREWS & CAR. BOLTS

24"

36"

24" TO 30"

2" X 6"

SPACE RACKS 24" TO 30" APART

SADDLE RACK

1" X 6"

WESTERN
SADDLE RACK

24"

1" X 4"

2" X 4"

12"

1" X 6"

18"

1" X 6"

34" 31"

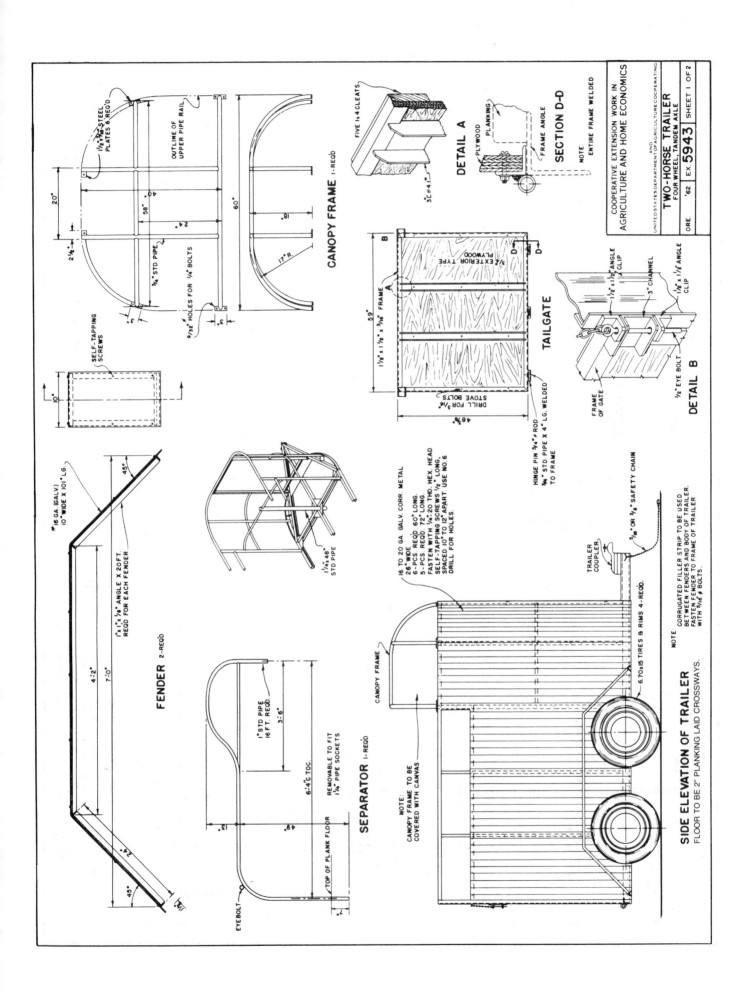

CANOPY FRAME 1-REQ'D

SELF-TAPPING SCREWS

FENDER 2-REQ'D

#16 GA (GALV) 10" WIDE X 10'1" LG

1" x 1" x 1/8" ANGLE X 20 FT. REQ'D FOR EACH FENDER

SEPARATOR 1-REQ'D

1" STD PIPE 16 FT. REQ'D

Removable to fit 1 1/4" pipe sockets

EYEBOLT

TOP OF PLANK FLOOR

1 1/4" x 48" STD PIPE

DETAIL A

FIVE 1x4 CLEATS

PLYWOOD

PLANKING

FRAME ANGLE

SECTION D-D

NOTE: ENTIRE FRAME WELDED

TAILGATE

3/4" EXTERIOR TYPE PLYWOOD

1 1/2" x 1 1/2" x 3/16" FRAME

DRILL FOR 5/16" STOVE BOLTS

HINGE PIN 3/4" ROD
3/4" STD PIPE x 4" LG. WELDED TO FRAME

DETAIL B

1/2" x 1 1/2" ANGLE CLIP

3" CHANNEL

1/2" x 1 1/2" ANGLE CLIP

FRAME OF GATE

1/2" EYE BOLT

SIDE ELEVATION OF TRAILER
FLOOR TO BE 2" PLANKING LAID CROSSWAYS.

16 TO 20 GA. GALV. CORR. METAL
26" WIDE
6-PCS. REQ'D. 60" LONG.
5-PCS. REQ'D. 72" LONG.
FASTEN WITH 1/4"-20 THD. HEX. HEAD SELF-TAPPING SCREWS 1/2" LONG, SPACED 10" TO 12" APART USE NO. 6 DRILL FOR HOLES.

CANOPY FRAME

NOTE:
CANOPY FRAME TO BE COVERED WITH CANVAS

TRAILER COUPLER

5/16" OR 3/8" SAFETY CHAIN

6.70x15 TIRES 8 RIMS 4-REQ'D.

NOTE: CORRUGATED FILLER STRIP TO BE USED BETWEEN FENDERS AND BODY OF TRAILER. FASTEN FENDER TO FRAME OF TRAILER WITH 5/16" ∮ BOLTS.

COOPERATIVE EXTENSION WORK IN
AGRICULTURE AND HOME ECONOMICS
AND
UNITED STATES DEPARTMENT OF AGRICULTURE COOPERATING

TWO-HORSE TRAILER
FOUR WHEEL, TANDEM AXLE

ORE. '62 EX. 5943 SHEET I OF 2

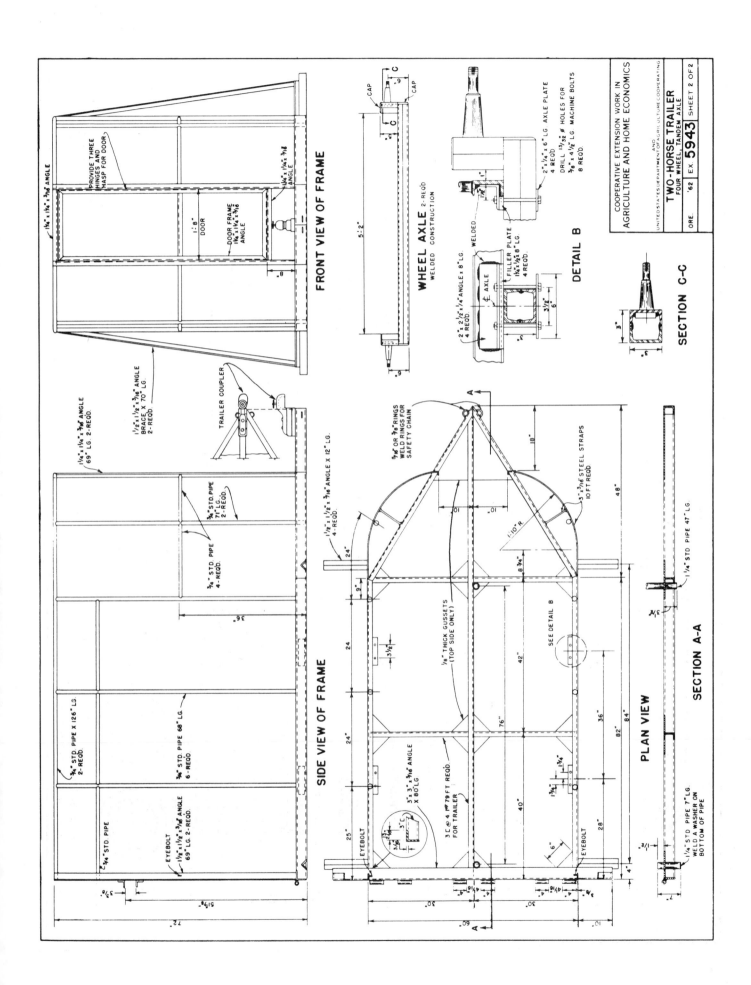

FRONT VIEW OF FRAME

SIDE VIEW OF FRAME

WHEEL AXLE 2-REQ'D.
WELDED CONSTRUCTION

DETAIL B

SECTION C-C

PLAN VIEW

SECTION A-A

COOPERATIVE EXTENSION WORK IN
AGRICULTURE AND HOME ECONOMICS
AND
UNITED STATES DEPARTMENT OF AGRICULTURE COOPERATING

TWO-HORSE TRAILER
FOUR WHEEL, TANDEM AXLE

ORE.   '62   EX 5943   SHEET 2 OF 2

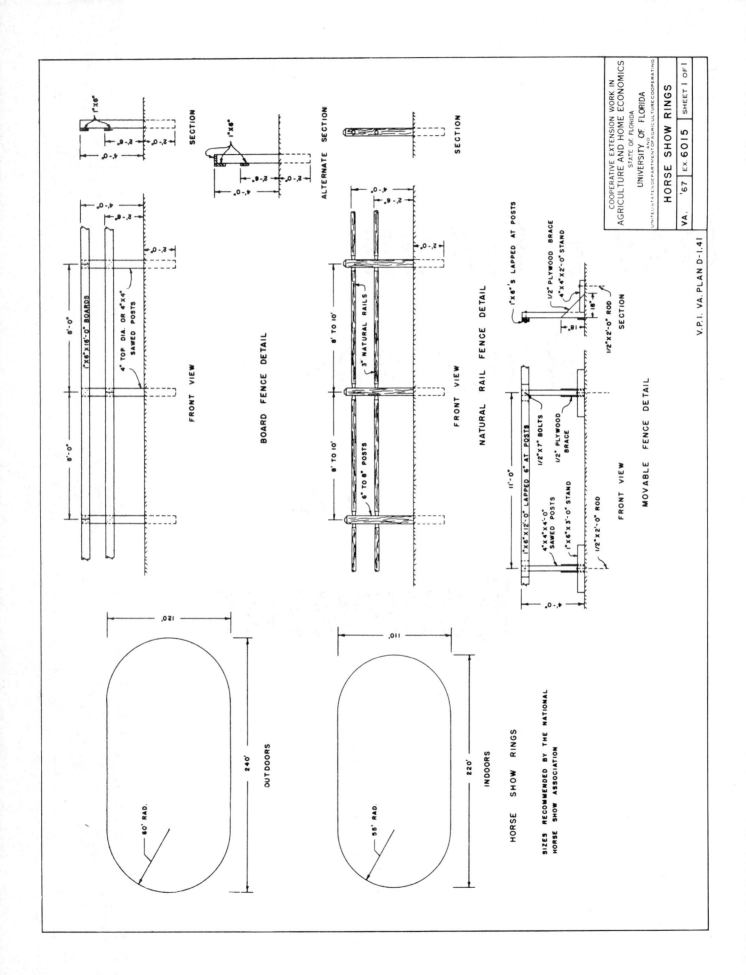

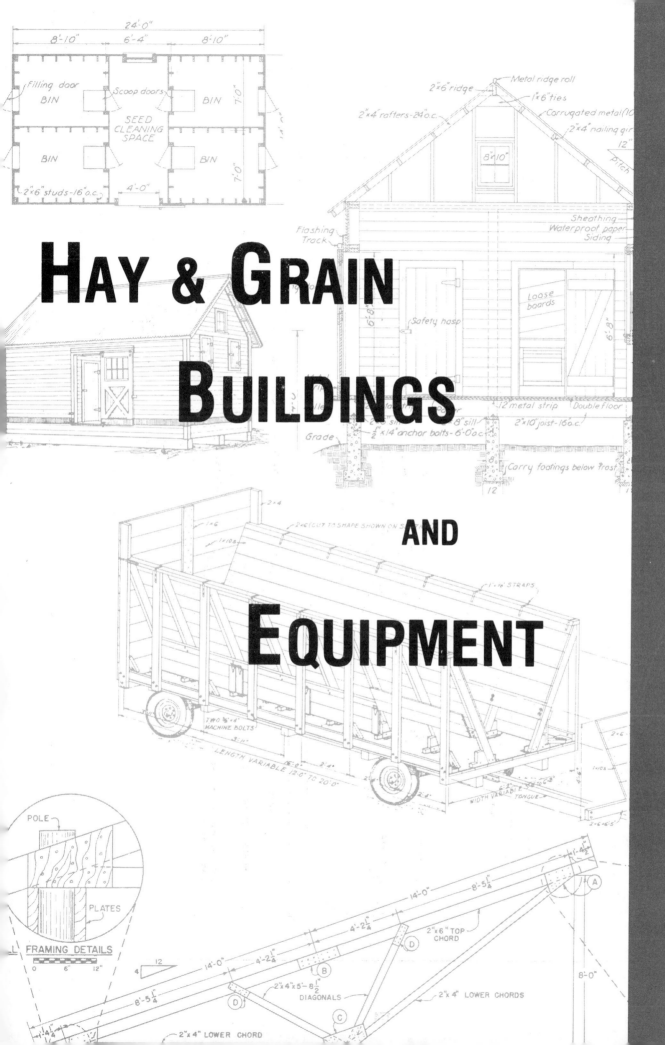

24'-0"

8'-10" 6'-4" 8'-10"

Fitting door
BIN

Scoop doors

BIN

SEED
CLEANING
SPACE

BIN

BIN

2"x6" studs-16" o.c.

4'-0"

7'-0"

7'-0"

2"x6" ridge

Metal ridge roll

1"x6" ties

Corrugated metal(10

2"x4" rafters-24"o.c.

2"x4" nailing gir

8'-10"

12

Pitch

Flashing
Track

Sheathing
Waterproof paper
Siding

Safety hasp

Loose
boards

6'-8"

12 metal strip

Double floor

Grade

2"x10" joist-16"o.c.

8" sill

½"x14" anchor bolts-6'-0"o.c.

Carry footings below frost

12

2"x4

2x6(CUT TO SHAPE SHOWN ON S

1"x6

1"x10 &

1"x1" STRAPS

POLE

TWO ⅜"x4"
MACHINE BOLTS

3'-0"

LENGTH VARIABLE 12'-0" TO 20'-0"

2'-4"

WIDTH VARIABLE

2"-6

1x10 &

TONGUE

2"-6"x6-5

PLATES

FRAMING DETAILS

0   6"   12"

14'-0"

8'-5¼"

A

4'-2¼"

D

2"x6" TOP
CHORD

8'-0"

12

14'-0"

4'-2¼"

B

4

2"x4"x5-8½"

DIAGONALS

2"x4" LOWER CHORDS

8'-5¼"

D

C

2"x4" LOWER CHORD

HAY & GRAIN
BUILDINGS
AND
EQUIPMENT

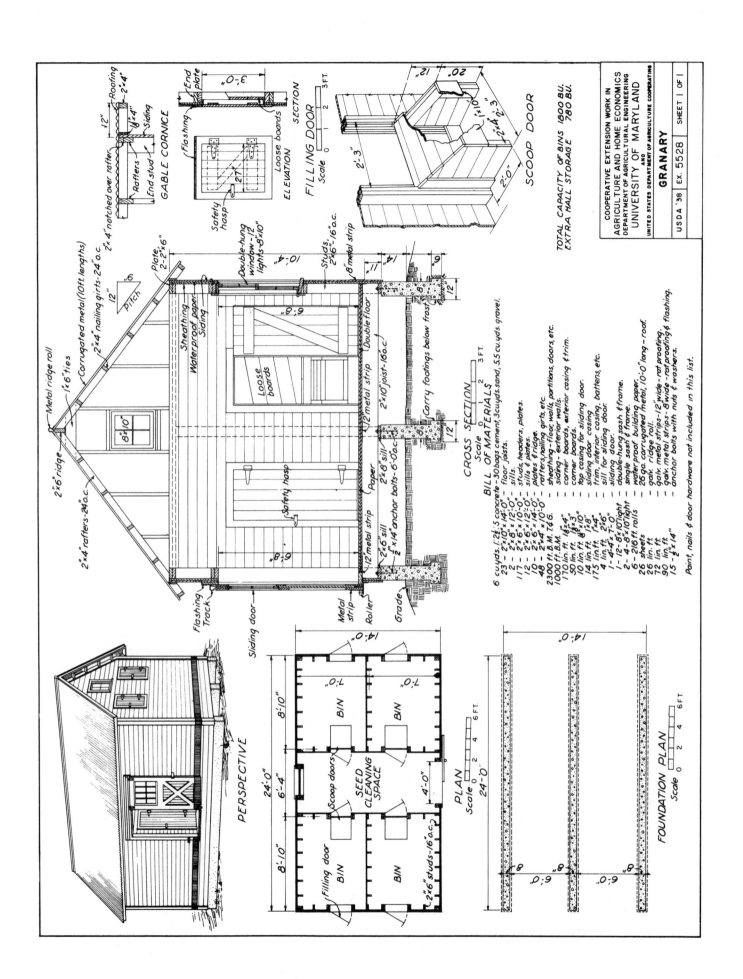

11

GABLE CORNICE

FILLING DOOR
SECTION
ELEVATION

SCOOP DOOR

GRANARY

COOPERATIVE EXTENSION WORK IN
AGRICULTURE AND HOME ECONOMICS
DEPARTMENT OF AGRICULTURAL ENGINEERING
UNIVERSITY OF MARYLAND
AND
UNITED STATES DEPARTMENT OF AGRICULTURE COOPERATING

TOTAL CAPACITY OF BINS 1800 BU.
EXTRA HALL STORAGE 780 BU.

USDA '38   Ex. 5528   SHEET 1 OF 1

CROSS SECTION
Scale ½" 2' 3 FT.

BILL OF MATERIALS

6 cu.yds. 1:2½:5 concrete - 30 bags cement; 3 cu.yds.sand; 5.5 cu.yds. gravel.
23 - 2"x4"x14'-0" floor joists.
 2 - 2"x8"x12'-0" sills.
117 - 2"x6"x12'-0" studs, headers, plates.
 12 - 2"x6"x12'-0" sills & plates.
 10 - 2"x6"x14'-0" plates & ridge.
 48 - 2"x4"x10'-0" rafters, nailing girts, etc.
2300 ft. B.M. T.&G. sheathing-floor, walls, partitions, doors, etc.
1000 ft. B.M. siding-exterior walls.
170 lin. ft. 1"x4" corner boards.
 30 lin. ft. 1"x3" corner boards, exterior casing & trim.
 10 lin. ft. 8"x10" top casing for sliding door.
 14 lin. ft. 1"x8" sliding door casing.
175 lin. ft. 1"x4" trim, interior casing, battens, etc.
  4 lin. ft. 2"x6" sill for sliding door.
 1 - 1'-4"x7'-0" sliding door.
 1 - 12-8"x10"light double-hung sash & frame.
 2 - 4-8"x10"light single sash & frame.
 26 - 216 ft. rolls waterproof building paper.
 26 - sheets 26 ga. corrugated metal, 10'-0"long-roof.
 72 lin. ft. galk. ridge roll.
 90 lin. ft. galv. metal strips-12"wide-rat proofing.
 15 - ½"x14" galv. metal strips-8"wide-rat proofing & flashing.
anchor bolts with nuts & washers.

Paint, nails & door hardware not included in this list.

PERSPECTIVE

PLAN
Scale 0 2 4 6 FT.

FOUNDATION PLAN
Scale 0 2 4 6 FT.

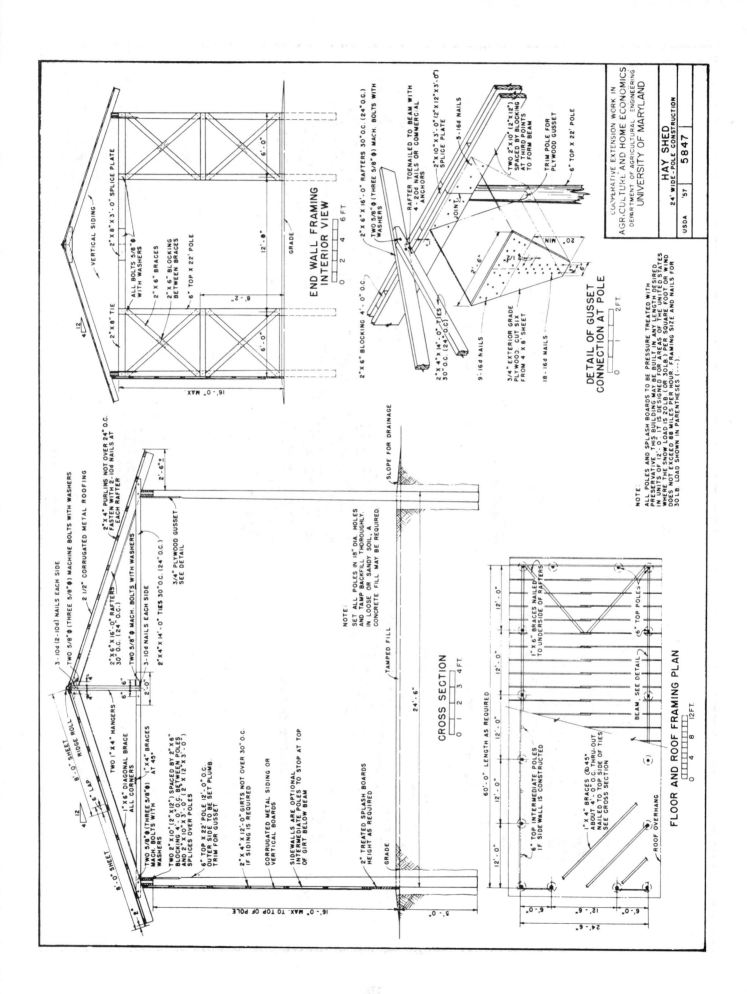

END WALL FRAMING INTERIOR VIEW

VERTICAL SIDING

2"X8"X3'-0" SPLICE PLATE

ALL BOLTS 5/8"ø WITH WASHERS

2"X6" BRACES

2"X6" BLOCKING BETWEEN BRACES

6" TOP X 22' POLE

2"X8" TIE

GRADE

16'-0" MAX.

2"X6" BLOCKING 4'-0" O.C.

2"X6"X16'-0" RAFTERS 30"O.C. (24" O.C.)

TWO 5/8"ø (THREE 5/8"ø) MACH. BOLTS WITH WASHERS

RAFTER TOENAILED TO BEAM WITH 4-20d NAILS OR COMMERCIAL ANCHORS

2"X10"X3'-0"(2"X12"X3'-0") SPLICE PLATE

5-16d NAILS

TWO 2"X10" (2"X12") SPACED BY BLOCKING AT THIRD POINTS TO FORM BEAM

TRIM POLE FOR PLYWOOD GUSSET

6" TOP X 22' POLE

2"X4"X14'-0" TIES 30"O.C. (24" O.C.)

9-16d NAILS

3/4" EXTERIOR GRADE PLYWOOD. CUT SIX FROM A 4 X 8 SHEET

18-16d NAILS

DETAIL OF GUSSET CONNECTION AT POLE

NOTE:
ALL POLES AND SPLASH BOARDS TO BE PRESSURE TREATED WITH PRESERVATIVE. THIS BUILDING MAY BE BUILT IN ANY LENGTH DESIRED IN UNITS OF 12'-0". IT IS DESIGNED FOR AREAS OF THE STATES WHERE THE SNOW LOAD IS 20 LB (OR 30 LB) PER SQUARE FOOT OR WIND DOES NOT EXCEED 88 MILES PER HOUR. FRAMING SIZE AND NAILS FOR 30 LB. LOAD SHOWN IN PARENTHESES (---).

3-10d (2-10d) NAILS EACH SIDE

2"X4" PURLINS NOT OVER 24" O.C. FASTEN WITH 2-10d NAILS AT EACH RAFTER

TWO 5/8"ø (THREE 5/8"ø) MACHINE BOLTS WITH WASHERS

2 1/2" CORRUGATED METAL ROOFING

2"X6"X16'-0" RAFTERS 30"O.C. (24" O.C.)

TWO 5/8"ø MACH. BOLTS WITH WASHERS

3-10d NAILS EACH SIDE

2"X4"X14'-0" TIES 30"O.C. (24" O.C.)

3/4" PLYWOOD GUSSET SEE DETAIL

8'-0" SHEET

RIDGE ROLL

TWO 1"X4" HANGERS

1"X6" DIAGONAL BRACE ALL CORNERS

1"X4" BRACES AT 45°

TWO 5/8"ø (THREE 5/8"ø) MACH. BOLTS WITH WASHERS

TWO 2"X10"(2"X12") SPACED BY 2"X6" BLOCKING 4'-0" O.C. BETWEEN POLES AND 2"X10"X3'-0" (2"X12"X3'-0") SPLICES OVER POLES

6" TOP X 22' POLE 12'-0" O.C. OUTER SIDE TO BE SET PLUMB. TRIM FOR GUSSET

2"X4" X 12'-0" GIRTS NOT OVER 30"O.C. IF SIDING IS REQUIRED

CORRUGATED METAL SIDING OR VERTICAL BOARDS

SIDEWALLS ARE OPTIONAL INTERMEDIATE POLES TO STOP AT TOP OF GIRT BELOW BEAM

2" TREATED SPLASH BOARDS HEIGHT AS REQUIRED

GRADE

8'-0" SHEET

6" LAP

16'-0" MAX. TO TOP OF POLE

5'-0"

NOTE:
SET ALL POLES IN 18" DIA HOLES AND TAMP BACKFILL THOROUGHLY. IN LOOSE OR SANDY SOIL, A CONCRETE FILL MAY BE REQUIRED

SLOPE FOR DRAINAGE

TAMPED FILL

24'-6"

CROSS SECTION

60'-0" LENGTH AS REQUIRED

12'-0"

12'-0"

12'-0"

12'-0"

12'-0"

1"X6" BRACES NAILED TO UNDERSIDE OF RAFTERS

6" TOP POLES

6" TOP INTERMEDIATE POLES IF SIDE WALL IS CONSTRUCTED

BEAM, SEE DETAIL

1"X4" BRACES @ 45° ABOUT 4'-0" O.C. THRU-OUT NAILED TO TOP SIDE OF TIES SEE CROSS SECTION

ROOF OVERHANG

6'-0"

12'-6"

6'-0"

24'-6"

FLOOR AND ROOF FRAMING PLAN

COOPERATIVE EXTENSION WORK IN
AGRICULTURE AND HOME ECONOMICS
DEPARTMENT OF AGRICULTURAL ENGINEERING
UNIVERSITY OF MARYLAND

HAY SHED
24' WIDE-POLE CONSTRUCTION

USDA '57 5847

178

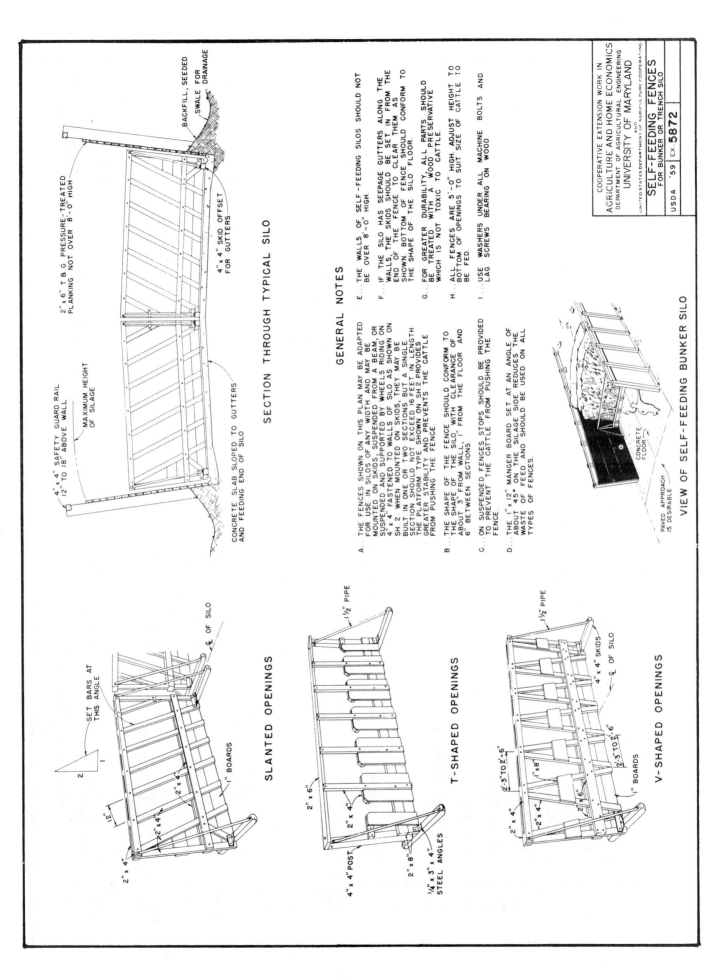

SECTION THROUGH TYPICAL SILO

2" x 6" T & G PRESSURE-TREATED PLANKING NOT OVER 8'-0" HIGH

BACKFILL, SEEDED SWALE FOR DRAINAGE

4" x 4" SKID OFFSET FOR GUTTERS

4" x 4" SAFETY GUARD RAIL 12" TO 18" ABOVE WALL

MAXIMUM HEIGHT OF SILAGE

CONCRETE SLAB SLOPED TO GUTTERS AND FEEDING END OF SILO

GENERAL NOTES

A... THE FENCES SHOWN ON THIS PLAN MAY BE ADAPTED FOR USE IN SILOS OF ANY WIDTH AND MAY BE MOUNTED ON SKIDS, SUSPENDED FROM A BEAM, OR SUSPENDED AND SUPPORTED BY WHEELS RIDING ON 4" x 4" FASTENED TO WALLS OF SILO AS SHOWN ON SH.2. WHEN MOUNTED ON SKIDS, THEY MAY BE BUILT IN ONE OR TWO SECTIONS, BUT A SINGLE SECTION SHOULD NOT EXCEED 16 FEET IN LENGTH. THE PLATFORM TYPE SHOWN ON SH.2 PROVIDES GREATER STABILITY AND PREVENTS THE CATTLE FROM PUSHING THE FENCE.

B... THE SHAPE OF THE FENCE SHOULD CONFORM TO THE SHAPE OF THE SILO, WITH CLEARANCE OF ABOUT 3" FROM WALL, 1" FROM THE FLOOR AND 6" BETWEEN SECTIONS.

C... ON SUSPENDED FENCES STOPS SHOULD BE PROVIDED TO PREVENT THE CATTLE FROM PUSHING THE FENCE.

D... THE 1" x 12" MANGER BOARD SET AT AN ANGLE OF ABOUT 45° ON THE SILAGE SIDE REDUCES THE WASTE OF FEED AND SHOULD BE USED ON ALL TYPES OF FENCES.

E... THE WALLS OF SELF-FEEDING SILOS SHOULD NOT BE OVER 8'-0" HIGH.

F... IF THE SILO HAS SEEPAGE GUTTERS ALONG THE WALLS, THE SKIDS SHOULD BE SET IN FROM THE END OF THE FENCE TO CLEAR THEM AS SHOWN. BOTTOM OF FENCE SHOULD CONFORM TO THE SHAPE OF THE SILO FLOOR.

G... FOR GREATER DURABILITY, ALL PARTS SHOULD BE TREATED WITH A WOOD PRESERVATIVE WHICH IS NOT TOXIC TO CATTLE.

H... ALL FENCES ARE 5'-0" HIGH. ADJUST HEIGHT TO BOTTOM OF OPENINGS TO SUIT SIZE OF CATTLE TO BE FED.

I... USE WASHERS UNDER ALL MACHINE BOLTS AND LAG SCREWS BEARING ON WOOD.

VIEW OF SELF-FEEDING BUNKER SILO

CONCRETE FLOOR

PAVED APPROACH IS DESIRABLE

SLANTED OPENINGS

SET BARS AT THIS ANGLE

℄ OF SILO

1" BOARDS

2" x 4"

12"

2" x 4"

T-SHAPED OPENINGS

1½" PIPE

2" x 6"

2" x 4"

2" x 8"

4" x 4" POST

¼" x 3" x 4" STEEL ANGLES

V-SHAPED OPENINGS

1½" PIPE

4" x 4" SKIDS

℄ OF SILO

1" BOARDS

2'-3" TO 2'-6"

2" x 8"

2" x 6"

2" x 4"

2'-3" TO 2'-6"

COOPERATIVE EXTENSION WORK IN AGRICULTURE AND HOME ECONOMICS
DEPARTMENT OF AGRICULTURAL ENGINEERING
UNIVERSITY OF MARYLAND
AND UNITED STATES DEPARTMENT OF AGRICULTURE COOPERATING

SELF-FEEDING FENCES
FOR BUNKER OR TRENCH SILO

USDA '59 EX. 5872

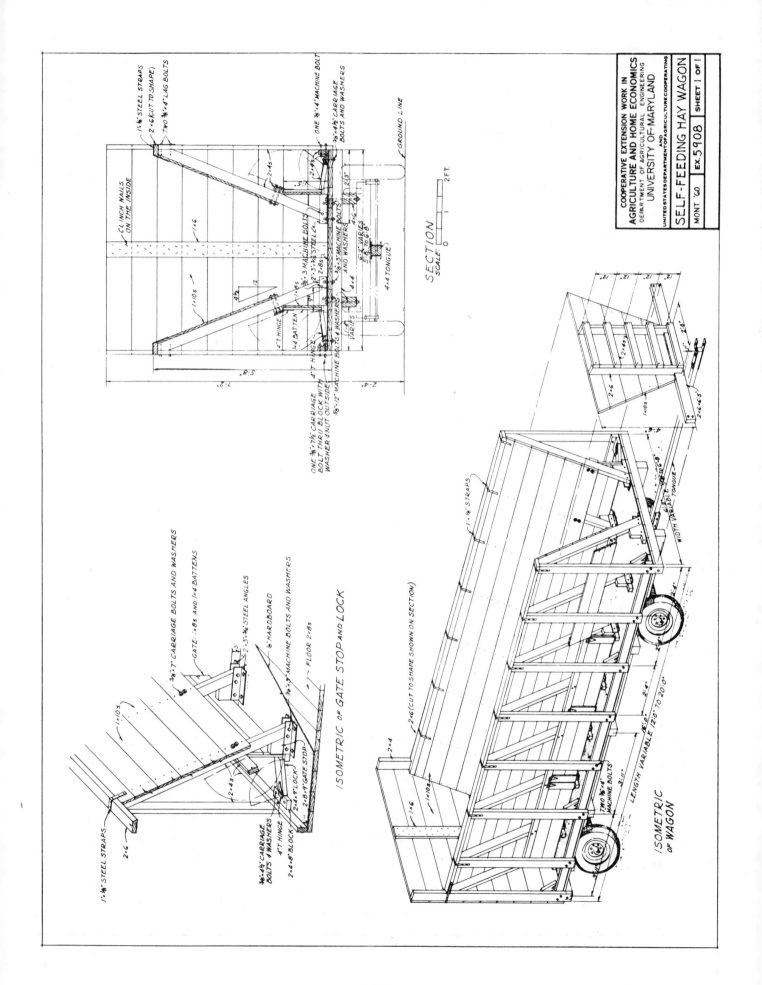

SECTION
SCALE: 0 | 1 | 2 FT.

ISOMETRIC OF GATE STOP AND LOCK

ISOMETRIC OF WAGON

COOPERATIVE EXTENSION WORK IN
AGRICULTURE AND HOME ECONOMICS
DEPARTMENT OF AGRICULTURAL ENGINEERING
UNIVERSITY OF MARYLAND
AND
UNITED STATES DEPARTMENT OF AGRICULTURE COOPERATING

SELF-FEEDING HAY WAGON

MONT. '60 | Ex. 5908 | SHEET 1 OF 1

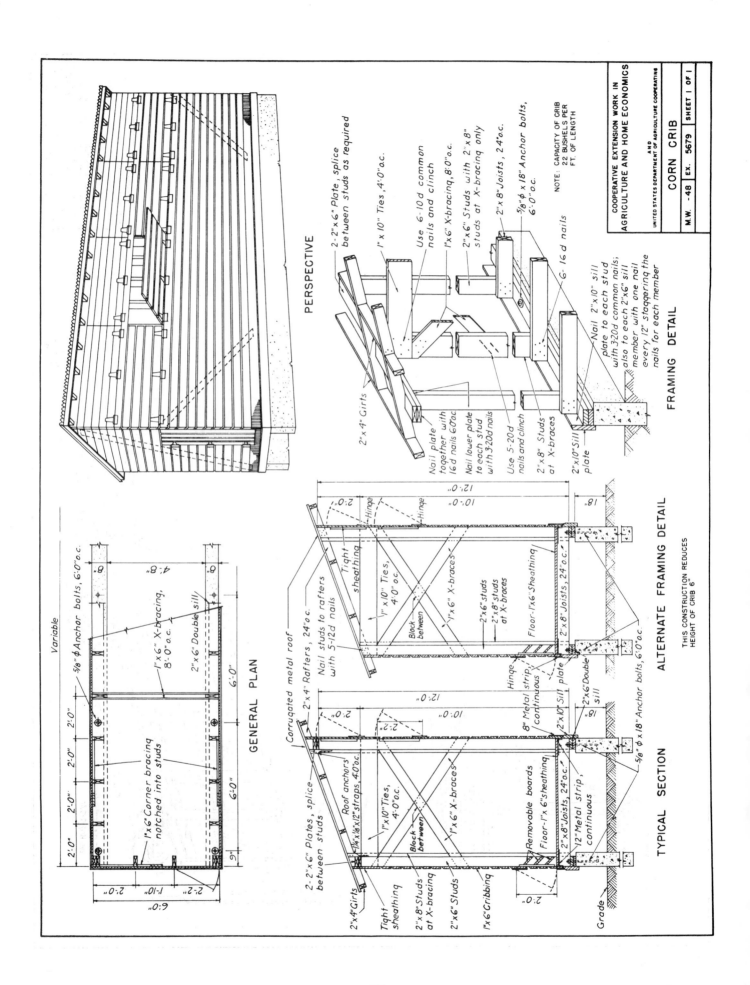

PERSPECTIVE

FRAMING DETAIL

2-2"x6" Plate, splice between studs as required

1"x10" Ties, 4'-0"o.c.

Use 6-10d common nails and clinch

1"x6" X-bracing, 8'-0"o.c.

2"x6" Studs with 2"x8" studs at X-bracing only

2"x8" Joists, 24"o.c.

5/8"⌀ x 18" Anchor bolts, 6'-0" o.c.

6-16 d nails

2"x4" Girts

Nail plate together with 16d nails 6'0.c.

Nail lower plate to each stud with 3-20d nails

Use 5-20d nails and clinch

2"x8" Studs at X-braces

2"x10"Sill plate

Nail 2"x10" sill plate to each stud with 3-20d common nails; also to each 2"x6" sill member with one nail every 12" staggering the nails for each member

COOPERATIVE EXTENSION WORK IN
AGRICULTURE AND HOME ECONOMICS
AND
UNITED STATES DEPARTMENT OF AGRICULTURE COOPERATING

CORN CRIB

M.W. -48 | EX. 5679 | SHEET I OF I

NOTE: CAPACITY OF CRIB 22 BUSHELS PER FT. OF LENGTH

GENERAL PLAN

Variable

5/8"⌀ Anchor bolts, 6'-0"o.c.

1"x6" X-bracing, 8'-0"o.c.

2"x6" Double sill

1"x6" Corner bracing notched into studs

2'-0" 2'-0" 2'-0" 2'-0"

6'-0"

8"

4'-8"

9"

2'-2" 1'-10" 2'-2"

6'-0"

2'-0"

ALTERNATE FRAMING DETAIL

THIS CONSTRUCTION REDUCES HEIGHT OF CRIB 6"

12'-0"

10'-0"

2'-0"

Hinge

Hinge

Tight sheathing

1"x10" Ties, 4'-0" o.c.

1"x6" X-braces

Block between

2"x6" studs
2"x8" studs at X-bracing

Floor-1"x6" Sheathing

2"x8" Joists, 24"o.c.

Hinge

8" Metal strip, continuous

2"x10" Sill plate

2"x6" Double sill

5/8"⌀ x 18" Anchor bolts, 6'-0"o.c.

18"

TYPICAL SECTION

Corrugated metal roof

2"x4" Rafters, 24"o.c.

Nail studs to rafters with 5-12d nails

2-2"x6" Plates, splice between studs

Roof anchors 1/4"x1-5/8"x12" straps, 4'-0"o.c.

1"x10" Ties, 4'-0" o.c.

Block between

1"x6" X-braces

2"x4" Girts

Tight sheathing

2"x8" Studs at X-bracing

2"x6" Studs

1"x6" Cribbing

Removable boards

Floor-1"x6"sheathing

2"x8"Joists, 24"o.c.

12"Metal strip, continuous

5/8"⌀ x 18" Anchor bolts, 6'-0"o.c.

Grade

12'-0"

10'-0"

2'-0"

2':2"

18"

2'-0"

181

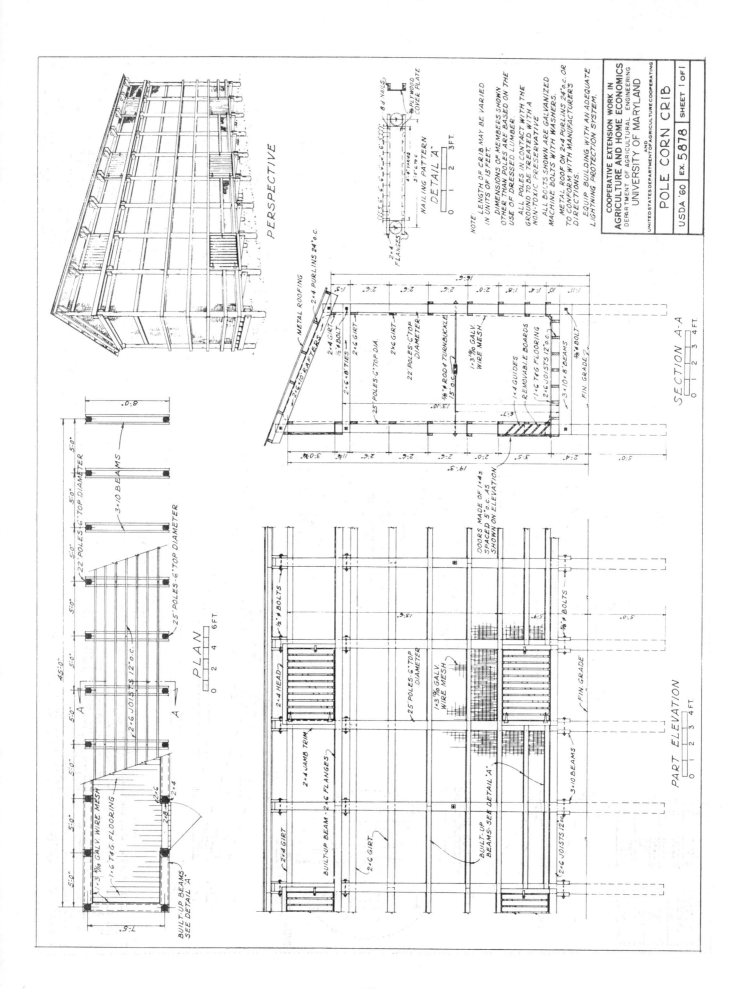

PERSPECTIVE

PLAN

SECTION A-A

PART ELEVATION

DETAIL "A"

NAILING PATTERN

NOTE: LENGTH OF CRIB MAY BE VARIED IN UNITS OF 15 FEET.

DIMENSIONS OF MEMBERS SHOWN OTHER THAN POLES ARE BASED ON THE USE OF DRESSED LUMBER.

ALL POLES IN CONTACT WITH THE GROUND TO BE TREATED WITH A NON-TOXIC PRESERVATIVE

ALL BOLTS SHOWN ARE GALVANIZED MACHINE BOLTS WITH WASHERS.

METAL ROOF ON 2x4 PURLINS 24"o.c. OR TO CONFORM WITH MANUFACTURERS DIRECTIONS.

EQUIP BUILDING WITH AN ADEQUATE LIGHTNING PROTECTION SYSTEM.

POLE CORN CRIB

COOPERATIVE EXTENSION WORK IN
AGRICULTURE AND HOME ECONOMICS
DEPARTMENT OF AGRICULTURAL ENGINEERING
UNIVERSITY OF MARYLAND
AND
UNITED STATES DEPARTMENT OF AGRICULTURE COOPERATING

USDA '60 | EX. 5878 | SHEET 1 OF 1

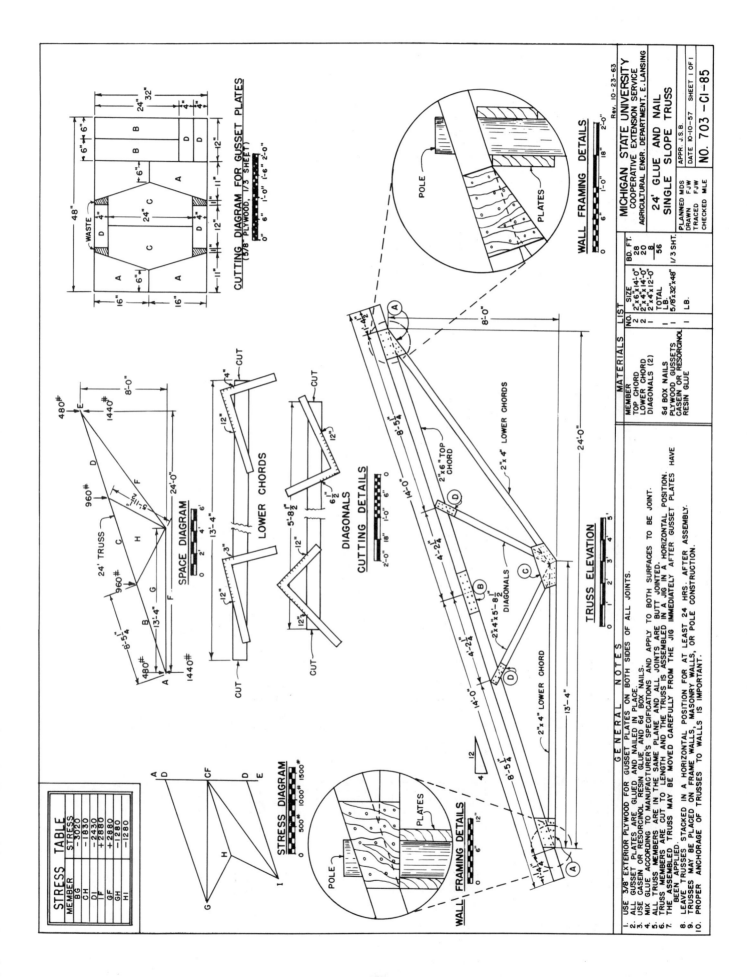

CUTTING DIAGRAM FOR GUSSET PLATES
(5/8" PLYWOOD, 1/3 SHEET)

WALL FRAMING DETAILS

Rev. 10-23-63

MICHIGAN STATE UNIVERSITY
COOPERATIVE EXTENSION SERVICE
AGRICULTURAL ENGR. DEPARTMENT, E. LANSING

24' GLUE AND NAIL
SINGLE SLOPE TRUSS

PLANNED MDS	APPR. J.S.B.
DRAWN FJW	DATE 10-10-57 SHEET 1 OF 1
TRACED FJW	
CHECKED MLE	NO. 703 -CI-85

MATERIALS LIST

MEMBER	NO.	SIZE	BD. FT.
TOP CHORD	2	2"x6"x14'-0"	28
LOWER CHORD	2	2"x4"x14'-0"	20
DIAGONALS (2)		2"x4"x12'-0"	8
		TOTAL	56
8d BOX NAILS		LB.	
PLYWOOD GUSSETS		5/8"x32"x48"	1/3 SHT.
CASEIN OR RESORGINOL			
RESIN GLUE		LB.	

SPACE DIAGRAM

LOWER CHORDS

DIAGONALS

CUTTING DETAILS

TRUSS ELEVATION

2"x6" TOP CHORD

2"x4" LOWER CHORDS

2"x4"x5'-8½" DIAGONALS

2"x4" LOWER CHORD

WALL FRAMING DETAILS

STRESS DIAGRAM

STRESS TABLE

MEMBER	STRESS
BG	-3020
CH	-1830
DI	-2430
IF	+2880
GF	+2880
GH	-1280
HI	-1280

G E N E R A L   N O T E S

1. USE 3/8" EXTERIOR PLYWOOD FOR GUSSET PLATES ON BOTH SIDES OF ALL JOINTS.
2. ALL GUSSET PLATES ARE GLUED AND NAILED IN PLACE.
3. USE CASEIN OR RESORCINOL RESIN GLUE, AND 6d BOX NAILS.
4. MIX GLUE ACCORDING TO MANUFACTURER'S SPECIFICATIONS AND APPLY TO BOTH SURFACES TO BE JOINT.
5. ALL TRUSS MEMBERS ARE IN THE SAME PLANE AND ALL JOINTS ARE BUTT JOINTED.
6. TRUSS MEMBERS ARE CUT TO LENGTH AND THE TRUSS IS ASSEMBLED IN A JIG IN A HORIZONTAL POSITION.
7. THE ASSEMBLED TRUSS MAY BE MOVED CAREFULLY FROM THE JIG IMMEDIATELY AFTER GUSSET PLATES
   HAVE BEEN APPLIED.
8. LEAVE TRUSSES STACKED IN A HORIZONTAL POSITION FOR AT LEAST 24 HRS. AFTER ASSEMBLY.
9. TRUSSES MAY BE PLACED ON FRAME WALLS, MASONRY WALLS, OR POLE CONSTRUCTION.
10. PROPER ANCHORAGE OF TRUSSES TO WALLS IS IMPORTANT.

183

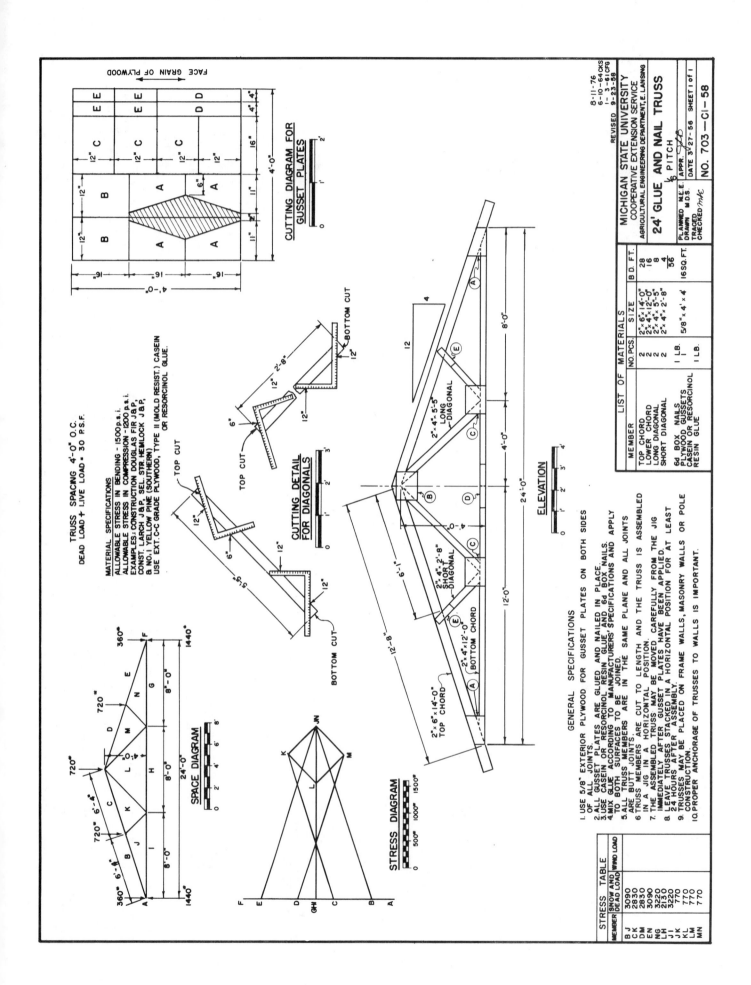

CUTTING DIAGRAM FOR GUSSET PLATES

FACE GRAIN OF PLYWOOD

CUTTING DETAIL FOR DIAGONALS

ELEVATION

TRUSS SPACING 4'-0" O.C.
DEAD LOAD + LIVE LOAD = 30 P.S.F.

MATERIAL SPECIFICATIONS
ALLOWABLE STRESS IN BENDING - 1500 p.s.i.
ALLOWABLE STRESS IN COMPRESSION - 1200 p.s.i.
EXAMPLES: CONSTRUCTION DOUGLAS FIR J&P,
CONST. LARCH J&P, SEL. STR. HEMLOCK J&P,
& NO.1 YELLOW PINE (SOUTHERN)
USE EXT. C-C GRADE PLYWOOD, TYPE II (MOLD RESIST.) CASEIN
OR RESORCINOL GLUE.

SPACE DIAGRAM

STRESS DIAGRAM

STRESS TABLE

MEMBER	SNOW AND DEAD LOAD	WIND LOAD
BJ	3090	
CK	2830	
DM	2830	
EN	3090	
LH	3220	
JI	2130	
JK	3220	
KL	770	
LM	770	
MN	770	

GENERAL SPECIFICATIONS

1. USE 5/8" EXTERIOR PLYWOOD FOR GUSSET PLATES ON BOTH SIDES OF ALL JOINTS.
2. ALL GUSSET PLATES ARE GLUED AND NAILED IN PLACE.
3. USE CASEIN OR RESORCINOL RESIN GLUE, AND 6d BOX NAILS.
4. MIX GLUE ACCORDING TO MANUFACTURERS' SPECIFICATIONS AND APPLY TO BOTH SURFACES TO BE JOINED.
5. ALL TRUSS MEMBERS ARE IN THE SAME PLANE AND ALL JOINTS ARE BUTT JOINTS.
6. TRUSS MEMBERS ARE CUT TO LENGTH AND THE TRUSS IS ASSEMBLED IN A JIG IN A HORIZONTAL POSITION.
7. THE ASSEMBLED TRUSS MAY BE MOVED CAREFULLY FROM THE JIG IMMEDIATELY AFTER GUSSET PLATES HAVE BEEN APPLIED.
8. LEAVE TRUSSES STACKED IN A HORIZONTAL POSITION FOR AT LEAST 24 HOURS AFTER ASSEMBLY.
9. TRUSSES MAY BE PLACED ON FRAME WALLS, MASONRY WALLS OR POLE CONSTRUCTION.
10. PROPER ANCHORAGE OF TRUSSES TO WALLS IS IMPORTANT.

LIST OF MATERIALS

MEMBER	NO. PCS.	SIZE	B D. FT.
TOP CHORD	2	2"×6"×14'-0"	28
LOWER CHORD	2	2"×4"×12'-0"	16
LONG DIAGONAL	2	2"×4"×5'-5"	8
SHORT DIAGONAL	2	2"×4"×2'-8"	4
			56
6d BOX NAILS	1 LB.		
PLYWOOD GUSSETS	1	5/8"×4'×4'	16 SQ. FT.
CASEIN OR RESORCINOL RESIN GLUE	1 LB.		

MICHIGAN STATE UNIVERSITY
COOPERATIVE EXTENSION SERVICE
AGRICULTURAL ENGINEERING DEPARTMENT, E. LANSING

24' GLUE AND NAIL TRUSS
⅙ PITCH

PLANNED N.E.E.	APPR.
DRAWN M.D.S.	DATE 3-27-56 SHEET 1 of 1
TRACED	
CHECKED	NO. 703—GI—58

8-11-76
6-10-64 CKS
1- 3-61 CFG
REVISED 9-23-58

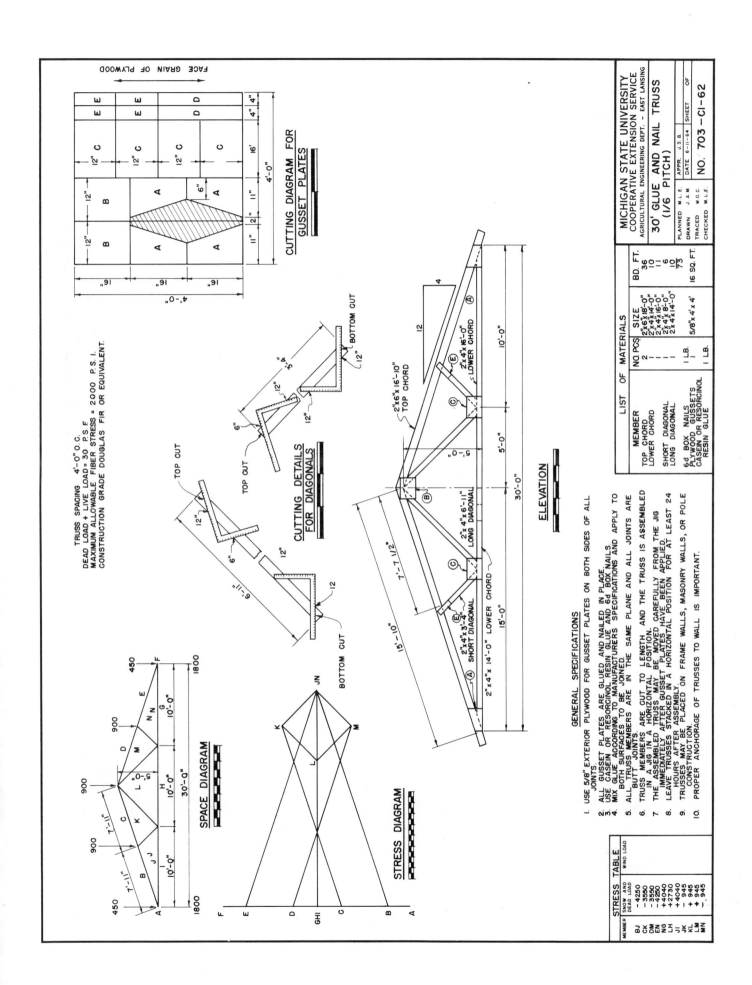

CUTTING DIAGRAM FOR GUSSET PLATES

FACE GRAIN OF PLYWOOD

CUTTING DETAILS FOR DIAGONALS

TOP CUT

BOTTOM CUT

TRUSS SPACING 4'-0" O.C.
DEAD LOAD + LIVE LOAD = 30 P.S.F.
MAXIMUM ALLOWABLE FIBER STRESS = 2000 P.S.I.
CONSTRUCTION GRADE DOUGLAS FIR OR EQUIVALENT.

ELEVATION

2"x6"x16'-10" TOP CHORD
2"x4"x16'-0" LOWER CHORD
2"x4"x6'-11" LONG DIAGONAL
2"x4"x3'-4" SHORT DIAGONAL
2"x4"x14'-0" LOWER CHORD

30'-0"

15'-10"

10'-0"

5'-0"

7'-7 1/2"

SPACE DIAGRAM

450 900 900 900 450
1800   1800

7'-11"   7'-11"
A B C D E F
J K L M N
G H N N
10'-0" 10'-0" 10'-0"
30'-0"

STRESS DIAGRAM

A B C D E F
K L M N
GHI
JN

GENERAL SPECIFICATIONS

1. USE 5/8" EXTERIOR PLYWOOD FOR GUSSET PLATES ON BOTH SIDES OF ALL JOINTS.
2. ALL GUSSET PLATES ARE GLUED AND NAILED IN PLACE.
3. USE CASEIN OR RESORCINOL RESIN GLUE AND 6d BOX NAILS.
4. MIX GLUE ACCORDING TO MANUFACTURERS' SPECIFICATIONS AND APPLY TO BOTH SURFACES TO BE JOINED.
5. ALL TRUSS MEMBERS ARE IN THE SAME PLANE AND ALL JOINTS ARE BUTT JOINTS.
6. TRUSS MEMBERS ARE CUT TO LENGTH, AND THE TRUSS IS ASSEMBLED IN A JIG IN A HORIZONTAL POSITION.
7. THE ASSEMBLED TRUSS MAY BE MOVED CAREFULLY FROM THE JIG IMMEDIATELY AFTER GUSSET PLATES HAVE BEEN APPLIED.
8. LEAVE TRUSSES STACKED IN A HORIZONTAL POSITION FOR AT LEAST 24 HOURS AFTER ASSEMBLY.
9. TRUSSES MAY BE PLACED ON FRAME WALLS, MASONRY WALLS, OR POLE CONSTRUCTION.
10. PROPER ANCHORAGE OF TRUSSES TO WALL IS IMPORTANT.

STRESS TABLE

MEMBER	SNOW AND DEAD LOAD	WIND LOAD
BJ	-4250	
CK	-3550	
DM	-3550	
EN	-4250	
NG	+4040	
LH	+2730	
JI	+4040	
JK	- 945	
KL	+ 945	
LM	+ 945	
MN	- 945	

LIST OF MATERIALS

MEMBER	NO. PCS	SIZE	BD. FT.
TOP CHORD	2	2"x6"x16'-0"	36
LOWER CHORD		2"x4"x14'-0"	10
		2"x4"x16'-0"	11
SHORT DIAGONAL		2"x4"x8'-0"	6
LONG DIAGONAL		2"x4"x14'-0"	10
			73
PLYWOOD GUSSETS		5/8"x 4'x 4'	16 SQ. FT.
6d BOX NAILS	1 LB.		
CASEIN OR RESORCINOL RESIN GLUE	1 LB.		

MICHIGAN STATE UNIVERSITY
COOPERATIVE ENGINEERING SERVICE
AGRICULTURAL ENGINEERING DEPT. - EAST LANSING

30' GLUE AND NAIL TRUSS
(1/6 PITCH)

PLANNED	M.L.E.	APPR.	J.S.B.	
DRAWN	J.A.M.	DATE	6-11-64	SHEET OF
TRACED	W.O.C.			
CHECKED	M.L.E.	NO. 703-CI-62		

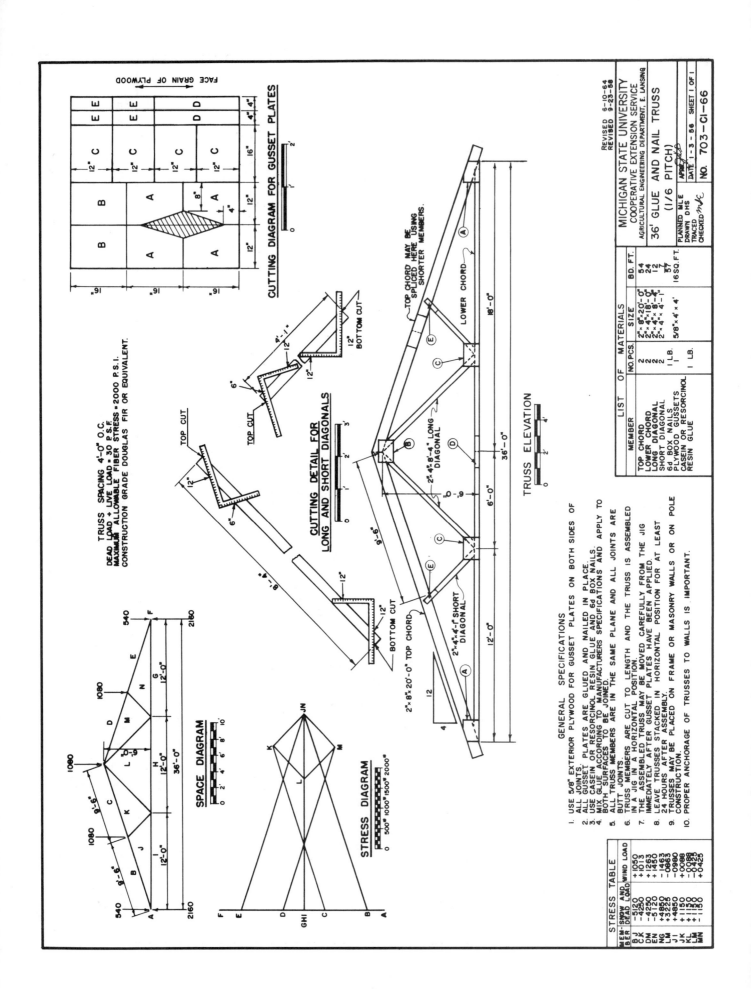

CUTTING DIAGRAM FOR GUSSET PLATES

FACE GRAIN OF PLYWOOD

CUTTING DETAIL FOR LONG AND SHORT DIAGONALS

TOP CUT

BOTTOM CUT

TRUSS SPACING 4'-0" O.C.
DEAD LOAD + LIVE LOAD = 30 P.S.F.
MAXIMUM ALLOWABLE FIBER STRESS = 2000 P.S.I.
CONSTRUCTION GRADE DOUGLAS FIR OR EQUIVALENT.

TOP CHORD MAY BE SPLICED HERE USING SHORTER MEMBERS.

LOWER CHORD.

2"× 4"× 8'-4" LONG DIAGONAL

2"× 4"× 4'-1" SHORT DIAGONAL

2"× 8"× 20'-0" TOP CHORD.

18'-0"

36'-0"

9'-0"

6'-0"

12'-0"

TRUSS ELEVATION

SPACE DIAGRAM

STRESS DIAGRAM

LIST OF MATERIALS

MEMBER	NO. PCS.	SIZE	BD. FT.
TOP CHORD	2	2"× 8"× 20'-0"	54
LOWER CHORD	2	2"× 4"× 18'-0"	24
LONG DIAGONAL	2	2"× 4"× 8'-4"	12
SHORT DIAGONAL	2	2"× 4"× 4'-1"	7
6d BOX NAILS	1 LB.		57
PLYWOOD GUSSETS	1	5/8"× 4'× 4'	16 SQ. FT.
CASEIN OR RESORCINOL RESIN GLUE	1 LB.		

GENERAL SPECIFICATIONS

1. USE 5/8" EXTERIOR PLYWOOD FOR GUSSET PLATES ON BOTH SIDES OF ALL JOINTS.
2. ALL GUSSET PLATES ARE GLUED AND NAILED IN PLACE.
3. USE CASEIN OR RESORCINOL RESIN GLUE AND 6d BOX NAILS.
4. MIX GLUE ACCORDING TO MANUFACTURERS SPECIFICATIONS AND APPLY TO BOTH SURFACES TO BE JOINED.
5. ALL TRUSS MEMBERS ARE IN THE SAME PLANE AND ALL JOINTS ARE BUTT JOINTS.
6. TRUSS MEMBERS ARE CUT TO LENGTH AND THE TRUSS IS ASSEMBLED IN A JIG IN A HORIZONTAL POSITION.
7. THE ASSEMBLED TRUSS MAY BE MOVED CAREFULLY FROM THE JIG IMMEDIATELY AFTER GUSSET PLATES HAVE BEEN APPLIED.
8. LEAVE TRUSSES STACKED IN HORIZONTAL POSITION FOR AT LEAST 24 HOURS AFTER ASSEMBLY.
9. TRUSSES MAY BE PLACED ON FRAME OR MASONRY WALLS OR ON POLE CONSTRUCTION.
10. PROPER ANCHORAGE OF TRUSSES TO WALLS IS IMPORTANT.

STRESS TABLE

MEMBER	SNOW AND DEAD LOAD	WIND LOAD
BJ	-5120	+1050
CK	-4250	+1013
DM	-4250	+1263
EN	-5120	+1450
NG	+4850	-1463
LM	+3225	-0863
JI	+4850	-0980
JK	+1150	+0088
KL	+1150	-0088
LM	+1150	-0425
MN	+1150	+0425

MICHIGAN STATE UNIVERSITY
COOPERATIVE EXTENSION SERVICE
AGRICULTURAL ENGINEERING DEPARTMENT, E. LANSING

36' GLUE AND NAIL TRUSS
(1/6 PITCH)

REVISED 6-10-64
REVISED 9-23-58

PLANNED MLE
DRAWN DHS
TRACED
CHECKED

DATE 1-3-56   SHEET 1 OF 1
NO. 703-CI-66

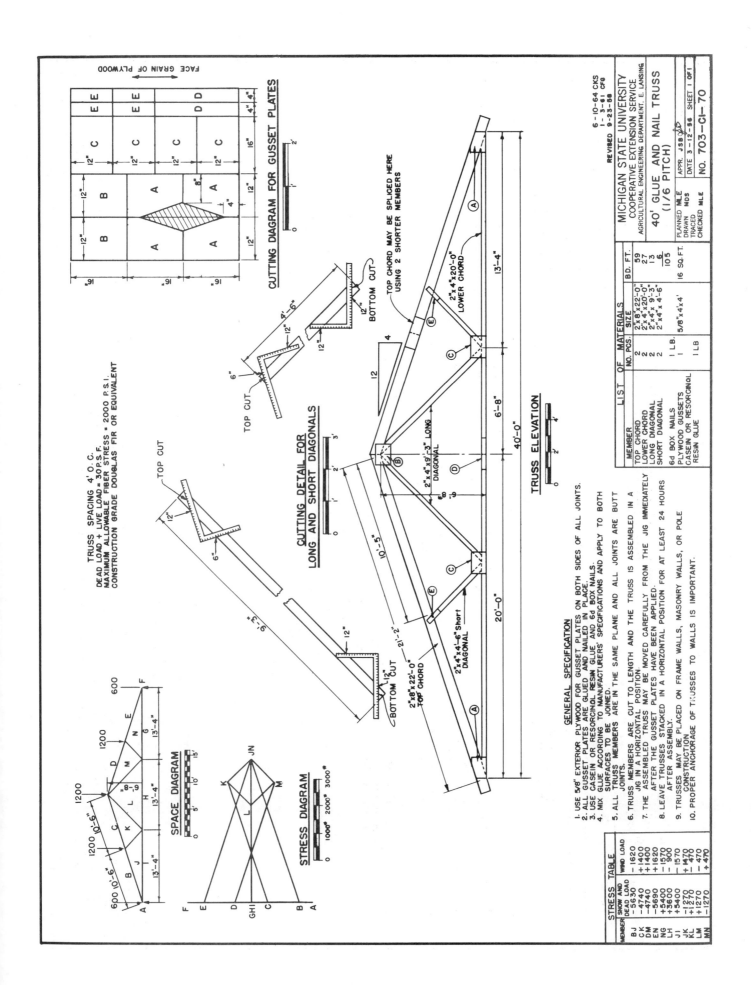

TRUSS SPACING 4' O. C.
DEAD LOAD + LIVE LOAD = 30 P.S.F.
MAXIMUM ALLOWABLE FIBER STRESS = 2000 P.S.I.
CONSTRUCTION GRADE DOUGLAS FIR OR EQUIVALENT

CUTTING DIAGRAM FOR GUSSET PLATES

FACE GRAIN OF PLYWOOD

CUTTING DETAIL FOR
LONG AND SHORT DIAGONALS

BOTTOM CUT

TOP CHORD MAY BE SPLICED HERE
USING 2 SHORTER MEMBERS

2"x4"x20'-0"
LOWER CHORD

13'-4"

6'-8"

40'-0"

20'-0"

2"x4"x9'-3" LONG
DIAGONAL

2"x4"x4'-6" Short
DIAGONAL

12" BOTTOM CUT
2"x8"x22'-0"
TOP CHORD

TRUSS ELEVATION

SPACE DIAGRAM

STRESS DIAGRAM

STRESS TABLE

MEMBER	SNOW AND DEAD LOAD	WIND LOAD
BJ	- 5630	- 1620
CK	- 4740	+ 1400
DM	- 4740	+ 1400
EN	- 5690	+ 1620
NG	+ 5400	- 1570
LH	+ 3600	- 900
JI	+ 5400	- 1570
JK	+ 1270	+ 1478
KL	+ 1270	+ 478
LM	- 470	- 470
MN	- 1270	+ 1270

GENERAL SPECIFICATION

1. USE 5/8" EXTERIOR PLYWOOD FOR GUSSET PLATES ON BOTH SIDES OF ALL JOINTS.
2. ALL GUSSET PLATES ARE GLUED AND NAILED IN PLACE.
3. USE CASEIN OR RESORCINOL RESIN GLUE AND 6d BOX NAILS.
4. MIX GLUE ACCORDING TO MANUFACTURERS' SPECIFICATIONS AND APPLY TO BOTH SURFACES TO BE JOINED.
5. ALL TRUSS MEMBERS ARE IN THE SAME PLANE AND ALL JOINTS ARE BUTT JOINTS.
6. TRUSS MEMBERS ARE CUT TO LENGTH AND THE TRUSS IS ASSEMBLED IN A JIG IN A HORIZONTAL POSITION.
7. THE ASSEMBLED TRUSS MAY BE MOVED CAREFULLY FROM THE JIG IMMEDIATELY AFTER THE GUSSET PLATES HAVE BEEN APPLIED.
8. LEAVE TRUSSES STACKED IN A HORIZONTAL POSITION FOR AT LEAST 24 HOURS AFTER ASSEMBLY.
9. TRUSSES MAY BE PLACED ON FRAME WALLS, MASONRY WALLS, OR POLE CONSTRUCTION.
10. PROPER ANCHORAGE OF TRUSSES TO WALLS IS IMPORTANT.

MICHIGAN STATE UNIVERSITY
COOPERATIVE EXTENSION SERVICE
AGRICULTURAL ENGINEERING DEPARTMENT, E. LANSING

40' GLUE AND NAIL TRUSS
(1/6 PITCH)

6 - 10 -64 CKS
1 - 3 - 61 CFG
REVISED 9-23-58

LIST OF MATERIALS			
MEMBER	NO. PCS.	SIZE	BD. FT.
TOP CHORD	2	2"x8"x22'-0"	59
LOWER CHORD	2	2"x4"x20'-0"	27
LONG DIAGONAL	2	2"x4"x 9'-3"	13
SHORT DIAGONAL	2	2"x4'x 4'-6"	6
			105
6d BOX NAILS	1 LB.		
PLYWOOD GUSSETS	1	5/8"x4'x4'	16 SQ. FT.
CASEIN OR RESORCINOL	1 LB		
RESIN GLUE			

PLANNED	MLE
DRAWN	MDS
TRACED	
CHECKED	MLE

APPR. JSB
DATE 3 -12-56   SHEET 1 OF 1
NO. 703—Cl—70

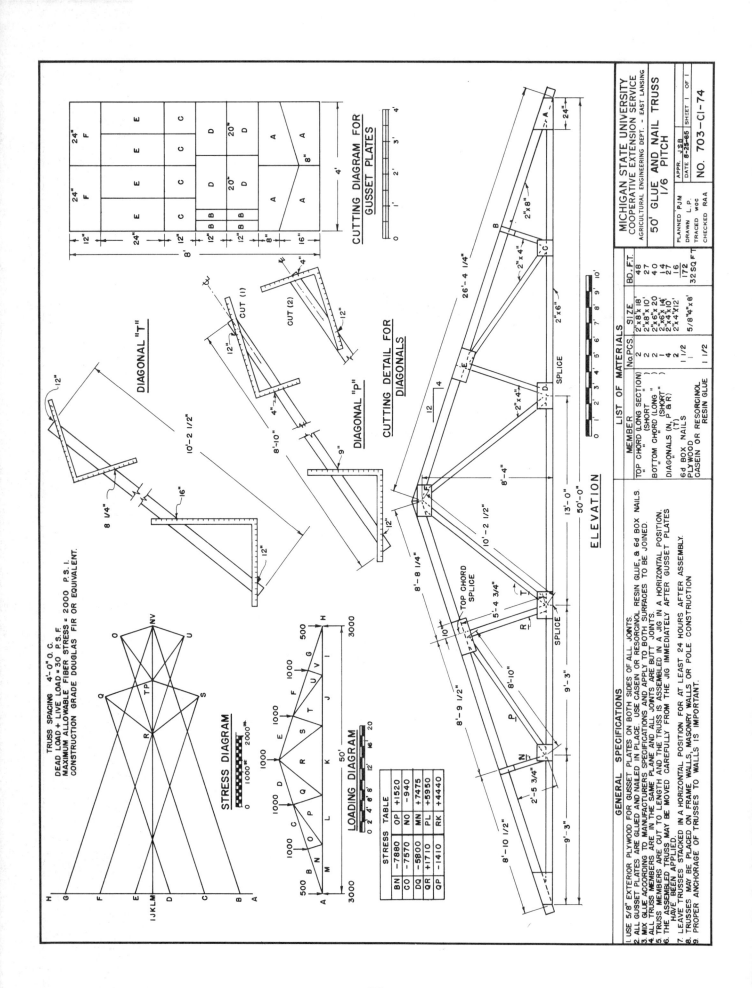

CUTTING DIAGRAM FOR
GUSSET PLATES

DIAGONAL "T"

CUT (1)
CUT (2)

DIAGONAL "P"

CUTTING DETAIL FOR
DIAGONALS

ELEVATION

STRESS DIAGRAM

LOADING DIAGRAM

STRESS TABLE

BN	−7880	OP	+1520
GO	−7570	NO	−940
DQ	−5800	MN	+7475
QR	+1710	PL	+5950
QP	−1410	RK	+4440

TRUSS SPACING 4'-0" O.C.
DEAD LOAD + LIVE LOAD = 30 P.S.F.
MAXIMUM ALLOWABLE FIBER STRESS = 2000 P.S.I.
CONSTRUCTION GRADE DOUGLAS FIR OR EQUIVALENT.

MICHIGAN STATE UNIVERSITY
COOPERATIVE EXTENSION SERVICE
AGRICULTURAL ENGINEERING DEPT. - EAST LANSING

50' GLUE AND NAIL TRUSS
1/6 PITCH

	APPR. JSB	
PLANNED PJM	DATE 8-25-65	SHEET 1 OF 1
DRAWN L.P.		
TRACED WDC		NO. 703−C1−74
CHECKED RAA		

LIST OF MATERIALS

MEMBER	No.PCS.	SIZE	BD.FT.
TOP CHORD (LONG SECTION)	2	2"x8"x18'	48
" (SHORT)	2	2"x8"x10'	27
BOTTOM CHORD (LONG)	2	2"x6"x20'	40
" (SHORT)	1	2"x6"x14'	14
DIAGONALS (N, P & R)	4	2"x4"x10'	27
" (T)	2	2"x4"x12'	16
6d BOX NAILS	1 1/2		172
PLYWOOD		5/8"x4'x8'	32 SQ FT
CASEIN OR RESORCINOL RESIN GLUE	1 1/2		

GENERAL SPECIFICATIONS

1. USE 5/8" EXTERIOR PLYWOOD FOR GUSSET PLATES ON BOTH SIDES OF ALL JOINTS.
2. ALL GUSSET PLATES ARE GLUED AND NAILED IN PLACE. USE CASEIN OR RESORGINOL RESIN GLUE, & 6d BOX NAILS.
3. MIX GLUE ACCORDING TO MANUFACTURERS SPECIFICATIONS AND APPLY TO BOTH SURFACES TO BE JOINED.
4. ALL TRUSS MEMBERS ARE IN THE SAME PLANE AND ALL JOINTS ARE BUTT JOINTS.
5. TRUSS MEMBERS ARE CUT TO LENGTH AND THE TRUSS IS ASSEMBLED IN A JIG IN A HORIZONTAL POSITION.
6. THE ASSEMBLED TRUSS MAY BE MOVED CAREFULLY FROM THE JIG IMMEDIATELY AFTER GUSSET PLATES HAVE BEEN APPLIED.
7. LEAVE TRUSSES STACKED IN A HORIZONTAL POSITION FOR AT LEAST 24 HOURS AFTER ASSEMBLY.
8. TRUSSES MAY BE PLACED ON FRAME WALLS, MASONRY WALLS OR POLE CONSTRUCTION
9. PROPER ANCHORAGE OF TRUSSES TO WALLS IS IMPORTANT.

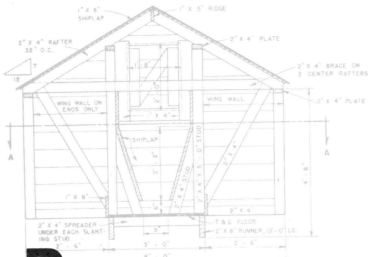

BEEF & DAIRY

BUILDINGS

AND

EQUIPMENT

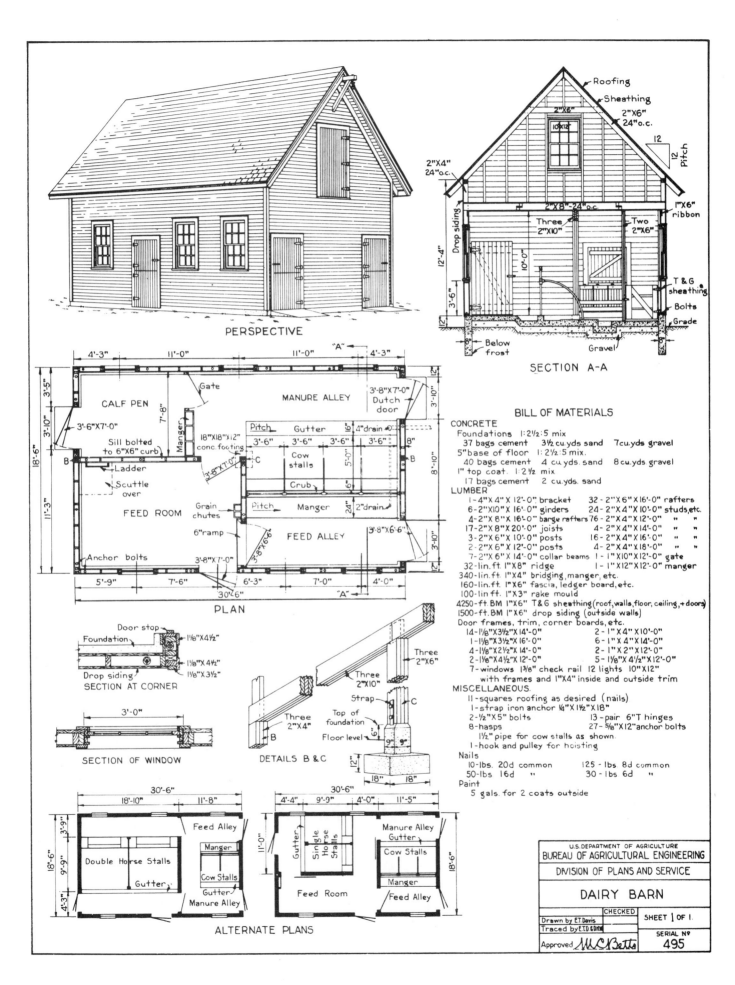

PERSPECTIVE

SECTION A-A

PLAN

4'-3" · 11'-0" · 11'-0" · "A" · 4'-3"

3'-5"

CALF PEN

MANURE ALLEY

3'-8"X7'-0" Dutch door

Gate

3'-10"

3'-10"

Manger

18"X18"X12" conc. footing

Sill bolted to 6"X6" curb

Pitch · Gutter · 16" · 4"drain

3'-6" · 3'-6" · 3'-6" · 3'-6"

3'-6"X7'-0"

Ladder

Cow stalls

5'-0"

8'-10"

Scuttle over

Crub

8"

FEED ROOM

18'-6"

Grain chutes

Pitch · Manger · 24" · 2"drain

6"

6"ramp

FEED ALLEY

3'-8"X6'-6"

11'-3"

Anchor bolts

3'-8"X7'-0"

6'-3" · 7'-0" · 4'-0"

3'-10"

5'-9" · 7'-6"

30'-6"

"A"

SECTION AT CORNER

Door stop
Foundation
1⅛"X4½"
Drop siding
1⅛"X4½"
1⅛"X3½"

SECTION OF WINDOW

3'-0"

DETAILS B & C

Three 2"X6"
Three 2"X10"
Three 2"X4"
Strap
Top of foundation
Floor level
C
B
9" 9"
12"
18" 18"

ALTERNATE PLANS

30'-6"
18'-10" · 11'-8"
3'-9"
Feed Alley
Manger
18'-6"
9'-9"
Double Horse Stalls
Cow Stalls
Gutter
4'-3"
Gutter
Manure Alley

30'-6"
4'-4" · 9'-9" · 4'-0" · 11'-5"
Gutter
Manure Alley Gutter
11'-0"
Single Horse Stalls
Cow Stalls
18'-6"
Feed Room
Manger
Feed Alley

BILL OF MATERIALS

CONCRETE
  Foundations 1:2½:5 mix
    37 bags cement   3½ cu.yds sand   7cu.yds gravel
  5"base of floor 1:2½:5 mix.
    40 bags cement   4 cu.yds. sand   8 cu.yds gravel
  1" top coat. 1:2½ mix
    17 bags cement   2 cu.yds. sand
LUMBER
  1-4"X 4" X 12'-0" bracket   32 - 2"X6"X16'-0" rafters
  6-2"X10"X 16'-0" girders   24 - 2"X4"X 10'-0" studs,etc.
  4-2"X 8"X 16'-0" barge rafters 76 - 2"X4"X18'-0" " "
  17-2"X 8"X20'-0" joists   4 - 2"X4"X14'-0" " "
  3-2"X 6"X 10'-0" posts   16 - 2"X4"X16'-0" " "
  2-2"X 6"X 12'-0" posts   4 - 2"X4"X18'-0" " "
  7-2"X 6"X 14'-0" collar beams   1 - 1"X10"X12'-0" gate
  32-lin.ft. 1"X8" ridge   1 - 1"X12"X12'-0" manger
  340-lin.ft. 1"X4" bridging,manger,etc.
  160-lin.ft. 1"X6" fascia, ledger board,etc.
  100-lin.ft. 1"X3" rake mould
  4250-ft. BM 1"X6" T&G sheathing(roof,walls,floor,ceiling,+doors)
  1500-ft. BM 1"X6" drop siding (outside walls)
  Door frames, trim, corner boards, etc.
  14-1⅛"X3½"X14'-0"   2 - 1"X 4"X10'-0"
  1-1⅛"X3½"X16'-0"   6 - 1"X 4"X14'-0"
  4-1⅛"X2½"X14'-0"   2 - 1"X 2"X12'-0"
  2-1⅛"X4½"X14'-0"   5 - 1⅛"X4½"X12'-0"
  7-windows 1⅜" check rail 12 lights 10"X12"
    with frames and 1"X4" inside and outside trim
MISCELLANEOUS.
  11-squares roofing as desired (nails)
  1-strap iron anchor ¼"X1½"X18"
  2-½"X5" bolts   13 - pair 6"T hinges
  8-hasps   27 - ⅝"X12"anchor bolts
  1½" pipe for cow stalls as shown.
  1-hook and pulley for hoisting
Nails
  10-lbs. 20d common   125 - lbs. 8d common
  50-lbs. 16d   "   30 - lbs 6d   "
Paint
  5 gals. for 2 coats outside

U.S.DEPARTMENT OF AGRICULTURE
BUREAU OF AGRICULTURAL ENGINEERING
DIVISION OF PLANS AND SERVICE

DAIRY BARN

Drawn by E.T.Davis   CHECKED   SHEET 1 OF 1.
Traced by E.T.D.&D.H.W.
Approved M.C.Betts   SERIAL N° 495

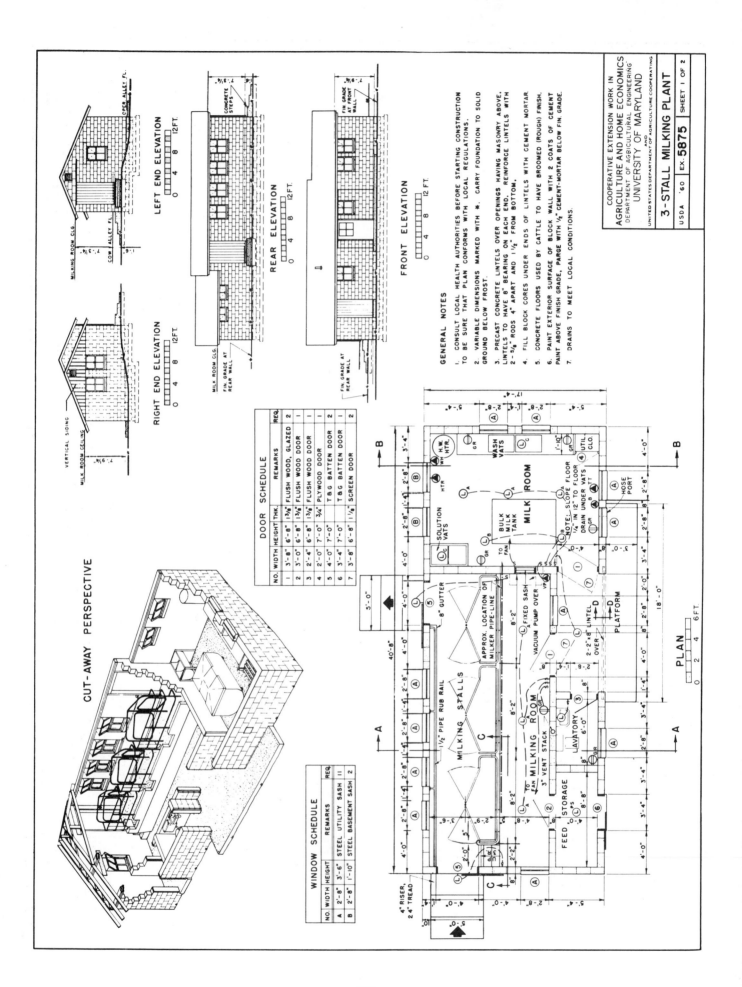

CUT-AWAY PERSPECTIVE

LEFT END ELEVATION

RIGHT END ELEVATION

REAR ELEVATION

FRONT ELEVATION

GENERAL NOTES

1. CONSULT LOCAL HEALTH AUTHORITIES BEFORE STARTING CONSTRUCTION TO BE SURE THAT PLAN CONFORMS WITH LOCAL REGULATIONS.

2. VARIABLE DIMENSIONS MARKED WITH ✷. CARRY FOUNDATION TO SOLID GROUND BELOW FROST.

3. PRECAST CONCRETE LINTELS OVER OPENINGS HAVING MASONRY ABOVE. LINTELS TO HAVE 6" BEARING ON EACH END. REINFORCE LINTELS WITH 2 - 5/8" RODS 4" APART AND 1 1/2" FROM BOTTOM.

4. FILL BLOCK CORES UNDER ENDS OF LINTELS WITH CEMENT MORTAR.

5. CONCRETE FLOORS USED BY CATTLE TO HAVE BROOMED (ROUGH) FINISH.

6. PAINT EXTERIOR SURFACE OF BLOCK WALL WITH 2 COATS OF CEMENT PAINT ABOVE FINISH GRADE. PARGE WITH 1/2" CEMENT-MORTAR BELOW FIN. GRADE.

7. DRAINS TO MEET LOCAL CONDITIONS.

DOOR SCHEDULE

NO.	WIDTH	HEIGHT	THK.	REMARKS	REQ.
1	3'-8"	6'-8"	1 3/8"	FLUSH WOOD, GLAZED	2
2	3'-0"	6'-8"	1 3/8"	FLUSH WOOD DOOR	1
3	2'-4"	6'-8"	1 3/8"	FLUSH WOOD DOOR	1
4	2'-0"	7'-0"	3/4"	PLYWOOD DOOR	1
5	4'-0"	7'-0"		T&G BATTEN DOOR	2
6	3'-4"	7'-0"		T&G BATTEN DOOR	1
7	3'-8"	6'-8"	1 1/8"	SCREEN DOOR	2

WINDOW SCHEDULE

NO.	WIDTH	HEIGHT	REMARKS	REQ.
A	2'-8"	3'-6"	STEEL UTILITY SASH	11
B	2'-8"	1'-10"	STEEL BASEMENT SASH	2

PLAN

MILKING STALLS

MILK ROOM

MILKING ROOM

FEED STORAGE

COOPERATIVE EXTENSION WORK IN
AGRICULTURE AND HOME ECONOMICS
DEPARTMENT OF AGRICULTURAL ENGINEERING
UNIVERSITY OF MARYLAND
AND
UNITED STATES DEPARTMENT OF AGRICULTURE COOPERATING

3-STALL MILKING PLANT

USDA '60 | EX. 5875 | SHEET 1 OF 2

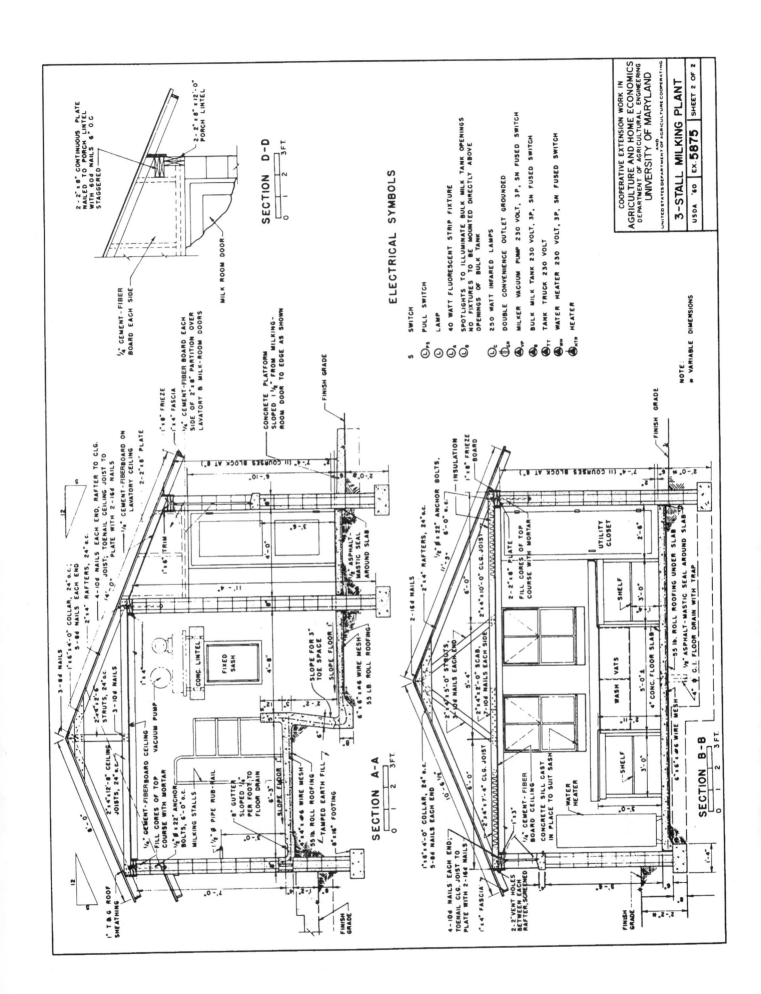

SECTION D-D

ELECTRICAL SYMBOLS

S   SWITCH
S_{PS} PULL SWITCH
L LAMP
L_A 40 WATT FLUORESCENT STRIP FIXTURE
L_B SPOTLIGHTS TO ILLUMINATE BULK MILK TANK OPENINGS NO FIXTURES TO BE MOUNTED DIRECTLY ABOVE OPENINGS OF BULK TANK
           230 WATT INFARED LAMPS
C_C DOUBLE CONVENIENCE OUTLET GROUNDED
CR MILKER VACUUM PUMP 230 VOLT, 3P, SN FUSED SWITCH
VP BULK MILK TANK 230 VOLT, 3P, SN FUSED SWITCH
B TANK TRUCK 230 VOLT
TT WATER HEATER 230 VOLT, 3P, SN FUSED SWITCH
WH HEATER
MTR

NOTE:
* VARIABLE DIMENSIONS

SECTION A-A

SECTION B-B

COOPERATIVE EXTENSION WORK IN
AGRICULTURE AND HOME ECONOMICS
DEPARTMENT OF AGRICULTURAL ENGINEERING
UNIVERSITY OF MARYLAND
AND
UNITED STATES DEPARTMENT OF AGRICULTURE COOPERATING

3-STALL MILKING PLANT

USDA '60 | EX. 5875 | SHEET 2 OF 2

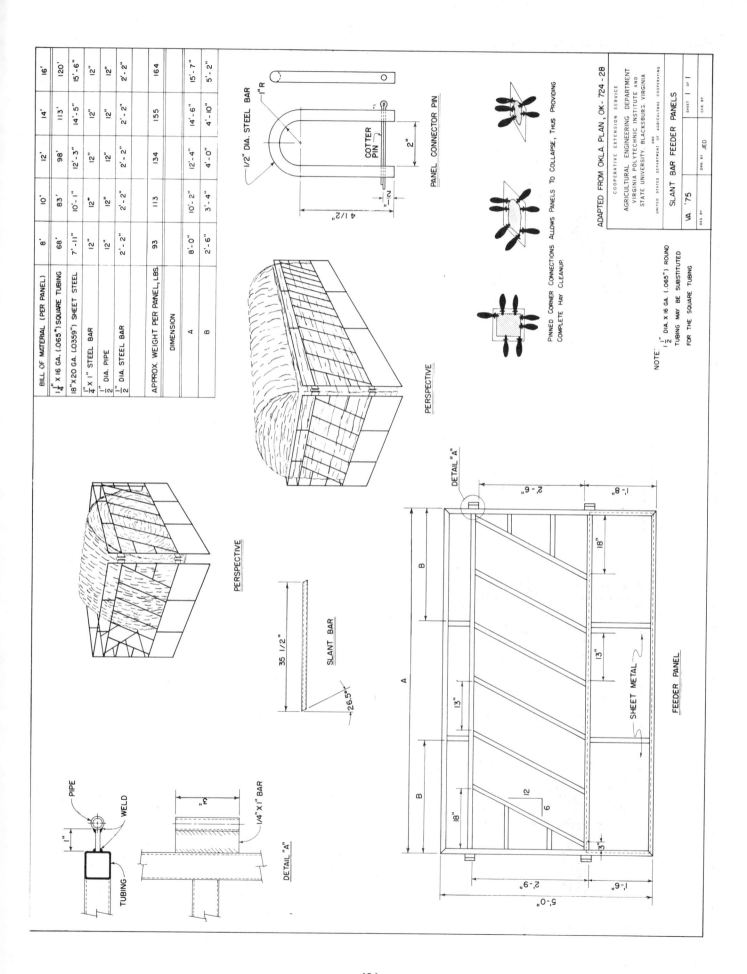

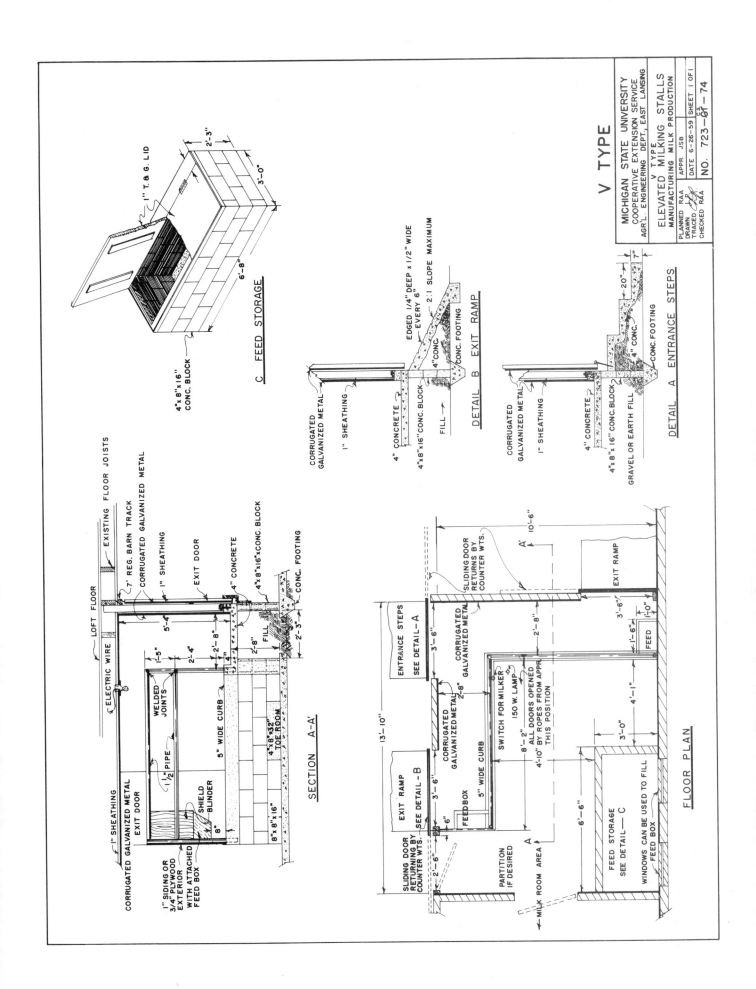

C FEED STORAGE

1" T. & G. LID

2'-3"

3'-0"

6'-8"

4"x8"x16"
CONC. BLOCK

DETAIL B EXIT RAMP

EDGED 1/4" DEEP x 1/2" WIDE
EVERY 6"

2:1 SLOPE MAXIMUM

CORRUGATED
GALVANIZED METAL

1" SHEATHING

4" CONCRETE

4" CONC.

FILL →

4"x8"x16" CONC. BLOCK

CONC. FOOTING

DETAIL A ENTRANCE STEPS

20"

7"

CORRUGATED
GALVANIZED METAL

1" SHEATHING

4" CONCRETE

4" CONC.

CONC. FOOTING

4"x8"x16" CONC. BLOCK

GRAVEL OR EARTH FILL

SECTION A-A'

EXISTING FLOOR JOISTS

LOFT FLOOR

7" REG. BARN TRACK

CORRUGATED GALVANIZED METAL

1" SHEATHING

EXIT DOOR

4" CONCRETE

4"x8"x16" CONC. BLOCK

CONC. FOOTING

ELECTRIC WIRE

1" SHEATHING

CORRUGATED GALVANIZED METAL EXIT DOOR

1" SIDING OR 3/4" PLYWOOD EXTERIOR WITH ATTACHED FEED BOX

1 1/2" PIPE

WELDED JOINTS

SHIELD BLINDER

8"

8"x8"x16"

5" WIDE CURB

4"x8"x32" TOE ROOM

5'-4"

2'-4"

1'-5"

2'-8"

2'-8"

2'-3"

FILL

FLOOR PLAN

ENTRANCE STEPS SEE DETAIL-A

SLIDING DOOR RETURNS BY COUNTER WTS.

CORRUGATED GALVANIZED METAL

EXIT RAMP

10'-6"

13'-10"

3'-6"

3'-6"

2'-8"

SWITCH FOR MILKER

150 W. LAMP

ALL DOORS OPENED BY ROPES FROM APPR THIS POSITION

8'-2"

4'-10"

4'-1"

3'-0"

3'-6"

1'-6"

1'-0"

FEED

2'-6"

6"

2'-6"

EXIT RAMP SEE DETAIL-B

FEEDBOX

5" WIDE CURB

SLIDING DOOR RETURNING BY COUNTER WTS.

PARTITION IF DESIRED

MILK ROOM AREA

FEED STORAGE SEE DETAIL-C

WINDOWS CAN BE USED TO FILL FEED BOX

6'-6"

V TYPE

MICHIGAN STATE UNIVERSITY
COOPERATIVE EXTENSION SERVICE
AGR'L. ENGINEERING DEPT., EAST LANSING

ELEVATED MILKING STALLS
MANUFACTURING MILK PRODUCTION

V TYPE

PLANNED RAA	APPR. JSB
DRAWN	DATE 6-26-59	SHEET 1 OF 1
TRACED	
CHECKED RAA	NO. 723-61-74

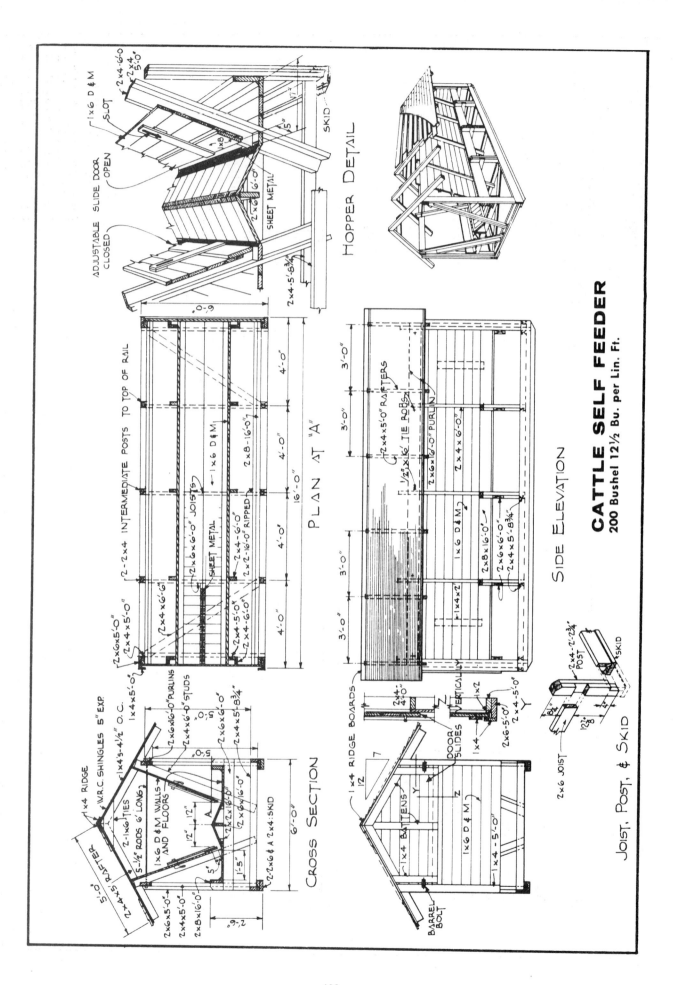

HOPPER DETAIL

PLAN AT "A"

CROSS SECTION

SIDE ELEVATION

JOIST, POST, & SKID

CATTLE SELF FEEDER
200 Bushel 12½ Bu. per Lin. Ft.

196

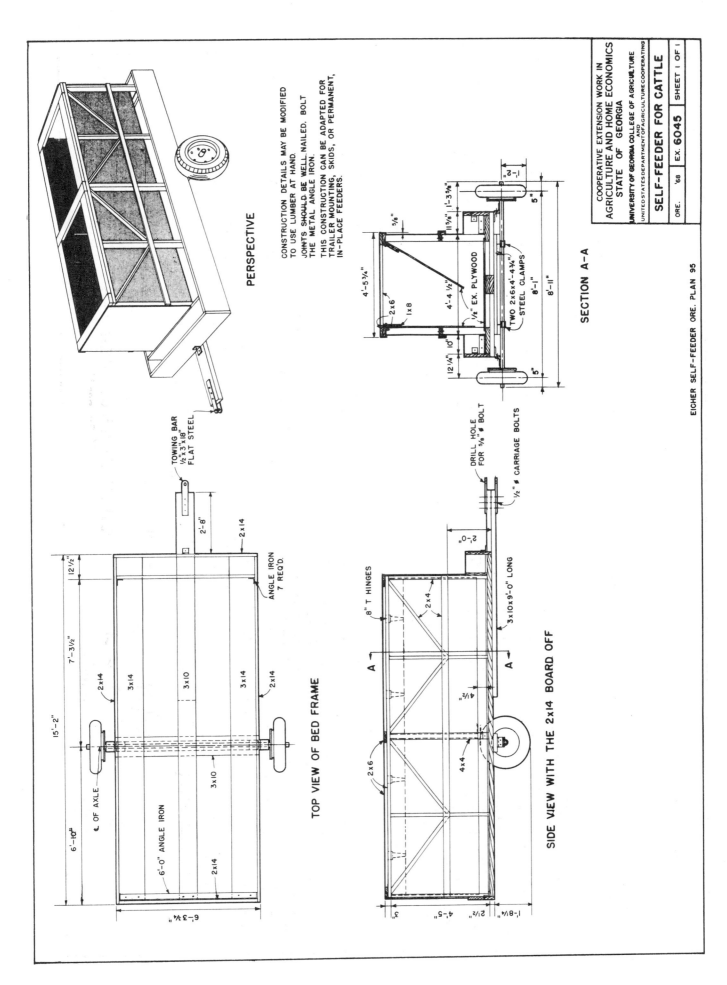

PERSPECTIVE

CONSTRUCTION DETAILS MAY BE MODIFIED
TO USE LUMBER AT HAND.

JOINTS SHOULD BE WELL NAILED. BOLT
THE METAL ANGLE IRON.

THIS CONSTRUCTION CAN BE ADAPTED FOR
TRAILER MOUNTING, SKIDS, OR PERMANENT,
IN-PLACE FEEDERS.

SECTION A-A

TOP VIEW OF BED FRAME

SIDE VIEW WITH THE 2x14 BOARD OFF

COOPERATIVE EXTENSION WORK IN
AGRICULTURE AND HOME ECONOMICS
STATE OF GEORGIA
UNIVERSITY OF GEORGIA COLLEGE OF AGRICULTURE
AND
UNITED STATES DEPARTMENT OF AGRICULTURE COOPERATING

SELF-FEEDER FOR CATTLE

ORE. '68 | EX. 6045 | SHEET I OF I

EICHER SELF-FEEDER ORE. PLAN 95

197

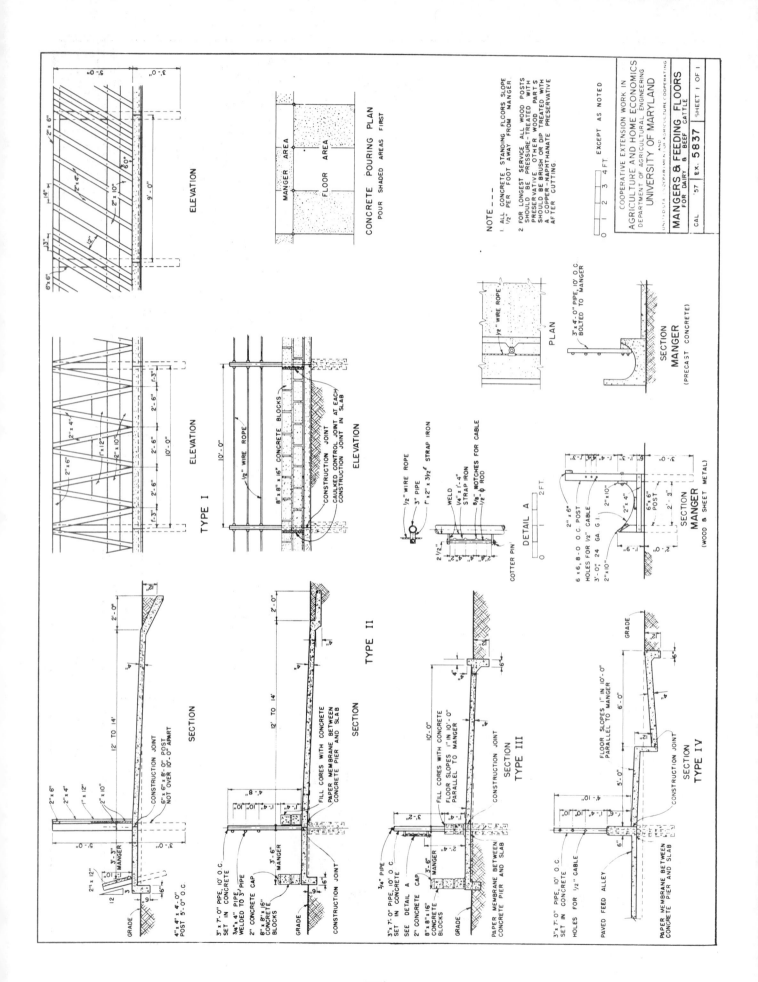

ELEVATION

CONCRETE POURING PLAN
POUR SHADED AREAS FIRST

MANGER AREA

FLOOR AREA

NOTE---
1. ALL CONCRETE STANDING FLOORS SLOPE
   1/2" PER FOOT AWAY FROM MANGER.
2. FOR LONGEST SERVICE ALL WOOD POSTS
   SHOULD BE PRESSURE-TREATED WITH
   PRESERVATIVE. OTHER WOOD PARTS
   SHOULD BE BRUSH OR DIP TREATED WITH
   A COPPER-NAPHTHANATE PRESERVATIVE
   AFTER CUTTING.

EXCEPT AS NOTED

0 1 2 3 4 FT

COOPERATIVE EXTENSION WORK IN
AGRICULTURE AND HOME ECONOMICS
DEPARTMENT OF AGRICULTURAL ENGINEERING
UNIVERSITY OF MARYLAND

MANGERS & FEEDING FLOORS
FOR DAIRY & BEEF CATTLE
CAL. '57 | Ex. 5837 | SHEET 1 OF 1

ELEVATION

TYPE I

1/2" WIRE ROPE

8"x 8"x 16" CONCRETE BLOCKS

CONSTRUCTION JOINT
CAULKED CONTROL JOINT AT EACH
CONSTRUCTION JOINT IN SLAB

ELEVATION

SECTION

TYPE II

SECTION

TYPE III

1/2" WIRE ROPE
3" PIPE

2 1/2"
COTTER PIN

WELD
1/4" x 1'-4"
STRAP IRON
5/8" NOTCHES FOR CABLE
1/2" ⌀ ROD

DETAIL A

0   1   2 FT

1/2" WIRE ROPE

PLAN

3"x 4'-0" PIPE, 10' O.C.
BOLTED TO MANGER

SECTION
MANGER
(PRECAST CONCRETE)

2"x 6"
6 x 6, 8-0 O.C. POST
HOLES FOR 1/2" CABLE
3'-0" 24 GA G I
2"x10" POST

2"x 4"
2"x10"
6"x 6"
POST

SECTION
MANGER
(WOOD & SHEET METAL)

GRADE

FLOOR SLOPES 1" IN 10'-0"
PARALLEL TO MANGER

CONSTRUCTION JOINT

SECTION
TYPE IV

3"x 7'-0" PIPE, 10' O.C.
SET IN CONCRETE

HOLES FOR 1/2" CABLE

PAVED FEED ALLEY

PAPER MEMBRANE BETWEEN
CONCRETE PIER AND SLAB

198

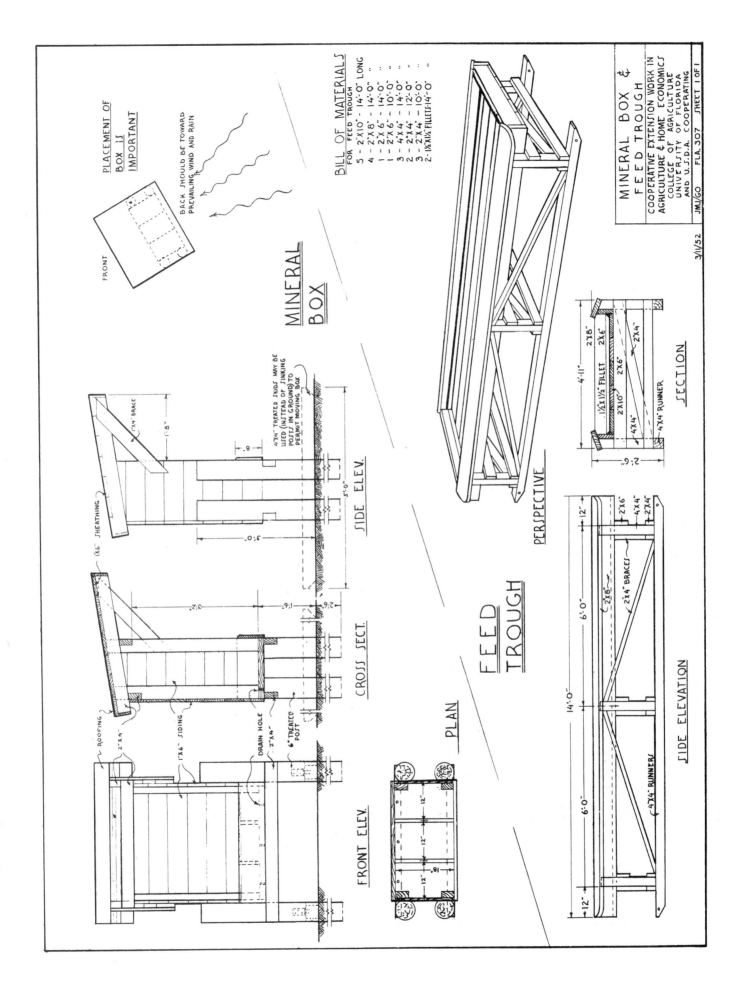

PLACEMENT OF
BOX IS
IMPORTANT

FRONT

BACK SHOULD BE TOWARD
PREVAILING WIND AND RAIN

BILL OF MATERIALS
FOR FEED TROUGH
5 - 2"X10" - 14'-0" LONG
4 - 2"X8" - 14'-0" "
1 - 2"X6" - 14'-0" "
3 - 4"X4" - 14'-0" "
2 - 2"X4" - 12'-0" "
3 - 2"X4" - 10'-0" "
2 - 1½X1½ FILLIT 14'-0"

MINERAL BOX

ROOFING

1"X6" SHEATHING

1"X4" BRACE

1'-8"

8"

5'-0"

3'-0"

SIDE ELEV.

4"X4" TREATED SKIDS MAY BE
USED (INSTEAD OF SINKING
POSTS IN GROUND) TO
PERMIT MOVING BOX

2"X4"

3'-0"

1'-6"

2'-6"

CROSS SECT.

2"X4"

1"X6" SIDING

DRAIN HOLE

2"X4"

6" TREATED POST

FRONT ELEV.

12"

12"

12"

18"

PLAN

FEED
TROUGH

PERSPECTIVE

4'-11"

1½X1½ FILLET   2"X6"

2"X10"   2"X6"

4"X4"

2'-6"

2"X4"

4"X4" RUNNER

SECTION

12"

6'-0"

14'-0"

6'-0"

12"

2"X6"

4"X4"

2"X4"

2"X8"

2"X4" BRACES

4"X4" RUNNER

SIDE ELEVATION

MINERAL BOX &
FEED TROUGH

COOPERATIVE EXTENSION WORK IN
AGRICULTURE & HOME ECONOMICS
COLLEGE OF AGRICULTURE
UNIVERSITY OF FLORIDA
AND U.S.D.A. COOPERATING

JMJ/GO   FLA. 307   SHEET 1 OF 1

3/1/52

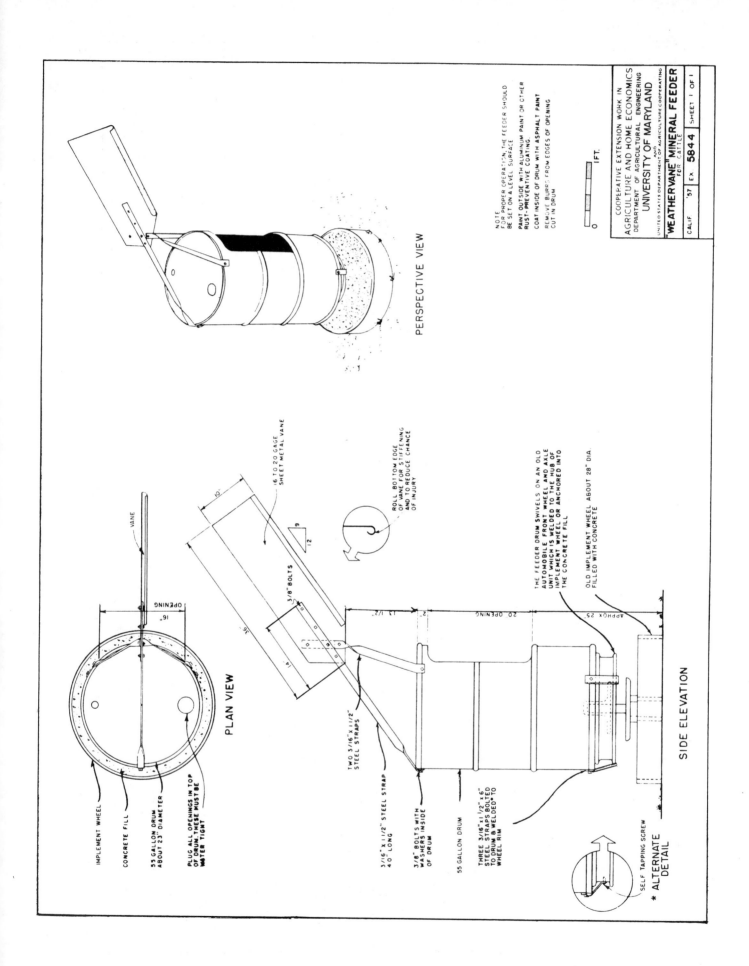

PLAN VIEW

PERSPECTIVE VIEW

SIDE ELEVATION

* ALTERNATE DETAIL

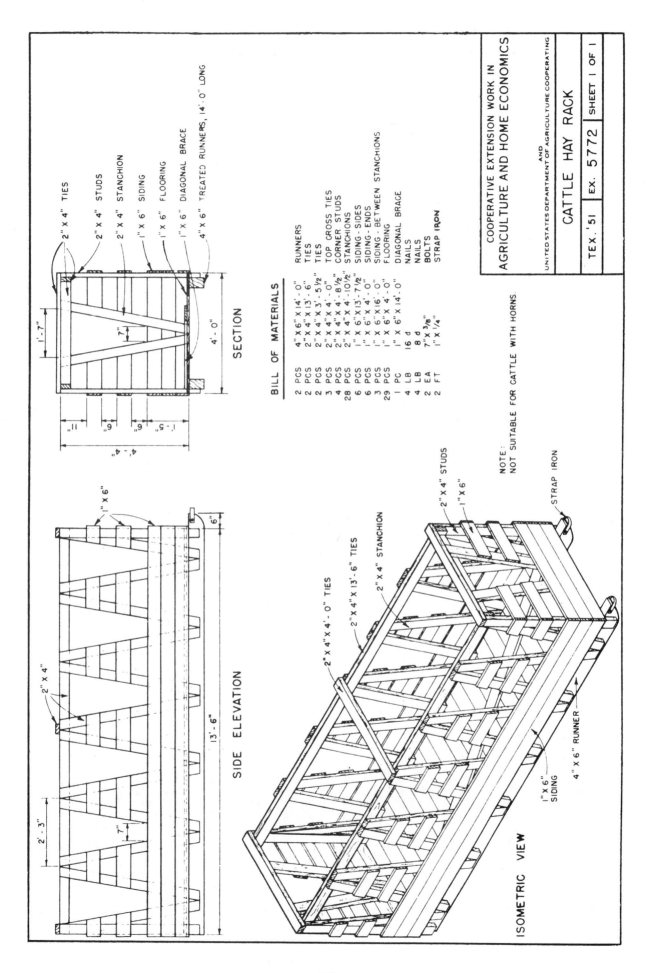

SECTION

2" x 4" TIES
2" x 4" STUDS
2" x 4" STANCHION
1" x 6" SIDING
1" x 6" FLOORING
1" x 6" DIAGONAL BRACE
4" x 6" TREATED RUNNERS, 14'-0" LONG

1'-7"
4'-0"
7"
11"
6"
6"
1'-5"
4'-4"

BILL OF MATERIALS

2 PCS	4" x 6" x 14'-0"	RUNNERS
2 PCS	2" x 4" x 13'-6"	TIES
2 PCS	2" x 4" x 3'-5½"	TIES
3 PCS	2" x 4" x 4'-0"	TOP CROSS TIES
4 PCS	2" x 4" x 4'-8½"	CORNER STUDS
28 PCS	2" x 4" x 4'-10½"	STANCHIONS
6 PCS	1" x 6" x 13'-7½"	SIDING-SIDES
6 PCS	1" x 6" x 4'-0"	SIDING-ENDS
3 PCS	1" x 6" x 16'-0"	SIDING-BETWEEN STANCHIONS
29 PCS	1" x 6" x 4'-0"	FLOORING
1 PC	1" x 6" x 14'-0"	DIAGONAL BRACE
4 LB	16 d	NAILS
4 LB	8 d	NAILS
2 EA	7" x ⅜"	BOLTS
2 FT	1" x ¼"	STRAP IRON

NOTE:
NOT SUITABLE FOR CATTLE WITH HORNS.

SIDE ELEVATION

1" x 6"
6"
2" x 4"
7"
2'-3"
13'-6"

ISOMETRIC VIEW

2" x 4" STUDS
1" x 6"
2" x 4" STANCHION
2" x 4" x 13'-6" TIES
2" x 4" x 4'-0" TIES
STRAP IRON
1" x 6" SIDING
4" x 6" RUNNER

COOPERATIVE EXTENSION WORK IN
AGRICULTURE AND HOME ECONOMICS
AND
UNITED STATES DEPARTMENT OF AGRICULTURE COOPERATING

CATTLE HAY RACK

TEX. '51 | EX. 5772 | SHEET 1 OF 1

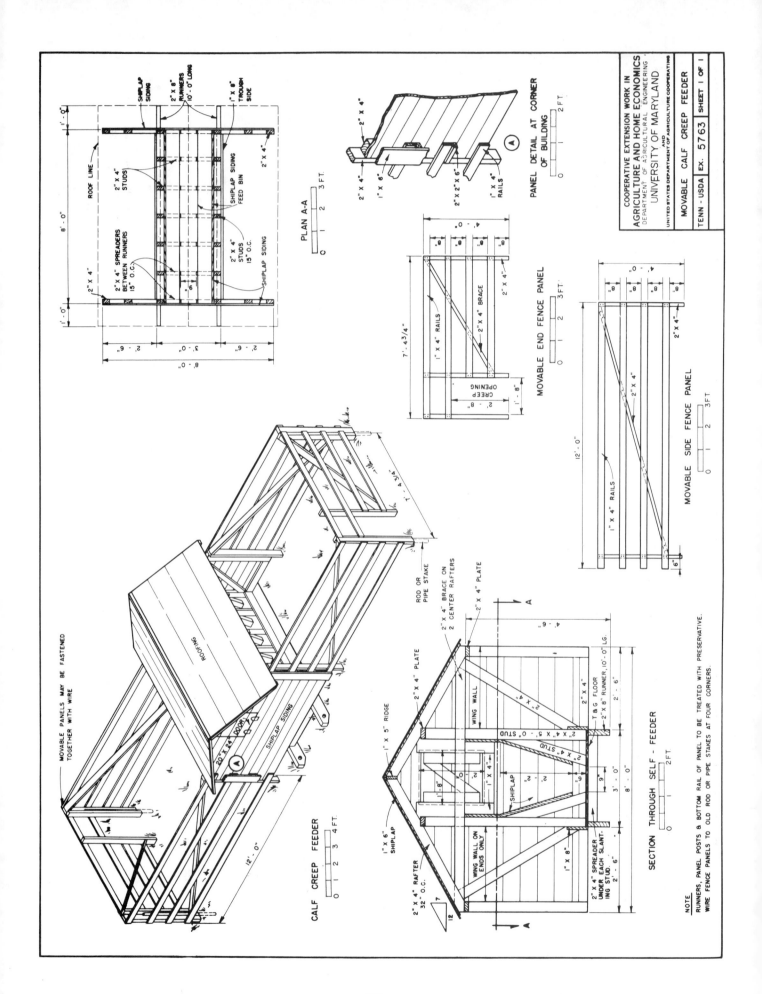

SHIPLAP SIDING

2" x 6" RUNNERS 10'-0" LONG

1" x 8" TROUGH SIDE

ROOF LINE

2" x 4" STUDS

SHIPLAP SIDING

FEED BIN

SHIPLAP SIDING

2" x 4" STUDS 15" O.C.

2" x 4" SPREADERS BETWEEN RUNNERS 15" O.C.

2" x 4"

2" x 4"

PLAN A-A

0 1 2 3 FT.

2'-6"   3'-0"   2'-6"

8'-0"

1'-0"   8'-0"   1'-0"

PANEL DETAIL AT CORNER OF BUILDING

0 1 2 FT

2" x 4"

1" x 6"

2" x 2" x 6"

1" x 4" RAILS

MOVABLE END FENCE PANEL

0 1 2 3 FT

1" x 4" RAILS

2" x 4" BRACE

2" x 4"

7'-4 3/4"

CREEP OPENING

8"

2'-8"

MOVABLE SIDE FENCE PANEL

0 1 2 3 FT

12'-0"

1" x 4" RAILS

2" x 4"

6"

COOPERATIVE EXTENSION WORK IN
AGRICULTURE AND HOME ECONOMICS
DEPARTMENT OF AGRICULTURAL ENGINEERING
UNIVERSITY OF MARYLAND
AND
UNITED STATES DEPARTMENT OF AGRICULTURE COOPERATING

MOVABLE CALF CREEP FEEDER

TENN - USDA | EX. 5763 | SHEET 1 OF 1

MOVABLE PANELS MAY BE FASTENED TOGETHER WITH WIRE

ROOFING

SHIPLAP SIDING

DOOR

CALF CREEP FEEDER

0 1 2 3 4 FT.

12'-0"

1" x 6" SHIPLAP

2" x 4" RAFTER 32" O.C.

ROD OR PIPE STAKE

2" x 4" BRACE ON 2 CENTER RAFTERS

2" x 4" PLATE

2" x 4" PLATE

1" x 5" RIDGE

WING WALL

2" x 4" STUD 5'-0"

2" x 4" STUD

1" x 4"

SHIPLAP

WING WALL ON ENDS ONLY

1" x 8"

2" x 4" SPREADER UNDER EACH SLANTING STUD

SECTION THROUGH SELF - FEEDER

0 1 2 FT

4'-6"

2'-6"

T & G FLOOR

2" x 8" RUNNER, 10'-0" LG.

2" x 4"

9"   3'-0"   9"

8'-0"

2'-6"

A

A

12

NOTE

RUNNERS, PANEL POSTS & BOTTOM RAIL OF PANEL TO BE TREATED WITH PRESERVATIVE.
WIRE FENCE PANELS TO OLD ROD OR PIPE STAKES AT FOUR CORNERS.

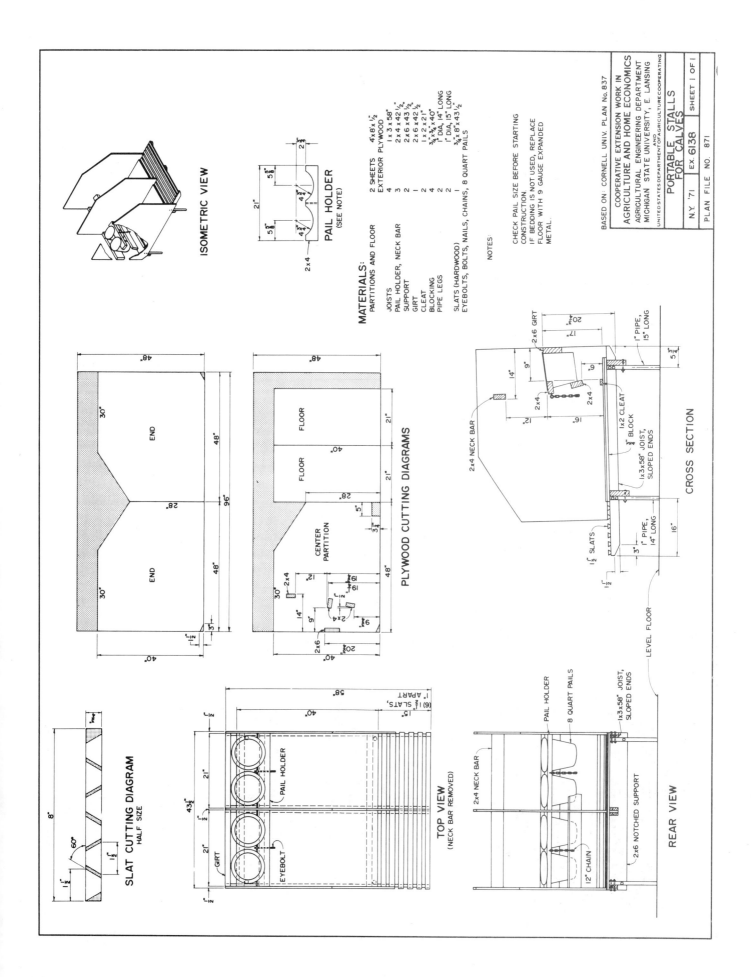

ISOMETRIC VIEW

PAIL HOLDER
(SEE NOTE)

MATERIALS:

PARTITIONS AND FLOOR	2 SHEETS	4'x8'x ½" EXTERIOR PLYWOOD
JOISTS	4	1 x 3 x 58"
PAIL HOLDER, NECK BAR	3	2 x 4 x 42 ½"
SUPPORT	2	2 x 6 x 43 ½"
GIRT	1	2 x 6 x 42 ½"
CLEAT	2	1 x 2 x 21"
BLOCKING	4	¾" x ¾" x 40"
PIPE LEGS	2	1" DIA, 14" LONG
	2	1" DIA, 15" LONG
SLATS (HARDWOOD)	1	¾" x 8" x 43 ½"
EYEBOLTS, BOLTS, NAILS, CHAINS, 8 QUART PAILS		

NOTES:

CHECK PAIL SIZE BEFORE STARTING
CONSTRUCTION.
IF BEDDING IS NOT USED, REPLACE
FLOOR WITH 9 GAUGE EXPANDED
METAL.

PLYWOOD CUTTING DIAGRAMS

END

END

FLOOR

FLOOR

CENTER PARTITION

CROSS SECTION

2x6 GIRT

2x4 NECK BAR

1x2 CLEAT

1x3x58" JOIST, SLOPED ENDS

1" PIPE, 15" LONG

1" PIPE, 14" LONG

SLATS

LEVEL FLOOR

SLAT CUTTING DIAGRAM
HALF SIZE

TOP VIEW
(NECK BAR REMOVED)

PAIL HOLDER

GIRT

EYEBOLT

(6) 1½" SLATS, 1" APART

REAR VIEW

PAIL HOLDER

8 QUART PAILS

2x4 NECK BAR

1x3x58" JOIST, SLOPED ENDS

2x6 NOTCHED SUPPORT

12" CHAIN

BASED ON: CORNELL UNIV. PLAN No. 837

COOPERATIVE EXTENSION WORK IN
AGRICULTURE AND HOME ECONOMICS
AGRICULTURAL ENGINEERING DEPARTMENT
MICHIGAN STATE UNIVERSITY, E. LANSING
AND
UNITED STATES DEPARTMENT OF AGRICULTURE COOPERATING

PORTABLE STALLS
FOR CALVES

N.Y. '71   EX. 6138   SHEET 1 OF 1

PLAN FILE NO.   871

203

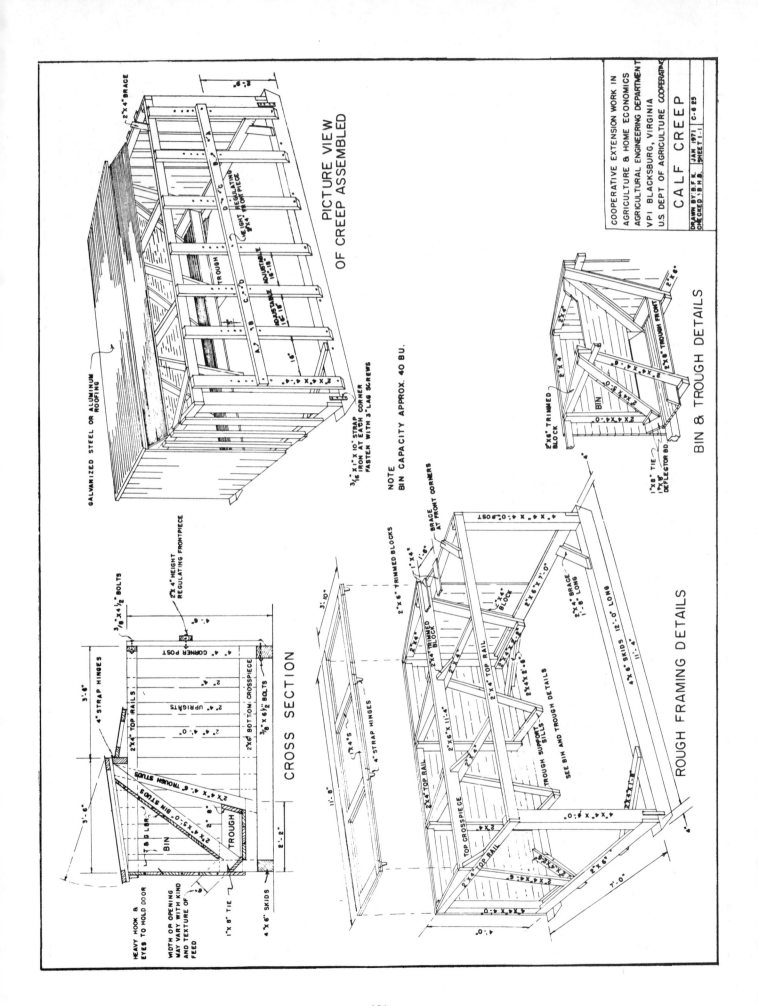

PICTURE VIEW
OF CREEP ASSEMBLED

CALF CREEP

COOPERATIVE EXTENSION WORK IN
AGRICULTURE & HOME ECONOMICS
AGRICULTURAL ENGINEERING DEPARTMENT
VPI BLACKSBURG, VIRGINIA
U.S. DEPT OF AGRICULTURE COOPERATING

DRAWN BY: B.F.K.   JAN. 1971   SHEET 1-1
CHECKED: B.H.B.   C-6.25

GALVANIZED STEEL OR ALUMINUM
ROOFING

NOTE
BIN CAPACITY APPROX. 40 BU.

3/16" x 1" x 10" STRAP
IRON AT EACH CORNER
FASTEN WITH 3" LAG SCREWS

BIN & TROUGH DETAILS

CROSS SECTION

ROUGH FRAMING DETAILS

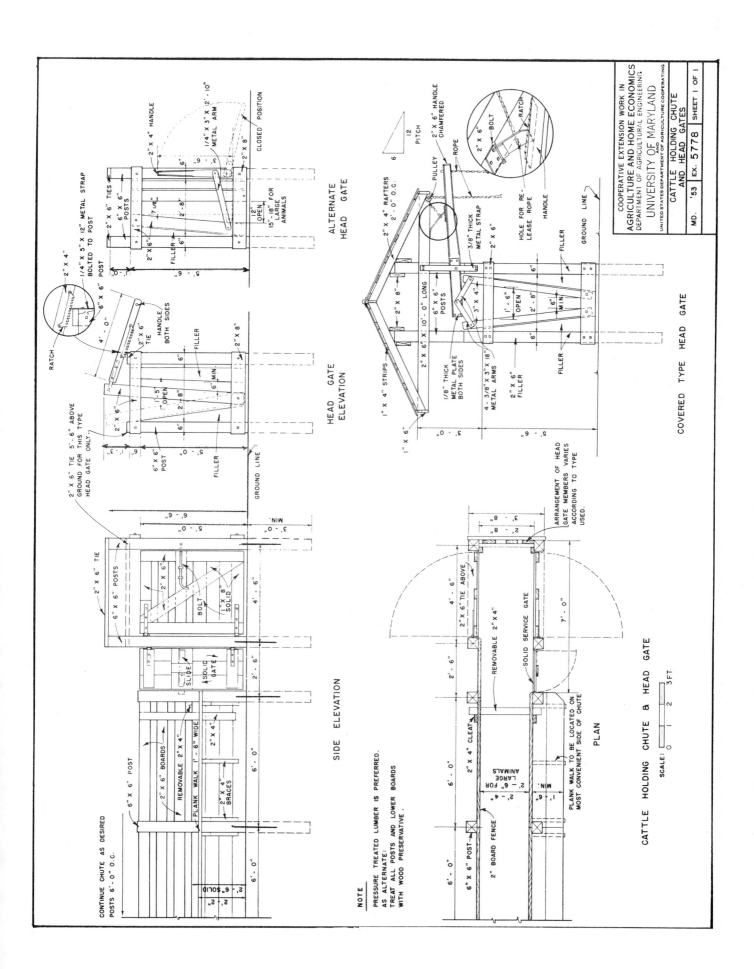

CATTLE HOLDING CHUTE & HEAD GATE

SCALE: 0 1 2 3 FT.

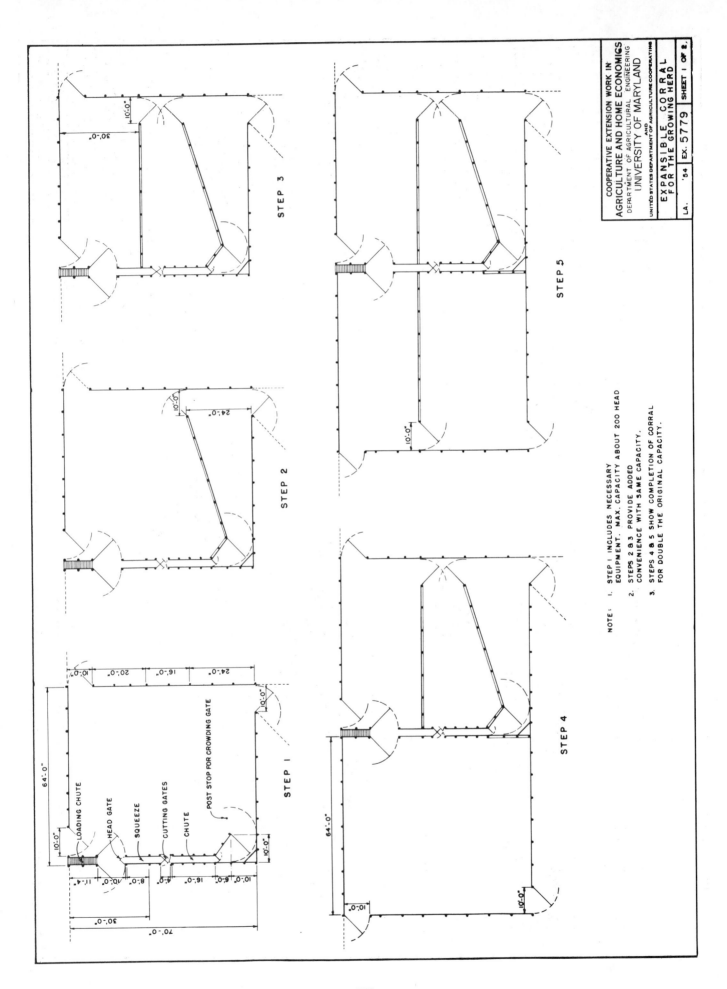

STEP 3

STEP 2

STEP 1

STEP 4

STEP 5

LOADING CHUTE
HEAD GATE
SQUEEZE
CUTTING GATES
CHUTE
POST STOP FOR CROWDING GATE

NOTE:
1. STEP I INCLUDES NECESSARY
   EQUIPMENT. MAX. CAPACITY ABOUT 200 HEAD

2. STEPS 2 & 3 PROVIDE ADDED
   CONVENIENCE WITH SAME CAPACITY.

3. STEPS 4 & 5 SHOW COMPLETION OF CORRAL
   FOR DOUBLE THE ORIGINAL CAPACITY.

COOPERATIVE EXTENSION WORK IN
AGRICULTURE AND HOME ECONOMICS
DEPARTMENT OF AGRICULTURAL ENGINEERING
UNIVERSITY OF MARYLAND
AND
UNITED STATES DEPARTMENT OF AGRICULTURE COOPERATING

EXPANSIBLE CORRAL
FOR THE GROWING HERD

LA. '54 EX. 5779 SHEET I OF 2.

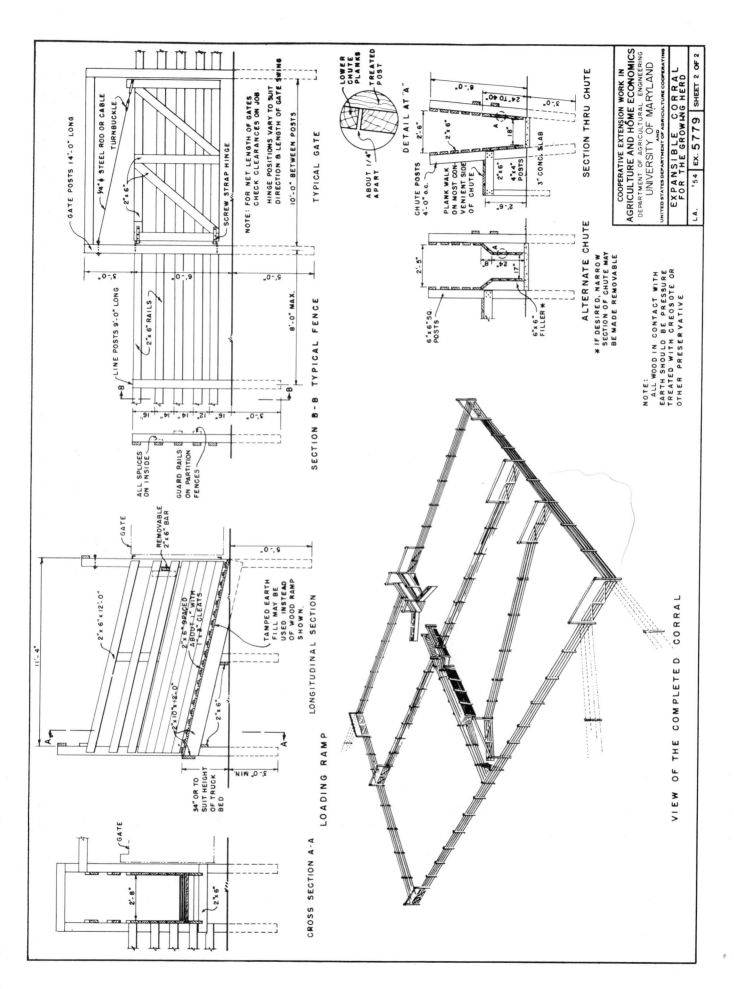

GATE POSTS 14'-0" LONG

¼" Ø STEEL ROD OR CABLE
TURNBUCKLE

2"×6"

SCREW STRAP HINGE

NOTE: FOR NET LENGTH OF GATES
CHECK CLEARANCES ON JOB.
HINGE POSITIONS VARY TO SUIT
DIRECTION & LENGTH OF GATE SWING

10'-0" BETWEEN POSTS

TYPICAL GATE

LINE POSTS 9'-0" LONG

2"×6" RAILS

ALL SPLICES
ON INSIDE

GUARD RAILS
ON PARTITION
FENCES

SECTION B-B TYPICAL FENCE

8'-0" MAX.

GATE

REMOVABLE
2"×6" BAR

2"×6"×12'-0"

2"×6" SPACED
ABOUT 1" WITH
1"×3" CLEATS

2"×10"×12'-0"

2"×6"

TAMPED EARTH
FILL MAY BE
USED INSTEAD
OF WOOD RAMP
SHOWN.

11'-4"

34" OR TO
SUIT HEIGHT
OF TRUCK
BED

3'-0" MIN.

LONGITUDINAL SECTION

LOADING RAMP

GATE

2"-8"

2"×6"

CROSS SECTION A-A

LOWER
CHUTE
PLANKS

TREATED
POST

ABOUT ¼"
APART

DETAIL AT "A"

CHUTE POSTS
4'-0" o.c.

PLANK WALK
ON MOST CON-
VENIENT SIDE
OF CHUTE

2"×6"

2"×6"

4"×4"
POSTS

3" CONC. SLAB

24" TO 40"

6'-0"

3'-0"

2'-6"

2'-6"

18"

SECTION THRU CHUTE

6"×6" SQ.
POSTS

6"×6"
FILLER *

2'-5"

24"

18"

17"

ALTERNATE CHUTE

* IF DESIRED, NARROW
SECTION OF CHUTE MAY
BE MADE REMOVABLE

NOTE:
ALL WOOD IN CONTACT WITH
EARTH SHOULD BE PRESSURE
TREATED WITH CREOSOTE OR
OTHER PRESERVATIVE

VIEW OF THE COMPLETED CORRAL

COOPERATIVE EXTENSION WORK IN
AGRICULTURE AND HOME ECONOMICS
DEPARTMENT OF AGRICULTURAL ENGINEERING
UNIVERSITY OF MARYLAND
AND
UNITED STATES DEPARTMENT OF AGRICULTURE COOPERATING

EXPANSIBLE CORRAL
FOR THE GROWING HERD

LA. | '54 | EX. 5779 | SHEET 2 OF 2

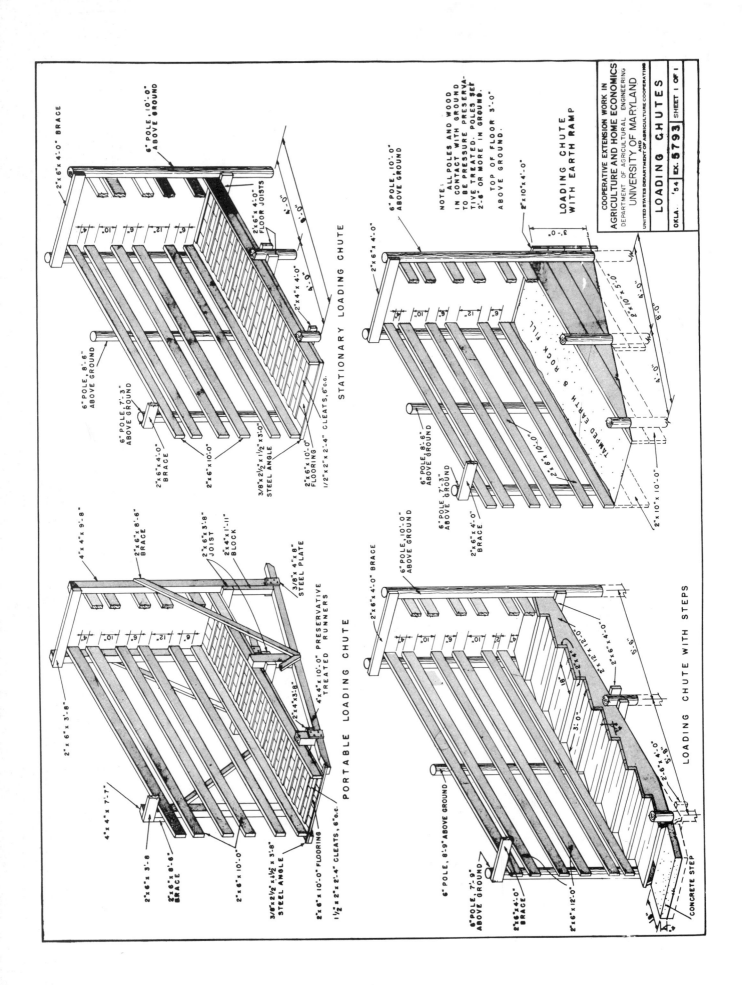

STATIONARY LOADING CHUTE

PORTABLE LOADING CHUTE

LOADING CHUTE WITH EARTH RAMP

LOADING CHUTE WITH STEPS

NOTE: ALL POLES AND WOOD IN CONTACT WITH GROUND TO BE PRESSURE PRESERVATIVE TREATED. POLES SET 2'-6" OR MORE IN GROUND. TOP OF FLOOR 3'-0" ABOVE GROUND.

COOPERATIVE EXTENSION WORK IN
AGRICULTURE AND HOME ECONOMICS
DEPARTMENT OF AGRICULTURAL ENGINEERING
UNIVERSITY OF MARYLAND
AND
UNITED STATES DEPARTMENT OF AGRICULTURE COOPERATING

LOADING CHUTES

OKLA. '54 | EX. 5793 | SHEET 1 OF 1

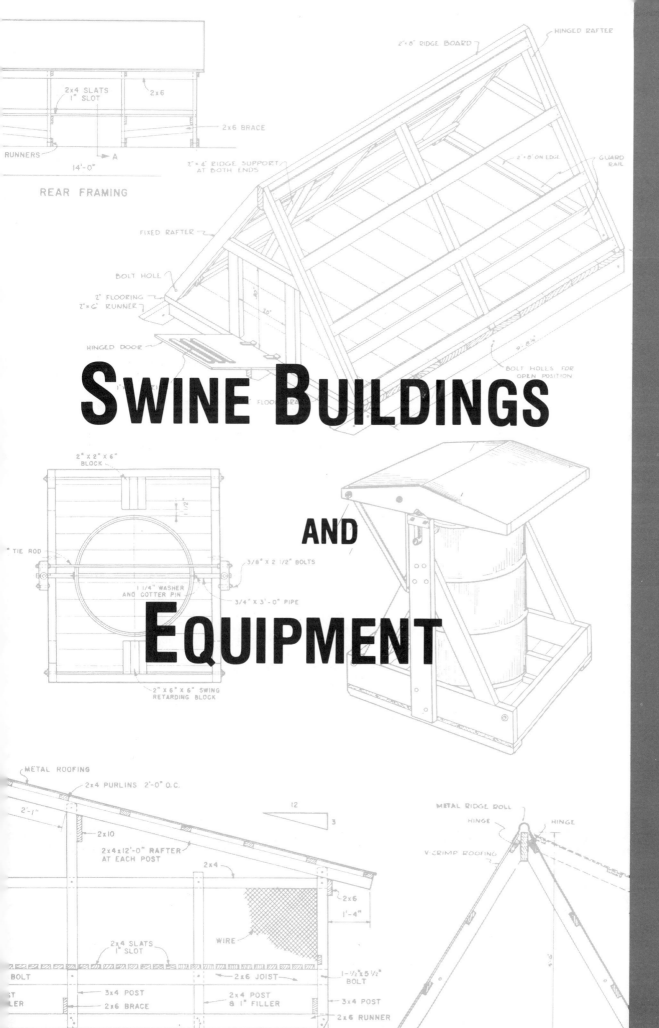

REAR FRAMING

2x4 SLATS 1" SLOT

2x6

2x6 BRACE

RUNNERS

14'-0"

A

2"x 4" RIDGE SUPPORT AT BOTH ENDS

2"x 8" RIDGE BOARD

HINGED RAFTER

2"x 8" ON EDGE

GUARD RAIL

FIXED RAFTER

BOLT HOLE

2" FLOORING 2"x 6" RUNNER

HINGED DOOR

10"

9'-8"

BOLT HOLES FOR OPEN POSITION

Swine Buildings

2" X 2" X 6" BLOCK

1 1/2"

" TIE ROD

3/8" X 2 1/2" BOLTS

1 1/4" WASHER AND COTTER PIN

3/4" X 3'-0" PIPE

2" X 6" X 6" SWING RETARDING BLOCK

and

Equipment

METAL ROOFING

2x4 PURLINS 2'-0" O.C.

2'-1"

2x10

2x4x12'-0" RAFTER AT EACH POST

2x4

2x4 SLATS 1" SLOT

WIRE

12

3

METAL RIDGE ROLL

HINGE

HINGE

V-CRIMP ROOFING

2x6

1'-4"

BOLT

3x4 POST

LER

2x4 POST 2x6 BRACE

2x6 JOIST

2x4 POST 8 1" FILLER

1-1/2"x 5 1/2" BOLT

3x4 POST

2x6 RUNNER

4'-0"

4'-0"

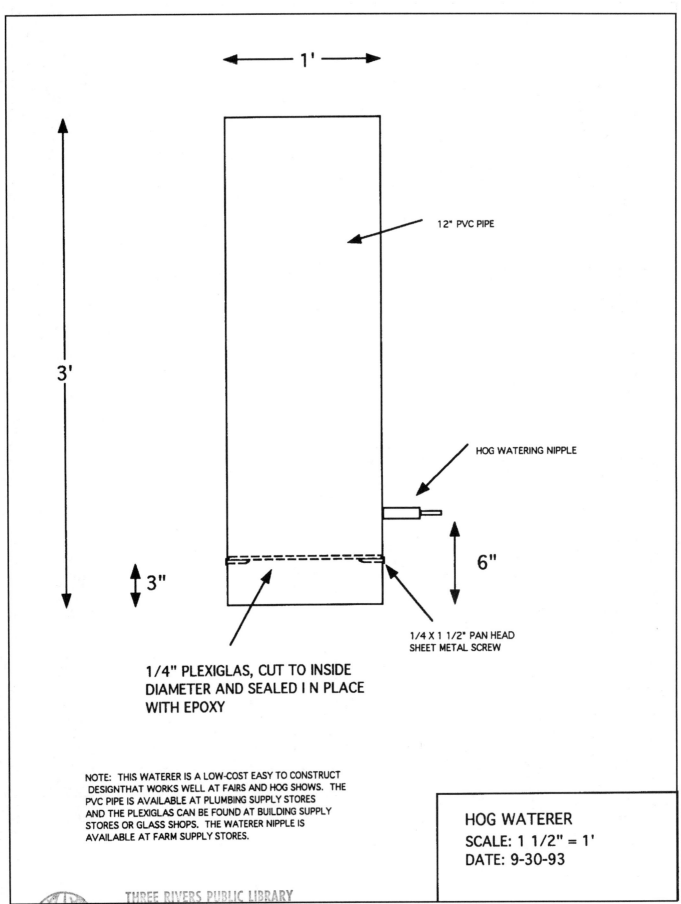

1'

3'

3"

12" PVC PIPE

HOG WATERING NIPPLE

6"

1/4 X 1 1/2" PAN HEAD
SHEET METAL SCREW

1/4" PLEXIGLAS, CUT TO INSIDE
DIAMETER AND SEALED I N PLACE
WITH EPOXY

NOTE: THIS WATERER IS A LOW-COST EASY TO CONSTRUCT
 DESIGNTHAT WORKS WELL AT FAIRS AND HOG SHOWS. THE
PVC PIPE IS AVAILABLE AT PLUMBING SUPPLY STORES
AND THE PLEXIGLAS CAN BE FOUND AT BUILDING SUPPLY
STORES OR GLASS SHOPS. THE WATERER NIPPLE IS
AVAILABLE AT FARM SUPPLY STORES.

HOG WATERER
SCALE: 1 1/2" = 1'
DATE: 9-30-93

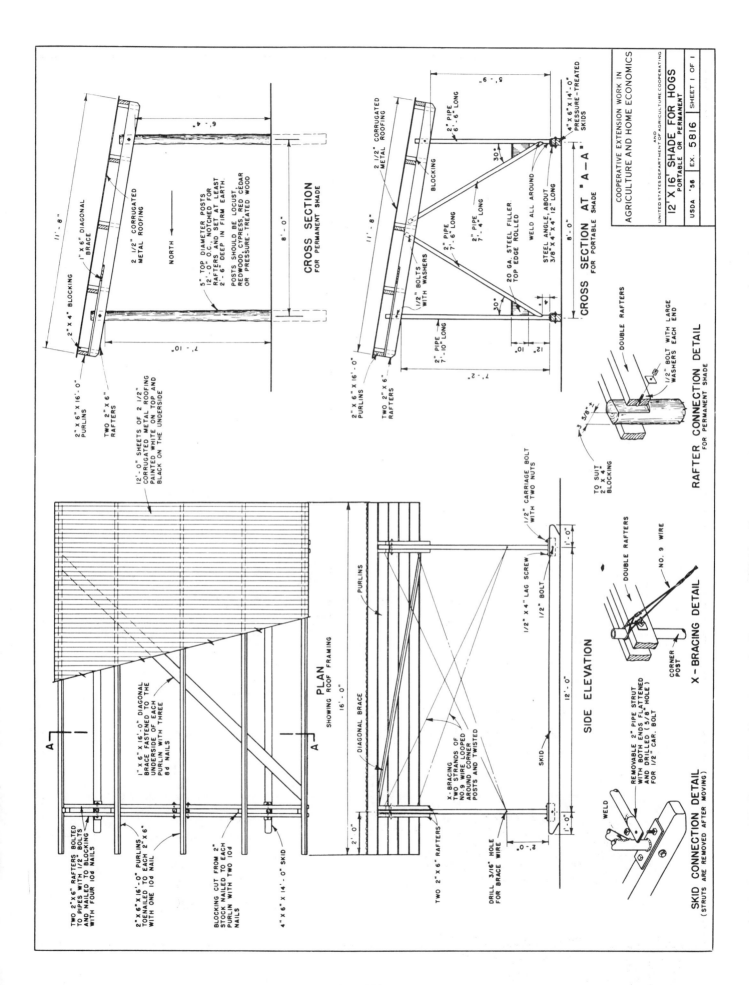

CROSS SECTION
FOR PERMANENT SHADE

NORTH

11'-8" DIAGONAL

1" x 6" BRACE

2" x 4" BLOCKING

2 1/2" CORRUGATED METAL ROOFING

9'-4"

8'-0"

7'-10"

5" TOP DIAMETER POSTS 12'-0" O.C. NOTCHED FOR RAFTERS AND SET AT LEAST 2'-6" DEEP IN FIRM EARTH.

POSTS SHOULD BE LOCUST, REDWOOD, CYPRESS, RED CEDAR OR PRESSURE-TREATED WOOD

2" x 6" x 16'-0" PURLINS

TWO 2" x 6" RAFTERS

12'-0" SHEETS OF 2 1/2" CORRUGATED METAL ROOFING PAINTED WHITE ON TOP AND BLACK ON THE UNDERSIDE

CROSS SECTION AT "A-A"
FOR PORTABLE SHADE

4" x 6" x 14'-0" PRESSURE-TREATED SKIDS

30°

2" PIPE 6'-6" LONG

2" PIPE 7'-6" LONG

2" PIPE 7'-4" LONG

20 GA. STEEL FILLER TOP EDGE ROLLED

WELD ALL AROUND

STEEL ANGLE, ABOUT 3/8" x 4" x 4" 12" LONG

30°

2" PIPE 7'-10" LONG

1/2" BOLTS WITH WASHERS

BLOCKING

2 1/2" CORRUGATED METAL ROOFING

11'-8"

5'-9"

6'-0"

7'-2"

10"

12"

2" x 6" x 16'-0" PURLINS

TWO 2" x 6" RAFTERS

DOUBLE RAFTERS

1/2" BOLT WITH LARGE WASHERS EACH END

TO SUIT 2" x 4" BLOCKING

3 5/8"

RAFTER CONNECTION DETAIL
FOR PERMANENT SHADE

DOUBLE RAFTERS

NO. 9 WIRE

CORNER POST

X-BRACING DETAIL

WELD

REMOVABLE 2" PIPE STRUT WITH BOTH ENDS FLATTENED AND DRILLED (5/8" HOLE) FOR 1/2" CAR. BOLT

SKID CONNECTION DETAIL
(STRUTS ARE REMOVED AFTER MOVING)

PLAN
SHOWING ROOF FRAMING

16'-0"

TWO 2" x 6" RAFTERS BOLTED TO PIPES WITH 1/2" BOLTS AND NAILED TO BLOCKING WITH FOUR 10d NAILS

2" x 6" x 16'-0" PURLINS TOENAILED TO EACH 2" x 6"

1" x 6" x 16'-0" DIAGONAL BRACE FASTENED TO THE UNDERSIDE OF EACH PURLIN WITH THREE 8d NAILS

BLOCKING CUT FROM 2" STOCK NAILED TO EACH PURLIN WITH TWO 10d NAILS

4" x 6" x 14'-0" SKID

A

A

SIDE ELEVATION

DIAGONAL BRACE

PURLINS

1/2" CARRIAGE BOLT WITH TWO NUTS

1/2" x 4" LAG SCREW

1/2" BOLT

X-BRACING TWO STRANDS OF NO. 9 WIRE LOOPED AROUND CORNER POSTS AND TWISTED

SKID

DRILL 3/16" HOLE FOR BRACE WIRE

12'-0"

2'-0"

3'-0"

1'-0"

1'-0"

TWO 2" x 6" RAFTERS

COOPERATIVE EXTENSION WORK IN AGRICULTURE AND HOME ECONOMICS
UNITED STATES DEPARTMENT OF AGRICULTURE COOPERATING
AND

12' X 16' SHADE FOR HOGS
PORTABLE OR PERMANENT

USDA '56   EX. 5816   SHEET 1 OF 1

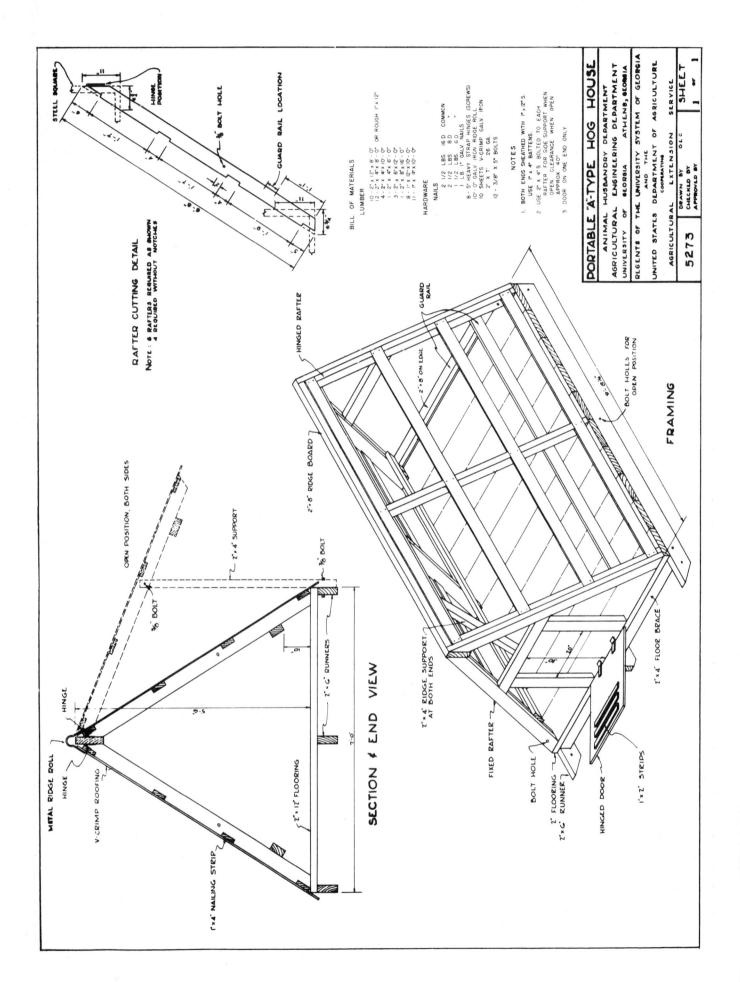

RAFTER CUTTING DETAIL

NOTE: 6 RAFTERS REQUIRED AS SHOWN
4 REQUIRED WITHOUT NOTCHES

SECTION & END VIEW

FRAMING

BILL OF MATERIALS

LUMBER

10 - 2" x 12" x 8'- 0"   OR ROUGH 1" x 12"
12 - 2" x 4" x 8'- 0"   "
4 - 2" x 4" x 10'- 0"   "
1 - 2" x 4" x 6'- 0"   "
3 - 2" x 6" x 12'- 0"   "
2 - 2" x 6" x 16'- 0"   "
8 - 1" x 12" x 10'- 0"   "
11 - 1" x 4" x 10'- 0"   "

HARDWARE

NAILS
    2 1/2 LBS. 16 D COMMON
    2 1/2 LBS. 8 D   "
    1 1/2 LBS. 6 D   "
    1 LB. 1" GALV. NAILS

8 - 5' HEAVY STRAP HINGES (SCREWS)
10'- 0" GALV. IRON RIDGE ROLL
10 SHEETS V-CRIMP GALV. IRON
    2' x 7'   26 GA.
12 - 3/8" x 5" BOLTS

NOTES
1. BOTH ENDS SHEATHED WITH 1" x 12"S.
   USE 1" x 4" BATTENS.
2. USE 2" x 4"S BOLTED TO EACH
   RAFTER FOR SIDE SUPPORT WHEN
   OPEN. CLEARANCE WHEN OPEN
   APPROX 40°
3. DOOR ON ONE END ONLY

PORTABLE "A"-TYPE HOG HOUSE

ANIMAL HUSBANDRY DEPARTMENT
AGRICULTURAL ENGINEERING DEPARTMENT
UNIVERSITY OF GEORGIA   ATHENS, GEORGIA
REGENTS OF THE UNIVERSITY SYSTEM OF GEORGIA
AND THE
UNITED STATES DEPARTMENT OF AGRICULTURE
COOPERATING
AGRICULTURAL EXTENSION SERVICE

DRAWN BY	OLC	SHEET
CHECKED BY		1 OF 1
APPROVED BY		

5273

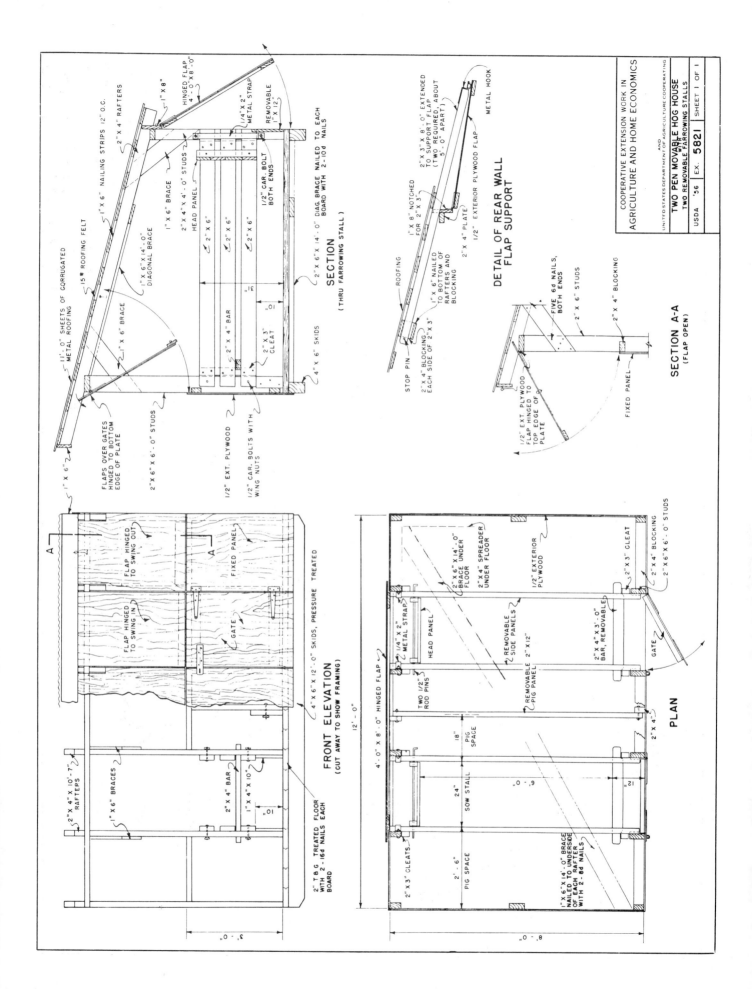

SECTION
(THRU FARROWING STALL)

11'-0" SHEETS OF CORRUGATED METAL ROOFING
15# ROOFING FELT
1" X 6" NAILING STRIPS 12" O.C.
2" X 4" RAFTERS
HINGED FLAP 4'-0" X 8'-0"
1/4" X 2" METAL STRAP
REMOVABLE 1" X 12"
1" X 6" X 14'-0" DIAGONAL BRACE
1" X 6" BRACE
2" X 4" X 4'-0" STUDS
HEAD PANEL
2" X 6"
2" X 6"
2" X 6"
1/2" CAR. BOLT BOTH ENDS
2" X 6" X 14'-0" DIAG. BRACE NAILED TO EACH BOARD WITH 2-10d NAILS
2" X 4" BAR
2" X 3" CLEAT
4" X 6" SKIDS

FLAPS OVER GATES HINGED TO BOTTOM EDGE OF PLATE
2" X 6" X 6'-0" STUDS
1/2" EXT. PLYWOOD
1/2" CAR. BOLTS WITH WING NUTS
1" X 6" BRACE
1" X 6"

DETAIL OF REAR WALL FLAP SUPPORT

2" X 3" X 8'-0" EXTENDED TO SUPPORT FLAP (TWO REQUIRED, ABOUT 5'-0" APART)
METAL HOOK
1" X 8" NOTCHED FOR 2" X 3"
ROOFING
1" X 6" NAILED TO BOTTOM OF RAFTERS AND BLOCKING
2" X 4" PLATE
1/2" EXTERIOR PLYWOOD FLAP
STOP PIN
2" X 4" BLOCKING EACH SIDE OF 2" X 3"

SECTION A-A
(FLAP OPEN)

FIVE 6d NAILS, BOTH ENDS
2" X 6" STUDS
2" X 4" BLOCKING
1/2" EXT. PLYWOOD FLAP HINGED TO TOP EDGE OF PLATE
FIXED PANEL

FRONT ELEVATION
(CUT AWAY TO SHOW FRAMING)

A
FLAP HINGED TO SWING OUT
FLAP HINGED TO SWING IN
FIXED PANEL
GATE
4" X 6" X 12'-0" SKIDS, PRESSURE TREATED
A

2" X 4" X 10'-7" RAFTERS
1" X 6" BRACES
2" X 4" BAR
1" X 4" X 10"
2" T & G TREATED FLOOR WITH 2-16d NAILS EACH BOARD
3'-0"

PLAN

12'-0"
4'-0" X 8'-0" HINGED FLAP
2" X 6" X 14'-0" BRACE UNDER FLOOR
2" X 4" SPREADER UNDER FLOOR
1/2" EXTERIOR PLYWOOD
1/4" X 2" METAL STRAP
HEAD PANEL
TWO 1/2" ROD PINS
REMOVABLE SIDE PANELS
REMOVABLE 2" X 12"
REMOVABLE PIG PANEL
2" X 4" X 3'-0" BAR, REMOVABLE
GATE
2" X 3" CLEAT
2" X 4" BLOCKING
2" X 6" X 6'-0" STUDS
2" X 3" CLEATS
PIG SPACE
2'-6"
SOW STALL
24"
18"
PIG SPACE
9'-0"
2" X 4"
12"
1" X 6" X 14'-0" BRACE NAILED TO UNDERSIDE OF EACH RAFTER WITH 2-8d NAILS
8'-0"

COOPERATIVE EXTENSION WORK IN AGRICULTURE AND HOME ECONOMICS
AND
UNITED STATES DEPARTMENT OF AGRICULTURE COOPERATING

TWO PEN MOVABLE HOG HOUSE
WITH TWO REMOVABLE FARROWING STALLS

USDA | '56 | EX. 5821 | SHEET 1 OF 1

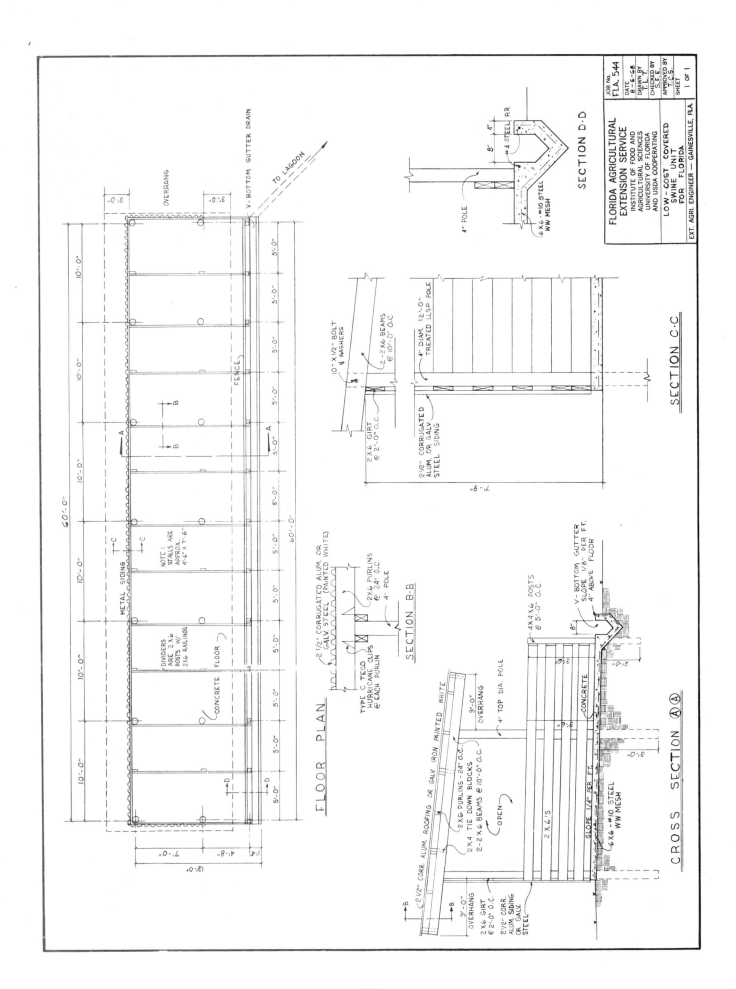

FLOOR PLAN

SECTION B-B

SECTION C-C

SECTION D-D

CROSS SECTION (A)(A)

NOTE:
STALLS ARE
APPROX.
4'-6" X 7'-6"

DIVIDERS
ARE 2X6
POSTS W/
2X6 RAILINGS

CONCRETE FLOOR

METAL SIDING

OVERHANG

V-BOTTOM GUTTER DRAIN

TO LAGOON

FENCE

2 1/2" CORRUGATED ALUM. OR
GALV. STEEL (PAINTED WHITE)

2X6 PURLINS
@ 24" O.C.

4" POLE

TYPE C TECO
HURRICANE CLIPS
@ EACH PURLIN

10" X 1/2" BOLT
& WASHERS

2-2X6 BEAMS
@ 10'-0" O.C.

2X6 GIRT
@ 2'-0" O.C.

2 1/2" CORRUGATED
ALUM. OR GALV.
STEEL SIDING

4" DIAM. 12'-0" LLSP POLE
TREATED

2 1/2" CORRUGATED
ALUM. OR GALV.
STEEL SIDING

#4 STEEL R.R.

4" POLE

6X6-#10 STEEL
WW MESH

2 1/2" CORR. ALUM. ROOFING OR GALV. IRON PAINTED WHITE

2X6 PURLINS - 24" O.C.

2X4 TIE DOWN BLOCKS

2-2X6 BEAMS @ 10'-0" O.C.

OPEN

OVERHANG

4" TOP DIA. POLE

4X4X6 POSTS
@ 5'-0" O.C.

V-BOTTOM GUTTER
SLOPE 1/8" PER FT.
4" ABOVE FLOOR

CONCRETE

2X6'S

6X6-#10 STEEL
WW MESH

SLOPE 1/4" PER FT.

2 1/2" CORR.
ALUM. SIDING
OR GALV.
STEEL

2X6 GIRT
@ 2'-0" O.C.

OVERHANG

FLORIDA AGRICULTURAL
EXTENSION SERVICE
INSTITUTE OF FOOD AND
AGRICULTURAL SCIENCES
UNIVERSITY OF FLORIDA
AND USDA COOPERATING

LOW-COST COVERED
SWINE UNIT
FOR FLORIDA

EXT. AGRI. ENGINEER — GAINESVILLE, FLA.

JOB No. FLA. 544
DATE 8-6-68
DRAWN BY L.T.
CHECKED BY S.F.
APPROVED BY T.C.S.
SHEET 1 OF 1

214

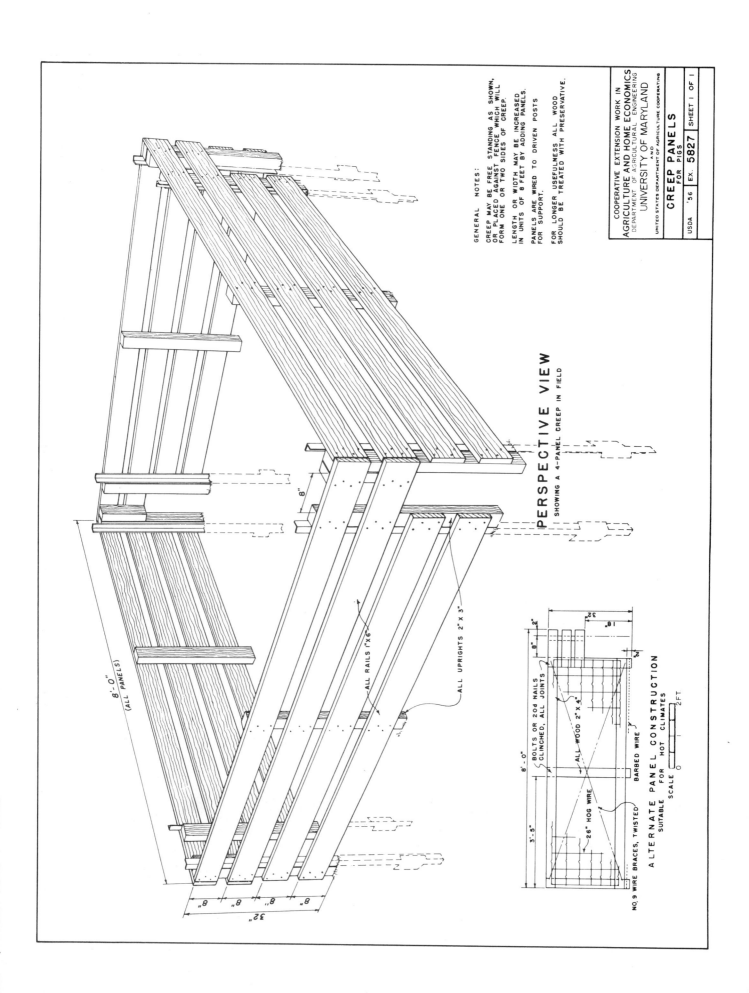

PERSPECTIVE VIEW

SHOWING A 4-PANEL CREEP IN FIELD

8'-0"
(ALL PANELS)

8" 8" 8" 8"
32"

ALL RAILS 1"x6"

ALL UPRIGHTS 2" x 3"

8"

GENERAL NOTES:

CREEP MAY BE FREE STANDING AS SHOWN,
OR PLACED AGAINST FENCE WHICH WILL
FORM ONE OR TWO SIDES OF CREEP.

LENGTH OR WIDTH MAY BE INCREASED
IN UNITS OF 8 FEET BY ADDING PANELS.

PANELS ARE WIRED TO DRIVEN POSTS
FOR SUPPORT.

FOR LONGER USEFULNESS ALL WOOD
SHOULD BE TREATED WITH PRESERVATIVE.

ALTERNATE PANEL CONSTRUCTION
SUITABLE FOR HOT CLIMATES

SCALE 0 1 2FT

8'-0"

3'-5"

NO. 9 WIRE BRACES, TWISTED

BARBED WIRE

26" HOG WIRE

ALL WOOD 2" x 4"

BOLTS OR 20d NAILS
CLINCHED, ALL JOINTS

32"

18"

2"

8"

COOPERATIVE EXTENSION WORK IN
AGRICULTURE AND HOME ECONOMICS
DEPARTMENT OF AGRICULTURAL ENGINEERING
UNIVERSITY OF MARYLAND
AND
UNITED STATES DEPARTMENT OF AGRICULTURE COOPERATING

CREEP PANELS
FOR PIGS

USDA '56 Ex. 5827 SHEET 1 OF 1

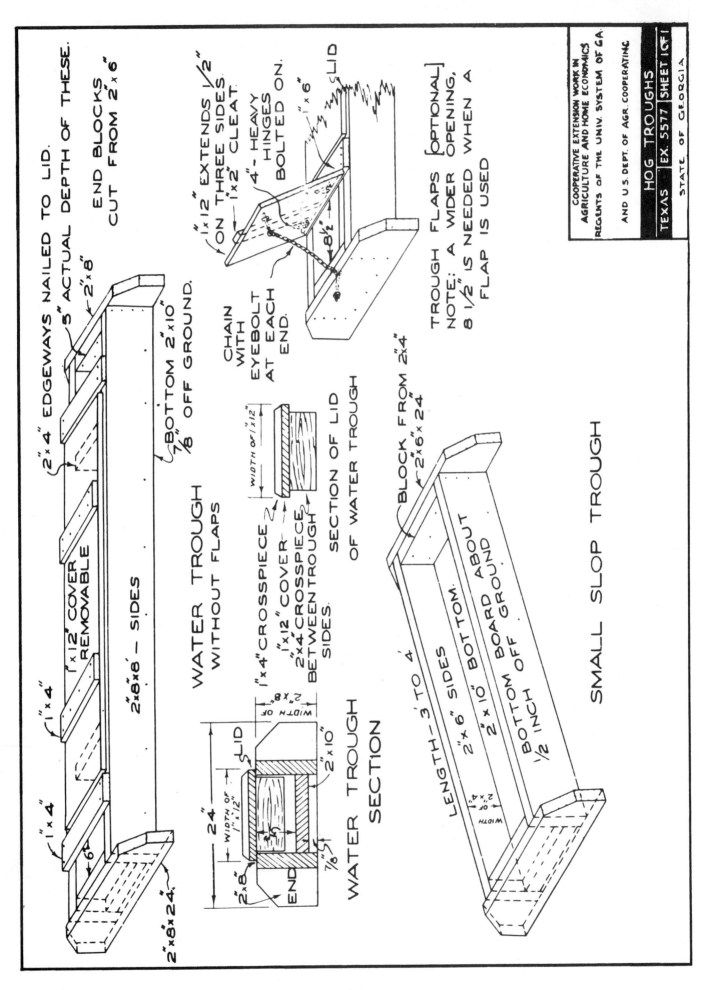

END BLOCKS CUT FROM 2"x6"

5" ACTUAL DEPTH OF THESE.

2"x4" EDGEWAYS NAILED TO LID.

2"x8"

1"x12" EXTENDS 1/2" ON THREE SIDES

1"x2" CLEAT

4"- HEAVY HINGES BOLTED ON.

1"x6"

LID

8 1/2"

CHAIN WITH EYEBOLT AT EACH END.

TROUGH FLAPS [OPTIONAL]

NOTE: A WIDER OPENING, 8 1/2" IS NEEDED WHEN A FLAP IS USED

BOTTOM 2"x10" 7/8" OFF GROUND.

1"x4"

1"x4"

1"x12" COVER REMOVABLE

2"x8"x8'- SIDES

6"

2"x8"x24"

WATER TROUGH WITHOUT FLAPS

WIDTH OF 1"x12"

1"x4" CROSSPIECE

1"x12" COVER

2"x4" CROSSPIECE BETWEEN TROUGH SIDES.

SECTION OF LID OF WATER TROUGH

BLOCK FROM 2"x4" 2"x6"x24"

WIDTH OF 2"x8"

LID

24"

WIDTH OF 1"x12"

2"x10"

7/8"

2"x8"

END

WATER TROUGH SECTION

LENGTH-3' TO 4'

2"x6" SIDES

2"x10" BOTTOM.

BOTTOM BOARD ABOUT 1/2 INCH OFF GROUND

WIDTH OF 2"x4"

SMALL SLOP TROUGH

COOPERATIVE EXTENSION WORK IN AGRICULTURE AND HOME ECONOMICS

REGENTS OF THE UNIV. SYSTEM OF GA.

AND U.S. DEPT. OF AGR. COOPERATING.

HOG TROUGHS

TEXAS | EX. 5577 | SHEET 1 OF 1

STATE OF GEORGIA

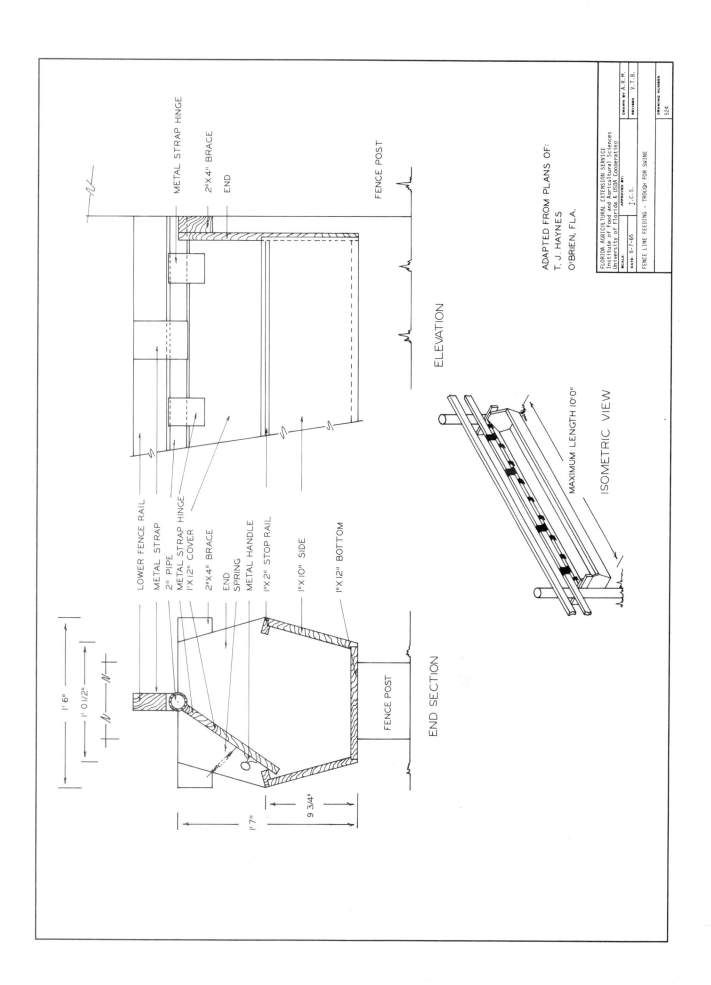

METAL STRAP HINGE

2"X 4" BRACE

END

FENCE POST

ELEVATION

LOWER FENCE RAIL

METAL STRAP

2" PIPE

METAL STRAP HINGE

I'X 12" COVER

2"X4" BRACE

END

SPRING

METAL HANDLE

I"X 2" STOP RAIL

I"X 10" SIDE

I"X 12" BOTTOM

MAXIMUM LENGTH 10'0"

ISOMETRIC VIEW

1' 6"

1' 0 1/2"

1' 7"

9 3/4"

FENCE POST

END SECTION

ADAPTED FROM PLANS OF:
T. J. HAYNES
O'BRIEN, FLA.

FLORIDA AGRICULTURAL EXTENSION SERVICE
Institute of Food and Agricultural Sciences
University of Florida & USDA Cooperating

SCALE:
DATE: 6-7-65
APPROVED BY:
J.C.S.

DRAWN BY: A.R.M.
REVISED   V.T.B.

DRAWING NUMBER
524

FENCE LINE FEEDING - TROUGH FOR SWINE

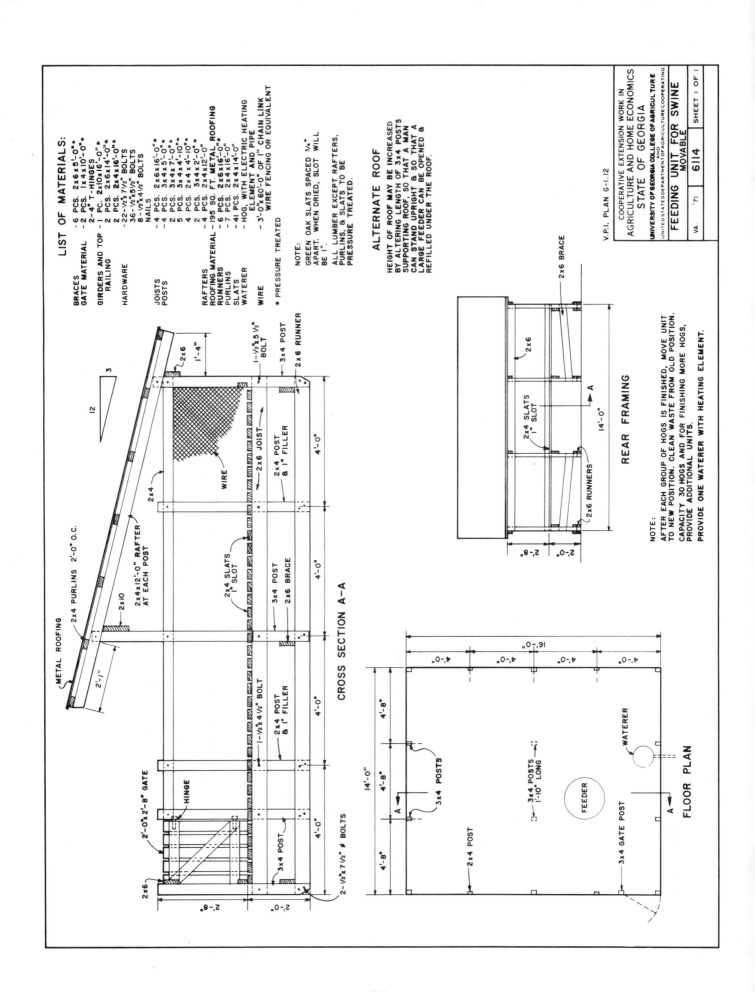

LIST OF MATERIALS:

BRACES	- 6 PCS. 2x6x5'-0"*
GATE MATERIAL	- 2 PCS. 1x4x10'-0"*
GIRDERS AND TOP RAILING	- 1 PC. 2x10x16'-0"*
HARDWARE	2 PCS. 2x6x14'-0"*
	2 PCS. 2x4x16'-0"*
	-22-1/2x7 1/2" BOLTS
	36-1/2x5 1/2" BOLTS
	8-1/2x4 1/2" BOLTS
	NAILS
JOISTS	- 4 PCS. 2x6x16'-0"*
POSTS	- 2 PCS. 3x4x5'-0"*
	2 PCS. 3x4x7'-0"*
	5 PCS. 3x4x4'-10"*
	4 PCS. 2x4x4'-10"*
	2 PCS. 3x4x2'-0"*
RAFTERS	- 4 PCS. 2x4x12'-0"*
ROOFING MATERIAL	- 195 SQ. FT. METAL ROOFING
RUNNERS	- 6 PCS. 2x6x16'-0"*
PURLINS	- 7 PCS. 2x4x16'-0"*
SLATS	-41 PCS. 2x4x14'-0"
WATERER	- HOG, WITH ELECTRIC HEATING ELEMENT AND PIPE
WIRE	- 3'-0"x60'-0" OF 1" CHAIN LINK WIRE FENCING OR EQUIVALENT

* PRESSURE TREATED

NOTE:

GREEN OAK SLATS SPACED 3/4" APART. WHEN DRIED, SLOT WILL BE 1".

ALL LUMBER EXCEPT RAFTERS, PURLINS, & SLATS TO BE PRESSURE TREATED.

2x4 PURLINS 2'-0" O.C.

METAL ROOFING

CROSS SECTION A-A

ALTERNATE ROOF

HEIGHT OF ROOF MAY BE INCREASED BY ALTERING LENGTH OF 3x4 POSTS SUPPORTING ROOF, SO THAT A MAN CAN STAND UPRIGHT & SO THAT A LARGE FEEDER CAN BE OPENED & REFILLED UNDER THE ROOF.

REAR FRAMING

NOTE:

AFTER EACH GROUP OF HOGS IS FINISHED, MOVE UNIT TO NEW POSITION. CLEAN WASTE FROM OLD POSITION. CAPACITY 30 HOGS AND FOR FINISHING MORE HOGS, PROVIDE ADDITIONAL UNITS.

PROVIDE ONE WATERER WITH HEATING ELEMENT.

FLOOR PLAN

V.P.I. PLAN G-1.12

COOPERATIVE EXTENSION WORK IN
AGRICULTURE AND HOME ECONOMICS
STATE OF GEORGIA
UNIVERSITY OF GEORGIA COLLEGE OF AGRICULTURE
AND
UNITED STATES DEPARTMENT OF AGRICULTURE COOPERATING

FEEDING UNIT FOR SWINE
MOVABLE

| VA. | '71 | 6114 | SHEET 1 OF 1 |

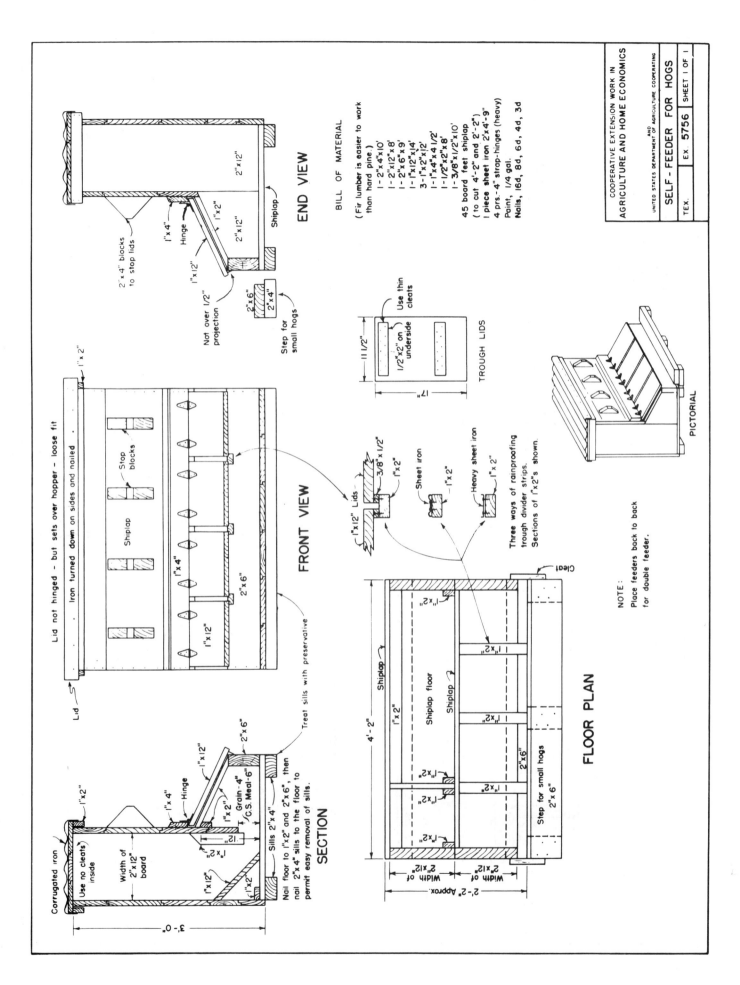

END VIEW

2"x12"

2"x4" blocks to stop lids

I"x4"
Hinge
I"x2"

2"x12"

Shiplap

Not over 1/2" projection

2"x6"   2"x4"

Step for small hogs

BILL OF MATERIAL

(Fir lumber is easier to work than hard pine.)
1 - 2"x4"x10'
1 - 2"x12"x8'
1 - 2"x6"x9'
1 - 1"x12"x14'
3 - 1"x2"x12'
1 - 1"x4"x41/2'
1 - 1/2"x2"x8'
1 - 3/8"x1/2"x10'
45 board feet shiplap
(to cut 4'-2" and 2'-2")
1 piece sheet iron 2'x4'-9"
4 prs.- 4" strap-hinges (heavy)
Paint, 1/4 gal.
Nails, 16d, 8d, 6d, 4d, 3d

Use thin cleats

11 1/2"

1/2"x2" on underside

17"

TROUGH LIDS

FRONT VIEW

Lid not hinged – but sets over hopper – loose fit

Iron turned down on sides and nailed

1"x 2"

Stop blocks

Shiplap

I"x 4"

2"x 6"

I"x 12"

Lid

Treat sills with preservative

3/8"x 1/2"
1"x 2"
1"x12" Lids

Sheet iron
1"x 2"

Heavy sheet iron
1"x 2"

Three ways of rainproofing trough divider strips. Sections of 1"x2"s shown.

SECTION

Corrugated iron

Use no cleats inside

Width of 2"x12" board

I"x 2"
I"x 4"
Hinge
1"x 12"
2"x 6"
1"x 2"
Grain- 4"
C.S. Meal- 6"

12"
I"x2"
I"x 2"
1"x 12"

Sills 2"x 4"

Nail floor to 1"x2" and 2"x6", then nail 2"x4" sills to the floor to permit easy removal of sills.

3'-0"

FLOOR PLAN

Cleat

1"x2"
Shiplap
4'-2"
1"x 2"
Shiplap floor
Shiplap
1"x12"
1"x2"
2"x6"
1"x2"
1"x2"
1"x2"
1"x2"
Step for small hogs
2"x 6"

Width of 2"x12"
Width of 2"x12"

2'-2" Approx.

PICTORIAL

NOTE:
Place feeders back to back for double feeder.

COOPERATIVE EXTENSION WORK IN
AGRICULTURE AND HOME ECONOMICS
AND
UNITED STATES DEPARTMENT OF AGRICULTURE COOPERATING

SELF - FEEDER FOR HOGS

TEX.   EX. 5756   SHEET 1 OF 1

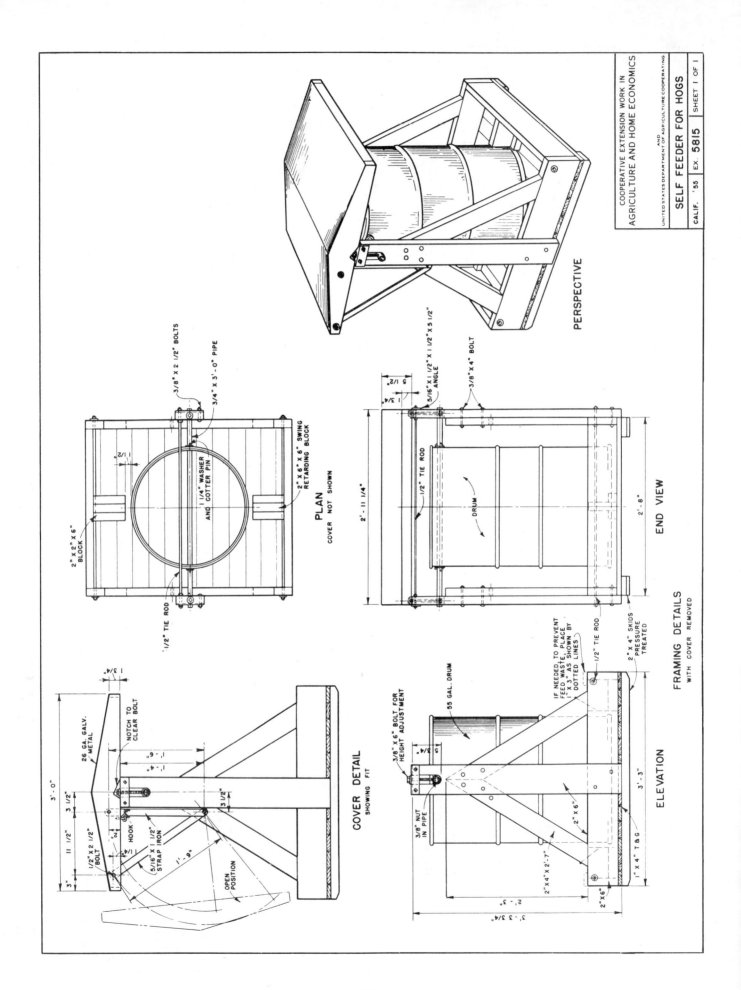

COOPERATIVE EXTENSION WORK IN
AGRICULTURE AND HOME ECONOMICS
AND
UNITED STATES DEPARTMENT OF AGRICULTURE COOPERATING

SELF FEEDER FOR HOGS

CALIF. '55   EX. 5815   SHEET 1 OF 1

PERSPECTIVE

PLAN
COVER NOT SHOWN

3/8" X 2 1/2" BOLTS
3/4" X 3'-0" PIPE
2" X 6" X 6" SWING RETARDING BLOCK
1 1/4" WASHER AND COTTER PIN
2" X 2" X 6" BLOCK
1/2" TIE ROD

END VIEW

5/16" X 1 1/2" X 1 1/2" X 5 1/2" ANGLE
3/8" X 4" BOLT
1/2" TIE ROD
DRUM
2'-11 1/4"
2'-8"

FRAMING DETAILS
WITH COVER REMOVED

COVER DETAIL
SHOWING FIT

26 GA. GALV. METAL
NOTCH TO CLEAR BOLT
3'-0"
3 1/2"
3 1/2"
11 1/2"
1/2" X 2 1/2" BOLT
HOOK
5/16" X 1 1/2" STRAP IRON
3"
1'-6"
OPEN POSITION
1'-9"

ELEVATION

55 GAL. DRUM
3/8" X 6" BOLT FOR HEIGHT ADJUSTMENT
3/8" NUT IN PIPE
IF NEEDED, TO PREVENT FEED WASTE, PLACE 1" X 3" AS SHOWN BY DOTTED LINES
1/2" TIE ROD
2" X 4" SKIDS PRESSURE TREATED
2" X 6"
1" X 4" T&G
2" X 4" X 2'-7"
2" X 6"
2" X 4" X 2'-7"
2'-3"
3'-3"
3'-3 3/4"

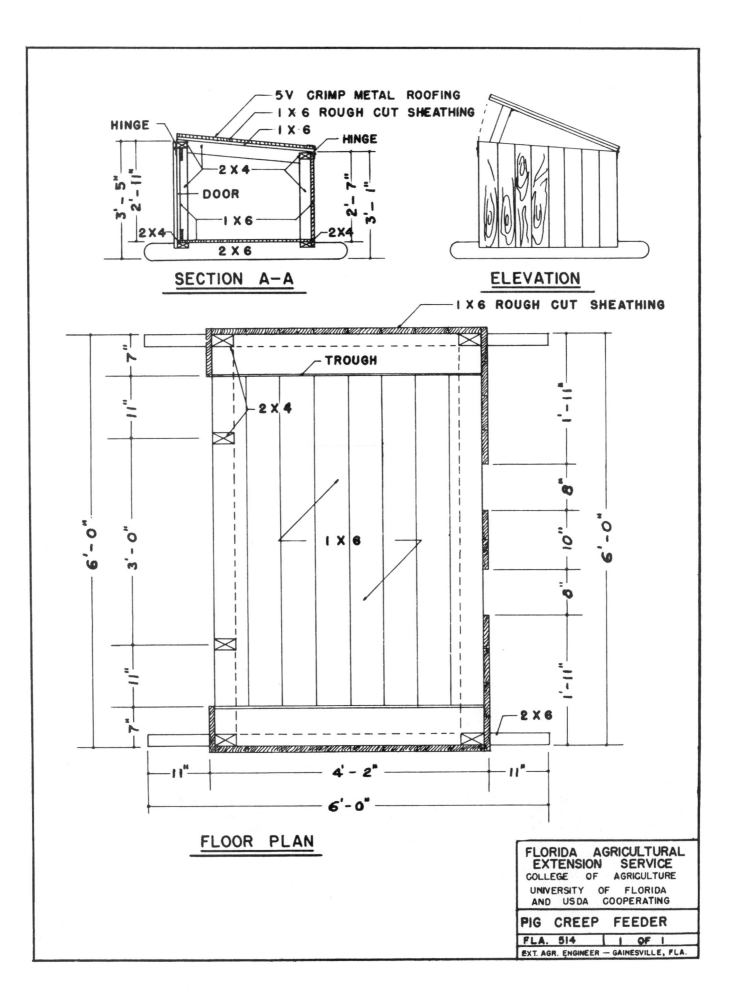

5V CRIMP METAL ROOFING
1 X 6 ROUGH CUT SHEATHING
1 X 6
HINGE
HINGE
2 X 4
3'-5"
2'-11"
DOOR
2'-7"
3'-1"
2 X 4
1 X 6
2X4
2X4
2 X 6

SECTION A-A

1 X 6 ROUGH CUT SHEATHING

ELEVATION

7"
TROUGH
2 X 4
1'-11"
11"
6'-0"
3'-0"
8"
10"
8"
1 X 6
6'-0"
11"
2 X 6
1'-11"
7"
11"
4'-2"
11"
6'-0"

FLOOR PLAN

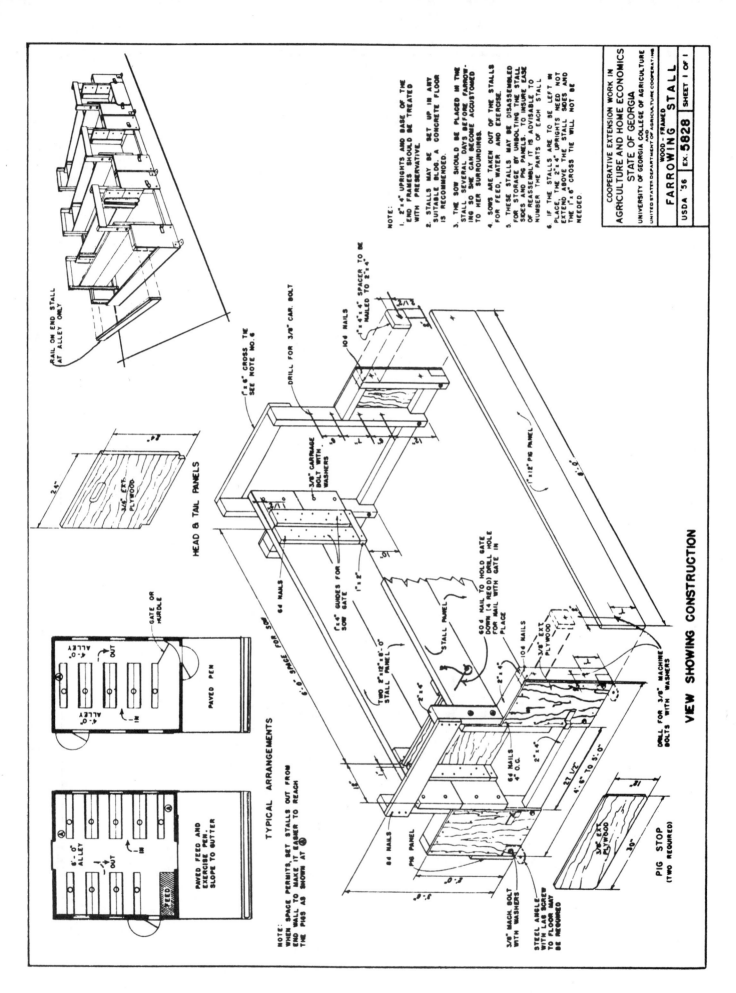

VIEW SHOWING CONSTRUCTION

RAIL ON END STALL AT ALLEY ONLY

HEAD & TAIL PANELS

3/4" EXT. PLYWOOD

2'-4"

TYPICAL ARRANGEMENTS

GATE OR HURDLE

ALLEY 4'-0"
OUT
IN
ALLEY 4'-0"

PAVED PEN

8'-0" ALLEY
OUT
IN
FEED

PAVED FEED AND EXERCISE PEN. SLOPE TO GUTTER

NOTE: WHEN SPACE PERMITS, SET STALLS OUT FROM END WALL TO MAKE IT EASIER TO REACH THE PIGS AS SHOWN AT Ⓐ

1"x6" CROSS TIE SEE NOTE NO. 6

DRILL FOR 3/8" CAR. BOLT

1"x4"x4" SPACER TO BE NAILED TO 2"x4"

10d NAILS

6-3/8" CARRIAGE BOLT WITH WASHERS

1"x4" GUIDES FOR SOW GATE

6d NAILS

6'-0" SPACE FOR SOW

1"x12" PIG PANEL

1"x12" STALL PANEL

6'-0"

TWO 2"x12"x6'-0" STALL PANEL

STALL PANEL

80d NAIL TO HOLD GATE DOWN (4 REQ'D) DRILL HOLE FOR NAIL WITH GATE IN PLACE

2"x4"

2"x5"

10d NAILS

3/8" EXT. PLYWOOD

6d NAILS 4" O.C.

2"x4"

27 1/2"

4'-6" TO 5'-0"

DRILL FOR 3/8" MACHINE BOLTS WITH WASHERS

6d NAILS
PIG PANEL

6'-0"

6'-0"

3/8" MACH. BOLT WITH WASHERS

STEEL ANGLE WITH LAG SCREW TO FLOOR MAY BE REQUIRED

31"

30"

3/4" EXT. PLYWOOD

PIG STOP
(TWO REQUIRED)

NOTE:

1. 2"x4" UPRIGHTS AND BASE OF THE END FRAMES SHOULD BE TREATED WITH PRESERVATIVE

2. STALLS MAY BE SET UP IN ANY SUITABLE BLDG. A CONCRETE FLOOR IS RECOMMENDED.

3. THE SOW SHOULD BE PLACED IN THE STALL SEVERAL DAYS BEFORE FARROWING SO SHE CAN BECOME ACCUSTOMED TO HER SURROUNDINGS.

4. SOWS ARE TAKEN OUT OF THE STALLS FOR FEED, WATER AND EXERCISE.

5. THESE STALLS MAY BE DISASSEMBLED FOR STORAGE BY UNBOLTING THE STALL SIDES AND PIG PANELS. TO INSURE EASE OF REASSEMBLY IT IS ADVISABLE TO NUMBER THE PARTS OF EACH STALL.

6. IF THE STALLS ARE TO BE LEFT IN PLACE, THE 2"x4" UPRIGHTS NEED NOT EXTEND ABOVE THE STALL SIDES AND THE 1"x6" CROSS TIE WILL NOT BE NEEDED

COOPERATIVE EXTENSION WORK IN
AGRICULTURE AND HOME ECONOMICS
STATE OF GEORGIA
UNIVERSITY OF GEORGIA COLLEGE OF AGRICULTURE
AND
UNITED STATES DEPARTMENT OF AGRICULTURE COOPERATING

WOOD-FRAMED
FARROWING STALL

USDA '56 | EX. 5828 | SHEET 1 OF 1

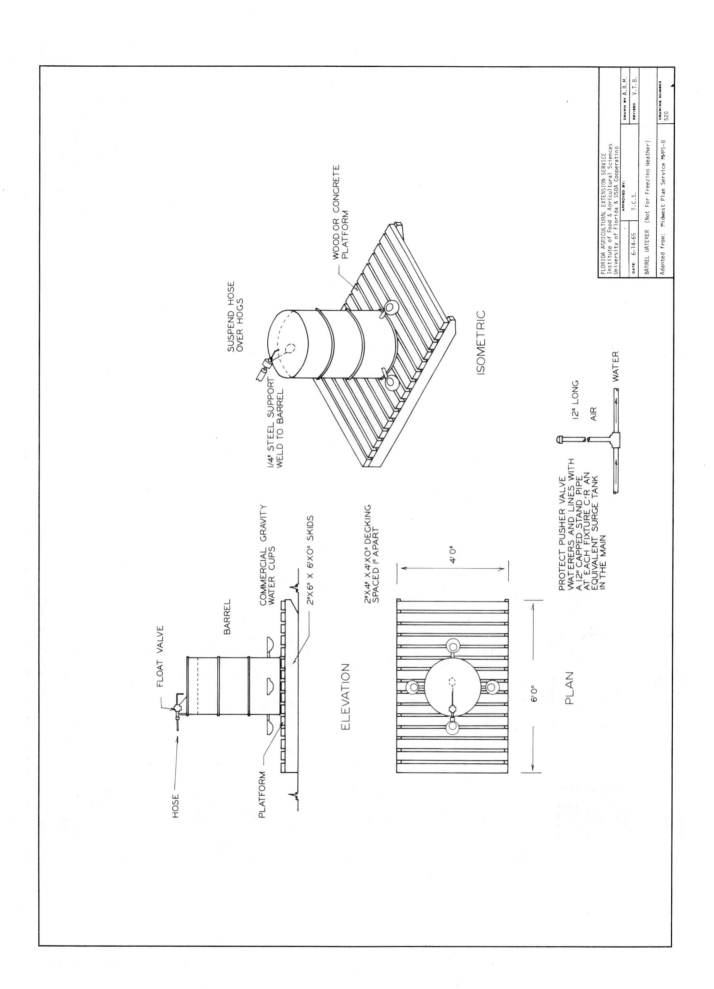

SUSPEND HOSE
OVER HOGS

1/4" STEEL SUPPORT
WELD TO BARREL

WOOD OR CONCRETE
PLATFORM

ISOMETRIC

FLOAT VALVE

BARREL

COMMERCIAL GRAVITY
WATER CUPS

2"X6" X 6'X0" SKIDS

2"X4" X 4'X0" DECKING
SPACED 1" APART

HOSE

PLATFORM

ELEVATION

PLAN

4'0"

6'0"

12" LONG

AIR

WATER

PROTECT PUSHER VALVE
WATERERS AND LINES WITH
A 12" CAPPED STAND PIPE
AT EACH FIXTURE OR AN
EQUIVALENT SURGE TANK
IN THE MAIN

FLORIDA AGRICULTURAL EXTENSION SERVICE
Institute of Food & Agricultural Sciences
University of Florida & USDA Cooperating

DRAWN BY: A.R.M.
REVISED: V.T.B.

APPROVED BY:

DATE: 6-14-65   T.C.S.

BARREL WATERER   (Not For Freezing Weather)

Adapted from: Midwest Plan Service MWPS-8

DRAWING NUMBER
520

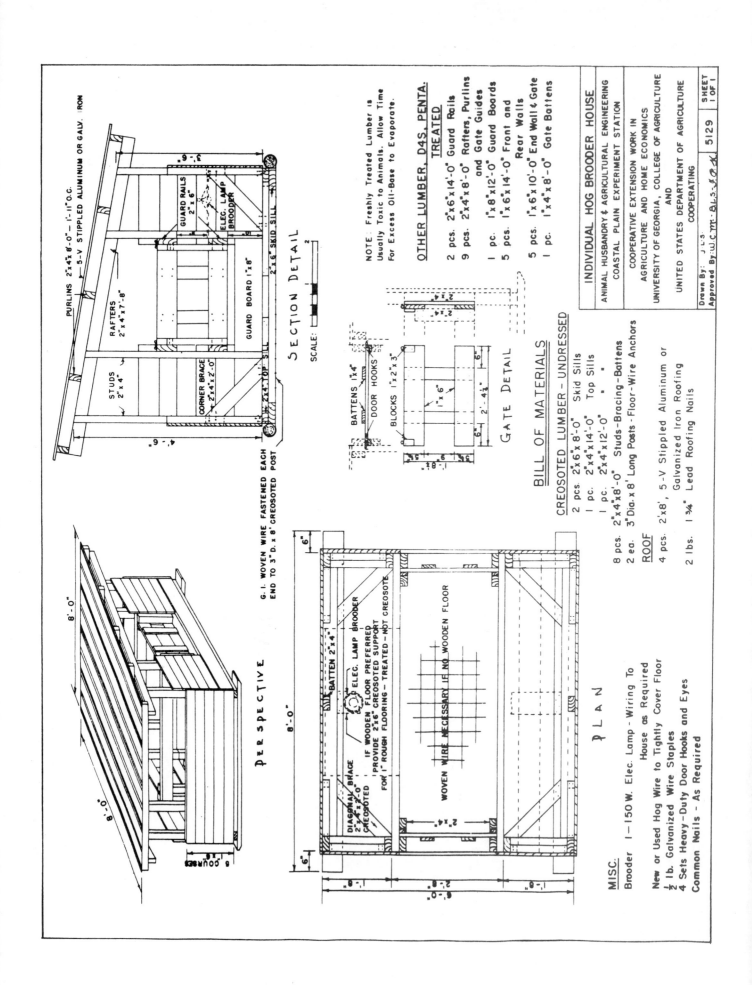

PURLINS 2"x4" 8'-0" – 1'-11" O.C.

5-V STIPPLED ALUMINUM OR GALV. IRON

GUARD RAILS 2" x 6"

ELEC. LAMP BROODER

RAFTERS 2"x4"x7'-8"

2"x6" SKID SILL

STUDS 2"x4"

CORNER BRACE 2"x4"x2'-0"

GUARD BOARD 1"x8"

1"x4"x6" TOP SILL

4'-6"

3'-0"

SECTION DETAIL

SCALE:

G.I. WOVEN WIRE FASTENED EACH END TO 3"D. x 8' CREOSOTED POST

BATTENS 1"x4"

DOOR HOOKS

BLOCKS 1"x2"x3"

1"x6"

6"

2'- 4½"

6"

6"

1'-8"

GATE DETAIL

NOTE: Freshly Treated Lumber is Usually Toxic to Animals. Allow Time For Excess Oil-Base to Evaporate.

OTHER LUMBER. D4S. PENTA. TREATED

2 pcs. 2"x6"x14'-0" Guard Rails

9 pcs. 2"x4"x8'-0" Rafters, Purlins and Gate Guides

1 pc. 1"x8"x12'-0" Guard Boards

5 pcs. 1"x6"x14'-0" Front and Rear Walls

5 pcs. 1"x6"x10'-0" End Wall & Gate

1 pc. 1"x4"x8'-0" Gate Battens

BILL OF MATERIALS

CREOSOTED LUMBER – UNDRESSED

2 pcs. 2"x6x 8'-0" Skid Sills

1 pc. 2"x4"x14'-0" Top Sills

1 pc. 2"x4"x12'-0" Studs-Bracing-Battens

8 pcs. 2"x4"x8'-0" Studs-Bracing-Battens

2 ea. 3"Dia.x 8' Long Posts - Floor-Wire Anchors

ROOF

4 pcs. 2'x8', 5-V Stippled Aluminum or Galvanized Iron Roofing

2 lbs. 1¾" Lead Roofing Nails

INDIVIDUAL HOG BROODER HOUSE

ANIMAL HUSBANDRY & AGRICULTURAL ENGINEERING
Coastal Plain Experiment Station

COOPERATIVE EXTENSION WORK IN AGRICULTURE AND HOME ECONOMICS
UNIVERSITY OF GEORGIA, COLLEGE OF AGRICULTURE
AND
UNITED STATES DEPARTMENT OF AGRICULTURE
COOPERATING

Drawn By: JCS
Approved By: W.C.M. BLS ЗФК   5129   SHEET 1 OF 1

8'-0"

8'-0"

8 COURSES

PERSPECTIVE

BATTEN 2"x4"

150 W. ELEC. LAMP BROODER

IF WOODEN FLOOR PREFERRED PROVIDE 2"x6" CREOSOTED SUPPORT FOR 1" ROUGH FLOORING – TREATED – NOT CREOSOTE

DIAGONAL BRACE 2"x 4"x 2'-0" CREOSOTED

WOVEN WIRE NECESSARY IF NO WOODEN FLOOR

2"x4"

6"

6"

1'-8"

2'-8"

1'-8"

6'-0"

PLAN

MISC.

Brooder 1 – 150 W. Elec. Lamp - Wiring To House as Required

New or Used Hog Wire to Tightly Cover Floor

½ lb. Galvanized Wire Staples

4 Sets Heavy-Duty Door Hooks and Eyes

Common Nails - As Required

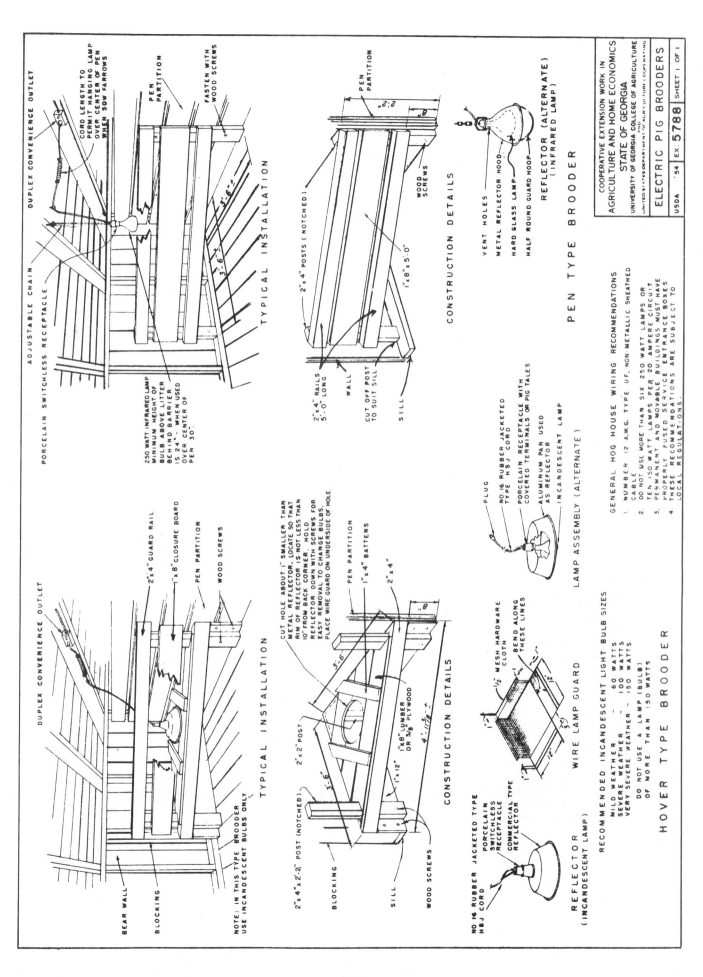

DUPLEX CONVENIENCE OUTLET

CORD LENGTH TO PERMIT HANGING LAMP OVER CENTER OF PEN WHEN SOW FARROWS

ADJUSTABLE CHAIN

PORCELAIN SWITCHLESS RECEPTACLE

PEN PARTITION

FASTEN WITH WOOD SCREWS

250 WATT INFRARED LAMP MINIMUM HEIGHT OF BULB ABOVE LITTER IS 24" BEHIND BARRIER WHEN USED OVER CENTER OF PEN 30".

3'-6"

3'-6"

TYPICAL INSTALLATION

PEN PARTITION

2"x2"

8"

2"x4" POSTS (NOTCHED)

2"x4" RAILS 5'-0" LONG

WALL

CUT OFF POST TO SUIT SILL

SILL

1"x8"x5'-0"

WOOD SCREWS

CONSTRUCTION DETAILS

VENT HOLES

METAL REFLECTOR HOOD

HARD GLASS LAMP

HALF ROUND GUARD WIRE

REFLECTOR (ALTERNATE)
(INFRARED LAMP)

PEN TYPE BROODER

COOPERATIVE EXTENSION WORK IN
AGRICULTURE AND HOME ECONOMICS
STATE OF GEORGIA
UNIVERSITY OF GEORGIA COLLEGE OF AGRICULTURE
AND
UNITED STATES DEPARTMENT OF AGRICULTURE COOPERATING

ELECTRIC PIG BROODERS

USDA '54 | EX. 5788 | SHEET 1 OF 1

DUPLEX CONVENIENCE OUTLET

2"x4" GUARD RAIL

1"x8" CLOSURE BOARD

PEN PARTITION

WOOD SCREWS

CUT HOLE ABOUT 1" SMALLER THAN METAL REFLECTOR. LOCATE SO THAT RIM OF REFLECTOR IS NOT LESS THAN 10" FROM BACK CORNER. HOLD REFLECTOR DOWN WITH SCREWS FOR EASY REMOVAL TO CHANGE BULBS. PLACE WIRE GUARD ON UNDERSIDE OF HOLE.

PEN PARTITION

2"x4" BATTENS

2"x4"

REAR WALL

BLOCKING

NOTE: IN THIS TYPE BROODER USE INCANDESCENT BULBS ONLY

TYPICAL INSTALLATION

3'-6"

2"x2" POST (NOTCHED)

3'-6"

1"x12"

1"x8" LUMBER OR 3/8 PLYWOOD

8"

4'-11 3/4"

2"x4"x2'-2" POST (NOTCHED)

BLOCKING

SILL

WOOD SCREWS

CONSTRUCTION DETAILS

PLUG

NO.16 RUBBER JACKETED TYPE HSJ CORD

PORCELAIN RECEPTACLE WITH COVERED TERMINALS OR PIG TALES

ALUMINUM PAN USED AS REFLECTOR

INCANDESCENT LAMP

LAMP ASSEMBLY (ALTERNATE)

1/2 MESH HARDWARE CLOTH

BEND ALONG THESE LINES

1"

12"

3"

12"

WIRE LAMP GUARD

NO.16 RUBBER JACKETED TYPE HSJ CORD

PORCELAIN SWITCHLESS RECEPTACLE

COMMERCIAL TYPE REFLECTOR

REFLECTOR
(INCANDESCENT LAMP)

RECOMMENDED INCANDESCENT LIGHT BULB SIZES

MILD WEATHER — 60 WATTS
SEVERE WEATHER — 100 WATTS
VERY SEVERE WEATHER — 150 WATTS

DO NOT USE A LAMP (BULB) OF MORE THAN 150 WATTS

HOVER TYPE BROODER

GENERAL HOG HOUSE WIRING RECOMMENDATIONS

1. NUMBER 12 A.W.G. TYPE UF, NON-METALLIC SHEATHED CABLE

2. DO NOT USE MORE THAN SIX 250 WATT LAMPS OR TEN 150 WATT LAMPS PER 20 AMPERE CIRCUIT

3. PERMANENT AND MOVABLE BUILDINGS MUST HAVE PROPERLY FUSED SERVICE ENTRANCE BOXES

4. THESE RECOMMENDATIONS ARE SUBJECT TO LOCAL REGULATIONS.

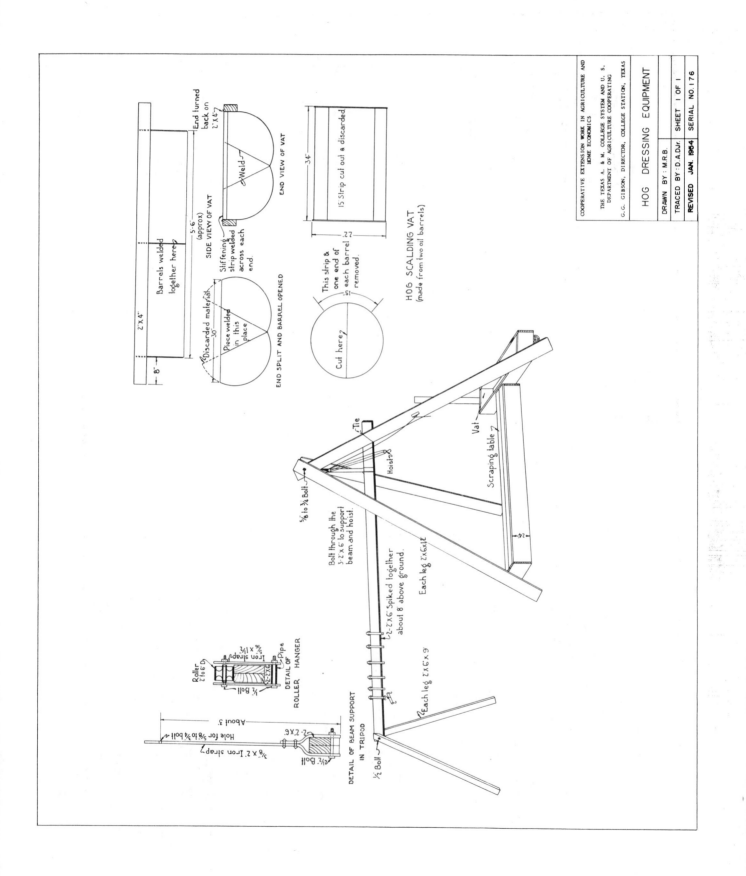

End turned back on 2" X 4"

END VIEW OF VAT

Weld

Barrels welded together here

2" X 4"

5'-6" (approx)

Stiffening strip welded across each end.

SIDE VIEW OF VAT

8"

Discarded material

30°

Piece welded in this place

END SPLIT AND BARREL OPENED

.34"

15 Strip cut out & discarded

.27"

This strip & one end of each barrel removed.

Cut here

HOG SCALDING VAT
(made from two oil barrels)

Tie

Hoist

Vat

Scraping table

24½"

5/8 to 3/4 Bolt

Bolt through the 3-2"x 6" to support beam and hoist.

2-2"x6" spiked together about 8 above ground.

Each leg 2"x6"x12'

Each leg 2"x6"x 9'

½ Bolt

Roller 2" to 6" D.

3/16 x 1½

Pipe

Iron strap

½ Bolt

2-2"x6"

DETAIL OF
ROLLER HANGER

Hole for 5/8 to 3/4 bolt

About 3'

3/8"x 2" Iron strap

2-2"x6"

2½" Bolt

½ Bolt

DETAIL OF BEAM SUPPORT
IN TRIPOD

COOPERATIVE EXTENSION WORK IN AGRICULTURE AND HOME ECONOMICS

THE TEXAS A. & M. COLLEGE SYSTEM AND U. S. DEPARTMENT OF AGRICULTURE COOPERATING

G. G. GIBSON, DIRECTOR, COLLEGE STATION, TEXAS

HOG DRESSING EQUIPMENT

DRAWN BY : M.R.B.

TRACED BY : D.A.DJr.   SHEET 1 OF 1

REVISED JAN. 1954   SERIAL NO. 176

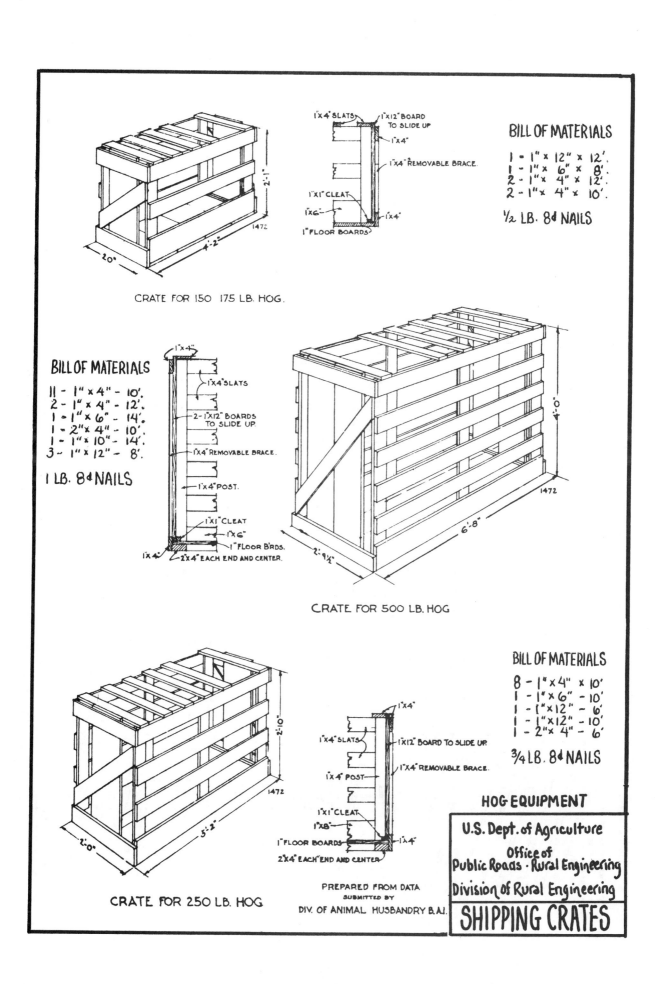

CRATE FOR 150 175 LB. HOG.

BILL OF MATERIALS

1 - 1" x 12" x 12'.
1 - 1" x 6" x 8'.
2 - 1" x 4" x 12'.
2 - 1" x 4" x 10'.

½ LB. 8ᵈ NAILS

1'x4' SLATS
1'x12' BOARD TO SLIDE UP
1'x4'
1'x4' REMOVABLE BRACE.
1'x1' CLEAT
1'x6'
1'x4'
1' FLOOR BOARDS

2'-1"
4'-2"
20"
1472

BILL OF MATERIALS

11 - 1" x 4" - 10'.
2 - 1" x 4" - 12'.
1 - 1" x 6" - 14'.
1 - 2" x 4" - 10'.
1 - 1" x 10" - 14'.
3 - 1" x 12" - 8'.

1 LB. 8ᵈ NAILS

1'x4'
1'x4' SLATS
2 - 1'x12' BOARDS TO SLIDE UP.
1'x4' REMOVABLE BRACE.
1'x4' POST.
1'x1' CLEAT
1'x6'
1' FLOOR B'RDS.
1'x4'
2'x4' EACH END AND CENTER.

CRATE FOR 500 LB. HOG

4'-0"
6'-8"
2'-9½"
1472

BILL OF MATERIALS

8 - 1" x 4" x 10'
1 - 1" x 6" - 10'
1 - 1" x 12" - 6'
1 - 1" x 12" - 10'
1 - 2" x 4" - 6'

¾ LB. 8ᵈ NAILS

1'x4'
1'x4' SLATS
1'x12' BOARD TO SLIDE UP.
1'x4' POST
1'x4' REMOVABLE BRACE.
1'x1' CLEAT
1'x8'
1' FLOOR BOARDS
2'x4' EACH END AND CENTER.
1'x4'

2'-10"
5'-2"
2'-0"
1472

CRATE FOR 250 LB. HOG

PREPARED FROM DATA
SUBMITTED BY
DIV. OF ANIMAL HUSBANDRY B.A.I.

HOG EQUIPMENT

U.S. Dept. of Agriculture

Office of
Public Roads · Rural Engineering

Division of Rural Engineering

SHIPPING CRATES

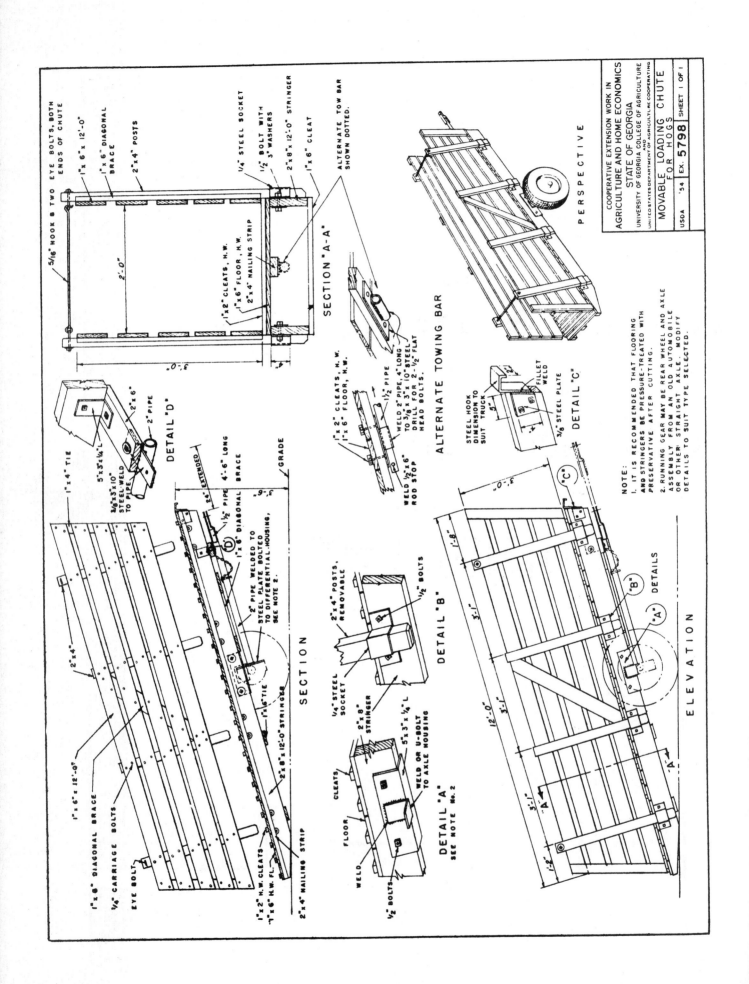

MOVABLE LOADING CHUTE FOR HOGS

PERSPECTIVE

SECTION "A-A"

ALTERNATE TOWING BAR

DETAIL "D"

DETAIL "C"

DETAIL "B"

DETAIL "A"
SEE NOTE No.2

SECTION

ELEVATION

DETAILS

NOTE:
1. IT IS RECOMMENDED THAT FLOORING AND STRINGERS BE PRESSURE-TREATED WITH PRESERVATIVE AFTER CUTTING.

2. RUNNING GEAR MAY BE REAR WHEEL AND AXLE ASSEMBLY FROM AN OLD AUTOMOBILE OR OTHER STRAIGHT AXLE. MODIFY DETAILS TO SUIT TYPE SELECTED.

COOPERATIVE EXTENSION WORK IN
AGRICULTURE AND HOME ECONOMICS
STATE OF GEORGIA
UNIVERSITY OF GEORGIA COLLEGE OF AGRICULTURE
AND
UNITED STATES DEPARTMENT OF AGRICULTURE, COOPERATING

USDA '54 EX. 5798 SHEET 1 OF 1

228

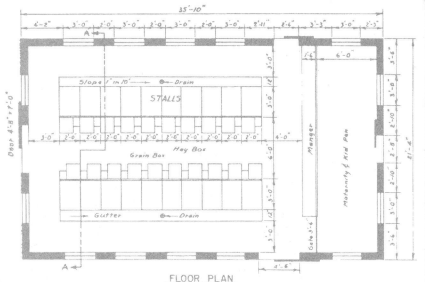

FLOOR PLAN

(labels within floor plan: STALLS, Hay Box, Grain Box, Gutter, Drain, Manger, Maternity & Kid Pen, Gate, Sloped 1" in 10', Deep 4'-8"-7'-0")

SHEEP & GOAT

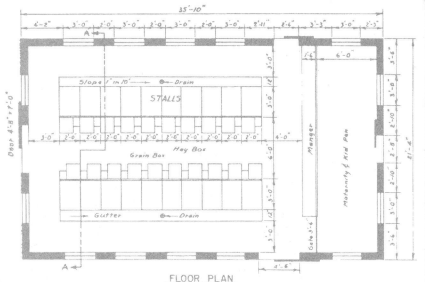

BARNS AND

EQUIPMENT

① BOX UNFOLDED, PAPER TWINE IN PLACE. LAY FLEECE FLESH SIDE DOWN WITH CLEAN TAGS & LOOSE ENDS IN THE CENTER.

② RAISE & HOLD SIDES

③ RAISE ENDS, CLOSING AND LOCKING THE BOX. TIE FLEECE.

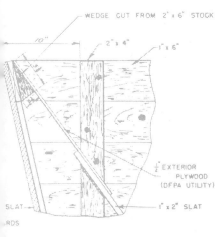

WEDGE CUT FROM 2" x 6" STOCK

2" x 4"

1" x 6"

½" EXTERIOR PLYWOOD (DFPA UTILITY)

1" x 2" SLAT

ENLARGED VIEW OF CORNER DETAIL

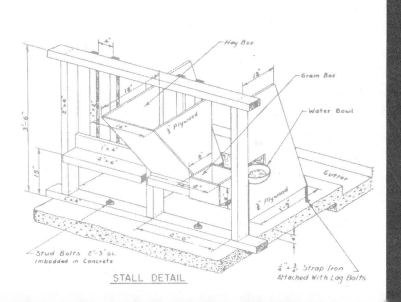

Hay Box

Grain Box

Water Bowl

Gutter

Plywood

Stud Bolts 2'-3" o.c. Imbedded in Concrete

¼" x ¾" Strap Iron Attached With Lag Bolts

STALL DETAIL

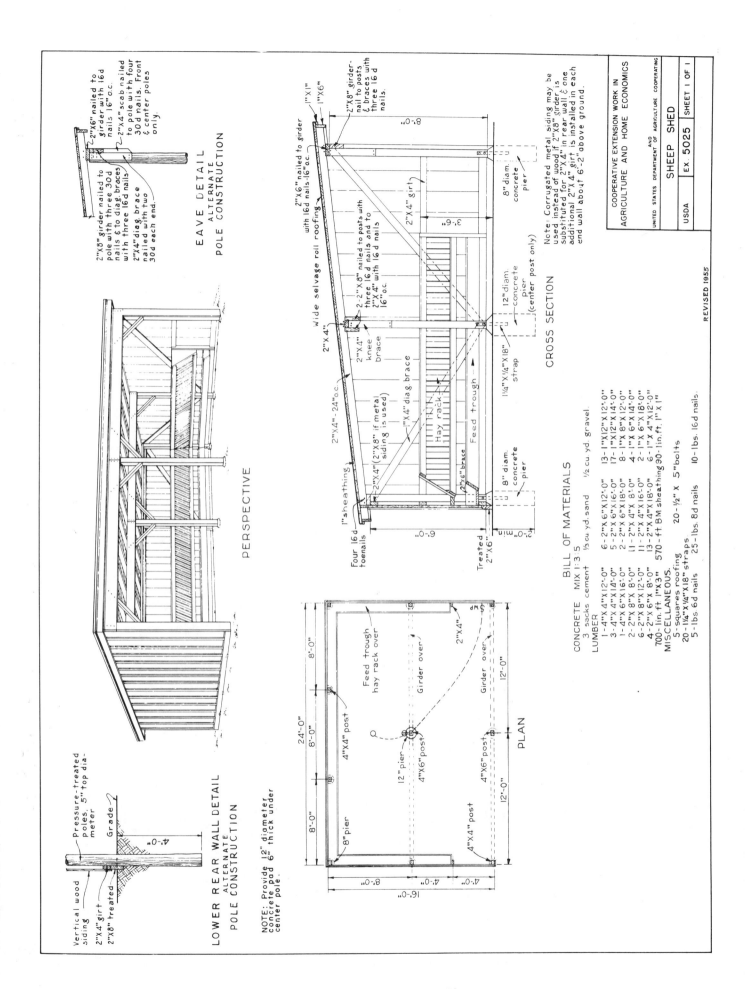

14

2"X6" nailed to girder with 16d nails 16" o.c.

2"X4" scab nailed to pole with four 30d nails. Front & center poles only.

2"X8" girder nailed to pole with three 30d nails & to diag. braces with three 16d nails.

2"X4" diag. brace nailed with two 30d each end.

EAVE DETAIL
ALTERNATE POLE CONSTRUCTION

PERSPECTIVE

Pressure-treated poles, 5" top diameter

Grade

Vertical wood siding

2"X4" girt

2"X8" treated

4'-0"

LOWER REAR WALL DETAIL
ALTERNATE POLE CONSTRUCTION

NOTE: Provide 12" diameter concrete pad 6" thick under center pole.

1"X1"
1"X6"

2"X8" girder—nail to posts & braces with three 16d nails.

8'-0"

2"X6" nailed to girder with 16d nails-16"o.c.

wide selvage roll roofing

2"X4"

2-2"X8" nailed to posts with three 16d nails and to 2"X4" with 16d nails 16" o.c.

2"X4" knee brace

1"X4" diag brace

Hay rack

Feed trough

1"X4"(2"X8" if metal siding is used)

2"X4"-24"o.c.

1" sheathing

2"X4"(2"X8" if metal siding is used)

Four 16d toenails

Treated 2"X6"

8" diam. concrete pier

12" diam. concrete pier (center post only)

1/4"X1/4"X18" strap

2"X6" brace

8" diam. concrete pier

2"X4" girt

3'-6"

8" diam. concrete pier

6'-0"

3'-0"

CROSS SECTION

Note: Corrugated metal siding may be used instead of wood if 2"X8" girder is substituted for 2"X4" in rear wall & one additional 2"X4" girt is installed in each end wall about 6'-2" above ground.

BILL OF MATERIALS

CONCRETE MIX 1:3:5
3 sacks cement 1/3 cu yd. sand 1/2 cu yd gravel.

LUMBER

1- 4"X 4"X12'-0"	6- 2"X 6"X12'-0"	13- 1"X12"X12'-0"
3- 4"X 4"X14'-0"	5- 2"X 6"X16'-0"	17- 1"X12"X14'-0"
1- 4"X 6"X16'-0"	2- 2"X 6"X18'-0"	8- 1"X 8"X12'-0"
2- 2"X 8"X 8'-0"	11- 2"X 4"X 8'-0"	4- 1"X 6"X14'-0"
6- 2"X 8"X12'-0"	11- 2"X 4"X16'-0"	2- 1"X 6"X18'-0"
4- 2"X 6"X 8'-0"	3- 2"X4"X18'-0"	6- 1"X 4"X12'-0"

700-lin. ft 1"X3" 570-ft BM sheathing 90-lin. ft 1" X 1"

MISCELLANEOUS.

5-squares roofing 20- 1/2" X 5"bolts
20- 1/4"X1/4"X18" straps
5- lbs 6d nails 25- lbs. 8d nails 10-lbs. 16d nails.

Feed trough
hay rack over

Girder over

12" pier

4"X4" post

4"X6" post

8" pier

4"X4" post

4"X6" post

2"X4"

Girder over

24'-0"
8'-0"
8'-0"
8'-0"

4'-0"
4'-0"
12'-0"

8'-0"
8'-0"
16'-0"

PLAN

COOPERATIVE EXTENSION WORK IN
AGRICULTURE AND HOME ECONOMICS
UNITED STATES DEPARTMENT OF AGRICULTURE COOPERATING
AND

SHEEP SHED

USDA | EX. 5025 | SHEET 1 OF 1

REVISED 1955

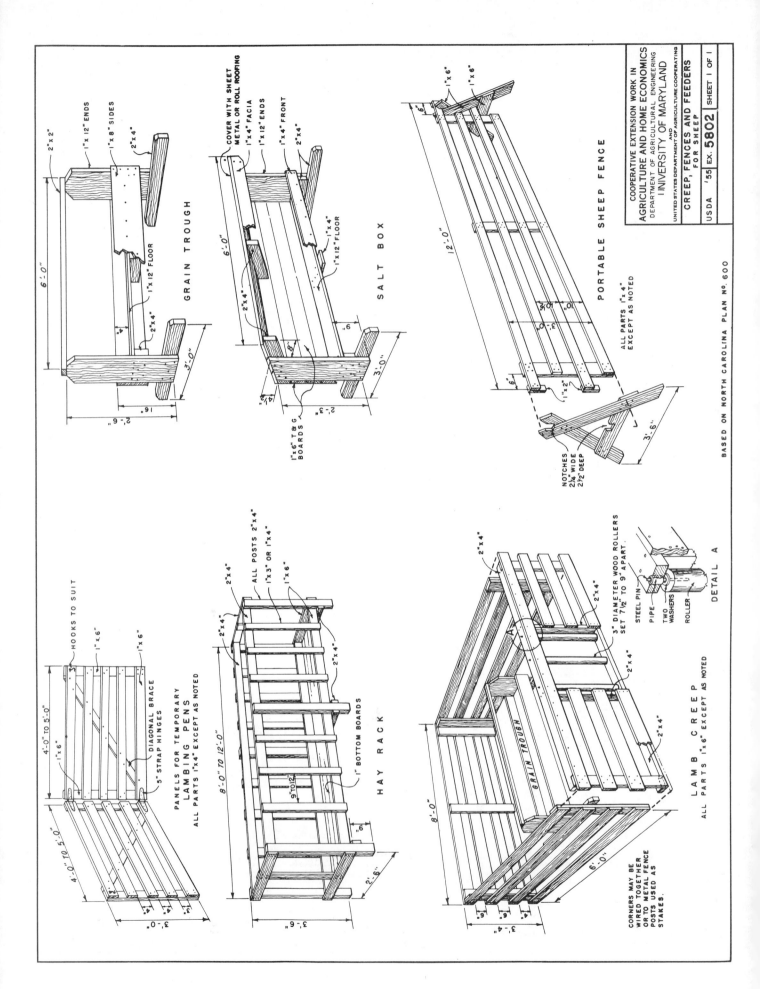

GRAIN TROUGH

2"x2"
1" x 12" ENDS
1" x 8" SIDES
2"x4"
1"x 12" FLOOR
2"x4"
6'-0"
3'-0"
16"
2'-6"

SALT BOX

COVER WITH SHEET METAL OR ROLL ROOFING
1"x4" FACIA
1"x12" ENDS
1"x4" FRONT
2"x4"
1"x4"
1"x12" FLOOR
2"x4"
1"x6" T&G BOARDS
6'-0"
8"
6"
4"
3'-0"
2'-3"

PORTABLE SHEEP FENCE

1"x6"
1"x6"
6"
12'-0"
3'-0"
10"
10"
6"
1"x2"
NOTCHES 2¼" WIDE 2½" DEEP
3'-6"

ALL PARTS 1"x4" EXCEPT AS NOTED

PANELS FOR TEMPORARY LAMBING PENS
ALL PARTS 1"x4" EXCEPT AS NOTED

HOOKS TO SUIT
1" x 6"
1"x6"
DIAGONAL BRACE
5" STRAP HINGES
4'-0" TO 5'-0"
1"x 6"
4'-0" TO 5'-0"
3'-0"

HAY RACK

ALL POSTS 2"x4"
1"x3" OR 1"x4"
1"x6"
2"x4"
2"x4"
2"x4"
1" BOTTOM BOARDS
8'-0" TO 12'-0"
9" TO 12"
6"
3'-6"
2'-6"

LAMB CREEP
ALL PARTS 1"x6" EXCEPT AS NOTED

2"x4"
2"x4"
2"x4"
2"x4"
2"x4"
3" DIAMETER WOOD ROLLERS SET 7½" TO 9" APART.
GRAIN TROUGH
8'-0"
6'-0"
6"
3'-6"
3'-4"

CORNERS MAY BE WIRED TOGETHER OR TO METAL FENCE POSTS USED AS STAKES.

DETAIL A

STEEL PIN
PIPE
TWO WASHERS
ROLLER

COOPERATIVE EXTENSION WORK IN
AGRICULTURE AND HOME ECONOMICS
DEPARTMENT OF AGRICULTURAL ENGINEERING
INIVERSITY OF MARYLAND
AND
UNITED STATES DEPARTMENT OF AGRICULTURE COOPERATING

CREEP, FENCES AND FEEDERS
FOR SHEEP

USDA '55 EX. 5802 SHEET I OF I

BASED ON NORTH CAROLINA PLAN NO. 600

232

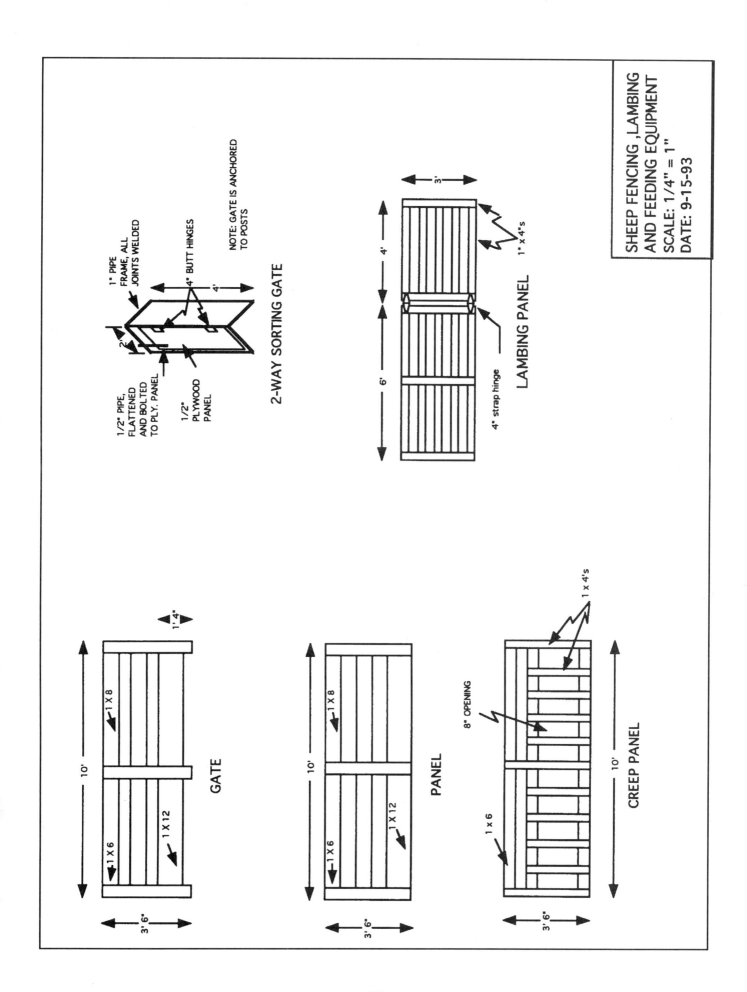

1" PIPE
FRAME, ALL
JOINT'S WELDED

4" BUTT HINGES

NOTE: GATE IS ANCHORED
TO POSTS

1/2" PIPE,
FLATTENED
AND BOLTED
TO PLY. PANEL

1/2"
PLYWOOD
PANEL

2'

4'

2-WAY SORTING GATE

3'

4'

6'

1" x 4"s

4" strap hinge

LAMBING PANEL

1' 4"

1 X 8

1 X 6

1 X 12

10'

3' 6"

GATE

1 X 8

1 X 6

1 X 12

10'

3' 6"

PANEL

1 x 4's

8" OPENING

1 x 6

10'

3' 6"

CREEP PANEL

SHEEP FENCING, LAMBING
AND FEEDING EQUIPMENT
SCALE: 1/4" = 1"
DATE: 9-15-93

233

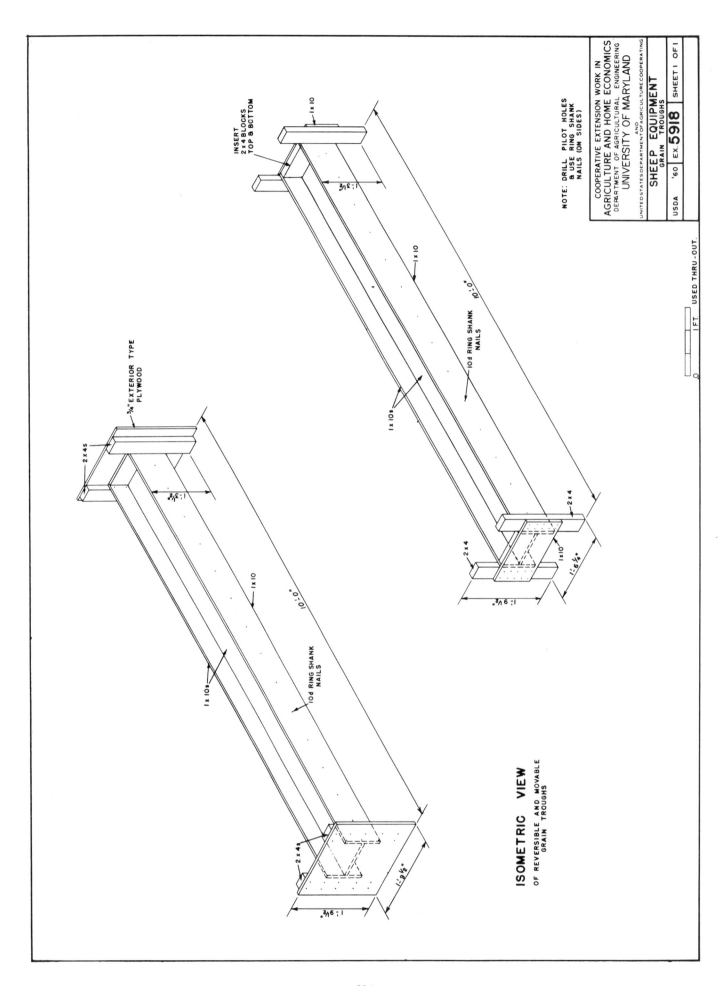

ISOMETRIC VIEW
OF REVERSIBLE AND MOVABLE
GRAIN TROUGHS

COOPERATIVE EXTENSION WORK IN
AGRICULTURE AND HOME ECONOMICS
DEPARTMENT OF AGRICULTURAL ENGINEERING
UNIVERSITY OF MARYLAND
AND
UNITED STATES DEPARTMENT OF AGRICULTURE COOPERATING

SHEEP EQUIPMENT
GRAIN TROUGHS

| USDA | '60 | EX. 5918 | SHEET 1 OF 1 |

NOTE: DRILL PILOT HOLES
& USE RING SHANK
NAILS (ON SIDES)

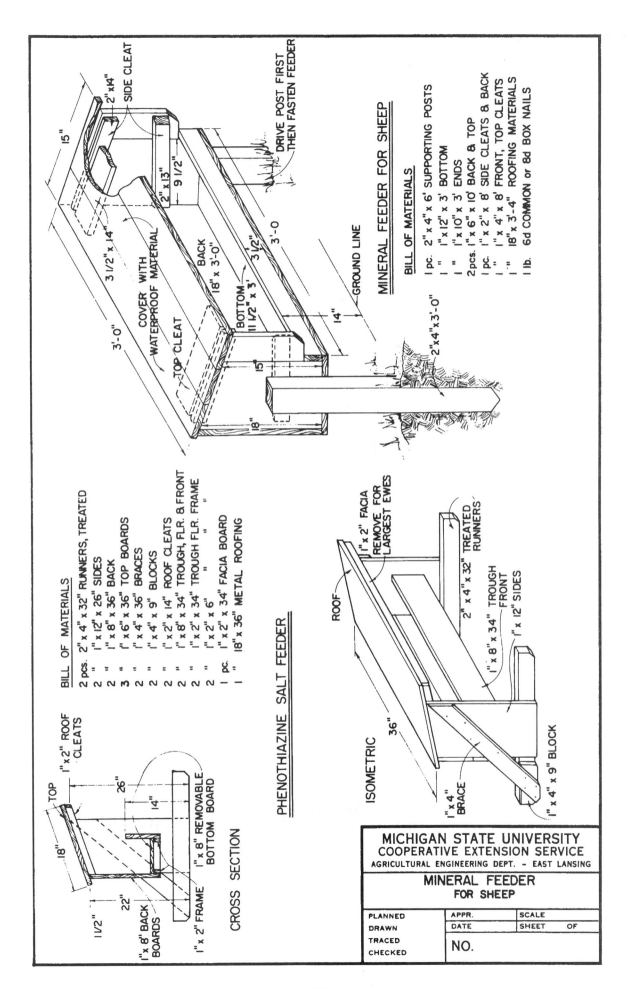

SIDE CLEAT

2" x 14"

15"

2" x 13"

9 1/2"

DRIVE POST FIRST
THEN FASTEN FEEDER

COVER WITH
WATERPROOF MATERIAL

3 1/2" x 14"

3'-0"

TOP CLEAT

BACK
18" x 3'-0"

BOTTOM
11 1/2" x 3'

3 1/2"

3'-0

15"

14"

GROUND LINE

2"x 4"x 3'-0"

18"

MINERAL FEEDER FOR SHEEP

BILL OF MATERIALS

1 pc.	2" x 4" x 6'	SUPPORTING POSTS
"	1" x 12" x 3'	BOTTOM
"	1" x 10" x 3'	ENDS
2 pcs.	1" x 6" x 10'	BACK & TOP
1 pc.	1" x 2" x 8'	SIDE CLEATS & BACK
"	1" x 4" x 8'	FRONT, TOP CLEATS
"	18" x 3'-4"	ROOFING MATERIALS
1 lb.	6d COMMON or 8d BOX NAILS	

PHENOTHIAZINE SALT FEEDER

BILL OF MATERIALS

2 pcs.	2" x 4" x 32"	RUNNERS, TREATED
2 "	1" x 12" x 26"	SIDES
2 "	1" x 8" x 36"	BACK
3 "	1" x 6" x 36"	TOP BOARDS
2 "	1" x 4" x 36"	BRACES
2 "	1" x 4" x 9"	BLOCKS
2 "	1" x 2" x 14"	ROOF CLEATS
2 "	1" x 8" x 34"	TROUGH, FLR. & FRONT
2 "	1" x 2" x 34"	TROUGH FLR. FRAME
2 "	1" x 2" x 6"	" "
1 pc.	1" x 2" x 34"	FACIA BOARD
1	18" x 36"	METAL ROOFING

CROSS SECTION

1" x 2" ROOF CLEATS

TOP

26"

14"

18"

22"

1 1/2"

1" x 8" BACK
BOARDS

1" x 2" FRAME

1" x 8" REMOVABLE
BOTTOM BOARD

ISOMETRIC

ROOF

1" x 2" FACIA
REMOVE FOR
LARGEST EWES

2" x 4" x 32" TREATED
RUNNERS

2" x 4" x 32" TROUGH
FRONT

1" x 8" x 34"

1" x 12" SIDES

36"

1" x 4"
BRACE

1" x 4" x 9" BLOCK

MICHIGAN STATE UNIVERSITY		
COOPERATIVE EXTENSION SERVICE		
AGRICULTURAL ENGINEERING DEPT. — EAST LANSING		
MINERAL FEEDER FOR SHEEP		

PLANNED	APPR.	SCALE	
DRAWN	DATE	SHEET	OF
TRACED	NO.		
CHECKED			

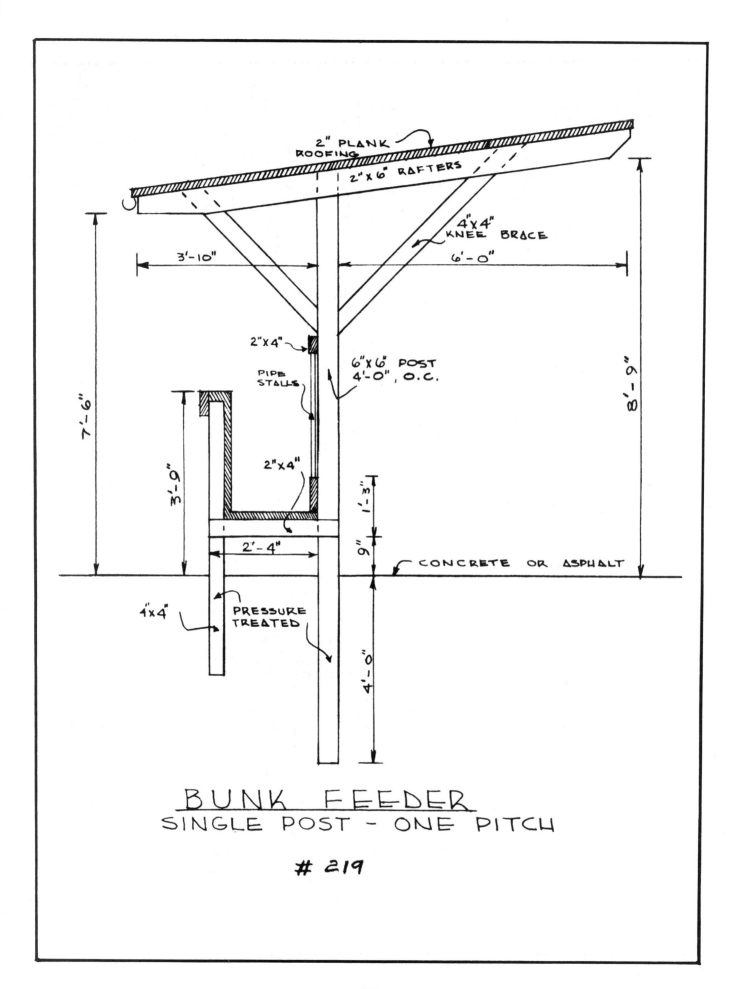

2" PLANK ROOFING

2" X 6" RAFTERS

4"X4" KNEE BRACE

3'-10"

6'-0"

2"X4"

PIPE STALLS

6"X6" POST 4'-0", O.C.

7'-6"

8'-9"

3'-9"

2"X4"

1'-3"

9"

2'-4"

CONCRETE OR ASPHALT

4"X4"

PRESSURE TREATED

4'-0"

BUNK FEEDER
SINGLE POST - ONE PITCH

219

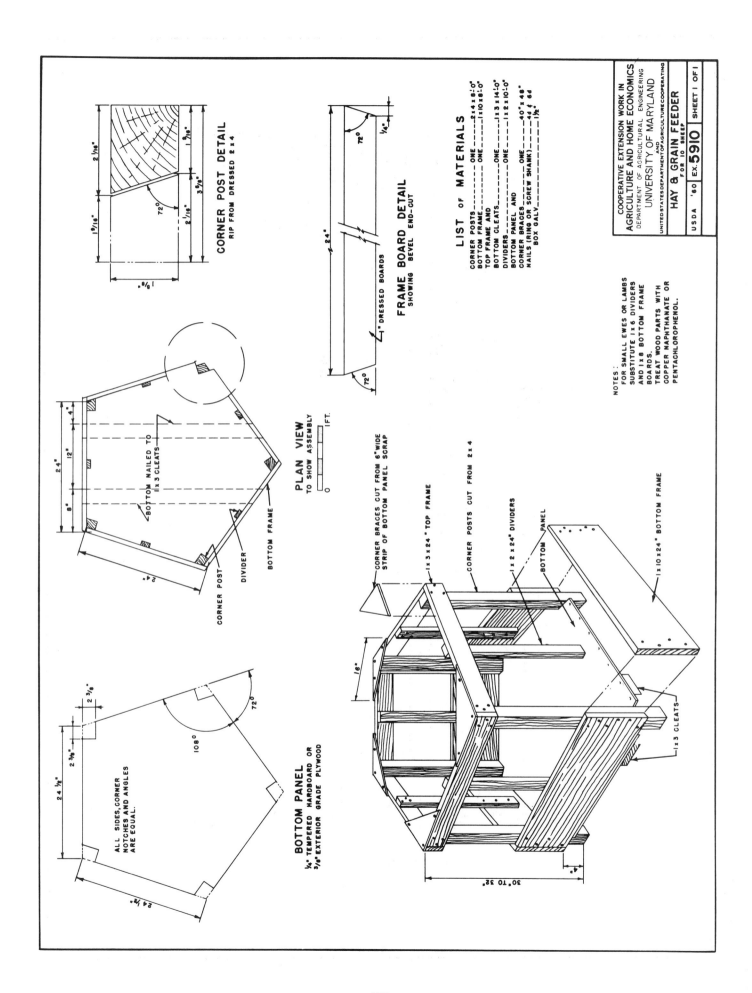

CORNER POST DETAIL
RIP FROM DRESSED 2 x 4

FRAME BOARD DETAIL
SHOWING BEVEL END-CUT

1" DRESSED BOARDS

LIST OF MATERIALS

CORNER POSTS _____ ONE _____ 2 x 4 x 8'-0"
BOTTOM FRAME _____ ONE _____ 1 x 10 x 8'-0"
TOP FRAME AND
BOTTOM CLEATS _____ ONE _____ 1 x 3 x 14'-0"
DIVIDERS _____ ONE _____ 1 x 2 x 10'-0"
BOTTOM PANEL AND
CORNER BRACES _____ ONE _____ 40" x 48"
NAILS (RING OR SCREW SHANK) _____ 4d & 6d
BOX GALV _____ 1½"

NOTES:
FOR SMALL EWES OR LAMBS
SUBSTITUTE 1 x 6 DIVIDERS
AND 1 x 8 BOTTOM FRAME
BOARDS.
TREAT WOOD PARTS WITH
COPPER NAPHTHANATE OR
PENTACHLOROPHENOL.

PLAN VIEW
TO SHOW ASSEMBLY
0   1 FT.

BOTTOM NAILED TO
1 x 3 CLEATS

BOTTOM FRAME

CORNER POST
DIVIDER

BOTTOM PANEL
⅛" TEMPERED HARDBOARD OR
⅜" EXTERIOR GRADE PLYWOOD

ALL SIDES, CORNER
NOTCHES AND ANGLES
ARE EQUAL.

108°
72°

CORNER BRACES CUT FROM 6" WIDE
STRIP OF BOTTOM PANEL SCRAP

1 x 3 x 24" TOP FRAME

CORNER POSTS CUT FROM 2 x 4

1 x 2 x 24" DIVIDERS

BOTTOM PANEL

1 x 10 x 24" BOTTOM FRAME

1 x 3 CLEATS

30" TO 32"

COOPERATIVE EXTENSION WORK IN
AGRICULTURE AND HOME ECONOMICS
DEPARTMENT OF AGRICULTURAL ENGINEERING
UNIVERSITY OF MARYLAND
AND
UNITED STATES DEPARTMENT OF AGRICULTURE COOPERATING

HAY & GRAIN FEEDER
FOR 10 SHEEP

USDA '60 EX. 5910 SHEET 1 OF 1

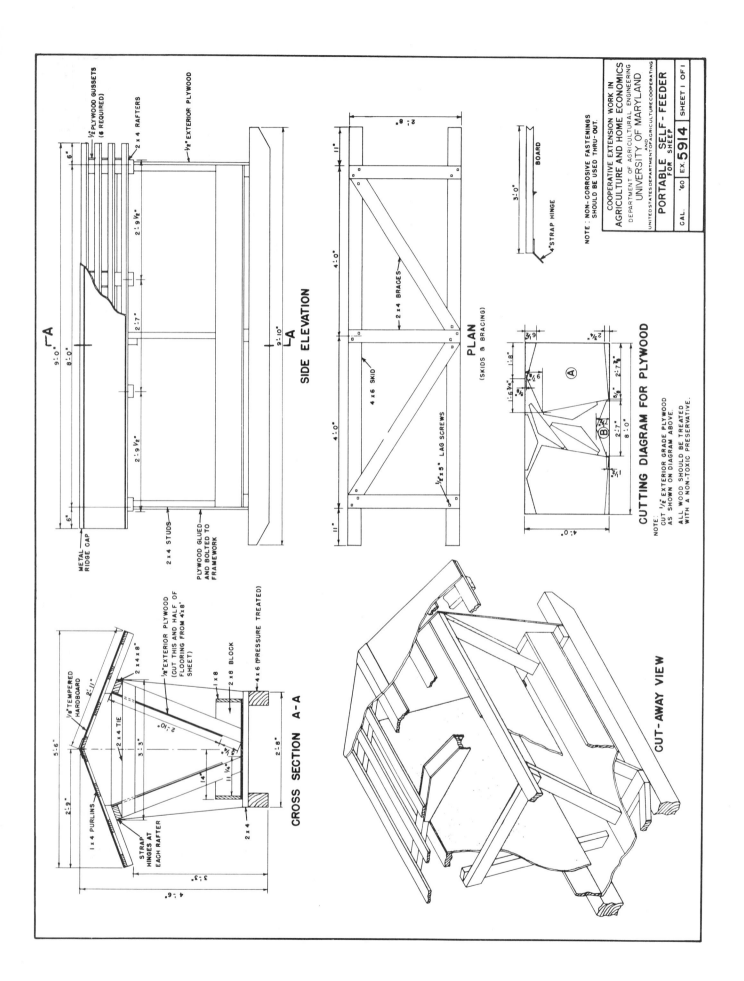

SIDE ELEVATION

PLAN
(SKIDS & BRACING)

CROSS SECTION A-A

CUTTING DIAGRAM FOR PLYWOOD

NOTE:
CUT 1/2" EXTERIOR GRADE PLYWOOD
AS SHOWN ON DIAGRAM ABOVE.

ALL WOOD SHOULD BE TREATED
WITH A NON-TOXIC PRESERVATIVE.

CUT-AWAY VIEW

NOTE: NON-CORROSIVE FASTENINGS
SHOULD BE USED THRU-OUT.

COOPERATIVE EXTENSION WORK IN
AGRICULTURE AND HOME ECONOMICS
DEPARTMENT OF AGRICULTURAL ENGINEERING
UNIVERSITY OF MARYLAND
AND
UNITED STATES DEPARTMENT OF AGRICULTURE COOPERATING

PORTABLE SELF-FEEDER
FOR SHEEP

CAL. | '60 | EX. 5914 | SHEET 1 OF 1

238

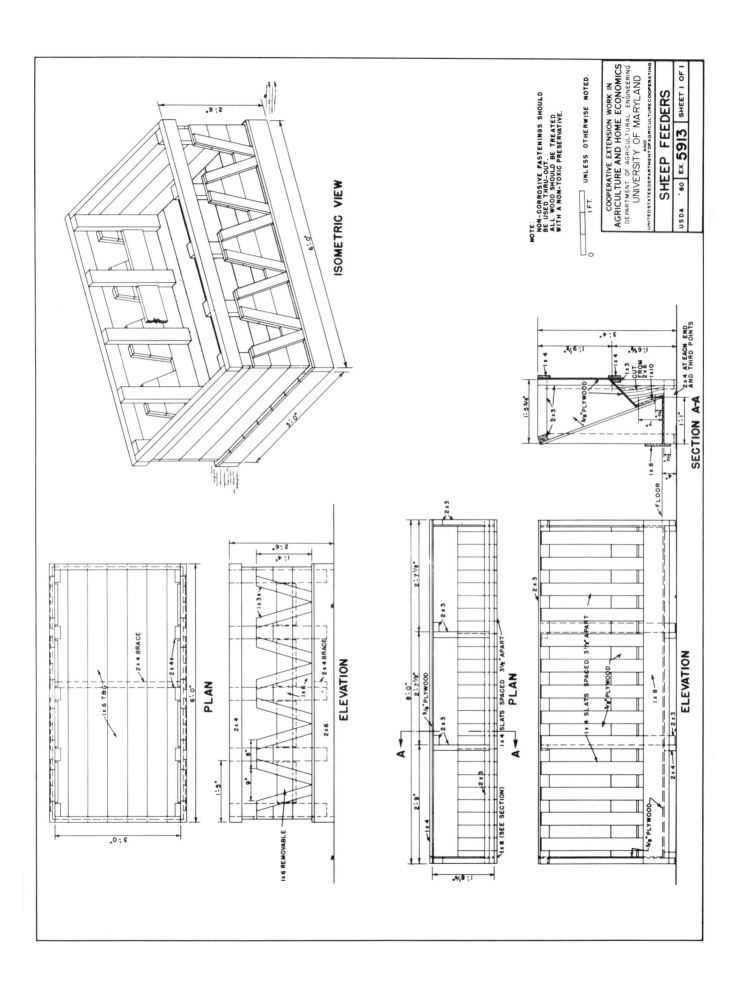

ISOMETRIC VIEW

PLAN

ELEVATION

PLAN

ELEVATION

SECTION A-A

NOTE:
NON-CORROSIVE FASTENINGS SHOULD
BE USED THRU-OUT
ALL WOOD SHOULD BE TREATED
WITH A NON-TOXIC PRESERVATIVE.

UNLESS OTHERWISE NOTED.

1 FT.

COOPERATIVE EXTENSION WORK IN
AGRICULTURE AND HOME ECONOMICS
DEPARTMENT OF AGRICULTURAL ENGINEERING
UNIVERSITY OF MARYLAND
AND
UNITED STATES DEPARTMENT OF AGRICULTURE COOPERATING

SHEEP FEEDERS

USDA '60 | EX. 5913 | SHEET 1 OF 1

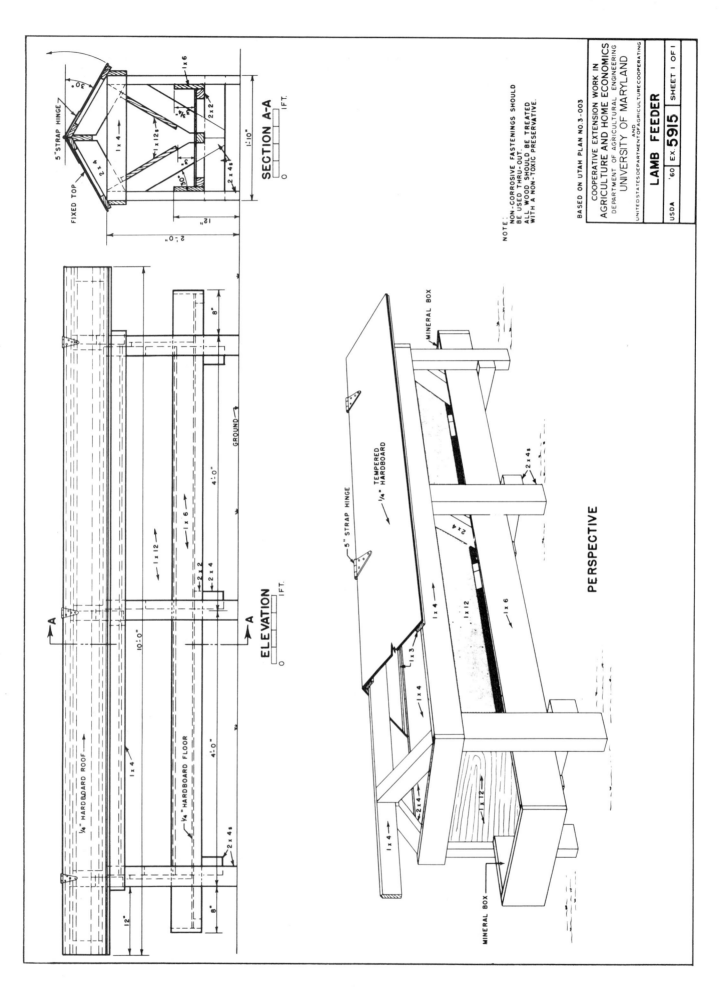

SECTION A-A

ELEVATION

PERSPECTIVE

5" STRAP HINGE

FIXED TOP

1 x 6

2 x 2

1 x 4

1 x 12s

2 x 4

30°

2 x 4s

12"

2'-0"

1'-10"

¼" HARDBOARD ROOF

1 x 4

1 x 12

2 x 2

2 x 4

1 x 6

¼" HARDBOARD FLOOR

10'-0"

4'-0"

4'-0"

8"

12"

8"

2 x 4s

GROUND

A

A

MINERAL BOX

5" STRAP HINGE

¼" TEMPERED HARDBOARD

2 x 4s

2 x 4

1 x 4

1 x 12

1 x 6

1 x 3

1 x 4

2 x 4

1 x 12

1 x 4

MINERAL BOX

BASED ON UTAH PLAN NO. 3-003

COOPERATIVE EXTENSION WORK IN
AGRICULTURE AND HOME ECONOMICS
DEPARTMENT OF AGRICULTURAL ENGINEERING
UNIVERSITY OF MARYLAND
AND
UNITED STATES DEPARTMENT OF AGRICULTURE COOPERATING

LAMB FEEDER

USDA   '60   EX. 5915   SHEET 1 OF 1

NOTE:
NON-CORROSIVE FASTENINGS SHOULD
BE USED THRU-OUT.
ALL WOOD SHOULD BE TREATED
WITH A NON-TOXIC PRESERVATIVE.

240

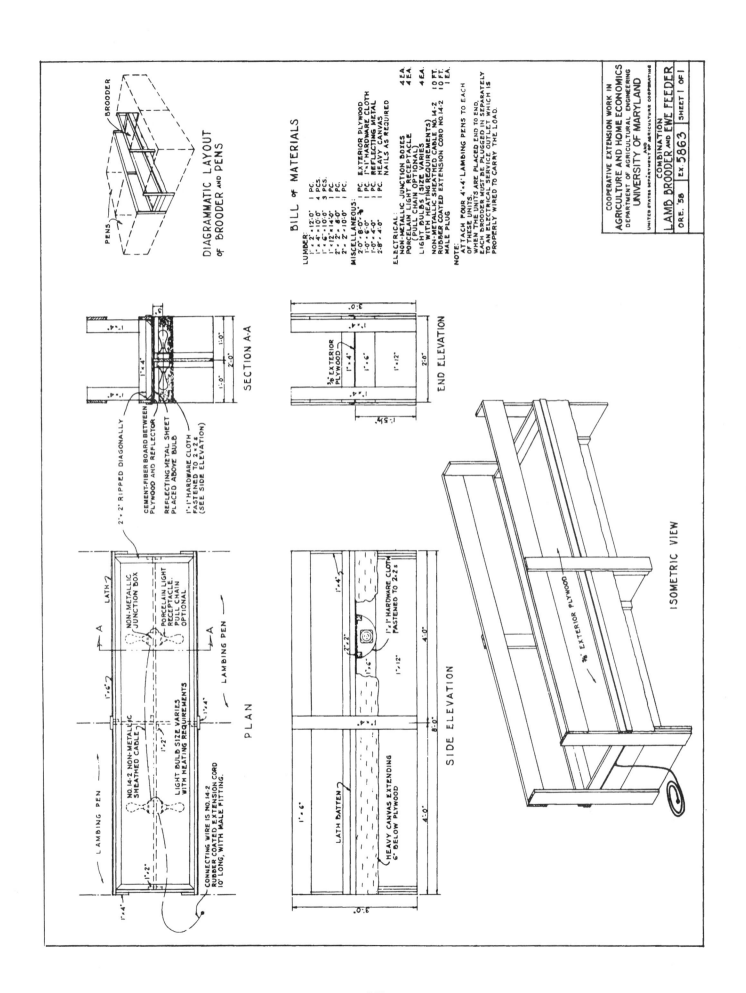

DIAGRAMMATIC LAYOUT
of BROODER and PENS

BILL OF MATERIALS

LUMBER:
1" x 2" x 12'-0"   1 PC.
1" x 4" x 10'-0"   4 PCS.
1" x 6" x 10'-0"   3 PCS.
1" x 12" x 4'-0"   1 PC.
2" x 2" x 4'-0"   1 PC.
2" x 2" x 10'-0"   1 PC.

MISCELLANEOUS:
2'-0" x 8'-0" x 3⁄8"   1 PC.   EXTERIOR PLYWOOD
1'-0" x 6'-0"   1 PC.   1" x 1" HARDWARE CLOTH
1'-0" x 4'-0"   1 PC.   REFLECTING METAL
2'-8" x 4'-0"   1 PC.   HEAVY CANVAS
                              NAILS AS REQUIRED

ELECTRICAL:
NON-METALLIC JUNCTION BOXES   4 EA.
PORCELAIN LIGHT RECEPTACLE   4 EA.
(PULL CHAIN OPTIONAL)
LIGHT BULBS SIZE VARIES   4 EA.
   WITH HEATING REQUIREMENTS)
NON-METALLIC SHEATHED CABLE NO. 14-2   10 FT.
RUBBER COATED EXTENSION CORD NO.14-2   10 FT.
MALE PLUG   1 EA.

NOTE:
   ATTACH FOUR 4'x4' LAMBING PENS TO EACH
   OF THESE UNITS.
   WHEN THE UNITS ARE PLACED END TO END,
   EACH BROODER MUST BE PLUGGED IN SEPARATELY
   TO AN ELECTRICAL SERVICE OUTLET WHICH IS
   PROPERLY WIRED TO CARRY THE LOAD.

2" x 2" RIPPED DIAGONALLY

CEMENT-FIBER BOARD BETWEEN
PLYWOOD AND REFLECTOR

REFLECTING METAL SHEET
PLACED ABOVE BULB

1" x 1" HARDWARE CLOTH
FASTENED TO 2 x 2s
(SEE SIDE ELEVATION)

SECTION A-A

END ELEVATION

3⁄8" EXTERIOR
PLYWOOD

LATH

NON-METALLIC JUNCTION BOX

PORCELAIN LIGHT
RECEPTACLE.
PULL CHAIN
OPTIONAL

LAMBING PEN

LAMBING PEN

NO. 14-2 NON-METALLIC
SHEATHED CABLE

LIGHT BULB SIZE VARIES
WITH HEATING REQUIREMENTS

CONNECTING WIRE IS NO. 14-2
RUBBER COATED EXTENSION CORD
10' LONG, WITH MALE FITTING.

PLAN

LATH BATTEN

1" x 1" HARDWARE CLOTH
FASTENED TO 2x2s

HEAVY CANVAS EXTENDING
6" BELOW PLYWOOD

SIDE ELEVATION

3⁄8" EXTERIOR PLYWOOD

ISOMETRIC VIEW

COOPERATIVE EXTENSION WORK IN
AGRICULTURE AND HOME ECONOMICS
DEPARTMENT OF AGRICULTURAL ENGINEERING
UNIVERSITY OF MARYLAND
AND
UNITED STATES DEPARTMENT OF AGRICULTURE COOPERATING

COMBINATION
LAMB BROODER AND EWE FEEDER

ORE. '56 | Ex. 5863 | SHEET 1 OF 1

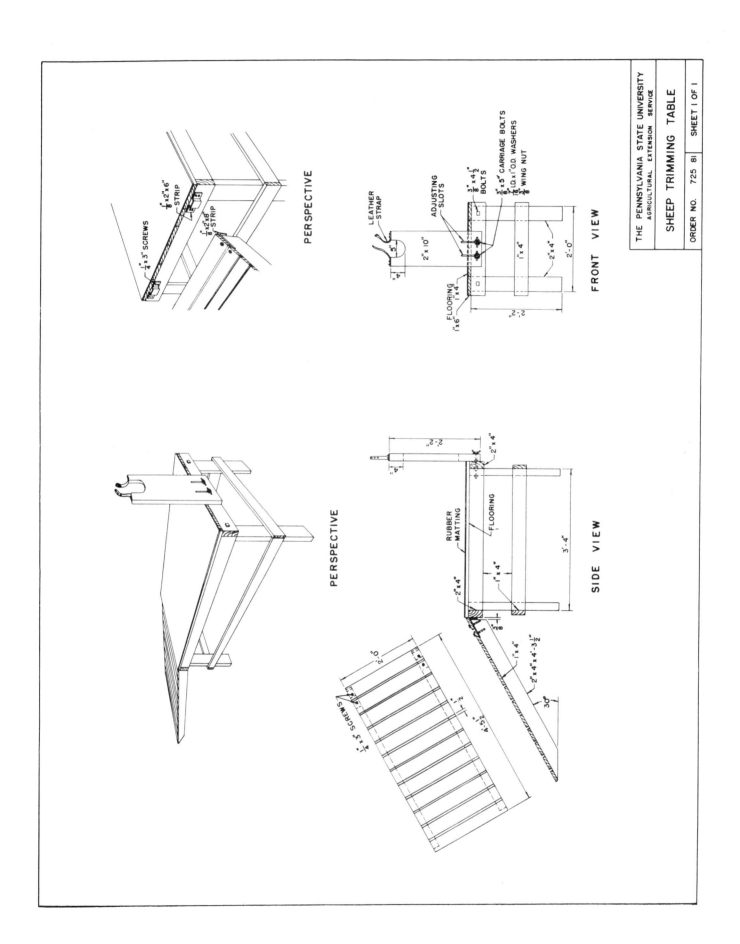

PERSPECTIVE

$\frac{1}{8}"x2"x6"$ STRIP

$\frac{1}{4}"x3"$ SCREWS

$\frac{1}{8}"x2"x8"$ STRIP

LEATHER STRAP

ADJUSTING SLOTS

$\frac{3}{8}"x5"$ CARRIAGE BOLTS

$\frac{3}{8}"x4\frac{1}{2}"$ BOLTS

$\frac{3}{8}"$ I.D. x I"O.D. WASHERS

$\frac{3}{8}"$ WING NUT

5"

2"x 10"

FLOORING
I"x4"

I"x6"

I'x 4"

2"x 4"

2'-0"

2'-2"

FRONT VIEW

PERSPECTIVE

2'-2"

2"x 4"

4"

RUBBER MATTING

FLOORING

2"x 4"

I"x 4"

$\frac{3}{8}"$

I"x 4"

2"x 4"x 4-3$\frac{1}{2}$"

3'-4"

SIDE VIEW

2'-0"

$\frac{1}{4}"x3"$ SCREWS

$\frac{1}{2}"$

4-5$\frac{1}{2}"$

30°

THE PENNSYLVANIA STATE UNIVERSITY
AGRICULTURAL EXTENSION SERVICE

SHEEP TRIMMING TABLE

ORDER NO. 725 81   SHEET I OF I

242

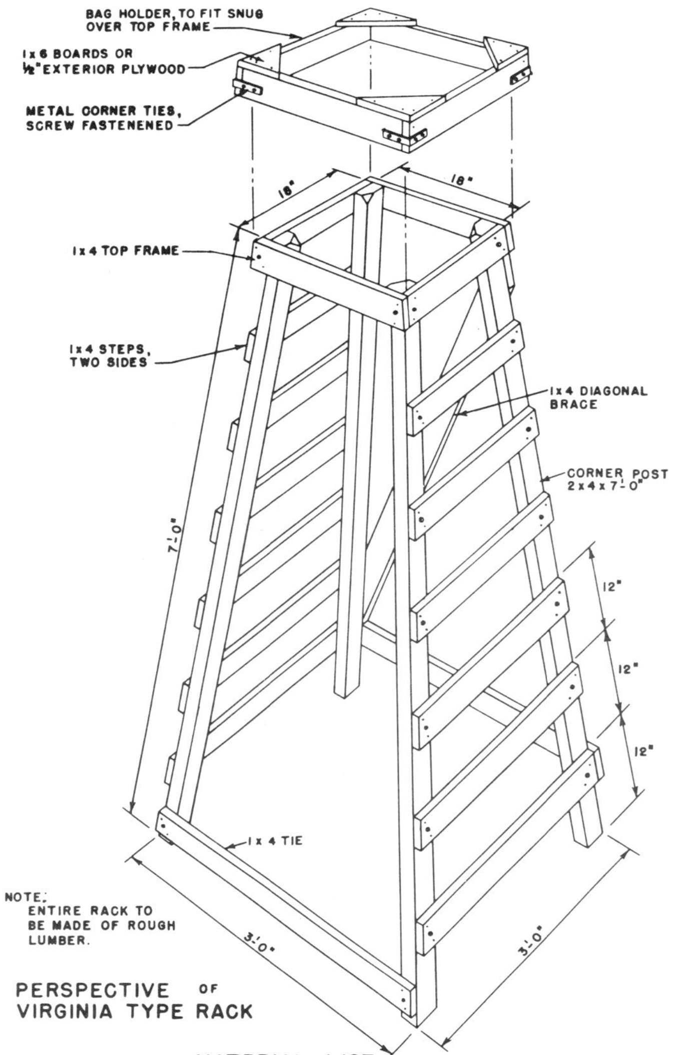
BAG HOLDER, TO FIT SNUG OVER TOP FRAME
1 x 6 BOARDS OR ½" EXTERIOR PLYWOOD
METAL CORNER TIES, SCREW FASTENED
18"
18"
1 x 4 TOP FRAME
1 x 4 STEPS, TWO SIDES
1 x 4 DIAGONAL BRACE
CORNER POST 2 x 4 x 7'-0"
7'-0"
12"
12"
12"
1 x 4 TIE
3'-0"
3'-0"

NOTE: ENTIRE RACK TO BE MADE OF ROUGH LUMBER.

PERSPECTIVE OF VIRGINIA TYPE RACK

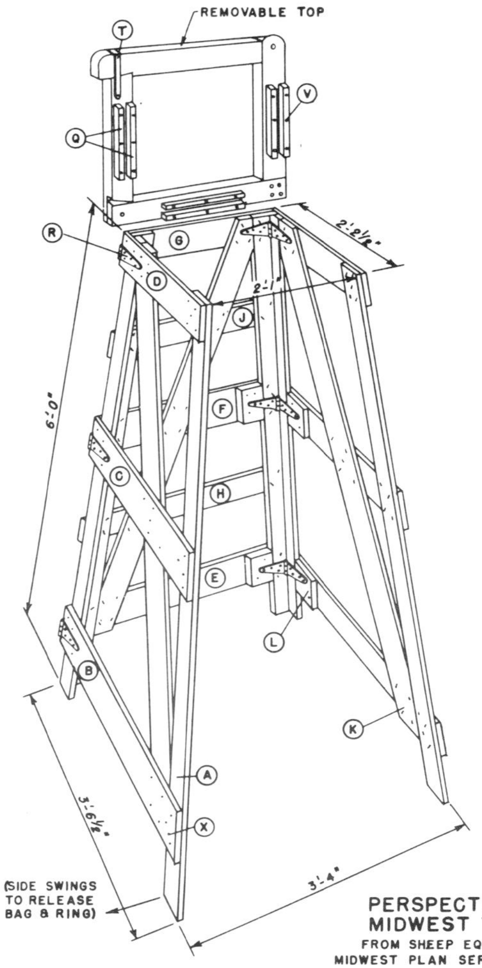
REMOVABLE TOP
T
V
Q
R
G
D
J
2'-2½"
2'-1"
6'-0"
F
C
H
E
L
B
K
A
X
3'-6½"
3'-4"
(SIDE SWINGS TO RELEASE BAG & RING)

PERSPECTIVE OF MIDWEST TYPE RACK

FROM SHEEP EQUIPMENT PLANS
MIDWEST PLAN SERVICE, AMES, IOWA.

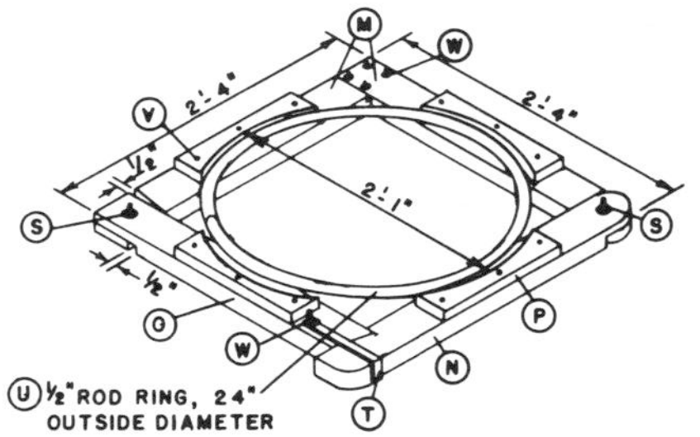
M
W
V
2'-4"
2'-4"
2'-1"
½"
½"
S
S
O
P
W
N
T
U ½" ROD RING, 24" OUTSIDE DIAMETER

REMOVABLE TOP

CUTTING LIST

ITEM	DESCRIPTION	QUANTITY
A	1 x 4 x 6'-0" CORNER POSTS	6
B	1 x 6 x 3'-6½" BOTTOM TIE	2
C	1 x 6 x 2'-11" MIDDLE TIE	2
D	1 x 6 x 2'-4" TOP TIE OR FRAME	2
E	1 x 6 x 3'-5" BOTTOM TIE OR STEP	1
F	1 x 6 x 2'-10" MIDDLE TIE OR STEP	1
G	1 x 6 x 2'-3" TOP TIE OR FRAME	1
H	1 x 4 x 2'-11" INTERMEDIATE STEP	1
J	1 x 4 x 2'-4" INTERMEDIATE STEP	1
K	1 x 4 x 6'-0" DIAGONAL BRACES	3
L	1 x 6 x 4" HINGE BLOCKING	4
M	2 x 4 x 2'-4" HARDWOOD FRAME	2
N	2 x 4 x 2'-6" HARDWOOD FRAME	1
O	2 x 4 x 2'-1" HARDWOOD FRAME	1
P	1 x 3 x 12" HARDWOOD (BAG HOLDER)	4
Q	1 x 1 x 12" HARDWOOD (CLAMPS)	6
R	6" STRAP HINGES (WITH SCREWS)	6
S	3/8" x 2 ½" BOLT	2
T	3/16" x ½" x 18" STRAP	1
U	½" x 6'-3½" ROD	1
V	1 3/4" - NO. 8 FLATHEAD WOOD SCREWS	30
W	¼" x 2 ½" BOLT	5
X	6d (RING OR SCREW SHANK) NAILS	1 LB.

NOTE: ENTIRE RACK TO BE MADE OF ROUGH LUMBER.

MATERIAL LIST

ITEM	SIZE	QUANTITY
CORNER POSTS	2 x 4 x 14'-0"	2
BAG HOLDER BRACE	1 x 6 x 1'-0"	1
STEPS (TWO SIDES)	1 x 4 x 8'-0"	4
DIAGONAL BRACE AND BOTTOM TIES	1 x 4 x 12'-0"	1
BAG HOLDER AND TOP FRAME	1 x 4 x 14'-0"	1
METAL CORNER TIES		4
WOOD SCREWS (FLATHEAD)	1" - NO. 10	16
	2" - NO. 10	38
NAILS (RING OR SCREW SHANK)	8d	1 LB.

USE OF THE WOOL PACKING RACK

FIRST, PLACE THE BAG IN THE RACK WITH THE MOUTH OF THE BAG FOLDED DOWN OVER THE TOP OF THE FRAME ABOUT 6" (IT MAY BE NECESSARY TO CUT THE SEAM OF SMALL-MOUTH BAGS ABOUT 4").

NEXT, PLACE THE BAG HOLDER DOWN OVER THE TOP OF THE RACK TO HOLD THE BAG SECURELY.

AFTER SHEARING EACH SHEEP, TIE THE FLEECE WITH PAPER TWINE. PACK THE FLEECES INTO THE BAG IN LAYERS OF 4 OR 5 BY CLIMBING INTO THE BAG AND TRAMPING THE WOOL.

WHEN THE BAG IS FILLED AND READY TO BE REMOVED PLACE A BOARD UNDER IT AND RAISE SLIGHTLY. THIS WILL RELEASE THE PRESSURE AT THE TOP SO THE BAG WILL NOT TEAR WHEN THE BAG HOLDER IS REMOVED. CAPACITY OF THE BAG IS ABOUT 200 POUNDS.

* DETAILS OF A WOOL BOX USED FOR TYING FLEECE - SEE PLAN EX. 5805

COOPERATIVE EXTENSION WORK IN
AGRICULTURE AND HOME ECONOMICS
DEPARTMENT OF AGRICULTURAL ENGINEERING
UNIVERSITY OF MARYLAND
AND
UNITED STATES DEPARTMENT OF AGRICULTURE COOPERATING

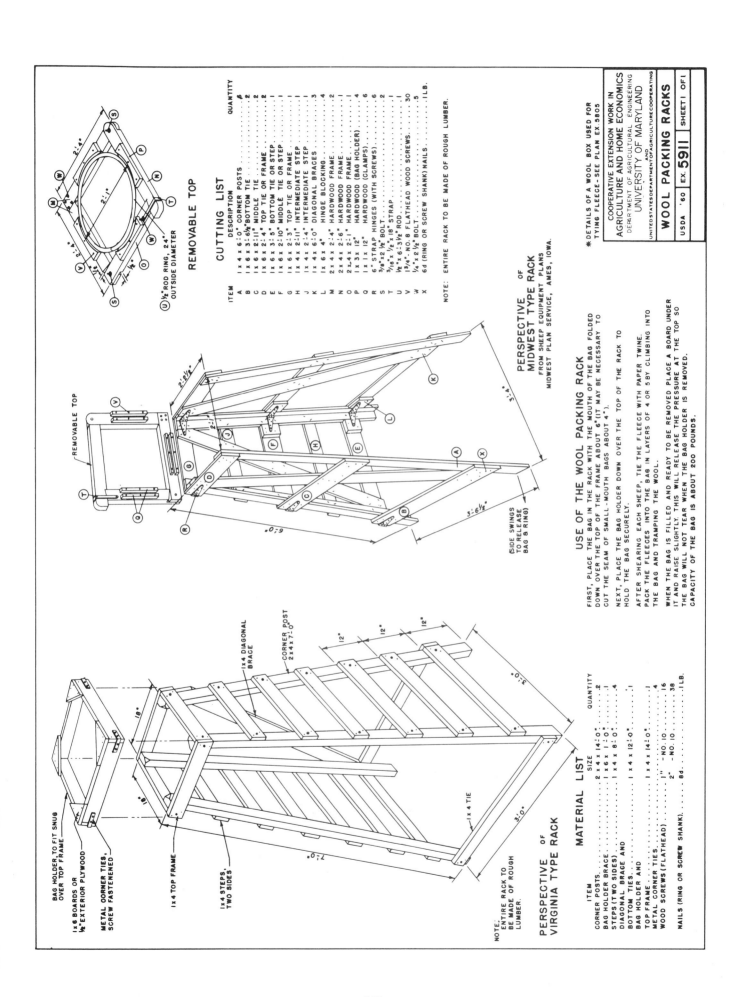

WOOL PACKING RACKS

USDA '60 | EX. 5911 | SHEET 1 OF 1

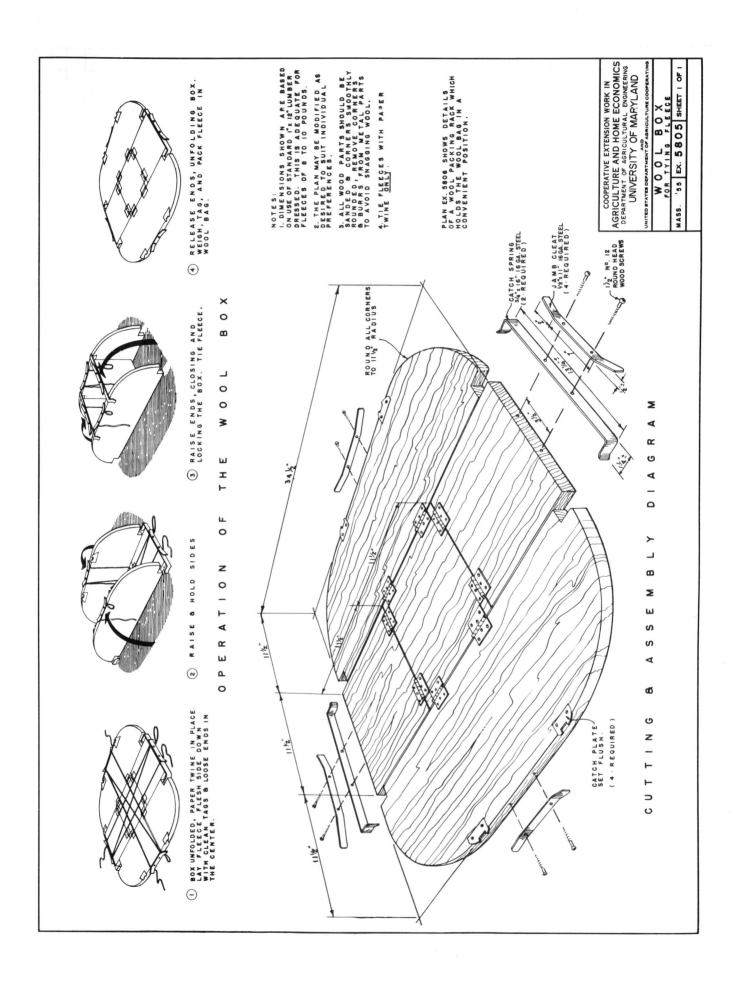

OPERATION OF THE WOOL BOX

① BOX UNFOLDED, PAPER TWINE IN PLACE.
LAY FLEECE, FLESH SIDE DOWN
WITH CLEAN TAGS & LOOSE ENDS IN
THE CENTER.

② RAISE & HOLD SIDES

③ RAISE ENDS, CLOSING AND
LOCKING THE BOX. TIE FLEECE.

④ RELEASE ENDS, UNFOLDING BOX.
WEIGH, TAG, AND PACK FLEECE IN
WOOL BAG.

NOTES:

1. DIMENSIONS SHOWN ARE BASED
ON USE OF STANDARD 1"x 12" LUMBER
DRESSED. THIS IS ADEQUATE FOR
FLEECES OF 8 TO 10 POUNDS.

2. THE PLAN MAY BE MODIFIED AS
DESIRED TO SUIT INDIVIDUAL
PREFERENCES.

3. ALL WOOD PARTS SHOULD BE
SANDED & CORNERS SMOOTHLY
ROUNDED, REMOVE CORNERS
& BURRS FROM METAL PARTS
TO AVOID SNAGGING WOOL.

4. TIE FLEECES WITH PAPER
TWINE ONLY.

PLAN EX. 5806 SHOWS DETAILS
OF A WOOL PACKING RACK WHICH
HOLDS THE WOOL BAG IN A
CONVENIENT POSITION.

CUTTING & ASSEMBLY DIAGRAM

ROUND ALL CORNERS
TO 11½" RADIUS

34½

11½"

11½

11½"

11½"

11½"

CATCH PLATE
SET FLUSH.
(4 REQUIRED)

CATCH SPRING
¾"x 16" (16 GA. STEEL)
(2 REQUIRED)

JAMB CLEAT
½"x 11" 16 GA. STEEL
(4 REQUIRED)

1½" NO. 12
ROUND HEAD
WOOD SCREWS

3¾"

1½"

COOPERATIVE EXTENSION WORK IN
AGRICULTURE AND HOME ECONOMICS
DEPARTMENT OF AGRICULTURAL ENGINEERING
UNIVERSITY OF MARYLAND
AND
UNITED STATES DEPARTMENT OF AGRICULTURE COOPERATING

WOOL BOX
FOR TYING FLEECE

MASS. '55 | EX. 5805 | SHEET 1 OF 1

244

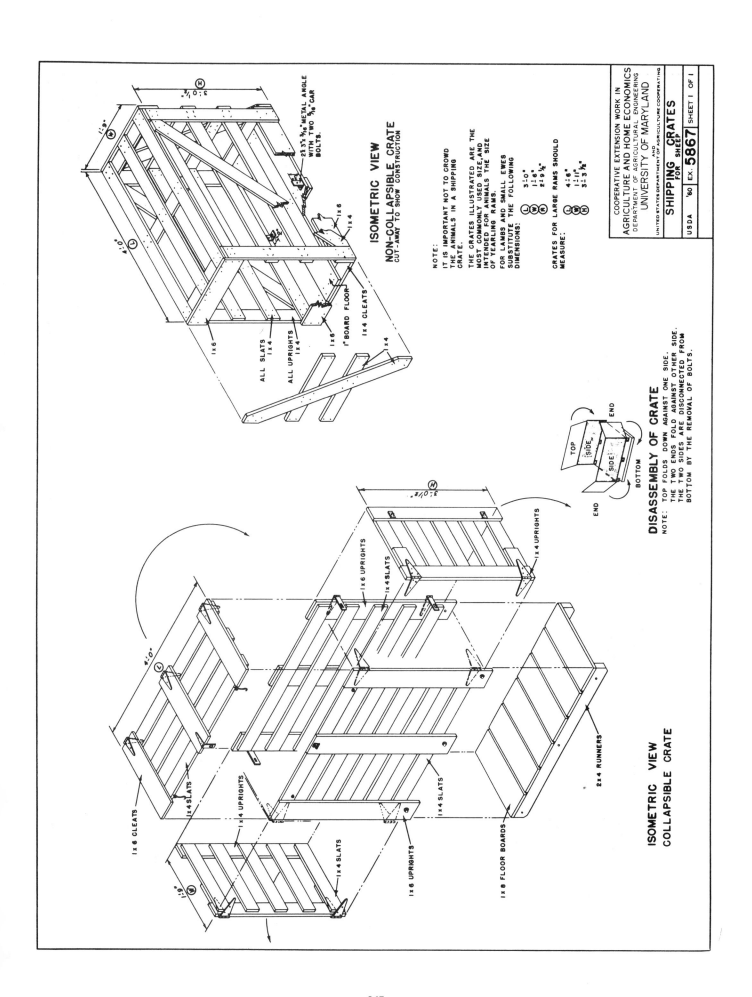

ISOMETRIC VIEW
NON-COLLAPSIBLE CRATE
CUT-AWAY TO SHOW CONSTRUCTION

2 1 3⁄4 X 3⁄16 METAL ANGLE
WITH TWO 5⁄16 CAR
BOLTS.

1 x 6

1 x 4

1" BOARD FLOOR

1 x 6

1 x 4 CLEATS

ALL SLATS
1 x 4

ALL UPRIGHTS
1 x 4

1 x 4

NOTE:

IT IS IMPORTANT NOT TO CROWD
THE ANIMALS IN A SHIPPING
CRATE.

THE CRATES ILLUSTRATED ARE THE
MOST COMMONLY USED SIZE, AND
INTENDED FOR ANIMALS THE SIZE
OF YEARLING RAMS.

FOR LAMBS AND SMALL EWES
SUBSTITUTE THE FOLLOWING
DIMENSIONS:

Ⓛ   3'-0"
Ⓦ   1'-6"
Ⓗ   2'-9½"

CRATES FOR LARGE RAMS SHOULD
MEASURE:

Ⓛ   4'-6"
Ⓦ   1'-11"
Ⓗ   3'-3¾"

DISASSEMBLY OF CRATE
NOTE: TOP FOLDS DOWN AGAINST ONE SIDE.
THE TWO ENDS FOLD AGAINST OTHER SIDE.
THE TWO SIDES ARE DISCONNECTED FROM
BOTTOM BY THE REMOVAL OF BOLTS.

TOP   END   SIDE   SIDE   BOTTOM   END

1 x 6 UPRIGHTS

1 x 4 SLATS

1 x 4 UPRIGHTS

1 x 6 CLEATS

1 x 4 SLATS

1 x 4 UPRIGHTS

1 x 6 UPRIGHTS

1 x 4 SLATS

1 x 6 FLOOR BOARDS

1 x 4 SLATS

2 x 4 RUNNERS

ISOMETRIC VIEW
COLLAPSIBLE CRATE

COOPERATIVE EXTENSION WORK IN
AGRICULTURE AND HOME ECONOMICS
DEPARTMENT OF AGRICULTURAL ENGINEERING
UNIVERSITY OF MARYLAND
AND
UNITED STATES DEPARTMENT OF AGRICULTURE COOPERATING

SHIPPING CRATES
FOR SHEEP

USDA   '60   EX. 5867   SHEET I OF I

245

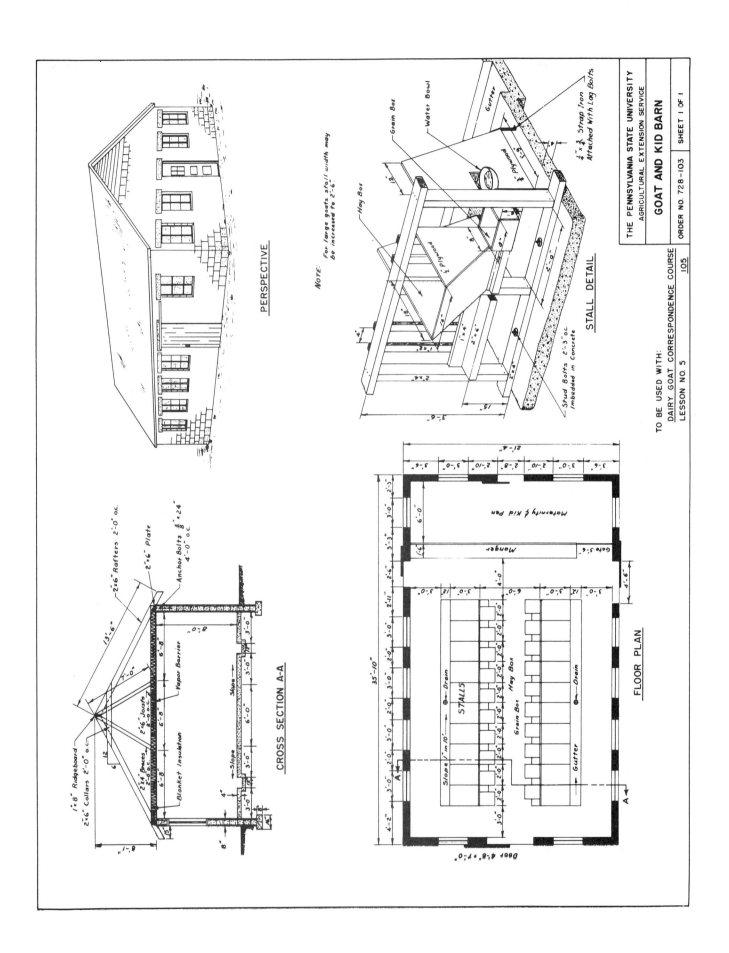

PERSPECTIVE

NOTE: For large goats stall width may be increased to 2'-6".

STALL DETAIL

Water Bowl
Grain Box
Gutter
Hay Box
½ Ply wood
½ Plywood
4"x ¾" Strap Iron Attached With Lag Bolts
Stud Bolts 2'-3" o.c. Imbedded in Concrete
1"x4"
2"x6"
2"x4"
2"x4"

CROSS SECTION A-A

1"x 8" Ridgeboard
2"x6" Collars 2'-0" o.c.
2"x 6" Rafters 2'-0" o.c.
2"x6" Plate
Anchor Bolts ⅝"x 24" 4'-0" o.c.
2"x6" Joists 2'-0" o.c.
2"x4" Braces 2'-0" o.c.
Vapor Barrier
Blanket Insulation
Slope
Slope

FLOOR PLAN

Maternity & Kid Pen
Manger
Gate 3'-6"
STALLS
Slope 1' in 10'
Drain
Drain
Hay Box
Grain Box
Gutter
Door 4'-8" + 1'-0"

THE PENNSYLVANIA STATE UNIVERSITY
AGRICULTURAL EXTENSION SERVICE

GOAT AND KID BARN

ORDER NO. 728-103   SHEET 1 OF 1

TO BE USED WITH:
DAIRY GOAT CORRESPONDENCE COURSE
LESSON NO. 5   105

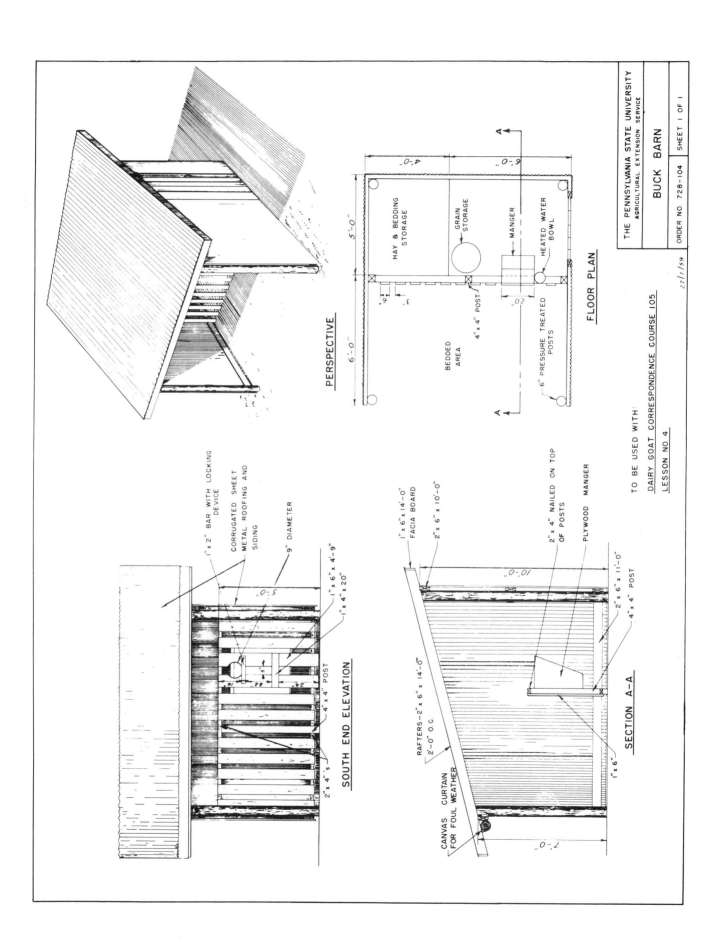

PERSPECTIVE

FLOOR PLAN

6'-0"
5'-0"
4'-0"
9'-0"

HAY & BEDDING STORAGE

GRAIN STORAGE

MANGER

HEATED WATER BOWL

BEDDED AREA

4" x 4" POST

6"
3'

20"

6" PRESSURE TREATED POSTS

A
A

SOUTH END ELEVATION

1" x 2" BAR WITH LOCKING DEVICE

CORRUGATED SHEET METAL ROOFING AND SIDING

9" DIAMETER

1" x 6" x 4'-9"

1" x 4" x 20"

5'-0"

4" x 4" POST

2" x 4" s

5"

SECTION A-A

1" x 6" x 14'-0" FACIA BOARD

2" x 6" x 10'-0"

2" x 4" NAILED ON TOP OF POSTS

PLYWOOD MANGER

RAFTERS—2" x 6" x 14'-0" 2'-0" O.C.

CANVAS FOR FOUL WEATHER

1" x 6"

2" x 6" x 11'-0" POST

4" x 4" POST

10'-0"

7'-0"

THE PENNSYLVANIA STATE UNIVERSITY
AGRICULTURAL EXTENSION SERVICE

BUCK BARN

ORDER NO 728-104   SHEET 1 OF 1

27/1/59

TO BE USED WITH:

DAIRY GOAT CORRESPONDENCE COURSE 105

LESSON NO 4

247

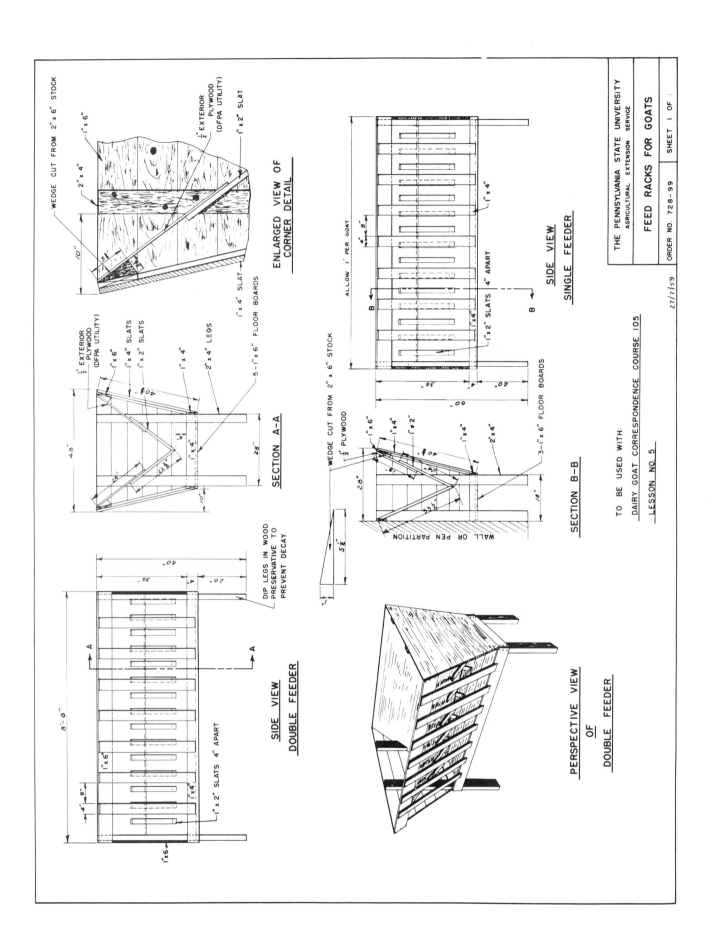

ENLARGED VIEW OF
CORNER DETAIL

WEDGE CUT FROM 2" x 6" STOCK
1" x 6"
2" x 4"
½ EXTERIOR PLYWOOD (DFPA UTILITY)
1" x 2" SLAT
10"
1" x 4" SLAT
1" x 4" FLOOR BOARDS

SECTION A-A

½ EXTERIOR PLYWOOD (DFPA UTILITY)
1" x 6"
1" x 4" SLATS
1" x 2" SLATS
1" x 4"
2" x 4" LEGS
5—1" x 6" FLOOR BOARDS
1" x 4"
40½"
48"
28"
10"

SIDE VIEW
DOUBLE FEEDER

8'-0"
60"
36"
20"
A   A
1" x 2" SLATS 4" APART
1" x 4"
8"
4"
1" x 6"
DIP LEGS IN WOOD PRESERVATIVE TO PREVENT DECAY.

SIDE VIEW
SINGLE FEEDER

ALLOW 1' PER GOAT
1" x 4"
8"
4"
1" x 2" SLATS 4" APART
B   B
36"
4"
20"
60"
1" x 4"

SECTION B-B

WEDGE CUT FROM 2" x 6" STOCK
½ PLYWOOD
1" x 6"
1" x 4"
1" x 2"
1" x 4"
2" x 4"
40½"
28"
18"
3—1" x 6" FLOOR BOARDS
18"
5⅝"
WALL OR PEN PARTITION

PERSPECTIVE VIEW
OF
DOUBLE FEEDER

THE PENNSYLVANIA STATE UNIVERSITY
AGRICULTURAL EXTENSION SERVICE

FEED RACKS FOR GOATS

ORDER NO. 728-99   SHEET 1 OF 1

TO BE USED WITH:
DAIRY GOAT CORRESPONDENCE COURSE 105

LESSON NO. 5

27/7/59

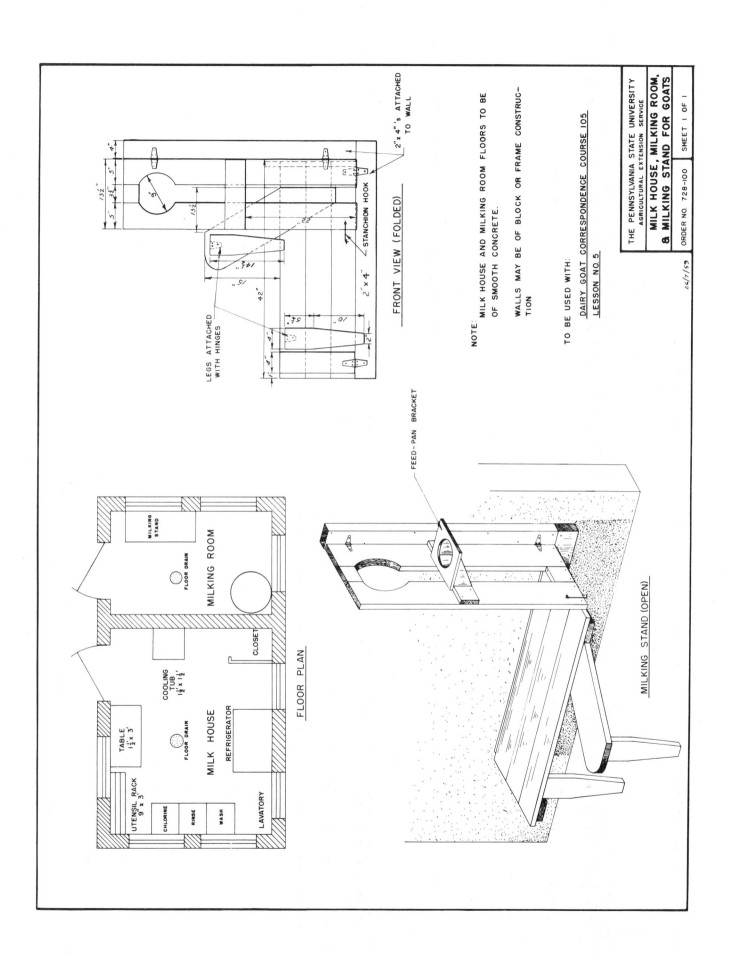

FRONT VIEW (FOLDED)

13½"
5" 3½" 5"
4"
6"
13½"
22"
14½"
15"
42"

STANCHION HOOK

2" x 4"'s ATTACHED
TO WALL

2" x 4"

LEGS ATTACHED
WITH HINGES

5½"
10"
4"
4"
2"

NOTE: MILK HOUSE AND MILKING ROOM FLOORS TO BE
OF SMOOTH CONCRETE.

WALLS MAY BE OF BLOCK OR FRAME CONSTRUC-
TION

TO BE USED WITH:

DAIRY GOAT CORRESPONDENCE COURSE 105
LESSON NO. 5

THE PENNSYLVANIA STATE UNIVERSITY
AGRICULTURAL EXTENSION SERVICE

**MILK HOUSE, MILKING ROOM,
& MILKING STAND FOR GOATS**

ORDER NO. 728-100 | SHEET 1 OF 1

24/7/59

FLOOR PLAN

MILKING ROOM

MILKING STAND

FLOOR DRAIN

CLOSET

COOLING
TUB
1½' x 1½'

MILK HOUSE

REFRIGERATOR

FLOOR DRAIN

TABLE
1½' x 3'

UTENSIL RACK
9" x 3'

CHLORINE

RINSE

WASH

LAVATORY

FEED-PAN BRACKET

MILKING STAND (OPEN)

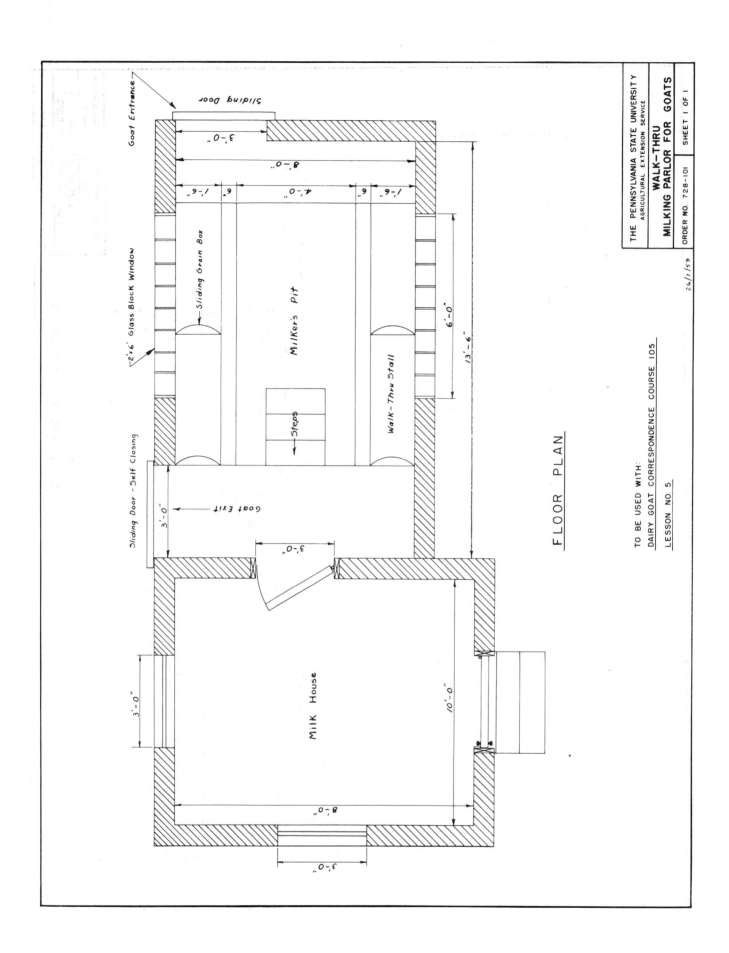

FLOOR PLAN

Goat Entrance

Sliding Door

3'-0"

8'-0"

1'-6" 6" 4'-0" 6" 1'-6"

2'x6' Glass Block Window

Sliding Grain Box

Milker's Pit

6'-0"

13'-6"

Walk-Thru Stall

Steps

Sliding Door - Self Closing

Goat Exit

3'-0"

3'-0"

Milk House

3'-0"

10'-0"

8'-0"

3'-0"

THE PENNSYLVANIA STATE UNIVERSITY
AGRICULTURAL EXTENSION SERVICE

WALK-THRU
MILKING PARLOR FOR GOATS

ORDER NO. 728-101   SHEET 1 OF 1

26/1/59

TO BE USED WITH:
DAIRY GOAT CORRESPONDENCE COURSE 105

LESSON NO. 5

250

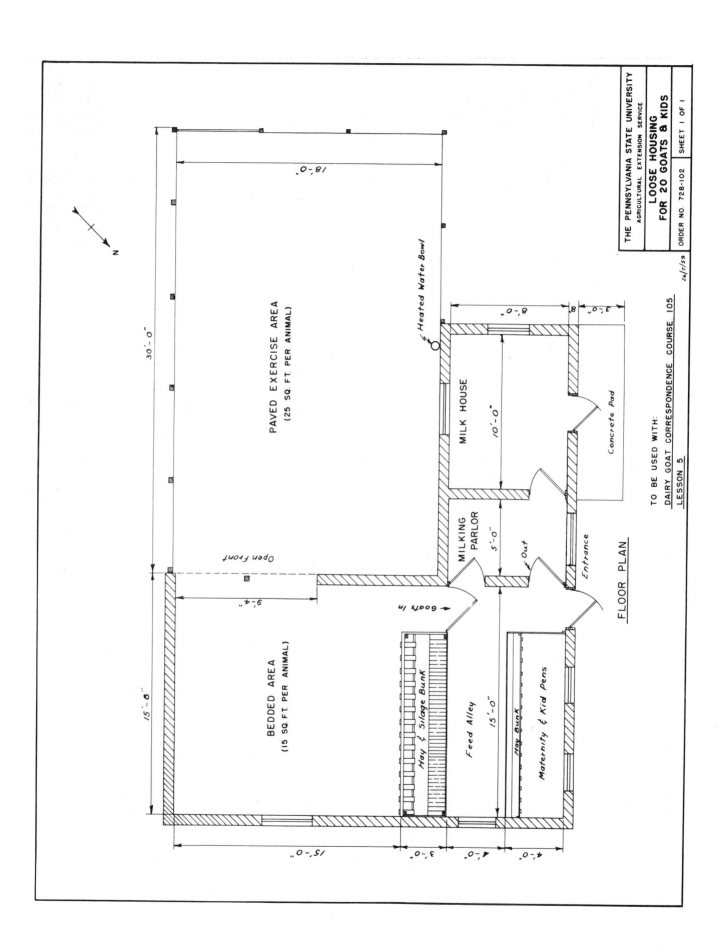

THE PENNSYLVANIA STATE UNIVERSITY
AGRICULTURAL EXTENSION SERVICE

**LOOSE HOUSING
FOR 20 GOATS & KIDS**

ORDER NO. 728-102   SHEET 1 OF 1

26/7/59

TO BE USED WITH:
DAIRY GOAT CORRESPONDENCE COURSE 105
LESSON 5

FLOOR PLAN

N

PAVED EXERCISE AREA
(25 SQ. FT. PER ANIMAL)

18'-0"

30'-0"

Open Front

Heated Water Bowl

MILK HOUSE

10'-0"

8'-0"

Concrete Pad

MILKING
PARLOR

5'-0"

Out

Entrance

Goats In

9'-4"

15'-8"

BEDDED AREA
(15 SQ. FT. PER ANIMAL)

Hay & Silage Bunk

Feed Alley

Hay Bunk

Maternity & Kid Pens

15'-0"

3'-0"

4'-0"

4'-0"

3'-0"

251

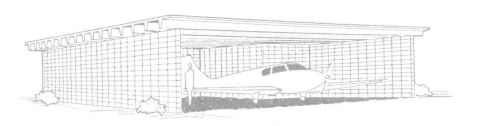

GENERAL VIEW

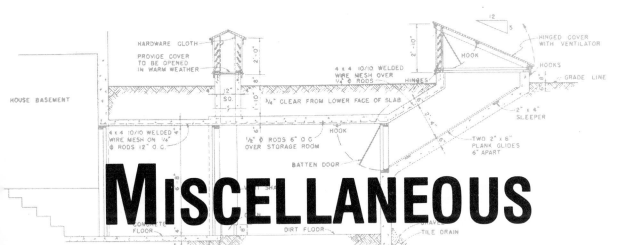

MISCELLANEOUS

STRUCTURES

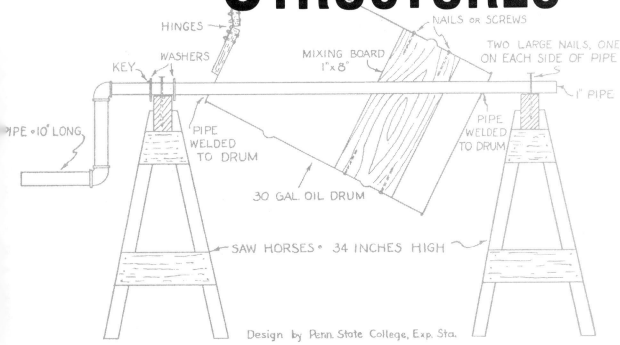

Design by Penn. State College, Exp. Sta.

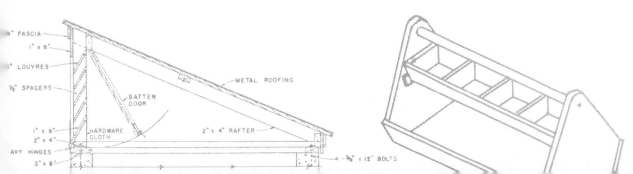

15

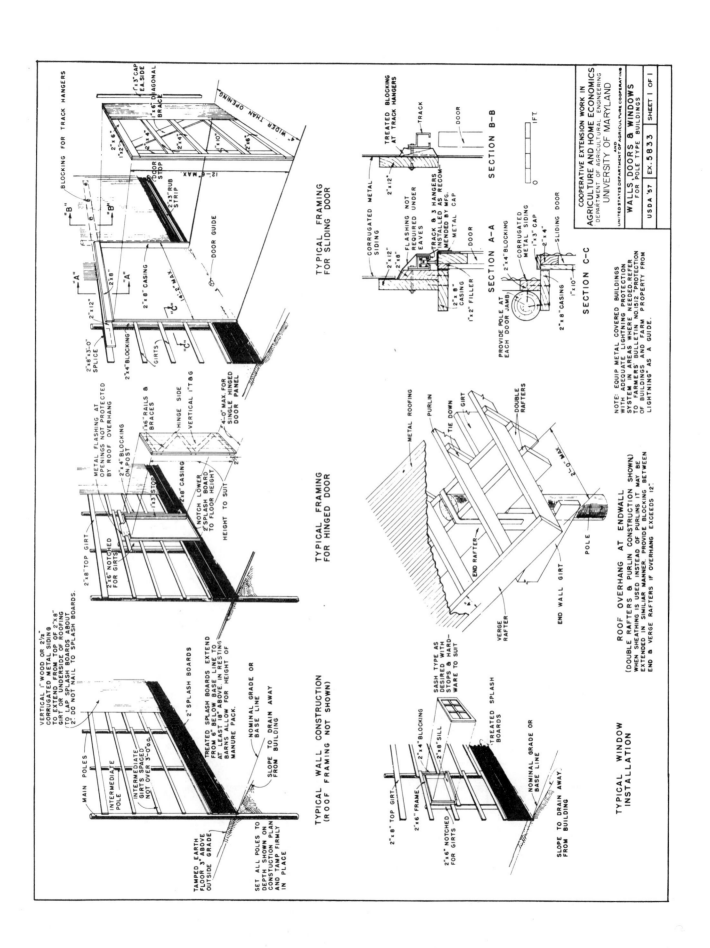

TYPICAL WALL CONSTRUCTION
(ROOF FRAMING NOT SHOWN)

TYPICAL FRAMING
FOR HINGED DOOR

TYPICAL FRAMING
FOR SLIDING DOOR

TYPICAL WINDOW
INSTALLATION

ROOF OVERHANG AT ENDWALL
(DOUBLE RAFTERS & PURLIN CONSTRUCTION SHOWN)
WHEN SHEATHING IS USED INSTEAD OF PURLINS IT MAY BE
EXTENDED IN SIMILIAR MANNER. PROVIDE BLOCKING BETWEEN
END & VERGE RAFTERS IF OVERHANG EXCEEDS 12".

SECTION A-A

SECTION B-B

SECTION C-C

NOTE: EQUIP METAL COVERED BUILDINGS
WITH ADEQUATE LIGHTNING PROTECTION
SYSTEM IN AREAS WHERE NEEDED. REFER
TO FARMERS' BULLETIN NO.1512 "PROTECTION
OF BUILDINGS AND FARM PROPERTY FROM
LIGHTNING" AS A GUIDE.

COOPERATIVE EXTENSION WORK IN
AGRICULTURE AND HOME ECONOMICS
DEPARTMENT OF AGRICULTURAL ENGINEERING
UNIVERSITY OF MARYLAND
UNITED STATES DEPARTMENT OF AGRICULTURE COOPERATING

WALLS, DOORS & WINDOWS
FOR POLE TYPE BUILDINGS

USDA '57   EX.5833   SHEET 1 OF 1

255

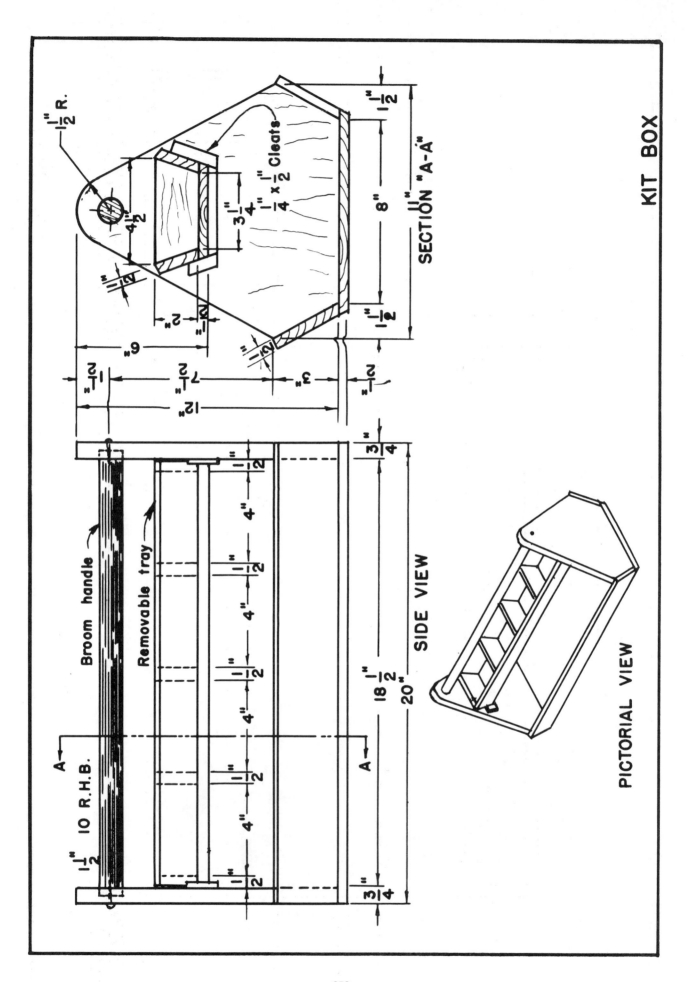

$1\frac{1}{2}$" R.

$1\frac{1}{2}$"

$4\frac{1}{2}$"

$3\frac{1}{4}$"

$\frac{1}{2}$"

2"

$\frac{2}{1}$"

$\frac{1}{2}$"

6"

$\frac{1}{4}$" x $\frac{1}{2}$" Cleats

8"

$1\frac{1}{2}$"

SECTION "A-A"

$1\frac{1}{2}$"

$7\frac{1}{2}$"

3"

$\frac{1}{2}$"

12"

$\frac{3}{4}$"

Broom handle

Removable tray

4"

$1\frac{1}{2}$"

4"

$1\frac{1}{2}$"

4"

$1\frac{1}{2}$"

$1\frac{1}{2}$"

$\frac{3}{4}$"

$1\frac{1}{2}$" 10 R.H.B.

A

A

$18\frac{1}{2}$"

20"

SIDE VIEW

PICTORIAL VIEW

KIT BOX

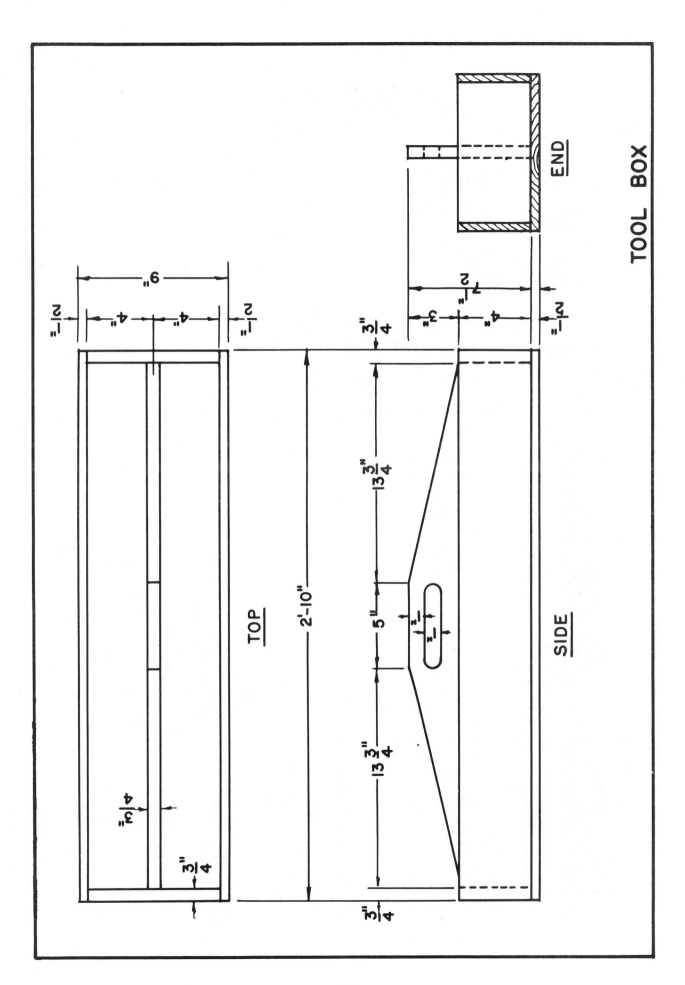

TOOL BOX

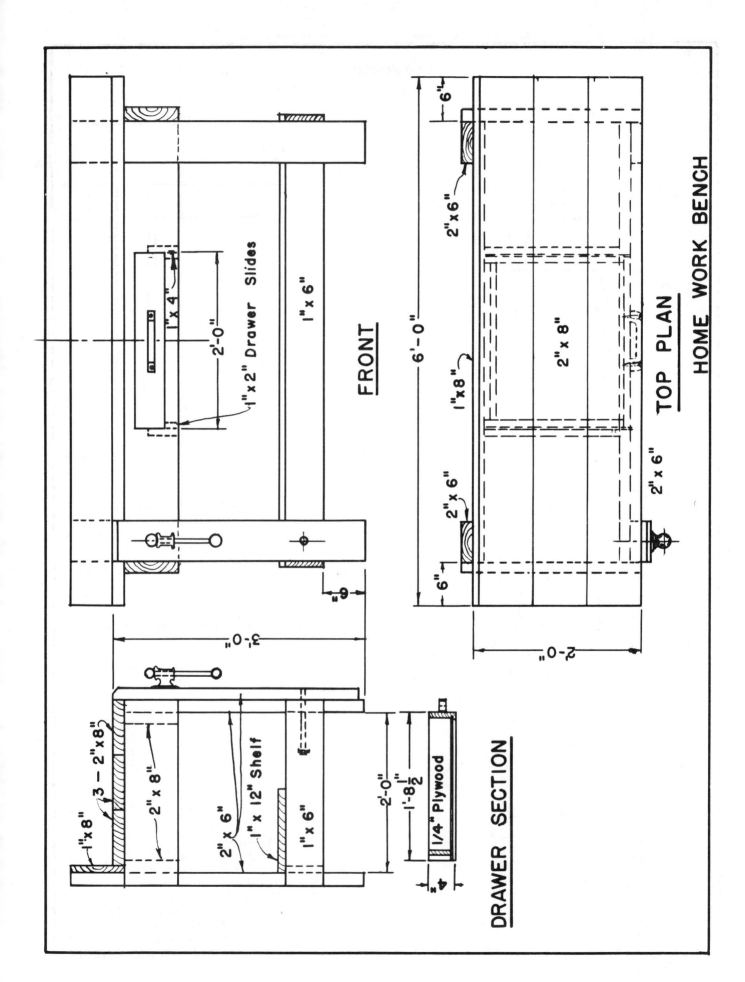

FRONT

I'x4"

2'-0"

I"x 2" Drawer Slides

I"x 6"

3'-0"

9"

3 - 2"x 8"

I"x 8"

2" x 8"

2" x 6"

I"x 12" Shelf

I"x 6"

2'-0"

I'-8½"

¼" Plywood

4"

DRAWER SECTION

6"

6'-0"

2"x 6"

I"x8"

2"x 8"

2" x 6"

6"

2'-0"

TOP PLAN

HOME WORK BENCH

SAW HORSES

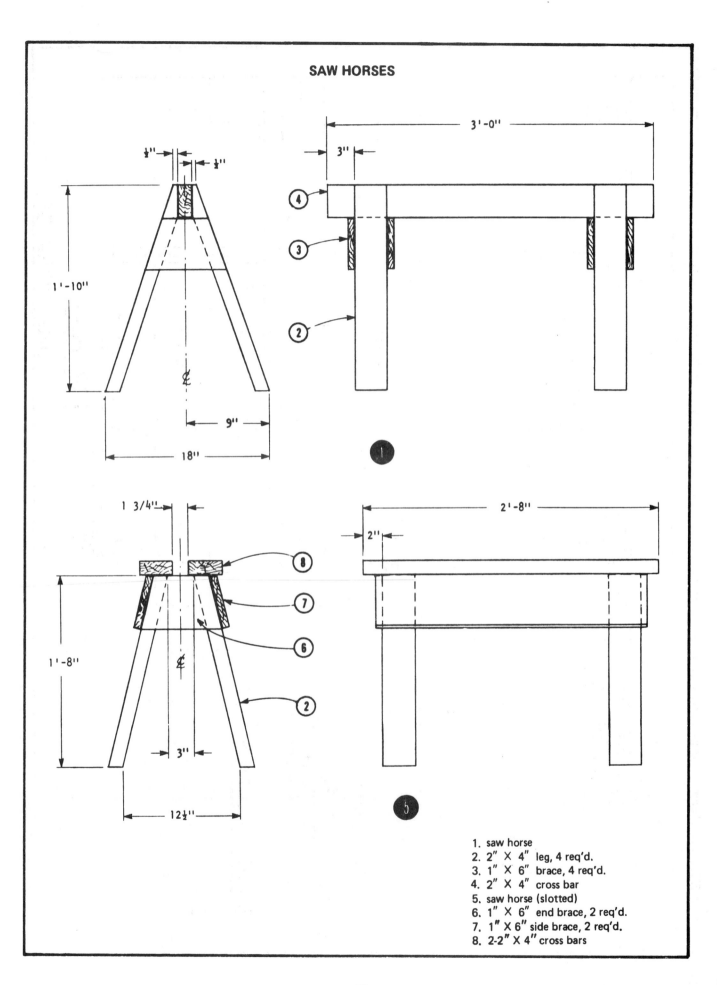

1. saw horse
2. 2″ × 4″ leg, 4 req'd.
3. 1″ × 6″ brace, 4 req'd.
4. 2″ × 4″ cross bar
5. saw horse (slotted)
6. 1″ × 6″ end brace, 2 req'd.
7. 1″ × 6″ side brace, 2 req'd.
8. 2-2″ × 4″ cross bars

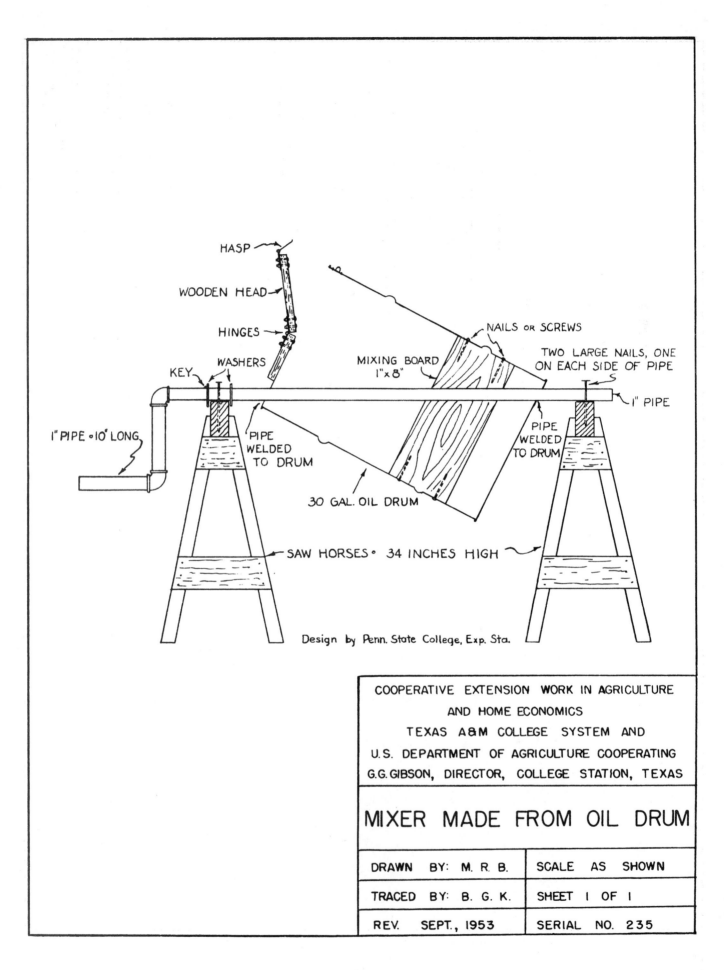

HASP

WOODEN HEAD

HINGES

WASHERS

KEY

NAILS OR SCREWS

TWO LARGE NAILS, ONE ON EACH SIDE OF PIPE

MIXING BOARD 1" x 8"

1" PIPE

1" PIPE ∘ 10" LONG

PIPE WELDED TO DRUM

PIPE WELDED TO DRUM

30 GAL. OIL DRUM

SAW HORSES ∘ 34 INCHES HIGH

Design by Penn. State College, Exp. Sta.

COOPERATIVE EXTENSION WORK IN AGRICULTURE
AND HOME ECONOMICS
TEXAS A&M COLLEGE SYSTEM AND
U.S. DEPARTMENT OF AGRICULTURE COOPERATING
G.G.GIBSON, DIRECTOR, COLLEGE STATION, TEXAS

MIXER MADE FROM OIL DRUM

DRAWN BY: M. R. B.	SCALE AS SHOWN
TRACED BY: B. G. K.	SHEET 1 OF 1
REV. SEPT., 1953	SERIAL NO. 235

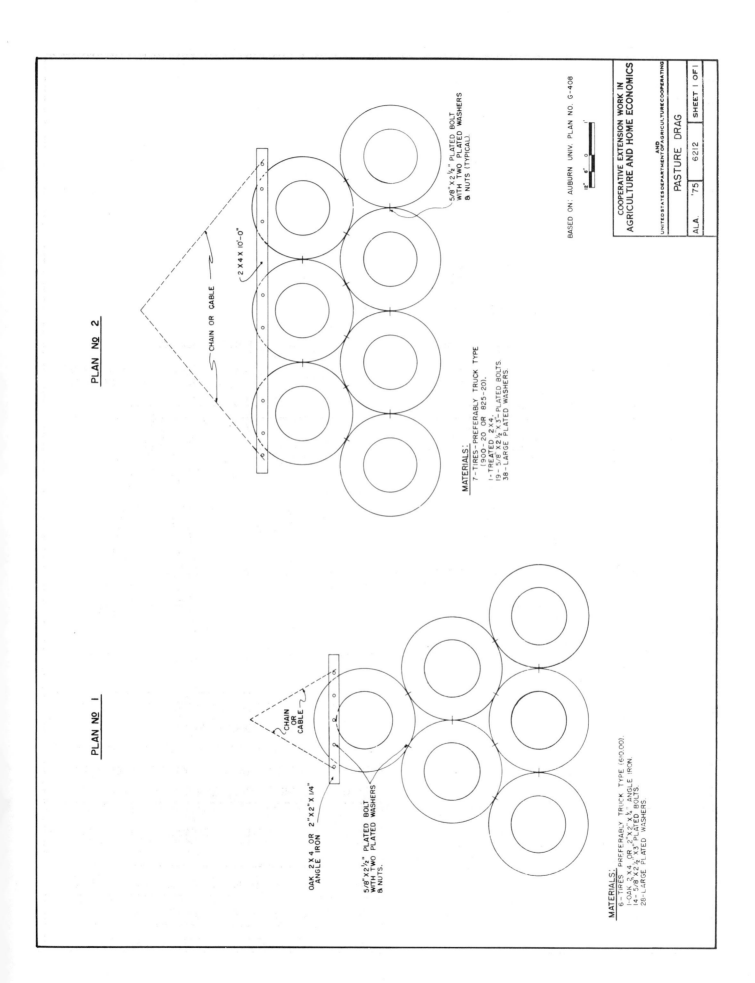

PLAN No 2

CHAIN OR CABLE

2 X 4 X 10'-0"

5/8" X 2 1/2" PLATED BOLT
WITH TWO PLATED WASHERS
& NUTS (TYPICAL).

MATERIALS:
7 - TIRES - PREFERABLY TRUCK TYPE
(900-20 OR 825-20).
1 - TREATED 2 X 4.
19 - 5/8" X 2 1/2" X 3" PLATED BOLTS.
38 - LARGE PLATED WASHERS.

PLAN No 1

CHAIN
OR
CABLE

OAK 2 X 4 OR 2" X 2" X 1/4"
ANGLE IRON

5/8" X 2 1/2" PLATED BOLT
WITH TWO PLATED WASHERS
& NUTS.

MATERIALS:
6 - TIRES - PREFERABLY TRUCK TYPE (610.00).
1 - OAK 2 X 4 OR 2" X 2" X 1/4" ANGLE IRON.
14 - 5/8" X 2 1/2" X 3" PLATED BOLTS.
28 - LARGE PLATED WASHERS.

BASED ON: AUBURN UNIV. PLAN NO. G-408

COOPERATIVE EXTENSION WORK IN
AGRICULTURE AND HOME ECONOMICS
AND
UNITED STATES DEPARTMENT OF AGRICULTURE COOPERATING

PASTURE DRAG		
ALA. '75	6212	SHEET 1 OF 1

12" 6" 0 1'

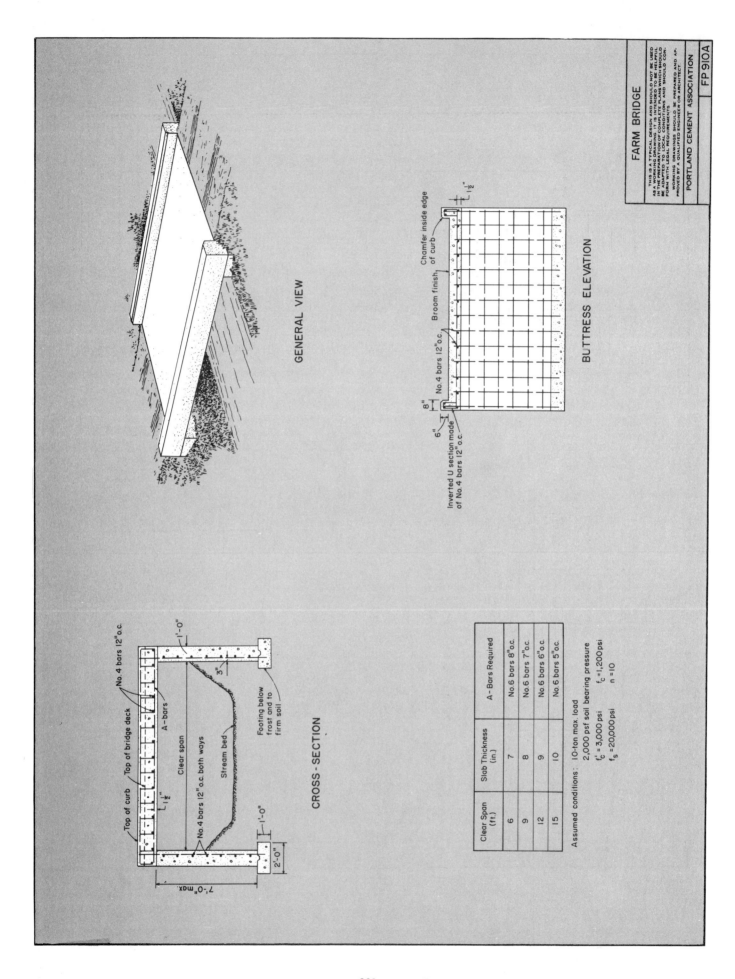

GENERAL VIEW

CROSS-SECTION

BUTTRESS ELEVATION

Clear Span (ft.)	Slab Thickness (in.)	A-Bars Required
6	7	No.6 bars 8"o.c.
9	8	No.6 bars 7"o.c.
12	9	No.6 bars 6"o.c.
15	10	No.6 bars 5"o.c.

Assumed conditions: 10-ton max. load
2,000 psf soil bearing pressure
$f'_c = 3,000$ psi $f_c = 1,200$ psi
$f_s = 20,000$ psi $n = 10$

FARM BRIDGE

THIS IS A TYPICAL DESIGN AND SHOULD NOT BE USED AS A WORKING DRAWING. IT IS INTENDED TO BE HELPFUL IN THE PREPARATION OF COMPLETE PLANS WHICH SHOULD BE ADAPTED TO LOCAL CONDITIONS AND SHOULD CON- FORM WITH LEGAL REQUIREMENTS.

WORKING DRAWINGS SHOULD BE PREPARED AND AP- PROVED BY A QUALIFIED ENGINEER OR ARCHITECT.

PORTLAND CEMENT ASSOCIATION

FP 910A

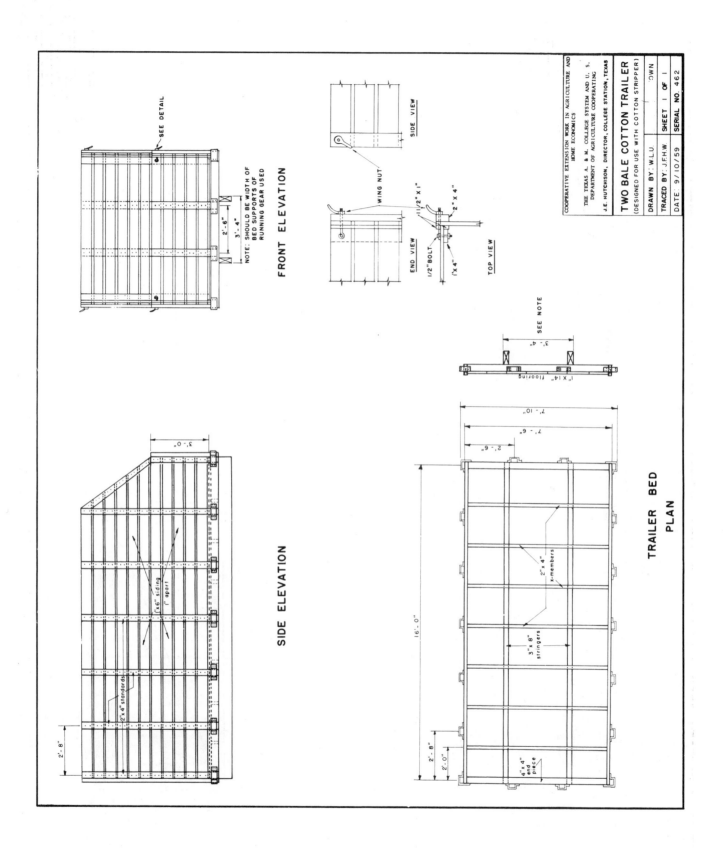

FRONT ELEVATION

NOTE: SHOULD BE WIDTH OF BED SUPPORTS OF RUNNING GEAR USED

SEE DETAIL

2'-6"
3'-4"

WING NUT

1 1/2" X 1"
2" X 4"
END VIEW
1/2" BOLT
1" X 4"
TOP VIEW
SIDE VIEW

SEE NOTE
3'-4"
1" X 14" flooring

SIDE ELEVATION

3'-0"
1" x 6" siding 1" apart
2" x 4" standards
2'-8"

TRAILER BED PLAN

7'-10"
7'-6"
2'-6"
16'-0"
2" x 4" x-members
3" x 8" stringers
2'-8"
2'-0"
4" x 4" end piece

COOPERATIVE EXTENSION WORK IN AGRICULTURE AND HOME ECONOMICS

THE TEXAS A. & M. COLLEGE SYSTEM AND U. S. DEPARTMENT OF AGRICULTURE COOPERATING

J.E. HUTCHISON, DIRECTOR, COLLEGE STATION, TEXAS

TWO BALE COTTON TRAILER
(DESIGNED FOR USE WITH COTTON STRIPPER)

DRAWN BY: W.L.U.   OWN
TRACED BY: J.F.H.W.   SHEET 1 OF 1
DATE: 9/10/59   SERIAL NO. 462

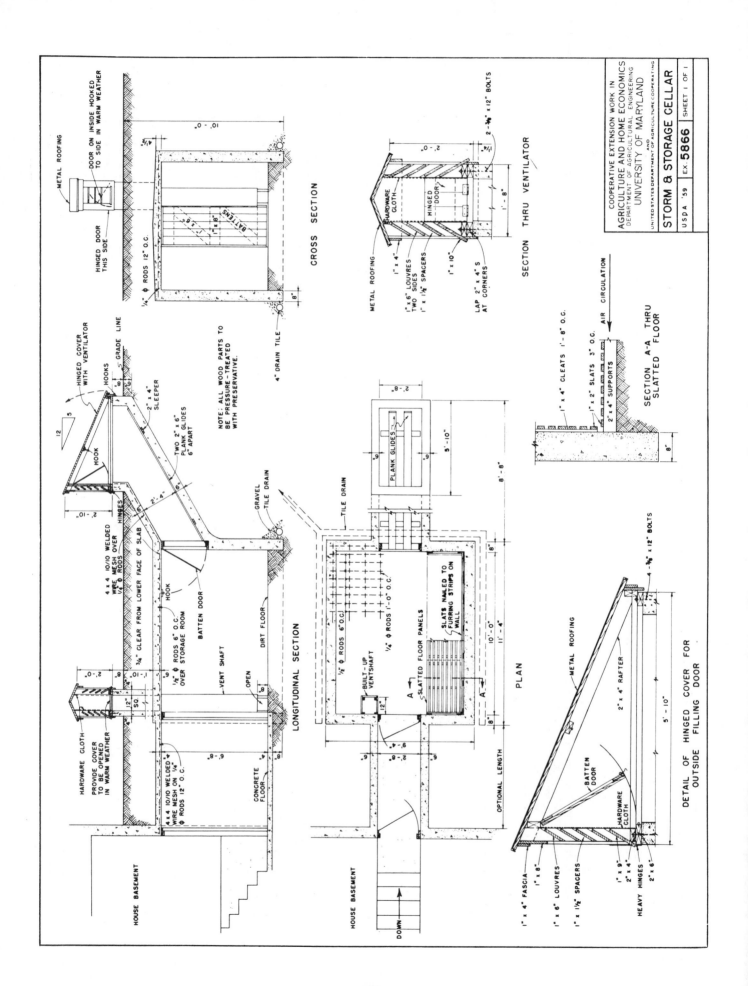

CROSS SECTION

SECTION THRU VENTILATOR

LONGITUDINAL SECTION

PLAN

SECTION A-A THRU SLATTED FLOOR

DETAIL OF HINGED COVER FOR OUTSIDE FILLING DOOR

NOTE: ALL WOOD PARTS TO BE PRESSURE-TREATED WITH PRESERVATIVE.

COOPERATIVE EXTENSION WORK IN
AGRICULTURE AND HOME ECONOMICS
DEPARTMENT OF AGRICULTURAL ENGINEERING
UNIVERSITY OF MARYLAND
AND
UNITED STATES DEPARTMENT OF AGRICULTURE COOPERATING

STORM & STORAGE CELLAR

USDA '59 | EX. 5866 | SHEET 1 OF 1

264

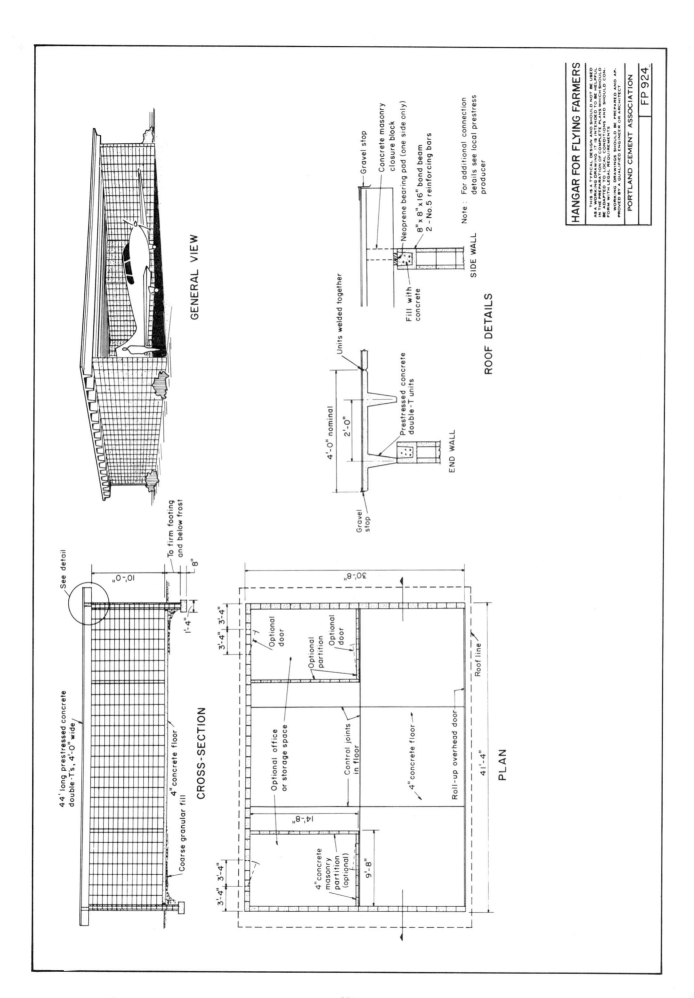

GENERAL VIEW

CROSS-SECTION

See detail

44' long prestressed concrete double-T's, 4'-0" wide

Coarse granular fill

4" concrete floor

To firm footing and below frost

10'-0"

1'-4"

8"

PLAN

Optional door

Optional partition

Optional door

3'-4" 3'-4"

Optional office or storage space

Control joints in floor

4" concrete floor

Roll-up overhead door

Roof line

4" concrete masonry partition (optional)

3'-4" 3'-4"

14'-8"

9'-8"

30'-8"

41'-4"

ROOF DETAILS

Units welded together

Prestressed concrete double-T units

4'-0" nominal

2'-0"

Gravel stop

END WALL

Gravel stop

Concrete masonry closure block

Neoprene bearing pad (one side only)

8" x 8" x 16" bond beam

2 - No.5 reinforcing bars

Fill with concrete

SIDE WALL

Note : For additional connection details see local prestress producer

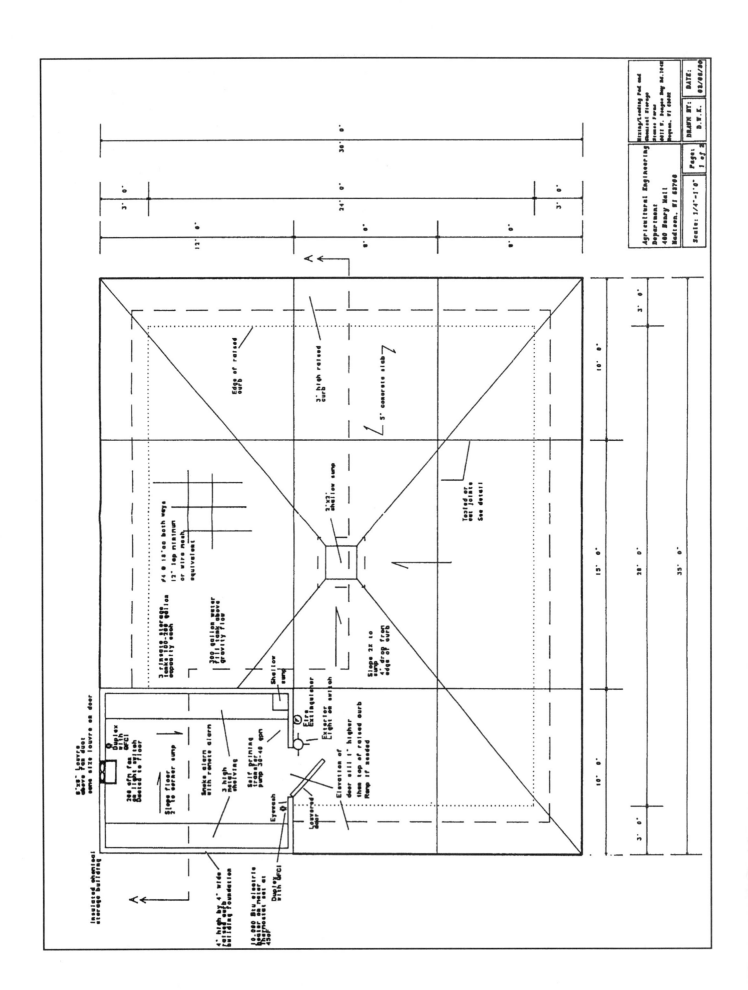

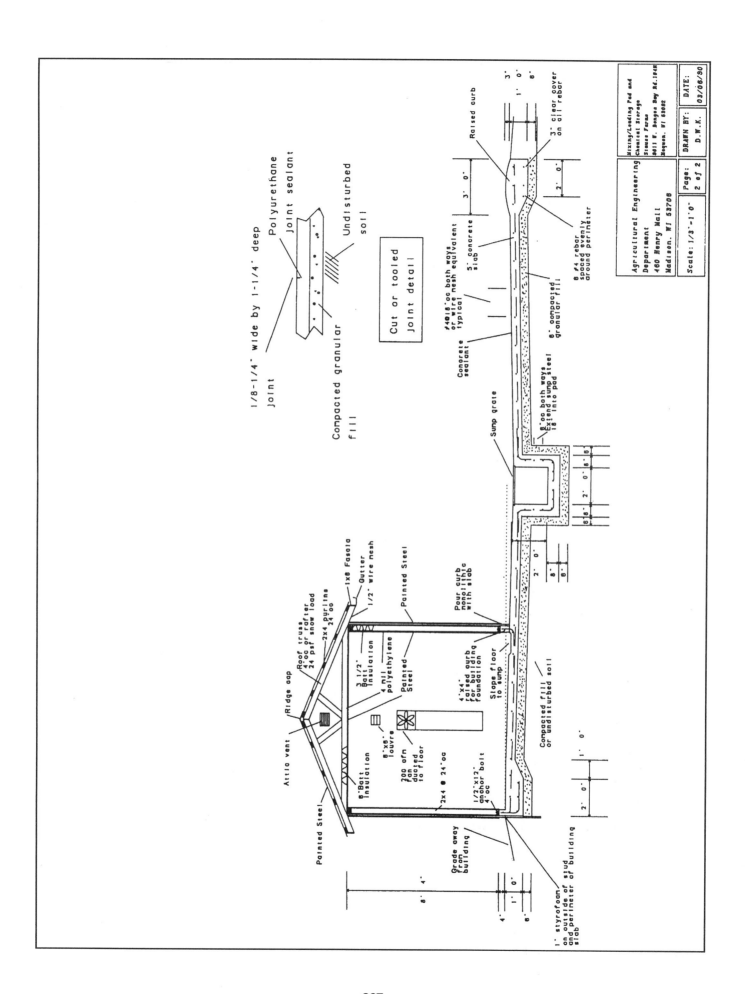

Polyurethane joint sealant

Undisturbed soil

1/8-1 1/4" wide by 1-1/4" deep joint

Compacted granular fill

Cut or tooled joint detail

Raised curb

3" clear cover on all rebar

#4@18"oo both ways or wire mesh equivalent typical

5" concrete slab

8 #4 rebar spaced evenly around perimeter

Concrete sealant

6" compacted granular fill

8"oo both ways Extend sump steel 18 into pad

Sump grate

Ridge cap

Attic vent

Painted Steel

Roof truss 4'oo or rafter 24 psf snow load

2x4 purlins 24 oo

1x8 Fascia

Gutter

1/2" wire mesh

3 1/2" Batt insulation

Painted Steel

4 mil polyethylene

Painted Steel

Pour curb monolithic with slab

6" Batt insulation

8"x8" louvre

200 ofm fan ducted to floor

4"x4" raised curb for building foundation

Slope floor to sump

2x4 @ 24"oo

1/2"x12" anchor bolt 4'oo

Compacted fill or undisturbed soil

Grade away from building

1" styrofoam on outside of stud and perimeter of building slab

Agricultural Engineering Department
460 Henry Mall
Madison, WI 53706

Mixing/Loading Pad and Chemical Storage
Stowe Farms
9611 W. Bonges Bay Rd.194M
Mequon, WI 69002

Scale: 1/3"-1'-0"

Page: 2 of 2

DRAWN BY: D.W.K.

DATE: 03/06/80

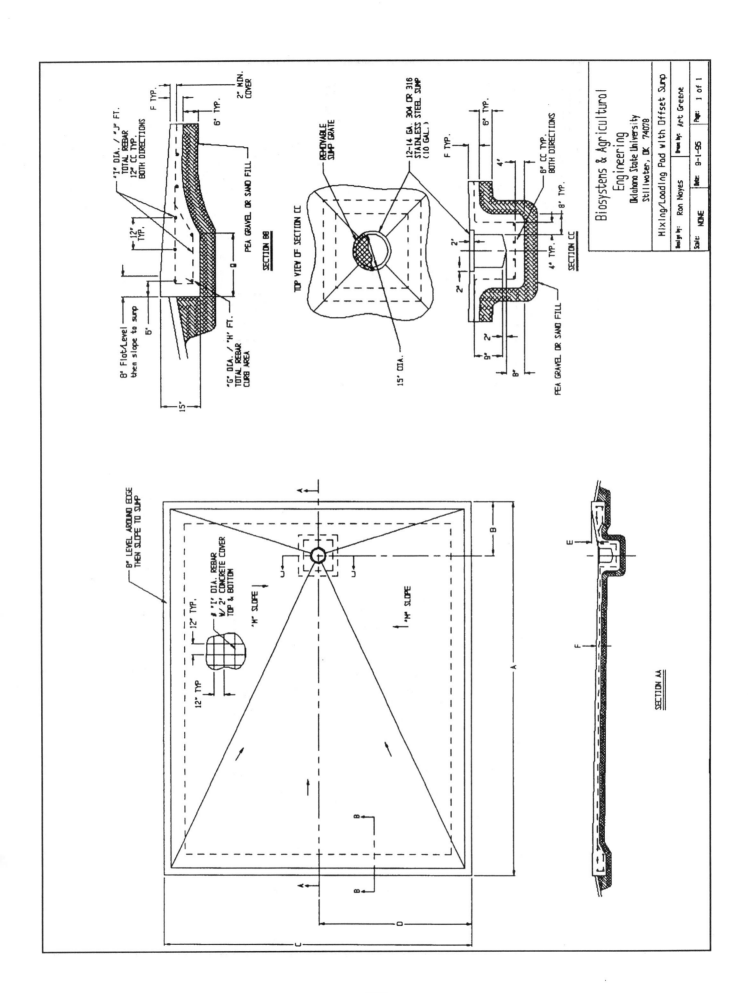

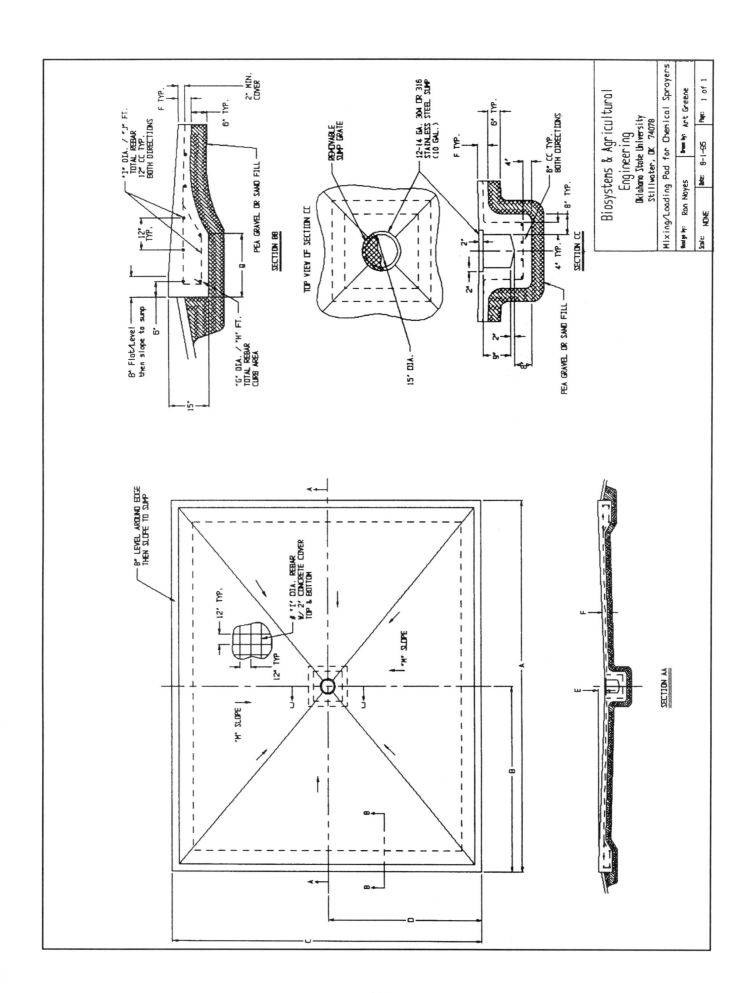

SECTION BB

2" MIN. COVER

F TYP.

6" TYP.

"I" DIA. / "J" FT.
TOTAL REBAR
12" CC TYP.
BOTH DIRECTIONS

12" TYP.

PEA GRAVEL OR SAND FILL

8" Flat/Level
then slope to sump

15'

G

5'

"G" DIA. / "H" FT.
TOTAL REBAR
CURB AREA

REMOVABLE
SUMP GRATE

12-14 GA. 304 OR 316
STAINLESS STEEL SUMP
(10 GAL.)

TOP VIEW OF SECTION CC

15' DIA.

F TYP.

6" TYP.

6" CC TYP.
BOTH DIRECTIONS

4"

8" TYP.

4" TYP.

2'

2'

2'

9"

8"

SECTION CC

PEA GRAVEL OR SAND FILL

8" LEVEL AROUND EDGE
THEN SLOPE TO SUMP

12' TYP.

"L" DIA. REBAR
W/ 2' CONCRETE COVER
TOP & BOTTOM

12' TYP.

"H" SLOPE

"H" SLOPE

A

B

D

C

SECTION AA

F

E

Biosystems & Agricultural
Engineering
Oklahoma State University
Stillwater, OK 74078

Mixing/Loading Pad for Chemical Sprayers

Design by: Ron Noyes   Drawn by: Art Greene   Page: 1 of 1
Date: 8-1-95
Scale: NONE

APPENDICES

Appendix A

State Cooperative Extension Service Offices that Provide Plans

The state universities that maintain offices for providing building and equipment plans are listed below. In some states, the service has been consolidated at a nearby state university, or with a regional plans service. Currently, several state universities are in process of consolidating cooperative extension services with other states. The following list reflects the latest information on the state universities that provide plans.

ALABAMA
Agricultural Engineering Extension
Auburn University
Auburn, AL 36849

ALASKA
Cooperative Extension Service
University of Alaska
Fairbanks, AK 99775

ARIZONA
Cooperative Extension Service
University of Arizona
Tucson, AZ 85721

ARKANSAS
Extension Agricultural Engineer
P.O. Box 391
Little Rock, AR 72203

CALIFORNIA
Biological and Agricultural Engineering
University of California
Davis, CA 95616

COLORADO
Cooperative Extension Service
Colorado State University
Fort Collins, CO 80523

CONNECTICUT
Extension Agricultural Engineer
University of Connecticut
Storrs, CT 06269

DELAWARE
Residents should write to the Connecticut
address

FLORIDA
Cooperative Extension Service
University of Georgia
Athens, GA 30602

HAWAII
Cooperative Extension Service
University of Hawaii
Honolulu, HI 96822

IDAHO
Agricultural Engineering Dept.
University of Idaho
Moscow, ID 83843

ILLINOIS
Agricultural Engineering Dept.
University of Illinois
Urbana, IL 61801

INDIANA
Agricultural Engineering Dept.
Purdue University
West Lafayette, IN 47907

IOWA
Agricultural Engineering Extension Iowa
State University Ames, IA 50011

KANSAS
Extension Agricultural Engineer
Kansas State University
Seaton Hall
Manhattan, KS 66506

KENTUCKY
Agricultural Engineering Dept.
University of Kentucky
Lexington, KY 40546

LOUISIANA
Cooperative Extension Service
Louisiana State University
Baton Rouge, LA 70803

MAINE
Residents should write: Midwest Plan
Service Iowa State University Ames, IA
50011

MARYLAND
Dept. of Agricultural Engineering
University of Maryland
College Park, MD 20742

MASSACHUSETTS
Residents should write to the Connecticut
address

MICHIGAN
Plan Service Secretary
Michigan State University
East Lansing, MI 48824

MINNESOTA
Extension Agricultural Engineer
University of Minnesota
St. Paul, MN 55108

MISSISSIPPI
Cooperative Extension Service
Mississippi State University
Mississippi State, MS 39762

MISSOURI
Agricultural Engineering Plan Service
University of Missouri
Columbia, MO 65211

MONTANA
Cooperative Extension Service
Montana State University
Bozeman, MT 59715

NEBRASKA
Agricultural Engineering Plan Service
University of Nebraska
Lincoln, NE 68583

NEVADA
Cooperative Extension Service
University of Nevada
Reno, NV 89557

NEW HAMPSHIRE
Cooperative Extension Service
University of New Hampshire
Durham, NH 03824

NEW JERSEY
Bioresource Engineering
Rutgers University
New Brunswick, NJ 08903

NEW MEXICO
Cooperative Extension Service
New Mexico State University
Las Cruces, NM 88033

NEW YORK
Dept. of Agricultural Biological
Engineering
Cornell University
Riley-Robb Hall
Ithaca, NY 14853

NORTH CAROLINA
Dept. of Biological and Agricultural
Engineering
North Carolina State University
Raleigh, NC 27695

NORTH DAKOTA
Extension Agricultural Engineer
North Dakota State University
Fargo, ND 58105

OHIO
Extension Agricultural Engineer
The Ohio State University
Columbus, OH 43210

OKLAHOMA
Cooperative Extension Service
Oklahoma State University
Stillwater, OK 74078

OREGON
Oregon State University
Corvallis, OR 97331

PENNSYLVANIA
Agricultural Engineering Dept
The Pennsylvania State University
Ag Engineering Building
University Park, PA 16802

PUERTO RICO
Cooperative Extension Service
University of Puerto Rico
Mayaguez, PR 00708

RHODE ISLAND
Residents should write to the
Connecticut address

SOUTH CAROLINA
Cooperative Extension Service
Clemson University
Clemson, SC 29634

SOUTH DAKOTA
MWPS Secretary
South Dakota State University
Brookings, SD 57007

TENNESSEE
Agricultural Extension Service
University of Tennessee
Box 1071
Knoxville, TN 37901

TEXAS
Agricultural Engineering
Texas A&M University
303 Ag Engineering Building
College Station, TX 77843

UTAH
Extension Agricultural Engineer
Utah State University
Logan, UT 84322

VERMONT
Residents should write to the
Connecticut address

VIRGINIA
Cooperative Extension Service
VPI & SU
Blacksburg, VA 24061

WASHINGTON
Cooperative Extension Service
Washington State University
Pullman, WA 99164

WEST VIRGINIA
Extension Agricultural Engineer
West Virginia State University
Morgantown, WV 26506

WISCONSIN
MWPS Secretary
Agricultural Engineering Dept.
University of Wisconsin
Madison, WI 53706

WYOMING
Residents should contact
Midwest Plan Service
Iowa State University
Ames, IA 50011

Appendix B

USDA and Regional Plan Service Sources

Agricultural Engineer: Extension Service
United States Department of Agriculture
Washington, DC 20250

Northeast Agricultural Engineering Service
152 Riley-Robb Hall
Cornell University
Ithaca, NY 14853

Midwest Plan Service
Iowa State University
Ames, IA 50011

Western Regional Agricultural Engineering Service
Oregon State University
Corvallis, OR 97331

Appendix C

Plans Available from the U.S. Department of Agriculture

POULTRY

Plan No.	Title
5845	Caged Layers
5871	Poultry House
5931	Cage Laying House
5936	Cage Laying House
5972	Broiler House
5990	Laying House
5996	Incinerator
6000	Poultry House
6001	Poultry House
6036	Broiler House
6053	Pullet Rearing House
6062	Cage Laying House
6084	Broiler House
6085	Poultry House
6087	Poultry House
6095	Egg Processing Plant
6131	Poultry House, Caged Layers
6134	Poultry House, Caged Layers
6140	Poultry House, Caged Layers
6166	Cage Laying House
6187	Poultry House, 25 to 40 Layers
6188	Poultry House, 50 to 80 Layers
6189	Layer House, 15,000 Birds

SHEEP

Plan No.	Title
5019	Sheep Shed
5733	Sheep Shed
5808	Sheep Feeder
5809	Sheep Chute
5811	Sheep Shed
5813	Sheep Shed
6058	Three-Way Cutting Gates
5861	Sheep Feeder
5863	Sheep Feeder
5867	Shipping Crate—Sheep
5874	Sheep Shed
5877	Sheep Crate
5905	Sheep Equipment
5910	Sheep Feeder
5911	Wool Packing Racks

SHEEP (Contd.)

Plan No.	Title
5912	Ewe Stanchion
5913	Sheep Feeders
5914	Sheep Feeder
5915	Sheep Feeder
5916	Mineral Feeder—Sheep
5917	Fences—Feeding Panels
5918	Grain Troughs
5919	Sheep Shed
5924	Loading Chute—Sheep
5926	Lambing Shelter
5999	Dipping Vat—Sheep
6006	Sheep Squeeze
6019	Corrals—Sheep
6043	Sheep Corral
6047	Sheep Chair
6096	Shearing Shed and Corral for Sheep
6142	Portable Footbath for Sheep

SWINE

Plan No.	Title
5756	Hog Feeder
5783	Breeding Crate
5798	Loading Chute
5799	Loading Chute
5814	Hog Feeder
5815	Hog Feeder
5816	Hog Shade
5818	Garbage Cooker
5820	Garbage Cooker
5821	Hog House
5825	Pig Production Plant
5826	Hog House
5827	Pig Creeps
5828	Farrowing Stall
5842	Hog Wallow
5870	Hog Shade
5873	Swine Unit
5907	Pig Brooder
5945	Hog Feeding Unit
5947	Hog Feeding Unit
5986	Feeding Floor

(Continued)

SWINE (Contd.)

Plan No.	Title
5988	Swine Feeder
5992	Farrowing House
5993	Swine Unit
6026	Farrowing House
6032	Farrowing House
6056	Portable Sow Feeders
6061	Farrowing House
6073	Two Hog Houses
6074	Hog House for Gestating Sows
6075	Hog House, Nursery and Finishing
6076	Hog House, Farrowing in Crates
6088	Farrowing House for Hogs
6089	Swine Finishing Parlor
6104	Finishing Floor to 400 Pigs
6105	Swine Nursery Building
6114	Feeding Unit for Swine
6115	Farrowing, House
6116	Hog House—Modified "A" Type
6122	Farrowing House
6125	Farrowing House for Sows
6127	Breeding Facilities for Swine
6130	Farrowing House for Sows
6135	Farrowing and Nursery Building
6144	Hog Feed—Stand-Up Type
6154	House for Dry Sows
6157	Hog Houses
6159	Finish Floor for Hogs
6169	Part Stat Feed Floor
6178	Finishing Parlor for Hogs

BEEF

Plan No.	Title
5974	Corral—Beef
5991	Corral—Beef
6012	Feed Bunks—Cattle
5932	Truck Scale Pen
6049	Corral
6065	Movable Calf Shelter
6077	Walk-through Headgate—Cattle
6091	Auction Yard for Livestock
6103	Breeding Chute for Beef Cattle
6106	Corral Layout and Equipment
6108	Cubed Hay Storage Feeder
6124	Cattle Feeder—Liquid Supplement
6129	Livestock Market
6133	Squeeze Chute for Cattle
6139	Curved Holding Chute
6141	Trailer for Cattle
6152	Corral and Breeding Chute
6153	Cattle Chute—Adjustable Type
6156	Confinement Beef Barn
6158	Confinement Beef Barn
6160	Confinement Beef Barn
6161	Cattle Corral Layouts

BEEF (Contd.)

Plan No.	Title
6167	Silage Feed Bunks
6172	Cattle Shed and Auction Barn
6183	Three-Tier Loading Chute
6184	Rodeo Arena
5465	Squeeze Chute
5681	Loading Chute
5740	Cattle Stock
5754	Cattle Shelter
5759	Mineral Box
5760	Bull Pen
6051	Cattle Guards
5761	Cattle Stocks
5763	Calf Creep
5764	Calf Creep
5768	Calf Creep
5769	Mineral Box
5772	Hay Rack
5776	Cattle Feeder
5777	Hay Racks
5778	Head Gates
5779	Corrals
5784	Cattle Stock
5789	Cattle Squeeze
5790	Corral
5791	Cattle Squeeze
5792	Cattle Stock
5793	Loading Chute
5794	Pole Barn
5835	Corrals
5837	Feeding Floors
5844	Mineral Feeder
5850	Cattle Chute
5852	Loading Chute
5853	Breeding Rack
5854	Fence Line Feeder
5862	Bunk Feeder—Cattle
5864	Bunk Feeder—Cattle
5876	Dipping Vat—Cattle
5906	Mineral Feeder—Cattle
5909	Watering Trough
5920	Feedlot—Beef
5925	Cattle Feeding Rack
5939	Cattle Feed Bunk
5940	Cattle Dipping Vat
5950	Fallout Shelter—Beef
5952	Range Corral
5959	Gates and Chutes
5960	Loading Ramp
5961	Gates and Fences

DAIRY

Plan No.	Title
5143	Bull Pen
5736	Milking Plant
5839	Screen Chamber

(Continued)

DAIRY (Contd.)

Plan No.	Title
5840	Artificial Breeding Stall
5846	Milking Stall
5851	Bull Barn
5868	Milking Plant
5875	Milking Plant
5885	Free Stall System—Dairy
5933	Calf Pens
5937	Fallout Shelter—Dairy
5938	Fallout Shelter—Dairy
5953	Stall Barn Fallout Shelter
5954	Free Stall Fallout Shelter
5955	Free Stall Fallout Shelter
5956	Free Stalls
5962	Tilting Calf Table
5969	Tilting Calf Table
5970	Calf Barn
5977	Dairy Equipment
5981	Manure Tank
5985	Free Stall System
5987	Manure Tank
6023	Free Stall System—Dairy
6025	Free Stall System—Dairy
6030	Free Stall Barn
6031	Free Stall System
6033	Milk House
6034	Free Stall Barn
6035	Free Stall System
6037	Crowding Gates—Dairy
6039	Free Stall Barn
6042	Free Stall Barn
6045	Self Feeder—Cattle
6050	Free Stall Barn
6052	Elevated Calf Pens
6057	Calf Tie Stalls
6063	Milk House
6066	Cattle Feeders
6067	Free Stall Shed
6078	Milkhouse
6092	Crowding Gate for Dairy Cattle
6102	Heifer Barn—Free Stall
6111	Free Stall Barn
6112	Pole Frame Dairy Barn
6113	Loose Housing Layout for Dairy Cattle
6126	Ventilation System for Cold Free Stall
6132	Milkhouse for Dairy Cattle
6138	Portable Stalls for Calves
6143	Wagon Rack for Silage Feeding
6146	Maternity Barn for Cows
6164	Dairy Calf Nursery
6165	Cow Kennels
6174	Milkhouse
6180	Movable Calf Pen
6186	Calf Barn
6194	Combination Breeding Stall and Box Stall

DAIRY (Contd.)

Plan No.	Title
6196	Dairy Barn—Economic Free Stall
6199	Elevated Calf Stall
6200	Elevated Calf Stall

HORSES

Plan No.	Title
5107	Box Stall Details
5175	Horse Stalls
5838	Riding Horse Barn
5943	Two-Horse Trailer
5994	Saddle Horse Barn
6010	Horse Barn
6011	Horse Barn
6014	Horse Equipment
6015	Horse Show Rings
6024	Horse Barn
6082	Portable Stable for a Horse
6107	Horse Barn
6118	Horse Barn, 2 Stall
6128	Horse Barn, Indoor Exercise Facilities
6148	Horse Barn—Capacity 88 Horses
6170	Horse Barn, 10 Stall
6171	Horse Barn and Arena

FEED STORAGE

Plan No.	Title
6009	50' Truss
6060	Machine Shed
5528	Four Bin Granary
5529	Granary
5532	Grain Elevator
5533	Corn Crib
5648	Sweet Potato House
5860	Fruit Cooler
5869	Drying Storage Shed
5872	Self-feeding Fences
5878	Corn Crib
5879	Hay Storage
5927	Potato Storage
5934	Fallout Shelter
5935	Storage Feeding Shed
5948	Fallout Shelter—People
5951	Fallout Shelter—Storage
5957	Fallout Shelter
5966	Fertilizer Shed
5979	Potato Storage
5989	Potato Storage
6016	Tobacco Barn
6017	Tobacco Barn
6018	Potato Storage
6021	Braced Wall Silo
6038	Potato Storage
6048	Bunker Silos—A, B and C
6055	Horizontal Silo

(Continued)

FEED STORAGE (Contd.)

Plan No.	Title
6059	Grain Storage Building
6068	Grain-Feed Handling Center
6069	Grain-Feed Handling Center
6070	Shed for Drying Hay
6072	Transportable Storage Bin
6081	Grain-Feed Handling Center
6086	Four Storage Sheds
6090	Grain Bin, 5,500 Bushel
6093	Storage Building for Garden Tools
6099	Movable Shed
6100	Utility Shed
6109	Wood Bunker Silo
6110	Concrete Trench Silo
6117	Fertilizer Storage
6119	Pallet Bin
6120	Pallet Bin
6121	Pallet Bin for Vegetables
6145	Storage Building for Fruit
6150	Machinery Shed
6168	Implement Shed
6175	Horizontal Silo

GREENHOUSES

Plan No.	Title
5189	Sash Greenhouse
5941	Greenhouse Cold Frame
5946	Greenhouse Plastic
5971	Hotbed
5980	Plant Growth Chamber
6029	Greenhouse
6064	Lath House
6080	Mini Hotbed and Propagating Frame
6094	Plastic-covered Greenhouse
6097	Tri-penta Greenhouse
6101	Propagation Unit for Plants
6163	Greenhouse Benches
6181	Home Greenhouse
6185	28' Greenhouse

BUILDINGS AND DETAILS

Plan No.	Title
5146	Farm Shop
5166	General Barn
5625	Rafter Framing
5626	Rafter Framing
5662	Gable Roof Frame
5663	Gambrel Roof Frame
5664	Gambrel Roof Frame
5669	Typical Walls
5670	Typical Walls
5671	Typical Walls
5680	Gambrel Roof Frame
5830	Pole Barn
5831	Pole Barn
5832	Pole Barn
5841	Machinery Shed

BUILDINGS AND DETAILS (Contd.)

Plan No.	Title
5847	Hay Shed
5848	Bunker Silo
5849	Machine Shed and Shop
5855-5	Shed Roof
5865	Bunker Silo
5921	36' Truss
5922	24' Truss
5923	24' Truss
5929	Garages
5930	Garages
5949	40' Roof Truss
5973	32' Utility Truss
5978	40' Truss
6005	Truss
6007	40' Truss
6008	48' Truss

VACATION BUILDINGS

Plan No.	Title
5184	Tourist Cabin for Two
5185	Tourist Cabin for Five
5186	Tourist Cabin for Four
5187	Summer Camp Building
5506	Five-Room Log Cabin
5507	Three-Room Cabin
5694	Bunk House
5928	Cabin
5964	24' A-Frame Cabin
5965	36' A-Frame Cabin
5968	Cabin
5997	Vacation House
5998	Adirondack Shelter
6002	Cabin
6003	A-Frame Cabin
6004	Cabin
6013	Dormitory Loft Cabin
7010	Two-Bedroom Cabin
7013	Two-Bedroom Log Cabin

MISCELLANEOUS STRUCTURES

Plan No.	Title
5188	Outdoor Fireplace
5192	Roadside Stand
5193	Roadside Stand
5197	Farm Spring House
5198	Incinerator
5505	Farm Gates
5614	Auto Bumper Gate
5695	Smoke House
5699	Roadside Stand
5824	Play Grounds
5833	Pole Barn Details
5908	Hay Wagon
5942	Irrigation Pipe Trailer

(Continued)

MISCELLANEOUS STRUCTURES (Contd.)

Plan No.	Title	Plan No.	Title
5963	Water Supply System	6083	Campground Comfort Station
5975	Boat Landing	6098	Incinerator
5982	Display Stands	6123	Comfort Station
5983	Roadside Stand	6137	Hutches for Rabbits
5995	Picnic Shelter	6147	Tank for Treating Wood
6020	Barbeque Pit	6149	Community Building
6022	Barbeque Pit	6151	Gate, Telescoping Type
6027	Roadside Market	6155	Sedimentation Tank
6028	Slot Ventilators	6162	Cable Fencing
6041	Corral Transport	6173	Wagon Rack for Tossed Bales
6046	Sprinkler Pipe Trailer	6177	Dock Bumper
6054	Pit-Type Privy	6190	Fan Ventilation Systems
6071	Wagon Box for Drying Hay	6191	Three-Point Hitch Boom
6079	Pavilion with Kitchen	6192	Pick-up Truck Racks

Appendix D

PLANS AVAILABLE FROM THE AMERICAN PLYWOOD ASSOCIATION 1119 A STREET TACOMA, WASHINGTON 98401

GENERAL INFORMATION

Number	*Description*
A40	Plywood Siding
A30	Plywood Sheathing for Walls and Roofs
Y110	Plywood Agricultural Construction Guide
V605	Plywood "How To" Book (how to buy and specify, work and finish information)
Y390	Guide to Plywood Grades

CATTLE — DAIRY AND BEEF

A500	Plywood Beef Cattle Feeder (4' x 7' portable unit)
P300	350-Bushel Cattle Feeder (8' x 16' portable unit)
U140	Liquid Supplement Cattle Feeder

FEED AND GRAIN STORAGE

M200	1,200-Bushel Portable Grain Bin (12' x 16' building)
W115	Overhead Bin for Feed, Grain or Fertilizer
N850	Four Compartment Bin for Farm Feed Mill (160 cu. ft./compartment)
T130	5,500-Bushel Grain Bin
X115	Plywood for Granular Storage

FERTILIZER

W115	Overhead Bin for Feed, Grain or Fertilizer
T115	Transportable Fertilizer Bin

MATERIALS HANDLING

Y205	Plywood Design Manual: Industrial and Agricultural Pallet Bins (48-page manual for design of bins for apples, pears, carrots, tomatoes, etc.)
N513	47" x 47" All Bolted Plywood Pallet Bin
R150	All Bolted Plywood Vegetable Pallet Bin
U165	47" x 40" All Bolted Plywood Pallet Bin
N511	Modified "Davis" Plywood Pallet Bin
M310	1-Ton Pallet Bin with Gravity Discharge
W110	490-Cubic Foot Bulk Hauler
	Case Histories:
R130	Plywood Pallet Bins Solve Peach Harvest Crisis
Y105	Of Note: Lemon Pallet Bin

(Continued)

PLYWOOD RIGID FRAME — BUILDING SYSTEM

Number	Description
H450	32' and 40' Rigid Frame Structure

POLE CONSTRUCTION — BUILDING SYSTEM

W120	Utility Buildings (28', 32', 36' and 40')

POULTRY ENTERPRISE

V130	USDA-6000 Poultry House Panel Construction — Floor Management
V115	USDA-6001 Poultry House Panel Construction — Cage Management

SWINE ENTERPRISE

K430	A-Type Hog House (6' x 6' portable units)
U155	Modified A-Type Hog House
K480	Swine Finishing Shed (open front end)
U670	Farrowing Shed (two 8' x 20' portable pull-together units)
U170	24' x 48' Farrowing House
U175	Farrowing Stall
Z115	Plywood in Swine Housing

MISCELLANEOUS

X495	Here's the All-Weather Wood Foundation System
Y800	Product Standard PS 1 for Construction and Industrial Plywood
S340	High Density Overlaid Plywood
U355	Medium Density Overlaid Plywood
Q30	MDO Plywood Siding (single-page data sheet on Medium Density Overlaid Plywood)
Q220	Pressure-Preserved Plywood (product data sheet)
V307	Finishing Plywood for Exterior Exposure (single sheet)
X440	Refinishing Plywood for Exterior Exposure (single sheet)
Z338	303 ® Product Data Sheet
U160	2-Stall Horse Barn
X505	Everything You Wanted to Know About Plywood

INDEX